THE PHILOSOPHICAL DIALOGUE

THE

PHILOSOPHICAL DIALOGUE

A Poetics and a Hermeneutics

VITTORIO HÖSLE

Translated by

STEVEN RENDALL

University of Notre Dame Press
Notre Dame, Indiana

Manufactured in the United States of America

Library of Congress Cataloging-in-Publication Data

Hösle, Vittorio, 1960–
[Philosophische Dialog. English]
The philosophical dialogue : a poetics and a hermeneutics /
Vittorio Hösle ; translated by Steven Rendall.
pages   cm
Previously published in German, under the title Der philosophische Dialog :
eine Poetik und Hermeneutik. München : Beck, c2006.
Includes bibliographical references and index.
ISBN 978-0-268-03097-1 (pbk. : alk. paper) —
ISBN 0-268-03097-9 (pbk. : alk. paper)
1. Philosophy. 2. Dialogue.   I. Rendall, Steven, translator.   II. Title.
B53. H6313   2012
101—dc23

2012037027

In Memory

of my beloved uncle

Josef Hösle

(1924–2005)

in gratitude for many conversations

in which his virtues were manifested

CONTENTS

ABBREVIATIONS

adult. libr. Orig. = *De adulteratione librorum Origenis* (Rufinus)

Ammonium (Ammon.)
   in Cat. = *In Aristotelis Categorias commentarius*

Aristophanes (Ar.)
   Ach. = *Acharnenses*

Aristotle (Arist.)
   Po. = *Poetica*
   Rh. = *Rhetorica*
   Metaph. = *Metaphysica*
   SE = *Sophistici Elenchi*
   Top. = *Topica*

Augustine (Aug.)
   C. acad. = *Contra academicos*
   Beat. vit. = *Beata vita*
   Conf. = *Confessiones*
   De civ. dei = *De civitate dei*
   De mag. = *De magistro*
   Ord. = *De ordine*
   Soliloq. = *Soliloquia*
   Retract. = *Retractationes*

Boethius
   Cons. = *Consolatio philosophiae*

Cicero (Cic.)
   Ac. Po. = Academica posteriori
   Ac. Pr. = Academica priora
   Att. = Epistulae ad Atticum
   De leg. = De legibus
   De or. = De oratore
   De rep. = De republica
   Fam. = Epistulae ad familiares
   Fin. = De finibus
   Lael. = Laelius
   De off. = De officiis
   Or. = Orator ad M. Brutum
   QF = Epistulae ad Quintum Fratrem
   Tusc. = Tusculanae disputationes

Demetrius Phaelereus (Demetr.)
   Eloc. = De elocutione

D.L. = Diogenes Laertius

Dionysius of Halicarnassus
   Dem. = De Demosthene
   Pomp. = Epistula ad Pompeium

Hermogenes
   Meth. = Peri methodou deinotētos

Horace
   Sat. = Satirae

Juvenal
   Sat. = Satiurae

Lactantius (Lact.)
   div. inst. = Divinae Institutiones

Longin. = Longinus

Lucian (Luc.)
Bis Acc. = Bis Accusatus
JTr. = Juppiter Tragoedus
Laps. = pro Lapsu inter Salutandum
Prom. Es = Prometheus es in verbis

Macrobius
Sat. = Saturnalia

Plato (Pl.)
Alc. I = Alcibiades I
Ap. = Apologia
Chrm. = Charmides
Cli. = Clitopho
Cra. = Cratylus
Cri. = Crito
Criti. = Critias
Ep. = Epistulae
Euthd. = Euthydemus
Euthphr. = Euthyphro
Grg. – Gorgias
Hp. ma. = Hippias major
Hp. mi. = Hippias minor
La. = Laches
Lg. = Leges (Laws)
Ly. = Lysis
Men. = Meno
Mx. = Menexenus
Phd. = Phaedo
Phdr. = Phaedrus
Plt. = Politicus (Statesman)
Prm. = Parmenides
Prt. = Protagoras

R. = Respublica (Republic)
Smp. = Symposium
Sph. = Sophista
Thg. = Theages
Tht. = Theaetetus
Ti. = Timaeus

Plutarch
  Mor. = Moralia

POxy = Oxyrhynchus Papyri

Proclus (Proc.)
  in Cra. = In Platonis Cratylum commentaria
  in Alc.= In Platonis Alcibiadem
  in Euc. = In primum Euclidis librum commentarius

Pseudo-Lucian
  Am. = Amores

Quintilianus
  Inst. = Institutio Oratoria

Thucydides (Th.)

Xenophanes
  DK = Diels-Kranz edition

Xenophon (Xen.)
  Mem. = Memorabilia
  Smp. = Symposium

But of all works of this kind, what is truly the most difficult is

a characteristical dialogue upon any philosophical subject:

to interweave characters with reasoning, by suiting to the

character of each speaker, a peculiarity not only of thought,

but of expression, requires the perfection of genius, taste,

and judgement.

—Henry Home Lord Kames,

Elements of Criticism (1851, 216)

The suspicion that the age in which we live is not one of the philosophically most productive eras of human history does not emerge solely from
an analysis of the content of contemporary philosophical production. It
also forces itself upon anyone who seeks to inventory the literary genres
that are currently used by philosophers: what a loss in literary diversity,
what a diminution of the possible modes of expression discovered and
created by two and a half millennia of philosophy! The absence of philosophical dialogue is particularly painful, indeed puzzling, in a period that
some people think is governed by the paradigm of intersubjectivity and
discourse.

I am aware, of course, that a proposal to revive the philosophical
dialogue comes with much better grace from someone who is capable
of writing one himself—someone like my friend Manfred Wetzel. But
even if one cannot do so, one can still advance the cause of philosophical dialogue by discussing systematically the possibilities of this genre.
At any rate, an intertextual awareness is characteristic of even the earliest dialogues, and a survey of what the philosophical dialogue has accomplished up to this point, indeed, of its essential traits, might inspire
new forms of this genre—and then this book would have truly fulfilled
its goal.

But even from a purely observational point of view, an analysis of
the philosophical dialogue seems to me rewarding for various reasons.
The literary genre of the philosophical dialogue reflects or transforms
a real phenomenon, philosophical exchange between different people.
This exchange is so essential to the essence of doing philosophy that an
analysis of the genre promises to shed light on the nature of philosophizing itself. Subjectivity and intersubjectivity are crucial fundamental

categories of philosophy, and in analyzing the philosophical dialogue, philosophy reflects on the connection of these categories in what it is itself: self-reflection and thinking through the fundamental categories are intensively combined in this analysis. In real conversations, arguments are exchanged, and the connections between the individual propositions that constitute arguments as such belong to the domain of logic. However, propositions are presented through speech acts, and their authors are persons. But relations between persons belong to the domain of ethics. Thus in the philosophical dialogue the two basic disciplines of theoretical and practical philosophy seem to be bound together in an especially close way.

However, actual philosophical exchange is only the starting point for the literary genre. What happens in the artistic transformation of the real starting point is governed by aesthetic rules, and hence a study of the philosophical dialogue will also produce insights into aesthetics and in particular into literary theory. The fact that many philosophers were clearly also great artists may be an encouragement; and it certainly has consequences for a theory of the relation between art and philosophy.

Finally, a theory of the literary genre of the philosophical dialogue will have something to contribute to the field of hermeneutics as well, for two reasons. First, actual dialogue between philosophers works only if they understand each other, and thus in every philosophical dialogue the problem of the mutual understanding between the literary characters who appear in it is an implicit, and frequently also an explicit, theme. Second, it is not just a matter of understanding the processes whereby these literary characters make themselves understood; it is also a matter of understanding the intentions of the author of the work. This is notoriously difficult, and perhaps some progress toward coping with it would be useful for the hermeneutics of philosophical and literary texts in general.

There are philosophical dialogues on almost every question, and although, of course, all these questions cannot be taken up here, because of the close relationship between the form and the subject of philosophical dialogue a certain familiarity with a multitude of philosophical disciplines is a precondition for a work like this one. There are also philosophical dialogues in all periods of the history of philosophy, even if they are distributed over time in a very interesting way that must itself be philosophically explained. No overall history of the philosophical dialogue has appeared since Rudolf Hirzel's two-volume study of the dialogue in general was published in 1895, and this book is not intended to be one, indeed, not even a history of the *philosophical* dialogue. (Nonphilosophical dialogues, especially if their authors are philosophers, will be occasionally cited if they present certain literary structures with particular clarity.) My book seeks only to present a *taxonomy and theory of the categories* of philosophical dialogue, and makes not the slightest claim to historical completeness; it is thus closer to Carlo Sigonio's *De dialogo liber* (1562), the first work on the genre and a masterpiece of Renaissance poetics, than to Hirzel's enormously learned work, which belongs to the age of historical positivism. Naturally, I have not read every philosophical dialogue that was ever written, nor have I even read *in toto* all the works to which I sometimes refer in this book; still less have I surveyed the whole secondary literature on the authors I discuss, even though I have looked into many more than I have cited. But it was not necessary to do so to grasp the essential characteristics of the genre. It is true that although I have limited myself to the realm of Western culture, I have sought to give examples from all periods, and in modern times from every century, partly to show the universality of the genre and partly to exemplify variations specific to a given period. The translations—often merely paraphrases—are, unless otherwise specified, my own—of course in this English language version themselves translated by Steven Rendall. Sometimes, however, I have thought it necessary to assume that the reader can cope with Latin and French.

This book combines theoretical reflections with examples that sometimes require intensive hermeneutic efforts in a way that will seem to some philosophers too literary-philological and to some students of literature and philologists too philosophical. In it, the contents and arguments of philosophical dialogues do not play a central role, nor does it seek to provide meticulously detailed, overall interpretations of individual texts. An admirer of Vico may be forgiven for attempting to connect philology and philosophy in this way. So far as the choice of texts is concerned, my goal was to make clear both the main lines of the genre's development and the contrasting ways in which the dialogue can be constructed. The preferred method is therefore comparison. Even if in this book, with the exception of two short works by Diderot, hardly a single philosophical dialogue is interpreted in toto, I harbor the hope that future complete interpretations of such dialogues will be able to make use of the categorial differentiations and case studies provided by this book.

Whitehead's famous remark that Western philosophy "consists of a series of footnotes to Plato" strikes many people as an exaggeration; but there is no doubt that it is true of the philosophical dialogue. No one who had access to Plato's works could have escaped his influence; even in the dark centuries his indirect influence can be seen. A book on the philosophical dialogue is thus inevitably also a book on the founder and greatest master of the genre. I wrote my first book about Plato, and this return to the philosopher who taught me what philosophy can be was a delightful experience. However, everyone who knows my earlier book will see how much my view of Plato has changed: my focus is now on the form of his dialogues, not their content, and thus on the early rather than the late dialogues. My awareness of how much in his philosophy belongs irremediably to the past has become clearer, but I am consoled by the certainty that no thinker has ever overcome the limits of his time as much as Plato did. Alongside Plato, Cicero (who is not an original thinker but is often a first-rate writer), and Augustine (whose Cassiciacum dialogues are particularly important for the inquiry pursued here), Hume and Diderot are heroes of this book, around whom numerous secondary figures are grouped.

After an introduction that is perhaps most innovative in seeking to use the categories of subjectivity and intersubjectivity to classify the plenitude of philosophy's modes of expression, this book is structured by the classical triad of the production, inner structure, and reception of the literary dialogue. The third part is deliberately left sketchy; the center of the book lies in the second part. That many of the categories of this second part apply to actual conversations no less than to the literary universe of philosophical dialogue not only explains why it is so detailed but also lends it a certain philosophical dignity.

It may be an excusable performative contradiction that this book does not itself take the form of a dialogue, but it would be inexcusable if it were not in large part indebted to conversations with teachers of literature and philosophy, students, friends, and colleagues. More than ever, the end of this preface must include thanks—to my father, Johannes Hösle, who introduced me early on to literary inquiry; to my teacher Imre Tóth, whose lectures on the philosophy of mathematics permanently shaped my approach to aesthetic issues; to my teacher Franz von Kutschera, whose systematic breadth and precision constantly spurred me on; to my teacher Dieter Wandschneider, without whose inexhaustible willingness to engage in conversation with me a quarter of a century ago I would not have found my philosophical way; to my teachers in Plato studies, Werner Beierwaltes, Konrad Gaiser, and Hans Krämer; to my friends and colleagues Pierre Adler, Wolfgang Braungart, Roland Galle, Rolf Geiger, Bernd Goebel, Bernd Gräfarth, Hans-Ulrich Gumbrecht, Jan-Lüder Hagens, Jens Halfwassen, Walter Haug, Christoph Horn, Christian Illies, Christoph Jermann, Friedhelm Marx, Walter Nicgorski, David O'Connor, Gretchen Reydams-Schils, Mark Roche, Kenneth Sayre, Péter Várdy, Matthias Wächter, Manfred Wetzel, Catherine Zuckert, and especially Dmitri Nikulin for many discussions on the subject of dialogue; to my students and colleagues who participated, in four seminars in Essen and Notre Dame on very different groups of philosophical dialogues, with expertise, intelligence, and enthusiasm (I am especially grateful to Andreas and Christian Spahn and Alfonso Flórez); to Nora Kreft, who as "Nora K." awakened me to the aesthetic potentialities of the dialogue in an epistolary conversation that went on for several years; and to the Erasmus Institute of the University of Notre Dame, at which I was able to begin thinking about this book during two research-leave semesters in 2001 and 2002. Writing the book, because of the difficulty of its subject, has taken far longer than I then thought it would. It was completed in 2004–5 during a year spent as a member of the Institute for Advanced Study in Princeton, which is probably in our own time the academic institution that in its universality and in the cultivation of space for independent thought, lively discussion, and civilized intellectual community most closely corresponds to the Platonic Academy. The friendliness and efficiency of the librarians Karen Downing, Gabriella Hoskin, Marcia Tucker, and Kirstie Venanzi, who met even my most recondite needs, were exceptional. I thank especially the ancient historian Glen Bowersock, the medievalist Caroline W. Bynum, the Islamic Studies scholar Patricia Crone, the sinologist Nicola Di Cosimo, the historian of science Noah Efron, the assyriologist Andrew George, the philosopher Hilary Gatti, the historian of science Peter Harrison, the physicist Piet Hut, the historian Jonathan Israel, the sinologist Thomas Jansen, the medievalist Joel Kaye, the historian of theology Yannis Papadoyannakis, the educationist Marisa Trigari, the classical philologist Heinrich von Staden, the political scientist Michael Walzer, the philosopher Morton White, the classical philologist Christian Wildberg, and the Egyptologist Katharina Zinn for all they have taught me and for their encouragement, which have made this book less inadequate than it would otherwise have been. In particular, Jonathan Israel's willingness to engage in discussion had Socratic dimensions and would be worthy of being preserved in a dialogue; without his help I could hardly have found the right approach to the eighteenth century. My greatest thanks, however, go to my wife, Jieon Kim, and our children, Johannes and Paul, who have supported me during this time with their daily conversation, which is not only the foundation of every family culture but ultimately also of every dialogue.

I am very grateful to Steven Rendall, who translated this book only a few years after its publication in German (2006), as with *Morals and Politics* doing a great job. I revised his translation carefully and decided not to integrate later secondary literature (only referring to some newer articles of mine when they clarified some points left vague in the book). I owe a particular debt to the University of Notre Dame for having financed with great generosity this translation, which I hope will prove useful to both philosophers and literary critics in the English-speaking world.

This book is dedicated to the memory of an intelligent and just man with whom it was always fascinating to converse, my beloved uncle Josef Hösle.

Introduction

Someone who describes the Pantheon, the *Boy with Thorn,* the frescoes of the Villa dei Misteri, Beethoven's Opus 111, Propertius's elegies, or Fellini's *E la nave va* (And the Ship Sails On) is often doing something useful, and occasionally indispensable, but he makes himself absolutely ridiculous if he claims that anyone who has read his descriptions no longer needs to see, listen to, or read these works of art. And this remains true even if nothing can be added to these descriptions, which is scarcely humanly possible. This has to do with the fact that the es-sence of a work of art consists not only in the satisfaction of conceptual thought but also of one of our senses or at least of the imagination, and that is precisely what cannot be done by the critic, who can never com-pete with his object. Wölfflin was not a painter, nor was Hanslick a composer. The case of the literary critic is somewhat different, how-ever, since he may sometimes succeed in producing first-class literature himself that either implicitly or explicitly competes with the work de-scribed. Plato's *Phaedrus* and Cicero's *De oratore* come to mind; they are not only significant philosophical analyses of oratory but also, seen from a rhetorical point of view, themselves first-rate; analogously, Frie-drich Schlegel's *Gespräch über die Poesie* (Conversation on Poetry) can itself claim to have poetic quality.[1] This implies that it will never be possible to describe these writings in such a way that reading them directly does not hold in store mental experiences that cannot be replaced by any summary and analysis, no matter how good.

The three works mentioned above are philosophical in nature, and that means that there are at least a few philosophical works that must be enjoyed as works of art, that is, to which justice is not rendered if only their argumentative content is analyzed.[2] To be sure, philosophical texts differ from other texts in the specific kind of truth claim they make, which is more direct and oriented toward verification through argumentative analysis than are works of art in the narrower sense (i.e., excluding philosophical texts), and certainly any intercourse with philosophical works goes radically off-track if it does not take seriously this special truth claim. It is also correct to say that there are philosophical texts in which the aesthetic dimension is minimal. In fact, every intersubjectively verifiable contribution to philosophy is necessarily formulated in language, and often in writing. To that extent, every contribution to philosophy observes the norms of linguistic communication, and at least some specifically aesthetic norms — such as clarity and density — also guide, at least in a diminished form, everyday communication. And yet it is incontestable that the aesthetic value of, say, Aristotle's *Metaphysics,* even the parts of it that avoid hiatus, is not very high. But that does not hold for all philosophical works; some philosophers have been first-rate writers, and a few have even been poets. This aesthetic quality of their works calls for an appropriate analysis that, as I have said, will in theory never be able to replace the theoretical analysis, but which the latter also does not make superfluous. We can speak of a *complementary* relationship between the two[3] — just as in a very analogous way works on political philosophy can

---

1. "Thus we can really speak of poetry only in poetry" (Schlegel 1967; 285). Ludoviko's plan to present in verse a system of false poetry (290) is thus superfluous, since in Schegel poetry does not presuppose verse — philosophical dialogues belong to the category of poetry (293, 304).

2. Conversely, there are also literary works in which philosophical ideas and discussions play an important role; for example, Schiller's philosophical poems or Musil's *Die Verwirrungen des Zöglings Törless;* however, in my book they are not thematic. Cf., e.g., C. Schildknecht and D. Teichert (1996).

3. The term plays a role in the important works of G. Gabriel; see, e.g., (1997).

be analyzed with regard to both their truth claims and their function in a political debate. Both kinds of observation are legitimate, but may also disregard each other, time and again. For example, both historians of philosophy and political historians have to read Cicero's *De republica;* the former will attend more to the arguments, the latter more to the function of these arguments in the political conflicts of the late Roman republic.

And yet the situation is even more complex and more interesting when the separation of the two modes of observation does not function properly. To return to my initial example of the complementarity of the - oretical and aesthetic observation, it becomes impossible to separate the two if without an aesthetic analysis the correct understanding of the philosophical work is impossible. This holds for various philosophical works belonging to entirely different genres. For instance, stylistic devices are used to show that certain thoughts are central; often they are an expression of a specific attitude, a life-feeling, only against the background of which certain arguments can be rightly understood. It is probably no accident that it is precisely philosophical revolutionaries like Heraclitus or Nietzsche who break with centuries-old tradition and write in a stylistically exciting way, which we would not claim of someone like Thomas Aquinas, who saw himself as part of a tradition. The attraction of Wittgenstein's *Tractatus,* without which its success among readers incapable of understanding its logical propositions cannot be explained, is also and precisely stylistic in nature; combining a logical order reminiscent of Spinoza with an aphoristic formulation reminiscent of Nietzsche, it is not only extremely original, but a splendid counterpart to its programmatic content, logical atomism, as well as to an extraordinary mastery of formal logic that simultaneously recognizes that very little can be grasped with logic alone.

This claim, that the argumentative analysis of a philosophical text is dependent on aesthetic considerations, holds particularly true for philosophical dialogues. Why? Because at least a significant number of philosophical dialogues—namely, those in which the author of the text is himself not one of the interlocutors—confront the reader with important hermeneutic problems. The author speaks in them in a way different from the way he speaks in a treatise, that is, not in the first person;[4] and before we analyze and evaluate his arguments, which cannot be simply identified with those of an interlocutor, we have to find out what the author actually wants to say.[5] Discovering this is not always easy, any more than it is easy to discover Shakespeare's own moral convictions—no matter how obvious it is that it is clearly not a good idea to attribute to him Richard III's or Lear's statements as his own just because he wrote them.[6] In reconstructing the theses to be attributed to a philosopher, and not solely to his literary creations, aesthetic tact is not the only condition, but it is an indispensable one, and anyone who lacks it will seldom correctly understand, even if he has great logical abilities, the arguments made by a philosopher writing a dialogue, because what he is analyzing is precisely not the argument, or at least not the complete argument, of the philosopher concerned.

Thus we have already determined a central reason why, in the framework of a literary theory of philosophy the philosophical dialogue plays an especially important role—especially important because in this case literary theory is relevant to philosophy in the strict sense. In order to explain more clearly what I mean by "philosophical dialogue," in the following I shall first deal with the specific traits of philosophical dialogue

4. The Greek term is *autoprosōpos;* cf. Luc. *JTr.* 29 and especially Ammon. *in Cat.* 4.14 ff. Busse, where, within Aristotle's syntagmatic writings, *dialogika* are distinguished from *autoprosōpa.* On this, see C. Sigonio (1993), 124. However, the term is misleading insofar as Aristotle appears in his own dialogues. By "in the first person," I refer not so much to the grammatical form as to the nature of the speech act, namely that the author himself seeks to assert something directly. Chapter 36 of Justin's *First Apology* is important in this regard: he interprets the prophets as masks of God and in explanation refers to pagan writers who are themselves the authors of the whole work but present several masks that converse with one another: *hena men ton ta panta suggraphonta onta, prosōpa de ta dialegomena parapheronta.*

Abbreviations of the Greek classics are given according to the list in H. G. Liddell and R. Scott, *A Greek-English Lexicon* (Oxford, 1961).

5. It is well known that the division of literary forms into authorial speech and character speech goes back to Plato (*R.* 392c ff.); see below, Part II, chap. 9. On the later history of this division see, e.g., P. von Moos (1997), 242 ff.

6. Cf. J.-J. Rousseau (1999), 157 ff. This situation may however lead one to deny a dramatist aesthetic views, for example, that are in fact his own: "My dear fellow, whatever you may say, it is merely a dramatic utterance, and no more represents Shakespeare's real views upon art than the speeches of Iago represent his real views upon morals," Vivian says to Cyril in Oscar Wilde's dialogue *The Decay of Lying* (1966; 981 f.).

in contrast to other literary forms of philosophy, its special status among them. Second, I shall distinguish the philosophical dialogue as a literary genre from actual philosophical conversation, and as a philosophical literary genre from nonphilosophical literary dialogues. Third and finally, I shall explain the connection between literary form and philosophical content in the philosophical dialogue.

CHAPTER 1

The Place of Philosophical Dialogue among the Literary Forms of Philosophy

A comprehensive literary analysis of philosophical texts must concentrate on their various linguistic building blocks—for example, on the choice of words, the use of rhetorical figures (among which metaphor deserves special interest), syntax, the arrangement of individual arguments, and the architectonics of the work as a whole. Of special importance, however, is the question to which genre the work concerned belongs, because the answer to it almost always has consequences for the analysis of the other questions.[1] Even if a text is composed of words, the choice of the words is influenced by the intention that guides the work as a whole; and as a rule this holistic intention selects the genre before it selects the individual words. Someone writing a philosophical didactic poem will use a style different from the one used by someone writing an essay—even though it may happen that an author decides on a certain genre because he is strongly attracted to the corresponding style. But that does not alter the fact that the choice of a specific genre is more general than, for example, the choice to use specific metaphors; it is, so to speak, the frame within which further decisions must be made,

---

1. My text (2005a) has been incorporated into this chapter, considerably abbreviated because of the differing context but also expanded.

precisely because it is not compatible with certain requirements. Someone dealing with works as different as Lucretius's *De rerum natura,* Des -
cartes's *Meditations,* or Plato's *Laches* can do them justice and understand them properly only if he recognizes the genre to which each of
them belongs.

A theory of philosophical genres may seem obsolete at a time when
there is a deep-seated mistrust of genre theories of any kind.[2] Certainly
twentieth-century critics have been skeptical about the nineteenth century's ingenious attempts at a theory of genres.[3] The grounds for this
skepticism are many and can be only touched upon here; but they must
be mentioned because without a brief discussion of them my adherence
to genre-theory categories might be branded as anachronistic. The uneasiness about genre theories has three roots. First, knowledge about
literature grew enormously during the twentieth century, also because
non-European cultures were taken into account. In view of this growth,
continuing to adhere, for example, to one of the most influential and
probably most complex theories of genre, that of Hegel, which sees epic,
lyric, and drama as the basic forms of literature, might easily be seen as
provincial and old-fashioned. The obvious objection to Hegel's theory is
that it is nothing more than a hypostatization of the contingent development of Greek literature. However, this objection is often made by literary scholars whose knowledge of the non-European world remains, despite the birth of entirely new cultural disciplines in the second half of
the nineteenth and in the twentieth century, considerably less extensive
than Hegel's was; but the anti-Eurocentric moral motive that drives it is
absolutely respectable. (I note in passing that it is still more respectable
when it is not connected, as it often is in many forms of postmodern intellectuality, with an anti-universalist position on the basis of which the
justification for the criticism of Eurocentrism is not easy to understand.)
Second, it is said that genre has repeatedly served to fetter poetic production, while significant and original literature is allegedly characterized by a break with typical generic norms. Third, however, criticism
of genre theory is in accord with the fundamental rejection of so-called

2. This uneasiness is already found in early Romanticism; it is described and
discussed in Schlegel's *Gespräch über die Poesie* (1967; 305 ff., 336 f.).
3. See, e.g., the essay collection by M. Dambre and M. Gosselin-Noat (2001).

essentialism in twentieth-century mainstream philosophy. It is at least as much a product of this rejection as it is a result of empirical discoveries.

Someone who analyzes the categories that dominate individual periods in the history of cultural studies will find that as a rule they do not emerge inductively from empirical research done by the scholars involved. For then it would amount on the one hand to an overgeneralization that could never be justified, and on the other hand it would be easy to explain causally why reference to a comprehensive category is recommendable on grounds of the politics of scholarship: it enhances the status of one's own work insofar as it relates it to something general, sometimes to the highest goals of humanity (the continuation of the narrative of the end of all great narratives may be among these goals); and it forms a banner under which academic alliances (e.g., the well-known "citation cartels") can be formed and attract the attention of the public to themselves. Discourse or Difference/Otherness are such concepts, and they function, as the pentagram did in ancient times, as interdisciplinary signs of recognition and even academic brand names around which scholars in the social sciences and cultural studies gather.

However, this merely shows that we cannot get along without categories. The question is not *if* categories should be used but *which* system of categories is most appropriate, and it is not obvious that difference is a more differentiating category than, for instance, the system of categories used by the essentialist tradition to which can be said to belong—especially for a philosophical study of literature—Plato, Aristotle, and Hegel, the canonical guiding figures of the present investigation. There is certainly a danger that in the night of that one category "difference" all cows will become black, because the mediating concepts that actually constitute the specific object under investigation disappear from view. But without concepts nothing is knowable; and the alleged upgrading of the individual through phrases such as "individuum est ineffabile" turns out in fact to be a disservice, because we cannot value positively what we do not know.[4] Thus it is surely correct that the conceptual framework established by nineteenth-century genre theory was too crude. But the sensible

4. A clever defense of the indispensability of conceptual knowledge even and especially in dealing with the individual is found in J. McDowell (1994), 56 ff., 104 ff.

reaction to it can only consist in developing a system of categories that is both more comprehensive and more fine-meshed, not in rejecting efforts to construct such a system. "While literature may move away from the old genres, it cannot move away from genre altogether without ceasing to be literature. It would neither communicate with readers nor have leverage on existing values."[5] Furthermore, in order to be appropriately interpreted, breaks with genres presuppose precisely the genres from which they distinguish themselves; and if a break with a genre is really significant, its greatest accomplishment will be only to contribute to the emergence of a new subgenre.[6] Aesthetic norms that are genre-specific, and in particular metrical norms, are, like most common norms, only prima facie norms subject to the supervision of higher principles; and thus just as we can be ironic, that is, say something untrue in order to cause someone to discover the truth himself, so can and should we deviate from iambic rhythm in order to make the reader feel the spurting-up of a jet of water, as C. F. Meyer does in his poem "Römischer Brunnen." But only someone who is familiar with iambic rhythms will feel it.

Does this mean a return to essentialism? That depends on how essentialism is defined. Here it will have to suffice to observe that the concept of natural kinds is a reasonable and even inevitable one.[7] Indeed, it is plausible that natural kinds can be defined only in relation to a systematic theory, but that is not a bad thing, insofar as one theory proves to be better than the alternatives, for instance, because it is simpler and has greater explanatory power. To give an example of a systematic theory that has made a decisive contribution to the general sense that there is a crisis of essentialism: the gradualism of the Darwinian theory of evolution has profoundly altered taxonomy, but it is hard to believe that the concept of species, or indeed all higher categories such as genera, and so on, should be regarded as arbitrary constructions.[8] For instance,

5. A. Fowler (1982), 278.

6. Cf. T. Todorov's excellent essay "L'origine des genres" (1987; 27–46), to which I owe much. Goethe anticipated this: 10.160 f.

7. See T. E. Wilkerson (1995).

8. Cf. E. Mayr 1997, 124 ff., esp. 131, in opposition to the nominalistic concept of species.

"bird" is a concept more fertile for biology than the one obviously ready-made for human needs: "animal comestible by humans." Analogously, for literary criticism "drama" is a natural and even indispensable concept, whereas "literary work consisting of more than two hundred thousand signs" is an artificial construct that might perhaps be useful in certain contexts but is not indispensable, if only because the limit drawn is arbitrary. Similarly, "tragedy" and "comedy" can be seen as genre concepts indispensable for literary studies, especially since this does not mean that there could not also be intermediate forms, and perhaps even a synthesis of the two.[9] In any case we have to distinguish not only genres but also modes such as "comic" and "tragic," because there are clearly comic novels. The naturalness of this classification does not depend solely on the fact that in Athens, for example, the two kinds of dramas were performed in different contexts and that none of the Greek dramatists wrote both comedies and tragedies. To be sure, such facts must be considered; social institutions' self-interpretations cannot be ignored by those who seek to understand them philosophically. But they are also not an ultimate criterion, because such facts vary culturally—which is shown, for instance, by the fact that in the modern period there are certainly writers who have written both comedies and tragedies. Moreover, in Athens the satyr play was institutionally connected with tragedy, because the tragic tension demanded relief (just as in the circus the clowns follow the acrobats); yet in a taxonomy of drama there is much to be said for classifying the satyr play with comedy, because both these forms of Greek drama, unlike tragedy, have to do with the anthropological constant of laughter.

How does one develop a plausible system of concepts? The empiricist view that concepts can be simply abstracted from reality is obviously a nonstarter: first of all, our minds are not passive with respect to reality; second, reality can be perceived only because it has already been categorized; and third, there are criteria that are immanent to thought, that is, not derived from experience, that make one conceptual classification appear simpler, for instance, than the conceivable alternatives. Even if the empirical view of concepts were correct, the problem of whether a con-

9. For a discussion of the *Versöhnungsdrama* (drama of reconciliation) already adumbrated in Hegel, cf. V. Hösle (1984b) and M. Roche (1997), 247 ff.

ceptual classification is complete or whether new concepts could in principle always be added to it would remain unresolved. When it is possible to do so, it is much more satisfactory to derive the individual subspecies of a concept from the possible combinations of basic concepts—then and only then can an integral whole be provided instead of an aggregate to which we can add at will. It is no argument against the plausibility of a conceptual system constructed in this way that often it is not fully instantiated everywhere. To return to genre theory: the notion that drama is a conceptually necessary category of literature is not contradicted by the fact that there are literatures in the world that have no drama. This shows only that drama has an especially complex set of presuppositions (it is a secondary speech genre, to use Mikhail Bakhtin's terminology); and this suggests the normative judgment that having a developed dramatic literature is one—but certainly not the only—criterion for judging the rank of the corresponding culture.

How can we best classify the literary genres of philosophy, and what place does philosophical dialogue occupy within them? Each philosophical work inevitably has three properties: it deals with one or more philosophical *themes;* it is written by one or more *authors,* whose view of the world claims to discover something new; and it is addressed to an *audience* that is supposed to be persuaded by this view, or at least to come to grips with it. These three aspects can easily be interpreted as manifestations of the fundamental philosophical categories of objectivity, subjectivity, and intersubjectivity; but this "upward" connection will not be explored in greater detail here. Instead, I will seek to connect it "downward," with the concrete genres. The differences between philosophical genres depend on which of these three properties is accented. Accordingly, we can speak of a "genre of objectivity," a "genre of subjectivity," and a "genre of intersubjectivity," depending on whether the object of philosophy, the producing subjectivity, or another subjectivity is foregrounded.[10] The claim of a classification grounded in this way is to represent all the decisive fundamental types, but I do not want to exclude the existence

---

10. C. Schildknecht (1990) discusses—without attempting to derive them—four forms, two of which I subsume under the "Genre of Objectivity": the dialogic form of philosophy (Plato), the monologic form (Descartes), the textbook form (Wolff), and the aphoristic form (Lichtenberg).

of further subspecies besides those discussed only as examples in the following. I would expressly point out that subspecies of one group may be connected with subspecies of another group, or with other subspecies of the same group: speeches can be embedded in a dialogue—think of Plato's *Symposium*—and dialogues can be inserted in an essay—think of Hume's two *Enquiries;* or conversation partners can undertake a critical commentary on a work, as for instance in Paul Feyerabend's "First Dialogue on Knowledge." And yet as a rule we can clearly see what the primary makeup of the text is: Feyerabend's work, as its title suggests, is first of all a philosophical dialogue; Leibniz's "Nouveaux essais sur l'entendement" is primarily a critical analysis of another work, and its dialogic form is, at least in the later parts, more or less pasted onto it.

1. Since philosophy differs from the individual branches of knowledge through its indispensable relation to the whole of being, the first subform of the genre of objectivity is surely the *philosophical system.* (Related is the philosophical encyclopedia, which resembles a system in its outward form, since the sequence of explanations is in this case not determined by a connection with their content but by the alphabet.) The system, which is essentially a modern genre, has evolved from the *philosophical didactic poem,* the most intellectual offspring of epic. Although the first Greek philosophical texts, those of the Milesians or Heraclitus, were written in prose, in a world in which education consisted essentially in appropriating the epic tradition, the didactic poem, such as those composed by Parmenides, Empedocles, and Lucretius, was an obvious way of imitating and at the same time undermining the traditional education. The contrast between the versified form and the conceptual content could lead to tensions: for example, Aristotle denies that Empedocles was a poet, claiming that he was a natural philosopher who had nothing in common with Homer but meter, which did not suffice to make him a poet.[11] But it is not just that true poetry may suffer in the poetic-philosophical mixture of the didactic poem, especially when the didactic poet has to communicate a worldview according to which all the beauties of nature, which he is able to describe in a way few others can rival, are nothing but

---

11. *Poetics* 1447b17 ff. A milder judgment is found in *Peri poiētōn*, frg. 1 Ross, where Empedocles' use of metaphor is praised.

accidental conjunctions of atoms, so that the real message of the work undermines any poetry, indeed, when the founder of the philosophy to be communicated by the poem was even hostile to poetry.[12] This may hold even for the philosophical content if, for example, the formal language of the epic suggests saying things that the philosopher actually wants to deny.[13] Because of this tension, the unshakable unity of the epic that Lukács lauds in some of his finest pages[14] does not characterize the philosophical didactic poem to the same extent as it does the poetic genre to which it is heir. And yet the didactic poem shares the epic's trust in the firmly established order of the world, within which the individual has to find his place. The individual is thematic only as part of the world, not insofar as it constitutes the world of epic or the didactic poem poetically or philosophically; and the problem of how to communicate the perspectives of different individuals does not yet really arise for him. The same holds as well for the great systems of modern times, those of Spinoza, Hegel, and Schopenhauer. It is hardly an accident that the ontology of all three of these systems is monist: true being is substance, the absolute idea, the will, and the individual is an object of the system only as its mode or accident.[15] In fact, with the loss of the poetry of the didactic poem and the emergence of "the thing itself," philosophizing individuality recedes entirely into the background; Spinoza and Hegel hardly refer to themselves, whereas Parmenides at least speaks about himself in the

12. Cf. M. R. Gale (2001), 16 ff. It is rather poignant that right in the middle of the work Lucretius nonetheless tries to provide a kind of pedagogical legitimacy for his enterprise (4.10 ff.)—as if it needed one.

13. Consider Xenophanes, whose only god is the greatest among gods and men (DK 21 B 23). On the other hand, in his proem, Parmenides refers, even if in an entirely different linguistic code, to themes that anticipate the content of divine revelation; see L. Ruggiu (1975), 9 ff., esp. 45 ff.

14. Lukács (1971), 21 ff.

15. *E contrario,* so to speak, through his failure, Spinoza shows his inability to practice the genre of dialogue in the two short dialogues (one between two personifications, the other between two individuals, Erasmus and Theophilus) at the end of the second chapter of the first part of the *Korte verhandelung van God, de mensch en des zelfs welstand* (*Opera* I 28–34). One of the very few passages in which a somewhat dialogic element appears in Hegel is §140 f. in the *Rechtsphilosophie* (7.279), where Hegel imitates modern ironists, and precisely where they address others. But Hegel does not speak in the first person.

proem to his didactic poem—but attributes legitimating power to the revealing divinity, not to himself.

Although the role of subjectivity is not yet itself an explicit subject of discussion, it inevitably increases in the subgenres of objectivity that have freed themselves from the system's claim to totality. The focus on one part of reality or on a single problem of philosophy also results from factors transcending the subject, such as the state of research; however, the individual inclination and talent of the philosophizing subject always plays a significant role. Depending on their scope, we can distinguish among the nontotalizing forms of objectivity the treatise, the inquiry, and the essay. A characteristic increase in the importance of the subjectivity factor is manifested in the genre of a collection of essays by a single author, in which a unifying factor, though only in the least satisfying cases the sole one, is the fact that they were all written by the same person. In Montaigne's special version of the essay the subjectivity of the writing philosopher is evident not only in the selection of themes and in the associative style but also in the increasing thematization of the thinker's own personality.

The form that most fully frees itself from the relation to the whole inherent in the claim to objectivity is the aphorism, which is given life by the individual style and characteristic idiosyncrasies of its author. And yet we are dealing with philosophical aphorisms only when the individual fragment calls upon the reader to fundamentally revise his relationship to the world, when the individual paradoxical remark requires him to distance himself from his own prejudices, usually in matters of morals. A single example may suffice: "Money is never more profitably used than when we allow ourselves to be cheated of it: for then we have traded it directly for prudence."[16] The statement seems at first almost self-contradictory, but the explanation after the colon draws our attention to the fact that in the long term no investment is as wise as an investment in one's own intelligence, and especially that certain insights can be gained *only* through painful personal experience. The melancholy of the second reason even points beyond the sphere of eudaemonist prudence—to which Schopenhauer sought to limit his *Aphorismen zur Lebensweisheit* (*The Wisdom of Life*)—toward the pessimism of his magnum opus.

16. A. Schopenhauer (1977), VIII 507 (= *Aphorismen zur Lebensweisheit* V 43).

2. It is tempting to begin the forms of subjectivity with a philosopher's notebook, because this kind of text, which is generally not intended for publication, serves primarily to clarify one's own thoughts, to sketch out publication plans and attacks on opponents that pull no punches. However, no matter how important this genre may be for the historian of philosophy, because it allows him to reconstruct the individual genesis of the work that will later appear in objective autonomy, as a rule the author does not thematize himself in them. That occurs in the philosophical journal, which cannot always be clearly distinguished from the notebook, but in which what is central is not so much sketches for projects as the observation of one's own stream of consciousness. An important subform of the genre of subjectivity is the meditation. It originated in the Middle Ages—for instance, Anselm's *Meditations*—but it reached its philosophical high point in the modern period, or more precisely with Descartes. Psychologically, the meditation is concerned not with observing one's own consciousness but with using it in a concentrated way to solve a problem. What characterizes, from a literary point of view, Descartes's *Medi-tationes de prima philosophia*? The answer is easy: most of the sentences have one or more verbal or pronominal forms in the first-person singular. The first word of the first meditation is *animadverti* (I became aware) and the first sentence has no fewer than five verb forms in the first-person singular. Not until the fourteenth sentence[17] do we find one in which no such form is found—although there is a verb in the first-person *plural (somniemus)*. The next sentence is the first that, like the two following ones, lacks any form in the first person; then there follow six more sentences with such (first-person) "meditative" forms; then again one without such a form; finally seven more with such forms. In the second and crucial meditation, this primacy of first-person forms is still more marked: it virtually swarms with first-person forms; and except for a few short sentences (eleven words at most) there are only two sentences without them.[18] All these "nonmeditative" sentences use verb forms in the third person; in the first two meditations there are no verbal and pronominal forms in the second person, while they can be found in the dedicatory

17. Even though after "negari?" (VII 18, 26), Charles Adam and Paul Tannery do not capitalize "nisi," I count the clause it introduces as a separate sentence.
18. VII 32, 21–23; 33, 26–29.

epistle to the members of the Sorbonne's theological faculty. The *Meditations* are as far removed from the self-forgetfulness of the system as they are from the courting of others that characterizes the third, intersubjective, genre. Since the *Meditations'* contribution to world history is the establishment of a new type of philosophy that seeks an unshakable foundation in subjectivity, the choice of the first person is naturally a deliberate stylistic one. Descartes's disinclination with regard to dialogue goes so far that even the forms of monologue are absent from his work,[19] whereas they so strikingly characterize a work like Wittgenstein's *Philosophical Investigations,* in which the author constantly carries on a conversation with himself, as it were, dividing himself and making possible objections to himself.[20] I will limit myself here to two well-known examples. "What is your aim in philosophy?—To shew the fly the way out of the fly-bottle" (I 309). The question of the fictive interlocutor, who is in fact part of the reflecting self, does not appear here between quotation marks, but the latter are used in I 307: "'Are you not really a behaviourist in disguise? Aren't you at bottom really saying that everything except human behaviour is a fiction?'—If I do speak of a fiction, then it is of a *grammatical* fiction."[21] The content of the second remark is directed against the type of philosophy that sees introspection as the privileged form of knowledge; and it makes sense that a methodological solipsist like Descartes—but not someone who helped found the "linguistic turn" and defends the impossibility of a private language—abhors the presence of the other so much that in his foundational text not even a fictive "you" is allowed to appear.[22]

The specifically human ability to relate to oneself as to another subject is also the basis for another subgenre of subjectivity—the philosophical autobiography, in which it is not the abstract "I" of the meditation but

19. A weak form of self-reference is found in the Second Meditation: "mihi persuasi" (VI 25, 2).

20. Cf. J. Heal (1995).

21. Wittgenstein (1980), 406 f.

22. The objectivist variant of the questioning, in which a reflection on one's own subject or another subject usually no longer occurs, even if the answered questions were sometimes really asked by others, is found in the so-called *erōtapokriseis* (the term goes back to twelfth-century Greek grammarians), that is, question-and-answer literature, a form that was favored by early Christian writers—for instance, by Ambrosiaster—and also played a major role in the Middle Ages. See A. Volgers and C. Zamagni (2004).

rather the concrete personality of the philosopher, and particularly its development, that is foregrounded—explicitly thematized, as is not the case in that of the journal, and at the same time in a form transcending the purely subjective that is seldom more genuine but sometimes more true than the journal, because it reveals general laws in the particular. A thinker's development cannot be described without reference to other people, because even if the reflecting "I" is able to conceive itself as an absolute, it has only become an absolute in the course of a life; its autonomy is something that has been achieved, not a given. However, it is no accident that in his *Discours* Descartes hardly acknowledges the significance of other people or traditions for his own development; and that Vico, in his *Vita . . . scritta da se medesimo*, protests against this fiction of a completely new intellectual beginning, partly explicitly and partly by elaborating an alternative kind of philosophical autobiography, gives his work its standing.

3. We can understand others only because we can mentally put ourselves in their position; indeed, even the user of a private language—whose existence can at least not be excluded on transcendental philosophical grounds—can be legitimately convinced to adopt a position in a conversation with himself only if he has thoroughly examined the objections to it. Real intersubjectivity functions only because the subject can replicate himself, see himself from the outside; but this ability is itself increased and refined by interaction with real other people. In the genre of intersubjectivity the other is an explicit and not merely implicit theme—at least the other is implicit if a work is addressed to other people; and even Descartes published his *Meditations*. An obvious subdivision of the genre of intersubjectivity might be made on the basis of whether the other is thematic in the third person, as in the commentary, or if he is—as in real or fictional speeches, sermons, lectures, personal letters, or, in the case of God, in philosophical prayers—addressed in the second person[23] or speaks "in his own voice," that is, in the first person, as

---

23. Sometimes this form is imposed from the outside on a work that is in reality a treatise, as the writer of the treatise on style *(Peri hermēneias)*, attributed to Demetrius Phalereus, already noticed about some pseudo-epistles (*Eloc.* 228; cf. Sigonio [1993], 130). Think, e.g., of E. Burke's *Reflections on the Revolution in France*. On the other hand, Anselm's *Proslogion* is essentially a prayer.

it were. But how can another person speak in the first person? In the literal sense, that is naturally impossible; it is (or rather: "it am") always only I who speaks in the first person. But I can allow others to speak in the first person by creating a literary universe in which I speak as the other, putting on his mask, as it were. The commentator often identifies himself with the master whom he is explaining; but in literary terms he must use the third person: "Gorgias writes that *p*." The linguistic distancing disappears, however, as soon as I deliver a speech or write a text as if I were Gorgias—for example, in a play or in a philosophical dialogue. This technique is obviously compatible with objective distancing, and can even express the latter to great extent. The ability to play the role of another, which is anthropologically rooted in the doubling of the (active) "I" and the (given) self, is often motivated by the Me, that is, the perception of the other's expectations. But it can also be enjoyed as an end in itself.[24] Without this ability there would be no theater, and also no philosophical dialogue. However, it is only a necessary, not a sufficient condition of the philosophical dialogue—because it is already exercised when I pretend to give the speech of another person, for instance. If Plato's *Menexenos* consisted solely of the speech attributed to Aspasia, it would remain a masterpiece; but it would not be a philosophical dialogue, just as his *Apology* is not one either. A dialogue involves at least two persons who speak with one another. A form of intersubjectivity is thus present not only in the creation of a literary universe by the writer of the dialogue, who must put himself in the place of another person; intersubjectivity is an essential element in the created literary universe itself. Intersubjectivity, we can say, both transcends the work and is immanent in it; it manifests itself both in the real relationship between the author and his literary creations, into which he breathes life, and in the ideal relationship between the fictional persons who people his literary construct and who speak to each other in the second person.

24. Cf. V. Hösle (1997), 320 ff.

CHAPTER 2

Conversation and Dialogue

Historical and Fictional Dialogue—Chat and Discussion— Philosophical and Nonphilosophical Dialogue

The objection to the preceding explanations is obvious: unlike a real exchange of letters, dialogue really has nothing to do with actual intersubjectivity.[1] The intersubjective relationships immanent in the work are purely fictional, and the relation between an author and his creation is merely a reveling in his own subjectivity, and certainly not anything intersubjective. Two responses can be made to this objection. First, even the relation between an important author and his literary work is not simply subjectively imaginary: what distinguishes the literary work from day or night dreams is not only that it emerges from the mind in external form but also that it meets demands that the writer experiences as inexorable. He cannot do just anything he wishes but is instead drawn on, as it were, by a *noēma* that he seeks to make clearer and clearer, but that preexists him—preexists not in the social world but in an ideal world. The relation between the author and his literary creations is thus only in a very limited sense analogous to that between an omnipotent

---

1. When Artemon calls the letter one of the two sides of a dialogue (Demetr. *Eloc.* 223), he confuses conversation and dialogue.

voluntarist God and a world that could be as it is or entirely different. The author can invent different literary universes, and as a rule he does, and in working on each universe there is a certain degree of freedom right at the beginning. But the smaller this degree of freedom, the greater the artistic value of the work. Sophocles' Antigone is not who she is because the poet made her so. He wrote his tragedy as he wrote it because he felt that it would best do justice to the *noēma* (whose content is the woman) that must have once enthralled him when he studied other representations of the mythical figure. He took the liberty of changing the myth, but precisely only because by making such changes he could do greater justice to the essence of this woman. This essence is seen with special clarity in her interactions with other characters in the drama (among these interactions in the broader sense of the word is also the absence of an explicit reference, for example, to Haemon); and to that extent the other fictional characters also participate in the necessity of the main character.

It might be objected that this necessity restricts the freedom of the creative artist; but it does not cancel the fictive nature of his characters. Sophocles' relation to Antigone is an intersubjective one only if one uses a so-called free logic as a base and grants that a *relatum* in such a relationship is a fictional subject; the relationship between Antigone and Ismene is intersubjective only if both *relata* can be fictional persons. The objection is doubtless relevant; and the problems some writers have with relationships in real life are perhaps an expression of this ontologically central difference. And yet this necessity that a significant literary universe has inevitably points to real intersubjectivity. One of its consequences is precisely that these characters and their relationships can be experienced as plausible by other real people, whom the writer inevitably addresses as his audience; and they were also plausible for the writer himself, partly because they reflected experiences of his own. Catullus's *Liber* is not a record of his love experiences; but he would never have been able to write his book had he not loved, and it could hardly have succeeded had others not loved.

In an entirely analogous way, there would be no philosophical dialogue if conversational philosophizing were not a social reality as familiar to the author of the dialogue as to his readers. The *logos Sōkratikos* does not represent any actual conversation of Socrates, and yet without his unfailing willingness to engage in conversation this genre would not have come into being.[2] Cicero really conversed with Quintus and Atticus, as did Gregory with Macrina, Augustine with Alypius, Licentius, and Trygetius, Anselm with Boso, Nicolas of Cusa with Peter of Erkelenz, Ficino with Cavalcanti, Galileo with Sagredo and Salviati, Diderot with d'Alembert and the French marshal's wife, and these conversations are echoed in their dialogues, and conversely, the decline of a philosophical culture of conversation is one of the causes of the crisis in philosophical dialogue. Even if for that reason the words are often used as if they were synonymous, in this book I want to make a rigorous distinction between them: "dialogue" designates a literary genre, while "conversation" designates a direct social interaction. This distinction seems to approximate the one made by Joseph de Maistre in his not fully completed dialogue published posthumously in 1821, *Soirées de Saint-Pétersbourg ou Entretiens sur le gouvernement temporel de la providence* (Saint-Petersburg Evenings, or Discussions on the temporal government of Providence). In the eighth discussion the Chevalier de B*** describes dialogue as fiction: "As for *dialogue,* this word represents a mere fiction; for it supposes a conversation that never took place. It is a purely artificial work: hence one can write as many of them as one likes; it is a composition like any other, which emerges wholly formed like Minerva from the writer's brain, and dialogues of the *dead,* which have made more than one writer famous, are just as real, and even as probable, as those of living people published by other authors."[3] The speaker is a young Frenchman whom the French Revolution—out of enmity to

---

2. Whereas a scholar studying Socrates is primarily interested in Socrates' real conversations and in the Platonic dialogues only insofar as they might make it possible to reconstruct the real conversations, a scholar studying Plato is interested in these conversations because he wants to understand how Plato transformed them into dialogues.

3. (1850), II 93. "Quant au *dialogue,* ce mot ne représente qu'une fiction; car il suppose une conversation qui n'a jamais existé. C'est une oeuvre purement artificielle: ainsi on peut en écrire autant qu'on voudra; c'est une composition comme une autre, qui part toute formée comme Minerve, du cerveau de l'écrivain, et les dialogues des *morts,* qui ont illustré plus d'une plume, sont aussi réels, et même aussi probables, que ceux des vivants publiés par d'autres auteurs."

which de Maistre's whole philosophy springs—has driven to St. Petersburg, where de Maistre was the king of Sardinia's ambassador from 1803 to 1817 and where the conversation is supposed to have taken place in 1809. In addition to the author (who speaks as "the Count") and the Chevalier there is a third conversation partner who is a member of the St. Petersburg Senate. The eighth conversation begins with the Chevalier's announcement that he can offer his friends "le procès-verbal des séances précédentes,"[4] that is, a transcript of the preceding sessions, which his exceptional memory has allowed him to prepare each time before retiring and which he has revised the following morning. However, he has left a wide margin so that his friends can correct his record. The Count is skeptical about the project of publishing the transcript. It is true, he says, that conversation—as he calls it, following Plato's *Phaedrus* (275d ff.)—allows interruptions, questions, and explanations; but for that very reason it is less suited to publication. The Chevalier disagrees; that might be true for convivial chat *(conversation)* but not for a discussion on a specific subject *(entretien)*. Both chat and discussion must be distinguished from dialogue, which, as we have seen, represents a fiction and is a purely artificial work. The Chevalier says that he has recently read Cicero's *Tusculan Disputations,* "une oeuvre de pure imagination," a work of pure imagination, in which the participants are identified solely by initials—and that cannot be said about him and his friends, for they are very real. "Nous ne sommes point des lettres majuscules; nous sommes des êtres très réels, très palpables: nous parlons pour nous instruire et pour nous consoler" (We are not initials; we are very real beings, very palpable: we talk to learn and to console ourselves). The Senator laughs and asks whether the Chevalier is planning to write down this chat about chatting as well, even though doing so would only make his project of publication still more difficult. The Chevalier emphatically affirms that that is his intention, and the Senator finally concedes that publication could do no great harm, at least if the foreword contained nothing like what is found in the foreword to Locke's *Essay.*[5] A careful reader of this text easily sees that the

4. II 89.
5. II 96, with an allusion to I 369, where the Count had demolished Locke.

Chevalier seeks to distinguish not so much between conversation and dialogue—in the terms used in this book—as between different forms of dialogue, because he certainly does not want to describe either the real discussion or the written record of his discussion with his friends as "dialogue." However, it is difficult not to see de Maistre's irony here; he himself is the author of his book, which was not edited by a real counterpart of the Chevalier.[6] The depreciation of dialogue takes place within what is—at least in the terminology I use here—itself a dialogue; and the protest against the fictional nature of characters in a dialogue is not without a subtle irony when voiced by such a character (even if de Maistre presumably preferred dialogues based on real conversations to purely fictional ones). As the Senator's laughter suggests, the author was aware of this irony—even conservatives can be witty, after all. In the terminology I have adopted in this book, an exact reproduction of a real conversation is also a "dialogue—a "historical dialogue" as distinguished from a "fictional dialogue."[7] My conceptualization is justified by the fact that the historical dialogue is also only a report of a conversation, not the conversation itself. The distinction between conversation and dialogue is surely indispensable when a dialogue is not merely an accurate record of a conversation; and there is no doubt that the overwhelming majority of dialogues neither are nor seek to be such records but are fictional instead. Authors of such works have repeatedly emphasized their fictional character, even in nonfictional texts such as real letters and prefaces; and in general the genre soon came to be

6. Although the dialogue is of course fictional, some of de Maistre's friends served as models for his characters. Tamara, Russia's former ambassador in Constantinople, was the model for the Senator, and the Marquis of Romance-Mesmon, the Count of Blacas, and the Chevalier de Bray were the models for the Chevalier. Cf. C. Lombard (1976), 54.

7. A remarkable intermediate form is represented by what can be called a "collage dialogue," such as the anonymous *Contra Philosophos*, which probably dates from the late Ostrogothic period. The latter is essentially a compilation of texts by Augustine, and thus in this sense a historical dialogue, since Augustine actually wrote the things that are attributed to him in this work. But he wrote them; he did not express them in a conversation, and certainly not in a conversation with Scipio, Varro, and Cicero, who are three of his interlocutors in this work, which is completely fictional in this regard. A fascinating modern example of the collage dialogue is I. Tóth (2000).

considered a fictional one.[8] But this distinction between dialogue and conversation must also be made when the dialogue is nothing but the transcript of a conversation. Such transcripts were made, for example, for theological controversies in the early Christian period: thus Origen's "Conversation with Heraclides" *(dialektos pros Hērakleidan)* is evidently such a transcript, probably slightly edited, of the main part of the corresponding controversy.[9] In the terminology used here, we can say "the conversation between Augustine and the Manichean Fortunatus took place on 28 and 29 August 392," but we cannot say "the dialogue took place on that day"—even though Augustine's "Acta seu disputatio contra Fortunatum Manichaeum" is presented as a transcript of this conversation, which was probably only slightly revised for publication.[10] Conversely, we can say "I have read Augustine's dialogue" but not "I have read his conversation"; and analogously, we should write "Plato had conversations, for example, with Eudoxus, and wrote dialogues, for the most part on Socrates' conversations." A modern example of a historical di-

8. See the letter Cicero wrote in July 45 B.C. to Varro, whom he represents in his *Academica* as one of the participants in a discussion with himself and Atticus: "feci igitur sermonem inter nos habitum in Cumano, cum esset una Pomponius. tibi dedi partis Antiochinas, quas a te probari intellexisse mihi videbar, mihi sumpsi Philonis. puto fore ut, cum legeris, mirere nos id locutos esse inter nos quod numquam locuti sumus, sed nosti morem dialogorum" (*Fam.* 9.8.1). This passage emphasizes that Cicero and Varro never had such conversations (even if Cicero believes that Varro actually held the position attributed to him; cf. also *Att.* 13.19.5: "aptius esse nihil potuit ad id philosophiae genus, quo ille maxime mihi delectari videtur"), but that is not required by the conventions of the genre ("mos dialogorum"). In *Cat.* 1.3, Cicero also makes it clear that the attribution to Cato of the discourse on old age is purely fictional, even if he tries to make it seem plausible by referring to Cato the Elder's Greek culture. Cf. also *Lael.* 1.3: "exposui arbitratu meo."

9. Cf. B. R. Voss (1970), 79 ff., who distinguishes between literary dialogues and records of debates—both private and synodal debates—in Origen's work. I have learned a great deal from Voss's important book. The conversational elements in the "Conversation with Heraclides," which first became known from a papyrus found in 1941 (see the introduction to J. Scherer's edition, 12–49, 47), seem rudimentary to us. The (more substantial) second part on Dionysius's question as to whether the soul is blood consists of a long speech by Origen (10.17–28.17), which is interrupted only once (24.18–20).

10. On Augustine's "records of debates"—including also "Contra Felicem"— cf. Voss (1970), 292 ff.

alogue is provided by the third part of Karl Popper and John Eccles's *The Self and Its Brain* (1977), a record of conversations between the two scientists, though it has the stylistic and compositional shortcomings of most historical dialogues.[11]

Often enough—and this is a further ground for my conceptualization—it is not clear whether we are dealing with a historical or a fictional dialogue—or rather, where exactly the work should be situated on the spectrum between historicity and fictionality.[12] This holds when the author himself leaves this question open;[13] but then it remains unclear even when the text is presented as a faithful record of a conversation, as in the

---

11. The physicist Piet Hut and the philosopher Bas van Fraasen have published (1977) an interesting form intermediate between historical and fictional dialogue that is itself—not solely the conversation on which it is based—a common work. They recorded their conversations in an idealized form, each of them also partly playing the role of the other. "It would be unsufferably frustrating to read an actual record, so we've written up the result as if we were developing a coherent flow of thought, though in practice we found ourselves backtracking repeatedly. This in itself had an interesting result: we could write it up in this form only by each playing the other's role from time to time, so that the labels indicating who says what are at this point an unknown permutation of the real story. We are now, as we try to recapture the past, two actors playing fictional characters into which we have turned ourselves by rewriting. That is only right, that a real experiment should have a fiction as outcome—at least from one point of view, as you'll see" (167). The final sentence is especially amusing, because it anticipates in the common foreword the opposition that occurs in the conversation subsequently represented, this opposition being, as we have previously seen, at least partly fictional. If a fictional dialogue is the common work of two authors—like David Lewis and Stephanie Lewis's *Holes*—the division of labor cannot involve each author writing the discourse of one of the literary characters, because that would destroy the aesthetic unity of the dialogue. See D. Lewis (1983), 9 n. 5. However, cf. below, p. 140.

12. In antiquity and the Middle Ages, this spectrum was more continuous than it is for us; even so "objective" a historian as Thucydides did not hesitate to rework the speeches of his statesmen. A new ontology, for which being is facticity and no longer an emanation of essences, underlies the modern sharp distinction between history and fiction. But modern historians also necessarily make selections in their material, and in doing so may be guided by aesthetic aims.

13. For example, F. Schlegel (1967), 286: "For me, talking about poetry with poets and poetically minded people has always been very exciting. Many conversations of this kind I have never forgotten; in others I cannot tell what belongs to imagination and what to memory; many things in them are real, others imagined. That is the case for the present one."

case of the "Soirées de Saint-Pétersbourg."[14] This kind of claim, made in the context of the dialogue, itself occurs within a literary work, and thus participates in the latter's bracketing of the usual claims to validity.[15] For that very reason it is hard to determine, for instance, whether or not the claim, made in all three of Augustine's Cassiciacum dialogues, that someone wrote down the conversations Augustine had with his friends is correct.[16] In the prologue to *Contra academicos* he already mentions a "notarius," that is, a secretary, who is supposed to have written down the conversation. But Augustine himself acknowledges that the remarks made by Licentius and Trygetius have been reworded: "Adhibito itaque notario, ne aurae laborem nostrum discerperent, nihil perire permisi. Sane in hoc libro res et sententias illorum, mea uero et Alypii etiam uerba

14. Cf. also Cic. *Tusc.* 5.41.121.

15. Because of the obviously literary character of the *Soirées,* we cannot speak of counterfeiting. On the other hand, this is appropriate in the case of alleged transcripts of debates that never took place, or in that of later alterations of correct transcripts. Rufinus handed down, in Latin translation, an extract from the fourth book of Origen's letters that shows that the great theologian had to suffer from both these types of counterfeiting: "Nam quidam auctor haereseos, cum sub praesentia multorum habita inter nos fuisset disputatio et descripta, accipiens ab his qui descripserant codicem, quae uoluit addidit et quae uoluit abstulit et quae ei uisum est permutauit, circumferens tamquam ex nomine nostro, insultans et ostendens ea quae ipse conscripsit. . . . Denique in Epheso cum me uidisset quidam haereticus et congredi noluisset neque omnino os suum aperuisset apud me, sed nescio qua ex causa id facere deuitasset, postea ex nomine meo et suo conscripsit qualem uoluit disputationem" (*adult. libr. Orig.* 7). To be sure, Rufinus translated *Peri arkhōn* not always faithfully, and omitted, for example, Origen's subordinationism, but there is no reason to doubt the authenticity of this letter.

16. See J. J. O'Meara (1951), who considered fictional, as did already Hirzel (1895; II 377 n. 3), all allusions—even though there are twenty of them—to the recording of the dialogue. However, his arguments are not conclusive. The constant repetition of this allusion seems to have no literary function; in addition, it is often found in the prefaces, which usually stand outside fictionality (see below, Part I, chap. 7). Even if the question cannot be definitively answered, I would prefer to assume that some of the conversations were actually written down but subsequently reworked. That also seems to be O'Meara's later position (1954; 193). Augustine is not de Maistre, who was still working on his dialogue eleven years after the conversation it is supposed to record but with his fiction of a transcript was probably thinking of the Church Father. A fortiori, the statement addressed to God in the *Confessions* (9.6.14) must be taken seriously, namely, that *De magistro* records actual conversations between Augustine and his son Adeodatus.

lecturus es" (1.1.4). The conversation on which *De beata vita* is based can have been transcribed very selectively at most.[17] And in the prologue to *De ordine* we read: "Ibi disserebamus inter nos, quaecumque uideban-tur utilia adhibito sane stilo, quo cuncta exciperentur … simul etiam, ut, si quid nostrum litteris mandare placuisset, nec aliter dicendi necessitas nec labor recordationis esset" (1.2.5). Here it is claimed that every use-ful discussion was recorded, to spare themselves later labors of express-ing oneself and remembering in the event that someone might decide to publish something of his own. Thus it is expressly stated that the de-cision to publish was made subsequently, and it is implied that what was written down provided only the basic material from which selections were made. Since the reported conversation begins in the darkness of a bedroom,[18] this first part was transcribed only the following morn-ing.[19] But even if these dialogues therefore cannot be verbatim records, a transcription of parts of the conversations was certainly made in Cas-siciacum and used in writing the dialogues. There is no doubt that the dialogues had as their starting point the real conversations between Augustine and his friends, relatives, and pupils on a patron's estate in Cassiciacum in the autumn and winter of 386/387, shortly before his baptism.[20] The number symbolism that underlies the division of the conversations in *De beata vita* and *De ordine* into three days each and those in *Contra academicos* into two periods of three days separated by an interruption of seven days (2.4.10) is still not a conclusive proof of the fictional status of this length, even if 3, 3 x 4 = 12, and 7 are sacred numbers for a Christian, because a real conversation can be organized in accord with symbolic concerns, as, for example, Ficino and his friends did.[21] (Similarly, the fact that the Evangelists attributed to Jesus state-ments that he was supposed to have made according to the "prophecies" of the Old Testament does not mean that he did not truly make them; if he conceived himself as the Evangelists interpreted him, it is even likely that these statements go back to him.) We can agree with J. J. O'Donnell:

---

17. Cf. 3.18: "quae uerba pueri sicut dicta erant cum conscribi mihi placuisset."
18. Cf. 1.3.6: "erant enim tenebrae."
19. 1.8.26.
20. Cf. *Conf.* 9.4.7 and *Retract.* 1.1.–3.
21. See below, Part III, chap. 19, 445.

"Even if we cannot aver that such-and-such words were spoken on such-and-such a day at Cassiciacum, the dialogues remain a vital record of one view of what went on there. . . . If A. were asked if the dialogues were 'historical,' he would probably say yes, and he would be telling the literal truth according to the standards of his times; but standards have changed, and the dialogues are rather to be viewed now as an unusually privileged form of historical fiction."[22] Even the Platonic dialogues that are perfectly elaborated works of art and whose anachronisms prevent us from seeing them as historical have a real starting point in Socrates' conversations and in Plato's discussions with his pupils and with friends of Eleatic or Pythagorean persuasion—a starting point that they leave behind in a quite different way, however, than Augustine's Cassiciacum dialogues leave theirs behind.

The distinction between conversation and dialogue is not necessarily one between orality and scripturality, though as a rule this is the case. Although a conversation is usually conducted orally, one can nevertheless imagine an exchange, for instance, between deaf persons, that is conducted in sign language or in writing; and an electronic "chat"—and in a certain sense any exchange of letters—is in the terminology of this book a conversation and not a dialogue.[23] Conversely, it would be conceivable (though it is not true of any text I know) that dialogues might be transmitted orally rather than in written form—but that would not make them into conversations even if tradition prescribed that they must always be presented with separate roles.[24] Modern linguistics rightly distinguishes between medial and conceptional orality and scripturality: a lecture given at a meeting is oral from a medial point of view but scriptural

22. (1992), III 87.

23. The philosopher is not bound by etymology; especially since the German word *Sprache* denotes written language as well, even though *sprechen* denotes an oral activity.

24. Plutarch tells us about children who gave performances of the simplest of Plato's dramatic dialogues, which they had learned by heart (*Mor.* 711C). Naturally, the dialogues were always also handed down in written form. G. Ryle's thesis that Plato's dialogues were originally published by oral presentation (1966; 21 ff.) is not provable, and his explanation of the shift from Socrates to the stranger from Elea in the *Sophist* is unacceptable (28 f.).

from a conceptional point of view; an interview published in a newspaper is scriptural from a medial point of view but often oral conceptionally. This differentiation is important for the theory of dialogue: historical dialogues are analogously conceptionally oral, while fictional dialogues are as a rule conceptionally written.[25] However, the last point is not necessarily valid: it is theoretically conceivable that there was a Homer of the dialogue who in conceiving his work dispensed with every means of writing and composed it only orally.[26] Reference to the usual stylistic distinctions between oral and written language[27] gets us only a little further: While it is true that there are dialogues that could never be spoken in the same form (e.g., Schelling's *Bruno*), in other cases even writers of fictional dialogues have quite deliberately sought to connect them with everyday language and have not hesitated to make use of the anacoluthons and ellipses that characterize every spoken utterance.[28]

25. On this distinction, see for instance L. Söll (1980) and H. Westermann (2002), 9 ff.

26. I am acquainted with the thesis that the author(s) of the *Iliad* and the *Odyssey* had access to writing. That is chronologically possible (and a fortiori, that his composition might have been written down by others during his lifetime), but in my opinion this is not likely. Even if he was brilliantly original, this author obviously came out of the culture of bardic singers, and nothing suggests that the early users of the alphabet were to be found in this group. In any case, it is clear that this assumption is not compelling. In a culture of orality the mind of exceptional individuals is capable of enormous compositional performances, even including the *Iliad*. This is not to deny that the introduction of writing profoundly altered the way our minds work and alone made possible certain literary and especially scientific and philosophical achievements; cf. W. J. Ong (1982).

27. These distinctions are valid only ideal-typically, not generally. A stylist's improvised speech that is conceptionally and medially oral may be closer to written language than a (conceptionally and medially written) exchange of letters between two uncultured persons.

28. Demetrius argues, in opposition to Artemon, that a dialogue imitating a conversation requires more improvisation than a letter, which as written and as a gift to another person demands a more elaborate style (*Eloc.* 223 ff.; see also *Eloc.* 21 on the specific clauses in dialogues). In contrast, see Sigonio (1993), 156; and especially T. Tasso (1586), 343 f. Ancient literary critics already noted that the rather colloquial style of the early Platonic dialogues differs sharply from the mannered style of the later ones. Dionysius of Halicarnassus's criticism of the style of the latter (*Dem.* 5–7; *Pomp.* 1–2) is famous. See also Longin. 4.6, 29.1, 32.7, all on passages from the *Laws*. Despite the striking stylistic change in Plato's work, his early dialogues are also

Finally, dialogues that are scripturally conceived and written down can be recited or staged, thus once again leaving the medium of scripturality without thereby becoming conversations. Iris Murdoch's first Acastos dialogue, "Art and Eros: A Dialogue about Art," was first performed in London in February 1980 as a National Theatre Platform Performance;[29] and a few of Diderot's philosophical dialogues, for example, have sufficient dramatic potential to be captivating on the stage. In comparison to existence in the form of a book, a performance has more reality, and theatrical performance is necessarily intersubjective. But this does not alter the "bracketing" that is part of the aesthetic; performed dialogues do not thereby become real conversations.[30] If we want to be precise, we should not say "I have witnessed the conversation between Socrates and Acastos" but rather, at most, "I have listened to the conversation between the actor Andrew Cruikshank playing Socrates and the actor Adam Norton playing Acastos."

This is the decisive point—that a dialogue reports a conversation or represents it, without thereby being itself a conversation, first of all because it is itself almost always the work of an individual. Since the form

---

composed in beautiful artistic prose. And they are accomplished works of art, perhaps dramatically all the more accomplished the less mannered their style. It is notable that in *Prt.* 359b Socrates does not quote verbatim Protagoras's earlier statement (349d), as one would do in a written work, but only paraphrases it—because that is what is done in a conversation, which is what the dialogue represents. Cf. A. Gide, "Corydon" (1935), 281 f., 290. In contrast, in Eberhard's *Dialogus Ratii et Everardi*, Ratius quotes accurately from memory whole paragraphs from authorities.

29. (1986), 10.

30. In the first part of *Wahrheit und Methode*, H. G. Gadamer criticizes the autonomization of the aesthetic in the neo-Kantians and in phenomenologists loyal to Husserl such as O. Becker (1960; 84 ff.), using interesting arguments, which basically only carry further Heidegger's criticism of Husserl's transcendental *epoché*. Gadamer skillfully begins with the arts that are directly important in the life-world, such as architecture (148 ff.), and then concentrates on those that are, like music and drama, intended for performance (105 ff.). We can certainly agree that the performance of a drama takes place in the real world—that holds true in general for every production and reception of a real work of art. But this does not alter the fact that a performance of a work of art that takes place in the real world stands for something ontologically different—a possible, because fictional, world. Without the—absolutely real—sense for possible worlds humans would not be human.

of language that makes use of graphic and not phonetic signs, and can be corrected before being communicated to other people, does not cease to exist after the moment in which it is produced,[31] it is less immediate and situation-dependent than speech, and therefore it is not surprising that after the development of a written language dialogues meant to remain available were primarily composed in writing, and thus the correlation of conversation with orality and dialogue with scripturality is well founded. But this is not a conceptually necessary correlation. Nonextensional contexts are already involved in the historical dialogue. In the latter as well, the author's truth claim is related not to the statements reported (at least when the author is not himself one of the conversation partners) but rather solely to the fact that these statements were made by the conversation partners. Drawing on Husserl's famous distinction between *noēma* and *noēsis,* we could say: the author's truth claim is related not to the *lekton* but rather to the *lexis.* Such a claim is made in an assertion like "The following conversation was conducted by A and B at such-and-such a time and at such-and-such a place"; the conversation itself will then be represented between quotation marks or in indirect discourse. Modern commentators on philosophical texts often understand their role in an analogous way; and if they themselves do not wish to or cannot adopt any position with regard to the issues involved, they are acting as pure historians and no longer philosophers. A philosophical dialogue is a contribution to philosophy only if its author takes his own position with regard to an issue, in whatever mediated way.[32] Paradoxically, this is more likely to happen when the author of the dialogue is freed from the historian's duty to respect the truth.[33]

31. However, this property of spoken language has been to some extent overcome through the development of sound recording during the past century.

32. Everyday language uses terms that are simultaneously intensional and extensional and that both attribute views and commit the speaker to their truth or falsity. Consider sentences like "He knows (he is deluded in believing) that p." See G. Frege (1976), 62 f.

33. There are the following possibilities: The author of a historical dialogue always asserts the truth of the *lexis,* and sometimes—but not necessarily—also that of the *lekton* of at least one of the conversation partners; the author of a fictional di-alogue does not assert the truth of the *lexis* but usually asserts at least the partial truth of the *lekton* of at least one of the conversation partners. However, a fictional dialogue

The author is freed from this duty in the fictional dialogue, which belongs to the domain of literature in the narrower sense,[34] to which we do not assign, for example, works of history.[35] Literature in the narrower sense is characterized by an aesthetic claim to validity that as a rule[36] entails an abandonment of the usual kind of truth claim that the historian still makes, even if the aesthetic claim is coupled in a complex way with ethical and also theoretical truth claims. The paradox of art is exactly this—that it promises a higher truth precisely because it lies, or rather, to

---

in which the author only represents opinions, without himself taking a position, is also conceivable, but then we can attribute to him at least an interesting skeptical point of view. Whenever not even this is the case, the author belongs at best to the history of literature, and certainly not to that of philosophy. To attempt to "free" someone like Plato from all truth claims is to insult his intelligence.

34. Aristotle, for whom verse, unlike mimesis in his sense of the word, is neither a necessary nor a sufficient condition for poetry, classifies dialogue (including Socratic dialogue) as poetry (*Poetics* 1447a28 ff.). In the dialogue *Peri poiētōn* frg. 4 Ross (= D. L. 3.37), however, the dialogue is situated between poetry and prose. This fragment may be absolutely reliable (the judgment of Empedocles, friendlier than in the *Poetics,* corresponds to it; see above, chap. 1, n. 11), and the deviation from the doctrine of the *Poetics* may be connected with the exoteric nature of the dialogue, which probably did not want to differ so sharply from linguistic usage. Cicero speaks of people who assign Plato's (and Democritus's) style, despite the lack of verse, rather than the style of the comedians, to the realm of poetry: "Itaque video visum esse non nullis Platonis et Democriti locutionem etsi absit a versu, tamen quod incitatius feratur et clarissimis verborum luminibus utatur, potius poema putandum quam comicorum poetarum" (*Or.* 20.67). Here the question concerns style, not fictionality, which cannot be attributed to Democritus's work. The abstract dialogue character named "Dialogue" in Lucian's *Bis accusatus* situates himself between prose and poetry, though only after his transformation in which Menippos and Lucian himself have a hand. On the ancient theory of dialogue, cf. M. Ruch (1958), 17 ff.

35. On the distinction between literature and historical writing, see Aristotle, *Poetics* 1451b5 ff. and in general the ninth, epistemologically central chapter. According to Cicero as well (*De leg.* 1.1.4), the relation to truth distinguishes historical writing from poetry, however much he concedes that in Herodotus and Theopompus there are countless fables.

36. This is not conceptually necessary: a work of art can be historically true, and so can an aesthetically accomplished philosophical dialogue, because in a rare moment of grace reality corresponded to artistic norms. But only someone who in the normal case in which they conflict chooses against historical facticity is an artist. Ultimately, this also holds in the notoriously anomalous case of the art of photography, which within facticity must at least be very selective.

put it better or more in accord with the truth, it abandons the conditions of normal discourse. Fictional discourse is the kind of nonassertive discourse that makes no claim to referentiality or satisfaction.[37] An actor who promises eternal love to his partner on the stage does not do so in reality; his speech act is not a promise but rather the representation of a promise.[38] And yet his *ethos*—if he has one (which is desirable, because there is certainly an ethics of fiction)[39]—is this: he seeks to communicate to his public insights, even and precisely of a moral nature, that they would hardly have gotten had he expressed his real feelings regarding the actress playing opposite him. In exactly the same way, the speech acts of someone who writes or recites a philosophical dialogue are not assertions, proofs, and so on, but rather representations of assertions, proofs, and so on. For the existence of society, it is of course essential to be able to distinguish between these two types of speech acts; and thus external forms have been developed that allow us to make this differentiation (analogously, irony, for example, is not allowed in certain contexts or with reference to certain emotions). Someone who says "I promise" on the stage, before a large audience, is not performing the speech act of promising; and someone who as the author of a philosophical dialogue writes "God does not exist" is not thereby declaring himself to be an atheist. He is not even asserting that the real counterpart of the literary character who makes this assertion—if there is such a counterpart—has made such an assertion. But why do we allow the author of a philosophical dialogue to disregard all the usual conditions for normal assertions? Only because it alone enables the best philosophical dialogues to give readers an especially intense and gratifying experience of philosophical truth.

37. Cf. G. Gabriel (1975), 28; as well as T. G. Pavel (1986). In his important article "Truth in Fiction" (1983; 261–80), which however ignores the specifically aesthetic element in literary universes, D. Lewis proposes an intensional operator "In such-and-such fiction . . . ," which can be inserted before a statement *f* in order to form a new statement (262). The question as to how far fiction can serve truth is touched upon in the third "Postscript" (278 f.).

38. Cf. Frege (1976), 26: "Just as thunder in the theater is not real thunder, and a theatrical fight only an apparent fight, so also a theater statement is only an apparent statement. It is only play, only poetry. In his role, the actor does not make statements, and he also does not lie, even when he says something that he is convinced is false."

39. Cf. W. C. Booth (1988).

How can this happen? Philosophical truths are essentially general: philosophy is interested not in the particular qualities of an ordinary John Doe but rather in what constitutes the essence of humans or at least of a human type. A *conditio sine qua non* of philosophizing is therefore a great capacity for abstraction, and the price that has to be paid for this is often high. Philosophers are, after all, concrete persons; and what they seek to understand—concepts and their characteristics—belongs ontologically to another order than the one to which they themselves belong. This can lead to a feeling of being lost in the world, and even to a self-alienation that makes philosophical existence painful. What makes the enjoyment of art so refreshing for the philosopher, perhaps even more than for other people, is that he is confronted by a relationship to the world that seems to merge the two sides of his existence—particular individuality and a relation to general concepts—into a unity that he cannot achieve himself, even though the category of unity undoubtedly plays a central role in the order of his concepts. Someone who reads *Don Quixote* gains an understanding of many things about human nature that the observation of his neighbor, or even himself, usually does not provide; and he can at the same time identify with the concrete hero of the novel, whereas it is not possible to identify with the essence of man. For making the universal available in sensible form, the fictional nature of the text is not too high a price to pay. Precisely because great art changes our perception of the general structures of reality, we accept the fact that it does not tell us anything true about a real person, or in the event that it happens to do so that is of no importance to it; for the inner coherence of the possible world that it outlines is art's true achievement. Simultaneously, this fictional world throws light on our world. How does it do so? On the one hand, the knowledge of norms that are not always instantiated in our world but ought to be respected is part of our real world; and reference—even if often indirect—to these norms is one of the sources of great art. People with the character of Sophocles' Neoptolemos are not commonly found in reality, but because an appeal to us proceeds from him, an appeal we are incapable of escaping even if we cannot do it justice, the *Philoctetes* offers us a deeper understanding of ourselves. On the other hand, rogues like Shakespeare's Richard III can also make fundamental characteristics of our real world evident in a

way that the latter itself cannot. The characters in aesthetically significant fictional universes, we might say, have few contingent properties
but mainly essential properties; and this is possible only because they are
underdetermined with respect to reality (and thus we need a three-value
logic in order to talk about them). The historical Macbeth was certainly
either Rh-positive or Rh-negative (very probably the former); but Shakespeare's Macbeth is neither, and any statement about the probability of
his being one or the other is meaningless, because in the fictional universe of Shakespeare's *Macbeth* there are witches but no laws regarding
the distribution of Rh factors.[40]

Since some of these general structures also pervade empirical reality,
art—including surrealist art—always stands in a certain relationship of
mimesis to reality; but since it is concerned with general structures, every
art—including realistic art—transcends empirical reality. To differing
degrees, mimesis and transfiguration characterize every work of art; and
often enough it is moral convictions that determine where the emphasis
falls: the victorious campaign of realism was connected with Christian
universalism.[41] However, a realistic work of art also constitutes a fictional
universe to which its statements refer and whose ontological status is of a
different kind from that of the work of art itself, which belongs to the real
world. This ontological difference is also present when a work of art,
for example, a historical novel, represents people from the real world.
"Napoleon" in Tolstoy's *War and Peace* does not refer to the Napoleon of
our world but rather to the Napoleon of an alternative world, and it is
only in the latter that Napoleon can encounter Andrey Bolkonsky. (We
do not need to decide here whether there is a transworld identity or only
a counterpart relationship between the two Napoleons.) This excludes
neither the possibility that the fictional Napoleon helps us better understand the real Napoleon nor the possibility that the author presupposes
that general assumptions regarding the real Napoleon will be transferred

---

40. However, D. Lewis rejects J. Heintz's theory of an underdetermined fictional world: "I do not know what to make of an indeterminate world, unless I regard
it as a superposition of all possible ways of resolving the indeterminacy—or, in
plainer language, as a set of determinate worlds that differ in the respects in question" (1983; 270 n. 11).

41. Cf. E. Auerbach (1946).

to his fictional Napoleon; the latter is even probable if he chooses a familiar name, and taking such assumptions into account results in an interesting twist.[42] In the third chapter I discuss how Plato, for example, alludes to historically known facts that thus belong to the fictional universe of his dialogues, even if they are not explicitly mentioned. Most fictional worlds are—at least in their creator's view—nomologically possible, and thus presuppose the same natural laws as our own world. In surrealistic literature, however, this is not the case; it deliberately concerns itself with only analytically possible worlds with other natural laws. But these can also help us, just like contrafactual thought experiments with alternative natural laws, better understand our real world—in the ideal case, its characteristics that are necessary or axiologically good. Few things reconcile us more with our mortality than the encounter with the immortal Struldbruggs in Jonathan Swift's *Gulliver's Travels*.

The cognitive achievement of great art does not depend solely on its subject, which combines the general and the particular in an ontologically fascinating way. Precisely because the nature of this combination is ambiguous, it requires special efforts on the part of the receiver; and the experience of the indispensability of arriving at one's own interpretation is a factor on the subjective side, without which there would be only the reception of other people's opinions, and no real knowledge. The irony encountered in everyday conversation is a casual intelligence test to which the conversation partners are subjected; and the fictionality of art is only an intensification of this irony. Following Theophrastus's *Peri lexeōs*, Demetrios writes that when the listener notices that something remains unsaid, he becomes a well-disposed witness of the speaker (this

---

42. Lewis writes pertinently (1983; 269): "Strictly speaking, it is fallacious to reason from a mixture of truth in fact and truth in fiction to conclusions about truth in fiction. From a mixture of prefixed and unprefixed premises, nothing follows. But in practice the fallacy is often not so bad. The factual premises in mixed reasoning may be part of the background against which we read the fiction. They may carry over into the fiction, not because there is anything explicit in the fiction to make them true, but rather because there is nothing to make them false." However, facts are later replaced by "overt beliefs," generally shared views regarding which it is generally known that they are generally shared (272). Furthermore, Lewis includes "carry-over from other truth in fiction . . . intra-fictional and inter-fictional" (274). Among the latter are, for example, genre conventions.

holds analogously for the writer and reader as well); for then he considers himself clever, since he has been given a chance to prove himself clever.[43] The artist communicates indirectly. He is saying something different from what he seems to say; in the fable he speaks about foxes and grapes, but he is talking about men. It may happen that what he means cannot be precisely determined, that there is not one interpretation (which would in any case have to include all legitimate interpretations). Here we may leave this question open. But there is certainly a multitude of nonsensical and banal interpretations, and if a hermeneutic theory can no longer exclude them, at least it cannot claim to be critical.

The fascination of the fictional universe of art is not without its dangers. It can make people prisoners in a world of illusion or appearance, when bad art is involved; but even great art can divert us from responsibility for the real world and lead to a loss of reality. That is precisely a subject of philosophical dialogues, whose writers have from Plato (*R.* 607b5 f.) onward often experienced in their own bodies the old conflict between philosophy and poetry, because writing good philosophical dialogues requires a twofold talent, philosophical and literary. The little community in Cassiciacum alternates philosophical discussions with readings from Virgil;[44] and all the participants do not rank the two activities in the same way. Augustine's most talented pupil, Licentius, has to be "converted" to philosophy; that is, he has to make an existential decision to shift his intellectual focus from poetry to philosophy.[45] Similarly, Philosophy expels Boethius's muses, but then itself speaks to him in verse.[46] One of Augustine's arguments against poetry is that it erects a wall between the poet and truth that is still more impenetrable than the one that separates Pyramus and Thisbe, about whom Licentius writes verses.[47] The metaphor is very well chosen, and shows that Augustine, a professor of rhetoric who has become a philosopher, does

---

43. *Eloc.* 222. Cf. also 288 and 297, with examples from Plato.

44. *Ord.* 1.8.26.

45. Augustine's twenty-sixth letter shows, however, that the conversion was short-lived. Cf. P. Brown (1969), 118 f.

46. *Cons.* 1.1.7 ff.

47. *Ord.* 1.3.8.: "uersus istos tuos . . . , qui inter te atque ueritatem inmaniorem murum quam inter amantes tuos conantur erigere."

not reject poetry and rhetoric but merely reorients them to put them in the service of philosophy, as had Plato before and Boethius after him.

However, residing in the fictional world can also prepare one for dealing with the real world. Even science cannot flower without imagination, that is, without the readiness to entertain at least apparently contrafactual assumptions and to elaborate possible worlds; and analogously, reveling in fantasy can prepare adults for reality, just as playing does the child. Precisely the bracketed space of the work of art can also allow people to have feelings that go much deeper than are normally possible in the reality determined by competition and the necessity of self-preservation. We may be deeply moved by Flaubert's novel, but who would want to have the Bovarys as his next-door neighbors? We can more easily empathize with tragic heroes on the stage than with people who in real life are a nuisance, or perhaps our opponents, or even our enemies; that is an anthropological fact that is certainly to be considered ambivalent. It can be a compensation for a "more of the same" in everyday life; however, at least in the middle term the development and education of the emotions through art may have the ability to reshape reality. In no case is identification with a literary hero an argument against the phenomenon of aesthetic "bracketing," but on the contrary a confirmation of it: it takes place more easily because of this bracketing. Only in very rare, exceptional cases does a spectator rush onto the stage in order to help a threatened character; in such cases we can speak of a "fading of the bracketing," when the separateness and ontological difference of the aesthetic realm is forgotten.

It is not difficult to apply to dialogue what I have said about art in general. The fact that in dialogues we see people arguing with and against one another produces a potential for identification that remains alien to a treatise. Philosophy deals essentially with propositions, of course, but propositions are produced by human beings through speech acts. It can be shown that abstracting from this fact leads to philosophical mistakes; and it is immediately evident that the limitation to propositions necessarily misses the sphere of the concrete that belongs to art. The terminally ill Macrina in Gregory of Nyssa's "On the Soul and Resurrection" elicits emotions of an entirely different kind from those elicited by Heidegger's discussion of the anticipation of death in *Being and Time;* and the near-

ness and distance of dialogue from real conversation both teaches us
to adopt a critical view with regard to the underlying social reality and
communicates stimuli to transform it. The difficulty of discovering the
intention of the author of philosophical dialogues, as in the case of a
dramatist, can help the reader gain autonomy in a way that only great art
can teach, and that the genre of objectivity in philosophy cannot. The
reader of a dialogue sees how the conversation partners are gradually led
to the truth; he is not confronted by a fully elaborated theory, which
might be more easily learned by heart but remains more foreign to him
precisely because it is not the result of his own efforts. Even though a
sharp distinction between conversation and dialogue is the crucial idea
in this section, we can even say that it is because of this indirectness of
communication that philosophical dialogue initiates—though in a mediated and necessarily asymmetrical way—a conversation between author and reader such as cannot be set in motion by a system. The reader
of the Platonic dialogues comes to them with interpretive hypotheses
whose collapse amounts to a kind of posthumous reply by the author
that triggers a new attempt to approach them.

So what is a dialogue, and what is a philosophical dialogue? The
lapidary definition found in Isidore of Seville—"dialogus est conlatio
duorum vel plurimorum, quem Latini sermonem dicunt" (dialogue is a
discussion between two or more persons, which the Latins would call
sermo)[48]—does not distinguish between conversation and dialogue.[49]

48. *Etymologiae* 6.8.2. The etymology of the word *dialegesthai* means "to discuss"
in the sense of an investigation that may be intersubjective but need not be. Cf. Pl. *Sph.*
263e3 ff. on *dianoia* and *dialogos;* in his work designated as a *dialogos* Justin speaks (3)
to Trypho about his "conversation with himself" *(ho dialogos pros hemauton).* See also
Aug. *De mag.* 1.2: "intus apud animum loqui." The terminological distinction drawn in
this book between conversation and dialogue was unknown throughout antiquity;
both *dialogos* and *sermo* could be used to designate either of them (cf. Pl. *Prt.* 335d3
and Arist. *Peri poiētōn* frg. 3 Ross and Cic. *De off.* 1.37.134 and *Or.* 44.151). On the
semantic field in Cicero, to which *collocutio, colloquium,* and *disputatio* also belong, cf.
G. Zoll (1962), 46 ff.

49. The same holds for the definitions given in Diogenes Laertius (3.48) and in
Albinos's *Prologos* (1), which has the further shortcoming that it includes in the *definiens* many conditions such as the art of characterization and discriminating style,
which characterize especially good dialogues but certainly not every dialogue.

In contrast, for Hirzel the dialogue "as an independent literary work" is a "discussion in the form of a conversation" *(Erörterung in Gesprächs-form).*[50] It is more appropriate to include the first determination in the *definiens* and then define the dialogue as a "literary genre that primarily represents a conversation." In Hirzel's definition, which aims at the individual work, not the genre, "independent" is necessary because other literary genres also represent conversations. The "dialogues" in novels, such as those of Dostoyevsky or Thomas Mann, are not independent but rather part of another literary genre. The conversations between Rodion Raskolnikov and Porfiry Petrovich or between Naphta and Settembrini have philosophical standing, but they draw their intensity from the murder of the pawnbroker and her sister or from Hans Castorp's seven-year-long confusions and the slow death of Joachim Ziemßen, and all this has no place in the representation of a simple conversation, a dialogue. Boccaccio's *Decameron,* Chaucer's *Canterbury Tales,* and Goethe's *Conversations of German Émigrés* are novella collections in dialogue form, not dialogues, because in them the primary focus is on the novellas, not on the interactions among the narrators. Even Werner Heisenberg's *Der Teil und das Ganze* (The Whole and Its Parts) is, despite its subtitle, *Gespräche im Umkreis der Atomphysik* (Conversations around Atomic Physics), not a dialogue; instead, it belongs far more to the genre of memoirs, or perhaps autobiography, because what holds the book together is Heisenberg's life and intellectual development, to which conversations certainly make a crucial contribution, but they are not the primary subject of the work. It is possible, of course, to work out a general theory of the dialogic in the drama, novel, satire, and dialogue— Bakhtin sought to do just that.[51] But this book, which is about the genre of dialogue, does not attempt to develop such a theory of the dialogic mode, even if positions that are part of such a general theory are repeatedly discussed.

Etymology already suggests a distinction between drama and dialogue: drama is primarily concerned with actions, dialogue with con-

50. (1895), I 7.
51. Cf. T. Todorov's classical introduction (1981), and, for example, the essay collection edited by R. Lachmann (1982). Cf. L. Pearce's more recent book on dialogics (1994).

versations.[52] Torquato Tasso, himself the author of elegant dialogues, begins his important *Discorso dell'arte del dialogo* with the idea that both people's actions and their reflections can be imitated. It is true that these cannot be sharply distinguished, since only a few actions would not be communicated at all and no reflection takes place without at least a mental action. And yet a sufficient difference is obvious, on which the differentiation between drama and dialogue is based: one imitates the deeds of active people, the other imitates the words of people talking with one another.[53] In a dialogue, the accompanying actions are a supplement whose omission would not destroy the genre.[54] Of course, there are forms intermediate between drama and dialogue: in Plato's *Symposium* the action is quite extensive and indispensable; on the other hand, in modern dramas the action is sometimes reduced to a minimum (consider Samuel Beckett's *En attendant Godot*). But even such a drama is essentially intended to be presented by professional actors, whereas in the case of dialogues performability is involved only contingently.[55] For that reason Diderot's *Le neveu de Rameau,* which is relatively easy to perform, is situated on the border between dialogue and drama, because for the author Rameau's psychology is just as important as his ideas; but since the work offers original ideas grounded in philosophical argument, it will be classified as a philosophical dialogue and not as a drama.

52. In the division of genres in Diomedes' *Ars grammatica* (Grammatici Latini I 482), dialogue is not mentioned as such, but mime is, which is classified under "poema dramaticum," along with tragedy, comedy, and satyr plays. A comparison of (Platonic) dialogue with drama is found in Maximus Tyrius 37.1.

53. "Nell'imitazione o s'imitano l'azioni degli uomini o i ragionamenti: e quantunque poche operazioni si facciano a la mutola, e pochi discorsi senza operazione, almeno dell'intelletto, nondimeno assai diverse giudico quelle da questi; e degli speculativi è proprio il discorrere, sì come degli attivi l'operare. Due saran, dunque, i primi generi dell'imitazione: l'un dell'azione, nel qual son rassomigliati gli operanti; l'altro delle parole, nel quale sono introdotti i ragionanti" (1586; 333). Analogously, in "A Defence of Poetry," P. B. Shelley says of Plato: "He sought to kindle a harmony in thoughts divested of shape and action" (1977; 484).

54. (1586), 335: "Ma ne' dialogi l'azione è quasi giunta de' ragionamenti; e s'altri la rimovesse, il dialogo non perderebbe la sua forma."

55. Cf. Tasso (1586), 336: "Ma nel dialogo principalmente s'imita il ragionamento, il qual non ha bisogno di palco: e quantunque vi fosse recitato qualche dialogo di Platone, l'usanza fu ritrovata dopo lui senza necessità." See also the concluding definition, 345.

Dialogues represent conversations; and the latter vary considerably in kind.[56] There seems to be an important difference between a conversation whose purpose is mainly to achieve a practical objective, as in a meeting to discuss something, and one whose purpose is chiefly to get acquainted with others, as in casual social chat.[57] In the first case, the conversation is only a means; in the second, it is a goal in itself. Naturally, there are slippery transitional cases. While buying an airline ticket one may, if no one else is standing in line, tell interesting travel stories, and casual small talk with a colleague at a party may in fact be a test conversation to find out if one wants to work more closely with him. And yet in many cases the difference is clear. Even if in the broad horizon of many conversations between two unattached young people of different sexes the possibility of an erotic relationship exists, such a conversation should normally be distinguished from making a pass, whose goal is clear enough. The charm of chat resides precisely in its purposelessness and openness to surprises of both a personal and a content-related kind: unexpected characteristics of the conversation partner as well as subjects may emerge;[58] abrupt changes of subject are acceptable in casual conversation, at the price of failing to pursue a point in depth.[59] In contrast to

56. The following trichotomy corresponds to that of F. D. E. Schleiermacher in his *Einleitung zur Dialektik:* practical, artistic, and pure thought and the three corresponding ways of conducting a conversation (1988; 117 ff., esp. 120 ff.).

57. Important texts on Western theories of chat are found in C. Schmölders (1986), who has written an elegant introduction to the volume (9–67). Henry Fielding's 1743 "Essay on Conversation" uses the concept in a much wider sense than I do in the following pages, namely, as meaning "pleasant intercourse," as his definition shows: "The Art of pleasing or doing Good to one another is therefore the Art of Conversation" (1972; 123). This art manifests itself in words and in deeds (124). It is shown not only in relations with other people but also in the relation to God and to oneself (121). Rules for chat in the sense in which I use the word are found only at the end of Fielding's essay (142 ff.).

58. For that very reason, the end of a chat is more or less arbitrary. Writing to Dontenville on January 20, 1934, Paul Valéry told him that when he received a contract for a text that was to consist of precisely 115,800 signs, he decided to write a (chat) dialogue: "Cette rigeur . . . l'a fait songer d'abord; trouver ensuite que la condition singulière à lui proposée pouvait être assez aisément satisfaite en employant la forme très élastique du *Dialogue*" (1945; 183).

59. In Diderot's *Le rêve de d'Alembert,* Bordeu complains that "we get to the bottom of nothing," and Mlle de l'Espinasse replies: "What does that matter? We're

public debates, where the goal is to impress outsiders, we are concerned with those with whom we are speaking and to whom we are often bound by friendship. Rhetorical rules play a small role.[60] Philosophical questions may arise in chats—usually ethical in nature, since the need to make judgments regarding occurrences in the immediate environment is common to all humans.[61] But the rules of politeness—which demand that so far as possible all those present be included, even if their contributions to the solution of a philosophical problem are very different in value, do not allow the conversation to get bogged down in a problem of detail (even if it is crucial), and prohibit explicit contradiction of others—are incompatible with concentrated philosophical discussion, that is, with a philosophical investigation undertaken by several people. Such a discussion is definitely goal-oriented; but in this case it is not a matter of achieving a practical goal but rather, even if questions of practical philosophy are discussed, one of achieving theoretical clarity, for example, regarding the question as to what a legitimate goal is. However, such a question is existential in a sense entirely different from that of booking the cheapest flight. Investigating philosophical questions, unlike investigating mathematical questions, can reveal what a human being is still more radically than chat, which is limited by considerations of power relationships, social conventions, and so on. Of course, a certain respect is required for the development of the conversation partners; but there are also conventions such as "religious questions are absolutely to be avoided" or "periodically go back to the neutral subject of the weather" that operate as a straightjacket that suffocates any more

---

not composing. We're talking" (Qu'importe? Nous ne composons pas. Nous causons) (1972; 222). Cf. Goethe, 9.481.

60. Cicero already recognized this in his ideal-typical opposition between "contentio" and "sermo." "Et quoniam magna vis orationis est eaque duplex, altera contentionis, altera sermonis, contentio disceptationibus tribuatur iudiciorum contionum senatus, sermo in circulis, disputationibus, congressionibus familiarium versetur, sequatur etiam convivia. Contentionis praecepta rhetorum sunt, nulla sermonis, quamquam haud scio an possint haec quoque esse" (*De off.* 1.37.132). The model is probably Pl. *Prt.* 336b1 ff.

61. Cf. Kant, *Kritik der praktischen Vernunft* (The Critique of Practical Reason) A 272 ff.

freewheeling investigation in which alone deeper levels of the personality can be uncovered.[62] Such an investigation is not incompatible with the development of friendships; on the contrary, it may promote them and in general presupposes a certain goodwill. The combination of a strict dedication to the subject under discussion transcending the contingent aspects of the conversational situation and very personal commitments to oneself and to others is what distinguishes a successful philosophical conversation from all other forms of conversation.[63]

The distinction I have made between forms of conversation corresponds to one between dialogues which, like many of Lucian's, focus primarily either on characterizing persons—often satirically—through their discussions or on the wittiness of cultured, convivial chat concerning practical objectives and, on the other hand, those that introduce persons primarily in order to clarify substantive issues. To go back to de Maistre's differentiation: the kind of conversation involved in the latter group of dialogues is a discussion of a problem, not a chat, which may include, for instance, telling stories.[64] For example, chat dialogues

62. The rules Fielding lays down at the end of his "Essay on Conversation" (see above, n. 57) are absolutely in accord with common sense, but the exclusion of serious debates ("Arguments"; 1972, 146)—especially when women are present—clearly marks the difference from discussion.

63. It is in accord with the spirit of our skeptical time that convivial chat *(Konversation)* often seems to be the ideal form of conversation—indeed, sometimes the word *conversation*—for instance, in contrast to *speech*—is taken to designate what is here called "chat" (e.g., by K. Stierle [1984]). In opposition to this, we must insist that a value-free, historically comprehensive phenomenological analysis encounters discussions and *Konversationen* as forms of intersubjectivity. To be more than a perpetuation of prejudices, their evaluation presupposes investigations that skeptics can seldom claim to have made.

64. In his reconstruction of ancient literary classifications, J. J. Donohue (1943; 85) distinguishes the dialogue from mime: "Outriders of the dramatic class were the Sicilian *mimes*, prose representations of familiar conversation, and the *dialogs*, prose representations of learned discussion." According to my categories, most of Lucian's dialogues and most of Erasmus's *Colloquia familiaria* are closer to mime than to the discussion dialogue, even if the level of their chat is elevated. Lucian himself offers an apt distinction between the chat dialogue and the philosophical dialogue, in his brilliant apology, the *Bis accusatus*, in which he has to defend himself first against rhetoric, from which he has turned away, and then against dialogue, which he has led away from Plato's sublime investigations. This text is itself a chat dialogue, and thus an instance of what is being theoretically defended. On this structure, cf. the following section of this introduction.

constitute the majority of ancient *symposion* and *deipnon* literature from Xenophon to Macrobius,[65] who explicitly distinguishes two forms of conversation and thereby implicitly distinguishes *symposion* literature from the more serious discussion dialogues.[66] The most brilliant satire on symposium literature is Petronius's *Cena Trimalchionis,* because it reveals the intellectual and linguistic vulgarity into which such a feast can sink.[67] Its satirical power no doubt makes the *Cena Trimalchionis* more interesting than the encyclopedia entries forced into dialogue form under the title *Deipnosophists (Deipnosophistai),* which we owe to Athenaeus; Petronius's sarcastic criticism of vulgarity is more fascinating than the tedious, and in a certain sense just as vulgar, display of a formless erudition in Athenaeus's work. A chat may in fact be included in a good discussion dialogue—for example, by Diderot—but it has to prepare the way for a discussion. In the middle, between the chat dialogue and the discussion dialogue, stands, for example, Schleiermacher's *Weihnachtsfeier.* Most of Plutarch's dialogues can also be situated in such a middle ground, because they lack philosophical precision: what they represent is more philosophical chat than philosophical discussion.

The philosophical dialogue is accordingly to be defined as a literary genre that represents a discussion of philosophical questions. A philosophical dialogue will almost always be written in prose, because philosophers do not hold discussions with one another in verse; but a fictional philosophical dialogue in verse is not fundamentally impossible. For example, Ramon Llull's *Desconhort* is, at least in the parts that

---

65. See J. Martin's valuable book, which refers to a symposium theory in Hermogenes (*Meth.* 36) and Athenaios (in Mansurius's remarks in the fifth book of the "Deipnosophistai") (1931; 1 ff.). It is interesting that in the text attributed to Hermogenes, *Peri methodou deinotētos,* the Socratic symposia are described as a genre *alongside* dialogue.

66. Cf. *Sat.* 1.1.2: "nam per omne spatium feriarum meliorem diei partem seriis disputationibus occupantes cenae tempore sermones conviviales agitant, ita ut nullum diei tempus docte aliquid vel lepide proferendi vacuum relinquatur: sed erit in mensa sermo iucundior, ut habeat voluptatis amplius, severitatis minus." Macrobius then refers to Plato's *Symposium,* which in fact differs from other dialogues of Plato in its casual tone and lesser argumentative intensity, but is nonetheless (just like Kierkegaard's "In vino veritas") not only an accomplished work of art, but also a first-rate philosophical achievement.

67. Cf. Horace *Sat.* 2.8 and Juvenal *Sat.* 5.

are less personal and deal with more general issues, a good example.[68] The author of a philosophical dialogue will be concerned not only with *lexis* but also with *lekton*, with the discussion among his characters as well as with the problems they (and through them, he himself) are trying to solve. A useful philosophical classification of dialogues can be made by asking whether the representation of the discussion has its own importance or whether the dialogue is focused almost entirely on the issue under discussion. For example, up to the first book of the *Republic* the Platonic dialogues belong to the first category, whereas starting with books II to X of the *Republic* they belong instead to the second category. But Plato's later dialogues are also centered—rather artificially—on a conversation. This is not the case for the popular genre of the diatribe, in which discussions are occasionally reported, but only in addition to long lectures.[69] For example, Arrian, in his *Diatribai* (the title may not be his), probably accurately recorded Epictetus's actual discourses, and even if dialogic elements occasionally enter into these discourses—as for example when Epictetus answers questions—the work is far removed from dialogue. Not only do the monologic sections, among which I count forms of soliloquy, far outweigh the dialogic ones,[70] but the conversation partners remain for the most part anonymous, and do not

68. Herodas's *Mimiamboi* (third cent. B.C.) are nonphilosophical dialogues in verse (hipponacteans), and despite their naturalistic coloring, which naturally captivated people when the papyruses on which they were written were discovered at the end of the nineteenth century, they are precisely for that reason fictional, indeed highly artificial dialogues. The contrast between vulgarity related to contemporary life and formal rigor must have fascinated Herodas's contemporaries. His contemporary Timon of Phlius's hexametric *Silloi*, which are extant only in fragments, are on the borderline between nonphilosophical literature and philosophy. The most important collections of fragments are still to be found in *Sillographorum graecorum reliquiae*, 89–187 (C. Wachsmuth provides an overview of the author and his work, 18–55), and in *Poetarum philosophorum fragmenta*, 173–206. Boethius's *Consolatio philosophiae* is prosimetric and thus continues the tradition of Menippean satire; a proximity to Seneca's tragedies has also been suggested (P. L. Schmidt [1977], 124). Giordano Bruno's "De gli eroici furori" consists essentially of poems and interpretations of them.

69. Cf. Hirzel (1895), I 369 ff. Xenophon's *Memorabilia* are also not a real dialogue (cf. Hirzel [1895], I 141 ff.) but rather memoirs with inserted dialogues—just as Xenophon's *Apology* is a report with inserted speeches.

70. Cf., e.g., 2.1.32, 3.13.7, 3.14.2, 4.4.26; and 30, 4.9.13.

represent another point of view that is of real interest but simply provide Arrian with an opportunity to refer to Epictetus's own views. Even the formally dialogic passages in many diatribes are closer to Wittgenstein's conversations with himself in his *Philosophical Investigations* than to a genuine dialogue with a real interlocutor. Seneca's so-called dialogues are also really diatribes.

Of course, the definition laid down here suffers from the fact that it uses the phrase "philosophical questions" in the *definiens* and does not explain it. But since this book is not a metaphilosophical study, the usual understanding may suffice: philosophical questions are questions that have to do with the principles of our knowledge and action. No one will claim that Varro's *De re rustica,* Richard Fitznigel's so-called *Dialogus de scaccario* (actually *De necessariis observantiis scaccarii*), Baldassare Castiglione's *Il Cortegiano,* Vincenzo Galilei's *Dialogo della musica antica, et della moderna,* and Galileo Galilei's *Dialogo . . . sopra i due massimi sistemi del mondo, tolemaico e copernicano* are philosophical dialogues, even if they are discussion dialogues that deal with general topics; the first is concerned with agriculture, the second with financial policy, the third with the norms of courtly culture, the fourth with musical theory, the fifth with astronomical questions.[71] To be sure, there are always problems of demarcation; and in this investigation I have included works that may seem to others more rhetorical, theological, or political than philosophical. But since in antiquity aesthetic questions were discussed by rhetoric, and in the Middle Ages questions of philosophy of religion were discussed by theology, and these problems are absolutely central for philosophy, and finally since even political occasional works can throw light on fundamental problems of political philosophy, I have not wished to exclude works such as Cicero's *De oratore,* Abelard's *Collationes,* and even Maurice Joly's *Dialogue aux enfers entre Machiavel et Montesquieu.* A fortiori, I have not ignored philosophical dialogues whose authors were not primarily professional philosophers—for one need not be a professional philosopher to produce good philosophy.

---

71. A biographical work like Satyrus's *Life of Euripides* was also written in dialogue form; cf. *POxy* 9, no. 1176; pp. 124–82.

CHAPTER 3

On the Relationship between Form and Content in the Philosophical Dialogue

One of the qualities that good art and good philosophy have in common is that the additive—the mere addition of information—runs counter to their nature. A great work of art and a major philosophical work strive to attain the form of unity that we usually call organic because the parts have been conceived in relation to one another and to the whole. More than ever, in a successful philosophical dialogue, which is ideally both a significant philosophical work and a beautiful work of art, we can expect form and content, genre and subject to be closely related. There are, of course, philosophical dialogues in which this is not the case and that could, for example, be transformed into a treatise without much being lost—but then it has not been worth the trouble to write a dialogue. Conversely, there are successful dialogues that skillfully represent a philosophical discussion but lack any intellectual originality.

Art, we saw, makes the universal available to the senses. By essence, a philosophical dialogue necessarily includes a philosophical question, argumentative efforts to answer it, their linguistic articulation, and a plurality of participants in the conversation. Accordingly, the philosophical dialogue has the task of clarifying the relation between certain kinds of people, certain philosophical views, and certain forms of debate, between certain arguments and the emotional reactions to them, between ways of thinking and ways of life, and also ideally between thoughts and language. I say "ideally" because only a few philosophers have succeeded in this—and fewer tragedians than one might at first think, because many tragedians, even great ones, proceed monolinguistically; that is, for the most part they maintain the same level of language, or in their work a change in linguistic level is based on themes, not persons: thus in the concluding speech of the *Gorgias,* Plato's Socrates adopts a more sublime style than in the foregoing conversation.[1] Yet Plato has skillfully imitated the stylistic characteristics of individual speakers. For example, in the *Protagoras* (337c f.) he parodies Hippias's style, and in the *Symposium* (194e ff.) he parodies that of Agathon. Sometimes, very much in the vein of polylinguistic comedy, he plays with conversation partners' dialectal peculiarities.[2] In the *Symposium,* when Eryximachos begins elaborately with the sentence "Hē men moi archē tou logou esti," he is imitating—perhaps unconsciously—*De arte* 4 from the *Corpus Hippocraticum;* in any case he thereby shows that he has internalized quotations from authorities. In Bruno's *La cena de le ceneri,* Prudenzio's frequent bits of Latin and quotations, as well as his mythological allusions, indicate this pedant's nature; and in *De la causa, principio e uno,* in connection with the *Cena* Armesso asks Filoteo, the character standing for Bruno, whether he is imitating the voice of an enraged and excited dog, and sometimes plays an ape, a wolf, a woodpecker, or a parrot, sometimes this animal, sometimes that.[3]

The relationship mentioned above can be positive—a harmony—or negative—an opposition or contradiction—in nature. This does not mean that successful dialogues favor contradictions; but they can teach us something important precisely by representing contradictions insofar as the latter make the untenability of a position experienceable through the senses, as it were. Philosophical ideas that are so abstract that they

1. See the anonymous "Prolegomena to Plato's Philosophy" (17.11 ff.).
2. Kebes' Boeotian dialect is famous; *Phd.* 62a8; cf. already Sigonio (1993), 176. On the other hand, it is doubtful whether *cheirourgēma* and *kurōsis* (*Grg.* 450b9) are Sicilianisms, as Olympiodor maintains in his commentary; but the terms might have been characteristic of Gorgias's style (cf. E. R. Dodds [1959], 196).
3. (1985), I 197.

have hardly any meaning for human life are among the least appropriate for a philosophical dialogue. Subjects in natural philosophy, for example, are especially unwieldy. Plato's *Timaeus* is surely one of his philosophically most important works; but dialogical passages are found only at the beginning, where the subject of natural philosophy has not yet been taken up. Similarly, Schelling's *Bruno*, which seeks to rival the *Timaeus*, is not a success as a dialogue. It is surely no accident that there have been only a few dialogues on questions in mathematics and natural philosophy; Eratosthenes' lost *Platōnikos*,[4] Galileo's previously mentioned *Dialogo*, and Leibniz's so-called *Dialogus de arte computandi* (the title is not his) come to mind. The fundamental importance for methodology and worldviews of the controversy over the heliocentric system, which can moreover be understood without much mathematics,[5] certainly contributed to the success of Galileo's dialogue—and similarly we can imagine a good dialogue on the consequences of Darwinism. In Leibniz's dialogue in the wake of Plato's *Meno*, the illustration of the nature of the process of learning mathematics is important.

Ethics is an especially obvious theme for dialogue, because its subject, right human conduct, can be represented in the dialogue itself by the conversational behavior of those taking part in it. Crito and Euthyphro in the Platonic dialogues of the same names, Jean-François Rameau and the Marshal's wife in the corresponding dialogues by Diderot, all think about moral questions the way they think about them because they are the persons they are; and if a change of mind can be produced in an ethical dialogue, that is usually because the corresponding persons undertake to change their behavior, in short, because something like a conversion occurs. A person whose character is as firmly established as that of Callicles in Plato's *Gorgias* or that of Rameau in Diderot's dialogue will not abandon his views. The attraction of Augustine's Cassiciacum dialogues consists precisely in the fact that they embed new philosophical

4. Cf. Hirzel (1895), I 405 ff. This dialogue apparently also touched upon, perhaps even dealt in large part with, the philosophy of mathematics.
5. "Ho poi pensato tornare molto a proposito lo spiegare questi concetti in forma di dialogo, che, per non esser ristretto alla rigorosa osservanza delle leggi matematiche, porge campo ancora a digressioni, tal ora non meno curiose del principale argomento," Galileo writes in his foreword (1998; 6).

convictions in a new way of life, whose appropriation is no less full of presuppositions than that of the new intellectual world. From this it follows that the philosophy of religion is an especially interesting subject for a philosophical dialogue, because religion is not solely a matter of the intellect but rather deserving the attention of the whole personality, and in fact dialogues on the philosophy of religion, and often interreligious dialogues, play an important role in late antiquity and the Middle Ages. Problems of metaphysics and epistemology are easier to depict in a dialogue if the various attempts at a solution are the expression of differing worldviews, and thus if these problems are not mere intellectual puzzles but have consequences for the way we lead our lives, for example, regarding the interpretation of our own scholarly or scientific activities or the nature of our moral duties. The debate with relativism and skepticism in Plato's *Theaetetus,* Cicero's *Academica,* and Augustine's *Contra academicos* varies greatly, but the choice of the dialogue form in all three makes sense because they attribute an existential meaning to the question. An ontological discussion like the one in the *Sophist* clearly becomes "dialoguable" (if this neologism is permitted) when it is made clear that the battle between idealism and materialism represents a "gigantomachy" (246a), and that an answer to this question is truly fateful.

In ethical dialogues the characters involved are almost always aware of the relation between the subject being discussed and the conversational procedure. This is also the case in aesthetic dialogues when, for example, the partners themselves discourse in aesthetically attractive ways, as does Socrates in Plato's *Phaedrus*.[6] The characters that act within a dialogue cannot, however, be aware of its overall design as an aesthetic achievement, because one may be able to govern aesthetically one's own statements, perhaps one's own appearance, but never, at least not completely, that of others. If there is a connection between the aesthetic norms set forth by an interlocutor in a dialogue and the principles on which the dialogue itself is constructed, this connection between form

---

6. Analogously, nondialogic aesthetic works have often exemplified the norms that they teach, at least when they are written in verse, like Horace's *De arte poetica,* but also occasionally works in prose as well. H. von Staden has impressively demonstrated this (1999; 368 ff.) regarding Longinus in connection with Pope's *Essay on Criticism* (v. 675 ff.). See my later essays (2009a) and (2010).

and content is therefore of a fundamentally different kind from the one initially discussed. We can describe these two types as "dialogue-internal" and "dialogue-external." Of course, sometimes the same statement may be related to both dialogue-internal and dialogue-external aspects, and thus seek to throw light on both the conversation partner who makes it and on the author of the dialogue.[7]

Many Platonic dialogues are doubtless among the best ever written, because the tension between idea and existence, between the truth of being and reality of life[8] permeates them just as it is a subject of Plato's real philosophy. The connection between form and content can be made particularly evident in these dialogues, both dialogue-internally and dialogue-externally. The *Phaedo* develops proofs of the immortality of the soul; and even if they are not among the most tenable in Plato's philosophy, the enormous influence of this work is based on the fact that they are offered by Socrates on the day of his execution, and the dialogue represents both his fearlessness and his intellectual efforts. Since the dialogue ends with an account of Socrates' death, the subject and the frame of the conversation are very closely related to each other—but in a conflictual way insofar as the vivid reality of Socrates' death is contrasted with the conceptually grounded belief in the immorality of the soul. However, because philosophizing itself is described by Socrates as a preparation for death (64a ff.), not only is the relation between the framing action and philosophical reflection on immortality conflictual, but his death is as it were only a continuation of this liberation from the bonds of the senses; and since in this great finale to his existence Socrates is given an opportunity to exemplify one of the virtues whose unity with knowledge he had constantly taught, courage (cf. 67b–69d), the way he dies is a confirmation of his life as well as his

---

7. The ancients were already clear about this distinction. Cf., e.g., Cic. *Or.* 13.42 on Plato's eulogy of Isocrates in *Phdr.* 278e ff., which he imitates at the end of *De oratore* and which is dialogue-internally a prophecy, dialogue-externally a compliment to a contemporary: "Haec de adulescente Socrates auguratur. At ea de seniore scribit Plato et scribit aequalis et quidem exagitator omnium rhetorum hunc miratur unum."

8. *Seinswahrheit und Lebenswirklichkeit.* From the second edition on, this is the subtitle of Friedländer's incomparable book on Plato.

theory.[9] Much the same can be said for the *Symposium,* whose formal
structure already makes it a twin of the *Phaedo.* The guests participating
in the banquet speak about love, and moreover there are erotic relationships among them; in fact the individual erotic relationships differ from
one another just as subtly as do their conceptions of love, which are set
forth in the seven speeches. In this context, Socrates has a special opportunity to display another virtue, temperance, which has as its crucial
part sexual self-control. All these are dialogue-internal harmonies, but
a dialogue-external harmony comes into play when at the end of the
Symposium Socrates forces the drunken Aristophanes and Agathon to
admit that the same person must be able to write both tragedies and
comedies (223d). This claim, which runs counter to the social reality of
Greek drama, finds no dialogue-internal confirmation—though it finds
confirmation if we transcend the fictional universe established by the
dialogue and consider the dialogue itself. It is clear that the author of the
dialogue, Plato, was capable of including comic elements in his work, such
as in the speech of the comic writer Aristophanes, as well as tragic ones
(among these we should count Alcibiades' love-hate for Socrates rather
than the tragedian Agathon's rhetorical gimmick).[10]

The *Phaedo* and the *Symposium* are philosophical dialogues with
an unusual amount of action; few others show us drunken lovers at a
party or philosophers being executed. This seems to represent a kind of
maximum of action; when fantastic stories are represented or reported,
such as Empedocles' resurrection of an apparently dead person in Heraclides Ponticus's *Peri tēs apnou,*[11] the philosophical quality of the work
suffers considerably, even if the story is related to the subject: the immortality of the soul. But this does not mean that dialogues with relatively little action cannot also represent the manifold relation between

---

9. Compared with the complexity of this relationship, the connection between Cato's age or Laelius's capacity for friendship and the subjects of the two Ciceronian dialogues named after them (Cic. *Lael.* 1.4 f.) seems rather simplistic.

10. On comic and tragic figures and scenes in Plato, see Tasso (1586), 333 ff.
Plato's claim influenced Bruno's dedicatory epistle to *La cena de le ceneri* (1985; I 15).

11. Cf. Frg. 76–89 Wehrli and the reconstruction in H. B. Gottschalk (1980),
13–36. Heraclides' dialogues apparently regularly introduced exotic and even mythical characters.

form and content, because both arguments and speeches are actions. A few examples taken from the works of the three most important ancient writers of dialogues should suffice.

In Plato's *Hippias minor,* one of his earliest dialogues, after a speech on Homer by the sophist Hippias, Socrates asks who is better in what quality, Achilles or Odysseus.[12] Hippias says that Achilles is the best man, but Odysseus is the wiliest (364c). That means, Socrates says, that Odysseus is false, and not because he does not know better; instead, he is wise in deception. However, in all the arts the ability to lie is combined in the same person with the ability to tell the truth. Achilles and Odysseus can therefore not be distinguished on the basis that one of them is truthful and the other false (369b). In response to Hippias's objection, Socrates shows that Achilles repeatedly utters falsehoods. When Hippias protests that although this is true, Achilles utters falsehoods unintentionally, whereas Odysseus does so intentionally, Socrates concludes that Odysseus must then be better than Achilles (371e). For in general a person who does something bad intentionally is better than one who does it unintentionally, since the former has an alternative. Thus a person who deliberately errs and does something shameful and wrong—if indeed there is such a person (376b)—is good. The limiting if-clause—like many other [*ei*] clauses in Plato—is crucial. One of the few statements that can be attributed with a high degree of certainty to the historical Socrates is the thesis that no one willingly does anything wrong. And since the condition that there is someone who willingly acts wrongly is unfulfilled, the conclusion regarding the good cannot be correct. This conclusion is in any case arrived at only by induction, and Plato certainly understood that when we move from value-neutral techniques to genuinely moral activities we move beyond the sphere in which induction is legitimate. Socrates thus leads Hippias into error—and he does so with such virtuosity because he knows the truth. Through his own behavior, Socrates confirms the thesis that he best deceives who knows the truth. This thesis, justified on the pragmatic level no less than on the semantic level, is also correct, and precisely because it is correct, the attentive reader is alerted to keep in mind that Socrates may deceive him: this deception is represented by his inductive argument in favor of the thesis that the good man deliberately

12. My interpretation follows essentially that of P. Friedländer (1964), II 125–34.

does wrong. But isn't Socrates, whom Plato surely considers good, intentionally doing something wrong when he intentionally deceives? No, because for Plato there is a legitimate kind of deception—for instance, the necessary and noble lies to which the inhabitants of the ideal state are exposed.[13] In Plato's *Hippias minor,* this is not expressly said but rather shown; and only someone who moves back and forth between the explicit statements in the dialogue and its action, only someone who takes into account both the pragmatic and the semantic dimensions, will be able to grasp what Plato wants to say in this apparently modest dialogue, which leads from a true statement about deception to a deception regarding the good, and in precisely that way shows that deception can sometimes be good.

Analogously, in the dialogues devoted to defining the virtues there are allusions to the fact that an appropriate search for a virtue displays this virtue itself: it follows from Plato's intellectualism that a philosophical existence is as such the highest norm of all morals; in Plato, the various virtues are therefore aspects of a philosophical existence. For example, in the *Laches,* which is concerned with courage, after refuting the general Laches' claim that courage is prudent steadfastness, Socrates remarks that their deeds are not in accord with their words, because the former are courageous but the latter seem not to be (193d f.). This is an ironic inversion of the bold general's longer speech, in which he declared that he likes those men in whom words and deeds are in harmony, the harmony of life itself, not that of the lyre or another entertaining instrument;[14] on the other hand, if he sees someone who speaks well but acts differently from the way he speaks, he is saddened and appears to be a *misologos,* a hater of discourse (188c ff.). Laches himself is someone who acts as he thinks, and he praises Socrates because he is at least courageous in his deeds.[15] But Socrates wants to make him see, and Plato wants to make the reader see, that achieving this harmony does not suffice to really

---

13. Cf. *R.* 414b.

14. To be precise, it should be mentioned that Laches praises Doric harmony in accord with the preference Socrates himself works out in the discussion of various harmonies in the *Republic* (398c ff). Augustine further develops the *Laches* passage, *Ord.* 2.19.50.

15. 181a7 ff. and 188e5 ff. In *Smp.* 221a7 f. Alcibiades emphasizes that after the defeat at Delion, Socrates' behavior was more appropriate than that of Laches.

possess a virtue; its possession depends on the quality of one's own thoughts. This becomes especially clear in the passage at 192d ff., in which the refutation of Laches' suggested definition begins. Socrates adduces several examples of imprudent, that is, highly risky, behavior, and asks whether it is more courageous than behavior that runs fewer risks in an analogous situation. The old warhorse maintains that it is, and must reluctantly admit the consequence that ignorant behavior is more courageous than intelligent behavior, which seems to contradict the normative distinction of courage (192c5 f.). (It is also presupposed that understanding, perhaps even prudence, is the highest value, and that could certainly be questioned, especially on the basis of a non-eudaemonist ethics, which Plato only rarely considers a possibility.) Especially important is the discussion (193a3 ff.) of the behavior of a military leader who prudently takes up a secure position and waits for promised reinforcements. Laches, of course, considers such a leader less courageous than one who fights under unfavorable conditions—and thus foreshadows his own defeat, for he fell in 418 at the battle of Mantineia after he had abandoned his position on a secure hill.[16] A false ideal of courage, to which he devoted his life, was thus responsible for his death. Plato thereby suggests that consistency is not a sufficient condition for the achievement of true virtue; in his view, a courageous man is only one who thinks about the consequences of his action and avoids unnecessary risks. Plato's conception of virtue does not exclude a moral consequentialism; he would not consider somebody like George Patton, for instance, as courageous (because, one might add on the basis of a universalist ethics, in marching on Messina he risked the lives of his soldiers without being forced to do so by any real military necessity, just to win fame for himself at Montgomery's expense).

The moralist Plato opposes Socrates to the sophists as someone whose acts are in accord with his teaching; but the intellectualist Plato also opposes him to the valiant defenders of Attic ethical life who were not capable of an intellectual understanding of morals. In fact, Laches' opponent Nicias, who was also a general, but who was already somewhat

---

16. Cf. Th. 5.65 ff. I owe some of my information on this point to W. T. Schmid (1992), 6 ff.

familiar with Socrates and his philosophy without really understanding his uniqueness, and takes an interest in him merely out of common curiosity, proposes an intellectualist definition that comes closer to the one intended by Plato. However, he also fails, for different reasons. Nicias acknowledges that ignorant beings—animals, but also women and children, as well as many men—cannot be said to be courageous. Fearlessness and courage are not the same thing,[17] and of the two only courage can be a virtue, because virtue presupposes knowledge. It is true that Laches protests that this view conflicts with common linguistic usage,[18] but the philosopher is not bound by the latter.[19] But Nicias is not able to clarify the relationship between courage and virtue in general (Protagoras also fails to do so in the dialogue to which he gives his name).[20] In particular, the atemporality of the object of knowledge is too much for him;[21] it cannot be clarified without metaphysical reflections. But Plato is not concerned merely to contrast Laches' and Nicias's intellects; he also wants to oppose their characters to each other. In fact, the dialogue contains not only an allusion to Laches' death but also to that of Nicias, who was executed in Syracuse in 413 after he failed to retreat in a timely manner when defeat was on the horizon; Thucydides reports that Nicias's belief in omens and augurs played a role in his self-destructive decision to stay.[22] Augurs are repeatedly mentioned in the *Laches;* and even if it is Laches who agrees with Socrates' decisive statement that the law commands that the augur must not give orders to the general, but the general to the augur,[23] Nicias does not simply not contradict him; he has previously made it clear, in a very Socratic way, that neither an augur nor a physician should be considered to have normative knowledge, the

17. 197b1 f.
18. 197c3 f.
19. Laches reluctantly alludes to the divinity of philosophers, 196a6 f., and deliberately to Socrates's conception of the philosopher-king, 197e1 f.
20. Plato alludes to the later dialogue, 190c8 ff., and to the connection between courage and prudence, 191d7 f.
21. 199b9 ff., where, however, Socrates wrongly moves on not only to all dimensions of time but also to all goods.
22. 7.50.
23. 199a1 ff. The hierarchy of forms of knowledge alluded to here is extended to include politics and philosophy in the *Euthydemus* (290b ff.).

latter being reserved for the philosopher.[24] But in the crisis of 413, Nicias forgot what he knew abstractly, which was not able to determine his behavior. Thus whereas Laches failed because he energetically followed a false idea, Nicias failed because he lacked the energy to act in accord with a true one. (However, for Plato's intellectualism that is possible only because his knowledge was not sufficiently grounded.) In the *Laches* Plato indicates that the great man combines the merits of Laches and Nicias—harmony between life and theory and philosophical insight, respectively—and thereby finally realizes them in their truth and that the correct definition of courage must include both generals' attempts at definition. Thus perseverance is required. He suggests this, for example, when in their aporia Socrates proposes to Laches that they tentatively accept the principle involved. Laches does not understand what he means, and asks what principle he is referring to. Socrates explains: "The principle of endurance. If you agree, we too must endure and persevere in the inquiry, and then courage will not laugh at our faintheartedness in searching for courage, which after all may be endurance" (194a).[25]

Thus despite his refutation of the definition of courage as prudent steadfastness, Socrates nonetheless maintains that a capacity for perseverance is part of the virtue, and that without it even the philosopher can make no progress toward achieving his goal.[26] The virtues are not only the topic of the philosophical quest but also its driving force; and only conversation partners who keep an eye on the conversational procedure itself have a chance of understanding them. The immediate application of the subject of conversation to the situation in which the conversation takes place is generally one of Socrates' most striking characteristics in the dialogues preceding the *Republic,* appearing, for example, in two passages in the *Gorgias:* Socrates asks Polus, who does not object to his definition of rhetoric as an art that produces pleasure,

---

24. 195c5 ff. The same distinction between normative and descriptive knowledge (the latter including knowledge of future facts gained through augurs) is found in *Chrm.* 173e10 ff.

25. Socrates' praise of the courage shown in conversation by Callicles (*Grg.* 494d3 f.) is ironic, to be sure, but it presupposes the validity of the standard, which Callicles respects only in a formal sense that misses precisely the essence of the virtue.

26. Analogously, we find *mē apokamōmen* in *Prt.* 333b7.

to produce pleasure while conversing with him (462d5 f.); and he reproaches Callicles for not allowing himself to be benefited by discipline, even though that was the subject of their conversation about temperance and the benefit of punishment. On the other hand, Charmides hesitates to agree with Critias's praise of his temperance, and thereby shows precisely through his bashfulness a certain form of temperance. No matter how much his blushing increases his grace,[27] it contradicts to a certain extent the ideal of reflective knowledge that the dialogue defends as the ultimate foundation of the virtue of temperance. The philosopher needs courage and self-control, and of course prudence, in order to pursue his search for knowledge; if he interacts with others in conversation, norms of justice are indispensable. And although it is not explicitly explained that a philosophical life is the highest form of worshiping the divine, that is the message dramatically presented in the *Euthyphro,* which appears to lead to an aporia only if we neglect the conversational event to focus solely on the propositions it communicates, forget pragmatics and consider only semantics.

At the beginning of the second book of Cicero's *De oratore,* Quintus Lutatius interrupts Catulus Antonius to remark that it is hardly surprising that an orator is best at praising eloquence, because in order to do so he has only to use the art that he is praising: "quod quidem eloquentem vel optime facere oportet, ut eloquentiam laudet; debet enim ad eam laudandam ipsam illam adhibere, quam laudat" (2.10.39). The subject of the conversation, rhetoric, is a driving force of the conversation in a different sense than the virtues are, but it, too, is a motive force and not only a subject of the conversation. It is clear that in his first dialogue, which has remained his best because he was writing about a subject with which he was completely familiar, Cicero was competing with Plato no less than in the two other dialogues of the trilogy, *De re publica* and *De legibus,* whose very titles recall Plato. In the first book of *De oratore,* Lucius Licinius Crassus, whose understanding of rhetoric comes closest to Cicero's, reproaches Plato for having become entangled in what we

---

27. 158c; temperance is later defined as modesty (160e), but this second attempt at defining it, which is based on introspection (160d6)—an initial form of reflexivity—also fails.

would now call a performative contradiction; and that is a reproach which, as we have seen, and as Cicero himself must have seen, would certainly have pained Plato had it been really justified. In Cicero's dialogue, Crassus says he cannot agree with those who want to exclude rhetoric from politics and science, as does the most important and eloquent of them, Plato, the founder of this kind of controversy. Crassus has read Plato's *Gorgias* in Athens under the supervision of the Academician Charmada, and admires Plato for it because in mocking the orators, Plato seems himself to be a consummate orator: "sed ego neque illis adsentiebar neque harum disputationum inventori et principi longe omnium in dicendo gravissimo et eloquentissimo, Platoni, cuius tum Athenis cum Charmada diligentius legi Gorgiam; quo in libro in hoc maxime admirabar Platonem, quod mihi [in] oratoribus inridendis ipse esse orator summus videbatur" (1.11.47). In an entirely analogous way, in the third book of *De oratore*, Catulus emphasizes that either the conversation in the *Gorgias* is completely invented or if Socrates really defeated Gorgias he did so only because he was the better orator.[28] It is true that Cicero's criticism of Plato is not justified insofar as in the *Phaedrus* Plato outlines a philosophically reformed rhetoric that differs little from Cicero's, and already in the *Gorgias* itself he alludes often enough to the possibility of a rhetoric in the service of philosophy.[29] Even if Crassus were justified in objecting that Socrates has rent asunder the original unity of tongue and heart, rhetoric and philosophy,[30]

---

28. "Ipse ille Leontinus Gorgias, quo patrono, ut Plato voluit, philosopho succubuit orator, qui aut non est victus umquam a Socrate neque sermo ille Platonis verus est; aut, si est victus, eloquentior videlicet fuit et disertior Socrates et, ut tu appellas, copiosior et melior orator" (3.32.129). Even if such a rhetoric is not the explicit subject of the earlier dialogue, we can certainly say that Plato was aware of the rhetorical qualities of the *Gorgias*. Crassus had again alluded to the *Gorgias* shortly before (3.31.129).

29. See below Part II, chap. 18, esp. n. 5.

30. "quorum princeps Socrates fuit, is qui . . . eisque, qui haec, quae nunc nos quaerimus, tractarent, agerent, docerent, cum nomine appellarentur uno, quod omnis rerum optimarum cognitio atque in eis exercitatio philosophia nominaretur, hoc commune nomen eripuit sapienterque sentiendi et ornate dicendi scientiam re cohaerentis disputationibus suis separavit; cuius ingenium variosque sermones immortalitati scriptis suis Plato tradidit, cum ipse litteram Socrates nullam reliquisset. Hinc discidium illud exstitit quasi linguae atque cordis, absurdum sane et inutile et reprehendendum, ut alii nos sapere, alii dicere docerent" (3.16.60 f.). Cf. 3.19.72.

he fails, first, to see that the explicit opposition of the two disciplines was an inevitable reaction to the Sophists' dissociation of persuasive discourse and its theory from the relation to truth that philosophy cannot abandon without betraying itself and, second, to recognize clearly enough that Plato, like Aristotle[31] after him, sought to overcome this separation, even if under the primacy of philosophy,[32] and to a large extent succeeded in doing so.

However, here we are not concerned with the fairness of Cicero's criticism of Plato. What matters far more is that Cicero is clearly aware of the transcendental nature of rhetoric: one can escape its demands in a convincing way only if one does them justice. The performative contradiction that Crassus and Catulus find in Plato's criticism of rhetoric is attributed to a character who does not himself appear as a conversation partner in the universe of the dialogue. But this character cannot be described as dialogue-external, because he absolutely belongs to this universe; at most he can be said to be "conversation-external," "conversation" being understood, of course, as referring to the one represented in the dialogue. But a related criticism is directed against one of the conversation partners in the dialogue as well: when, after the arrival of Catulus and his half brother Gaius Julius Caesar Strabo, Crassus elegantly seeks to avoid having to give a speech, Caesar replies that he nonetheless is not sorry he came, because the refusal to speak was already a pleasing speech: "Tum Caesar 'equidem,' inquit 'Catule, iam mihi videor navasse operam, quod huc venerim; nam haec ipsa recusatio disputationis disputatio quaedam fuit mihi quidem periucunda" (2.7.26). In the second book, a similar witticism punctuates the long speech delivered by Marcus Antonius, who, unlike Crassus, sees philosophical theory and the appropriation of the Greek intellectual world as being of no use to rhetoric. Caesar notes how well Antonius knows Greek historical writing; and Catulus adds that, admiring Antonius's erudition, he no longer wonders how someone who is allegedly uncultured could be such a good

---

31. To whose *Rhetoric* Antonius appreciatively refers, 1.10.42.

32. Crassus also defends this primacy in the event of a conflict: "quorum si alterum sit optandum, malim equidem indisertam prudentiam quam stultitiam loquacem" (3.35.142).

orator.[33] The major opponents, Crassus and Antonius, thus demonstrate their eloquence and culture precisely in seeking to escape the former or deny the latter's relevance.

But it is not only for dialogue-internal characters that eloquence has a conversation-shaping power in addition to being the topic of the conversation. Cicero alludes on several occasions to the largely fictional nature of his dialogue—saying in the proem to the first book that the conversation represented in *De oratore* was only reported to him by Caius Aurelius Cotta.[34] Cicero repeats this claim in the proem to the third book and urges, not his brother Quintus, to whom the work is dedicated and who in any case has only the highest opinion of Cicero, but rather his other readers, to imagine Crassus as still better than he is represented—just as the readers of Plato's dialogues, which are marvelously, even divinely well composed, imagine Socrates to be even greater than he appears to be in those dialogues.[35] This passage seems to be a moving expression of humility: the author seeks to efface himself entirely behind his hero (or rather heroes, since he later mentions Antonius as well). However, anyone who knows that humility is not the most obvious of Cicero's virtues should reread this passage. By once again noting that he was not present during these conversations and that Cotta transmitted to him only the *topoi* and basic propositions, he indirectly suggests that the rhetorical organization of the speeches given by his conversation partners is his own work; the praise given them dialogue-

---

33. "'Id me hercule' inquit Catulus 'admirans illud iam mirari desino, quod multo magis ante mirabar, hunc, cum haec nesciret, in dicendo posse tantum'" (2.14.59; cf. 2.89.362). Similarly, Crassus unmasks Antonius's lack of education as mere pretention (2.86.350). Cf. 2.1.4, where Cicero speaks explicitly of Antonius's intentional concealment of his education.

34. 1.7.24; 1.8.29.

35. "Neque enim quisquam nostrum, cum libros Platonis mirabiliter scriptos legit, in quibus omnibus fere Socrates exprimitur, non, quamquam illa scripta sunt divinitus, tamen maius quiddam de illo, de quo scripta sunt, suspicatur; quod item nos postulamus non a te quidem, qui nobis omnia summa tribuis, sed a ceteris, qui haec in manus sument, maius ut quiddam de L. Crasso, quam quantum a nobis exprimetur, suspicentur. Nos enim, qui ipsi sermoni non interfuissemus et quibus C. Cotta tantum modo locos ac sententias huius disputationis tradidisset, quo in genere orationis utrumque oratorem cognoveramus, id ipsum sumus in eorum sermone adumbrare conati" (3.4.15 f.).

internally is thus also to be read dialogue-externally. And since Cicero connects his efforts to get the reader to imagine Crassus as still greater than he appears in the dialogue itself with the usual reaction to the Socrates of the Platonic dialogues, he is comparing himself with a model who fills others with anxiety and regarding whom it is later said that he (Plato) made Socrates, who never wrote anything, immortal[36]—so Cicero analogously immortalized Crassus.[37] Cicero is completely aware of the self-praise implied in the passage cited from the proem; he at least indirectly urges his reader to think as highly of him as Quintus does. Finally, the preference given Crassus over Antonius is noteworthy; it arises from the fact that Crassus's and not Antonius's conception of rhetoric is closer to Cicero's own as it is developed, in a nondialogic form, in the *Orator,* for example. We have to concede that such a clever concealment of self-praise behind a caring gesture of humility with regard to a predecessor is a considerable rhetorical achievement.[38] And since this occurs in a text written in the first person and situated outside the fictional universe, namely, in a proem, we have no ground for doubting that at least this achievement sprang from Cicero himself, and this may lead us to admire all the more the creative power he displayed in writing the speeches of his dialogue characters. Presumably Cicero actually wanted the attentive reader to follow such lines of thought. Is that an overinterpretation? Hardly, if we consider that one of the work's maxims, repeated no fewer than seven times, is that art should not be noticed as such.[39] By revealing

36. 3.16.60.

37. Cf. G. Zoll (1962), 77: "Cicero is the *Latin Plato* and Crassus is a *Roman Socrates.*" Zoll correctly notes that by situating the conversation in the past, Cicero opted for the Platonic rather than the Aristotelian model; he wants to make his "memoria veterum" understood as a work of gratitude (75 ff.). However, Zoll underestimates Cicero's awareness of the fact that the remembering person is at least as important as the one remembered.

38. See my analysis of a similarly situated passage (*De rep.* 2.1.21 f.) in Hösle (2004b), 156 ff. One of the more attractive traits of Cicero's vanity is that it occasionally led him to write more creatively. Bruno's vanity, on the other hand, is always cumbersome.

39. 2.35.148 f.; 2.36.153; 2.37.156; 2.41.177; 2.50.203; 2.77.310; 3.50.193. This is a topos of ancient rhetoric and poetic theory that Castiglione reworked in the theory of *sprezzatura,* which is not only discussed in his *Il Cortegiano* (1.4.82 ff.) but also illustrated in the conversational conduct of that dialogue.

this maxim, Cicero winks to the reader to indicate that his rhetorical art should be followed as closely as possible.

Another passage in which the subject of conversation and the procedure of conversation coincide probably influenced the last dialogue to be considered in this chapter. Catulus interrupts Antonius to warn him that in his speech about oratory he has forgotten the order *(ordo)* and arrangement *(dispositio)* of the proofs, an area in which he is a past master. With great urbanity, Antonius at first behaves as if he were a Monsieur Jourdain of eloquence—once again an apparent gesture of humility that nonetheless actually confirms what Antonius has said insofar as it corresponds to his general thesis that eloquence is acquired by practice or even by accident, and not a form of theoretical knowledge: " 'Vide quam sim' inquit 'deus in isto genere, Catule: non hercule mihi nisi admonito venisset in mentem; ut possis existimare me in ea, in quibus non numquam aliquid efficere videor, usu solere in dicendo vel casu potius incurrere'" (2.42.180). After he has added that hardly anything is more important than the order of a speech, he says, in a sudden about-face, that it is not really yet time for a discussion of this subject. The order of the conversation requires, it is more implied than said, another place for the subject of arrangement. Order is both the subject of conversation and its guiding force in the dialogue of a thinker who in his youth was introduced to philosophy by Cicero's dialogue *Hortensius,*[40] but was a professor of rhetoric for a long time before he became a Christian neo-Platonist and thus learned to practice philosophy with a quite different degree of intensity. I am speaking, of course, of Augustine and his *De ordine,* the most important of the Cassiciacum dialogues.[41]

The conversation reported in *De ordine* begins at night, in a bedroom where Augustine and his young friends have already gotten into bed. However, Augustine is unable to go to sleep, partly because he cannot tear himself away from his thoughts and partly because the unusually

40. *Beat. vit.* 1.4; *Conf.* 3.4.
41. In *Contra academicos* the connection between cognitive activity and epistemological theme is hardly reflected; but see 1.4.11, where Augustine remarks, concerning Licentius's observation that the previous day's discussion was interrupted when they were seeking a definition of error: "Hic plane . . . non erras, quod ut tibi omen sit ad reliqua, libenter optauerim."

loud sound of water flowing in a nearby canal is keeping him awake, especially since he cannot explain it to himself. When Licentius suddenly shoos mice away, Augustine sees that he, too, is awake; and the third person in the room, Trygetius, also shows that he is awake. Licentius has a simple explanation for the phenomenon that is disturbing Augustine: the fallen autumn leaves have stopped up the canal. Augustine is impressed and explains that now he knows why Licentius himself hadn't been surprised by it. However, Licentius is surprised — in a further coincidence of the activity of thinking and its object[42] — that Augustine is surprised: "modo plane dedisti mihi magnum mirari. — Quidnam hoc est? inquam. — Quod tu, inquit, ista miratus es" (1.3.8). Whereas Plato (*Tht.* 155d) and Aristotle (*Metaph.* 982b12 ff.) see wonder *(thaumazein)* as the beginning of philosophy, Augustine describes astonishment *(admiratio)* as a vice *(vitium);* and yet it is only the astonishment that a man like Augustine is subject to this vice of astonishment that gets the conversation going. The cause of astonishment, Augustine says, is something unfamiliar that happens outside the apparent causal order: "res insolita praeter manifestum causarum ordinem." Licentius agrees, but only because Augustine said "apparently" *(manifestum)* — for nothing can happen outside the order: "nam praeter ordinem nihil mihi fieri uidetur."

Licentius then develops a theory of an all-encompassing causal order, a theory that is influenced by both the Stoic doctrine of *heimarmenē* and by Virgil's conception of *fatum* (which is given a Christian interpretation: 1.4.10) and whose high degree of abstraction is worthy of Spinoza. That nothing happens without a cause is a priori true, even if we do not know the concrete cause of an event. This also holds for human behavior. Chance exists only relative to our lack of knowledge; as such, it does not exist: "Et hic respondebo nos parum uidere; nam temerariam quae illas genuit nequaquam esse naturam. Quid plura? Aut aliquid sine causa fieri docear aut nihil fieri nisi certo causarum ordine credite" (1.4.11; cf. 1.5.14). Licentius is so overwhelmed by this thought that he would also attribute a factual refutation of his position to the general order: "Tantum enim eum (sc. ordinem) animo imbibi atque

---

42. This is a type-, not a token-coincidence, for Licentius is not astonished by his own astonishment but by Augustine's.

hausi, ut, etiamsi me quisquam in hac disputatione superarit, etiam hoc nulli temeritati sed rerum ordini tribuam. Neque enim res ipsa, sed Licentius superabitur" (1.3.9). Here we can object that Licentius gives causes precedence over reasons, and that is never permissible: the context of reasons may be uncircumventable, but if it leads us to reject the idea of a comprehensive causal order as unacceptable, then we must simply no longer rely on it. At least we must distinguish between a concept of order as theoretical validity and the concept of a causal order, and Licentius is thinking primarily of the latter when to Trygetius's astonishment he defends error as causally necessary and thus part of the order (1.6.15). In fact, in the second book one of the main problems discussed will be whether a stupid person, for instance, acts in accord with the order. In this question Augustine sees, as he says, a pitfall: if it is answered in the affirmative, then the definition of order as the structure in accord with which God directs everything is endangered; if it is answered in the negative, then there seems to be something outside order; and we cannot wish either of these. Hence the warning not to upset everything by defending order, that is, not to create disorder.[43]

The associated problem of whether the comprehensive, deterministic context of order is purely causal or teleological is not sufficiently discussed (1.5.12). As Christians, all the conversation partners assume, without adequate arguments, that it is teleological, and thus Augustine attributes to the leaves blown by the wind and floating on the water the function of reminding people of the order of things; and in the series of accidents that has gotten their conversation going, Licentius sees with fascination the ordering hand of God, whom he addresses directly: "Quis neget, deus magne, inquit, te cuncta ordine administrare? Quam se omnia tenent! quam ratis successionibus in nodos suos urgentur! quanta et quam multa facta sunt, ut haec loqueremur! quanta fiunt ut te inueniamus!" (1.5.14). This is even more the case because not only our conversations with others but also our own insights do not depend on us; an order transcending us underlies them.[44] That the opportunity for discussion of order itself proceeds from the divine order is empha-

43. 2.4.11.
44. Cf., in addition to 1.5.14, 1.3.6, 1.8.21, and 1.8.23.

sized several times.[45] At the end of the dialogue, for instance, we read that Alypius's laudatory reference to Pythagoras—which the aged Augustine was to regret[46]—was made in accord with a hidden divine order: "Quod autem Pythagorae mentionem fecisti, nescio quo illo diuino ordine occulto tibi in mentem uenisse credo" (2.20.54).

At first sight, *De ordine* seems to fail in two ways, as a dialogue and as a philosophical project. As a dialogue it fails because it ends with Augustine's long discourse on educational theory, which completely overwhelms the conversational exchange, although it has, as is said, its own order.[47] And it fails as a philosophical project because it offers no satisfactory answer to the admittedly not simple question of the extent to which evil in all its forms, for example, moral and intellectual, is compatible with the divine order. (In the later dialogue *De libero arbitrio*, Augustine was to discuss this problem further with a more mature conversation partner, Euodius.) And yet *De ordine* is able to save itself because it explains why the question itself remains open from the point of view of the theory of order: without the acquisition of foreknowledge, without answers to preliminary questions, the great metaphysical problems cannot be resolved in an orderly way. Someone who rushes into them without having made his way through the right order of the disciplines will become curious instead of eager, credulous instead of learned, unbelieving instead of cautious: "Illud nunc a me accipiatis uolo, si quis temere ac sine ordine disciplinarum in harum rerum cognitionem audet inruere, pro studioso illum curiosum, pro docto credulum, pro cauto incredulum fieri" (2.5.17). That there is a pedagogically necessary order is subsequently repeated no less than five times before the end of the dialogue.[48]

---

45. 2.2.7: "cum deus ipse oportunitatem ordine dederit"; 2.3.8: "cetera, ut iam sese habet ordo ille, prouenient"; 2.4.12: "Quam magna, inquam, quam mira mihi per uos deus ille atque ipse, ut magis magisque credere adducor, rerum nescio quis occultus ordo respondet"; 2.7.22: "Nam ut primum nobis istam de ordine quaestionem nescio quis ordo peperit." Analogously, in Shaftesbury's *The Moralists*, Theocles addresses the genius of Nature as the "author and subject of these thoughts!" (1999; 110).

46. *Retract.* 1.3.3.

47. 2.10.29.

48. 2.7.24., 2.14.39, 2.17.46, 2.18.47, 2.19.51. In *Retract.* 1.3.1, Augustine explains that at the end of *De ordine* he switched from the divine order to the easier question of the order of study.

The insistence on this point naturally reminds us of Plato;[49] but with the important difference that Augustine, no less as the author than as a conversation partner in the dialogue, presents this education as something that for him is still to be worked out. In the dialogue *De magistro* (probably written in 389), Augustine seems to have become a teacher in a fuller sense of the word, one who makes what happens in the conversation represented—teaching—itself a theme.[50] However, the work's point is entirely Platonic: the true teacher is already within, namely God in us.

Plato's dialogues, Cicero's *De oratore,* and Augustine's *De ordine* differ from each other thematically no less than they do in the group dynamics of the characters in the dialogues. And yet they have one thing in common: one and the same subject is both the theme of the investigation and its guide. *De ordine* is not, as I have said, new in that regard; but what is new in it is that the subject is not, as in the case of the virtues or eloquence, something immanent to the speakers but rather a power that transcends them in moving toward the whole. This shows that Augustine stands at the end of the ancient world and on the threshold of the Middle Ages. Turning the gaze away from the dramatically interacting conversation partners toward the unified order that underlies them is one of the reasons for the decline of the dialogue form.

49. For instance, consider the comprehensive educational program for philosopher-kings in the seventh book of the *Republic* but also passages like *La.* 182b5 ff., *Euthd.* 282e1 f. and 288c6 ff., *Grg.* 454c1 ff., and *Men.* 82e12 f., frequently with the important word *hexēs* (see also *Mx.* 241a6), which corresponds to *ordine.*

50. Cf. esp. 12.40: "Velut si abs te quaererem hoc ipsum quod agitur, utrumnam uerbis doceri nihil possit."

PART I

The Production of
Philosophical Dialogue

CHAPTER 4

The Stages of the Philosophical
Dialogue's Historical Development

The philosophical dialogue[1] was not invented by the Greeks.[2] We might
mention *The Conversation of a World-Weary Man with His Soul* (if it
can be called "philosophical"); the so-called "Babylonian Theodicy";
the *Upanishads,* for example, the famous discussion between Uddālaka
Āruni and his son Śvetaketu in the seventh chapter of the "Chandogya-
Upanishad"; the *Analects,* which report Confucius's conversations; the
central part of the Book of Job (3:42.6); the "Suttapiṭaka" in the *Tipiṭaka,*
which reproduces the Buddha's conversations as well as his didactic

---

1. The goal of the following section is to indicate lines of development, not to
name all the important philosophical dialogues (not to mention nonphilosophical dialogues). For that, see Hirzel or, for readers seeking a briefer overview, the third part of
S. Guellouz (1992; 165–250). Still shorter are the useful articles by H. Görgemanns
(1997) and M. Grosse (1999), from which I have derived much information.

2. This holds a fortiori for the chat dialogue. One example among many is the
formally fascinating Babylonian *Dialogue of Pessimism* (c. seventh century B.C.), which
takes up the master-servant problematics in a satirical vein, the servant constantly
finding arguments for the contradictory courses of action his master proposes. There
is an English translation by B. R. Forster (1993), 815 ff. On Sumerian literary dialogues,
see B. Alster (1990), and on the subgenre of dialogue within the genres of Old Egyptian
literature, see R. B. Parkinson (1996).

discourses—texts that have their origins in Egypt, Mesopotamia, Brahmanic India, China, Israel, and Buddhist India. Even if in a few cases their precise dates are debatable, some of these works are as old as those of classical Greece, and some are much older. *The Conversation of the World-Weary Man with His Soul* was written around 2000 B.C., the "Babylonian Theodicy" in the first half of the first century B.C. at the latest, the "Chandogya Upanishad" around 600 B.C., the *Analects* probably in the second generation of Confucius's pupils, that is, in the fifth century B.C., the dialogic part of the Book of Job, unlike the older frame story, between the sixth and the fourth century B.C.; and there are good reasons for continuing to think that the extant version of the "Suttapitaka" was completed in the first century B.C. and contains a great deal of material that is considerably older—even if the Buddha lived later than has traditionally been assumed.

In all the aforementioned cultures the dialogue, and especially the philosophical dialogue, has existed for a long time. A few examples may suffice. The Chinese debate with Buddhism, for instance, occasionally took a dialogic form; only consider Fan Zhen's Qi dynasty anti-Buddhist text "Shenmie lun" (On the Extinction of the Spirit, c. A.D. 500), which discusses at an amazingly high level and with extraordinary philosophical density the arguments for and against the identity of body and mind.[3] One of the most important texts that is not part of the *Tipitaka* but is nonetheless a semicanonical text of Theravada Buddhism is the *Milindapañha* (Menander's Questions), a dialogue in Pali between the Buddhist monk Nagasena and the Greco-Indian king Milinda/Menander of Bactria, a historical figure of the second century B.C. who may have actually converted to Buddhism. The dialogue probably dates from the first or second century A.D. and may have originally been composed in Sanskrit. The *Bhagavad Gita,* one of the most important and influential

---

3. There is a German translation in T. Jansen (2000), 235–46. On the dialogic elements in the Chinese discussion of Buddhism, cf. H. Schmidt-Glintzer (1976), 132 ff. For example, Mou Tzu's apology for Buddhism, *Li-huo lun,* from the second century A.D. is dialogic (see the partial translation in W. T. de Bary, W. Chan, and B. Watson [1960], 314 ff.); and the texts with paradoxical questions or answers, the so-called *kōans,* are also dialogic; see, for example, the one by Pen-Chi from the ninth century (partially translated in de Bary, Chan, and Watson [1960], 403 ff.).

texts of Hinduism, presumably also dates from the first two centuries A.D., and has the form of dialogue (indirect and not self-standing, because it was inserted into the sixth book of the *Mahabharata*). The Sanskrit text *Prabodhacandrodaya*, written by Kṛṣṇa Miśra in the eleventh century and translated early on into German (1842), is not a dialogue but an allegorical philosophical drama, in which philosophical positions are represented. In the Islamic world, the dialogue form is used only rarely;[4] one of the few and best examples is Ja'far b. Mansur al-Yaman's Ismaili's *Kitab al-'Alim wa'l-ghulam*, from the early tenth century.[5] The Jew Solomon ibn-Gabirol's "Fons vitae," written in Arabic and extant in toto but only in Latin translation, is a teacher-pupil dialogue from the eleventh century. Finally, Jehuda Ha-levi's *Kusari*, also written in Arabic and dating from the twelfth century (translated into Hebrew by Judah ben Saul ibn Tibbon in the same century) is one of the most important medieval dialogues on the philosophy of religion. Unfortunately, none of these texts are discussed in this book, not because they are unimportant, but because my ignorance of non-Indo-European languages would make my treatment of them much too dilettantish. Precisely when the literary qualities of a text are concerned, reading it in the original language is indispensable. Even in the case of texts that I have read in the original, such as the "Chandogya-Upanishad," or the *Bhagavad Gita*, a competent analysis would be too extensive and go beyond the framework of this book. I therefore limit myself to occasional allusions to these works.

The spread of philosophical dialogue in the high cultures that have produced philosophical texts shows that it is a natural form. Philosophizing originally took place in conversation, whether among like-minded friends or—in premodern cultures the asymmetrical relationship is the

---

4. This may be connected with the differing nature of the Islamic debate as compared with the Western; see T. Huff (1993), 159.

5. See J.W. Morris's introduction to his edition and translation, esp. pp. 6 ff. On a didactic dialogue by Abū Muqātil from the late eighth century, cf. J. Schacht (1964), which paraphrases it in part. The lack of interest in the dialogue form shown by Islamic culture may have to do with the fact that Plato's philosophy was known chiefly in translations of paraphrases (e.g., Galen's), even though a complete and literal translation of the *Republic* was made; cf. D. C. Reisman (2004).

rule—between a teacher and his pupils, and it was tempting to mirror this social reality even after the transition from orality to scripturality. The growing need to legitimate socially valid traditions at least partly through autonomous reason, felt in many parts of world during the period between 800 and 200 B.C. (which Karl Jaspers called the "axial age"), was favorable to the dialogue form because it did not simply confront the addressee of the text with the author's authority, but let him participate in the questions asked by the interlocutors. Despite the many dialogues in other cultures we can maintain that the Greeks succeeded in elevating the genre to a new level, among other reasons because alternatives to the teacher-pupil dialogue were discovered. Certainly it is not completely impossible that non-Greek texts influenced the genesis of the Greek genre.[6] But first, this is far from proven;[7] and second, even if there really was an influence, exercised by whatever intermediaries, it would not affect the novelty of the Greek achievement, which was produced by both literary and philosophical innovations.

With regard to literary innovation, the drama is certainly one of Greece's most original creations. Of course, some other cultures also have dramas—but not all of them; for instance, Semitic cultures do not (and that is why an interpretation of the Song of Solomon as a drama is scarcely plausible, despite its dialogic elements). But what distinguishes the classical Greek drama of the fifth century—both tragedy and comedy—from that of India is the unique intensity of the moral quest, the deepening

6. This is the thesis of C. Fries (1933).

7. Fries's essay suffers from the fact that he gives too little attention to Vico's great discovery of a typological but not genealogical affinity (however, see 152). The analogies that he points to between the reports of the Buddha's discourses and Plato's dialogues are in fact extensive, but they can easily be derived from a culture of debate common to Greece and India but which arose independently. If we accept the recent later dating of the Buddha originally proposed by Heinz Bechert, an influence of Buddhist texts on Plato's dialogues is impossible, but in any case it is improbable; if anything, the *Upanishads* would be a more likely source of influence. However, Indian influence on Plato has not been demonstrated, and even in the case of the assumption of Persian influence on Plato we must be cautious; see J. Kerschensteiner (1945). More likely, given Menander's Greek ancestry, though also far from established, is a certain influence of the specifically Greek form of dialogue on the *Milindapañha,* which none - theless contains not a single idea taken from Greek philosophy.

of the individual by questioning the accepted moral norms. It is no accident that "tragic" has become a concept not only in aesthetics but also in ethics. Similarly, from a formal point of view it is clear that dramatic dialogue in general and stichomythia in particular were the great school of philosophical dialogue: characterization through the exchange of differing worldviews, and sometimes the arguments that support them, most succinctly in stichomythia, paved the way for philosophical dialogue. A relative straight trajectory leads from the prologue to Sophocles' *Antigone* (1 ff.) or the *agōn* of just and unjust speeches in Aristophanes' *The Clouds* (889 ff.) through Thucydides' Melian dialogue to the *logoi Sōkratikoi*. R. Hirzel, from whom I have borrowed heavily in the following remarks, traced the prehistory of Greek dialogue in all its details.[8] He notes the dialogic structures already found in the epic, as well as in the lyric and particularly the choral lyric; reminds us of the "Contest of Homer and Hesiod" (whose basic idea goes back to Alcidamas and probably presupposes an even older tradition); discusses, so far as they can be deduced from the few, partly disputed fragments that remain, the Sicilian comedy of Epicharmus and the mime of his fellow Sicilian Sophron, which appear to have had a certain influence on Plato;[9] discusses reports of conversations as they are found, for example, in the founder of memoir literature, Ion of Chios, and probably also in Critias's *Homiliai;* examines the dialogic passages in the historical works of Herodotus and Thucydides, as well as the objections that orators occasionally make to themselves by introducing a fictive opponent;[10] and finally discusses the hypothesis, still sometimes entertained today but unproven, that the work "The Constitution of Athens," attributed to Xenophon but certainly dating from the fifth century, must originally have been read as a dialogue. However, one thing is clear: this work stands on the threshold of dialogue, "because in it discussion is driven forward on

---

8. (1895), I 11–67.

9. According to repeated references in the ancient biographies of Plato; cf., e.g., D. L. 3.9–18. Epicharmus is quoted in Plato, *Grg.* 505e1 and *Tht.* 152e5. On Sophron and Xenarchus, said to be Sophron's son, cf. M. Pinto Colombo (1934). On Epicharmus's and Sophron's influence on Plato, cf. the important book by J. M. S. McDonald (1931), esp. 117–41.

10. A good example is Antiphon 3.2.3.

the basis of objections that seem not to be the writer's own objections, but rather those of others."[11]

However, no matter how much literary development may have prepared the way for the dialogue, the latter still seems to owe its ultimate birth to a phenomenon that was precisely not literary in nature, the unique personality of Socrates. So far as we know, no earlier philosopher had ever written dialogues, although dialogic elements certainly appeared in philosophical treatises.[12] How could Socrates become the midwife for the new genre? In simple terms, we can say that the ability to critically examine one's own mores that characterized Greek drama in a still unreflective way was raised in Socrates to full self-consciousness. In him ancient tradition already recognized the founder of practical philosophy, in which the Greeks were even more original than in theoretical philosophy. Important metaphysical speculations were also made in India—but not the comprehensive attempt to ground in reason, and solely in reason, the norms that guide our conduct. With the Sophists this kind of need begins to be expressed; but it was Socrates who through his life and death no less than through his philosophizing first showed how it might be possible to give a positive answer to the question regarding the rational basis for our moral convictions. The central idea that we can attribute to the historical Socrates is that the truly moral demand is not that we unreflectively follow the customs of our culture but rather that we base our actions on reason.[13] However, this presupposes that there is a kind of practical reason, that is, a rational answer to the question about our ultimate goals. The first duty is to give a rational explication of our own moral duties, and since practical reason is generally valid, that is, for each[14] and all,[15] every person must be

11. (1895), I 52.

12. See, e.g., DK 68 B 125, where Democritus has the senses speak to the understanding. The report that Zeno of Elea was the first to write dialogues (D. L. 3.48) can hardly be right, and is easily explained by the fact that he was considered the founder of dialectic. The dialogic elements in the *Dissoi logoi* can be explained by Socratic influence. Cf. V. Hösle (1984a), 288 ff.

13. Cf. *Cri.* 46b4 ff.

14. *Ap.* 38e6 f.

15. *Ap.* 30a2 f.

encouraged to determine his own duties in a rational way. These duties cannot be imposed upon him; he must discern them with his own *logos*. But most people have to be urged to perform this act of autonomy; and the sole framework in which this can happen is a conversation in which they are motivated to engage in such an effort by learning to see how little they actually know (which in no way implies that for Socrates the ultimate conclusion of wisdom is that we cannot know anything). It is this existential dimension that distinguishes Socratic conversation from the Sophists' public debates and mock intellectual battles. In the *Prota-goras* Plato has Socrates say, probably echoing the historical person, that he does not examine solely propositions but also people; not only the truth but also us.[16] This is expressed, for example, in the fact that all the Platonic dialogues are named after one of Socrates' interlocutors—with the exception of five works *(Symposium, Republic, Sophist, States-man,* and *Laws)*. Socrates' mission lies in this kind of examination, which he justifies religiously in the Platonic *Apology* as service to the divinity,[17] and that is also categorically valid even if Socrates makes enemies for himself with it; indeed, he cannot give it up even if he could thereby escape being condemned.[18]

To what extent Plato's *Apology* is a historical document need not be discussed here. It probably records the historical Socrates' way of life and self-conception—no matter in how idealized a form—more than does the literary genre that is named after Socrates, the *logos Sōkratikos.* Even if there is much to be said for the view that the first works in this genre were written during Socrates' lifetime, it did not really flourish until after his death, with the twofold goal of keeping the memory of the master alive and of continuing his mission with one's own means—that is, partly as historical, partly as fictional dialogue. After Socrates' execution, the *logos Sōkratikos*—a mirroring of the Socratic ethos (Arist. *Rh.* 1417a–16b ff.) in a new medium, that of writing, which had remained alien to Socrates himself—represented a kind of revenge taken by his students on those

16. 333c 7 ff. and 348a 5.

17. *Ap.* 30a6 f., 30e3 ff. On the concept of *hypēresia,* which Socrates or Plato borrows from tragedy, cf. C. Wildberg (2002), esp. 102 ff.

18. *Ap.* 21e, 28b f., 29c f.

who had thought that by doing away with Socrates the individual they had also killed his program. However, this revenge entailed a change in medium—from conversation to dialogue (even if the beginning of Plato's *Symposium* suggests that alongside dialogue an oral tradition of Socratic conversations continued to exist at least for a time). The change in medium lay in the spirit of the time, which in general shifted its focus from the oral to the written—although not without resistance and critical remarks, not only on the part of orators like Alcidamas,[19] but also on that of the greatest of all authors of *logoi Sōkratikoi*, Plato himself, as we see in the conclusion of the *Phaedrus*. It can be presumed that the historical Socrates would also have seen the triumph of the dialogue as a two-edged sword: the spread of the influence of Socratic ideas was purchased at the price of a decline of living conversation and thus of a subtle transformation of those ideas. Ideas are not always neutral with regard to the medium used to communicate them.

Aristotle names Alexamenus of Teos as the first author of dialogues.[20] We know nothing else about him. Even if the wording of the Aristotle fragment found in Athenaeus (XI 505b f.) designates Alexamenos as the author of *logoi Sōkratikoi*, Nicias of Nicaea and Sotion, and analogously Favorinus in Diogenes Laertius (3.48), evidently interpreted Aristotle to mean that Alexamenos was the very first author of (discussion) dialogues. That motivated some philologists to emend the text in order to make it clear that Alexamenos's dialogues were not Socratic in nature.[21] However, we should avoid conjectures when they are not absolutely necessary; it is simpler to assume that these authors were concerned with the origin of dialogue in general, and only abstracted from the Socratic

19. The discourse *On the authors of written speeches or on the Sophists (Peri tōn tous graptous logous graphontōn ē peri sophistōn)* is best consulted in F. Blass's edition of Antiphon.
20. *Peri poiētōn* frg. 3 Ross, who however gives the Athenaeus text with the textual change (not based on any mansucript) discussed in following note.
21. In his critical apparatus on this passage in his edition of Athenaeus, G. Kaibel writes (III 116): "fort. *tous proteron graphentas tōn Sōkratikōn dialogous,* neque enim Socraticos Alexamenus, sed dialogos primus scripsisse traditur, cfr. Diog. L. 3, 48." Even the first fragment of a work transmitted in an Oxyrhynchus papyrus dating from the second century A.D., probably about Plato (*POxy* 45, no. 3219, pp. 29–39) does not solve the problem, as W. M. Haslam has correctly noted (36).

nature of Alexamenos's dialogue without denying it.[22] However that may be, even if the first discussion dialogues were not Socratic in nature, they are completely overshadowed by the multitude of *logoi Sōkratikoi* that began to appear around the turn of the fourth century. We do not know whether all the authors to whom such works are attributed really wrote them or whether they are later counterfeits; the list of works attributed to Crito in D. L. 2.121 arouses serious doubts; the same goes for Glaucon, Simmias, and Cebes (2.124 f.). In the case of Simon the Shoemaker (2.122 f.), who is not mentioned by either Xenophon or Plato, we cannot even know whether he really existed or whether the traditional claim that he wrote down the conversations he had with Socrates in his cobbler's shop is merely a clever invention.[23] However, the notion that in addition to Plato and Xenophon, whose writings are the only ones extant, Antisthenes and Aeschines wrote *logoi Sōkratikoi* was not challenged by Panaetius himself, who also thought that the Socratic dialogues attributed to Phaedo and Eucleides of Megara might be genuine (D. L. 2.64).[24]

In any case, more important than the quantity of *logoi Sōkratikoi* was the quality of the best of them. Socrates' most gifted pupil was not the first Greek to create the philosophical dialogue, but he did put it into a form that has never ceased to be paradigmatic over the past 2,400 years. On the one hand, this is because Plato is probably the greatest of all philosophers—at least for originality and wealth of ideas no one has ever rivaled him. But on the other hand, and no less important, Plato was a literary genius. The report that in his youth Plato wrote poetry—lyrics as well as tragedies (D. L. 3.5)—is certainly plausible. At least he must have appropriated through theoretical study the most important

22. Cf. P. Natorp (1893) and R. Hirzel (1895), I 100 f., n. 2.

23. The shoemaker's house that D. B. Thompson excavated (1960) is, of course, no proof of his existence; first, the kylix bearing the name "Simon" found in immediate proximity to the house need not have belonged to the owner of the house, and second, even in that case it would only prove that there was a shoemaker by this name in fifth-century Athens, not that he was the author of Socratic writings. On the other hand, Wilamowitz's claim that this shoemaker did not exist (1879; 187) is also not sufficiently grounded.

24. A recent edition of the fragments of the Socratics has been published by G. Giannantoni. On possible works by Aristippus, see Giannantoni's reflections: *Socraticorum Reliquiae,* III 143–55.

literary techniques of Greek drama, for instance, since he transferred them to the new genre of the philosophical dialogue in a virtuoso way.[25] I will have occasion later to discuss a few of these techniques, on which Plato's masterful characterization[26] and the organic unity of his dialogues,[27] which has seldom if ever been equaled by other authors, are based. It has been said that "anonymity" is characteristic of Platonic dialogue:[28] even if Plato's works were published under his name, he appears neither as an interlocutor nor as the writer of a preface in which the author speaks to the reader. Perhaps one of the secrets of Plato's success is that the most important mask of this mysterious and introverted man was Socrates, one of the most extroverted figures in the history of the world. The mask of the Athenian in the *Laws* is admittedly thin, but it is still a mask: Plato's name is not used. He is named twice in the nondialogic *Apology*;[29] in the dialogues just once, and then only to explain that he was *not present* at Socrates' death because he was ill. Phaedo's statement is vague: "I believe that Plato was ill";[30] and even if it absolutely makes sense dialogue-internally that Phaedo does not remember precisely the reason for Plato's absence, dialogue-externally this indeterminacy is, of course, perplexing, and only a clear confirmation of Plato's wish to efface himself—even where he is referred to. It seems at first that Plato's absence because of illness is mentioned chiefly in order

25. That Plato, despite all his criticism of poetry, was actually in competition with Homer, was already rightly seen by the ancients (cf. Longinus, 13.4).

26. Proclus rightly praises Plato as *mimētikōtatos,* as the one who took mimesis (especially of persons) the furthest (*in Cra.* XIV; 5, 17 Pasquali).

27. The close connection between the prologue and the actual discussion in Plato's dialogues is emphasized, for instance, by Basil in his letter 167 (in the Benedictine edition, letter 135), and by Proclus in his commentary on the *Parmenides* (658, 32 ff. Cousin).

28. Cf. the well-known article by L. Edelstein (1962), who sees in it partly a tribute to the teacher that reminds us of the Pythagoreans and partly a deliberate retreat of the individual in the face of general reason: "In this way Platonic anonymity symbolizes the objective element in his philosophy, the universality of reason" (21). In a later article, M. Frede (1992) connected the anonymity of Plato with the aporetic nature of many of his dialogues, which he, in my opinion incorrectly, interprets as reflecting a real skepticism.

29. 34a1, 38b6.

30. *Phd.* 59b10: *Platōn de oimai ēsthenei.*

to contrast his absence with the unexcused absence of Aristippus and Cleombrotus, who were not far away, namely in Aegina—a criticism that is all the sharper because it is not directly expressed.[31] And in fact of all the Socratics none was more distant from Plato than Aristippus, in both nature and ideas.

However, this withholding of his own position did not prevent Plato from occasionally revealing himself, clearly for initiates, by having his dramatis personae make statements that produce meaning when related to Plato himself dialogue-externally.[32] In particular, Plato's reserve does not mean that he had no position of his own; indeed, according to the conception I consider the only right one, even the early so-called aporetic dialogues do not end in an aporia for their writer, or even for the main participant in the conversation. The irony of the Platonic Socrates with regard to his interlocutors and that of Plato with regard to his readers is obvious for any unprejudiced reader, and it is one of the main reasons not only for the hermeneutic difficulties but also the attraction of Plato's works. It is clear that both the Platonic Socrates and Plato himself "hold back" a great deal, and even someone who is not inclined to assume that there is any esoteric doctrine transcending the dialogue oeuvre cannot deny that many dialogues foreshadow later ones and "save out" something to be explained in subsequent dialogues—or, in my view, sometimes only in oral teaching.[33] But that means that at least the majority of Plato's dialogues form a single literary universe, even if there are breaks between some of the dialogues; I examine these in Part II, chapter 8. Since a development-history reconstruction of Plato has proven to be far more difficult than was long thought, the idea of a pedagogical plan suggests itself, a plan that underlies the sequence of the dialogues and that Plato

31. Demetr. *Eloc.* 288.
32. See Part II, chap. 18 (p. 435 ff.).
33. Discussion of this was initiated by H. J. Krämer's splendid dissertation (1959) and significantly developed by K. Gaiser (1963). My defense of the so-called Tübingen school was consistent from (1984a) to (2004a); perhaps the present book shows that such a defense need show no lack of sensitivity to the dialogue form. H. Gundert presciently foresaw (1968; 57) that given the complexity and innovativeness of Krämer's and Gaiser's research, decades of work on the new problems of method and content would be necessary.

probably worked out early on and, even if no doubt with modifications, carried out over decades—far more successfully than five-year economic plans. Therefore it is more indispensable in his case than in that of any other author of dialogues to keep the whole of his work in view, even if we seek to interpret only one dialogue. He had great staying power, and demands as much of his intelligent readers.

In view of the perfection of his work, which later writers of philosophical dialogues have often experienced as a spur, but also repeatedly as crippling because they find it hard to believe that anything can still be added to the genre, the question inevitably arises as to how the dialogue genre could continue to be practiced at all after Plato. After the fifth century, there was no Greek tragedy worth passing on to later generations; and another cultural soil, the Roman one, was required for it to sprout again, and almost two millennia to produce a tragedy that was aesthetically of the same rank. Shouldn't we expect the philosophical dialogue to undergo an analogous fate? First of all, the answer to this question is yes; Hirzel titled the third section of his book, which deals with Aristotle and his contemporaries, "Der Verfall" (The Decline, following "Essence and Origin of the Dialogue" and "The Blossoming," of which Socrates and the Socratics, including Plato, are the subject). It is no accident that since the first century B.C. the transmission of the Aristotelian text has concentrated on the didactic writings—in them was recognized, after they became accessible again, the greater philosophical value, and people did not believe that high literary quality compensated for the lesser philosophical density of the exoteric writings, most but not all of which were dialogues. Cicero[34] and Quintilian[35] might rightly praise the stylistic qualities of the Aristotelian dialogues, which probably avoided the hiatus more than did the Platonic dialogues[36] and whose long speeches corresponded more closely to rhetorical norms than to the rapid-fire, stichomythic exchanges of Plato's early dialogues. But the true merit of a dialogue depends only to a small extent on its rhetorical qualities.

34. *Ac. Pr.* 2.38.119: "veniet flumen orationis aureum fundens Aristoteles."
35. *Inst.* 10.1.83.
36. Cf. Cic. *Or.* 44.151.

What most distinguished Aristotle's dialogues from those of Plato, with which they compete thematically, and even partly in their titles,[37] was the break with "anonymity." It is very possible that Aristotle was the first to have introduced himself as an interlocutor in a philosophical dialogue;[38] there is no doubt that he appeared in many of his dialogues as a conversation partner, and in some played the leading role.[39] We can go still further: Aristotle wrote proems, as did Cicero after him, in which he spoke as author to the reader; that is, he wrote prefaces.[40] Although the numerous fragments of Aristotle's exoteric writings allow the reconstruction of many of the ideas developed in them, the way in which

37. I refer to the *Menexenus,* the *Symposium,* the *Sophist,* and the *Statesman.*

38. Cf. Hirzel (1895), I 292. The fact that Xenophon on one occasion represents himself speaking to Socrates (*Mem.* 1.3.8 ff.) does not contradict this, on the one hand because the *Memorabilia,* as already noted (chap. 2, n. 69), is not a dialogue and on the other because the passage is minute in comparison with the work as a whole. It is striking that Xenophon speaks of himself in the third person.

39. See, in addition to Cic. *Fam.* 1.9.23: "scripsi igitur Aristotelio more . . . tris libros in disputatione ac dialogo 'de Oratore'" (which evidently refers to the nondramatic element in Aristotle's dialogues, that is, the long speeches, since Cicero does not himself appear in *De oratore*), Cic. *Att.* 13.19.4: "quae autem his temporibus scripsi, *Aristoteleion* morem habent, in quo ita sermo inducitur ceterorum ut penes ipsum sit principatus."

40. That clearly emerges from Cic. *Att.* 4.16.2: "quoniam in singulis libris utor prohoemiis ut Aristoteles in iis quos *exōterikous* vocat." The most obvious interpretation of the passage is that Aristotle, like Cicero, wrote prefaces to the individual books of his dialogues (cf. Hirzel [1895], I 298 f., n. 1). The passage in Basil's letter already cited (above, n. 27), according to which Aristotle and Theophrastus immediately entered upon their subjects, can along with the passage in Cicero be interpreted only as meaning that "the Aristotelian 'prooemia' were not, as in the case of Plato, dramatic expositions interwoven with the conversation, but were, like Cicero's, separated from the latter as genuine 'prefaces'" (J. Bernays [1863], 137). How correctly Bernays answered in his book many philologically difficult questions in research on Aristotle, again and again elicits admiration. Hirzel drew attention chiefly to the Basil passage (I 275), but his later reference to the Cicero passage (I 295, n. 2) shows that he shared Bernays's interpretation. On the other hand, G. Zoll (1962; 87 f., n. 17) sought to reconcile the two passages so that Aristotle wrote only short proems. This is unsatisfactory and is based on a lack of distinction between dialogue-internal and dialogue-external proems, namely prologue and preface. In the passage just mentioned Cicero uses the term *prohoemiis* to refer to dialogue-external proems, while in *R.* 357a2 Socrates uses the term *prooimion* to refer to something that is (seen from our perspective) dialogue-internal, namely the conversation represented in the first book of the *Republic,* which prepares the way for the systematic representation in the second to tenth books.

the dialogues are conducted can be deduced from them only to a limited extent, since very few of the fragments reproduce exchanges between two persons.[41] As in most of Plato's late dialogues the contribution made by one of the interlocutors is limited to approbative clichés—"Certainly," "You are right," and so on. In general no one who studies the fragments can escape the impression that the crucial tendency of the Aristotelian dialogue was toward the loss of the indirectness of communication. In his dialogues as well, Aristotle wanted to make himself immediately understood; and since they were addressed to a broader audience, he tried to proceed less allusively and technically than in his treatises based on lectures. Naturally, Plato's dialogues, as distinct from his teaching in the Academy, only rarely seem to presuppose technical knowledge; but it would be a mistake to think that they are therefore easy to interpret. Plato's play of masks and the inscrutable irony of the Platonic Socrates are the reasons why down to the present day intelligent and learned readers do not agree whether the *Laches* or the *Charmides* ends in a genuine aporia. In contrast, a play of masks is hardly possible for an author who appears in his own work. Even if irony is not denied to such an author, and even if we must in principle distinguish the author of a dialogue from his like-named counterpart acting as a conversation partner within the dialogue, we have not the slightest ground for assuming that Aristotle adopted an ironic posture or exploited this distinction; the writing of prefaces suggests the contrary. The absence of scenic prologues deprives the Aristotelian dialogue of the possibility, so characteristic of Plato's dialogues, of highlighting aesthetically fascinating relationships between actions that are external to the philosophical discussion, such as encounters and greetings, and the real substantive conversation; instead of offering an organic unity of prologue and discussion, in Aristotle the text is divided into preface and genuine dialogue.[42] That drawing characters can

---

41. *Eudēmos,* frg. 6 Ross; and *Peri eugeneias,* frg. 2 Ross. The fragment shows that the dialogue was an indirect one; the reporter was Aristotle himself, comparable to Socrates in the *Republic.*

42. This reminds us of the external addition of the prologue in Euripides' tragedies, whose function is to avoid burdening the subsequent representation of affects with the task of communicating information necessary for the comprehension of the play. See F. Nietzsche, *Die Geburt der Tragödie* 12 (1988; 1.85 f.). Plato's art is made

hardly have been a concern for Aristotle, as it was for Plato, is shown by the fact that the titles of most of the latter's dialogues are just proper names, whereas this is true of only two of Aristotle's.[43] The origin of dialogue in living conversation, of which the Socratics were still very aware, was farther away for Aristotle—discussion in school had replaced chats in the gymnasium or the agora. Nor did classical Greek tragedy live on in Aristotle. He sought to archive tragedies, to reflect on them theoretically, but he no longer strove to incorporate them into his philosophy. Only someone who no longer feels tragic emotions puts himself onstage—or has himself appear in a dialogue.[44] Only the genre of comedy allows the author to represent himself.[45] Not being able to resist expressing one's own opinion is ultimately an expression of the decline of aristocratic forms, of which the techniques of distancing are always part.

And yet one aspect of Aristotelian dialogue points toward the future. Even if Aristotle gave himself the lion's share of the conversation in many of his dialogues, and even if he was doubtless convinced that he was intellectually superior to his interlocutors, in his dialogues something is missing that characterizes almost all the earlier philosophical dialogues in Greece: the daemonic figure of Socrates. The asymmetry between this stonemason who paid with his life for his pleasure in philosophizing, which he experienced as a duty, and his interlocutors is far greater than that between the first professor—who was, as we know, Aristotle—and

clear, for example, in the *Phaedo,* in which the last actions of the dying Socrates are described in no less detail than his last arguments. In contrast, Gregory recounted the life (including the death) and the teaching of Macrina in two different works. There are also scenic elements in the account of Macrina's death in *On the Soul and the Resurrection,* but because of the earlier *Vita* not in a detail comparable to that of Plato's *Phaedo.*

43. I refer to the *Menexenus* and the *Nerinthus* (D. L. 5.22, it being debated whether the title of the latter has been accurately handed down and really represents the name of a person). The *Gryllus, Eudemus,* and *Alexander* have subtitles ("On the Art of Oratory," "On the Soul," and "For the Colonies") which are Aristotle's, whereas the subtitles of Plato's dialogues were all added later.

44. Cf. Hirzel's excellent comparison of the decline of tragedy with that of dialogue (1895; I 294–300).

45. Consider Kratinos's *Putinē* (Bottle), in which the great comedian mocked his own drunkenness so brilliantly that he was victorious over Aristophanes' *The Clouds.* The praetexta *Octavia* attributed to Seneca cannot have been written by him, precisely because Seneca appears in it.

his pupils, colleagues, and perhaps also monarchs.[46] Even the cleverest professor remains just a professor; Socrates was something different and greater. In particular, he acquires a heroic, not to say divine, majesty in the work of Plato, who represents him—and thus himself—as almost omniscient, as the paragon of all virtues, and also as underestimated by his closest friends, such as Crito, whose intellects and personalities cannot match his, and to whom he therefore reveals, as Plato does to readers of his dialogues, only part of what he knows. The profound loneliness of the Platonic Socrates—at least the Socrates of the dialogues preceding the *Republic*, to whom it is never granted to have a pupil named Plato, whereas in the later dialogues he instructs a Theaetetus and converses with figures such as the stranger from Elea and Timaeus who are of equal if not superior intellectual ability—is the price to be paid for the enormous asymmetry of the relationship between Socrates and his interlocutors in the dialogues preceding the *Republic*.[47] It is this asymmetry against which the whole development of the philosophical dialogue after Plato at least implicitly protests and that was never to return. To be sure, the teacher-pupil conversations of the Middle Ages are also asymmetrical—but none of them presents a comparable decline. If we seek something analogous, we must go back to the Gospels, because such an asymmetry is bearable only in religion, not in philosophy.

This provides an answer to the question asked earlier as to how the dialogue could continue to exist after Plato. It counts in favor of the plausibility of this answer that it is in accord with the answer to the question as to what was new in Hellenistic philosophy, which did not attain the same intellectual level as classical Greek philosophy. It is indeed inferior, but Hellenic philosophy paved the way for ethical universalism, which was still foreign to Plato and Aristotle but is essentially characteristic of modern ethics.[48] The establishment of a symmetrical relation-

46. G. Gaiser (1985) has interpreted a passage in Philodemus's *Rhetoric* as indicating that Philip II of Macedon was a conversation partner in one of Aristotle's dialogues, and suggests that the latter was the *Eudemus*, in which he is supposed to have conversed with the eponymous protagonist. But this reconstruction remains hypothetical.

47. See the apt title of the essay by T. A. Szlezák (1988).

48. This universalism also includes a reevaluation of relationships within the family, as G. Reydams-Schils (2005) has shown. We need only contrast Plato's *Phaedo* with Musonius Rufus.

ship between the interlocutors in the philosophical dialogue is related to the effort made by the Stoics, for example, to give ethics a universalist content. This is entirely compatible with a tendency toward the private: whereas in the market or on the playing field no craftsman or youngster was safe from the unique questioning and humiliation dished out by the one-of-a-kind Socrates, whose philosophizing was essentially public and was practiced almost everywhere,[49] now minds of equal rank meet in the private seclusion of their country estates. The Peripatetic Praxiphanes is probably the first to whom we owe such a "villa dialogue"—in *Peri poiētōn* (or *Peri poiēmatōn*) Isocrates and Plato met on an estate and spoke about the art of poetry and its theory (D.L. 3.8).[50] The point of this dialogue was that the two contemporaries, who assigned different values to the emotions, did not vie before a large audience but talked in a friendly way with each other and assumed that they were fundamentally equals. Anyone who considers the mutual animosity between the Academy and the school of Isocrates, and recalls that certainly the *Euthydemus* (304d ff.) and perhaps even the *Phaedrus*, with its benevolent but nonetheless slightly condescending praise (279a f.), represent a certain distancing from Isocrates, will doubt that Plato would have appreciated this symmetricalization. But there is no doubt that it corresponded to the spirit of the time, and with the villa dialogue Praxiphanes created a subgenre of the philosophical dialogue that foreshadowed its future development.

This becomes particularly clear in the dialogues of the next great figure in the history of the genre, Cicero. To be sure, Cicero was also influenced by Marcus Junius Brutus's villa dialogues in the three books of *De jure civili*,[51] in which the Greek influence is hard to determine—in the discussion of law as well as in the fact that the conversation takes place between father and son, we see something typically Roman, namely the importance of law and family. But whatever Brutus's knowledge of Greek models in general and of Praxiphanes in particular might have been, Cicero's intimate knowledge of these models, especially Plato, some of

---

49. Cf. C. Sigonio (1993), 192: "ut ad virtutem inserendam et vitia ex animis hominum evellenda nullum tempus importunum, nullum locum alienum existimaret."
50. Cf. frg. 11–17 Wehrli.
51. Cf. *De or.* 2.55.223 f.

whose works he translated,[52] is evident. As I shall repeatedly show, Cicero demonstrated a very high degree of literary creativity that far outstrips his specifically philosophical achievement. For instance, some of his adaptations of Platonic themes are examined in Part II, chapter 11; here I must limit myself to a few remarks on the nature of his villa dialogues. All Cicero's dialogues take place in private spaces, for the most part on country estates where leading Roman politicians visit each other.[53] In comparison to the socially diverse background of the conversation partners in the *logoi Sōkratikoi,* a narrowing has taken place that becomes particularly problematic when Cicero has statesmen and generals discuss problems of theoretical philosophy in which they never took any interest. They might speak convincingly of the art of oratory and politics, but hardly of epistemological subtleties. Even if in his *De fato,* which consists mainly of his speech and of which only fragments are extant, Cicero was able to make a competent presentation of Stoic determinism, one can say the same of few Roman Optimates. We know that this is the reason why Cicero abandoned the last two parts of the "Hortensius-Catulus-Lucullus" trilogy and replaced them by the four books of the *Academici libri,* in which the eponymous consuls were replaced as Cicero's conversation partners first by Cato and Brutus and finally by Varro and Atticus. Simply adding explanatory prefaces to the first version—strangely enough, the preface to *Lucullus* has, like the rest of the dialogue been well preserved—had proved insufficient.[54] Since Varro's erudition was not in doubt, it made sense to bring him in, even

---

52. "Platonis aemulus" Quintilian calls Cicero (10.1.123). Similarly, Lact. *div. inst.* 1.5.16 and 3.25.1. Though Cicero did adopt the Aristotelian innovations, his best dialogues are the ones in which he subtly varies Platonic themes. See Hösle (2008a).

53. Cf. C. Sigonio (1993), 162: "Neque enim apud eum fere loquitur quisquam nisi aut consularis aut senator aut certe in luce reipublicae vivens. Saepe etiam qui memoria patrum maiorumque floruerunt dignitate principes civitatis et gloria colloquentes facit, ut summae eorum auctoritati atque amplitudini par prope dictionis verborumque magnificentia ac maiestas iure attribuenda fuerit."

54. Cf. *Att.* 13.13.1: "commotus tuis litteris . . . totam Academiam ab hominibus nobilissimis abstuli, transtuli ad nostrum sodalem"; 13.16.1; 13.19.3: "sane in personas non cadebant; erant enim *logikōtera* quam ut illi de iis somniasse umquam viderentur"; and 13.32.3. It cost Cicero—or rather his friend and publisher Atticus—something to make this change in the book, which was already in production (*Att.* 13.13.1).

though Cicero had never discussed skepticism with him.[55] This erudition was able to compensate for the fact that Varro was not a "vir consularis," that is, not a former consul (he rose only as far as the rank of praetor), unlike the quartet in the first version of the trilogy. We are only too aware of how proud Cicero was of having become a consul: he even went so far as to refer to the more "respectable" philosophers as *consulares philosophos*,[56] a kind of class consciousness that was completely alien to Socrates and at which less prejudiced people can only smile.

And yet Cicero's pomposity, which we find so tedious, as many of his contemporaries no doubt also did, was, as is usually the case in life, only a compensation for the inner insecurity that he felt, as a *homo novus*, with regard to the patricians, and as a Roman, with regard to the Greeks. Cicero wanted to "belong" to the Roman political elite and to the Greek intellectual elite; he may also have wanted to be recognized by them as especially talented—but no more. Plato would have considered this laughable petty ambition; his goal was entirely different: to transform the political and intellectual world of his time with the Ideas in view, to turn his interlocutors' souls around,[57] that is, to convert them. The existentially demanding, testing, probing Socrates of Plato's dialogues has no equivalent in Cicero's works. There were certainly rank differences within the elites, and when Cicero himself appears as a conversation partner, or even in the prefaces,[58] he repeatedly satisfies his irrepressible vanity, usually more clumsily than in the passage from the preface to the third book of *De oratore* analyzed above.[59] But he does not

---

55. *Fam.* 9.8.1 (see above, chap. 2, n. 8).

56. Hortensius frg. 114 Grilli. On the extraordinary importance of former consuls for Cicero, see, e.g., *De or.* 1.40.182.

57. *R.* 518d.

58. Prefaces are lacking only in *De legibus*, which was, however, never completed, and in the *Academica posteriora*.

59. In addition to the direct self-praise of the conversation partner Cicero, Cicero also likes to have himself praised by other interlocutors—probably in the hope that the reader does not see that this is also a form of self-praise on the part of the author. Two passages may suffice to show this: "aut num propterea nulla est rei publicae gerendae ratio atque prudentia, quia multa Cn. Pompeium, quaedam M. Catonem, non nulla etiam te ipsum fefellerunt?" (div 1.14.24); and "equidem etiam in te saepe vidi et, ut ad leviora veniamus, in Aesopo, familiari tuo, tantum ardorem vultuum atque motuum"

represent something categorically different, as Socrates does. In dialogues where Cicero is not himself involved—and these are as a rule his better ones—he succeeds in describing an urbanely charming world characterized by symmetry. This symmetricalization was presumably made easier by Cicero's membership in the Academy—in an Academy that, unlike the old Academy of Plato and his immediate successors, had since Arcesilaus and Carneades been marked by a skeptical spirit that Cicero considered Socratic; he did not support Antiochus of Ascalon's effort to return to the old Academy by giving it a Stoic twist. This skeptical spirit is reflected in Cicero's way of allowing the interlocutors to make speeches, mostly long ones, pro and con, and sometimes as *advocati diaboli*, that is, contrary to their own convictions, as for example Lucius Fu-

---

(div. 1.37.80). In both passages, Quintus is speaking to his brother, and whereas the second is merely tactless (the "lightweight" Clodius Aesopus, was after all Cicero's teacher in delivery, the first, which ranks Cicero's skill as a statesman higher than those of Pompey and Cato, is embarrassing—as was presumably also the attribution of this remark precisely to his brother who had not appreciated Cicero's indecisive behavior during the civil war against Caesar but was later reconciled with him. In his essay "Of the Rise and Progress of the Arts and Sciences," David Hume acknowledged: "I have frequently been shocked with the poor figure under which he [sc. Cicero] represents his friend ATTICUS, in those dialogues, where he himself is introduced as a speaker. That learned and virtuous ROMAN, whose dignity, though he was only a private gentleman, was inferior to that of no one in ROME, is there shewn in rather a more pitiful light than PHILALETHES'S friend in our modern dialogues. He is a humble admirer of the orator, pays him frequent compliments, and receives his instructions, with all the deference which a scholar owes to his master" (1987; 128 f.). Although the reference to the *Tusculanae* in Hume's corresponding footnote is an error, since "A" in the later manuscripts does not stand for "Atticus," the observation is essentially correct, and we can particularly agree with the later addition (1987; 623) that the "tolerable equality maintained among the speakers" in *De oratore* has to do with the fact that Cicero does not himself appear in it. (But Antonius's prophecy that an orator might still appear who will outdo even Crassus [1.21.95] can only refer to Cicero himself; the same thing can be said of 3.21.80 and 3.24.95, where Crassus speaks. Thus Cicero even has two John the Baptists. It will be conceded that Plato's use of Socrates to predict Isocrates'—not his own—achievement [*Phdr.* 278e ff.] is subtler. Cicero imitates this passage at the end of his dialogue and refers to Hortensius: 3.61.228 ff.; yet the reader of *Brutus* knows that Cicero considers himself superior to Hortensius as well.) However, my basic thesis, which is comparative in nature and emphasizes a greater symmetry in Cicero's dialogues than is found in Plato's, is not thereby challenged; but we can add in passing that in the eighteenth century the need for symmetry had become still greater.

rius Philus does in *De re publica*. The stylistic technique of long speeches is influenced by Aristotle, whereas the opposition of two positions is influenced by Carneades[60] and goes ultimately back to the Sophists, in particular to Protagoras. But that certainly does not mean that for Cicero all positions were equally justified. To be sure, his Academic skepticism implied a special openness to other schools; Cicero took Aristotelianism and Stoicism seriously. But he did not consider Epicureanism a legitimate position in either theoretical or practical philosophy. However, that did not prevent him from treating either Caius Velleius in *De natura deorum* or Lucius Manlius Torquatus in *De finibus bonorum et malorum* with respect, and the Epicurean Atticus was his best friend.[61] No reader of *De oratore* can doubt that Cicero prefers Crassus's ideas to Antonius's (even if all the conversation partners repeatedly represent Cicero's own views)—and yet, what tact he shows with regard to Antonius as well![62]

The special grace of this work lies in the fact that the assembled speakers, who have often battled each other in court,[63] are able, in the nonhierarchical situation of the villa conversation, to recognize how much they admire and are even willing to support an opponent who had once cost them a victory or at least tried to defeat them, and whom they have occasionally feared or avoided. The competitive situation in the Forum is based on a general consensus that underlies it, and even on personal friendships. A particularly good example of the way Antonius and Crassus bat the ball back and forth, approaching each other's positions,

60. See *De rep.* 3.5.8. and 3.6.9.

61. In J. Bodin's *Colloquium heptaplomeres,* which intensifies Cicero's liberal perspectivism, after Senamus has said that a consensus, based in love, regarding divine and human matters is the best bond of harmony among friends and citizens, Curtius objects that this statement of Cicero's (*Lael.* 6.20) is contradicted by his own behavior, especially his friendship for Atticus, and deeds are more important than opinions. "Ista quidem est ficta verbis M. Tullii sententia, quam suis ipsis factis oppugnavit, ut minus quaerendum sit, quid sentiat, cum appareat, quid fecerit. Quis enim Epicuraeos magis coluit, quam Atticus? Cui tamen mortalium Cicero magis amicus, quam Attico, extitit unquam? At nihilominus Cicero sectam Academicorum secutus est, quamdiu vixit, Epicuraeos scriptis omnibus lacerans . . ." (1857; 115).

62. On the urbanity of *De oratore,* and the modesty and mutual respect shown by the main speakers, cf. Sigonio (1993), 254 ff. (e.g., in reference to 1.21.96 ff.).

63. 1.39.178, 1.48.207, 2.21.89, 2.23.98, 2.47.197 ff.

playing with their rivalry, is found in the middle of Book II. When the subject of wit comes up, Antonius asks the young Gaius Julius Caesar Strabo to discuss it, because he surpasses all others in wit.[64] Caesar begins his disquisition on the subject (one of the most important in the history of theory of the comic) but then interrupts himself to ask Antonius why he attributed superiority in witty speech to him rather than to Crassus, who is more deserving of this accolade. Antonius's answer is itself witty. He did so, he says, only because he is envious of Crassus, who manages to combine his first-rate wit with gravity and dignity.[65] Crassus laughs (Antonius's generous praise shows, as does indeed the whole tone of the conversation, that envy really plays no role among these friends), and Antonius goes on to offer a criticism of Caesar's thesis that there is no art of wit:[66] Caesar has himself proposed an utterly convincing rule of this art. Thus Antonius defends Crassus's basic tendency to seek rules, which he has just rejected precisely with reference to wit.[67] Yet instead of now declaring himself the winner, Crassus contradicts him—there is no art of oratory.[68] Rules cannot make someone an orator—otherwise anyone could become one—but only help us discern after the fact what is sound or weak in what nature and practice have taught us. Thus instead of glorying in Antonius's recognition that he is right, Crassus makes a broad concession to Antonius's position. Conversely, later on Antonius acknowledges that an orator has to know the virtues,[69] which was Crassus's initial thesis.[70] The latter reacts to this by noting that Antonius has shown himself to be "a master of the art" *(artificem)* even if he has heretofore dissimulated his knowledge. His defense of a reduced conception of rhetoric was also ironic, Crassus says. This is combined with thanks to Antonius for having left him little to discuss and having done the lion's share of the task. But Antonius turns this around: it is Crassus

---

64. 2.54.216.

65. 2.56.228.

66. 2.56.229.

67. 2.54.216.

68. In the first book Crassus had already said that whether or not there was an art of oratory depended on how "art" is defined, and Antonius agreed (1.23.107 ff.). Cf. Crassus's remark, 3.50.159.

69. 2.85.348 f., in contrast to 1.49.213.

70. 1.11.48 and 1.15.68 f.

who is playacting, because the most important part of the discussion has now been handed over to him.[71] At the end of the dialogue, Antonius finally declares that he has accepted Crassus's ideal of the orator, which he had challenged in his own work.[72] Thereby the opposition between the approaches of the "practitioner" Antonius and the "theoretician" Crassus is largely overcome; it is more a question of where the accent falls than of a fundamental contradiction, and they have shown a remarkable ability to think their way into each others' positions. With a magnanimity that recalls that in cantos 11 and 12 of Dante's *Paradiso,* in which Thomas and Bonaventure each praise the other's order and lament the decline of their own, each declares the other to be the greater orator.[73]

Cicero succeeded in writing dialogues between peers differently than Plato did; and even if his probabilistic skepticism presumably made this change easier for him, he did not represent the banal meta-position according to which everyone can think what he wishes, since there is no truth anyway. Genuine issues are wrestled with seriously, and sometimes with good arguments, in his dialogues; but the liberal skeptic Cicero leaves the individual interlocutors considerable freedom. If we seek a twentieth-century philosopher who comes close to Cicero's conversational culture and understanding of the truth, we can mention Gadamer. The Hortensius in Cicero's dialogue of the same name, of which only fragments are extant, was very probably "converted" to philosophy, but to philosophizing as such, not to a specific school. At the end of *De divinatione,* Cicero makes his "athletic" understanding of philosophical conversation clear: he has criticized the Stoics so explicitly only because their arguments are so astute; his real goal is to avoid citing authorities and leave the audience's judgment free and uninhibited.[74] In *De natura deorum,* it

71. 2.86.350 f. See above, chap. 3, n. 33.
72. 3.49.189.
73. 2.89.364, 3.9.32 ff. It is unfortunate that in his later dialogues Cicero did not take to heart Crassus's statement that what is most difficult is rightly to assess oneself.
74. "cum quibus omnis fere nobis disceptatio contentioque est, non quod eos maxume contemnamus, sed quod videntur acutissime sententias suas prudentissimeque defendere. cum autem proprium sit Academiae iudicium suum nullum interponere, ea probare, quae simillima veri videantur, conferre causas et, quid in quamque sententiam dici possit, expromere, nulla adhibita sua auctoritate iudicium audientium relinquere integrum ac liberum, tenebimus hanc consuetudinem a Socrate traditam" (div. 2.72.150).

is artfully left open whether the author, Cicero, leans more toward the Stoic Quintus Lucilius Balbus or the Academic Caius Aurelius Cotta.

The chief threat to the Ciceronian philosophical dialogue is obvious: even as it succeeds in realizing the nature of symmetrical exchange, the dialogue risks becoming a chat dialogue. Most of Plutarch's dialogues— perhaps with the exception of the *Dialogue on Love* (*Erōtikos*)—are of this kind; they lack both complex philosophical arguments and an existentially intensive quest. In contrast, Lucian's dialogues continue the literary experiment of Menippean satire and intentionally combine the traditional dialogue with comedy to form a structure that has great satirical power. Lucian is fully aware of the innovativeness of his achievement in bringing the dialogue down from heaven to earth, as the dialogue "The Double Indictment" *(Dis katēgoroumenos)* and the prolalia "To One Who Said 'You're a Prometheus in Words'" *(Pros ton eiponta, Promētheus ei en logois)* show.[75] But no matter how certain it is that he has a place in the history of literary forms and no matter how much he sarcastically mocks the philosophy of his time, he is himself not a real philosopher. Nonetheless, in particular with his *Dialogues of the Dead*—discussions among the dead in the underworld, some of whom were philosophers—he represented something that came to have an interest for more philosophical minds as well: Fontenelle's *Nouveaux dialogues des morts* and Joly's *Dialogue aux enfers entre Machiavel et Montesquieu*, for example, would be inconceivable without the model provided by Lucian. The dialogues written by his most important German translator, Christoph Martin Wieland—especially "Peregrinus Proteus" and "Göttergespräche"— were also clearly influenced by him.

Among the targets of Lucian's satires were the followers of the new Christian religion. The latter very early seized upon the literary form of the dialogue and once again gave it a profundity that was, if not intellectual, at least existential, and that it had lacked since the *logoi Sōkratikoi*. The adoption of important components of Platonic metaphysics explains why the Platonic dialogues were a model that was emulated, even if critically; for example, Methodius emulated the *Symposium* in his dialogue with almost the same title, *Symposium or on Virginity (Symposion*

75. See esp. *Bis Acc.* 32–34 and *Prom. Es* 6.

ē peri hagneias), and Gregory of Nyssa emulated the *Phaedo* in his *On the Soul and Resurrection (Peri psykhēs kai anastaseōs).*[76] What is new, however, is the subgenre of the conversation among adherents of different religions: Justin's Greek *Dialogue with the Jew Tryphon (Pros Tryphōna Ioudaion dialogos),* the oldest extant Christian dialogue (c. 150),[77] and its counterpart in Latin literature, Marcus Minucius Felix's *Octavius,* in which a pagan is converted to Christianity,[78] are the best-known examples. Some of the interreligious dialogues and even more of those among Christians represent real theological debates without any literary pretensions. The philosophical content of these dialogues is seldom high. This changes with Augustine. Of his many dialogues only the three previously mentioned Cassiciacum dialogues have a fully elaborated setting; they are his most ambitious from a literary point of view. Formally, they are also villa dialogues; yet characteristically, the villa in Cassiciacum does not belong to any of the friends who have gathered there but rather to an absent friend, Verecundus.[79] Those who meet there are not senators or *viri consulares* but rather young men, of whom the most successful, Augustine, is on the brink of a radical reorientation, both professional and personal. Even if there is no doubt about the Christian orientation of the Cassiciacum dialogues, at the time when they were written Augustine had not yet been baptized. A spirit of sincere searching blows through them, unlike the later writings of the church father a spirit that is all the more moving because it is able to found a sense of community. Augustine dominates the conversation, but his acknowledgment that he is not wise[80]

---

76. Cf. H. M. Meissner (1991), 384–94.

77. The older *Dialogue between Jason and Papiscus* by Aristo of Pella has been lost; in it a Jewish Christian converted an Alexandrian Jew. Cf. M. Hoffmann (1966), 9 f.

78. Regarding the question of the temporal relation of this work to Tertullian's *Apologeticum* there is no established consensus, because it can hardly be definitively answered—despite the most striking correspondences between the two works. It seems to me as to most contemporary scholars that because of his superior intellect it is more likely that Tertullian's work was written first. Minucius Felix was a talented writer but not an original philosophical mind. In addition, the harsh polemic is not appropriate in a conversation among friends; Minucius Felix must have taken it from an apologetic author, and Tertullian is a good candidate. Thus a date around 200 is plausible.

79. *Ord.* 1.2.5.

80. *Ord.* 2.2.7, 2.3.9.

is sincere; and although the Platonic Socrates claimed only the honorary title of philosopher, not that of a wise man,[81] this is compatible with the very wide-ranging asymmetry of the relationship between him and Phaedrus (an asymmetry that helps us understand why Plato could not make himself appear as an interlocutor). The thanks Augustine offers to his fellow discussants at the end of *De beata vita* for having fed him, the host,[82] is Ciceronian in spirit, not Platonic, and the role played by a woman, his mother, Monica, in the dialogues implies something that goes beyond even Cicero (I return to this subject in Part II, chapter 16). The community in Cassiciacum reminds us of the original Christian community;[83] it also includes nonintellectuals like Augustine's cousins Lartidianus and Rusticus, who are in fact uneducated but on whose *sensus communis* Augustine relies.[84] In one respect, however, Augustine is closer to Plato than to Cicero: for him, what is at stake are not rhetorical exercises but his own life, his own mores, his own self.[85]

It is the seriousness of his search that leaves Cicero's cultivated conviviality far behind and reminds us of Plato. This has to do with the fact that Augustine, after passing through a skeptical phase, rejects skepticism in *Contra academicos,* and thus decides for Plato and against Cicero, avoiding, however, a break with the skeptical Academy by defending the—historically untenable—thesis that its skepticism was only an exoteric, ironically intended game.[86] At the end of the dialogue, his friend and opponent Alypius agrees: perhaps the Academicians had really wished to be defeated by their progeny.[87] The young listeners are disappointed that Alypius gives in and that the conversation is over, but Au-

81. *Phdr.* 278d3 ff.
82. 4.36. Cf. 2.16 on the temporary inequality of the conversation partners.
83. It is probably not too much to suggest that the lack of an experience of community comparable to that of the Christians is one of the reasons for the almost complete absence of the dialogue form among pagan Neoplatonists.
84. *Beat. vit.* 1.6.
85. *C. acad.* 2. 9.22: "non ego istam disputationem disputandi causa susceptam uolo. . . . De uita nostra de moribus de animo res agitur." Cf. 3.1.1 and 3.2.3: "ipsam uitam, propter quam sapientia quaeritur." In *Ord.* 2.8.25 life and education are described as the two parts of the discipline at stake.
86. 2.10.24, 2.13.29, 3.17.37–3.20.43.
87. 3.20.44.

gustine urges them to read Cicero's *Academici libri* and there to find "unconquered" arguments against Augustine's position, which has now been adopted by Alypius as well, and which is described as a "jest" *(nugae).* The friends laugh, and Augustine concludes the work by saying that they have found a more moderate and rapid end to the controversy than he had expected—although whether it is also a truly well-grounded one, he does not know.[88] This conclusion, which seems to acknowledge that skepticism is right, is certainly ironic; yet this irony is essential, because it urges the youngsters to study the opponent; it seeks to make Alypius defend the newly achieved position on his own, and leaves it to the reader to judge how well founded the refutation of the skeptics is. That the aged Augustine, who can be accused of many things, but not humor, rejects this irony[89] does not do him credit. But the dogmatism of the later writings cannot diminish the attraction of the early dialogues. Of all the extant ancient dialogues, only Plato's and Augustine's radiate a "You must change your life" that exhorts the reader to make a choice but does not force him to do so. That Augustine does not have the same superiority over his interlocutors as that enjoyed by Plato's Socrates, because for him the role of model is already occupied by Christ, may seem to some a weakness, and to others a strength. In any case, it is clear that only someone who, like Augustine, is prepared to let his own weaknesses be seen could found the genre of autobiography.[90] Deepening Platonism by taking a new interest in the finite subjectivity of human beings, indeed of all human beings, remains Augustine's contribution to world

88. 3.20.45. "Legite Academicos et, cum ibi uictorem—quid enim facilius?—istarum nugarum Ciceronem inueneritis, cogatur iste a uobis hunc nostrum sermonem contra illa inuicta defendere. Hanc tibi, Alypi, duram mercedem pro mea falsa laude restituo.—Hic cum arrisissent, finem tantae conflictionis—utrum firmissimum nescio—modestius tamen et citius, quam speraueram, fecimus." (The edition cited has "ista," but that must be a typographical error for "iste," as a glance at the Stromata edition, also by W. M. Green, confirms.)

89. *Retract.* 1.1.4.

90. Cf. B. R. Voss (1970; 303) on Augustine's dialogues: "They are personal in the highest degree. What is crucial is not that he talks about himself, his experiences, and his wishes, but rather that though he does not expressly say so, we can tell that he is moved by the subject and the development of the conversation, in which intellectual life has found an exceptionally powerful expression. Augustine's dialogues are the apogee of early Christian dialogue literature."

history, and it manifests itself precisely in the form of his early dialogues. It is no accident that in his *De secreto conflictu curarum mearum,* the founder of humanism, Petrarch, chose as his interlocutor Augustine, who had worked through experiences not unlike his own: "multu tu, dum corporeo carcere claudebaris, huic similia pertulisti."[91]

In late antiquity philosophical-theological dialogue remained a favored genre, as is proven by Aeneas of Gaza's *Theophrastus* and Bishop Zacharias of Mytilene's *Ammonius,* which date from the late fifth century and early sixth century, respectively. These two works, which are not intellectually outstanding, defend the Christian rejection of the theory of metempsychosis and the doctrine of the creation of the world in time against the pagan philosophies of Plato and Aristotle, but in doing so they constantly allude to the Platonic art of dialogue and make use[92] of central Platonic theorems. Within the dialogues of the Middle Ages, two groups stand out: the didactic, that is, teacher-pupil dialogues, and the interreligious dialogues.[93] In the first group, the conversation often seems mechanical, even when, as in Alcuin's *Disputatio de rhetorica et de virtutibus* and *De dialectica,* the pupil is Charlemagne—but there is no individual characterization.[94] If some of these dialogues were transformed into treatises, little would be lost. However, that is not true of Anselm of Canterbury's *Cur deus homo,* in which he converses with his favorite pupil, Boso, and in which both characters are masterfully drawn. Since the dialogue deals with one of the two central dogmas that are specifically Christian, Anselm prepares the way for the subgenre of the interreligious dialogue in a broader sense of the word. (A work like Gilbertus Crispinus's *Disputatio Christiani cum Gentili* mediates between the two types of dialogue.)

The most famous interreligious dialogues of the Middle Ages represent encounters between Christians, Jews, Muslims, and/or pagans;

91. (1955), 24.
92. Cf. the *hypothesis* of the *Ammonius* (93, 13 ff. Minniti Colonna).
93. Cf. K. Jacobi's classification (1999), 12. A list of philosophical and theological dialogues in prose from the Latin Middle Ages can be found in M. von Perger (1999).
94. Especially in *De dialectica,* the questions that the royal pupil asks (e.g., 958 C) are anything but psychologically plausible for a person with Charlemagne's educational background. In the eighth century, Alcuin was the most learned man in the West, but he was neither an original philosopher nor a gifted writer of dialogues or poet.

among the most important works in the subgenre we should mention, in addition to the already mentioned *Kusari* of Jehuda Ha-levi and Gilbertus Crispinus's "Disputatio Iudei et Cristiani," Abelard's *Collationes* (also known as *Dialogus inter philosophum, Judaeum et Christianum*), Ramon Llull's *Llibre de gentil e dels tres savis,* and Nicholas of Cusa's *De pace fidei,* from the twelfth, thirteenth, and fifteenth centuries respectively. Llull and Nicholas of Cusa wrote many other dialogues and in general are probably the most original producers of philosophical dialogues in the Middle Ages. Llull's originality is shown, for example, in his choice of language: he was the first Western philosopher to write in a vernacular, namely Catalan (and also in Latin, and perhaps in Arabic as well).[95] Nicholas of Cusa stands on the threshold between the Middle Ages and the Renaissance: when in the *Idiota* dialogues he introduces the character of a layman in order to question presumed certainties, he is clearly going back to the figure of Socrates. However, that the layman's opponent is an orator is itself a jibe against the values of Renaissance culture, which the layman's demand for a quantitative science transcends, even pointing toward the scientific revolution of the seventeenth century.

The Renaissance is without doubt one of the most important periods in the history of the dialogue, which became, in deliberate imitation of the ancient models of Plato, Cicero, and Lucian, one of the favorite genres in Italy, Spain, and France.[96] Someone who shares the opinion that from the point of view of foundational efforts, Renaissance philosophy represents a low point between medieval and post-Cartesian philosophy will tend to conclude that the number of first-class, specifically philosophical dialogues is not high. In addition to Lorenzo Valla's *De vero falsoque bono* and *De libero arbitrio,* which Leibniz rated so highly that he cited it at length at the end of his *Essais de théodicée,* Thomas More's *Utopia,* and Tommaso Campanella's *La Città del Sole,* Jean Bodin's *Colloquium heptaplomeres de abditis rerum sublimium arcanis* deserves a prominent place among the philosophical dialogues of the Renaissance. What is new about this dialogue on the philosophy of religion, whose

95. On Llull's dialogues, see R. Friedlein (2004), esp. 259–86, where twenty-six dialogues are listed and characterized formally.
96. Cf. V. Cox (1992), J. Gómez (1988), A. Rallo Gruss (1996), and especially, on the humanistic dialogue of the Quattrocento in the wake of Petrarch, D. Marsh (1980).

relation to its medieval predecessors resembles that between Cicero's dialogues and Plato's, is the skeptical twist it gives to the subgenre, which ultimately led to the latter's decline.[97] Whereas medieval authors, even when they left the conclusion of the conversation open, clearly indicated what they themselves considered to be the truth, Bodin no longer believes in the one true religion but is obviously of the opinion that God is best served by a plurality of religions. The arguing friends respect each other, even if no one is converted, and in fact the whole project of a religious conversation is ultimately abandoned.[98] If like Bakhtin we maintain that the truly dialogic involves an irreducible plurality of voices, then Bodin's dialogue is dialogic, but Plato's are not.

The Renaissance's contribution to the theory of dialogue is as important as the dialogues it produced.[99] To be sure, Plato already had an implicit theory of the dialogue that can be inferred from his scattered meta-dialogic comments; to be sure, an author like Lucian reflected on the transformation of the dialogue form that he completed; and from Aristotle's *Poetics* on, we find numerous remarks on the theory of the dialogue in antiquity. But Carlo Sigonio was the first to devote a whole book to the genre of the dialogue, with his *De dialogo* (published in 1562), a work that triggered a controversy with Francesco Robortello, and was republished in Germany later in the sixteenth century and in the early seventeenth century, and again in the eighteenth century in Italy.[100] The material on which theory building is based includes Plato's, Xenophon's, and Cicero's dialogues—even Augustine was ignored, not to mention medieval dialogues. The poetological categories, especially that of *imitatio* (mimesis) proceed in large measure from Aristotle's *Poetics,* which began to be commented upon and to be grasped only in the Renaissance; in antiquity it was almost entirely unknown, and even if in the Middle Ages there were Arabic and Latin translations of it, at that time the works to which Aristotle refers were unknown. Like Aristotle,

97. Cf. V. Hösle (2004c).
98. (1857), 358.
99. On this subject, see the fundamental works of J. R. Snyder (1989) and C. Forno (1992), from which much of the following information is taken. D. Gilman (1993) deals not only with the Italians but also the French author Louis Le Caron.
100. See F. Pignati in the bilingual edition of Sigonio's work (1993), 109 ff.

Sigonio wants to establish aesthetic norms—that is, he wants to distinguish good from bad dialogues and set forth rules for this purpose. His concentration on the proems to the dialogues and his high praise for the urbanity of the interlocutors is remarkable, and points to an implicit ethics of dialogue, and certainly also reflects the norms of the real conversational culture of the Renaissance. Sigonio's book influenced Torquato Tasso's short but dense and influential *Discorso dell'arte del dialogo* of 1585 (published in 1586). Like Tasso, the third Renaissance theoretician of the dialogue, his elder acquaintance Sperone Speroni, also wrote dialogues of his own (he also appears as an interlocutor, together with Sigonio, in F. Patrizi's unfinished dialogue *L'amorosa filosofia,* published in 1577); and his wide-ranging and quite associative *Apologia dei dialoghi* in four parts was written in 1574 in response to the Inquisition's suspicions regarding his dialogues (it was first published posthumously in 1596). Right at the beginning of this work he tells how he explained to the Magister Sacri Palatii of the Holy Office, who was criticizing his youthful dialogues, that dialogues are like comedies; one cannot make their authors responsible for the vices or erroneous statements made by the characters; on the contrary, their errors are a sign of the quality of a literary work.[101]

In fact, there is no doubt that one of the causes of the favor shown the dialogue form from the Renaissance to the eighteenth century was the hope that it would allow authors to propose audacious theses without having to take responsibility for them, and in this way to avoid problems with the censors. However, writing dialogues—in addition to which they also wrote nondialogic works—did not keep either Giordano Bruno or Lucilio (Giulio Cesare) Vanini from being burned at the stake; and it is

101. Cf. S. Speroni (1989), 267: "ho meco colla ragione la autorità di Basilio, che ogni dialogo sente non poco della commedia. dunque siccome nelle commedie varie persone vengono in scena, e molte d'esse non molto buone, ma tutte quante a buon fine, e però admesse dalla città; . . . e parla ognuno da quel che egli è, o pare essere; e se parlasse altrimenti, non ostante che egli dicesse di buone cose, male farebbe il suo officio e spiacerebbe al teatro: così il dialogo ben formato, siccome è quel di Platone, ha molti e varii interlocutori, che tal ragionano, quale è il costume e la vita, che ciascun d'essi ci rappresenta. Per li quali ragionamenti chi conchiudesse, che 'l buon Platone fusse ignorante e reo uomo, o mala cosa li suoi dialoghi, per avventura farebbe invalido sillogismo, e mostrarebbe di non sapere che cosa fusse dialogizzare."

well known that Galileo Galilei's deliberate use of the dialogue form in his *Dialogo . . . sopra i due massimi sistemi del mondo, tolemaico e copernicano,* did not prevent him from being condemned either, especially since the irony in Salviati's acceptance of the instrumentalist theory of truth proposed by Simplicio, who obviously wants only to preserve his belief in authority, is palpable.[102] Bodin's *Colloquium heptaplomeres,* written in 1588, was not published until 1857 (by Ludwig Noackin the only edition that has yet appeared); in 1720 the authorities had halted the printing of the book in Leipzig, which was already under way. Thus the stratagem certainly did not always work; the inquisitors were not necessarily less perceptive than their contemporaries who correctly understood the dialogues. And on the other hand, the dialogue form was not the only way of speaking "in a roundabout way." In a treatise, distancing from dangerous theses was more credible because it took place in the first person, and yet the author could always include enough winks to the wise to ensure that he would be correctly understood. A classic example, at least in my view, is Descartes's *Principia philosophiae,* in which the restriction of his own cosmological theory to the status of a pure construction can hardly have been seriously meant, in view of what we know about his theory of science and his dismay regarding Galileo's fate.[103]

This explains why despite the persistence of censorship a continued flourishing of philosophical dialogue was not guaranteed. Several reasons explain the genre's clear decline in the course of the seventeenth century. First, the Renaissance dialogue was connected with humanistic values, esteem for rhetoric and a form of skepticism from which the new conception of science, at least in Descartes, turned sharply away.[104]

102. Simplicio makes his motive clear in his remark, "ritenendo sempre avanti a gli occhi della mente una saldissima dottrina, che già da persona dottissima ed eminentissima appresi ed alla quale è forza quietarsi," and Salviati reacts to this confession of limitation with the highest praise: "Mirabile e veramente angelica dottrina" (1998; 504). However, Bruno's criticism of instrumentalism in "La cena delle ceneri," his dialogue in defense of Copernicanism, was not ironic but direct (1985; I 87 ff.); and the sole function of Frulla, who characteristically has no equivalent in Galileo, is to make fun of Prudenzio, the precursor of Simplicio in Bruno's work.

103. Also, 3.53—right before the relativization of his own construction, 3.54 ff.— is a clear hint at Descartes's own position.

104. Even the new conception of philosophy proposed by Petrus Ramus, whose mind is clearly inferior to Descartes's, is hostile to the dialogue; cf. W. Ong (1979).

The spirit of system is not easy to combine with that of dialogue: one cannot imagine a philosophy like that of Spinoza's *Ethics* being set forth in dialogue form.[105] If this is true for a philosophy that does not take finite subjectivity as its basis—and this is the second point—it certainly holds for a thought like that of Descartes, which sees the *cogito* as its foundation. We have already shown that the meditation is the appropriate form for representing this project. Descartes was not, of course, a dogmatic solipsist; his conversation with Burman, conducted in Latin on April 16, 1648, which Burman wrote down four days later (together with Clauberg), presumably on the basis of notes he took during the interview,[106] shows, just as much as his replies to the objections to the *Meditations,* how seriously he took others' criticism and how carefully he responded to it. But this does not change the fact that Descartes's central, foundational idea is not compatible with the dialogue form: someone who doubts everything, even the existence of his own body and that of other minds, cannot presuppose the existence of other people, which is, however, the presupposition of any conversation, and thus also that of any dialogue representing such a conversation. This is demonstrated with particular clarity by the only dialogue Descartes wrote—we do not know when, perhaps in the last months of his life[107]—even though characteristically he did not finish it: "La recherche de la verité par lumiere naturelle."

105. Cf. the letter from Pamphilus to Hermippus at the beginning of Hume's *Dialogues Concerning Natural Religion* (1947; 127), the frame conversation in K.W.F. Solger's *Erwin* (1971; 3), and Hegel's brusque judgment of this same dialogue: "The best way to make the content of *Erwin* more understandable would be simply to set it forth in an uninterrupted speech; . . . then it would be easy to grasp what one can hardly figure out with the hard work of reading through the conversations" (11.268 f.). According to Hegel, the best dialogues—which for him include Plato's *Timaeus* but not the *Phaedo* or the *Symposium*—are those that are "most distant from any chatty manner" (269). The charm of episodes interwoven with the investigation is "all too often so seductive that many readers stop with the introductions, but are fatigued by the dryness of the logical abstractions and their development, which contrast so strongly with the introductions, and do not go into them, though they still think that they have read Plato and have mastered his philosophy" (270).

106. Republished in Adam and Tannery's edition, V 144–79.

107. It is in any case far more probable that Descartes wrote this dialogue late in life than in the 1630s; but it is not impossible that the work was composed relatively soon after the *Meditations,* that is, around 1642, as S. Gaukroger suggests (1995; 362 f.).

This work is a villa dialogue in two books, in which Eudoxe, whose views are similar to those of Descartes, entertains two of his friends, the uneducated man of the world Poliandre and the scholastically trained Epistemon, at his country estate. There is, of course, a subtle irony in the fact that the name of the Scholastic, who thinks in an unscientific way, implies a claim to knowledge *(epistēmē)*, whereas the true philosopher seems content with good opinion *(doxa)*.[108] But this irony is tempered by his hero bearing the name of Eudoxus of Cnidus, who was certainly the greatest mathematician of antiquity except for Archimedes, and who may even have excelled the latter. Against Epistemon's resistance, Eudoxus tries to convince Poliandre of the fundamental principles of his new philosophy based not on tradition but solely on reason. As is well known, methodological doubt is a crucial part of this philosophy. Whereas Epistemon compares the task of understanding with the correction and painting-over of a bad picture, Eudoxe is more radical: the first picture has to be completely wiped away and started over from the beginning.[109] Using an analogous metaphor, shortly afterward Eudoxe says that a badly built house must be torn down and a new one built; he does not want to be one of those craftsmen who limit themselves to repairing old works with a sponge because they do not feel capable of undertaking new ones.[110] It is true that twentieth-century architectural history suggests the objection that a city planner who succeeds in bringing new ideas organically out of the substance of old buildings is more im-

---

108. This may be contrasted with the differently situated irony in Galileo's *Dialogo,* in which the name of the Aristotelian Simplicio explicitly alludes to the great Simplicius (1998; 7), on the one hand, and, on the other, to a certain simplemindedness; whereas Galileo ultimately has in mind the *meaning* of the name, Descartes has in mind the qualities of the most important *bearer* of the name.

109. "Vostre comparaison découvre fort bien le premier empeschement qui nous arrive; mais vous n'adjoutés pas le moyen duquel il se faut servir, affin de s'en garder. Qui est, ce me semble, que, comme vostre peintre feroit beaucoup mieux de recommencer tout à fait ce tableau, ayant premierement passé l'esponge par dessus pour en effacer tous les traits qu'il y trouve, que de perdre le temps à les corriger . . ." (V 508).

110. "Et par consequent, je seray non seulement incertain si vous estes au monde, s'il y a une terre, s'il y a un soleil; mais encore, si j'ay des yeux, si j'ay des oreilles, si j'ay un corps, & mesme si je vous parle, si vous me parlez, & bref de toutes choses . . ." (V 509).

portant than one who comes in with a bulldozer; but here we are concerned only with understanding Descartes: completely unlike Hegel in the *Phänomenologie des Geistes,* he does not consider his own position the culmination of a tradition; not only should a diachronic intersubjectivity not be constituted, it should be swept away. But with this starting point, how is a synchronic intersubjectivity in a conversation among different people conceivable? It is simply part of the logic of the Cartesian approach that this is fundamentally questioned. After Eudoxe has explained to Poliandre, in part with the help of the dream argument, the fundamental unreliability of our sense knowledge—despite the protests of Epistemon, who fears they are getting into deep waters in which one can only drown—Poliandre finally accepts the position of problematic idealism. But this means that he now doubts not only the existence of the earth, the sun, and his own body but also that of his conversation partner and the fact that a real conversation has taken place at all: "And consequently, I shall be unsure not only whether you are in the world, whether there is an earth, whether there is a sun, but also whether I have eyes, whether I have ears, whether I have a body, & even whether I am speaking to you, whether you are speaking to me; in short, I shall be unsure about everything."[111]

It is surely an accident, but one of those accidents that could not have happened more cleverly had it been planned, that it is precisely with these words that the extant French original (in the form of the transcript prepared by Tschirnhaus) breaks off. To be sure, another segment of the unfinished dialogue has survived in Latin translation; Descartes thus continued his work beyond the passage just cited (though he completed only a small part of what he announced at the outset). But wouldn't it make sense for Descartes to actually break off his dialogue at the passage in question? How can one pursue further a conversation if one doubts the existence of the interlocutor? Here one cannot object by referring to dreams. In a dream we do not doubt the existence of our dreamed interlocutor; we think he is real, and that is why we go on

---

111. V, 514. "And consequently, I shall be unsure not only whether you are in the world, whether there is an earth, whether there is a sun, but also whether I have eyes, whether I have ears, whether I have a body, & even whether I am speaking to you, whether you are speaking to me; in short, I shall be unsure about everything . . ."

dreaming. (However, it is possible to dream that one has just slept and dreamed a conversation; dreams within dreams are not rare.) It is true that in the Latin version Eudoxe is delighted by Poliandre's statement cited above: that is just the position to which he wanted to lead him.[112] But to be consistent, shouldn't he now conclude and say farewell? Fichte is certainly more consistent when in the second part of *Die Bestimmung des Menschen* he has the idealist arguments presented to the "I," not by a fellow human being, but by a "spirit" whose ontological status remains vague and who withdraws at the end of this part of the work, because the "I" alone must arrive at the crucial insight, and in fact, in the third part the "I" is just as alone as he is in the first. Those who seek, like Descartes, the early Fichte, or Husserl, to ground philosophy in egological reflections would do better to abandon the dialogue form or limit themselves to the reduced form they can find in Fichte. "La recherche de la verité par la lumiere naturelle," shows that Descartes did develop a playful interest in the dialogue form, probably at the end of his life,[113] but it is by nature just as contradictory to the spirit of his philosophy as the axiomatic presentation of his program at the end of the second of his *Replies*[114] is to the basic foundational notion of the *cogito,* which rests on the principle of performative consistency, but precisely not in an intersubjective context. It was a brilliant instinct that led Descartes to adopt for his main philosophical work the sole form that corresponded to its content—the meditation.

The crisis of Cartesianism did not prevent philosophers of the seventeenth and eighteenth centuries who rejected the *cogito* as a starting point—whether because as materialists they rejected the idea that the soul was a special kind of substance, or because they put God at the apex of their system—from writing dialogues: consider for example Hobbes's *Dialogue between a Philosopher and a Student of the Common-Laws of England,* Leibniz's *Nouveaux essais sur l'entendement,* Malebranche's *Conversations chrétiennes,* and Berkeley's *Three Dialogues between Hylas and*

112. "En te quàm optimè comparatum, atque eò tantùm te perducere constitueram" (V 514).
113. See A. Baillet's "Vie de Monsieur Des-Cartes" (quoted in Adam and Tannery's edition, V 529).
114. VII 160–70.

Philonous.[115] Even in Berkeley's case, this does not contradict what I said earlier, since Berkeley did not extend his idealistic reinterpretation of reality to other minds, of which we have, according to him, no "ideas" that would make this reinterpretation absolutely necessary, but only "notions"—a purely terminological way out that conceals the crucial problem rather than solving it, but to which we nonetheless owe some stimulating dialogues (including the later *Alciphron: or, the Minute Philosopher*). However, one cannot help but note that none of these works comes close to the best of the ancient models. In none of them is character drawing really a central interest, and this is shown for example by the fact that the conversation partners are indicated either by mere common nouns or even letters ("A" and "B" in Hobbes's *Behemoth*), or else fictitious proper names that stand for the positions that they represent. Hylas believes (at first) in the existence of matter *(hylē)*, while Philonous, the friend *(philos)* of the mind *(nous)*, is, like Berkeley, an immaterialist—there is here no trace of the irony that we have seen in the names Descartes gives his characters. It is true that there are anonymous interlocutors in ancient dialogues as well: think of the *hetairos* in the frame dialogue of Plato's *Protagoras* or of Cicero's *Tusculan Disputations;* and in medieval dialogues names like "Judaeus" and "Idiota" are common nouns.[116] It is also possible that some of the names in Plato's dialogues that are not attested anywhere else, are, like "Eudicus" in the *Hippias minor*[117] or "Philebus" in the dialogue that bears his name, aptronyms for wholly invented characters.[118] (The view occasionally put forth to the

115. In his Appendix to Leibniz's *Dialog zur Einführung in die Arithmetik und Algebra* (1976; 178 ff.), E. Knobloch mentions, in addition to four (paraphrasing) translations of dialogues, twenty-one dialogues by Leibniz himself, some of which, however, were never completed.

116. A fictitious proper name that stands for a concept is found in the fascinating *Dialogus Ratii et Everardi* by Eberard of Ypres, a Cistercian monk and pupil of Gilbert de la Porée who wrote the dialogue in the late twelfth century, to whose exceptional literary and sometimes comic qualities P. von Moos (1989) drew attention. Ratius from Athens—the son of Ratio and the brother of Sophia (245, 252)—is clearly not a historical person but rather reason personified.

117. Cf. P. Friedländer (1964), II 133.

118. In Methodius's *Symposion,* "Arete" and probably also "Agathe" are suchaptronyms, even if Thecla, Paul's companion, is certainly a person whom Methodius

effect that Plato presented only real characters in his dialogues[119] cannot be proven for all his characters; indeed, with regard to a rather literary name like "Philebus"[120] it is even, in my opinion, unlikely.) However, the great majority of the characters in the dialogues of Plato, Cicero, and Augustine do represent real persons; and should the Callicles in the *Gorgias*, who is not found anywhere else, turn out to be invented—which is improbable but not impossible[121]—he is nonetheless a flesh-and-blood character. The first statement (447a1 f.) made by this man, who is basically an opportunistic weakling (481e1 ff.), reveals his fascination with violence.

The situation is quite different, for example, in Leibniz's brief *Dialogus inter Theologum et Misosophum*, which was probably written in 1678–79 but first published in 1948. Here the characters' names are more common nouns than fictitious proper nouns.[122] Misosophus— "the hater of wisdom"[123]—is a fideist with a deep mistrust of reason, while Theologus is a rationalist. It is noteworthy that Leibniz manages to show in a few pages the circularity of any fideistic grounding of belief as well as the untenability of the claim that metaphysical and logical truths do not hold for God; but that does not change the fact that his dialogue lacks the psychological depth of Plato's *Euthyphro*. In a few strokes, Plato masterfully shows what is morally problematic about the eponymous interlocutor in this dialogue; anything analogous will be sought in vain in Leibniz. However, in his interdenominational *Dialogue entre Poliandre et Théophile*, written at about the same time but first published only in 1905, Leibniz succeeded in capturing the pathological element in the figure of the Catholic dignitary Poliandre—for whom Nikolaus Steno,

---

considers to be historical, even if she probably is not. In Galileo's *Dialogo*, "Simplicio" is an aptronym but may stand for a real person. His interlocutors are two of Galileo's dead friends. The three interlocutors in the *Dialogo* reappear in Galileo's *Discorsi e dimostrazioni matematiche*.

119. Cf., e.g., J. Barnes (1987), 882: "all of these are real historical persons."

120. Cf. D. Nails (2002), 238.

121. Dodds's arguments (1959; 12 ff.) are plausible but not compelling.

122. This is indicated from the outset by the salutation "o Theologi" (1999; 2213).

123. In this name we hear an echo of Plato's concept of the *misologos* (cf. *Phd.* 89d1).

the major Danish anatomist, a convert and apostolic vicar in Hannover, was the model; for example, when Poliandre, who openly acknowledges his ignorance of the church fathers, describes the Jansenists as "heretics" and indeed the whole French clergy as "semi-heretics," suggesting that the pope will, at the appropriate time, act against them because the papal court is cunning and able to conceal its intentions but knows how to drop its mask and strike when the opportunity presents itself.[124] Compared with the moral purity of his Protestant interlocutor—whose name "Theophile" means "beloved of God" and perhaps also "God-loving,"[125] recurs in several other dialogues by Leibniz (e.g., in the *Nouveaux essais*), and is also familiar to us from Bruno and Spinoza—Poliandre's lack of spirituality and the pleasure he takes in worldly shrewdness (but which he fails to show when he heedlessly reveals the Curia's hidden intentions) are nothing less than shameful. And yet despite its powerful satire of Poliandre and his intellectually simplistic and morally clumsy attempts to convert his interlocutors, the dialogue is disappointing because, first, it is more theological than philosophical in nature, and second, because it does not end, as a Platonic dialogue would, in a confrontation or crisis but rather in mutual goodwilll.[126] This is very Christian; and Leibniz's irenic nature, which he indicates by using the name "Pacidius" in various dialogues, makes his character as attractive as his unique intelligence makes his mind venerable.[127] However, dramatic talent does not develop under

124. "Le Pape n'attend qu'un temps favorable. Il y aura peut estre un jour quelque minorité en France, ou quelque Cardinal ministre, ou quelque Roy qui en voudra au clergé, et la cour de Rome qui est fine, et qui sçait dissimuler, et lever le masque quand il faut, fera quelque Nouveau Concordat avec le Roy, qui luy soûmettra ces esprits remuans, au dépens de leur bourse" (1999; 2225; cf. 2223).

125. In addition to its original passive meaning, the Greek *theophilēs* also has an active meaning.

126. Leibniz also argued with Steno in notes to the latter's second letter to Johannes Sylvius and also in two fictional letters (1999; 2179–2202), and even if he considers accusing him of subjective dishonesty, he ultimately refrains from making this insulting reproach (2189 f.).

127. Hirzel rightly emphasizes this: "No matter how little effort Leibniz devoted to the dialogue, it seems that a great man can do nothing without putting his characteristic stamp on it: the dialogue . . . became for his far-ranging and elevated mind what it had probably never been before at least to this degree—a way of achieving reconciliation and balance" (1895; II 398).

these conditions, and therefore an essential presupposition for a good dialogue is lacking.

In the history of the philosophical dialogue, Hume's *Dialogues Concerning Natural Religion* (published posthumously in 1779) have a central place. Only a few philosophical works of such originality and significance have been written in dialogue form since Plato, and Hume's is as perfect artistically as it is intellectually. To be sure, the two dialogues that Hume included in his *Enquiries*—one in the eleventh chapter of the *Enquiry Concerning Human Understanding,* the other as an appendix to the *Enquiry Concerning the Principles of Morals*—are graceful and elegant; but they alone would not have established Hume's place of honor in the history of the genre. Hume, whose character was even more attractive than that of Leibniz—if that is possible—because he was not even vain but instead treated himself with the same good-humored irony that characterized his relation to the world, wrote on August 15, 1776, ten days before his death, to Adam Smith, regarding the *Dialogues Concerning Natural Religion:* "On revising them (which I have not done these 15 years) I find that nothing can be more cautiously and more artfully written."[128] This judgment should be taken seriously, because the fact that Hume could also judge himself objectively is shown by the distance he takes on himself in his autobiography, which is almost sui generis, and was also written in the year of his death. In a letter to William Strahan of June 8, 1776, Hume notes, "Some of my Friends flatter me that it [sc. *Dialogues*] is the best thing I ever wrote,"[129] and his friends were right, at least from a literary point of view. What is marvelous about this dialogue (the first draft of which was composed in 1751) is that it demolishes, with enormously astute arguments, a central element of the rational theology founded by Plato, the teleological proof of God's existence; but at the same time it is, despite its Ciceronian trappings, more Platonic than almost any other dialogue, and indeed in a certain sense more than the dialogues of Plato himself. The remarkable intermediate position occupied by Hume, who is one of the most radical innovators in theoretical philosophy but a conservative in practical philosophy, also becomes evi-

128. *Letters,* II 334.
129. *Letters,* II 322.

dent in the *Dialogues.* Nothing shows more clearly how "classically" Hume conceived the dialogue than the contrast with the dialogues written by his contemporary and acquaintance Denis Diderot. As revolutionary as Hume's dialogue is from the viewpoint of the philosophy of religion, his attribution of superior insight to a single conversation partner remains traditional. Hume does everything he can to pull the wool over the reader's eyes—for example, because of the preface, which is not written in the first person, contrary to what we find in Aristotle and Cicero, but whose similarity to the model of *De natura deorum* nonetheless awakens false expectations, and because of the astonishing change Philo seems to undergo in Part 12. Hume succeeded in this attempt to lead his readers astray—even if a few of his contemporaries already correctly interpreted the work, in the nineteenth century Hume's position was largely identified with that of the physicotheologist Cleanthes, whose name reminds us of the famous Stoic. Only in the twentieth century did scholars come to agree—for the time being—that Hume's spokesman is rather Philo, whose name makes us think of the founder of the fourth Academy.[130] Philo is just as much a sage as the Platonic Socrates was—a man of outstanding intelligence whom his contemporaries did not correctly understand and inevitably underestimated, but who was able to cope with this ironically. It is no accident that in Hume's philosophy the term used to refer to the masses is "the vulgar"—it corresponds entirely to the Platonic *hoi polloi.* Whether an epistemology like Plato's is more likely to allow one to speak of an opposition between the wise man and

130. See N. K. Smith's excellent introduction in D. Hume (1947), 1–123, especially 57 ff. I am familiar, naturally, with later, opposing interpretations, among which the brilliant one by J. Dancy (1995) stands out. But no matter how clever his idea of connecting the reader's difficulty in interpreting Hume's text with the failure of the interpretation of the world as an expression of a divine intention, and no matter how right he is that Part 12 exhibits the contradiction between the (untenable) physicotheological argument and the naturalness, that is, the inevitability, of the corresponding belief, this does not imply that Hume's text is uninterpretable (46 f., 51, 55). Rather, the fact that this contradiction is ultimately manifested in Philo himself shows that he and his author have the same awareness of the complexity of the problem. And Hume knew, of course, that our experience with texts encourages us to assume that their creators are authors, whereas we have no comparable experience with the world as a whole.

the masses than is Hume's skepticism is an absolutely legitimate question, but one that will not be answered here. Here I am concerned only to indicate that Hume goes Plato one better, because although Plato and his Socrates also hold something back, no halfway intelligent reader can doubt Socrates' superiority. However, the enormous force of Hume's arguments was acknowledged only long after his death. Therein lies the subtle irony of Hume as an author, but it is a classical irony because it does not question the existence of arguments that are not catchy but are nevertheless cogent. According to Hume, these arguments demolish the worldview that Plato significantly helped to establish, or rather Hume claims that his counterarguments show conclusively that the physico-theological argument does not work, although Hume and Philo do not deny that it is based on an ineradicable reflex of the human mind. But a true Platonist cannot be satisfied with this concession.[131]

The Enlightenment brought a revival of the dialogue in general and the philosophical dialogue in particular—think, for example, of Fontenelle, Shaftesbury, Lessing, Herder, Hemsterhuis, Voltaire, Rousseau, and especially Diderot.[132] Even if Diderot was not, like Plato and Hume, a philosopher who distinguished himself through his investigations on foundational questions, his is nonetheless one of the most multifaceted minds in the history of philosophy, and since he is also one of the most innovative masters of narrative form—in the explosive force of its social criticism and also in its reflexivity, its destruction of dramatic illusion, and its revelation of the associative nature of our stream of conscious-

---

131. In a letter to Gilbert Elliot written on February 18, 1751, Hume insists that in practical philosophy one can be satisfied with a feeling, but not in theoretical philosophy: "But in Metaphysics or Theology, I cannot see how either of these plain & obvious Standards of Truth can have place. Nothing there can correct bad Reasoning but good Reasoning: and Sophistry must be oppos'd by Syllogism" (*Letters,* I 151). Cf. his next letter to Elliot: "We must endeavour to prove that this Propensity is somewhat different from our Inclination to find our own Figures in the Clouds, our Face in the Moon, our Passions & Sentiments even in inanimate Matter. Such an Inclination may, & ought to be controul'd, & can never be a legitimate Ground of Assent" (I 155). This is true even if we strongly desire, when the doubts first arose in adolescence, to believe in the physicotheological proof, as Hume declares was his own case (I 154).

132. On the dialogue in the Enlightenment, cf T. Fries (1993).

ness, *Jacques le fataliste et son maître* is superior even to Laurence Sterne's *Tristram Shandy*[133]—it is hardly surprising that the literary quality of his dialogues is unparalleled. No one since Plato had gone so deeply into the connection between character and worldview, or had produced so many "round" characters;[134] no one had managed to let it grow with such elegance existentially urgent questions out of everyday chat; no one had been comparably original in experimenting with the formal possibilities of the genre. The literary universes created by Diderot are populated by nightmare-tormented philosophers whose utterances while asleep are written down and discussed, eccentric immoralists with exceptional mimetic abilities, Polynesian noble savages, honest knifesmiths, and charming Catholic noblewomen with a coquettish interest in atheists. But what is really fascinating is that Diderot, like only Bodin before him, seems to see truth in the irreducible perspectivism of the dialogue partners.[135] Just as in *Le neveu de Rameau*, "Lui," not "Moi," has the last word, so the *Entretien d'un père avec ses enfants* and the *Entretien d'un phi - losophe avec la Maréchale de *** end with a rebuke delivered to the first-person narrator by his pious interlocutors. The latter are—completely unlike the Catholic and Calvinist clergymen in the sarcastic *Dialogues chrétiens* of 1760, which almost certainly derive from Voltaire—not described as unlikable and sanctimonious but rather, on the contrary, as people of outstanding dignity and grace: few eighteenth-century texts make the greatness of Catholicism so clear as these two dialogues by the materialist Diderot, who undoubtedly belongs to the radical wing of the Enlightenment so masterfully described by Jonathan Israel. And yet Diderot's openness has a flipside: in *Le neveu de Rameau* the goal is not, as it is for instance in Plato's *Gorgias,* to convert the immoralist or at least to refute his arguments; instead, his position is supposed to be represented in all its brilliance and misery, and even if it seems to the reader in many respects more interesting than that of the interlocutor designated as "Moi," each character's primary interest in the other is purely

133. An early comparison between the two works is found in Schlegel's *Gespräch über die Poesie* (1967), 330 f.

134. I refer to E. M. Forster's distinction between "flat" and "round" characters (1974; 46 ff.).

135. Cf. R. Galle (1980), esp. 223.

descriptive: they do not seek to learn *from* one another, but *about* one another. This objectivizing attitude becomes still clearer in the trilogy devoted to d'Alembert: the latter has his most interesting ideas not in his conversation with Diderot but in his dream, which is listened to and written down; and the real discussion of this dream takes place in his absence, between Mlle de l'Espinasse and Bordeu. D'Alembert is a kind of idea-producing machine; he is no longer an interlocutor in his own right.

The tendency to doubt the possibility of a generally binding knowledge of the truth is presumably one of the factors that contributed to the decline of the dialogue form that began in the early nineteenth century with alarming rapidity and from which the genre has still not recovered. A further, associated factor is the triumph of Romantic subjectivity. Descartes's subjectivity was on the one hand isolated, even unique; on the other hand, it was supposed to provide the foundation for something universally valid: the new science. In contrast, with Romanticism the abyssal depths of the individual "I" are opened up to large groups of people, and what they discover is an extremely specific particularity that no longer seeks to subordinate itself to a general project like that of modern science (or the later project of the Enlightenment). Someone who regards his own position, qua his own, as absolute, will hardly put much effort into understanding the different intellectual project or even the differing views of another person; in fact, he will even take pride in his inability to do so.[136] This necessarily leads to the transformation, indeed the collapse, of the culture of convivial conversation that is the basis of dialogue.[137] Friedrich Schlegel's *Conversation on Poetry* (*Gespräch über die Poesie,* 1800) is characteristic of this decline. A large part of the conversation reported consists of the presentation of previously written essays. A contrast with Plato is helpful here. To be sure, in the *Symposium* conversational exchange also plays a limited role—and in this respect, the *Symposium* is not typical of Plato's dialogues—but nothing is simply read out, and the seven speeches given by the participants are all impro-

---

136. As Schlegel's Camilla puts it, "the less capable someone is of understanding what someone else wants, the more he usually considers himself unique" (1967; 339).
137. Cf. J. Wertheimer (1990), esp. 57–90; and G. Kalmbach (1996).

vised. The speech given by Socrates in the *Menexenus* is purported to have been learned by heart; it, too, is not read. The first speech in the *Phaedrus* is read out, but not the far more important second and third speeches, which Socrates gives extempore. Schlegel's interlocutors are, on the other hand, literary critics—that is, they are professional readers—and such persons are not always gifted conversation partners. Indeed, it is precisely the ideology of fully unforced chat proceeding without procedural rules that requires the use of the written form when more complex arguments are to be presented. One of the essays in Schlegel's dialogue takes the form of a letter that was written after a conversation and that is now read out in the main conversation; in it we read: "And moreover, I find it more natural, when necessary, to give written lessons than oral ones, which seem to me to profane the sacred character of the conversation."[138] It is no less symptomatic that the most substantial dialogue from the period of German idealism also offers a *reading* of a dialogue within a brief framing conversation, Solger's *Erwin* of 1815.

Hardly any work shows the fate of dialogue more clearly than one of the few important dialogues of the nineteenth century, Søren Kierkegaard's "In Vino Veritas" (1845), the first part of *Stadier paa livets vei* (Stages on Life's Way) and the only dialogue written by this writer and philosopher, who was so innovative formally, and whose pleasure in playing with masks resembles Plato's. That Kierkegaard wrote only one dialogue is hardly surprising if we consider that his pseudonymous works appeared under names such as "Victor Eremita" and "Johannes de Silentio" and that the third part of the *Stadier* contains a commentary by Frater Taciturnus on Quidam's diary, which he claims to have accidentally fished out of a lake into which it had been dropped in a chest[139]—a diary that makes literary use of Kierkegaard's unhappy engagement to Regine Olsen. The failure of communication is Kierkegaard's central personal and philosophical theme, and his third or religious stage is characterized by a withdrawal into his own subjectivity, in which alone God can be experienced. In the literary plan of the *Stadier,* which proceeded from the combination of two works that were originally conceived as

138. (1967), 329.
139. 8.11 ff.

independent (the later third part and a work consisting of the first two parts, with the planned title *Vrangen og Retten* [Wrong and Right]), the dialogue form corresponds to the lowest stage, that of the aesthetic; the ethical stage is represented by the treatise form (Assessor Vilhelm's treatise on marriage), and the religious by the (commented upon) diary form. Convivial conversation in common is the realm of what Kierke-gaard calls "the aesthetic," that is, morally irresponsible pleasure, and thus precisely not the place where the divine can be experienced; indeed, it is not even the place where interpersonal intimacy is experienced. The participants in Plato's banquet not only speak about love but also show it in their relationships to each other; and even if Methodius's virgins chose a celibate way of life, they still experience together their common love for God. Kierkegaard's banquet is exclusively male, but since same-sex love was taboo in the nineteenth century the object of the partici-pants' desire has to be external to the group itself. However, since the five men who have gathered together are, for very different reasons, neither capable of love nor religious, their reflections on women become one of the most impressive monuments to misogyny in European intellectual history, a misogyny that is not even compensated by a common feeling of male solidarity: what could connect a cynic like Johannes the Seducer with the suffering young man? Love was the favorite subject of sympo-sium literature from the outset, and it is no accident that the last original work in the subgenre takes as its theme the failure of erotic relationships. If love, which was a subject about which one could once speak convivially because it was part of a general order of being and the first step in the as-cent to the principle of all being, becomes a highly private relationship between two and only two people, it can no longer be the subject of a symposium. Indeed, love cannot be discussed by even two people when it has become as forced and distorted as Kierkegaard's relationship to Regine, about which he was never able to speak with her. But we owe to his inability to engage in real conversation the literary work through which he tried to establish indirect communication with her, and even though he failed in this attempt, he succeeded in communicating with readers long after his death.

The diminished form in which dialogue survives is shown, for ex-ample, by Schopenhauer's work, which structures mainly chapter 15,

§174, of the second volume of *Parerga und Paralipomena,* "Ueber Religion," as a conversation between Demopheles ("Benefit of the People") and Philalethes ("Friend of Truth"; short dialogic pieces can be found in chapters 3, 8, 10, and 14, i.e., §§ 60, 112, 141, and 172). In chapter 1 of the same volume, "Ueber Philosophie und ihre Methode," Schopenhauer justifies his distrust of the genre in a very Cartesian way, and he even uses a Romantic opposition between intersubjectively valid but deficient concepts and a private but epistemologically superior intuition:

> Our own, earnest meditation and intimate observation of things is related to a conversation with another person on the same subjects as the machine is related to a living organism. . . . One wholly understands only oneself; others one only half understands, because all that can be achieved is a commonality of concepts, not the intuitive comprehension that underlies them. Therefore deep philosophical truths are probably never brought to light by means of joint thinking, in conversation. . . . As a way of communicating philosophical thoughts, the written dialogue is appropriate only when the subject allows of two or more entirely different or even opposed views, concerning which either the judgment is left up to the reader or which taken together complement each other to produce a full and correct understanding of the subject: the first case also includes the refutation of objections raised.[140]

---

140. "Zu unserer eigenen, ernstlichen Meditation und innigen Betrachtung der Dinge verhält sich das Gespräch mit einem Andern über dieselben wie eine Maschine zu einem lebendigen Organismus. . . . Nur sich selbst nämlich versteht man ganz; Andere nur halb: denn man kann es höchstens zur Gemeinschaft der Begriffe bringen, nicht aber zu der diesen zum Grunde liegenden anschaulichen Auffassung. Daher werden tiefe, philosophische Wahrheiten wohl nie auf dem Wege des gemeinschaftlichen Denkens, im Dialog, zu Tage gefördert werden. . . . Als Form der Mittheilung philosophischer Gedanken ist der geschriebene Dialog nur da zweckmäßig, wo der Gegenstand zwei, oder mehrere, ganz verschiedene, wohl gar entgegengesetzte Ansichten zuläßt, über welche entweder das Urtheil dem Leser anheimgestellt bleiben soll, oder welche zusammengenommen sich zum vollständigen und richtigen Verständniß der Sache ergänzen: zum erstern Fall gehört auch die Widerlegung erhobener Einwürfe" (1977; IX 13 f.).

Schopenhauer's Italian contemporary, Giacomo Leopardi, who expressed in poetic form the same sense of life,[141] structured as dialogues several of the texts collected in his *Operette morali;* his model is Lucan, and it is more sentiments than arguments that are communicated. Nor is Nietzsche a writer of dialogues—even *Also sprach Zarathustra* is not a dialogue but rather partly a diatribe, partly a parody of the Gospels. The failure of attempts to write dialogues is significant.[142] Since the beginning of the nineteenth century it is chiefly writers who have written dialogues that constantly touch upon philosophical questions—in addition to Leopardi, Oscar Wilde (*The Decay of Lying* and *The Critic as Artist*, 1891), André Gide (*Corydon*, 1920—the 1911 first edition, twelve copies, having disappeared into a drawer), and Paul Valéry (*Eupalinos ou l'architecte* and *L'âme et la danse,* 1921). It is not without importance that Wilde's *The Decay of Lying* is a discussion of an essay whose reading constitutes a large part of the conversation; it thereby artfully combines, like Schlegel's *Conversation on Poetry,* the dialogue and the essay. As might be expected, given the crisis in the genre, in the twentieth century authors deliberately returned to the most influential model of the genre—Plato. Gide's *Corydon* has as its subtitle *Quatre dialogues socratiques;* even if the dialogue takes place in the present, it nonetheless deals

141. However, the differences between their political ideas are enormous, as F. De Sanctis was the first to note, in 1858, in his brilliant dialogue "Schopenhauer e Leopardi," in the *Rivista contemporanea* (1986; 117–60).

142. Thus in 1914 Lukács originally intended to write his *Die Theorie des Romans* as a "series of dialogues," as he acknowledges in the foreword published in 1962: "A group of young people withdraws from the war psychosis of their environment, just as the story-tellers of the *Decameron* had withdrawn from the plague; they try to understand themselves and one another by means of conversations which gradually lead to the problems discussed in the book—the outlook on a Dostoevskian world" (*The Theory of the Novel,* trans. A. Bostock [Cambridge MA: MIT, 1971], 11–12). In 1944–45, toward the end of the war, Martin Heidegger wrote three dialogues, which were, however, published posthumously only in 1995; one part of the longest dialogue—"*Agkhibasiē*. Ein Gespräch selbstdritt auf einem Feldweg zwischen einem Forscher, einem Gelehrten und einem Weisen" (A Triadic Conversation on a Country Path between a Researcher, a Scholar, and a Sage) was published in 1959 under the title *Zur Erörterung der Gelassenheit—Aus einem Feldweggespräch über das Denken.* Plans for continuations found in Heidegger's literary remains show that he planned more dialogues. I confess, however, that I am not sorry that these works remained at the planning stage.

with homosexuality, which was then still a very risky Platonic theme. As in the case of Wilde, Gide's Corydon bases his explanations on an (un-completed) book manuscript. In Valéry, the conversation partners are Socrate, Phèdre, and Ériximaque, familiar to us from Plato's *Symposium* and *Phaedrus*. In her two *Acastos* dialogues, first published in 1986, Iris Murdoch presents, in addition to the eponymous young man, Socrates and Plato, whose appearance together is, however, just as un-Platonic as the opposition between their positions—despite the subtitle *Two Platonic Dialogues*. In contrast to Murdoch, Paul Feyerabend situated his three dialogues in the present—but the best of them, the "First Dia-logue" (which was actually written last, in 1990), takes place in a semi-nar room at a well-known university (one thinks of Feyerabend's own university, Berkeley), where Plato's *Theaetetus* is discussed. Thus here as well, Plato remains an interlocutor in the broadest sense of the word. Might other examples of the genre in contemporary philosophy[143] lead to its general revival?

143. Cf. R. L. Purtill (1975), I. Lakatos (1976), K. Popper and J. C. Eccles (1977; 76–81), J. Perry (1978), C. F. von Weizsäcker (1981; 9–14), D. Lewis (1983; 3–9), R. Scruton (1993), P. Engel (1997), E. Tugendhat (1997), D. Bell (2000), J. F. Rosen-berg (2000), P. Clavier (2002), and especially M. Wetzel (2001 ff.), who also uses the form in other works and offers an overview of postwar German philosophy. On this, see V. Hösle (2001). Hackett Publishing Company had a special series, Dialogues, in which Perry's dialogue and others have appeared.

CHAPTER 5

Social Presuppositions and Obstacles

At first sight, the distribution of the philosophical dialogue over the ages is surprising. To be sure, Greek and Roman—including Christian—antiquity is a period especially rich in dialogues, whose high point occurred in the time of Plato. Important philosophical dialogues were also written during the Middle Ages but relatively fewer than in antiquity; with the renewed interest in antiquity during the period of Humanism and the Renaissance, the dialogue genre flourished again. During the Enlightenment it enjoyed great popularity, until it largely faded away in the course of the nineteenth century. Hirzel writes, "The dialogue has appeared in large numbers in only three periods, all of them during revolutionary periods in world history, as a sign of their intellectual battles and a means of waging them. The first time, its youth, included the period of the Soph - ists and the following decades; then it returned and dominated literature when the Renaissance and Reformation set in; and the third time, and up to now last, great droves of them appeared and contributed to Frederick the Great's Enlightenment, Storm and Stress, and the Romanticism of our literature, as well as to the English and French Revolutions."[1]

Hirzel's observation rightly points to the origin of philosophical dialogue in times of crisis. The least fascinating subgenre, the teacher-

1. Hirzel (1895), II, 443 f.

pupil dialogue, can be used, and is, during periods when tradition is transmitted in a normal way, and it was thus favored in the Middle Ages, for instance, whereas dialogues like Plato's *Gorgias,* Augustine's *Contra academicos,* Bodin's *Colloquium heptaplomeres,* and Hume's *Dialogues Concerning Natural Religion* are all monuments to radical breaks with tradition. A fundamental change in perspective is expected of their readers, who are compelled to give up positions that have for centuries been considered the true ones, and that are still considered true by most people of the same social class. This is not easy; and since the writer of dialogues represents the resistance that such an expectation necessarily elicits, he can teach the reader to cope productively with his own emotional resistance. At least he shows that he is aware of these reactions, which do not surprise him, and are perhaps even an argument in favor of his theory, because they are consequences of its truth. Collisions between different cultures are analogous to breaks with tradition; they also encourage dialogues. I have already discussed the interreligious dialogues of late antiquity and the Middle Ages; the otherness of the worldview characteristic of the Far East has led to various Western dialogues, ranging from Malebranche's pro-Christian *Entretien d'un philosophe chrétien et d'un philosophe chinois* and Voltaire's *Entretiens chinois* through Martin Heidegger's *Aus einem Gespräch von der Sprache. Zwischen einem Japaner und einem Fragenden* to Daniel Bell's *East Meets West: Human Rights and Democracy in East Asia.*[2] If these were the only relevant parameters, the present would have to be particularly favorable to philosophical dialogue: there have been few periods in which so many intercultural encounters have taken place while at the same time so many cultures have been subjected to an internal transformation.

In addition, contemporary Western societies have something that not all periods have: a public sphere. But dialogue as logos Sōkratikos has its roots in the public sphere, because Socrates claimed the right to

---

2. Engel (1997) depicts a conversation—and letters—between three Frenchmen, a "continental," an "analytical" philosopher, and a reporter, but the conversation takes place in Hong Kong. "Quel meilleur endroit pour réfléchir sur le destin de la philosophie de l'Occident, que celui où sa culture se fond dans celle de l'Asie et du troisième millénaire?" (What better place to reflect on the fate of philosophy in the West than the one where its culture merges with that of Asia and of the third millenium?).

participate in every conversation in the agora. Someone who seeks conversation is not satisfied with his own views but instead wants in part to subject them to criticism and test them in conversation and in part to become acquainted with and also test other people's ideas. This involves not only an interest in truth but also a pleasure taken in intellectual competition, in measuring one's intellectual powers against those of others. This was rightly emphasized by Shaftesbury in his dialogue *The Moralists: A Philosophical Rhapsody,* which first appeared in 1705 under the title *The Sociable Enthusiast; a Philosophical Adventure Written to Palemon* and was later included in the *Characteristics:* "This is that academic discipline in which formerly the youth were trained; when not only horsemanship and military arts had their public places of exercise, but philosophy too had its wrestlers in repute."[3] Similarly, Nietzsche writes: "I have indicated how Socrates could be repulsive: the fact that he did fascinate people needs all the more explaining. That he discovered a new kind of agon and was its first fencing master for the noble circles of Athens is one point. He fascinated by stirring up the agonal drive of the Hellenes—he introduced a variation into the wrestling match between young men and youths."[4] Plato already taught that a conviction that cannot be defended in conversation is not a real insight, and in the Laches, for instance, he has Socrates maintain that what one knows one must also be able to say.[5] Laches agrees with him, but later explains that he really thought he knew what courage was, even if he could not say it, and he is himself upset about this discrepancy.[6] Knowledge differs from mere opinion because it is capable of competently reacting to criticism; thus someone who really wants to know whether he knows something or only thinks he does will seek conversation.[7] Cultures in which a rigid tradition

3. (1999), 9. This is contrasted with the contemporary decline of the culture of discussion (6).

4. *Götzen-Dämmerung. Das Problem des Sokrates* 8 (1988; 6.71). Translation modi fed from D. Large, *The Twilight of the Idols, Or How to Philosophize with a Hammer* (Oxford, 1988), 14. Plato's *Laches* is the best proof of Nietzsche's thesis.

5. *Oukoun ho ge ismen kan eipoimen dēpou ti estin* (190c6).

6. 194a8 ff. Cf. *Euthphr.* 11b6 f. and *Hp. ma.* 296d7 ff., where it is assumed that the soul wanted to say something that it did not say.

7. Cf. Augustine, *C. acad.* 3.20.45, where Alypius is asked to offer his own defense of what he has learned.

claims a monopoly on truth and that have no critical openness at all can hardly produce dialogues.

And yet at the same time the dialogue is not addressed only to the public. Unlike the meditation, for instance, it represents the public—and therein lies a potential for criticism of the public. First, Plato already knew and showed that not all conversational structures serve to discover truth, for example, in the *Euthydemus*. Second, Plato already described conversations in closed, private spaces (as did the later villa dialogue). In private spaces a structure develops on which the flourishing of dialogue is crucially dependent: the culture of cultivated chat, which the ancient Greeks, the Italians of the Renaissance, and the salons of the French Enlightenment enjoyed to such a great extent.[8] P. von Moos correctly asked whether the dialogue, like every work of art, not only mirrors reality but also compensates for its shortcomings, "so that behind dialogic texts we might find an unsatisfied need for real conversations, and that an increase in cultivated chat and conviviality is accompanied by a withering away of the dialogue as an art form."[9] But even if this is so in part for certain periods, at least in the medium term we can assume a positive relation between conversation and dialogue: important chats will inspire persons with a talent for literature; and conversely in a period in which chat is not cultivated, a need for conversation dialogues can hardly be widespread, even if the decline of a chat culture may cause those who have experienced its splendor to be nostalgic and lead them to make compensatory efforts in the form of dialogues. But not only do dialogues grow out of the humus of conversation; they can fertilize it by establishing a model such as Baldasar Castiglione's dialogue *Il cortigiano,* which provides a theory of a way of life decisively shaped by chat and at the same time exemplifies it in a literary form (the thematically related "Galateo" by the cleric Giovanni della Casa is not a dialogue but rather a fictional speech given by an old man to a young one).

Individual freedom of speech, even if not necessarily in the legally guaranteed form found in most developed countries today, is surely a

8. The fact that German culture had this to a smaller degree is one of the reasons why there are few philosophical dialogues in the German language. Cf. Hirzel (1895), II 441 f.

9. (1997), 238.

necessary presupposition for fruitful chat: totalitarian states have produced no dialogues. But it is not a sufficient condition. First, legally guaranteed freedom of speech is compatible with social taboos that significantly restrict the subjects that can be discussed intelligently in a society: there is a kind of liberalism that is no less averse to bringing up the question of God than religiosity is to an unprejudiced discussion of atheism. Second, freedom of speech does not by itself mean that one knows how to speak well or even has something to say; on the contrary, general freedom of speech can be interpreted in such a way that all contributions to a discussion are treated as being of equal importance, which seldom raises the level of chat. Third, good chat presupposes not only good speakers but also good listeners. However, we have seen that Romantic subjectivism does not favor good listeners; and even if Romantic ideals such as religion and love have largely broken down, that does not mean that the ability to listen well has been revived. Fourth, a culture of cultivated discussion has certainly fallen victim to the surge of new media. Just as the rapid exchange of e-mails has dealt a death blow to the culture of letter-writing, surfing the net is putting an end to sociable groups, which require a considerably greater individual commitment. Even where people still gather for philosophical conversations, there is always the inexorable danger that someone's cell phone will ring. And when the conversation takes place in a professional context, for example, a discussion group at a conference, the predetermined time framework and the audience's expectations of a show seldom encourage originality.

It would even be possible to defend the provocative claim that certain forms of censorship have favored the dialogue. We have already seen that in times of censorship dialogue has been a favorite form of evasion—although a risky one, alongside which there were also other forms of literary disguise. That Hume would allow his *Dialogues* to be published only posthumously,[10] and that Diderot's most famous dialogues were not published until the nineteenth century (the adventure of the manuscript of *Le neveu de Rameau* has been so often recounted

---

10. However, Hume seems to have wanted them to be published earlier, even if he ended up following his friends' advice to delay their publication. Cf. his letter to Gilbert Elliot, March 12, 1763 (*Letters,* I 380).

that it can be assumed to be familiar here), shows that despite the form they had chosen they anticipated problems—certainly they no longer feared that they would be burned as heretics, but they did fear ostracism. This danger also existed in times without formal censorship; and it has been argued that Plato used his irony and that of his Socrates to conceal his own oppressive intellectual superiority, which could be a serious problem in a democratic society in which ostracism was institutionalized. However, Plato never sought to conceal his rejection of Attic democracy; and Socrates' ironic gestures of humility are not very difficult to see through. Presumably only later generations misinterpreted them, as crassly as those Athenians who had the funeral oration in the *Menexenus,* one of the most trenchant critiques of Attic imperialism, delivered as a eulogy of Athens.[11]

Therefore what is involved in Plato's choice of the dialogue form is less a fear of persecution than the desire to reveal his true views only to intelligent readers. The aristocratic system of values in general favors indirect communication that can be deciphered only by initiates; and even if Plato transformed the aristocracy of social status into an aristocracy of the mind, both are essentially based on a kind of elitism that deems only certain carefully tested individuals worthy of learning the central tenets. The composition of dialogues is not a substitute for but rather a functional equivalent of the *peira* of which the *Seventh Letter* speaks (340b5): this should also not be denied by advocates of a Platonic esotericism, who rightly point out that this cannot be reduced, as for instance Schleiermacher[12] and Hegel[13] thought, to the difficulties encountered in interpreting the dialogues but rather consists in a special oral teaching within the Academy to which the dialogues nonetheless constantly allude and which they partly reveal.[14] Hume was not the leader of a school, and in his case one cannot really speak of esotericism. But the conviction that those who misunderstood his *Dialogues*—like the reporter of the conversation, Pamphilus—deserve their fate and should be left in their lack

11. Cf. Cic. *Or.* 44.151.
12. (1996), 34.
13. 19.21 f.
14. Cf. Hösle (2004a), 51 f.

of understanding is an aristocratic consciousness in a broader sense that scorns the forms of hawking publicity. The dialogue highlights an inter-subjective event, but paradoxically it may thereby make it harder to understand the author, who wants to be understood by fewer people than does the author of a diatribe.

In Plato the use of the dialogue form was already based on a certain ideal of education. In his view, we cannot begin philosophy at just any point; we must pass through certain steps, and even commit certain errors, because only in that way can we learn. "Acute quidam falleris," "You are mistaken in an astute way," Augustine says to Adeodatus.[15] When Adeodatus later asks Augustine to explain precisely where he committed an error (which involved a confusion of the word and what is designated by the word), his father refuses to tell him; instead, he asks the same question again, so that Adeodatus will find out by himself where he went wrong. The son is grateful to his father for this.[16] The mathematical error made by the slave in the *Meno* suggests itself; because it is presented and criticized, the reader learns more than if the right result had been immediately given to him.[17] The boy in Leibniz's *Dialogus de arte computandi* makes an analogous error (even if Charinus's question is actually wrongly formulated); but Charinus warns him not to reply too hastily, and the boy realizes his mistake.[18] It can also be said in a treatise that one must not read the second chapter before the first; but that would not suffice to show what it means to proceed in the correct order—or not to so proceed. Still more important is the conviction of a large part of the tradition that a philosophical education is more than a transfer of information: it is training in a way of life. This training is shown and taught by the dialogue, just as it naturally puts forth certain propositions to whose transmission the treatise limits itself. Even the teacher-pupil dialogue, which comes closest to the treatise, usually presupposes a personal relationship between the teacher and the pupil

15. *De mag.* 5.14.
16. 8.22. When Augustine later asks whether he should draw a conclusion from an admission of Adeodatus's, the latter answers that he would rather do it himself (8.24). He has thus learned to proceed on his own.
17. See *Men.* 82bff. Cf. above, chap. 3, n. 49.
18. (1976), 78.

that could flourish under the conditions of traditional societies more easily than in the bureaucratized knowledge industry in modern industrial countries. In Plato's dialogues, Socrates is concerned with the knowledge of the truth, but he is no less concerned with the "souls" of at least a few of his interlocutors; that is why the *Phaedrus* can end with a common prayer (279b6 ff.). Augustine's Cassiciacum dialogues and Anselm's *Cur deus homo* are also based on this personal concern with the Other, which obviously underlies interreligious dialogues as well, and this contributes to their special attraction. That in Hume's *Dialogues* Pamphilus is a pupil, and as it were Cleanthes' adopted son, whereas the superior mind, Philo, has no personal relation to the sole young participant in the conversation, is a subtle inversion of the Platonic roles and points *e contrario* to Philo's splendid and at the same time tragic isolation.

It is well known that in Plato this interest in the Other is connected with the homoerotic educational culture of his time.[19] The erotic tension is evident not only in the *Symposium* and *Phaedrus* but also, especially, in the three palaestra dialogues, *Lysis, Charmides,* and *Euthydemus,* since the nakedness of the young male body in the sports arena is particularly likely to awaken erotic desire. However, Plato desexualized the homoerotics of his time; according to him, the pleasure taken in the Other's body should be transformed into an interest in his soul, and ultimately in the supra-personal idea of the Good. Plato's Socrates often seems only to feign a sexual interest in a young interlocutor in order to capture his attention; when he is particularly insistent—for example, when he tells Menexenus that since they are alone he would disrobe and dance before him, if he were only asked to do so (236c11 ff.)—the irony is obvious. But this interest remains the starting point without which the personal relationship and thus also the common philosophizing would not get under way at all. The relationship between Anselm and Boso is free of any sexuality; but their friendship is so exclusive that one would not want to deny it of its erotic traits.[20] In Marsilio Ficino's *De amore,* a dialogic commentary on Plato's *Symposium,* discreet allusions to homoerotic love affairs

19. Cf. the fundamental work by K. J. Dover (1989), esp. 153 ff.
20. Cf. B. Goebel and V. Hösle (2005), 191, with respect to *Ep.* 174 and 209.

among those present can be found.[21] The predominance of homosexual over heterosexual erotics in the philosophical dialogues of antiquity results from the fact that in them women play no central role, as we will see. Diderot, however, gives women a more important place: in the *Entretien d'un philosophe avec la Maréchale de* ***, which represents the marshal's wife at her bath, the heterosexual flirting is emphasized. The flirting keeps within the bounds of the seemly, in part because of the difference in rank, but it continues throughout the conversation. In the modern age homosexual love is largely taboo; Gide can discuss the subject but not represent it in the dialogue. Only in Murdoch's *Acastos*, especially in the second dialogue, "Above the Gods," is the erotic relationship clearly less Platonic than it is in Plato's dialogues or in Ficino.[22]

In the preceding paragraphs factors have been mentioned that explain why after the decline of Cartesianism and the idea of a system, indeed, why even after the rise of a philosophy that claims to be determined by the principle of intersubjectivity, hardly any dialogues have been written. Neither the dialogic philosophy of Martin Buber,[23] for example, in the first half of the twentieth century, nor the hermeneutic philosophy of Hans-Georg Gadamer or the discourse theory of Karl-Otto Apel and Jürgen Habermas, in the second half of the same century, have led to a revival of the genre.[24] R. Casali (2005) has rightly distinguished Habermas's abstract, purely cognitive ideal of communication from the chat paradigm on which the educational model of the Italian Renaissance is based. The latter is concerned with emphasizing indi-

---

21. "Dicam equidem, et si vereor ne quis vestrum hec audiens erubescat," Giovanni Cavalcanti says in his second speech (1984; 58).

22. One has only to read the ending, where Socrates goes off arm in arm with Alcibiades, and Timonax arm in arm with Antagoras, who is infatuated with him, and from whom he wants to buy a slave in whom he is interested not primarily on humanitarian grounds (97, 129 f.), while Acastos—as Antagoras has already done (117)—reproaches Plato for his jealousy of Alcibiades but finally manages to put his arm around his hip (121).

23. According to my terminology, this trend has to be called a "philosophy of conversation."

24. The interview that the 101-year-old Gadamer gave Silvio Vietta (2002) is not a fictional dialogue. Nor did the conversation between Jürgen Habermas and Joseph Cardinal Ratzinger, the later pope Benedict XVI, in January 2004 in Munich lead to a fictional dialogue.

vidual moral differences no less than differences in social rank, with training pupils to live in a way that is supposed to lead to a happy existence, and also with leading them to identify with a tradition that has to be slowly appropriated and deciphered. Modern egalitarianism can endanger one aspect of the chat culture: if everyone has become equal, spending time together can no longer help people complement each other by participating in a conversation. In particular, however, the "scientification" of philosophy, its becoming technical, makes it more remote from everyday chat, in which the discussion dialogue must also have one of its roots. If philosophy has become so technical that it requires, for example, extensive formalization, one can hardly imagine writing a philosophical dialogue. To be sure, a dialogue, especially an indirect one, can describe someone interrupting a conversation to go to the blackboard and write something down; something analogous happens in the passage in the *Meno* mentioned above. But it happens only once.[25] In Galileo's *Dialogo sopra i due massimi sistemi,* there are several calculations, tables, and drawings, but they are introduced by the conversation partners' own speech acts.[26] If, on the other hand, things have to be constantly written down, as in Leibniz's *Dialogus de arte computandi,* then conversation and its representation in a dialogue are no longer the right media for philosophizing. It is no accident that not only did Leibniz's dialogue remain unfinished, but even the part that was finished fails as a dialogue: the last quarter of the text, which deals with algebraic formulas, consists of a long lecture given by Charinus,[27] and it is hard to see how an adult—not to mention a child—could follow it without writing down the formulas and slowly examining them.

"Scientification" goes hand in hand with the detachment of philosophy from a way of life that supports it. One of the paradoxes of twentieth-century philosophy is that the philosophy of existence has not changed this in any way: it writes about forms of existence but has not presented

25. The later, mathematically difficult passage, 86e ff.—correctly interpreted by K. Gaiser (1964)—is only spoken and implies no change in medium.

26. Cf., e.g., (1998), 221 f., 352 f., 383: "come adesso vi mostro disegnando questa terza figura."

27. In Knobloch's bilingual edition, Charinus speaks without interruption from p. 136 to p. 174.

an impressive existence that is comparable even to Wittgenstein's (not to mention Socrates'), and still less has it been able to make forms of existence visible in the genre of the philosophical dialogue. Why? The answer is not hard to find: a philosophical existence cannot be sought *intentione recta;* it arises from the effort to appropriate a truth that transcends the subject. If one does not believe in such a truth, there can be no philosophical existence worthy of being represented in a philosophical dialogue.

CHAPTER 6

Individual Presuppositions
and Obstacles

If there are also ages and philosophical orientations that are more favorable for dialogue than others, not all philosophers of those ages and
orientations have made use of the dialogue form. The Enlightenment was
well disposed toward the dialogue, and Kant's work is, especially in the
area of theoretical philosophy, the German equivalent of Hume's. And yet
Kant wrote no dialogue: we would hardly be inclined to call "dialogue"
the short conversation between Caius and Titus after proposition IX
in the *Principiorum primorum cognitionis metaphysicae nova dilucidatio*
or the "Fragment of a moral catechism" in the "Ethical didactics" at the
end of the second part of the *Metaphysics of Morals*.[1] A severe moralism
is typical of Kant, for whom this "catechism" is concerned with nothing
other than raising the child to an autonomous knowledge of ethical duty.
This contrasts sharply with Palamedes' subtle irony in the "Dialogue" that
appears at the end of Hume's second *Enquiry*. Palamedes' report on the
land of Fourli and its unusual customs—including homosexuality, suicide, and regicide, which are generally admired there—alludes to the
familiar world of Greco-Roman antiquity, but precisely in view of this

---

1. *Metaphysische Anfangsgründe der Tugendlehre*, §52, n.; 8.620 ff.

world's fame it is still more well suited for challenging the Enlightenment conviction that its own norms are universal. Hume ultimately wants to defend this conviction, though he limits it to general principles;[2] but that he is able to play ironically with it is typical of his nature and is surely a necessary presupposition for writing fascinating dialogues. In Kant, this presupposition is not fulfilled; the experience of the unconditional nature of the moral law prevented him from thinking his way into other value systems in an unprejudiced manner. Someone who considers lying categorically forbidden would presumably find intolerable even the temporary disguise that a writer accepts when he speaks in the voice of another person. In particular, it would have torn Kant apart internally to mount the most eloquent, seductive, and plausible defense he could for a position that he himself considered categorically forbidden.

It is possible to maintain that this is to Kant's honor; and perhaps a similar structure of personality explains why some other first-rate thinkers, such as Plotinus, Thomas Aquinas, Vico, and Husserl, wrote no dialogues. The writer of dialogues must be able to think by indirection; not everyone is capable of doing so, and it is in any case not a general presupposition for good philosophy. However, two important qualifications must be added. First, immoralists may also be incapable of writing dialogues; an egomaniac like Nietzsche lacked the ability to abstract from himself and observe himself from the outside, without which he could write *The Antichrist* and *Ecce Homo* but not a dialogue. Someone who philosophizes with a hammer will have difficulty writing philosophical chamber music. Second, the example of Plato shows that a

---

2. Gilbert Elliot correctly saw this; in a letter of February 1751 he expresses his relief on finding that Hume, despite the skeptical beginning of the dialogue, comes back to common sense at the end: "In the first part of this work, you have given full scope to the native bent of your genius. The ancients and moderns, how opposite soever in other respects, equally combine in favour of the most unbounded skepticism. Principles, customs, and manners, the most contradictory, all seemingly lead to the same end; and agreeably to your laudable practice, the poor reader is left in the most disconsolate state of doubt and uncertainty. When I had got thus far, what do you think were my sentiments? I will not be so candid as to tell you; but how agreeable was my surprise, when I found you had led me into this maze, with no other view, than to point out to me more clearly the direct road. Why can't you always write in this manner?" (J. H. Burton [1846], I 323).

writer of dialogues can be convinced of the unconditional binding force of moral norms. However, there are good grounds for suspecting that Plato was able to represent someone like Callicles so convincingly only because he himself had for some time been inclined to believe that "might makes right," a view that seemed obvious for someone of his generation and social standing, and one from which the historical Socrates presumably weaned him. Plato's moralism is more strained and reflective than Kant's, which seems almost innate—but that means that it is less naive, and precisely for that reason it was capable of becoming the foundation for the composition of the most important dialogues in the history of philosophy.

Naturally, another individual presupposition for writing philosophical dialogues is the author's artistic talent. We have already mentioned Plato's probable attempts at drama; and we know that Diderot wrote dramas as well. Cicero was a first-rate orator and a master of the language; Llull was one of the best poets and prose writers of the Middle Ages; Kierkegaard and Murdoch were undoubtedly talented both as philosophers and as writers. In Feyerabend as well, the artistic vein is clear, and perhaps stronger than the specifically philosophical one. Hume's receptive aesthetic sensitivity at least was developed, as is shown by his essays on the theory of literature, one of which, *Of the Standard of Taste,* has an important place in the history of aesthetics. The combination of a talent for philosophy and a talent for writing is not common, and this explains why there are not many philosophical dialogues that are truly successful in both respects—because the countless didactic dialogues do not belong to this small group. A good dialogue, like a good drama, has two presuppositions, one of which is the writer's interest in, or even empathy with, individuals who defend other positions, a quality that is not to be found in monists like Spinoza and Hegel. At the same time, however, the dialogue also presupposes a readiness to allow different positions to collide with each other powerfully. We have already seen (p. 109 f.) that the irenic mind of Leibniz, who believed in a plurality of substances, was detrimental to the quality of his dialogues. Plato, in contrast, is so great an artist because he allows the weaknesses of his characters to come boldly into relief. This might be thought cruel, but then we have to admit that a certain cruelty is inseparable from the artistic enterprise.

I have already discussed the relation between eros and chat; it varies not only with the culture but also with the individual.[3] If the colors and sounds made by many animals play a role in sexual selection, it is hardly surprising that the talent for artful and intelligent speaking is made to serve erotic goals. Conversely, however, a spiritual person quickly learns to subject his erotic energy potential to intellectual goals. The poet writes such good lyrics because he has fallen in love; but he has fallen in love because he wants to write poetry. Something analogous might hold for Plato. In a letter full of Platonic reminiscences that Diderot wrote to his friend Sophie Volland, probably on October 12, 1759, he tells her that although she was not present, she nonetheless inspired his chat:

> I was full of the tenderness that you had inspired in me when I appeared amid our guests; she shone in my eyes; she gave life to what I said; she controlled my movement; she manifested herself in everything. I seemed to them extraordinary, inspired, divine. . . . We spent an evening full of enthusiasm of which I was the center. . . . I spoke to d'Alembert like an angel. . . . I went back to Montami's place, and he could not help telling me as I left him: "O, my dear sir, what pleasure you've given me!"; and I replied in a low voice to the cold man whom I had moved: "It's not I, it's she, it's she who was acting in me."[4]

Feyerabend is so gallant as to conclude his "First Dialogue" with the appearance of an "attractive lady with curly hair and a heavy Italian accent" named Grazia, who, as always, arrives too late and self-confidently explains that she would certainly have had something to contribute to the discussion[5]—an allusion to Feyerabend's last wife, Grazia Borrini.

3. Cf. Hirzel (1895), I 31 ff.
4. *Correspondance* II 269 f. "J'étois plein de la tendresse que vous m'aviez inspirée quand j'ai paru au milieu de nos convives; elle brilloit dans mes yeux; elle échauffoit mes discours; elle disposoit de mes mouvements; elle se montroit en tout. Je leur semblois extraordinaire, inspiré, divin. . . . Nous avons passé une soirée d'enthousiasme dont j'étois le foyer. . . . J'ai parlé à d'Alembert comme un ange . . . je suis rentré chez le Montami qui n'a pu s'empêcher de me dire en me quittant: 'O, mon cher monsieur, quel plaisir vous m'avez fait!'; et moi je répondois tout bas à l'homme froid que j'avois remué: 'Ce n'est pas moi, c'est elle, c'est elle qui agissoit en moi.'"
5. (1991), 45.

Dialogues are, as I have repeatedly said, more difficult to interpret than treatises, especially when the author does not appear in them. In order to choose this genre, the writer of dialogues must therefore have an interest in masks and disguises; as a rule, he will be an ironic or even mysterious person or at least want to be one. As the example of Kierkegaard shows, the dialogue is not the only genre that is available to such a person; but it is a particularly obvious option. However, an author who conceals himself behind his text wants to be recognized for who he is by at least a select few; otherwise, he would not take the trouble to write at all but rather keep silent. Nonetheless it may happen that he is content not to be understood until after his death. In fact, many of Plato's allusions were correctly interpreted only two millennia after his death, and a few of them still await correct interpretation. That Plato, unlike Nietzsche,[6] never publicly stated that he did not want to be read by his contemporaries does not invalidate the assumption that he was aware to what extent his dialogues would remain incomprehensible for many of his contemporaries and also for later readers; it only shows that he was more noble than Nietzsche. But how can an interpreter claim in good faith that he has understood Plato, for example, and deciphered his text?

---

6. *Götzen-Dämmerung. Streifzüge eines Unzeitgemässen* 51 (1988; 6.153).

CHAPTER 7

The Problem of Authorial Intention

Interpreting Plato is so difficult because he wrote—except for the *Apology* and a few of the letters attributed to him—only dialogues. The interpreter has it easier when the writer composed not only dialogues but also treatises or other nonfictional works in the first person. If these are historical works, they can help us determine which historical event underlies his dialogues as their core: Gregory of Nyssa's *Life of Macrina* proves that Gregory conducted religious conversations with his dying sister, even if it also makes it clear that they could not have had the philosophical density that they assume in his dialogue *On the Soul and Resurrection*. If on the other hand the author has written philosophical treatises, the interpreter must take them into account if he wants to understand correctly the point of the dialogues or, better, if he wants to reconstruct the *mens auctoris*, the author's intention. I say "better" because the reconstruction of the *mens auctoris* is not the only legitimate form of understanding. In fact, one of the achievements of Gadamer's hermeneutics is to have reminded us that understanding cannot be reduced to the reconstruction of authorial intention. This holds even for scientific texts: a scientist can, for instance, intend to refute a theory and to this end derive from it consequences that he considers so paradoxical that he regards the theory as disproven. However, later developments may con-

firm these consequences; and then this scientist may acquire the reputation of having involuntarily been the first to have further developed
the theory that he actually wanted to destroy. This case may seem surprising, but it is basically only a further application of a familiar outcome of the theory of action, namely, that the consequences of an act
may deviate from the intention that produced them. *Noēmata* have
their own logic, which may deviate from the characteristics of the *noēsis* that first discovered them. Analogously, truth and truthfulness are
two different things; someone may say something true, even if he himself thinks that what he has said is false, but for whatever reason wants
it to be thought to be true.[1]

Even more than for scientific texts, this holds for literary texts. Unconscious processes of creation obviously play an essential role in the
exact sciences, including mathematics, as we have known at least since
Poincaré and Hadamard; but the ability to bring the results of these
processes into the light of consciousness and subject them to critical
analysis is also an essential part of science.[2] The writer does not always
need to have this ability; he can unconsciously do the right thing, instinctively use certain means of representation that achieve an aesthetic end in a perfect way, without knowing that they do it, and a fortiori without having any idea of why they do it; jokes are much older than
the theory of jokes. Indeed, the writer may even realize by his means of
representation an effect that runs counter to the intended one. He may
intend to represent the irresponsibility of an adulteress who in his hands
becomes so lovable, whose behavior toward the husband patronizing
her seems so excusable and whose punishment seems so inhuman, that
his work helps change his culture's judgment regarding adultery, even
if this was far from being his intention. That was, in a very simplified
form, what happened in the case of Fontane's novel *Effi Briest*. Such examples may be relatively rare, but at least this experience is common to
every writer that his own work surprises him by transcending him. In
the preface to the *Laelius*, Cicero writes that the authority of Cato in
the eponymous dialogue influences him so much that in reading his

1. Cf. Augustine, *De mag.* 13.41.
2. Cf. J. Hadamard (1996), 56 ff.

own work he sometimes has the feeling that Cato and not he himself is speaking.[3]

Although a comprehensive interpretation of a text, and thus also of a philosophical dialogue, is not bound to what its author intended, it remains important to distinguish between the reconstruction of the author's meaning and an interpretation of his text that explicitly goes beyond it. We should concede that the latter can be far more important than philologically meticulous interpretations of the *mens auctoris,* but only insofar as there is a consensus regarding which activity one is engaged in. We can understand how earlier ages that were able to justify truth claims only by appealing to authorities could read into authoritative texts, in what was often a subjectively honest way, their own views regarding the subjects concerned; and no corpus invited that so much as Plato's dialogues, in which the author himself does not speak in the first person. But in a post-Enlightenment age there is no longer any justification for proceeding in this way, even if, for example, a few Heideggerians and Straussians are still addicted to it.

What allows the interpreter to reconstruct the views of the author of a dialogue? As already indicated, it is always necessary to study the non-dialogic writings of the author, insofar as they are available. These may be of a public nature—for example, autobiographies or meditations— or of a private nature—for example, letters or journal entries. Anyone who has read Cicero's *Orator* knows that in *De oratore* Crassus rather than Antonius represents Cicero's position; anyone who has studied Descartes's main works will not for an instant doubt, on reading *La recherche de la verité par la lumiere naturelle,* that it is Eudoxe behind whom the author is hidden. However, it is possible to object that statements in works written in the first person can also be insincere; and to that extent we lack a criterion for the interpretation of dialogues. Such a suspicion is particularly strong when in his public writings an author takes a position whose negation entails significant social sanctions. It is legitimate to pursue

3. 1.4: "genus autem hoc sermonum positum in hominum veterum auctoritate et eorum inlustrium plus nescio quo pacto videtur habere gravitatis; itaque ipse mea legens sic adficior interdum ut Catonem, non me loqui existimem." Similarly, he asks Atticus to now imagine that Laelius, not Cicero, is speaking: "tu velim a me animum parumper avertas, Laelium loqui ipsum putes" (1.5).

such a suspicion—but only when the corresponding position is not immunized against criticism because every contradictory bit of evidence that might be adduced can be countered by saying, "That is also a disguise." Then we are dealing with what Karl Popper has called "reinforced dogmatism"—that is, a position that can no longer be refuted, although (it has to be added) its negation is not semantically or performatively self-contradictory. An author may believe naively in the dogmas of his time; but when he says things that are in contradiction to those dogmas—and the discrepancy cannot be resolved in terms of historical development, for instance, which is often possible—the assumption that he does not believe in those dogmas has a prima facie plausibility, even though he loudly professes his adherence to them. But this is only a prima facie plausibility, because the author need not be aware of the contradiction, may have repressed it through self-censorship mechanisms or resolved it in the framework of a theory of double truth (which admittedly is often only a pretext). After all, the overwhelming majority of persons, even very intelligent ones, hold incompatible beliefs without realizing it. However, if the corresponding contradiction is generally discussed in the environment and if the theory of double truth directly contradicts other epistemological views held by the author to be interpreted, this suspicion becomes stronger and can even become a certainty. But then, too, as interpreters we must take great care that when we arrive at the well-founded conclusion that in a given passage an author is speaking against his own conviction, we do not conclude that for that reason he has already adopted our own view—because there may very well be a third and even many more possibilities. If for example a seventeenth-century author suggests that he does not believe in the divinity of Christ, that is far from meaning that he is an atheist: he can still be a deist, or even a theist.

What we have said holds for public texts written in the first person. In the case of private letters, especially when they are addressed to close friends whom the author considers to be more or less his intellectual equals, or a fortiori in the case of journal entries, dissimulation is not likely—unless the author lives in a totalitarian state in which both mail and private diaries are subject to surveillance. But then, too, we can normally assume that letters are written in such a way that only the censor, and not the friend, is deceived. Hume's letter to Gilbert Elliot of March 10, 1751, throws light on the interpretation of the *Dialogues Concerning Natural Religion;* it is hard to deny that Philo speaks for Hume far more than Cleanthes does when we read:

> I have often thought, that the best way of composing a Dialogue, wou'd be for two Persons that are of different Opinions about any Question of Importance, to write alternately the different Parts of the Discourse, & reply to each other. By this Means, that vulgar Error woud be avoided, of putting nothing but Nonsense into the Mouth of the Adversary: And at the same time, a Variety of Character & Genius being upheld, woud make the whole look more natural & unaffected. Had it been my good Fortune to live near you, I shou'd have taken on me the Character of Philo, in the Dialogue, which you'll own I coud have supported naturally enough: And you woud not have been averse to that of Cleanthes.[4]

This text is one of the most interesting on the theory of the dialogue, because it simultaneously addresses the internal problematics of the genre—the fact that the dialogue represents intersubjectivity but is nonetheless the product of a single individual. Many writers of dialogues have succumbed to the danger of not doing justice to the position distant from their own, but a few of them were well aware of this. When Cicero wrote his *Academica,* he represented as his philosophical opponent Varro, a man who was still alive and who was not so close to him as his brother Quintus or Atticus, for example; that was risky. Therefore in a letter to Atticus he proudly emphasizes that Philo's position, which he attributes to himself, does not appear to be superior to Antiochus's critical view of skepticism, which Varro defends; the latter view is inherently plausible, he says, and he has carefully expressed it through his stylistic abilities, if he has any.[5] In another letter, however, he acknowledges that he often

4. *Letters* I 154.
5. "ut non sim consecutus ut superior mea causa videatur. sunt enim vehementer *pithana* Antiochia; quae diligenter a me expressa acumen habent Antiochi, nitorem orationis nostrum, si modo is est aliquis in nobis" (*Att.*13.19.5).

seems to see the face of Varro, who complains—unjustly—that in the *Academica* Cicero's position was more comprehensively defended than his own.[6] In Bodin's *Heptaplomeres,* the Jew Salomo similarly complains that in his *Dialogue with the Jew Tryphon* Justin represents the latter as so inexperienced and incompetent that he, Salomo, was very irritated by reading it and by the banality of the arguments made by Justin, who trumpets his own victory like a *miles gloriosus* in the theater.[7] Thus Bodin lets the reader know dialogue-externally that he himself intends to avoid this error. Similarly, in a note Leibniz observed that dialogues were usually so written that the author favored one side. But it is part of a truly philosophical dialogic art that both sides fight with equal strength and everything that the most acute opponent could say is said. Thus the triumph of the dialogue would be the triumph of the topic. However, in the belief that a synthetic philosophy could overcome the conflict of perspectives—a belief that is typical of him—Leibniz adds that the author of the dialogue is like a judge or mediator in a legal proceeding.[8]

It speaks for the intellectual honesty of Cicero, Bodin, and Hume that they did not wish to allow any objection like that made by Salomo to be made against them; and precisely because of this moral quality their

6. "ita mihi saepe occurrit vultus eius querentis fortasse vel hoc, meas partis in iis libris copiosius defensas esse quam suas, quod mehercule non esse intelleges" (*Att.* 13.25.3).

7. "Et quidem memini legisse me in Justini Martyris dialogo cum Tryphone Judaeo, quem adeo imperitum et ineptum fingit, ut me lectionis et ineptiarum scriptoris valde pigeat (victoriam enim dialogistes, quasi miles gloriosus in theatro stans, decernit)" (127). Cf. 148, where Salomo also quotes Justin, whose ideas he recognizes in Toralba's objection. Bodin did not know the sixth-century anonymous Greek *Dialogus cum Iudaeis,* in which still less of the dialogic spirit is to be found, since the Christ simply talks at the Jews. As J. H. Declerck writes in his introduction, the work is addressed not to Jews but to Christians. "If the goal of anti-Jewish literature had really been to convince the Jews to have themselves baptized, works such as our *Dialogos* would certainly have not been very effective means for achieving that end" (XXIX, n. 14).

8. "Dialogi ita scribi solent ut autor faveat parti. Artis dialogisticae vere philosophicae foret ita scribere, ut utrinque pari parte pugnetur, utque dicantur quae acerrimus adversarius dicere posset. ita demum triumphus dialogi foret triumphus causae. Esset enim velut colloquium, congressusque litigantium judiciarius, autore Dialogi quasi judice aut si mavis praeside atque moderatore." Leibniz MS. in the Niedersächsische Landesbibliothek Hannover 4 III 5e f. 29; quoted in E. Knobloch's appendix to Leibniz (1976), 183.

dialogues are often hard to interpret. Even if Hume's *Dialogues* did not become a collaborative work—which is generally difficult, and Elliot could not hold a candle to Hume—we can grant him that he made the opposing position as strong as it could be made in his time. (Hume could not have known that the revolution in epistemology carried out by Kant and German idealism would give proofs of God's existence new opportunities.) Despite these efforts, however, Hume could not avoid representing Philo's superiority, because he was truly imbued by it. That in Cleanthes he created a respectable character honors him and distinguishes him from Philo, who by no means can be regarded as Cleanthes' creator. Philo takes part in a conversation; but he is not writing a dialogue.

Philo is not identical with Hume because they differ in ontological status; and for this nonidentity the difference in names is neither necessary nor sufficient. Even if a character bearing the author's name appears in one of his fictional dialogues, he is still not identical with him: the same propositions can have different truth values depending on whether they refer to the author or to the like-named character in the dialogue.[9] The ontological difference does not imply, of course, that the like-named conversation partner cannot be the author's spokesman, and thus the author cannot identify with him; finally, as we have seen, a conversation partner with an entirely different name can be to a large extent spokesman for the author, as is Eudoxe in Descartes's dialogue and Philo in Hume's.[10] A representative can be the spokesman for his master in the real world as well, although two different persons are involved. But it is possible that the author of a dialogue does not want to take responsibility for what the like-named interlocutor within the conversation says: Diderot the author, for instance, may not want to be responsible for the position of

9. This does not hold, of course, for all statements: Cicero the author and Cicero the interlocutor in the trilogy that begins with the *Hortensius* were both consuls. But only the latter engaged in epistemological discussions with Hortensius, Catulus, and Lucullus.

10. This may even be expressly said in the dialogue. "Or che dirrò io del Nolano? Forse, per essermi tanto prossimo, quanto io medesmo a me stesso, non mi converrà lodarlo?," Teofilo asks in the frame conversation in Bruno's *La cena de le ceneri* (1985; I 29 f.), and thus indicates that he is the spokesman for Bruno, whose ideas set forth in the main conversation he faithfully presents.

the first-person narrator in *Le neveu de Rameau* or in the two *Entretiens*. In this case the author does not really speak in the first person in the statements that he attributes to the like-named interlocutor or narrator, because the conversation and the narrative are subject to aesthetic bracketing. However, the author must have something to do with the position that is attributed to him (or should one say "that he attributes to himself"?). It would be tactless to give the name "Edmund Husserl" to a radical skeptic in a dialogue, because despite the extensive autonomy of the aesthetic universe, a complex web of connotations connects it with the real world, which one can misappropriate only when one wants to show an interesting point of view to its best advantage. And this would be tactless even on the part of Husserl himself, who might thereby not have violated a duty to himself but would have certainly violated duties toward his readers. However, the author may let it be understood that he thinks more comprehensively than the like-named conversation partner, who may correspond more to a widespread image of the author than to his reality. Precisely when the conversation is set in the past, this difference is indicated: Cicero, for instance, writes at the end of *De natura deorum* only about what seemed to him more convincing immediately after the fictional conversation, more than thirty years before the composition of the dialogue—namely, the Stoic position, as opposed to the skeptical one.[11] Since in the (dialogue-external) preface the author Cicero continues to adhere to the skeptical Academy (1.3.6), it is tempting to interpret this as suggesting that the author Cicero does not identify with the impression the silent interlocutor who bears his name had more than thirty years earlier.[12] Since in a preface under his own name, unlike in a

11. "Haec cum essent dicta, ita discessimus ut Velleio Cottae disputatio verior, mihi Balbi ad veritatis similitudinem videretur esse propensior" (3.40.95).

12. However, see J. Leonhardt (1999), 17, 22, 29 f., 38, 61 ff., who in his interpretation gives the concluding sentence priority. In my opinion, it is possible that Cicero recognized the social function of Stoic theology but opposed it skeptically in theory: one should be religious and at the same time recognize that this position is not grounded in reason. "Et enim ipse Cotta sic disputat, ut Stoicorum magis argumenta confutet quam hominum deleat religionem" (div. 1.5.8). It is also conceivable that Cicero really could not decide whether despite the Academic criticism, Stoic theology might be saved— possibly by means of new and better arguments.

prologue, an author generally speaks outside the fiction,[13] statements made in it have the same status as those in nondialogic writings such as treatises and letters, and thus do not participate in aesthetic bracketing. They are therefore essential aids to interpretation. For example, Cicero writes explicitly at the beginning of the *Cato* that what the eponymous character says fully expresses his opinion,[14] and we may, indeed must, take this statement absolutely literally.

Nonetheless, this holds only for prefaces that are external to the dialogue and under the author's own name.[15] Proems that are internal to the dialogue, that is, prologues, are also subject to aesthetic bracketing. The first-person narrator of a dialogue—for example, that of the three previously mentioned dialogues by Diderot—belongs, like that of a novel, to the fictional world, and is thus not to be identified with the author.[16] It has even sometimes been claimed that such a first-person narrator should be distinguished not only from the author but also from the like-named interlocutor within the dialogue. To be sure, the conversation partner and the narrator play different roles and address a different audience; but this is still no argument for challenging their identity—since ultimately every person plays different roles without losing his identity. Analogously, Socrates, the narrator of the conversation in the *Protagoras*, even if he shows some different character traits,[17] is identical with the Socrates who is Protagoras's conversation partner in the same dialogue, but surely not with the historical Socrates. The ontological differenti -

13. The same holds for an afterword, as in Feyerabend (1991), 163–67, and for footnotes, as in Rousseau's *Rousseau juge de Jean-Jacques* or Gide's *Corydon*. The boundary between preface and prologue is not always sharp; "Al discreto lettore" in Galileo's *Dialogo sopra i due massimi sistemi* (1998; 5–7) is a preface, but first, its last paragraph constitutes the prologue, and second, the irony of the genuine preface is unmistakable: the author speaks, but he is not straightforward.

14. "iam enim ipsius Catonis sermo explicabit nostram omnem de senectute sententiam" (1.3).

15. If written by the author, synopses of the dialogue that are external to it have an analogous status, as for instance at the beginning of Aeneas's *Theophrastus*, and so do chapter titles, as in Cusanus's *Idiota de mente*.

16. Only in such an atypical dialogue as Fichte's *Sonnenklarer Bericht* is this otherwise; on this, see below, Part II, chap. 13.

17. Irony is, however, a constant that characterizes not only Socrates the conversation partner but also Socrates the narrator (e.g., *Ly.* 218c5 f.).

ation is meaningful only if the first-person narrator reports a dreamed conversation, because even in this case the same propositions can have different truth values, depending on whether they relate to one or the other: the first-person narrator for instance lay in bed and snored while the dreamed (or, depending on the theory of the "I," the dreaming) "I" went for a stroll and talked.

The condition that the preface be in the author's own name was mentioned because there can also be dialogue-external prefaces that do not belong to the same fictional universe as the dialogue but are themselves clearly designated as fictional, for instance through the use of a pseudonym.[18] This is, as it were, a case complementary to the one just mentioned—the iteration of the bracketing takes place not inside but outside the dialogue. The classical example is the invention of an editor who claims to have come across the dialogue in a surprising way. It is well known that Kierkegaard was a master of such fictional prefaces. The fictional editor of his only work containing a dialogue is a cheerful (and intellectually unsophisticated) bookbinder with the aptronym Hilarius Bogbinder, who in this case does not really understand what he is editing—a manuscript written by a man of letters who has died in the interim, which he has been given to bind, which has lain about in his shop, and which his children have used to learn to read and write—until a seminarian and philosopher who tutors Bogbinder's son realizes the importance of the manuscript and recommends its publication, suggesting that it might have been written by several hands.[19] The latter supposition, which is reflected in the subtitle of *Stadier paa livets vei, Studier af Forskjellige,* that is, *Studies by Various,* is clearly false from a point of view outside the text, since Kierkegaard was the only author of the work. But it is important because it indicates that in addition to the short dialogue in the first part, the work as a whole, like *Enten-Eller* (Either/Or), has a dialogic character. "Dialogic" absolutely in the Bakhtinian sense of a polyphony of voices that partly drown out the author's voice, which

---

18. Pseudonyms have two quite different functions—protecting the author, who wants to remain unknown, and "bracketing" what a known author says. Here we are concerned with the latter case.

19. 7.11 f. Hilarius's shoulder-shrugging indifference with regard to this supposition, "Selv har jeg derom ingen Mening," is amusing.

speaks to us certainly not in the preface, but at most in the figure of the writer of the diary edited and commented upon by another editor in the third part of *Stadier*. Or should one rather say, restrictively, "wants to speak"? Some readers of Kierkegaard cannot get over the feeling that his true genius is shown not in the ethical and religious voices of his pseudonymous works, and certainly not in those of the treatises and sermons published under his own name, but rather in the texts written by the "aesthetes" condemned by his conscious "I." At the least one has to say that we take Kierkegaard's critique of the aesthetic way of life so seriously because we sense how deeply this suffering artist has grasped it from within.

No reader of the *Stadier* has ever been tempted to interpret Bogbinder as Kierkegaard's spokesman; he is simply too naive and too unphilosophical. A preface by a simple editor must be clearly distinguished from one by an author. On the other hand, the preface to the *Dialogues Concerning Natural Religion* reminds us, in style and content, of Cicero's prefaces to his dialogues. Here, the use of the dialogue form is justified in a way that can easily be attributed to Hume himself. At the outset, we are told that although modern philosophers have made less use of the dialogue than the ancients did, it is a genre that is appropriate for them in two cases: first, when a theory is obvious and at the same time important, because "the novelty of the manner can compensate for the triteness of the subject"; and second, when a question is obscure and uncertain. "Reasonable men may be allowed to differ, where no one can reasonably be positive: Opposite sentiments, even without any decision, afford an agreeable amusement: And if the subject be curious and interesting, the book carries us, in a manner, into company; and unites the two greatest and purest pleasures of human life, study and society."[20] Fortunately, we are told immediately afterward, "these circumstances are all to be found in the subject of Natural Religion," since the existence of God is obvious and important, while the attributes of God and the nature of his Providence are obscure. Here, however, the reader familiar with Hume's treatises stops short: neither this claim nor the rhetorical tone reminds us of Hume's familiar style, of his characteristic voice marked by

20. (1947), 128.

an unmistakable combination of irony and sobriety. In case the reader has skipped the beginning, he should go back and take a closer look at it. Immediately after the title he will find "Pamphilus to Hermippus." This preface in the form of a fictional letter is, despite the difference in intellectual level, just as pseudonymous as Bogbinder's; and the name of its fictional author, which means "everyman's friend," is a warning signal.[21] The following conversation was not fabricated by him but is faithfully reported by him; to be precise, one would have to say that the book offers a fiction of the narrative of a historical dialogue. Within the literary universe to which he belongs, Pamphilus claims that he has not invented anything[22] — whereas Bogbinder knowingly publishes a fictional work. Pamphilus's report contains repeated interpretations of modes of behavior that throw more light on him than on the corresponding persons; this is examined in Part II, chapter 9. In addition, the concluding judgment in favor of Cleanthes[23] is made by Pamphilus, not by Hume — just as the young Cicero's judgment at the end of *De natura deorum* must be distinguished from that of the mature author. Pamphilus does not say himself that he has in Cleanthes almost an adoptive father and is thus, considering his youth, prejudiced in his favor, but this emerges from the statements by Demea which he reports.[24] In short, in spite or precisely because of the echo of classical prefaces in which from Aristotle onward authors speak in the first person, the preface to the *Dialogues*

21. A contrast with Shaftesbury's *The Moralists* is worthwhile. This dialogue also takes the form of a letter (from Philocles to Palemon); but the first of the three parts summarizes a conversation between Philocles and Palemon himself, at the end of which there is a promise of a letter about a conversation between Philocles and Theocles, whose aptronym ("God's glory") indicates that his theory is that of the author himself. In addition, Theocles is explicitly said to be Shaftesbury's friend, and he defends Shaftesbury's *Inquiry Concerning Virtue and Merit* against the accusation of atheism (1999; 50 ff.).

22. "My youth rendered me a mere auditor of their disputes; and that curiosity, natural to the early season of life, has so deeply imprinted in my memory the whole chain and connection of their arguments, that, I hope, I shall not omit or confound any considerable part of them in the recital" (1947; 129).

23. "I cannot but think, that PHILO's principles are more probable than DEMEA's; but that those of CLEANTHES approach still nearer to the truth" (1947; 228). This judgment corresponds in some extent to that of Hermippus (128).

24. (1947), 130.

is a brilliant deception by which many readers have been taken in. But through the name "Pamphilus," Hume provides a clear hint to its correct interpretation.[25]

An important corollary must be added. There is no external identifying mark that makes it possible to distinguish automatically between true and mendacious speech; and even if there were one, lies would immediately imitate it. An expression such as "Now I'm really telling the truth" seldom elicits trust. Analogously, this holds for fictional speech, which has one of its sources in imitation. For that very reason a formal demarcation between first-person speech and fictional speech can never be conclusive; it is part of the essence of fiction to undermine such formal demarcations. The formal boundaries established by one period may be rejected by the next one: Alfred Hitchcock's *Stage Fright* failed in part because he not only had a character tell a story that was false (within the film's universe), but made the fictitious events visible while they were being narrated. This violated the film grammar of the time but is now quite common. Thus one can of course also imagine that an author might write a theoretical preface in his own name that in reality is meant fictionally. But he would have to provide signals that allow this to be seen. What kind of signals could these be?

Resort to internal characteristics is inevitable. It is well known that Davidson and Gadamer, although they come from very different positions, defend the claim that understanding is possible only if we assume that the interpretandum states the truth, not in every respect, but still in a fundamental respect. In Davidson, this claim is connected with the problem of radical interpretation: basically, even in the case of speakers of our own language we do not know what meaning they associate with their statements—that is, whether they are really speaking our own language. (Nonetheless most senders have an interest in being understood, because the behavior they desire usually ensues only if the receiver recognizes their intention). In the case of speakers of a completely unknown language the sole possibility of understanding them consists—not for em-

---

25. Analogously, the "Avant-propos de Mésothète" in Engel (1997) points to the fictional character of the reported dialogue, even if the last two sentences are real acknowledgments by the author.

pirical but for transcendental reasons—in assuming that they referred to an event that actually occurred at a given point in time, if they made a specific statement at this point and not at another. That is in principle correct; but since transcendental arguments can easily show us that we can also understand false statements, one of the foundations on which a theory of understanding has to be based is a psychological theory that explains why certain errors, whether individual or, in certain periods, general, are natural.[26] These errors can follow necessarily from the background as assumptions; that is, they can be rational in a certain sense of the term. The quantity of errors can be large; but a human being who had absolutely no contact with reality would cease to be human.

Davidson's theory concerns chiefly the primary meaning of linguistic texts; but it can easily be extended to secondary, indirect meanings. What does this mean? To give a simple example: in an ironic statement such as "How wise this man is!" the primary meaning is obvious—that this man is wise. But the speaker hopes that the intelligent listener will understand that the opposite is meant. However, it would be completely false to say that the primary meaning of "How wise this man is!" is that this man is stupid; for then the speaker would have to say "How stupid this man is!" On the contrary, the speaker absolutely wants the intelligent listener to understand both—that he has said something that means that this man is wise, but in this particular case attention should be directed to his stupidity. How can we decipher irony? The normal case is surely the one in which the statement is obviously false, and thus in our example refers to a clearly stupid or at least untalented person (such as the compliments Socrates addresses to the charlatans Euthydemus and Dionysodorus in Plato's *Euthydemus,* or Frege's compliments to the mathematician Schubert in his "Über die Zahlen des Herrn H. Schubert," a work of unsurpassably subtle irony). However, in addition to the subject matter, the speaker's intellectual capacities (and in some cases those of the addressee, since irony often but not always seeks to be understood) must also be taken into account; thus it can certainly happen that a stupid man says of a wise one, "How wise this man is!," but means it ironically, because he cannot see the latter's wisdom. Whether an isolated

---

26. Cf. V. Hösle (2004d).

statement, for instance, praise for an author, is ironically meant or not quite often cannot be determined: to decide, we would need a significant corpus of statements made by such a speaker, just as generally speaking only words attested several times can be interpreted.

Analogously, in reconstructing the intentions of the author of a dialogue we have to assume first of all that the author stands behind the position that comes closest to the truth or is better grounded. Cotta's arguments against Stoic theology are often strong, and they are not rejected in *De natura deorum*—and this strengthens the presumption that the author Cicero did not identify with the Stoic position. But this is only a prima facie argument, since even major intellects have repeatedly made errors and identified with positions that are false or poorly grounded. Llull's arguments for the two specific dogmas of Christianity in his *Llibre del gentil e dels tres savis* are important but not compelling. Yet he considered them compelling, as everyone familiar with his treatises and his biography knows. However, not only can a philosopher overestimate an achievement that may in fact be the relative best in the framework of his period, but nonetheless not correspond to the truth; in principle, he may even juxtapose two positions of his time and consider the more poorly grounded one to be the correct one. However, in this case it is unlikely that he has really understood the arguments in favor of the better position; and we will be able to determine this from the way in which they are presented. Thus the victory of a position at the end of a dialogue is generally—but not always—an indication that its author considered this position the right one. But the fact that a dialogue ends in an aporia does not mean, as we shall see, that its author was not clear about the question concerned or at least thought he was not. One of the reasons for choosing the dialogue form has very often been respect for the reader's autonomy; he is supposed to react to the reading by examining the quality of the arguments exchanged. If he succeeds in doing so, he may, if he does not have sufficient knowledge of intellectual history and psychology, still misunderstand the *mens auctoris;* but he has nonetheless done philosophy a service.

I began this section by asking how we can understand Plato—the most difficult author of dialogues, precisely because he wrote almost exclusively dialogues. First we have to examine the quality of the arguments exchanged in his dialogues. If they are not compelling, this may be a genuine error in Plato; if an erroneous argument is repeatedly made and nowhere rejected, this hypothesis is even natural, because it is hard to see any point in the repetition. Or else Plato can have intentionally committed the error, which must then no longer be described as an error.[27] A reason for this may be that Plato wanted to teach the reader to be vigilant. Because he himself does not appear in his dialogues, Plato has to attribute this error to one of the conversation partners; and the latter can commit this error unwittingly, allowing Plato to indicate his intellectual level, or wittingly, as Plato's Socrates sometimes seems to do, because he, like his author, thinks he has a right to test some of his fellow humans, indeed, even to deceive them—as we already saw in chapter 3.

Second, all Plato's texts have to be studied. They can be interpreted only as a whole, never in isolation. If, for example, only the *Hippias minor* were extant, there would be hardly any chance of understanding the *mens auctoris;* and this holds a fortiori for individual passages in a dialogue. Since Socrates, the Eleatic stranger, Timaeus, and the Athenian stranger say many intelligent and original things, it is plausible to assume that to a significant extent they represent Plato's own philosophy.[28] The unity of Plato's work does hardly allow the interpreter to dissociate Plato from certain positions taken by these four figures (which might easily be ascribed, as far as we know the history of philosophy, to Plato himself) solely because the interpreter does not like them, while at the same time claiming that the good arguments made by these same figures are Plato's own.[29] However, this is compatible with two different points. On the one hand, Plato may assign thematic emphases to his four conversation leaders, which implies that their creator is more comprehensive

27. Cf. E. Heitsch (2000), 183 ff.

28. This was already the opinion expressed by the author of the work, presumably about Plato, transmitted in the *Oxyrhynchus Papyrus* (*POxy* 45, frg. 2). Cf. also D. L. 3.52, although he does not seek to identify directly the Eleatic stranger and the Athenian stranger with Parmenides or with Plato.

29. D. Sedley aptly comments, "Some interpreters have even used this device to rescue Plato from subscribing to arguments which they judge unworthy of him, although it is much rarer to find him being similarly absolved of having to believe the good arguments" (2004; 6).

than any one of them alone. On the other hand, in choosing the dialogue as his medium, though he was also competent in others, such as lecturing and conversing, Plato took into account his receivers, who, because they could not be determined, were not necessarily specialists; and his conversation partners do the same: like their creator, they hold some things back;[30] and they adapt to the intellectual level of their interlocutors, which is not the same in the context of a banquet in honor of a poet as in a conversation among trusted pupils of a dying teacher, some of whom have traveled long distances, or in a confrontation with representatives of opposing schools, in which the latter might sometimes find their own weapons turned against them.

Third, we must gather as much background knowledge as possible about Plato, his language, and especially the philosophy, literature, and science of his time, to which Plato reacts, and the investigations pursued in his school, the Academy. If there is an indirect tradition about Plato's oral teachings, which were presented in the first person and to which the dialogues themselves refer, it is of greatest value, because it provides us with an Archimedean point on the basis of which the indirect mode of communication of the dialogues can be deciphered.

---

30. The famous "deliberate gaps" that H. J. Krämer (1959) discovered should be interpreted as being both internal and external to the dialogues. Not only Plato but also the Platonic Socrates is an esotericist, as T. A. Szlezák (1985; 2004) has persuasively shown.

PART II

The Universe of
the Philosophical Dialogue

The central, second part of this book analyzes only a few of the recurring categories with which every interpreter of a dialogue has to work.[1] First, we will be concerned with determinations such as the unity and plurality of the literary universe, dramatic and narrative presentation, and reality and possibility within the literary universe, that is, with a formal ontology of the dialogue. Then we will turn to what might be called, following Kant's first *Critique,* the "aesthetics" or physics of the dialogue— that is, the theory of space and time within which a conversation takes

---

1. The following categorization has certain points in common with that in the "elements of the dialogue" in the anonymous *Prolegomena* (16 f.; cf. Procl. *in Alc.* 10, 3–16 Creuzer) but is based on an entirely different principle of subdivision.

place. The interpersonal fabric indispensable for conversation and the moral norms that regulate it will be discussed in connection with the social theory and ethics of the dialogue. The forms of consensus building are the subject of the logic of the dialogue, which deliberately follows the ethics of the dialogue, in which it has its origin. Finally, reflections on the artistic character of the dialogue constitute the peculiar aesthetics of the dialogue—"aesthetics" in another sense of the word than the one used above. But isn't the whole second part an aesthetics of the work of art? Yes—but from the point of view of the interpreter. The last chapter in Part II concerns the aesthetic reflections expressed in the dialogue itself.

CHAPTER 8

Individual Dialogues and
Groups of Dialogues

Even if the philosophical dialogue, like any work of art, has to be produced by an author, it is still autonomous insofar as it represents a possible world that has its own properties, which must be considered independently of its author's intentions. In principle, every philosophical dialogue constitutes its own world: different dialogues, even if they are written by the same author and represent persons with the same names, do not necessarily refer to the same possible world, so that no problems of consistency arise when they assert contradictory states of affairs; an author's hands are not tied by statements made in an earlier dialogue.[1] On the other hand, there are series of dialogues comparable to Aeschylus's *Oresteia* or Schiller's Wallenstein trilogy, that refer to the same possible world—that is, to be precise, to periods of time in the same possible

---

1. Even if there are no contradictions between two literary works by the same author, presumably it is better to assume that they belong to two different literary universes, insofar as there are no relations between the objects and the events of the two works. However, this does not hold when, for instance, in a single novel parallel actions are represented that do not intersect even at the end (as in William Faulkner's *The Wild Palms*); the contrast between the parallel actions shapes the character of the whole work and the universe it represents.

world that are different but belong together. Berkeley's *Three Dialogues between Hylas and Philonous, in Opposition to Sceptics and Atheists,* were not only published as a single book but obviously constitute a single universe. (The former is neither a sufficient nor a necessary condition for the latter: an author may combine within a single volume dialogues that refer to entirely different worlds,[2] and he may publish over a period of years dialogues that are understood as continuations of the earlier ones.) Augustine's Cassiciacum dialogues, Nicholas of Cusa's three *Idiota* dialogues (in four books), and Diderot's three dialogues, *La suite d'un entretien entre M. d'Alembert et M. Diderot, Le rêve de d'Alembert,* and *Suite de l'entretien précédent,* refer respectively to a single literary universe, just as does Cicero's trilogy "Hortensius," "Catulus," and "Lucullus." These works were conceived from the outset as a unit. The same goes for the three conversations represented in Cicero's *De finibus bonorum et malorum,* even though they do not directly follow one another but rather take place at different points in time—50 B.C. for the one with Torquatus, which is dealt with in the first two books, 52 B.C. for the one with Cato, to which the next two books are devoted, and 79 B.C. for the conversation represented in the last book. But Cicero is present in all three conversations; thus they relate to the same world and in fact were composed one with the other in mind. However, it may also happen that the idea of writing another dialogue connected with an earlier one may not occur to an author until after the latter has been published. The conversation reported in Cicero's *Laelius* is supposed to have taken place a few days after Africanus's death (1.3), an event that the conversation represented in *De re publica* immediately preceded; and since the close friendship between Laelius and Africanus that is depicted in the earlier work is thematic in the later one, it is obvious that both works must be interpreted as belonging to the same literary universe.

The question regarding Plato's dialogues is harder to answer. Even if Socrates appears in all of them except the *Laws,* it can hardly be denied that his personality changes over the decades of Plato's literary activity. The chronology of the production of the dialogues does not at all correspond to the fictional chronology in which the represented conversa-

2. Of Feyerabend's *Three Dialogues on Knowledge,* only the second and third refer to a common literary universe.

tions take place, and we can scarcely assume that the Socrates who explains in a brief intellectual autobiography shortly before his execution that he never found a teacher who offered him a teleological interpretation of nature (*Phd.* 96a ff.) belongs to the same world as the Socrates who, according to the fictional chronology of the much later *Timaeus,* listened, as a mature man, to the speech of the Pythagorean Timaeus— even if he characteristically simply listened without saying something on the subject himself.[3] Conversely, the narrator and conversation leader of the *Republic* is almost omniscient; and that cannot be easily reconciled with the reduced role played by Socrates in the later dialogues dealing with metaphysics and natural philosophy, in which, in my opinion, Plato clearly signals that his philosophy has not only Socratic but also Eleatic and Pythagorean roots. But as important as this may be for the historian of philosophy who is interested in the historical Socrates and in Plato's development, it is difficult to harmonize with the image of Socrates in the dialogues up to and including the *Republic,* in which he seems to have no intellectual equals. The assumption that the dialogues deal with different literary universes is therefore tempting at first sight. And yet there are, as I have already indicated (p. 81 f.), groups of dialogues that have been conceived as a unit, just like those mentioned in the preceding paragraph: consider the group *Theaetetus-Sophist-Statesman* or the group *Timaeus-Critias.* It is interesting that in both cases a further dialogue is announced that was never written—the *Philosophos* (*Sph.* 217a3, 253e8 ff.; *Plt.* 257a4 f., c1) and the *Hermokrates* (*Ti.* 20a7 ff.; *Cri.* 108a5 ff.), respectively.[4] This can be interpreted as meaning either that Plato abandoned his original intention or that an extant dialogue (e.g., the *Parmenides*) stands for the *Philosophos,*[5] or else that he deliberately

---

3. In the *Phaedo* the theory of the Ideas is attributed to Socrates, but expressly not an axiological philosophy of nature (99c6 ff., 108d5 ff.), which Plato thus claims as his own achievement, influenced by the Pythagoreans. See J. Stenzel (1956), 32–47, esp. 36 ff.

4. Herein surely lies the origin of the grouping of Plato's dialogues into tetralogies that Thrasyllus took as the basis for his edition (D. L. 3.56)—and he was probably not the first to do so.

5. Against this thesis it can be noted that none of the late dialogues points to itself even allusively as being the *Philosophos.* The identification of the *Philosophos* with the *Parmenides,* as proposed for instance by E. A. Wyller (1970), 7 f., is incompatible with the most plausible relative chronology of the late dialogues.

intended to omit it in order to point to a gap (i.e., to unwritten doc-trines).[6] In the first case, the lack would only shed light on the change in the author's intention; in the third case it would itself be, so to speak, an element of the literary universe that is intended, like the deliber-ately fragmentary nature of some of Rodin's statues, to be carefully inter-preted. Here we are not concerned to decide which interpretation is the correct one; in view of the uncompleted nature of the *Critias,* the first possibility is more likely with regard to the second group than with re-gard to the first. We must also consider the related possibility that Plato's death prevented him from completing the second planned trilogy. Even if the *Laws* was probably his last work,[7] Plato may have put off working on the second trilogy. Moreover, this shows the artwork's radical onto-logical dependence on its author before its completion: it can outlive him but only when death has not made it impossible for him to finish it.

However, the situation is particularly complex in the case of the *Timaeus,* because it refers not only to the still-to-be-written works but also back to Plato's major work: *Timaeus* 7c ff. sums up central themes in the *Republic.* But not all the themes are mentioned. This does not indicate that Plato wrote different versions of the *Republic,* as has been claimed;[8]

6. Friedländer's suggestion (1964; I 162) that in the *Sophist* and the *Statesman,* as well as in announcing the *Philosophos,* Plato wanted to draw attention to the "word-less irony" of the present but silent Socrates suffers from the assumption that Plato al-ways remained a Socratic. In reality, early on he was already more than a Socratic.

7. As D. L. 3.37 seems to suggest.

8. This is the thesis proposed by H. Thesleff (1982), 101 ff., who is followed, for instance, by D. Nails (1995), 116 ff. But the arguments for an Ur-*Republic* that was differ-ent from the *Thrasymachus* are far from compelling, especially since the *Timaeus* is a work of Plato's old age, and thus could hardly allude to an early version of the *Republic.* Gellius 14.3.3 f. also fails to prove the point in question. At most we can concede that from the first dialogues on, Plato had in mind an Ur-*Republic,* that is, a comprehensive theory combining metaphysics, ethics, and politics, on the basis of which and in order to articulate it in a major work Plato wrote the individual early dialogues. The decisive argument against the idea that Plato continually updated his dialogues after their pub-lication is not that this would make it impossible for us to reconstruct the history of Plato's development, because one can hardly assume that this has to be possible. In-stead, it has to do with the nature of these works, which—unlike manuscripts for lec-tures like Aristotle's, to which it is always possible to add something new—are organic wholes (cf. *Phdr.* 264c) that do not consist of pieces that can be added on and were probably published only when their author was satisfied with their organicity. Further-more, Plato would then have deleted some of the contradictions between the dialogues.

the transition from the philosophy of the state to the philosophy of history, which is the subject of the beginning of the *Timaeus* (19b f.), does not require the epistemological and metaphysical explanations which, furthermore, Plato had already given in the earlier trilogy and deepened in the dialogues dedicated to the theory of principles, the *Parmenides* and the *Philebus*. Moreover—and this is the crucial point—at the beginning of the *Timaeus* Socrates cannot be referring to the conversation represented in the *Republic* because Timaeus, Critias, Hermocrates, and the unnamed fourth guest did not take part in it. Plato suggests instead that on the day before the conversation represented in the *Timaeus*, Socrates shared with these friends his ideas about political philosophy; and that these ideas do not essentially differ from those developed in the *Republic* follows from the fact that we are dealing with the same Socrates who appears in Plato's other dialogues.

In actuality it is clear that in general Plato wanted his Socratic dialogues to be interpreted as a whole; the correspondences and cross-references among the dialogues are too numerous to think otherwise. For example, that the *Symposium* and the *Phaedo* represent complementary virtues of the true philosopher, who likes to live and dies with dignity, has often been remarked; but they are only complementary if they refer to the same individual. Plato repeatedly gives the impression that his Socrates avoids the extremes that are found in other people. The *Euthyphro* and the *Crito,* for example, which are both connected with Socrates' trial, preceding and following it, respectively, represent in their eponymous heroes two people who want to be entirely different from the rest of humanity[9] or exactly like others, respectively;[10] and Plato opposes these caricatures of "morality" and "ethical life," as it might be put in Hegelian terms, to the truly moral Socrates, who neither wants to follow the crowd[11] nor considers it an achievement when he is laughed at.[12] Analogously, Diotima is the counterpart of Aspasia, and the sophisms in the *Euthydemus* mirror the insights in the *Meno*. The knowledge that the Socrates of the early dialogues holds back is, as it were, paid out in the

---

9. Cf. *Euthphr.* 3b9 ff., d3 f., 4b3, e9 ff.
10. Cf. *Cri.* 44b9 ff., d1 f., 45d8 ff.
11. *Cri.* 44c6 f., d6 ff., 46bff.
12. *Euthphr.* 3c6 f.

Republic, the late dialogues, and the teachings within the Academy; and that means that from the outset Plato intended to write a nonaporetic dialogue that would resolve the apparent aporias of the early dialogues. In conceiving his work, Plato had even greater staying power than Thomas Mann did in writing his Joseph novels, in which many allusions in *Die Geschichten Jaakobs* (The Stories of Jacob) become comprehensible only in the last novel of the tetralogy, which appeared a decade later. But precisely because Plato worked on the literary representation of his philosophy over several decades, it is hardly surprising that, unlike in Mann's Joseph novels, there are inconsistencies and implausibilities in the work of an author that probably seeks to refer to a single literary universe; the reader must therefore discreetly overlook them.

In addition, the death of Socrates was for Plato a central biographical event; three of the works connected with this death are probably early ones. Thus Plato did not have an opportunity to sketch a development of Socrates that somehow paralleled his own (if he was aware at all of the latter, whose crucial steps may have been taken before the publication of his first dialogue). He began the representation of the literary Socrates from the end of the latter's life, so to speak. Furthermore, the still relatively young Socrates of the *Protagoras,* which takes place in 433–432, seems already enormously superior to the old Sophist, even if at the end the latter condescendingly tells his younger competitor that he greatly admires *him,* especially among people of his age, and says that he would not be surprised if Socrates became a leading philosopher.[13] So far as I can see, there is however one passage in Plato's work—in addition to the already mentioned passage in the *Phaedo* (96a ff.), where Socrates looks back on his own intellectual development—in which a change in Socrates is represented. I am referring, of course, to the first part of the late dialogue *Parmenides,* which is about the earliest conversation— according to its fictive chronology—represented by Plato. Here Socrates is still young, and he proves to be incapable of refuting Parmenides' objections to the theory of Ideas. He is now himself in the position of a young man who is eager to learn but not yet sufficiently educated—the position in which his interlocutors in the dialogues written earlier found

13. *Prt.* 361e2 ff.

themselves. Parmenides scolds and encourages him at the same time, saying that he has begun to make decisions regarding ethical concepts too soon, without being trained in dialectic. Socrates' impulse is admirable and divine, Parmenides says, but he has to practice if the truth is not to escape him.[14] As we have seen, this contrasts in a witty way with the image that the earlier dialogues give of Socrates' later conversations; for example, in a passage in the *Euthydemus* (301a1 ff.), Socrates alludes to one of the difficulties that Parmenides mentions (*Prm.* 130e4 ff.)—a passage that is rightly adduced by those who are skeptical about a discontinuous development of Plato but which at the same time proves that the Platonic Socrates develops. However, we cannot exclude the possibility that the criticism of Plato's young Socrates, which is absolutely meaningful in dialogue-internal terms (here I use "dialogue-internal" as referring to the totality of all the previous Platonic dialogues, as well as to the *Parmenides*), should be understood dialogue-externally as the author Plato's initial distancing from his literary character and its real model— a distancing that is continued in the later dialogues and culminates in the *Laws.*

Cervantes's *Don Quixote* is rightly considered one of the most brilliant works of the modern age. In different fields, Machiavelli, Mandeville, and Malthus recognized that good intentions can have dreadful consequences and good consequences can be the result of dreadful intentions; at the beginning of the first volume of his novel, Cervantes takes up this insight, which essentially characterizes the modern period, but he unintentionally transforms it into a steadily increasing admiration for his hero, who through the manifold complications in the inn finally does more good than he himself can understand, but precisely *not* more than he wanted. The modernity of the second volume of the work is perhaps still more extensive, even if it is perhaps less poetic; Don Quixote now has to cope with two books about him, the first volume of *Don Quixote* and a lamentable forgery. The literary reflexivity of the second volume of *Don Quixote* is generally known; what is less well known is the fact that the explicit thematization of an earlier literary work in a further literary work of the same genre had already played a role in the

14. *Prm.* 135c8–d6.

philosophical dialogue in antiquity. This device can be shown to exist
in Cicero's works, where it first may have been used. Neither *De legibus*
nor *De divinatione* is a dialogue that represents—like the *Laelius,* for
instance—a conversation that continues an earlier one depicted in another dialogue; instead, it represents a conversation that presupposes
dialogues written earlier, namely, *De re publica* and *De natura deorum,*
respectively. This is possible because their author, who does not participate in the conversation depicted in *De re publica* and is only a mute listener in that depicted in *De natura deorum,* becomes himself an interlocutor. In *De divinatione* it is Quintus's annoyance with the third book
of *De natura deorum* that is the occasion of the new conversation.[15] On
the other hand, at the beginning of *De legibus,* Cicero's friend Atticus
tells him that because with *De re publica* he had already competed with
Plato, he should now write a counterpart to the latter's *Laws;* Cicero responds by asking whether Atticus wants a conversation on public institutions and the best laws.[16] Thus following his model, Plato's Phaedrus, he
moves from a written work—which is, instead of Lysias's speech, his own
dialogue—to the live conversation but within the fictional space constituted by a written work. Nicholas of Cusa's *De ludo globi* provides an analogous example from the Middle Ages. The first book represents a conversation between the Cardinal and Duke John of Mosbach-Neumarkt, the
second book another conversation between the Cardinal and the young
Duke Albrecht IV of Bavaria-Munich. The latter read the dialogue that
reproduces the first conversation after he saw Duke John reading it; but
he did not understand it sufficiently.[17] Consequently, in the conversation
Nicholas of Cusa discusses the themes of his earlier dialogue—in a conversation that itself becomes the content of a second dialogue.[18]

15. "Perlegi, [ille] inquit, tuum paulo ante tertium de natura deorum, in quo
disputatio Cottae quamquam labefactavit sententiam meam, non funditus tamen
sustulit" (1.5.8).

16. 1.5.15.

17. IX 73 f.

18. A conversation by an author (Lucian) who takes a text of his own—*The
Death of Peregrinus* (*Peri tēs Peregrinou teleutēs*)—as his point of departure and in fact
converses with its subject is represented by Wieland's dialogue of the dead *Peregrinus
Proteus,* but the author of the dialogue is not identical with the author of that text.

CHAPTER 9

Introductory Taxonomy

Direct, Indirect, and Mixed Dialogues

In antiquity efforts were already made to categorize philosophical di-alogues, especially Plato's. The best known of these are the taxonomies in Diogenes Laertius (3.49–51), in Albinus (*Prologos*, 3), and in the anonymous sixth-century *Prolegomena to Plato's Philosophy* (17.19–29). The precise relationships of dependency are disputed, but these divisions *(diaereses)* probably go back to a common source that divided dialogues at a first level into "guiding" *(hyphēgētikos kharaktēr)* and "investigative" *(zētētikos kharaktēr),*[1] the latter being subdivided into "exercising" *(gumnastikos)* and "disputatious" *(agōnistikos kharaktēr).* The classification can be plausibly connected with Aristotle's *Topics,*[2] and because Aristotle's didactic writings had been missing for some time, this gives us a probable terminus post quem for the dating of our division, which was already used by Thrasyllos (D. L. 3.57–61), thus giving us a terminus ante quem.[3] The "guiding" dialogues were divided into speculative and

---

1. The author of the *Prolegomena* adds to these two categories a "mixed" *(miktos)* type.
2. Cf. esp. *Top.* 159a25 ff. and 161a21 ff. The "exercising" aspect of the conversation is still mentioned by Augustine (*C. acad.* 1.9.25).
3. Cf. O. Nüsser (1991), 136 ff.

practical, and then subdivided, the former into natural and logical, the latter into ethical and political; the "exercising" into "maieutic" *(maieutikos kharaktēr)* and "tentative" *(peirastikos kharaktēr),* the "disputatious" into "demonstrative" *(endeiktikos kharaktēr)* and "distinctive" *(anatreptikos kharaktēr).* Since Schleiermacher,[4] the defects of this division, which confuses the way of conducting a conversation with the subject of the dialogue and cannot clearly distinguish the subspecies of the "investigative" dialogue from one another, are well known; and it can therefore be set aside.[5]

Considerably more interesting is the alternative division, which Diogenes Laertius qualifies as "more tragic [i.e., literary] than philosophical" and mentions only in passing—a division into dramatic, narrative, and mixed dialogues.[6] The significance of this division has been enormous down to the present day. At first sight, it seems to go back to Plato himself; in the third book of the *Republic,* in the context of his theory of poetry, after giving priority to the discussion of problems of content he has Socrates raise the question of form (392c6 ff.).[7] Adimantus does not understand what he means by that. Socrates explains that poets tell us about something that is past, present, or future, and then asks: "Do not they proceed either by pure narration or by a narrative that is effected through imitation, or by both?"[8] Once again, Adimantus cannot follow him, and Socrates resorts to examples to make himself understood. He quotes the beginning of the *Iliad,* where the poet at first speaks in his

4. (1996), 45.

5. However, Albinus's thesis (3), that the didactic dialogue is concerned primarily with matters of fact, and the searching dialogue with persons, is interesting.

6. 3.50: *legousi gar autōn tous men dramatikous, tous de diēgēmatikous, tous de meiktous.*

7. The effort to make connections between the classification of dialogues and Plato's own observations is particularly clear in Proclus, in *R.* I 14 ff. Kroll. However, precisely because he takes Plato's division seriously, Proclus has to define the three types of dialogue differently from Diogenes, and classify the *Republic* as a mixed form. Cf. below, p. 176 f., where the divergence between Plato's division and the one following Diogenes is examined.

8. 392d5 f.: *Ar' oun ouchi ētoi haplēi diēgēsei ē dia mimēseōs gignomenēi ē di'amphoterōn perainousin.* Whether a difficult passage in Aristotle (*Po.* 1448a19 ff.), which is corrupt at the end, indicates an analogous tripartite division, as some interpreters think, or rather a bipartite division, as Nüsser (1991), 182 ff., tries to make plausible with the help of other passages from the *Poetics,* is a question that I will leave open here.

own voice but then has Chryses speak; and this latter is an example of narrative through mimesis. The concept of mimesis is thus used here in a narrower sense than elsewhere in Plato, who sees (e.g., in the tenth book of the *Republic*) all art as mimesis in the broader sense.[9] Then Socrates shows, counterfactually, how Homer could have avoided mimesis (in the narrower sense), and he recounts—without meter, because he is not a poet[10]—the Chryses episode, using only indirect discourse. Finally, he generalizes his example, seeing in tragedy and comedy the paradigm for mimetic literature, in the dithyramb the model for narrative (diegetic) literature, and in epic the model for a poem that combines both modes of representation (394b8 ff.). This passage is so interesting because it is almost inevitable that it will also be read dialogue-externally: in it, Plato gives obvious hints as to how to understand his own dialogues, of which a few are dramatic, others diegetic, and still others a mixing of the two forms. In my opinion, Plato wanted the intelligent reader to apply these statements about literary theory to his own work, and this is shown by Socrates' clearly ironic remark that he is not a poet.[11] That Plato was aware of the aesthetic qualities of his work is not a mere assumption; it is clearly suggested by the conclusion of the *Symposium* (223d; see above, p. 53), where Plato proudly refers to the novelty of his literary creation.[12] Stefan Büttner (2000) has persuasively shown how Plato constantly presupposes three basic types of poets, the traditional, who is guided by empirical facts, the enthusiastic, and, as the most elevated, the philosophical writer, whom he himself exemplifies. This observation may even be intended to indicate that verse is not a necessary (or sufficient) condition for poetry—an Aristotelian insight that I have already discussed[13] and that, like some other discoveries that first appear explicitly in Aristotle,

---

9. Cf. G. F. Else (1986), 22 ff.

10. 393d8: *phrasō de aneu metrou; ou gar eimi poiētikos.*

11. In 378e7 f. Socrates says only that he and Adimantus are not poets at that moment *(en tōi paronti).*

12. The passage *Ti.* 21c4 ff. should also be read reflexively, that is, as alluding to the fact that with the *Timaeus* and the *Critias* Plato entered into competition with Homer and Hesiod. Similarly *R.* 366d7 ff., 540c3 f., *Phdr.* 247c3 f., *Ti.* 19d2 ff., *Criti.* 108b3 ff., *Lg.* 811c6 ff., 817b3 ff., 858c f.; even if *Mx.* 239c3 ff. is obviously false, given the work of Phrynichus, Aeschylus, Simonides and Pindar, and thus ironically proves that the orators are lying, the passage nonetheless refers to Plato's literary innovativeness.

13. Cf. above, chap. 2, n. 34.

may go back to Plato. In my view, another statement should be read re -
flexively. Shortly before his admission that he is not a poet, Socrates says
that poetry could get along without mimesis and would become pure
narrative if the poet did not seek to conceal himself anywhere.[14] This statement is odd, because up to this point the category of self-concealment
has not been used in relation to poets. However, by contraposition the
statement says that if a poet uses mimesis, he wants to conceal himself. It
is one of the peculiarities of Plato's work, including the *Republic,* that unlike that of most of his philosophical predecessors it makes extensive use
of mimesis (in the narrower sense of the word). Doesn't this require us to
conclude that Plato is someone who wants to conceal himself? (My argument assumes, I think rightly, that Plato sees himself as a poet.) After all,
this hint, which at first sight seems to contradict itself performatively, is
extremely discreet: not every reader will notice it.

The distinction between dramatic (direct), narrated (indirect), and
mixed dialogues (narrated within a dramatic frame) covers Plato's works
very well, even if it can be further differentiated.[15] Among the dramatic
dialogues are probably Plato's earliest dialogues like *Hippias minor, Ion,*
and the *Crito,* and also all those after *Theaetetus* (with the exception of
Parmenides, if it is later, though after 137c4 it becomes purely dramatic).
In view of Plato's presumed beginnings as a writer of tragedies, there is
something to be said for the claim that he discovered the potential of
indirect and mixed dialogues only later on;[16] and obviously after *Par-*
menides he felt that he had exhausted it, and therefore lost interest in this
form of dialogue more ambitious literarily and also more laborious.
Within the dramatic dialogue it makes sense to distinguish dialogues that
consist in large part of a long speech, like the *Menexenus, Timaeus,* and
Critias (at least in its extant form); and also Cicero's *Cato* and *Laelius,*
which have, however, a preface. In the case of narrative dialogues, we can

14. 393c11 ff.: *ei de ge mēdamou he auton apokruptoito ho poiētēs, pasa an autōi
aneu mimēseos he poiēsis te kai diēgēsis gegonuia einē.*

15. I follow O. Nüsser's excellent classification (1991; 238 ff.).

16. However, it has to be considered that older Socratics already wrote indirect
and mixed dialogues; cf. below, p. 394 f. The anecdote in D. L. 2.60, according to which
Menedemos accused Aeschines of having published Socrates' dialogues under his own
name, is more easily explainable if we assume that Aeschines' dialogues had Socrates
as narrator (this was pointed out to me by K. Döring).

differentiate between those in which the narrator—who in most of these dialogues, but not in *Parmenides,* is Socrates—expressly addresses an audience, for example, an unnamed friend, as in *Charmides,*[17] and those in which this is not the case, as in *Lysis* or the *Republic* where, however, first-person forms that repeatedly make the reader aware of the narrator are used right up to the end of the text.[18] In mixed dialogues the main conversation is reported in a dialogue between the narrator and another person. Consider for example the *Protagoras,* where, however, as in Plutarch's *Erōtikos,* the frame conversation takes place only briefly at the beginning, so that the difference from an indirect dialogue is not great; or the *Euthydemus* and *Phaedo,* in which Socrates and (since no one can report his own death) Phaedo are the reporters, respectively. The *Symposium* is a mixed dialogue whose frame conversation reminds us of that in the *Protagoras,* but in which the narrator, Apollodorus, unlike Socrates and Phaedo in the dialogues just mentioned, has not himself taken part in the conversation but only heard it from others—from Aristodemus and in part from Socrates himself.[19] The structure of iterated narrative is also familiar from the *Parmenides,* in which the narrator Cephalus tells how he and his compatriots from Clazomenae came to Antiphon to learn from him about the conversation that Parmenides, Zeno, Socrates, and Aristotle once had and that Antiphon himself, who was then not yet born, had heard about from Pythodorus, who was at that time hosting the Eleatic philosophers. Since Cephalus initially recounts a short conversation he had with Antiphon's half brother (and Plato's full brother), Adimantus, the dialogue has some traits of a mixed conversation even if the last perspective on the dialogue is diegetical. Reported speeches are included not only in a diegetic and mixed dialogue like the *Symposium,* in which even in the main conversation Socrates reports a speech by Diotima, but also in dramatic dialogues like the *Menexenus,* in which Socrates repeats Aspasia's oration, and in the *Timaeus,* at the beginning of which Critias tells a story his like-named grandfather had heard from his own father, Dropsides, who in turn had heard it from

17. 154b8, 155c5, d3.
18. Cf. *Ly.* 223b4 and *R.* 614b2.
19. *Smp.* 173a f. 172a ff. refers to other narratives and narrators of the main conversation.

Solon.[20] Finally, the *Phaedrus* takes as its starting point the analysis of a written version of a speech that is attributed to Lysias, and that probably is actually one of his, since the attribution and especially the stylistic criticism of the speech[21] would otherwise be pointless.

The *Theaetetus,* in which Plato announces his return to the dramatic form, has a special status. The dialogue consists of an introductory conversation between Euclides and Terpsion, in which the former tells the latter that he has just met the dying Theaetetus and remembered how Socrates once told him about the conversation that he had with Theaetetus (and Theodorus) shortly before his death. At that time he, Euclides, had written down Socrates' report of this conversation shortly after hearing it, and also repeatedly asked Socrates whenever he had forgotten something. He now has a slave read from this transcript; the following dialogue is a recitation from it. It is interesting that we have here a multiple change in medium: the original Socrates-Theaetetus-Theodorus conversation; Socrates' report of this conversation to Euclides; Euclides' transcription; the transcription's correction on the basis of a conversation between Euclides and Socrates; the oral recitation of the transcript by a slave, in the presence of Euclides and Terpsion. Of particular importance in our context is Euclides' explanation that he had decided—despite the fact that the conversation was reported to him by Socrates—to write it down in dramatic form. "I wanted to avoid in the written account the tiresome effect of bits of narrative interrupting the dialogue, such as 'and I said' or 'and I remarked' wherever Socrates was speaking of himself, and 'he assented,' or 'he did not agree,' where he reported the answer. So I left out everything of that sort, and wrote it as a direct conversation between the actual speakers."[22] In fact, the inclusion of such reportorial formulas can be annoying; with the same argument and similar words, Cicero, in the *Laelius,* where the eponymous hero converses with his two sons-in-law,[23] Petrarch in "De secreto conflictu curarum

20. *Ti.* 20d ff.
21. *Phdr.* 234e ff.
22. *Tht.* 143b8–c5.
23. *Lael.* 1.3: "quasi enim ipsos induxi loquentes, ne 'inquam' et 'inquit' saepius interponeretur atque ut tamquam a praesentibus coram haberi sermo videretur." Cf. *Tusc.* 1.4.8: "Sed quo commodius disputationes nostrae explicentur, sic eas exponam, quasi agatur res, non quasi narretur."

mearum," where he speaks with Augustine,[24] and Valla in *De libero arbitrio,* where he speaks with his friend Antonius Glarea, all opt for direct dialogue. Valla repeats Cicero verbatim, but Valla thinks Cicero's words would apply only to "Valla's" situation, since only "Valla," and not "Cicero," is an interlocutor in the respective conversations represented; in fact, even in Quintus Mucius Scaevola's later presentation of this conversation Cicero could have done nothing more than listen.[25] Valla is right but probably does not realize that Cicero's error arises from his imitation of the beginning of the *Theaetetus,* which Cicero, for whom Plato was the constantly present model, obviously had in mind more than his own work.

Despite the additional effort required, authors continued to deviate from the direct dialogue form; and that can be explained only if indirect and mixed dialogues have advantages that compensate for this additional effort. What are these advantages? First, the narrator adds a new point of view. This is especially true when he himself is not one of the interlocutors; however, then the question as to how he can know about the conversation arises. There are two possibilities: the narrator can be, like the nameless one in the *Colloquium heptaplomeres* or Pamphilus in the *Dialogues Concerning Natural Religion,* a mute witness to the conversation;[26] or else he can have heard the conversation from someone else who either took part in it himself or heard about it from someone else who . . . ; the structure is repeatable at will, but after being used a few times it loses its aesthetic interest as well as its credibility.[27] Certainly one

24. (1955), 26: "Hunc nempe scribendi morem a Cicerone meo didici; at ipse prius a Platone didicerat."
25. (1987), 60 ff.: "cuius disputationis verba in libellum retuli, exponens illa quasi agatur res, non quasi narretur: ne 'Inquam' et 'Inquit' saepius interponeretur; quod se fecisse Marcus Tullius, vir immortali ingenio, cur dixerit in libro quem inscripsit Laelium, equidem non video. Nam ubi auctor non a se disputata, sed ab aliis recitat, quonam modo 'Inquam' interponere potest? veluti est in Laelio Ciceronis, in quo disputatio continetur habita a Laelio cum duobus generis, G. Fannio et Q. Scaevola, recitataque ab ipso Scaevola, Cicerone cum nonnullis familiaribus audiente, et, ut illa aetate, vix ausuro disputare et colloqui cum Scaevola, quandam prae se vel aetatis vel dignitatis religionem ferente."
26. The Greek term is *kōphon prosōpon;* cf. Cic. *Att.* 13.19.3.
27. The author of the *Prolegomena* wants to limit the number of interlocutors or reporters to four, in accord with the Neoplatonic theory of hypostases (20). Cf. Proclus, in *Prm.* 682, 16 ff. Cousin.

of the functions of the introduction of one or even several narrators is to make the conversation credible, especially if the narrator has the same name as the author. This authentification is, of course, merely fictional, but not within the literary universe (even if we cannot exclude the possibility that the author might sometimes want to use an especially long series of narrators to indicate ironically the fictional nature of his work). Precisely when the series of narrators consists of two or three members, the impression of the enduring intellectual influence of the conversation, indeed, of the construction of a tradition, is communicated. The beginning of Plato's *Symposium* shows the continuing interest in Socrates' conversations; the beginning of the *Parmenides* shows that people traveled from as far as Ionia to find out what was discussed in Athens almost seven decades earlier. That these people came from Clazomenae, the city where Anaxagoras was born,[28] is surely no accident but rather points to the theme of the second part of this most difficult of Plato's dialogues, which in my opinion outlines the theory of the two principles that stood at the center of the unwritten doctrine and obviously should be interpreted as a synthesis of Eleatic and Ionian philosophy.[29] By separating the two journeys to Athens—that of the Eleatics to the east, that of the Clazomenaeans to the west—the claim to produce a synthesis is, however, not openly declared but only alluded to.[30] That Antiphon, from whom Cephalus and his friends hear about the conversation, has in the meantime been raising horses and is telling a smith how to mend a bridle when they encounter him must also contain an allusion to the following conversation, for example, to the notion that the dialectic of the principles can help improve the theory of Ideas, whose problems are discussed in the first part of the dialogue.[31] In addition, there is an ironic suggestion that simply learning profound conversations by heart does not prevent one from living an unphilosophical life. Another example of the function

28. *Prm.* 126a1.
29. Cf. V. Hösle (1984), 461 ff., in connection with Proclus, in *Prm.* 625, 12 ff; 629, 24 ff. Cousin.
30. Plato's dialogues do what Heraclitus says of the Delphic Apollo (DK 22 F 93)—it neither says nor conceals but rather gives a sign: *oute legei oute kruptei alla sēmainei.*
31. Cf. C. F. von Weizsäcker (1981; 21), who is following G. Picht.

of intermediate narrative steps is found in Cicero's *De re publica*. Cicero says that he heard about the conversation between Scipio and his friends, which allegedly took place in 129 B.C., some fifty years later, from a participant in the conversation, Publius Rutilus Rufus, who was then a young man—and where? In Smyrna,[32] which, as is well known, claimed to be Homer's birthplace, and is certainly one of the Ionian cities with the richest tradition. By mentioning Smyrna, which would of course have had no place in a dramatic version of the dialogue, Cicero achieves two things: first, he refers to the fact that this place is part of the Roman Empire, whose mission the dialogue praises; and second, Greek culture is thereby granted a role in communicating purely Roman culture—a friendly if somewhat condescending gesture in view of the text's general intention to represent the superiority of Roman policy.[33]

The second main advantage of indirect and mixed dialogues is especially important in a literature that does not include stage directions (such as those of which Murdoch, for example, makes ample use). The narrator can describe extralinguistic conversational behaviors and the paralinguistic elements that are usually left out in a direct dialogue,[34] or even mention the hidden motives behind a speech act, and thus give the represented world a new dimension. On the other hand, he may reproduce certain exchanges in an abbreviated form, because they are summarized in the report. A few examples should suffice. In the *Protagoras,* Socrates tells how the eponymous hero struggles to admit that he has been

---

32. *De rep.* 1.8.13.

33. A variation on the structure of the repeated narrative is found in Xenophon's *Oeconomicus (Oikonomikos)*. Xenophon reports, as the narrator, a conversation between Socrates and Critobulus, which he says he himself witnessed; from chapter 7 on, however, Socrates tells Critobolus, who doesn't say another word, about a conversation he had with Ischomachus, who himself reports on conversations with his wife. According to Sigonio (1993; 176), by introducing Ischomachus, Xenophon increases the authority of Socrates, whose fame was not based on the augmentation of his property.

34. It is conceivable, of course, that one interlocutor directly addresses the outward behavior of the other, as in the first sentence of Nicholas of Cusa's *Dialogus de deo abscondito duorum, quorum unus gentilis, alius Christianus:* "Video te devotissime prostratum et fundere amoris lacrimas, non quidem falsas sed cordiales" (IV 3). But one can only begin a conversation by conveying such observations; one cannot constantly burden it with them.

refuted: "He agreed, though most reluctantly,"[35] and again, "he could no longer bring himself to assent, but was silent."[36] In a direct dialogue Plato would have found it harder to express Protagoras's silence; an interlocutor would have had to mention it explicitly, which might seem tactless.[37] In the same way, only in an indirect dialogue can Socrates express a hypothesis as to why Protagoras asked Prodicus and Hippias to join in the conversation—namely, because it would give him an opportunity to show off his rhetorical skill,[38] or refer to the pleasure Thrasymachus takes in speaking, which the latter conceals by claiming that he want to hear Socrates' answer;[39] only in an indirect dialogue can he speak, though ironically, about his fear that his opponent might be right[40] and about his attempt to gain time.[41] It is delightful when in the *Lysis* Socrates says that Lysis repeatedly looked at him and the group assembled around him, which included his lover, Hippothales, but even if it was obvious that he wanted to join them, he held back until Menexenus went over to Socrates and he was able to follow his friend without attracting attention.[42] How could a direct dialogue express Lysis's gradual approach, which throws a significant light on his noble nature, since he does not want to impose himself on anyone and has already learned that one has to let a lover stew in his own juice? How could a direct dialogue represent Hippothales' unrestrained but wordless joy after Socrates has shown Lysis and Menexenus that the beloved must love a true lover—a joy that demonstrates Hippothales' limited understanding of Socrates' remarks, which charac-

---

35. *Prt.* 333b3. Cf. 332e2 ff.

36. *Prt.* 360d6.

37. In the *Gorgias,* however, Socrates does this repeatedly (468c7 f., d6, 475d, 5 ff., 489a4 ff., 509e2 ff., 515c3 f., 519d5 ff.), and this contributes to the impression that the dialogue is less subtle than the *Protagoras.* But we must be wary of drawing chronological conclusions, since the desire to be as direct as possible—which is appropriate in a direct dialogue—might have been triggered by a personal or political event that escapes us.

38. *Prt.* 317c f. Cf. *Prt.* 335a9 f.: Protagoras is dissatisfied with his own last answers.

39. *R.* 338a5 ff.

40. *Prt.* 339c8 f.

41. *Prt.* 339e3 ff. In contrast, Licentius seems to be trying seriously: Aug. *Ord.* 2.1.3.

42. Cf. *Ly.* 207a5 ff.

terize someone like him precisely not as a true lover, just as Lysis's silence testifies to his great intelligence, which has foreseen the aporia.[43] In the *Charmides,* Critias's annoyance, manifested only in facial expressions and gestures, after the eponymous hero, smiling, has cast a meaningful glance at him, correspondingly shows that the inept definition of prudence as "doing one's own business" is his own—and it sheds light on his character, which is focused on gaining recognition and not primarily on resolving the issue at hand.[44] The exchange of looks and smiles between Parmenides and Zeno shows the delight they take in the young Socrates and at the same time confutes Pythodorus's expectations.[45] Moreover, as narrator, Socrates observes not only direct behavior but also the observations of others.[46]

Augustine also reports his observations of the conversation partners, for instance, their—and his—tears,[47] their concentration,[48] their wish to express something,[49] and their silence, which says more than words could.[50] In the paralinguistic elements that characterize a living conversation, such as the exchange of glances, he sees a favorable advantage over reading a simple dialogue (which, he implies, has to neglect these elements).[51] To Bruno we owe extremely witty descriptions of displays of gestures and facial expressions intended to impress other people.[52] However, the most comprehensive account of body language in the history of the philosophical dialogue goes back to Diderot. This

43. Cf. *Ly.* 222a4–b2.
44. Cf. *Chrm.* 162b10 ff.
45. *Prm.* 130a3 ff.
46. Cf. *Chrm.* 154c ff., *Ly.* 207b5 ff., and *Euthd.* 273b5 f. Also in the *Ion,* the eponymous hero reports that he observes his audience, but he is concerned only with money (535c).
47. *C. acad.* 2.7.18.
48. *Ord.* 1.10.28.
49. *Ord.* 2.2.5.
50. *Ord.* 1.8.24.
51. *C. acad.* 2.7.17: "ut aliquando uos audiam disserentes et, quod plus est, uideam, quo mihi spectaculo nihil potest felicius exhiberi. . . . legere etiam uos licebit; sed nescio quo modo, cum admouentur oculis idem ipsi, quos inter sermo caeditur, bona disputatio si non utilius, at certe laetius perfundit animum."
52. (1985), I 85, 108, 127 f.

holds for *Le rêve de d'Alembert,* even if it is a direct dialogue. But it is constructed in such a special way that it nonetheless has traits of an indirect
dialogue: Mlle de l'Espinasse tells the physician Bordeu what d'Alembert,
who continues to sleep during most of the conversation, had said during his earlier dreams and how his body behaved; we will return to this
in chapter 10. It is true that what is reported is only the monologue of a
dreamer; but because it is triggered by a real conversation (with Diderot),
Mlle de l'Espinasse's report reminds us of an indirect dialogue or rather,
since it occurs in a meta-conversation, of a mixed dialogue. Gestures can
replace explicit assent—in the *Entretien d'un père avec ses enfants* Denise
silently presses her brother's hand.[53] In particular, however, *Le neveu de
Rameau* offers the most detailed depiction of body language one can
imagine: the poor nephew can react to the internal tensions caused by his
musical and intellectual mediocrity, his constant humiliations in society,
and his lack of moral fiber only through a mimetic play that is virtually
unparalleled in the history of world literature; Rameau is able to represent even silence through his sounds.[54] Even if the main part of the work
consists of a direct verbal exchange between *Moi* and *Lui,* and even if
Diderot has thus stripped away the tiresome aspects of indirect di -
alogue, as Plato did in the *Theaetetus, Le neveu de Rameau* is doubtless
an indirect dialogue, for the narrator speaks not only in the long introduction, but repeatedly, chiefly in order to describe his interlocutor's
body language.[55]

The mixed dialogue adds to the advantages of the indirect dialogue
the possibility of allowing different perspectives to react in a conversation. When the interlocutor interrupts the reporter, he thereby indicates
especially important passages in the conversation; for example, Echec -
rates strengthens the impact of Cebe's objections by adopting them,[56]
and conversely he increases our sense of the significance of Socrates'
makeshift or "second voyage" *(deuteros plous)* argument when he turns
to Phaedo again, and for the last time, and tells him that what Socrates

53. (1972), 271: *"Ma soeur se taisait; mais elle me serrait la main en signe d'ap-
probation."*
54. (1972), 107.
55. Analogously, *Eberhard's Dialogus Ratii et Everardi* is also an indirect dialogue.
56. Cf. *Phd.* 88c ff.

has just said had a marvelous effect not only on those who were present at the time but also on those who were then absent but are now listeners.[57] It seems clear that the passage is to be read dialogue-externally and thus reflexively; because the same impression is supposed to be made on readers of both the main conversation and the meta-conversation. In the case of the *Euthydemus,* the meta-conversation takes place at the beginning, in the middle, and at the end of the dialogue. Crito's protest against the attribution of such a complex philosophy of mathematics to Clinias has, in my opinion, the function of calling attention not only to the Platonic Socrates but also to Plato himself;[58] the repetition in the frame conversation of the aporia in which Socrates' protreptical discourse has become entangled—Crito proves to be just as incapable of resolving it as Clinias—indicates its enormous importance.[59] Crito's account at the end of the dialogue of a criticism of the main conversation gives Plato an opportunity to distinguish his conception of philosophy from that of Isocrates, because only the latter can be meant in the passage at 304d ff. Methodius's *Symposium* is also a mixed dialogue; and it absolutely makes literary sense that the author puts at the end the discussion of the philosophically interesting question whether a chastity that knows temptations stands higher than its unreflected form, and even places it within the frame conversation.[60] The festive mood of the speeches of the virgins would be dampened if they themselves reported their struggles with the flesh. An especially successful mixed dialogue is Zacharias's *Ammonius;* it is interesting that Zacharias is designated in the frame conversation as "Λ" and in the reported conversation as *"Christianos"* (Christian). In the early modern period, Bruno's *La cena de le ceneri,* in which the main conversation with Bruno is commented upon at length in the very long frame conversation, and Solger's *Erwin* are well-known mixed dialogues; however, the most original mixed dialogue is certainly Diderot's *Supplément au voyage de Bougainville ou dialogue entre A. et B. sur l'inconvénient*

57. Cf. *Phd.* 102a3 ff.

58. Cf. *Euthd.* 290e, and on this and on an analogous function of Diotima's speech, see below, p. 436.

59. Cf. *Euthd.* 291b ff., and on this, V. Hösle (2004e), 272 ff.

60. 293 ff. in the canonical Allatius pagination, which will also be used for further citations of this text.

d'attacher des idées morales à certaines actions physiques qui n'en compor-
tent pas (first published posthumously in 1796). Nonetheless, the frame
conversation, in contradistinction to Plato but in agreement with the
reflective tendency of modernity, is almost as important as the main conversation it comments on, and at which, moreover, neither A nor B was
present, but which was instead presented to them only in written form, in
the shape of a—fictional—complement to the famous travel account
Voyage autour du monde by Bougainville, who tells how he took possession of Tahiti for France during his voyage around the world. The first
part of Diderot's dialogue reproduces a conversation between "A" and
"B," while the second part reproduces a speech by an old man from
Tahiti from that complement, which is commented upon by A and B,
and the bulk of the third part as well as the fourth part represent a conversation between the native Orou and the French chaplain, which is
also commented upon by "A" and "B" at the end of the third part and in
the fifth part of the dialogue. Thus there is a constant oscillation between the two levels of conversation, which is facilitated by the fact that
the old man and Orou have ideas about the world that contradict those
of the Europeans, but they nonetheless argue in an astonishingly European way. "A" himself notes that Orou's speech is "un peu modelé à
l'européenne."[61]

Up to this point, I have proceeded as if the classification into direct,
indirect, and mixed dialogues corresponded to Plato's classification of
literary forms in the third book of the *Republic*. Doubtless there is a parallel between them, and yet there is also a crucial difference, because
Plato's point is to distinguish between personal and authorial speech.
In Plato, the narrator is never Plato himself—that is, the author—but
someone else, for the most part Socrates, though he may also be Cephalus and in the mixed dialogues Phaedo or Apollodorus. This is surprising
because Plato seems to criticize mimetic narrative (*R.* 394e ff.); "despite
Socrates' profession of the preferability of narration to *mimēsis* there is
no authorial, no non-mimetic narrative voice in the dialogue."[62] Sigonio
already noted that although in fact Cicero wrote diegetic dialogues, con-

---

61. (1972), 324.
62. L. A. Kosman (1992), 83.

trary to what Diogenes Laertius said, Plato did not.[63] However, no matter
how justified this criticism is, it nonetheless overlooks the fact that the
author cannot be simply identified with the first-person narrator—as
I already said in Part I, chapter 7. This is not the place to go into the
ever-subtler refinements of modern theory of narrative;[64] without offering further arguments, I would like to propose that the fundamental distinction is that between the "implied author" and the "dramatized narrator" (to use W. Booth's terms), and that as a rule the first-person narrator
is only an especially interesting case of the dramatized narrator.[65] Among
indirect philosophical dialogues there are a few with anonymous authorial narrators. Leibniz's *Dialogus de arte computandi* is one apt example, which also shows that even in such a dialogue one of the interlocutors (in this case, Charinus) can stand to a large extent for the author.
Another example is Nicholas of Cusa's *De pace fidei*. On the other hand,
most dialogues have a narrator who bears a name that is either, as always in Plato, different from the author's or, as sometimes in Cicero,
the same as the author's. However, this distinction is not particularly
important in two cases, namely, when both first-person and other narrators are guarantors of objectivity or both clearly introduce their own
particular, nongeneralizable points of view. That as a narrator Plato's
Socrates, just like Cicero, enjoys almost authorial omniscience (and that
behind this mask Plato himself can sometimes be recognized) is just as

63. "Ut autem non probem haec me ratio impellit, quod universa ea Socratis
narratio sit, non Platonis. Neque enim dialogus numerari ullus potest, in quo Plato
ipse narrationem ullam instituat, nisi forte Socratem pro Platone velimus accipere"
(1993; 164; cf. 182). It may be the case that the writer of the previously repeatedly
mentioned work preserved on an Oxyrhynchus papyrus already understood this—
according to O. Nüsser (1991), 189.
64. W. C. Booth (1983) remains fundamental, esp. 149 ff. I am particularly in
agreement with the two following statements: "Perhaps the most overworked distinction is that of person" (150) and "Perhaps the most important differences in narrative effect depend on whether the narrator is dramatized in his own right and on
whether his beliefs and characteristics are shared by the author" (151).
65. This does not exclude a triadic classification of narrative forms in accord with
the basic categories of objectivity, subjectivity, and intersubjectivity; to the authorial
and personal forms of narrative I would add a third in which several personal narrators
take turns. But I know of no philosophical dialogue that makes use of this last possibility, since an analogous effect can best be achieved by means of a mixed dialogue.

obvious as that in contrast, the first-person narrator in *Le neveu de Rameau* has his own, limited point of view. Anyone who begins his account by acknowledging that "J'abandonne mon esprit à tout son libertinage. . . . Mes pensées, ce sont mes catins" (I let my mind rove wantonly . . . my ideas are my trollops)[66] does not exactly encourage readers to trust in his objectivity. This dialogue is consequently far more distant from an authorial point of view than the *Republic,* even if only the former seems to be diegetic. That is what is so fascinating and at the same time oppressive about this dialogue: even if Diderot as narrator and interlocutor rejects the Enlightenment's shift into immoralism, as author he shows such fascination with this possibility, or at least an awareness of the fact that it is a not improbable outcome of the destruction of all moral authorities, that he is far more interesting than his homonymous interlocutor. However, he allows himself to be identified with Rameau far less than with the first-person narrator. On the other hand, in Gide's *Corydon* there is a factual identification of the author, not with the first-person narrator, but rather with his interlocutor. Not only does the former have none of Gide's outward features, but the mixture of homophobia and voyeurism that characterizes him make him appear to be petite bourgeois and self-righteous (he does not even hesitate to use nationalistic and anti-Semitic commonplaces);[67] in contrast, Corydon appears to be superior and straightforward. It is immediately obvious that the "I" *(je)* in the footnotes, in which the author speaks, cannot be identical with the "I" of the first-person narrator, but this is hardly necessary to prevent a halfway intelligent reader from identifying Gide with the first-person narrator. Were it possible to doubt where Gide stands, he would not have had to delay publication so long. But since the reader has a natural tendency to identify with a first-person narrator, Gide's literary device may lead the reader—at least a reader in the first half of the twentieth century—to initially internalize the homophobic position, which is more familiar to him, and become uncomfortable with it only in the course of reading the dialogue.

The function of the description of the interlocutors' conversational behavior can be exercised by any indirect dialogue. But if it is marked by

66. (1972), 31.
67. (1935), 212 f., 282, 293 f.

a personal point of view, the reader must reckon with the possibility that the dialogue offers an interpretation that is highly questionable. The remarks made by Hume's Pamphilus regarding the paralinguistic behavior of the conversation partners are the best example of this; the contrast between their smart-alecky false objectivity and their failure to grasp the real state of affairs makes them positively comic. This can escape the reader, however, because Pamphilus sometimes offers absolutely correct interpretations. I will begin with one such example. It is well known that the three participants in the conversation represent three different positions with regard to rational theology: Demea defends a negative theology and believes in the possibility of a priori, apodictic arguments—which are, however, never precisely set forth[68]—whereas Cleanthes and Philo both defend an empirical epistemology. The difference between them consists in the fact that Cleanthes is convinced that the physicotheological proof of God can be defended on this basis, whereas Philo does not share this view; his demolition of this proof occupies most of the dialogue. The epistemological presupposition shared by Cleanthes and Philo is important for a philosophical criticism of Hume, because it opens up the possibility of reconstructing the physicotheological proof on an a priori basis, for example, in combination with the ontological proof of God, which Hume rejects, and the moral proof, which he does not know. However, Cleanthes is not aware of this possibility, which may, indeed must, be ignored in an immanent interpretation.

What is almost malicious in Philo's behavior is that at the beginning of the dialogue he presents himself as a devout person who takes a special interest in the religious education of Demea's children—especially in this godless age!—which Demea wants to carry out by making them familiar with a healthy skepticism on the basis of which he can establish a fideistic philosophy of religion. "Your precaution, says PHILO, of seasoning your children's minds with early piety, is certainly very reasonable; and no more than is requisite, in this profane and irreligious age."[69] Philo goes on to say that "the vulgar" have contempt for philosophy because of its many controversies, and entrust themselves all the more to theology. It is only the half-educated, he says, who are intoxicated by the

68. (1947), 143 ff., 188 ff.
69. (1947), 131.

achievements of science and "profane the inmost sanctuaries of the temple." In this situation there is a proven means of leading people back to religion—strengthening skepticism. "When these topics are displayed in their full light, as they are by some philosophers and almost all divines; who can retain such confidence in this frail faculty of reason as to pay any regard to its determinations in points so sublime, so abstruse, so remote from common life and experience?" Pamphilus now remarks that this speech caused Philo's two interlocutors to smile—though in different ways: "That of DEMEA seemed to imply an unreserved satisfaction in the doctrines delivered: But in CLEANTHES's features, I could distinguish an air of finesse; as if he perceived some raillery or artificial malice in the reasonings of PHILO." This observation is already interesting from a formal point of view: it directs our attention to the facts that, first, the same speech can be interpreted differently, and second, that a similar expressive behavior—for example, a smile—can have different causes. Thereby Hume points on the one hand to the dialogue's central subject: the existence of the world can be explained in different ways. On the other hand, he anticipates the dialogue's conclusion. In the end, the worthy Demea will remark with horror that Philo's skepticism in no way provides a foundation for fideism but instead undermines the latter by leading, like Spinoza's philosophy, to the view that no moral properties can be attributed to God. (A theological grounding of ethics therefore slips away; Hume avoids ethical relativism only by appealing—very much in the vein of Shaftesbury's practical philosophy—to our moral feelings, whose validity is simply presupposed.)

According to Philo, there are four possibilities. The first causes of the world are either perfectly good or perfectly evil, or they are, as in Manichaeism, morally opposed to each other or else amoral.[70] That the world is morally mixed excludes the first two possibilities, and the uniformity and constancy of general laws excludes the third possibility; the fourth is thus by far the most plausible. This means that neither benevolence nor righteousness in a sense comparable to the human one can be attributed to the highest being. This holds in particular if there is more moral evil than good, more natural evil than good; but even if the rela-

70. Contrast Shaftesbury (1999), 109 f.

tionship were turned around, we would have to find a cause for evil whose existence is a fact, and this could ultimately only be the first cause. Here Demea cries out and shortly afterward leaves the group on a pretext: "Hold! Hold! cried DEMEA: Whither does your imagination hurry you? I joined in alliance with you, in order to prove the incomprehensible nature of the divine Being, and refute the principles of CLEANTHES, who would measure everything by a human rule and standard. But I now find you running into all the topics of the greatest libertines and infidels; and betraying that holy cause, which you seemingly espoused. Are you secretly, then, a more dangerous enemy than CLEANTHES himself?" That Demea's eyes are opened only at this point does not testify to his intellectual brilliance, and in fact there is no doubt that both Philo and Hume take Cleanthes more seriously than Demea. Even Pamphilus seems to have grasped the real situation from the outset, though his remarks cited above might be the result of a "memory" influenced by the discussion's final result.

Cleanthes ironically asks Demea if he is just now understanding that from the beginning Philo has been amusing himself at their expense. He thereby takes advantage of the "injudicious reasoning of our vulgar theology," which emphasizes the weaknesses of human reason, the unknowablility of divine nature, and the misery and wickedness of the human race. "In ages of stupidity and ignorance, indeed, these principles may be safely espoused . . . But at present . . ." Here Philo interrupts him with unsurpassably acid sarcasm: "Blame not so much, interposed PHILO, the ignorance of these reverend gentlemen. They know how to change their style with the times . . . When religion stood entirely upon temper and education, it was thought proper to encourage melancholy; as indeed, mankind never have recourse to superior powers so readily as in that disposition. But as men have now learned to form principles, and to draw consequences, it is necessary to change the batteries, and to make use of such arguments as will endure, at least some scrutiny and examination." What is mischievous in this passage, which mirrors in a single paragraph Philo's change in the course of the dialogue, consists first in the fact that at the beginning Philo defends worthy clerics against Cleanthes' intellectual criticism—but only in order to show that these gentlemen are not more sincere but rather more crafty and opportunistic than they at first seemed. They are absolutely capable of reacting to changes in their clientele's level of education. The second kind of mischief consists, of course, in the fact that Cleanthes himself is just such an enlightened theologian. Philo thus lets him know what he thinks of him morally and intellectually; indeed—and this is a particularly painful blow for a certain kind of person—he lets him know that his theology is in no way more developed than that of the age but instead merely reproduces what most contemporary clerics say.[71] Cleanthes, it is thus implied, is not ahead of his time; it is Demea who is limping after it.[72]

I just used twice the expression "he lets him know." Does he really do that? Cleanthes is not upset (and Demea's departure immediately afterward certainly has more to do with the earlier deception); he continues to chat in a friendly way with Philo and even allows himself to be fooled by the fideism that Philo serves up at the end of the conversation— absolutely in the style of proponents of radical enlightenment like Pierre Bayle.[73] This interpretation of mine of the conclusion is thoroughly compatible with the view that Philo's statement, *"that the cause or causes of order in the universe probably bear some remote analogy to human intelligence,"* is sincere, because since it is, as Philo says, ambiguous or at least undefined, saying it seriously does not mean much. If something is meaningless, one no longer needs to lie about it.[74] But the narrator of the conversation that concerns us here demonstrates his intellectual innocence with the following simple commentary on the mischievous passage just cited: "Thus PHILO continued to the last his spirit of opposition, and his censure of established opinions." This sentence corresponds to Cleanthes' observation cited in the following paragraph and thus shows once again the narrator's intellectual dependency on his teacher. Cleanthes says to Philo: "Your spirit of controversy, joined to your abhorrence of vulgar superstition, carries you strange lengths, when engaged in an argument; and there is nothing so sacred and venerable, even in your own

71. A good example of optimistic theology is, in addition to Leibniz, Shaftesbury; cf. (1999), 57 ff., 71 f., 85.
72. (1947), 212 f.
73. On this, see J. Israel's convincing interpretation (2001; 331 f.), even if many scholars disagree with him.
74. (1947), 227.

eyes, which you spare on that occasion."[75] That is a reproach, and Cleanthes draws from it the conclusion that in the future he should discuss theological questions with Philo and Pamphilus separately (and it is against this background that Philo's apparent fideistic retraction begins). And yet Cleanthes' words are marked by a certain goodwill that on the one hand represents him as congenial and on the other clearly proves one thing: Cleanthes has understood Philo just as little as Crito understood Socrates in the *Phaedo*. The originality and power of Hume's arguments, which still occupy philosophy today, simply roll off him. The same goes for the narrator. Philo's decisive arguments against the physicotheological proof occur quite early in the dialogue, namely, already in the second part. On the one hand, he shows that in this world reasonable planning is only one of four different types of causes of order—the others are instinct and reproduction in plants and animals—so why then should it be made the model for the order of the world as a whole?[76] On the other hand, Philo emphasizes that inferring an architect from a house makes sense only because we have already seen many people build houses—but we have never watched God while he was creating a world. "But how this argument can have place, where the objects, as in the present case, are single, individual, without parallel, or specific resemblance, may be difficult to explain. . . . To ascertain this reasoning, it were requisite, that we had experience of the origin of worlds." This comment by the narrator is highly significant: "PHILO was proceeding in this vehement manner, somewhat between jest and earnest, as it appeared to me."[77] On the one hand, Pamphilus repeats, parrotlike, Philo's expectation, expressed shortly before, that he would probably be described as a "rallier"; on the other hand, Pamphilus misunderstands the nature of Philo's peculiar mixture of seriousness and irony. The seriousness is related to his arguments, the mockery to the difficulties the overwhelming majority of people, including his conversation partners, have understanding them. These difficulties are confirmed by Cleanthes' following declamations, which show that he has absolutely failed to grasp the weight of the two

75. (1947), 214.
76. (1947), 147 ff., 178.
77. (1947), 149 f.

arguments; and even if the reader owes to this circumstance the agreeable consequence that in the following Philo explains and expounds his arguments and in doing so develops marvelously witty ideas such as that of a series of generations of universes, this circumstance nonetheless casts a humiliating light on Cleanthes. However, Pamphilus's reaction is still more revealing. Philo's embarrassed silence after Cleanthes' outburst is commented upon this way: "Here I could observe, HERMIPPUS, that PHILO was a little embarrassed and confounded: But while he hesitated in delivering an answer, luckily for him, DEMEA broke in upon the discourse, and saved his countenance."[78] Pamphilus is absolutely correct in observing that Philo is silently embarrassed; but he misses the fact that Philo keeps quiet because he does not know how he should react to Cleanthes' intellectual blunders. That Pamphilus even thinks that Demea's contribution has saved face for Philo shows such a misjudgment of the intellectual ranking of the interlocutors that the intelligent reader can only laugh. Hume's irony is, moreover, analogous to that of Philo, who, after Demea quotes Malebranche, whom Hume did not hold in high regard, seems to lay down his arms: "After so great an authority, DEMEA, replied PHILO, as that which you have produced, and a thousand more, which you might produce, it would appear ridiculous in me to add my sentiment."[79] Through the introduction of the narrator's point of view, Hume seems to humiliate himself as much as Philo; insofar as he points to the latter's irony, however, he also points to his own, and in addition makes it clear that Philo is the character who most stands for him. "Le bon David," as Hume was called, was thoroughly aware of his own superiority to his intellectually simpler contemporaries.

Indirect and mixed dialogues often have more room for the description of the scene of the conversation than direct dialogues do; but while there are countless nonscenic direct dialogues, which represent, as it were, a naked exchange of blows, Plato's *Phaedrus,* for example, shows that a direct dialogue can also be scenic. However, before we examine the place and time of the dialogue more closely, the reality content of the literary universe of different dialogues must be analyzed.

78. (1947), 155.
79. (1947), 142.

CHAPTER 10

The Modal and Ontological Status
of the Literary Universe —
Personification and the Problem of
Realism — Dream and Dialogue

The literary universe represented in a work of art, including philosophical dialogues, is autonomous. Nonetheless, both the producers and the receivers of dialogues belong to the real world, and they constantly ask themselves whether the represented universe could belong to their own world, that is, whether it is nomologically possible, whether it is governed by the same natural laws as the real world.[1] If that is the case, then we speak of "realistic dialogues," a category to which most philosophical dialogues doubtless belong. If it is not the case, then we are dealing with nonrealistic dialogues. However, there are certainly transitional

---

1. Analytically impossible worlds are usually not created by a philosophical dialogue. If it contains contradictions — as does for example Diderot's *Le neveu de Rameau,* where Jean-Philippe Rameau is sometimes said to be still alive and sometimes said to be already dead — these are more likely to be attributed to the still unfinished status of the work than to an intention on the part of the author, whose point would escape me at least. On this problem, see Lewis (1983), 277 f.

cases, because it is not always clear whether a variation of only one element of our world or of a natural law has occurred.

A good example of such a transitional dialogue is Plato's *Menexenus,*
one of his most brilliant writings. Socrates encounters Menexenus, who is
politically ambitious; he has just come from the Council of 500, which is
electing a new orator for funeral eulogies. By a fortunate accident, just the
day before Socrates has learned such a speech from his rhetoric teacher,
Aspasia, Pericles' wife, which uses clichés taken from the famous *logos epi-
taphios* that Pericles delivered but which Socrates believes she wrote for
him; she threatened to beat him if he did not learn it by heart, he says, and
he now presents it.[2] The speech is a masterpiece of satire, because it lays
bare the empty rhetoric of patriotic propaganda and the shameless falsifi-
cations of history that go along with it. At the beginning of the dialogue
Socrates, with a sarcasm that reminds us far more of the German avant-
garde of the 1920s than of the image of Plato purveyed by German secondary school teachers in the time of National Socialism, had already remarked with regard to such a speech that it showed that it is advantageous
to die in battle, especially since a poor man would receive a costly funeral
and a bad man have an elaborate eulogy made over him.[3] His ironic praise
of the funeral orators who so captivate him that he only comes back to
himself three days later and sees again how things really are on earth[4] is
later retracted with the comment, which mocks every speech glorifying
one's own community, that praising Athenians in the Peloponnese and
Peloponnesians in Athens may be a rhetorical achievement but praising
the same people from whom one hopes to win recognition for one's own
speech is not.[5] Thus Socrates' or Aspasia's speech does not contain solely
praise—or rather, to be precise, it contains prima facie almost solely
praise, but most of it, if by no means all, in a poisoned form. No sentence
shows the ambiguity of Plato's relation to Athens better than the one that
says that even today the Athenians remain unconquered by the Peloponnesians because they have conquered themselves and were defeated by
themselves.[6] In view of Athens's defeat in the Peloponnesian War, which

2. *Mx.* 236a ff.
3. *Mx.* 234c.
4. *Mx.* 235b f. Cf. *Ap.* 17a2 f.
5. *Mx.* 235d3 ff.
6. *Mx.* 243d5 ff.

put an end to its hegemony forever, such a sentence is incredibly brazen and in fact shows that Attic democracy is based on *doxa,* that is, mere opinions, which are not necessarily true.[7] And yet this sentence has a deeper meaning—because the notion that Athens's military defeat was due not really to exogenous factors but rather to faulty political decisions and a faulty understanding of politics is one that Plato has Socrates defend in the *Gorgias* and the *Meno* as well. But the details of this splendid speech and its representation of the mechanisms of patriotic constructions of history do not concern us here. What is crucial in the context of this chapter is that Socrates sketches an outline of Attic history down to the so-called Peace of Antalcidas. This occurred in 386, that is, thirteen years after Socrates' execution; Aspasia, the year of whose death is unknown, probably died earlier. Anachronisms are common in Plato and in other authors of philosophical dialogues; I examine this issue again in chapter 12. The writer of a fictional text has a sovereign right to commit such anachronisms, and as a rule they are only variations on individual events within our world; the author does not want them to be seen as anachronisms. But in this case the anachronism is so blatant that one cannot avoid the impression that Plato is drawing attention to it—he wants the reader to perceive it. But then we are dealing with something spectral: the funeral oration on Athens is delivered by a dead man inspired by a dead woman, and in such a way that his interlocutor does not even notice. Like the recycling of a speech almost half a century old, this is splendidly suited to the description of Athens's decline. The nineteenth-century inclination to deny the text's authenticity is thus impossible, not only because Aristotle cites the text,[8] but also because it is based on a misunderstanding of its point.[9] However, the latter indicates that the *Menexenus* is Plato's only dialogue that is not truly realistic, but it is also not overtly unrealistic, because the anachronism can be interpreted as naive.

7. Cf. *Mx.* 238d2, d5, d8, and 243d2 ff.
8. *Rh.* 1367b8 f., 1415b30 ff.
9. The occasionally proposed rejection of just the passage 244b3–246a4, on the ground that it is an interpolation (see, e.g., D. Nails [2002], 319 f.) is also unacceptable, if only because the expression *oi basilea eleutherōsantes* (246a1) is unsurpassably brilliant—Athens's alliance with the Persian king (cf. 244d5 ff.) is presented as a further extension of democracy, which is known to have been the pretext for Attic imperialism (cf. 242a7, b5 ff.).

In the passage quoted above (p. 21), de Maistre has the Chevalier de B*** ironically cite the dialogues of the dead as real, that is, as actually the paradigm of nonrealistic dialogues. In fact, at least in the part of our world that is accessible to us, the dead cannot speak; dialogues of the dead thus depict a nomologically impossible world. However, a conversation between persons of differing periods or on subjects that became current only after their death should not be seen as nomologically impossible if the age in which someone lives is considered a contingent, not an essential fact; there are no natural laws that exclude the possibility of a conversation about Napoleon III's undermining of the constitutional state between someone who thinks about political questions exactly as Machiavelli does and someone who thinks about them exactly as Montesquieu does. Maurice Joly's *Dialogue aux enfers entre Machiavel et Montesquieu* would immediately lose its nonrealistic character if the two interlocutors were replaced by two characters who voiced exactly the same opinions but were described as "a nineteenth-century follower of Machiavelli" and "a nineteenth-century follower of Montesquieu." However, Joly had sound reasons for choosing the other appellations, which both give his interlocutors a more interesting status and lend his criticism of the present the appearance of a detached point of view, because the dead cannot intervene in the present. However, Napoleon III's police suspected that the detached literary universe that the book depicts did not prevent the book from having an influence.

Fables in which animals speak to each other can clearly no longer be regarded as realistic literature, but neither can philosophical dialogues in which the interlocutors are mythical figures or personified abstractions. The Peripatetic Aristo of Ceos had the mythical Tithonus deliver a lecture on old age—but in his *Cato* Cicero decided to introduce a historical person, so that the speech would have more authority.[10] Among the works attributed to Diogenes of Sinope,[11] a few titles allow us to suspect

10. "omnem autem sermonem tribuimus non Tithono ut Aristo Cius (parum enim esset auctoritatis in fabula), sed M. Catoni seni, quo maiorem auctoritatem haberet oratio" (*Cat.* 1.3). Cf. also Cicero's criticism of Ariston fin. 5.5.13.1.

11. D. L. 6 80. On the difficult question as to what Diogenes himself might have really written, see K. Döring (2006), 21.

the presence of mythical interlocutors. But dialogues with personifications are particularly widespread. All the interlocutors may be personi -
fications, as in Petrarch's *De remediis utriusque fortune* and in the brief
first dialogue at the end of the second chapter of the first part of Spinoza's *Korte verhandelung van God, de mensch, en des zelfs welstand,* or
they may constitute at least the great majority of the interlocutors, as in
Kṛṣṇa Miśra's *Prabodhacandrodaya* or Llull's *Liber natalis pueri parvuli
Christi Iesu.*[12] However, only one interlocutor may be a personification.
In Llull's *Llibre del gentil e dels tres savis,* the three sages representing Judaism, Christianity, and Islam are real persons, just like the pagan—but
the Lady Intelligence ("dona Entallegencia") whom they encounter in
the "prologue" to the work surely is not. In Petrarch's *De secreto conflictu curarum meum,* we should interpret allegorically the personified
Lady Truth who prepares him for Augustine's appearance and is present
throughout the conversation between them, although she remains silent,
so that Petrarch seems to hear in Augustine the voice of truth itself.[13] Of
course, both Truth and Augustine are figures with which Petrarch could
not really speak—but for different reasons, because while the passage
just cited makes Augustine the spokesman for truth, he nonetheless remains a real individual, though from a past age. A conversation between
a person and a personification is also represented in Leopardi's *Dialogo
della natura e di un islandese,* in which nature shows itself to be completely indifferent to the suffering of its sensitive creatures, which are
called into being without their having desired it; the dialogue ends with
the Icelander's being eaten by hungry lions or with his death in a sand-
storm; in the latter version, his mummy ends up satisfying the curiosity
of European museumgoers.[14]

The best-known example of a personification in a philosophical dialogue is surely "Philosophy" in Boethius's *Consolatio philosophiae,* who
is the model for Truth in Petrarch's dialogue. Her first appearance to
Boethius when he is in prison, awaiting execution and consoling himself

12. In addition to six allegorical figures and the mythical figure of Mary,
Ramon Llull himself appears at the end (*ROL* VII 72 f.).

13. "ut tamen quicquid ex te audiet ex me dictum putet, presens adero" (1955; 26).

14. (1956), 534 f.

by writing verses dripping with world-weariness and self-pity, character-izes her as superhuman: her eyes glow; her glance is more penetrating than is usual among humans; her strength is inexhaustible, despite her great age; her size varies—sometimes she is of human size, sometimes she reaches the heavens, indeed beyond them—and her robe, made of an indissoluble material, has the patina of great age; while the letter *Pi* on its lower border and the letter *Theta* on its upper border allude to the ascent by stages from practical to theoretical philosophy. In a few places her robe has been torn by rough men. In her right hand she carries books, in her left a scepter.[15] All this can, indeed should, be read allegori-cally. It refers to characteristics of philosophy as an intellectual activity that mentally penetrates reality; rises above the mass of humanity yet must make use of human powers of understanding; is old and at the same time inexhaustibly vital; entertains ideas that are indestructible but have a long history; in its disciplines is hierarchically structured and reaches its apex in theory, to which Boethius now devotes himself, after long political activity, for which he must pay with his life; is subject to all schools' attempts to monopolize it[16] but is ultimately dominant through the power of the mind and its tradition. In the conversation with such a figure there can be no symmetry; it need not first knock and request a conversation but instead imposes itself. With harsh words it drives away the muses among whom Boethius had sought consolation, and who now suddenly appear personified in the form of a chorus. Boethius is weeping so much that he cannot tell who this lady with such command-ing authority is, and looks silently down at the floor.[17] But she is not only commanding, she is also motherly; she sits down close to the bed and, after she has shooed away the muses by words in prose, speaks to him for the first time in verses that describe his torpor. Then she mentions the medical art to him and and reminds him that he was nourished and grew up on her milk. She gave him the weapons that would have kept him safe, had he not cast them away. But Boethius still seems not to rec-ognize her and remains silent, whether because he is ashamed (which

15. *Cons.* 1.1.1–6.
16. Cf. *Cons.* 1.3.7.
17. *Cons.* 1.1.13.

she would prefer) or because his stupor oppresses him. He has forgotten himself, she tells him, but he will remember himself once he has recognized her. Then she touches his breast with her hand and dries his tears with her robe.[18] Now Boethius is finally able to shake off his deep depression and recognize his visitor as Philosophy. He is surprised that she, the teacher of all virtues, has descended from her heights and joined him in the loneliness of his isolation: "Et: Quid, inquam, tu in has exsilii nostri solitudines, o omnium magistra virtutum, supero cardine delapsa venisti?" She replies that Philosophy is not allowed to leave an innocent person unaccompanied along the way, and reminds him that he is not the first philosopher who is to die an unjust death. It is not surprising that it is precisely philosophical people whom the dishonest find extremely alien to their interests and who therefore encounter their hatred, which cannot, however, reach the heaven of philosophy.[19] Here Boethius finally overcomes his paralysis and adopts what the most modern psychology also sees as the only way to produce catharsis in such a situation: he talks about himself, about the political activities he has undertaken in accordance with Plato and Philosophy,[20] and his dreadful fall. This has cost him not only his position, his honor, and his property—"ego quidem bonis omnibus pulsus, dignitatibus exutus, existimatione foedatus";[21] it awakes in him the suspicion that the world is ruled by Fortune, not by Reason. This leads to the substantial part of the dialogue, but only after Philosophy, unmoved by Boethius's complaints and with a calm countenance, has reminded him of his true, spiritual homeland. What is crucial here is her idea that Boethius no longer knows who he is, because he does not know what the purpose of things is; only a reconciliation with the ordered structure of the world will be able to bring him back to himself.[22]

Boethius, who had planned to translate and comment upon not only Aristotle but also Plato, certainly had the *Crito* in mind as he was writing this work. In both works philosophers are in prison, awaiting

---

18. *Cons.* 1.2.1–7.
19. *Cons.* 1.3.1–14.
20. *Cons.* 1.4.5–7.
21. *Cons.* 1.4.45.
22. *Cons.* 1.5.1 ff., 1.6.10 ff.

their execution. But what a contrast! Although Socrates also occupies himself with poetry, after completing a poem on Apollo he versifies Aesop's fables; it is religious and moral themes that concern him.[23] In contrast, Boethius's introductory poem focuses on his own suffering. He is in deepest despair, and only with difficulty can Philosophy get his attention. Crito also has to wait a long time before Socrates turns to him, but only because Socrates is sound asleep. In both the *Crito* and the *Phaedo* it is Crito who is greatly upset; Socrates does not lose his unshakable composure for even a moment. Of course, this also has to do with the fact that the Platonic Socrates does not bear the same name as his author; someone who, like Boethius, is representing himself cannot idealize himself in the same way. Boethius's behavior is probably more common than Socrates'; and therefore we can describe the *Consolatio philosophiae* as the more realistic work. Precisely because its human hero is weaker, more fallible, and more emotional than Plato's Socrates, he requires a superior interlocutor who, if he (or she) is not to discourage Boethius too much, cannot be human. Paradoxically, the introduction of a personification that makes this dialogue nonrealistic is precisely the consequence of a greater realism—in a different sense of the word, of course. This seems wrong-headed, but it is familiar to every admirer of Auerbach's *Mimesis,* one of the greatest works of literary scholarship. Medieval literature, despite its many personifications and allegories, is more realistic than ancient literature, because it moves beyond the aristocratic ideology of antiquity and recognizes, on the basis of its new idea of God, something worth depicting in the creaturely nature of human beings.

It seems to me that here we find the right answer to the old question as to whether the *Consolatio* is a Christian work at all. Valla already reproached Boethius for failing to mention Christ or the Christian religion and its rules anywhere in his dialogue; out of an excessive admiration for philosophy, Valla suggest, he has allowed his ship to go aground on barbaric coasts.[24] Boethius's theological writings show that he considered himself a Christian, and nothing in the *Consolatio* is incompatible with Christianity. But for Boethius, as for many other authors of late

23. *Phd.* 60c ff.
24. (1987), 136.

antiquity, being a Christian does not seem to have meant very much: the core of his own intellectual convictions is a Neoplatonism that shows itself open to the dogmas of Christianity without allowing them to penetrate this core area. In an existential crisis like the one in which Boethius found himself, a person concentrates on his intellectual core. But even if Boethius differed from Augustine in that Christology was scarcely part of his intellectual core, his sensibility was certainly shaped by Christianity, whether he knew it or not. A pagan philosopher could hardly have brought himself to offer the kind of unsparing depiction of his own stupor that Boethius presents at the outset; it presupposes Augustine's *Confessiones*. For pagans, philosophy is divine; but the maternal quality it has in Boethius is something new and surprising, and seems to suggest that a temporary loss of autonomy is not a disgrace but something thoroughly human. In chapter 16 (p. 397 ff.), I show that Christianity enhanced the status of women in philosophy; but Boethius even goes so far as to feminize the abstract personification of philosophy, of course also because of the grammatical gender of the Greek and Latin words. Here too we see how precisely the loss in realism brings parts of reality into view to which the Platonic or Ciceronian dialogue was blind.

Eloquent personifications also occur in Plato; the personification of the Laws in the *Crito*[25] is the most famous but not the sole example.[26] But this does not alter the fact that all of Plato's dialogues (with the partial exception of the *Menexenus*) represent a nomologically possible universe, because they are introduced as deliberate fictions within the conversation—just as Plato's Socrates in the *Apology*,[27] still alive, imagines possible conversations among the dead in the underworld. The human ability to imagine the nomologically impossible is definitely part of our real world; and in dreams it becomes something actualized daily—or rather nightly. An author can transform something nomologically impossible into something possible by having his heroes dream inside the literary universe—that is, not by having them simply relate a

25. 50a–54d.
26. At *Prt.* 361a–c. Socrates imagines that the outcome of the discussion speaks and mocks the conversation partners.
27. 40e–41c.

real dream in the course of a conversation, as Plato has Socrates do in the *Crito*[28] or as Cicero has Scipio do at the end of *De re publica*.[29] Scipio Aemilianus makes every possible effort to give a rational explanation for his erstwhile dream, which he finally relates. Because the preceding evening he had spoken with the Numidian king Masinnisa about Scipio Africanus, his grandfather (by adoption), the latter appeared to him that night, just as Ennius dreamed of Homer: "fit enim fere ut cogitationes sermonesque nostri pariant aliquid in somno tale, quale de Homero scribit Ennius, de quo videlicet saepissime vigilans solebat cogitare et loqui."[30] However, the report of the dream itself takes place in a trance-like state: when his friends cry out when Aemilianus alludes to his possible murder by relatives, he merely smiles sweetly and asks them to listen calmly and not awaken him from his sleep.[31] Thus the narrative of the dream, which is itself dreamlike, mediates between the dream and the sleep of death that is soon to come.

In contrast, in the "Prohemium" to his *Secretum*, Petrarch expressly excludes the possibility that he has dreamed: "contigit nuper ut non, sicut egros animos solet, somnus opprimeret, sed anxium atque pervigilem mulier quedam inenarrabilis etatis et luminis, formaque non satis ab hominibus intellecta, incertum quibus viis adiisse videretur."[32] This distinguishes him from Nicholas of Cusa, who seems to frame realistically his dialogue *De pace fidei*, which is anything but realistic, by reducing the event depicted to the status of a vision. Depending on how one understands the nature of this vision (as a mere subjective event, a real seeing, or as a subjective experience in which an objective truth is revealed), one can interpret the universe of the dialogue as nomologically

---

28. 44b f.

29. A modern example is K. W. F. Solger's *Der Traum* (1972; 96–179), a mixed dialogue at the end of which Adelbert reports, in the frame conversation, a long dream (171 ff.).

30. 6.10.10. This "day residue" theory, as we may call it following Freud, arises from critical common sense itself without requiring much talent for observation; it is also found div. 2.68.140.

31. 6.12.12: "Hic cum exclamavisset Laelius ingemuissentque vehementius ceteri, leniter arridens Scipio: 'st! quaeso' inquit 'ne me e somno excitetis, et parumper audite cetera.'"

32. (1955), 22.

possible—in the first as well as in the third case (which is in my opinion the one intended)—or impossible—in the second case. Nicholas of Cusa goes to some lengths to make the occurrence of this vision psychologically plausible. His narrative is conducted authorially, that is, not in the first person, although the man it is about reminds the reader of the author, since it is said that he was once in Constantinople, which is also true of Nicholas of Cusa, though of only a few of his Latin contemporaries. This man is supposed to have been profoundly shaken by the news of the fall of Constantinople in 1453 and the horrors committed during it, and to have resorted, sighing, to prayer. His prayer is characteristically not for revenge; God, who is described as the creator of all men, is asked instead, in his benevolence, to limit the persecutions, which are raging more violently than usual because of the differing religious rites—a prolepsis of the dialogue's crucial message that the one religion does not exclude a difference in rites, and is in fact only enriched by their plurality.[33] Probably because of his continued daily meditation, we are told in a sentence that could satisfy a modern specialist in the psychology of religion as well as a religiously naive person, after a few days this pious man had a vision through which it became clear to him that a consensus among wise men who were familiar with the different religions of the world could be achieved, and thereby a perpetual religious peace.[34] The central content of this vision is ultimately only a vivid explication of the moral and religious idea with which this pious man reacts to a dreadful political event: not hatred for the perpetrators, but rather compassion for the victims and an awareness of the fact that religious persecution is widespread, but hardly in accord with the God who

33. Cf. VII 7 and 62.

34. "FUIT EX HIIS, quae apud Constantinopolim proxime saevissime acta per Turkorum regem divulgabantur, quidam vir zelo Dei accensus, qui loca illarum regionum aliquando viderat, ut pluribus gemitibus oraret omnium creatorem quod persecutionem, quae ob diversum ritum religionum plus solito saevit, sua pietate moderaretur.

Accidit ut post dies aliquot, forte ex diuturna continuata meditatione, visio quaedam eidem zeloso manifestaretur, ex qua elicuit quod paucorum sapientum omnium talium diversitatum quae in religionibus per orbem observantur peritia pollentium unam posse facilem quandam concordantiam reperiri, ac per eam in religione perpetuam pacem convenienti ac veraci medio constitui" (VII 3 f.).

is considered the father of all human beings. Even if it is not made explicit, Nicholas of Cusa's formulation implies that any persecution on religious grounds, even Christian ones, is contrary to God's will.[35] The content of the vision is now that the pious man is transported to the height—but, it is explicitly said, to an intellectual height *(ad quandam intellectualem altitudinem)*. There he sees God in the court of the dead and saints; angels bring the news of religious persecutions, and an archangel asks God to put things right. At first, God bristles—after the prophets, he has sent his Word to Earth; what more can be done? Now it is the Word Himself that emphasizes that because of their free will humans need to be told more often; the various religions should, since there is only one truth, be led through divine intervention to a single orthodox belief. God agrees with this idea, and thus intellectual representatives of all the important religions and nations are summoned. The conversation among them is initially moderated by the Word (chaps. IV–X), then by Peter (chaps. XI–XV), and finally by Paul (chaps. XVI–XIX). The discussion in Heaven—in a Heaven of the understanding, as Nicholas writes at the end, in order to stress the allegorical nature of the conversation[36]— begins with a reflection on the wisdom presupposed by all and ends with the divine demand that the representatives of the religions return to their own peoples to lead them to the unity of the true worship of God and then meet in Jerusalem, in order to found in the name of all a perpetual peace on the basis of a common belief. Thereby it is made clear that the real work remains to be done: as in Plato's allegory of the cave, the ascent has to be followed by a descent. What is represented is an ideal model, not a real conversation in space and time. However, the reader wonders how such a conversation could succeed when the authority of the Word, Peter, and Paul is no longer presupposed.

---

35. Cf. also these later statements, which are not limited to any particular religion: "ob religionem plerosque in invicem arma movere et sua potentia homines aut ad renegationem diu observatae sectae cogere aut mortem inferre" (VII 4) and "et quia omnes, qui hanc aut faciunt aut patiuntur persecutionem, non aliunde moventur nisi quia sic saluti credunt expedire et suo creatori placere, misertus est igitur Dominus populo" (VII 10). However, this does not prevent Petrus from making an anti-Judaic remark (VII 39).

36. "in caelo rationis" (VII 62).

The bracketing of a conversation by stating that it took place in a vision or dream is not permissible solely when the conversation represented is nomologically impossible: one can, after all, also dream something nomologically possible. In Abelard's *Collationes,* neither the conversation between the philosopher and the Jew nor that between the philosopher and the Christian represents anything impossible; but they nonetheless take place within a dream. "Aspiciebam in uisu noctis: et ecce uiri tres, diuerso tramite uenientes, coram me astiterunt," we read in the opening sentence of this work.[37] It is not easy to understand the function of this sentence; the clear rational argumentation that follows is not oniric in any way, and after the "prefatio" the notion that the whole is a dream is never again mentioned. Obviously, the opening sentence plays on Daniel 7:13, a passage that Christians liked to relate to the coming of Christ. John Marenbon has proposed that Abelard is distancing himself ironically from the dream visions of the Middle Ages—and perhaps also from those in the Old Testament and their interpretations—and opposes the authority of arguments to that of nocturnal visions: "The contrast between the dramatic continuation of the biblical passage and the down-to-earth tenor of Abelard's description suggests, rather, that the readers are being deliberately teased: having their expectations raised only to be let down almost as quickly. Perhaps Abelard wants to underline the fact that, although technically a dream, his *Collationes* are sober, wide-awake discussions, and that it is through such careful, argumentative procedures, rather than from sudden revelation, that we should expect to increase our understanding."[38] I would suggest three further possible grounds for Abelard's choice of the dream form. First, the second sentence of his dialogue is "Quos ego statim, iuxta uisionis modum, cuius sint professionis uel cur ad me uenerint interrogo." Thus Abelard immediately asks his visitors, as is usual in dreams, about their religion and the reason for which they have come. Thus he indicates that a greater directness is possible in a dream than in reality, which is characterized by social constraints; in a dream, one can immediately come to the point. Second, we have to consider the possibility that Abelard wanted to draw

37. (2001), 2.
38. Abelard (2001), xxxvii f.

attention to the fact that the quality of an argument, which is for him the real question, is not increased by its visionary character—but is also not eradicated by its dream character. An argument is valid or invalid, no matter by whom it is made, or indeed whether it is perceived awake or in a dream.[39] Third, by introducing himself from a dialogue-internal point of view as the creator of the whole conversation, Abelard may have wanted to indicate that from a dialogue-external point of view he is the author of the dialogue. For he remains its creator even if he takes little part in it. The small role played by Abelard the *iudex* is, as it were, compensated through the omnipresence of Abelard the dreamer, which reminds us of the creative achievement of Abelard the writer. In view of Abelard's subtle humor and his vanity, which is generally acknowledged, even by himself,[40] it is also possible that he wants to point self-ironically to the ambivalence of his feelings when he rejects the compliments of the philosopher who speaks to him as the representative of the three, though these compliments are nonetheless very flattering.[41] When Cicero has his interlocutors praise him, perhaps he represses the fact that as the author he is praising himself;[42] but the dreamer is closer to the speakers than the author, because he is a dialogue-internal character, so that Abelard was probably aware of the paradox involved in his rejection of praise that originated in himself. Since this brilliant philosopher, theologian, and writer was vain, he may even have relished this paradox. Vain people also find their own weaknesses, including their own vanity, interesting.

To be sure, the transcendent God of medieval philosophy, who rips the soul out of the cosmos and puts it in front of himself, prepared the way for the Cartesian turning point, in which the dream argument plays a central role. If everything can be a dream, how can we be sure that there is an external world? It is well known that in Descartes, only belief in God's truthfulness—a belief that is not easy to reconcile with his theological voluntarism—justifies our natural trust in the existence of a *res extensa*. What is brilliant about Diderot's d'Alembert trilogy is that it

39. This important idea is expressed by Augustine with respect to mathematical and moral propositions: *C. acad.* 3.11.25 and 12.28.
40. See only chapters 2 and 3 of *Historia calamitatum mearum*.
41. (2001), 4 ff.
42. Cf. above, chap. 4, n. 59.

makes the most radical counterposition to subjective idealism, materialism, proceed from a dream, that is, precisely from the basis of Cartesianism. This is possible, of course, only if the dream is not, as it is in Abelard, the metaphysical place within which the conversation takes place;
instead the conversation takes place in external reality, and the dream is,
as it were, observed from without and objectified. And this in turn presupposes that the dream is not private, but instead the dreamer speaks
and thus allows others to share his hidden thoughts. However, this communication situation is anomalous and morally questionable, because
the dreamer does not know that someone is listening to him, and the
person who is listening probably violates an obligation to be discreet.
This is all the more true when the listener reads out to another waking
person her transcript of these statements made in the dream. Such behavior is excusable only if this person is motivated by friendly care. Her
waking interlocutor will then be a physician to whom she turns for help.

This is precisely the situation in Diderot's trilogy, which he wrote
during the summer of 1769 but later added to and revised. The first part,
La suite d'un entretien entre M. d'Alembert et M. Diderot, begins, as the
title suggests, in medias res: d'Alembert grants Diderot, who has apparently already spoken about sensibility as a general property of matter,
that it is difficult to imagine a being that is not extended but nonetheless
occupies space, that is essentially different from matter but nonetheless
united with it, that moves without being itself moved. "Un être dont je
n'ai pas la moindre idée; un être d'une nature aussi contradictoire est
difficile à admettre."[43] But anyone who denies such a being finds himself ensnared in other difficulties. Diderot defends his central thesis: The
phenomenon of metabolism shows how inorganic matter can become
organic, and thus capable of feeling; and the gap between marble, for instance, and a sensible being is greater than that between a feeling and a
thinking being—this is a notoriously dangerous consequence of the
Cartesian revolutionizing of ontology, which Descartes himself parried
when he denied that animals have feelings.[44] With characteristic directness, Diderot examines the production of d'Alembert himself, who was

43. (1972), 161.
44. (1972), 164.

the abandoned illegitimate son of Mme de Tencin and the Chevalier Destouches-Canon. Diderot describes d'Alembert's procreation, the implantation of the fertilized egg, its development into a fetus, his birth and abandonment, and finally his first-rate achievements in mathematics and physics, such as his theory of precession. In a witty satire of the language of both alchemy and theology, which are thereby given equal scientific status, we read: "Voici en quatre mots la formule générale. Mangez, digérez, distillez in vasi licito, *et fiat homo secundum artem*." The sequence moves from lifeless matter to sensible matter and from there to thinking matter, and then finally with death, back to lifeless matter: "un être inerte, un être sentant, un être pensant, un être résolvant le problème de la précession des équinoxes, un être sublime, un être merveilleux, un être vieillissant, dépérissant, mourant, dissous et rendu à la terre végétale."[45] Diderot's programmatic materialistic explanation of consciousness is diametrically opposed to the two-substance theory: "vous en voulez à la distinction des deux substances," d'Alembert says to him, and he agrees.[46] Like Hume,[47] Diderot rejects the notion that mental properties are indivisible in a different sense from physical ones, and sees the relation between cause and effect as contingent in all cases.[48] Using the model of a harpsichord capable of sensation, Diderot tries to show how several ideas can be simultaneously present to the mind, and how one idea can draw another behind it.[49] He absolutely grants that according to this theory there can be no genuine activity on the part of the subject. When d'Alembert asks how one could draw conclusions in his system, he replies, "C'est que nous n'en tirons point: elles sont toutes tirées par la nature."[50] A high point of his theory is certainly the claim that it can also explain the opposite theory, the solipsist one (Diderot was probably thinking of Berkeley), which therefore no longer remains an external threat. "Il y a un moment de délire où le clavecin sensible a

---

45. (1972), 165.
46. (1972), 169.
47. *Treatise*, 1.3.6 and 1.4.5.
48. (1972), 172 f.
49. (1972), 168 ff.
50. (1972), 174.

pensé qu'il était le seul clavecin qu'il y eût au monde, et que toute l'harmonie de l'univers se passait en lui."[51] D'Alembert would now like to go to bed, but Diderot warns him: he will dream about their discussion. D'Alembert tries to take refuge in his skepticism, but Diderot seeks to show him that one is never in the situation in which opinions are of exactly equal weight; instead, one always leans toward one of two opposed positions—but not always the same one. Finally, Diderot says farewell with a reminder of death, which is not so anxiety producing if one can only double the life span. "Vous verrez ce qui en arrivera." But d'Alembert does not want to deal with this question; he just wants to sleep.[52]

Diderot does not appear in the following two parts of the trilogy; and in a certain sense it could be said that d'Alembert is also no longer an interlocutor, even though he is absolutely present in the second part of the trilogy, *Le rêve de d'Alembert* (though not in the third part). But by far the majority of what he says here he expresses when he is asleep. He exemplifies what he has denied: his inner harpsichord plays and in spite of itself produces sounds after Diderot has bumped into it; despite his absence he thereby remains the master of the conversation. That the most interesting arguments for materialism are proposed by someone who rejects it as a conscious subject, and are thus precisely not a product of a planning subjectivity, is a fascinating correspondence between the subject of the conversation and the conversational procedure, which, as was shown above in chapter 3, characterizes the best philosophical dialogues. It is particularly witty when the dreaming d'Alembert is able to persuade himself of the unity of his consciousness only by touching *himself*—that is, of course, *his body:* "car je suis bien un, je n'en saurais douter . . . (en disant cela, il se tâtait partout)."[53] However, the inevitability of a conscious interlocutor in a dialogue is shown, this time in defiance of Diderot, by his introduction of the physician Bordeu, whom Mlle de l'Espinasse calls in because she is deeply upset by what d'Alembert has said while asleep, apparently in the course of a kind of nightmare. Bordeu is soon able to calm d'Alembert's woman friend, assuring

51. (1972), 174.
52. (1972), 177.
53. (1972), 181.

her that the philosopher is not seriously ill, and he shows interest when she begins to read him her record of his nightly statements. Bordeu shows his scientific sense when he asks whether one of the sentences spoken by Mlle de l'Espinasse comes from her or from the dreamer. He quickly understands with which ideas d'Alembert is grappling, and claims that he can anticipate some of d'Alembert's next statements. Mlle de l'Espinasse asks mockingly whether he himself is dreaming[54] but has to acknowledge, to her amazement, that Bordeu is really capable of doing this. At first she thinks there is some kind of trick, but after her servant tells her that he has communicated nothing to Bordeu she cannot maintain this hypothesis.[55] Bordeu's congeniality to d'Alembert's muse Diderot is not surprising, because in the dialogue as well as in reality, Bordeu is a well-known vitalist materialist. The real Diderot was his friend and admirer, and owed him many of his ideas.

However, Diderot indulges in a wicked jest here, since the real Théophile de Bordeu was not d'Alembert's personal physician. His physician was Michel Bouvard, one of Bordeu's bitterest enemies, who even managed to get him removed from the register of Paris physicians.[56] While through Mlle de l'Espinasse Bordeu becomes familiar with the night thoughts of d'Alembert, who was more a skeptic than a Cartesian, but certainly not a materialist, the latter becomes, as it were, a transmission belt, if not almost a guinea pig, in the conversation between the two materialists. This is absolutely tactless with regard to d'Alembert, who had been Diderot's friend during their collaboration on the *Encyclopédie;* however, since their quarrel in 1759 their relationship had remained cool. Nonetheless, Diderot had visited d'Alembert during his severe illness in the summer of 1765 and on that occasion became acquainted with Julie de l'Espinasse, who was caring for d'Alembert; this memory probably inspired the conception of the trilogy. At the time the latter was written, d'Alembert, who had earlier lived with his foster mother, had moved to Mlle de l'Espinasse's home, where he was the

54. (1972), 183. Cf. 194.
55. (1972), 185 f. On the other hand, there is a real deception in Diderot's philosophically less interesting dialogue *Mystification.*
56. Cf. P. N. Furbank (1992), 325.

leading figure in her salon. The relationship between the two was notoriously complex: d'Alembert was infatuated with his hostess, who was
fifteen years younger than he, but they were lovers for a short time at
most. Soon d'Alembert had to be content with being Julie's friend, even
if he learned how strong her relationships with other men had been only
after her death in 1776: she died of a broken heart because of her unre-
quited love for the Count de Guibert. All this has to be mentioned here
because Diderot, who knew Julie only briefly, and may in fact have met
her only once,[57] seems to have immediately understood the nature of
their relationship. His diagnostic eye very quickly grasped the most diverse forms of sexuality (including their inhibitions), even those that de-
viated from his own, which was direct and sensuous.

Diderot's Mlle de l'Espinasse is d'Alembert's caregiver, no more; her
real interlocutor is Bordeu, with whom she dines alone in the third part
of the trilogy, the *Suite de l'entretien précédent,* because d'Alembert has
gone out to dine elsewhere. She and Bordeu discuss the boldest sexual and
bioethical ideas of their time: the moral permissibility of masturbation,
which is socially useful, homosexuality, and even the creation of half-
animal, half-human mixed beings that could be used as servants. (This
last point shows the modern reader that there was an inherent potential for inhumanity in the emancipatory ideals of the Enlightenment.)[58]
Especially important in this discussion is the discovery that being contrary to nature is not a moral criterion, since nothing can happen that is
unnatural[59]—a discovery that would be easier to accept if a plausible
alternative moral criterion were proposed. Even in the second part, in
which d'Alembert is present—at first asleep, then awake—there is no
real conversation between Mlle de l'Espinasse and d'Alembert. Mlle de
l'Espinasse has a natural curiosity to learn from Bordeu, and she increasingly outgrows the role of the concerned friend of the patient and takes on
that of a full-fledged conversation partner who is capable of learning and

57. Furbank (1992), 322 ff.
58. In the eighteenth century bioethical questions were actively discussed;
Hume's well-known essay "Of Moral Prejudice" is about the impregnation of a
woman who wants a child but not a husband, and the legal problems arising there-
from (1987; 538–44).
59. (1972), 245.

is almost Bordeu's intellectual peer. She is more open intellectually than d'Alembert was in the conversation with Diderot, and Bordeu takes her seriously in a way that d'Alembert obviously never has. In one of the most audacious passages in the *Rêve,* Diderot alludes to the lack of a sexual relationship between Julie and d'Alembert and at the same time to d'Alembert's love for Julie and his painful relationship to his own sexuality.

Mlle de l'Espinasse repeatedly reports on the body language of the sleeping d'Alembert; for instance, during the discussion of alternative methods of reproduction, whose fantastic character seems to be the individual pendant to Hume's self-reproducing worlds, he moves his hands as if he were imitating laboratory instruments.[60] He even quotes Virgil's Fourth Eclogue, which is interpreted, however, not as an anticipation of the birth of Christ, as it was in the Middle Ages, but rather of a materialistic program. Then we read:

> Puis il ajoutait en soupirant: Ô vanité de nos pensées! ô pauvreté de la gloire et de nos travaux ! ô misère, ô petitesse de nos vues! Il n'y a rien de solide, que de boire, manger, vivre, aimer et dormir . . . Mademoiselle de l'Espinasse! où êtes-vous? – Me voilà. – Alors son visage s'est coloré. J'ai voulu lui tâter le pouls; mais je ne sais où il avait caché sa main. Il paraissait éprouver une convulsion. Sa bouche s'était entrouverte. Son haleine était pressée. Il a poussé un profond soupir; et puis un soupir plus faible et plus profond encore. Il a retourné sa tête sur son oreiller et s'est endormi. Je le regardais avec attention, et j'étais toute émue sans savoir pourquoi. Le coeur me battait, et ce n'était pas de peur. Au bout de quelques moments, j'ai vu un léger sourire errer sur ses lèvres. Il disait tout bas: . . . Dans une planète où les hommes se multiplieraient à la manière des poissons, où le frai d'un homme pressé sur le frai d'un femme . . . J'y aurais moins de regret. Il ne faut rien perdre de ce qui peut avoir son utilité. Mademoiselle, si cela pouvait se recueillir, être enfermé dans un flacon et envoyé de grand matin à Needham . . . (Docteur, et vous n'appelez pas cela de la déraison?)[61]

60. (1972), 188.
61. (1972), 189.

What is tasteless but also fascinating about this passage is that Mlle de l'Espinasse is describing d'Alembert's ejaculation as he apparently dreams of her, but she herself seems not to understand what has happened. Her comment that she could not find his hand in order to take his pulse would otherwise be too mischievous; but it is naive,[62] just as are the questions she asks Bordeu. This is not in contradiction to the fact that she is emotionally shaken by this event; one can absolutely be moved by others' emotions whose nature one does not understand but whose power one nonetheless feels. That she does not understand what is going on can only mean, within the literary universe constructed by Diderot, that Mlle de l'Espinasse at least has no sexual relation with d'Alembert and does not know what nocturnal emissions are. Regarding d'Alembert, the story tells us that he definitely has sexual feelings, that he desires Mlle de l'Espinasse—but that this desire dares to live itself out only in dreams, among other reasons because it is a way of later sleeping better and deeper. D'Alembert apparently does not have even sexual dreams often: he needs to be inspired by a materialistic theory that awakens doubts about his theoretical ideas and fame, and turns his attention to earthly pleasures in order to have an ejaculation. Immediately thereafter, he is tormented by regrets: for him, the emission of semen is not an end in itself; he would have liked the semen to be put to use; he envies the external fertilization of fish. It is hard not to think of Wagner's verses in Goethe's *Faust:* "wie sonst das Zeugen Mode war, / erklären wir fur eitel Possen."[63] Later on, d'Alembert expresses his melancholy, which is so different from Diderot's unbounded vitality, by saying that if the inhabitants of Saturn had more sensitivity and thoughts than he, they would be only that much unhappier.[64]

Diderot's treatment of his friend's sex life might be considered shameless, but first of all we should not be surprised by his indiscretion. The author of *Les bijoux indiscrets* had already given it a trial run in

---

62. This is also shown by her curt answer to Bordeu's question about her sexual sensations as a subspecies of haptic sensations: "Je vous entends. Non. Celle-là est toute seule de son espèce; et c'est dommage" (1972; 203).

63. Goethe, *Faust* II, v. 6838 f. "Begetting in the former fashion / We laugh to scorn beside the new" (trans. W. Arndt [New York, 1976]).

64. (1972), 194.

1748, and in *Le neveu de Rameau* there is a passage that Goethe deliberately omitted from his classic translation, which Hegel cited three times
in his *Phänomenologie des Geistes*,[65] and which recounts a kind of rape
of the financier Bertin by his demanding and plump lover, the actress
Hus—an account given by Rameau's nephew, who is a member of
Bertin's household and his parasite, and who thus is guilty of a special
breach of trust.[66] The protest made by *Lui* does not alter the fact that the
author Diderot commits an offense against taste similar to Rameau's. It
is understandable that the real de l'Espinasse and d'Alembert were furi-
ous when people who had read the text, which at that point existed only
in manuscript form, told them what was in it; and also that d'Alembert
absolutely demanded of him that it be burned.[67] In a letter to d'Alembert dating from late September 1769, Diderot says that in the meantime he had torn up the text, of which he was particularly proud, and
now, at his request, had tried to reconstruct it from a few fragments but
was only partly successful.[68] But for whatever causes and—conscious or
unconscious—motives, the dialogue survived in its complete version,
and we can hardly be sorry that it did. For we must, second, grant that
the dialogue is mad but profound,[69] and that in particular Diderot brilliantly connected the sexual episode in *Le rêve de d'Alembert* with both
the kind of relationship between the interlocutors and the subject of the
conversation. In this case at least he was not guilty of pornography, if
the latter consists in the representation of sex acts as an end in itself. The
most impressive description of nocturnal emission is probably found in
a philosophical work that was the greatly admired model for the materialists of the seventeenth and eighteenth centuries, Lucretius's *De rerum
natura*.[70] There, however, it occurs in a didactic poem, the first genre of
objectivity, which did not prevent Lucretius from describing the sexual
fantasies that cause the emission, that is, not only the production of

65. 3.365, 387, 403.
66. (1972), 94 f.
67. *Correspondance*, IX 156.
68. *Correspondance*, IX 156 ff.
69. *Correspondance*, IX 140: "Il n'est pas possible d'être plus profond et plus fou"
(Letter to Sophie Volland, September 11, 1769).
70. 4.1030 ff.

sperm but also the inner point of view, though authorially. In Diderot, the emission is depicted within a conversation, that is, personally, not authorially, and in fact from the external point of view of a person who has no direct access to the inner life of the dreamer, and who fails to perceive the primary phenomenon that expresses the event, the ejaculation—though she does perceive the accompanying phenomena. The point of the whole passage is that Mlle de l'Espinasse is herself the cause of the phenomenon, which she cannot or will not perceive. Bordeu's reaction to her report is typical of him: he immediately sees what has happened and also understands the meaning of the sleeping d'Alembert's remarks, but he avoids taking a position with regard to it. He replies to Mlle de l'Espinasse's question quoted above only by saying, "Auprès de vous, assurément." She does not understand this reference to her own perspective, and misinterprets the proposition in local sense: "Auprès de moi, loin de moi, c'est tout un, et vous ne savez ce que vous dites." Then she tells him that she had hoped that d'Alembert would now have a more peaceful night, and the physiologist coolly observes, "Cela produit ordinairement cet effet," the pronoun *cela* referring, of course, to the emission.

I am not concerned here to discuss the abundance of ideas that come up in the further course of the conversation: on the basis of a critique of essentialism,[71] a deterministic theory grounded in part by denying transworld identity,[72] some thought experiments,[73] and many anecdotes about unusual cases such as Siamese twins, psychic illnesses, and autosuggestion that remind us of Oliver Sacks's books, Bordeu develops a materialistic theory of the mind, according to which, for example, given other neural pathways sense organs entirely different from those we know would be possible,[74] and, in contrast to what Descartes thought, an interruption of consciousness occurs.[75] Genius consists—as Bordeu himself acknowledges, daydreaming and in agreement with Diderot's

71. Cf. (1972), 196.
72. (1972), 232.
73. (1972), 204.
74. (1972), 202. Cf. the related text of Lessing, "Daß mehr als fünf Sinne für den Menschen sein können" (1966; II 686–88).
75. (1972), 231.

theory of acting developed in the *Paradoxe sur le comédien*—in control over one's own sensibility, a control that itself has, of course, a material basis.[76] Abstract knowledge is interpreted purely syntactically.[77] Consciousness is said to be a function of a material network that is also able to produce religious phenomena such as deliverance from pain by concentrating on a Cross, phenomena that Bordeu does not deny but instead seeks to explain materialistically.[78] Dreams should be explained in the same way, including dreams whose rigor is no less than that of waking thought and dreams that lead to emissions such as d'Alembert acknowledges to have had the preceding night.[79] Thus his behavior in the dream is connected with the theoretical content of the dialogue; a vital excitement also ultimately underlies thought. The practical consequences of the materialist turn will be discussed in the third part, whose central theme is the decoupling of sexuality and reproduction. Bordeu teaches, among other things, that masturbation is permissible—a subject that was not an easy one in the eighteenth century,[80] and that was prepared for by d'Alembert's unconsciously performed masturbation. It is striking that Bordeu, like Hume in his second *Enquiry,* traces moral duties to the pleasant and the useful, whether for oneself or for others,[81] but he draws from this radical consequences that challenge the mores of the time, and that the socially and politically conservative Hume avoids. The cautious d'Alembert is absent from this discussion as well: when he is awake he resists theoretical materialism, and it is only when he is asleep that he is drawn into it and satisfies his sexual needs; but when he wakes up he refuses to even discuss practical materialism. Apparently Diderot wants to suggest, as Wilhelm Reich later did, that one of the things preventing the development of a vitalistic materialism is the fear of one's own sexuality. That is, of course, no philosophical argument in

76. (1972), 226 ff.

77. (1972), 237.

78. Cf. (1972), 223.

79. (1972), 229 f.

80. Cf. T. Laqueur (2003). In his impressive monograph on Diderot published in 1866, K. Rosenkranz still had to justify not keeping silent about this subject (II 255, with reference to II 250).

81. (1972), 241.

favor of materialism, but it is seductive as an invitation to sexual revolution, because the latter is extolled as the gateway to new insights. There is an obvious relation to Freud, who on several occasions, for instance at the end of the twenty-first lecture in the *Vorlesungen zur Einführung in die Psychoanalyse,* refers, not, it is true, to the *Rêve de d'Alembert,* but rather to the following sentence from *Le neveu de Rameau,* which anticipates the theory of the Oedipus complex: "Si le petit sauvage était abandonné à lui-même; qu'il conservât toute son imbécillité et qu'il réunît au peu de raison de l'enfant au berceau, la violence des passions de l'homme de trente ans, il tordrait le col à son père, et coucherait avec sa mère."[82] The development of a theory of dreams that on the one hand conceives the dream as the site of astonishing because uncensored creativity and on the other hand transforms it from an argument for idealism into a perfect example of a biologistic conception of the soul is one of Freud's most fateful achievements; and Diderot, thanks to d'Alembert's emission, certainly preceded him in adopting this line of attack. However, whether the truth claim inevitably associated with intelligent creativity can be justified materialistically or biologistically is a question that neither Diderot nor Freud can really answer—or even understand.

82. (1972), 117.

CHAPTER 11

The Space of Conversation

The dialogue artist's capacity for abstraction gives him the right to represent the conversation in such a way that it seems to take place between two pure minds, that is, beings who cannot be assumed to have bodies and thus necessarily occupy a space. Although every artwork is underdetermined in comparison with reality, corporality is not an indispensable characteristic of a person, but it is such a familiar one that the artist does well to explicitly represent it. However, this inevitably raises the question about the space of the conversation and requires that a scenic dialogue be written. Nonetheless, the author can attribute the process of abstraction, which he himself could undertake from the outset, to his interlocutors, who consciously decide to abstract from the place where they are and begin an inward journey. The place in which Boethius encounters the personified Philosophy in the *Consolatio philosophiae* is, like that of the *Crito* and the *Phaedo,* a prison, and he contrasts it with the place where they previously met, a library in his own house, where they often discussed the knowledge of human and divine things.[1] But this opposition between the present and the remembered place is less important to his

---

1. 1.4.3: "haecine est bibliotheca, quam certissimam tibi sedem nostris in laribus ipsa delegeras, in qua mecum saepe de humanarum divinarumque rerum scientia disserebas?"

interlocutor, Philosophy, than that between external locality in general and the inner space of the mind. In her long speech, she reminds Boethius that he has not been exiled from his homeland but has moved away from it himself; the true, that is, the spiritual, homeland is such that someone who resides within its boundaries in no way deserves to become an exile; but someone who voluntarily leaves it by that very act ceases to be worthy of it. "Therefore what moves me is not the sight of this place so much as the sight of your countenance, nor do I seek the library whose walls are adorned with ivory and glass so much as the seat of your mind, in which I have put not books but what constitutes the value of books, namely the maxims of my books of old."[2] Philosophy is concerned with neither libraries nor books but rather with mind and ideas.

The renunciation of outward things is easy for her because she is not a real person, and Boethius's conversation with her thus increasingly becomes a conversation with himself. Where the otherness of the interlocutor continues to exist, however, the question of space arises. Even the souls of the damned, the penitent, and the blessed in Dante's *Divina commedia* all find themselves in a place: the complex relationships among them are mirrored by their spatial relationships, among other things, and Dante's detailed topography of the Beyond constantly sheds light on their respective moral levels. The space may be the underworld of the dialogues of the dead; it may be the oniric space of dialogues that represent a dreamed conversation; it may be an allegorical space, like that in Llull's *Llibre del gentil e dels tres savis,* for instance—but it always remains a space. In Paul Valéry's dialogue of the dead, *Eupalinos,* Phèdre complains that Socrate has separated himself from others—and this is probably a spatial relation. Socrate thereupon draws Phèdre's attention to a river—an object that is primarily spatial, but which Socrate describes as the river of time, which carries everything away with it except for souls, which it casts up upon the bank of the realm of the dead.[3]

2. 1.5.6: "Itaque non tam me loci huius quam tua facies movet nec bibliothecae potius comptos ebore ac vitro parietes quam tuae mentis sedem requiro, in qua non libros sed id quod libris pretium facit, librorum quondam meorum sententias collocavi."
3. (1945), 9 ff.

However, their timelessness does not alter the fact that they can speak with each other—an event that one can hardly imagine as beyond time.

The uninhabitable forest in which Llull the pagan gets lost and into which the wise representatives of the three monotheistic religions withdraw as a neutral place is initially characterized with all the attributes of a realistic *locus amoenus*.[4] It contains springs and brooks, numerous beautiful trees bearing fruit, wild animals such as deer and stags, gazelles, hares, and rabbits, as well as birds of various kinds that sing wonderfully. Thus at first the pagan thinks that an excursion to this place with all there is to see, hear, and smell will overcome his depression, which arises from his suddenly awakened fear that after death he will be nothing. But he soon has to acknowledge that the thought of death cannot be repressed: "Con lo gentil se volc consolar e alegrar en so que vesia e oya e odorava, lo pensament li venc de la mort e l'anitchilament de son esser, e adoncs muntiplicá son coratge en dolor e en tristicia."[5] Nor does anything change when he satisfies another sense and begins to taste the delicious fruits on the trees: as soon as he begins to think of death, his suffering only grows. Only the encounter with the three wise men, who prove to him the existence of God and the Resurrection, frees him from his depression. What matters is arguments, not the beauty of nature, no matter how great it is—that is the point of the prologue to the dialogue. However, Llull bridges the gap between the beauty of nature and the conclusiveness of the arguments by introducing allegorical figures. I have already mentioned Lady Intelligence (p. 189); she appears to the three wise men (before their encounter with the pagan), elegantly clothed and on horseback, in a beautiful meadow with a spring from which the horse drinks. The spring waters five trees, whose peculiarity makes this space into an allegorical one. On the blossoms of the trees letters are written, something that does not occur in nature. These letters stand for the uncreated virtues of God, as well as for the created virtues and the capital vices (which Llull identifies with the *peccats mortals*). Lady Intelligence teaches the wise men to combine these letters in certain ways. Llull thought his combinatory *Ars* (which is still at an initial stage in this early

4. Cf. E. R. Curtius (1961), 202 ff.
5. (1993), 7.

work of his) was a necessary and sufficient foundation for a proof of all Christian dogmas. Here we are not concerned to analyze the rules for combining and excluding communicated by Lady Intelligence and their use in the course of concrete arguments in the philosophy of religion in the four main parts of the dialogue; here we are interested only in the allegorical function of the trees. As was already the case in the famous Porphyrian tree and will be the case in Llull's other works, such as the late work *Arbre de sciencia,* and on down to Descartes, the tree stands for knowledge: a single trunk that branches out into limbs from which blossoms sprout refers to the systematic nature of a comprehensive interpretation of reality. The blossoms, Lady Intelligence says in conclusion, are principles and doctrine for the guidance of erring humans, and the despairing can be consoled by knowledge of this tree.[6]

However, most of the localities depicted in dialogues are realistic, not allegorical, in nature. But the realistic character of a literary representation never prevents it from pointing to something else at the same time, though it does so in a discreet way that does not violate the laws of reality. No path to the place of a philosophical conversation has ever been described in greater detail than the one in the second dialogue of Bruno's *La cena de le ceneri.* The crossing of the Thames in a boat rowed by two ferrymen, one of whom resembles Charon, wading in a muddy puddle that is compared with Avernus, and moving around in circles[7] are all described very precisely; no less realistic is the description of the London rabble. And yet Bruno wants us to read the text allegorically at the same time; in the epistolary preface *(proemiale epistola)* he emphasizes that his description of the steps taken and the crossings made will probably be judged by everyone as more poetic and tropological than historical; Bruno speaks of "moral topography" and compares himself with a painter obsessed with details.[8] Apparently he wants to suggest that his path to his own philosophy has gone to contradictory philosophical schools that are imprisoned in circular reasoning and are doomed to

6. (1993), 11.

7. (1985), I 54, 58, 60.

8. (1985), I 10 f.: "secondo, una descrizion di passi e di passaggi, che piú poetica e tropologica, forse, che istoriale sarà da tutti giudicata; terzo, come confusamente si precipita in una topografia morale."

death. The spaces that are depicted in Plato's *Protagoras* are those of contemporary Attic culture; but they allude to the descent into the underworld *(Nekyia)* in Homer and foreshadow the metaphysical topography
of the Allegory of the Cave. At daybreak, Socrates is awakened by the
young Hippocrates, who brings him news that Socrates already knows,
namely, that Protagoras is sojourning in Athens (310a) and in fact at Callias's, where the two of them head after a long walk and conversation in
Socrates' courtyard. In the passage at 311a6–7, it is twice emphasized that
as a rule, Protagoras stays "inside" *(endon)*; in contrast, Socrates takes his
friend first into the courtyard and then into the city—in both cases, out
into the open; and while they are still in the courtyard they see the sun
come up, which allows Socrates to see Hippocrates blush.[9] However, in
order to engage Protagoras in conversation, they have to go back into a
closed space, and that is not made easy for them. Since they discuss a
question in front of the entrance to Callias's house until they arrive at
a consensus, the doorkeeper—a eunuch, significantly—takes them for
Sophists and will not let them go in; he finally opens the door, reluctantly,
and only after Socrates has explained that he is not a Sophist (314c ff.)—
a bit of information given by Plato to the reader no less than by Socrates
to the eunuch. The two express quotations from the eleventh book of the
Odyssey (315b9, c8) throw light on the function of this impeded entry: it
is the equivalent of a journey to the underworld, or, in the language of the
Republic, a descent into the cave of appearances. And the introduction of
a eunuch points to the fact that the world whose entrance he guards lacks
any pedagogical eros, which Socrates knows about better than any other.
What Socrates sees inside the house is overwhelmingly comic: the three
main Sophists, Protagoras, Hippias, and Prodicus, in three different positions. The first is moving about, followed by a large entourage consisting of foreigners and Athenians whom he has enchanted like Orpheus

---

9. 312a2 f. This suggests, of course, that the ability to blush is like the dawn of
moral daylight—in agreement with the importance of shame in Protagoras's speech
(322c1 ff.). With this brief comment on Hippocrates' body language, Plato shows, in
my opinion, that he stands behind this part of Protagoras's remarks. The crucial conversation depicted in the third part of Shaftesbury's *The Moralists* (1999; 95 ff.), in
which the phenomenon of shame is used as an argument for moral realism (139 f.),
also begins at daybreak.

and bound to him. No one wants to get in his way, and that leads his entourage to engage in peculiar contortions every time he has to turn around. In contrast, Hippias sits on a throne like a judge in the underworld and answers questions as if he were handing down the law. Finally, Prodicus is still lying in his room, wrapped up in a blanket, teaching those who are sitting at his bedside. It is only too bad that Socrates cannot understand what they are talking about, because Prodicus's booming voice echoes within the room (314e ff.). Prodicus's situation expresses in extreme form the fundamental peculiarity of sophistic space: the space is not open but is characterized by power relationships and pretentious behavior (Protagoras being the most dynamic and Prodicus the most lethargic of the three); free and comprehensible communication is not possible in it. It is the space of the cave in the later allegory, which Plato had probably already imagined at the time he wrote the *Protagoras*.[10]

An obvious way of classifying conversational spaces, which is guided by the categories of objectivity, subjectivity, and intersubjectivity, is to divide them into natural, private, and public ones. Since these are to be conversational spaces, all of them involve a plurality of subjects, but to different extents: the public space has no sharp boundaries; the private space excludes. But like the public space, the private space is man-made, while the landscape has the attraction of the nonhuman, the other, and is both relaxing and challenging. I begin with examples of public spaces. The court in which Plato's *Euthyphro* takes place is such a space. But Euthyphro is surprised that Socrates—who is there only because he has been charged—is not in the Lyceum, a gymnasium (2a1 ff.) in which the conversation in *Euthydemus*, for instance, takes place.[11] In general, a space of which Plato was especially fond as the site of Socrates' conversations is the palaestra, that is, the wrestling school. In chapter 5 I noted the homo - erotic intensity of this space. It grows still stronger in the dressing room, which Plato mentions twice: both the conversation in the *Euthydemus* (272e2) and that in the *Lysis* (206e6 f.) take place in such an

10. Cf. Friedländer (1964), I 169 f., II 3. In II 125 the *endon* (*Hp. mi.* 364b5) is similarly interpreted: Hippias's speech is given in a closed space, but the conversation takes place outside.

11. The main conversation in the *Theaetetus* apparently takes place in a gymnasium that is not further specified (144c1 ff.).

apodutērion.[12] Whether Plato's interest in wrestling schools is based on the fact that he himself was a wrestler—and such a good one that he had competed at the Isthmic Games[13]—or whether this anecdote is based instead on the situation of various of his conversations in the palaestra is far less important than the literary function of this place: Plato appeals to the Greeks' agonal instinct and shows that philosophy is a more demanding and worthy form of sport than wrestling. At the same time, Plato subtly transfers to the psychic realm the erotic attraction to which young men will have been repeatedly exposed while wrestling, especially in a culture like the Attic, and which represents a peculiar counterweight to the situation of competition and even of physical fighting. There is a famous scene in the *Charmides* in which the eponymous hero, surrounded by admirers, enters the palaestra of Taureas, where the dialogue is to take place: all eyes are drawn to him, and not only those of Socrates, who confesses to find all young men of this age group pleasing—even the youngest child looks at Charmides (154c6 ff.). If we are not inclined to assume a pre-Freudian theory of childhood sexuality, the function of this remark is probably to indicate that joy in beauty does not presuppose sexual desire. And that is precisely the state that Socrates seeks for himself; in this respect he seems to want to become like a child. When Chaerephon points out to him that Charmides' naked body is still more beautiful than his face, Socrates requires only "one other slight addition" (154d8), which in Plato is always a signal that something is particularly important—that he have a noble soul as well. To make sure of this, he wants to see Charmides' soul rather than his body; but the metaphor remains athletic-erotic: he wants to *undress* his soul (*apedusamen* e5). When Charmides sits down on the bench between Socrates and Critias— everyone on the bench moves aside, hoping Charmides will sit next to him, so that the man sitting on one end has to stand up and the one on the other end falls to the ground—Socrates seems to lose his composure,

---

12. In Plutarch's *Erōtikos,* Bakchon's cousin Anthemion accuses Bacchon's lover, Peisias, of opposing his cousin's marriage because he wants to keep him for himself as long as possible, just as fresh as he is when undressing in the wrestling schools (*Mor.* 749 F).

13. D. L. 3–4, with reference to Dicaearchus.

and his desire increases still more when he gets a glimpse under Charmides' robe (155d f.). But apparently he quickly gets hold of himself, because his capacity for argumentation and abstract discussions does not
visibly suffer from the proximity of the beautiful young man—on the
contrary. In *Lysis* (207b1 ff.) and in *Euthydemus* (273b1 f.) as well, the
boys desired by everyone, Lysis and Clinias, sit next to Socrates, as if mag-
netically drawn to him, whereas their lovers, Hippothales and Ctesippus,
stand opposite them—Plato thus showing their uncontrolled sexual tension, whereas Socrates radiates inner peace. In the *Euthydemus* the two
sophists sit on either side of Socrates and Clinias (271a f.), thus framing them. On the one hand, this makes it look as though Socrates were
caught in their pincers;[14] on the other hand, he occupies a middle position that is, according to Plato, an excellent one.[15] Is it going too far to
interpret the comic episode of the characters at the ends of the bench
standing up and falling down as indicating that Socrates remains, regarding verticality as well, unshakably in the middle? However, although
sexual self-control distinguishes the Platonic Socrates, we cannot deny
that his relationship to his interlocutors is erotic, if curiosity about deeper
levels of another person, a mutual opening up, and even a mutual unveil-
ing and disrobing is part of the erotic. That the Platonic Socrates and his
author reveal themselves only to a limited extent, however, is the foundation of their enduring erotic attraction.

In Athens, the palaestra is a *public place,* in which a free man can take
part in a conversation at least as a listener and a member of a claque:
figures like the two specialists in eristic in the *Euthydemus* are accompanied by a large entourage. In modern times, the place that most corresponds to it is the café, which serves as a central meeting place for urban
intellectuals, although it lacks the athletic and homoerotic dimension.
At least the café in which Diderot and Rameau converse is a kind of
arena, because even if only *Moi* and *Lui* speak, Rameau's loud coughing[16]

---

14. Compare the sitting arrangement in Bruno's *La cena de le ceneri* (1985; I 82).

15. Athens is in the middle between Elea and Magna Graecia (see above, p. 170);
the Greek nation occupies the middle between the Thracians and the Egyptians
(*R.* 435e f.).

16. (1972), 74.

and especially his pantomimes increasingly interest the chess players around them and finally even the passersby, who lean on the windows from the outside. Rameau is no exhibitionist; he is so involved in his performance that he seems not to notice the interest others take in him or even the loud laughter he provokes. "Tous les poussebois avaient quitté leurs échiquiers et s'étaient rassemblés autour de lui. Les fenêtres du café étaient occupées, en dehors, par les passants qui s'étaient arrêtés au bruit. On faisait des éclats de rire à entrouvrir le plafond. Lui n'apercevait rien."[17]

The public nature of this place is in stark contrast to the seclusion of the dining room in which Diderot's *Suite de l'entretien précédent* occurs; indeed, the real conversation between Bordeu and Mlle de l'Espinasse begins only after the servants have withdrawn.[18] Analogously, Gide's *Corydon* takes place in a private apartment, which is filled with books that prove the breadth of the host's intellectual horizon. Similarly, a bold conversation that challenges not the moral but the religious ideas of its own time, such as the one in Bodin's *Colloquium heptaplomeres,* can be conducted only in a private space: arguments in favor of an open society can initially be made only in closed groups. Only slowly, after discussing questions of natural philosophy (including parapsychology), do the seven friends approach the subject of the philosophy of religion, which first appears at the end of the third book and is discussed in the three longer and more fascinating books that follow. The host, the Venetian Catholic Coronaeus, breaks off the third day's conversation, which is beginning to venture into dangerous areas, by arguing that they have to postpone until the following day the question whether a good man is allowed to speak about religion at all; for it is not permissible to mix the sacred and the profane.[19] And then the subject is very cautiously approached, by way of general reflections on the function of dissent and conflict and of remarks on religious wars, tolerance in Islam, and the

17. (1972), 106.
18. (1972), 239.
19. (1857), 111: "Et quoniam a physicis quaestionibus ad metaphysica delapsi sumus, ne sacra profanis misceantur, die crastino decernendum nobis, an viro bono de religione disserere liceat."

possibility of several religions. Only after all this does Coronaeus return to his question of the day before.[20] With subtle irony, Bodin shows how most of the participants initially oppose discussion on various grounds—the Platonist Toralba because human reason is not adequate to the task, the Jew Salomo because no one's religious conviction should be challenged, the skeptic Senamus because the social cost of religious change is too high—until the Lutheran Fridericus defends the view that public discussions of the recognized religion is dangerous and pernicious if they are not based on divine authority, as in the case of Moses, or on military power, as in the case of Mohammed. But private discussions among learned men, he maintains, are extremely fruitful.[21] This is ironic, because Fridericus is by far the most intolerant of the friends, as his remark about Mohammed already suggests and as is clearly demonstrated by his subsequent attack on Salomo, who has up to this point always evaded his attempts to argue about religion with him. However, what Fridericus has in mind is attempts to convert his interlocutors— attempts that are even less palatable because he himself is not prepared to subject his own belief to common examination. But no matter how questionable his motives may be, the correctness of his basic thesis is confirmed by this as well as by the other dialogues on the philosophy of religion that take place either in a dream space, as in Abelard and Nicholas of Cusa, or in the seclusion of an allegorical forest, as in Llull, but never in a public place. Coronaeus's house is an especially appropriate space not only because of the host's intellectual openness; the first-person narrator of the dialogue, who functions as a reader during meals, initially describes Coronaeus's countless books and mathematical and musical instruments, and even his "pantotheca," a large cabinet that contains all of reality's forms of being, whether in actuality or in representation— a man-made microcosm that fits well with the encounter of the most important religions.[22]

20. (1857), 125.
21. (1857), 126: "Et quoniam a physicis quaestionibus ad metaphysica delapsi sumus, ne sacra profanis misceantur, die crastino decernendum nobis, an viro bono de religione disserere liceat."
22. (1857), 2 f.

In antiquity private spaces were already important sites for philosophical conversation. Callias's house has already been mentioned, but
the stream of visitors makes it almost a public space like an adult education center. Similarly, Gorgias's residence in Callicles' house transforms
it at least partly into a public space.[23] The private can be constituted as
such only where there are specifically public spaces; where these are
lacking or limited to state functions, private rooms have to be made regularly available for quasi-public purposes. Agathon's banquet is probably a private affair; however, the unexpected appearance of Aristodemus
and Alcibiades, as well as Agathon's remarks at *Symposium* 174e5 ff. and
212d1 f., shows that at least at a victory celebration people of the same social standing could not be turned away without giving any reason. In general, the uninvited and the belated guest are *topoi* of *deipnon* and *symposion* literature; they produce dramatic movement.[24] The Hellenistic villa,
on the other hand, is truly a private space, among other reasons because
it is remote from the center of public life, that is, the city. Only invited
guests or real friends look in; the rivalry that can easily arise before an
audience—sometimes even an unknown one—such as characterizes,
for example, Socrates' duels with Protagoras and Gorgias, is absent here.
As was shown in chapter 4 (p. 87 f.), the villa dialogue corresponds to the
ethical innovations of the Hellenistic period, especially its individualism
and the high value it put on symmetrical relationships. It is significant
that in his villa dialogues Cicero even takes pains to overcome the asymmetry that remains in this genre—that one of the interlocutors is the
host, and the other or others the guests who must go to him. Cicero,
Hortensius, Catulus, and Lucullus all had their villas in the Campania;
that suggests the fiction that the friends had invited each other for conversations on three successive days. Interestingly, the dialogue called
Hortensius takes place in Lucullus's villa, *Catulus* in that of Catulus, and
Lucullus in that of Hortensius: this suggests that the host—usually but
not necessarily—is not himself the leader of the conversation. This also
explains why Cicero does not set any of the discussions in his own villa:
he can thus ensure that he has the lion's share in the conversation in the

23. Cf. *Grg.* 447b7 f.
24. Cf. Xen. *Smp.* 11 f.

trilogy as a whole.[25] In the revised version of the work, Varro becomes Cicero's (and Atticus's) interlocutor, and Cicero goes to great lengths to show how on the one hand he and his friend Atticus, who is staying with him, and on the other hand Varro all take pains to seek one another out (Varro was older, but only Cicero was a *vir consularis*). As soon as Cicero and Atticus hear that Varro has arrived at his own nearby estate the preceding evening, and that only the fatigue of the trip has prevented him from immediately visiting them, they hasten to go there. When they are not far from his villa they see him coming toward them, apparently on his way to Cicero's estate; they return with him to his own house, where the conversation takes place.[26]

In the third book of *De finibus*, written in the year 45 after Cato's suicide, the encounter between Cicero and Marcus Porcius Cato takes place in a neutral place—in the library at the villa of a third person, the young Lucius Licinius Lucullus, the son of the previously mentioned statesman and general. Cicero has come from his estate in Tusculum in order to borrow books, and in fact he is looking for Aristotle's didactic writings;[27] there he happens to meet Cato, who immediately tells him that he would have already visited him had he known that he was residing at Tusculum. With a few deft strokes Cicero makes clear the difference in character and intellect that separates him from Cato, who is surrounded *(circumfusum)* by books by the Stoics and "devours" *(helluari)* them. Cicero does not scold Cato for his enthusiasm for reading, in which he has also indulged in the Curia, because his devotion to the state has not suffered from it, and he has rightly ignored the judgment of the masses.[28] His participation in the upbringing of his nephew Lucullus is also positively depicted, even if that of Cicero, who is not a relative of the boy, was no less important. And yet it is impossible to overlook Cicero's slightly condescending tone; despite his eulogy "Cato," he clearly considers himself enormously superior to the bookworm: partly as a man of the world, but also partly as

25. Presumably, however, Hortensius and Catulus decide, together with Cicero, during a visit to the latter's villa reported at the beginning of the trilogy, to go together to Lucullus's villa, which has many works of art (frg. 1 Grilli).

26. *Ac. Po.* 1.1.1.

27. 3.3.10.

28. 3.2.7.

an intellectual, who on the one hand structures his reading more distinc-
tively and selectively and on the other is more curious and does not allow
adherence to a school to determine what he should read. However, Cato
is disappointed that Cicero has not come to borrow any Stoic writings.
The villa in which Augustine and his friends philosophize in the Cassiciacum dialogues is simpler; there is no mention of a library. Instead, the
conversation in *De beata vita* begins on a cold November day,[29] in a warm
bath, but ends in a meadow after the weather warms up.[30] On the other
hand, the meta-conversation in Zacharias's *Ammonius* takes place in a
church—the cathedral of Berytos (Beirut).[31] The site is, of course, deliberately chosen, and not only because a church is generally suitable for a
religious subject and provides an appropriate contrast to the *Mouseion* in
Alexandria, where the second of the reported main conversations takes
place,[32] but also because the main subject of the dialogue is the proof that
the world was created by God—*theou dēmiourgēma*.[33] However, the architect of the cathedral whose beauty is praised is mentioned twice;[34] and
this prepares the way for the thesis that despite its splendor the world
cannot be identified with God.

One of the advantages of the villa as a place for philosophical discussion is its distance from Rome and the sometimes life-threatening
politics practiced there. Cicero repeatedly notes that the political type to
which he considers himself to belong does not engage in politics out of a
desire for power or a lack of intellectually fulfilling alternatives but rather
out of a sense of responsibility, and that his real interests are at least as
theoretical as practical in nature. The "otium cum dignitate" for which
the noble villa symbolically stands is opposed to political "negotium."[35]
After Caesar's rise to dictatorial power, there is something compensatory
in this leisure, and Cicero was honest enough to see and acknowledge

29. 2.6.
30. 4.23.
31. Among the pagan dialogues, the first book of Varro's *De re rustica* takes
place in a temple (that of Tellus).
32. 107, 36 ff. Minniti Colonna.
33. 94.5 Minniti Colonna.
34. *dēmiourgou* 96, 56, and 62 Minniti Colonna.
35. Cf. Zoll (1962), 136.

that.[36] For example, Atticus interrupts Cicero when the latter wants Varro to tell him the news from Rome. The subject is too depressing, he says (the dialogue takes place in the summer of 45, that is, during Cicero's forced political inactivity), and it would be more interesting to hear what Varro himself is writing about at the moment.[37] But also in *De fato*, which takes place after Caesar's murder, the conversation between Cicero and the designated consul, Aulus Hirtius, quickly moves to the abstract heights of the problem of determinism and the logical and other questions connected with it. The political crisis is dangerous; and the two statesmen consider how it can be overcome and how peace and leisure can be maintained, as their legal duty almost requires them to do.[38] But "otio" is probably the cue that moves Hirtius to ask Cicero about his rhetorical and philosophical works. It is hardly surprising that both men would die a violent death shortly afterward; anyone who is discussing three-valued logic on the eve of a civil war will necessarily succumb to the brutal will to power of a man like Mark Antony. And yet we ought not deny the dignity of this behavior.

In *De oratore* Scaevola, seeing a plane tree, turns to his son-in-law and asks why they should not imitate Socrates in the *Phaedrus* and sit down on the grass; with its spreading branches, Crassus's plane tree casts no less shadow than that of Socrates, which owes its eminence less to the "little rivulet" described by Plato than to Plato's eloquence.[39] The latter remark refers to the literary character of Plato's text; and it goes without saying that Cicero seeks thereby to allude to the fictional nature of his own work.[40] By citing Plato's *Phaedrus* at the beginning and at the end of the work (3.61.228 ff.), Cicero presents *De oratore* as a Roman counterpart to the Greek model. However, his changes are worth noting. That

36. Div. 2.2.4 ff.

37. *Ac. Po.* 1.1.2: "<Tum> Atticus 'Omitte ista quae nec percunctari nec audire sine molestia possumus quaeso' inquit 'et quaere potius ecquid ipse novi.'"

38. "cum ad me ille venisset, primo ea, quae erant cotidiana et quasi legitima nobis, de pace et de otio" (1.2).

39. 1.7.28: "Cur non imitamur, Crasse, Socratem illum, qui est in Phaedro Platonis? Nam me haec tua platanus admonuit, quae non minus ad opacandum hunc locum patulis est diffusa ramis, quam illa, cuius umbram secutus est Socrates, quae mihi videtur non tam ipsa acula, quae describitur, quam Platonis oratione crevisse.

40. Cf. above, p. 62 f.

224 The Universe of the Philosophical Dialogue

Crassus has cushions brought in points to the higher level of urbanization in his time as compared with that of Socrates and Plato. But precisely because it is more urban, classical Roman culture is much more sentimental than Attic culture was; it longs for nature, into which Socrates merely follows Phaedrus, rather than deliberately withdrawing into it. In Plato, the overwhelming majority of Socrates' conversations take place in the city. Even if the two men being on the banks of the Ilissos is appropriate to the erotic theme of the dialogue and even if through Socrates Plato offers one of the most enchanting descriptions of a landscape in all of Greek literature, which appeals in a few lines to the senses of sight, smell, taste, and hearing (230b2–c5), Phaedrus expresses his astonishment that Socrates, like a foreigner, does not know the place at all. Socrates replies that that is because he is eager to learn, and only people in the city, not fields and trees, can teach him things (230d3 ff.). He is interested less in myths, like the one about Boreas's rape of Oreithyia, and rationalistic criticism of it, than in self-knowledge (229c ff.). This remark is not egocentric because shortly before Socrates had made it clear that knowledge of himself also implies knowledge of Phaedrus (228a5 f.). Socrates' anthropocentrism does not prevent him, however, from allowing himself to be inspired by the magic of the place.[41]

The excursion into nature remains exceptional for Plato's Socrates. On the other hand, in Plato's sole dialogue without Socrates, the Laws, the Athenian stranger, Clinias and Megillus slowly move through a Cretan landscape whose unevenness is mentioned at the beginning of the discussion of the subject and related to the light weapons carried by the Cretans (625c). This might be seen as the beginning of geostrategic science—but no matter how much the latter requires observation of the nature of the land, one cannot fail to recognize that its true interest concerns its political consequences. The introductory remarks concerning the walk to be taken do mention the trees that cast shade, but the goal remains crucial: the grotto and temple of Zeus (625a f.)—an artifact with religious significance. In Cicero, in contrast, there is a genuine interest in untouched nature. The noble villa outside Rome is certainly also a status symbol; but in moving words in the prologue to the first

41. 238c9 ff., 262d2 ff., 263d5 f.

and second books of *De legibus,* Cicero, unlike the Platonic Socrates, expresses his hope that the encounter with nature will lead to a regeneration of his soul. However, the relation is sentimental insofar as nature interests him only because of its effects on human beings—its moral no less than its aesthetically inspiring effects. The first clash in *De legibus,* a three-way dialogue among Cicero, his brother Quintus, and Atticus that takes place near Arpinum, the two brothers' hometown, brilliantly expresses the dialectic between nature and its poetic fashioning. Atticus recognizes the grove and the oak that Marius is said to have planted—because it is familiar to him from Cicero's poem "Marius" on the other great man from Arpinum. "Lucus quidem ille et haec Arpinatium quercus agnoscitur, saepe a me lectus in Mario: si enim manet illa quercus, haec est profecto; etenim est sane vetus." Thus he makes his identification subject to the reservation that that oak is still alive; and Quintus reacts to this by remarking that it is alive and will always be alive, because it was sown by the mind, and no tree can be sown by a farmer that is as enduring as that sown by a poet's verse: "Manet vero Attice noster et semper manebit: sata est enim ingenio. Nullius autem agricolae cultu stirps tam diuturna quam poetae versu seminari potest." Atticus sees this as praise for his brother, which Quintus acknowledges, and adds that this oak of Marius's will not fail to be at this place so long as Latin literature remains alive. Even when age and storms have destroyed it, it will survive—thanks to the power of Cicero's poetry; for through the power of memory many things can persist in many places longer than in reality: "multaque alia multis locis diutius commemoratione manent quam natura stare potuerunt."[42] Only here does Atticus turn to Marcus Tullius Cicero to learn whether the anecdote that Marius himself planted this oak is true. Cicero refuses to give a direct answer, and asks instead whether it is true that not far from Atticus's home in Rome the Romulus who became Quirinus met Proculus Julius, and that not far from Atticus's home in Athens Aquilo, that is, Boreas, raped Oreithyia. Atticus stubbornly repeats his question, which is also asked by others, and Cicero has to explain what his counterquestion meant—that the poet is not a witness but should not be seen as mendacious for that reason: "Et mehercule

42. 1.1.1.f.

226 The Universe of the Philosophical Dialogue

ego me cupio non mendacem putari, sed tamen nonnulli isti Tite noster faciunt inperite, qui in isto periculo non ut a poeta sed ut a teste veritatem exigant."[43] This provides the occasion for observations concerning the difference between poetry and historiography and for Atticus's request that Cicero write a historical work.

A comparison with the beginning of the *Phaedrus*, to which Cicero's text clearly alludes,[44] is worthwhile here. Certainly, the author Cicero's self-praise is striking: the conversation begins with a reference to his poem—now lost, probably fortunately—and quickly returns to him and his further literary plans. Thus nature appears refracted through contemporary poetry, whereas in Plato it appears refracted through an ancient myth. Socrates is not interested in a rationalistic interpretation of this myth—not because it would be false, but because it would be a distraction from more important tasks; in contrast, Cicero clearly indicates that myths do not concern truth. He mentions several myths, both Greek and Roman, whereas Plato limits himself to one; and he also subordinates recent Roman history to the sovereign right of poetry, from which myth building is not distinguished. Cicero agrees with Plato in maintaining that poetry immortalizes, and he takes the metaphor of sowing from the *Phaedrus* (276e7). However, it has lost any sexual connotation (just as Cicero's *Laelius* eliminates any homoerotic dimension from the ideal of friendship).

De legibus is a literary work that deals with law and politics. Whereas the prologue to the first book moves nature into the context of poetry, and thus must be read reflexively, the prologue to the second book is concerned with the relations between nature and politics, which is the true subject of the dialogue. Atticus suggests that they continue their conversation on an island in the little river Fibrenum. Cicero agrees, because he likes to go there to think, write, or read. The encounter with nature in the first book had already had a beneficial effect on Atticus. He had, contrary to his Epicurean profession of faith, granted Cicero that nature is guided by a divine spirit, and even added that he was not afraid

43. 1.1.4.

44. 1.1.3 refers to *Phdr.* 229c ff., 2.3.6 to *Phdr.* 230b5 ff. In 1.5.15 the *Laws*, the thematic model of *De legibus*, is explicitly cited.

that one of his fellow Epicureans might hear him, because of the bird-song and the rushing of the river.[45] The voice of nature thus drowns out the pressure of society. There is something purifying about it, because it throws a person back on himself, and allows him to deepen his subjectivity by temporarily distancing him from others. Atticus cannot get enough of nature, and rejects the splendid villas with their marble floors and paneled ceilings. Indeed, he sees a connection between the subject and the setting of the conversation. Cicero's philosophy of law is based on the theory of natural law; "natura" was already mentioned in 1.5.16 and 1.6.18. Just as in his observations on law Cicero rightly traces everything back to nature, so nature rules over everything that is needed for resting and refreshing the mind. "Itaque ut tu paulo ante de lege et de iure disserens ad naturam referebas omnia, sic in his ipsis rebus quae ad requietem animi delectationemque quaeruntur, natura dominatur."[46] However, Atticus is surprised that Cicero enjoys the place so much. Cicero mentions its beauty and its value for health, and also emphasizes that it is his and Quintus's true home. Here are their sacred objects and many traces of their ancestors, here is the house inhabited by his grandfather and rebuilt by his father, in which he himself was born; he is happy to show Atticus his cradle. Atticus is astonished that Cicero calls Arpinum his true home, and he asks ironically if Cicero has two hometowns. Cicero emphatically agrees: everyone born in a *municipium* has two hometowns, a natural one and a political one, his birthplace and Rome. We must prefer the latter, which as a whole state bears the name of *res publica;* we have to be willing to die for it, to devote ourselves to it. But the homeland where we were born is no less sweet than the other. Never will he deny it the name of "home," even if the other is greater.[47] To be sure, Cicero's remarks have their starting point in the complex

---

45. 1.7.21.

46. 2.1.2.

47. 2.2.5: "Ego mehercule et illi et omnibus municipibus duas esse censeo patrias, unam natur<ae, alter>am civitatis . . . sed necesse est caritate eam praestare <e>qua rei publicae nomen universae civitatis est, pro qua mori et cui nos totos dedere et in qua nostra omnia ponere et quasi consecrare debemus. Dulcis autem non multo secus est ea quae genuit quam illa quae excepit. Itaque ego hanc meam esse patriam prorsus numquam negabo, dum illa sit maior, haec in ea contineatur."

constitutional structure of the Roman republic. But they can easily be generalized: the relationship between local, national, and global dimensions remains a central theme in every political philosophy. One can only admire Cicero for having situated the conversation in Arpinum, thereby representing the dimension of nature that complements, as it were, *De re publica.* The earlier work ends with Scipio's dream and its glance into the immense cosmos that includes and transcends even the Roman state: from the point of view of the universe, the earth seems small, and so, a fortiori, does the Roman Empire;[48] the desire for glory is relativized in a salutary way.[49] *De legibus,* on the other hand, is concerned with the small units out of which this state is composed. In small things as in great, it is nature that supports the state—the rivers and birds of the homeland no less than the stars in the heavens.

In addition to the earth and the firmament, there is another, broader space that can inspire philosophical thoughts, the sea. The view of its immensity and the movement of its waves provides the context of Minucius Felix's *Octavius.* The dialogue begins with three friends' excursion to Ostia, where they take a walk on the beach at daybreak.[50] It is autumn, thus no longer so hot, and they enjoy the breeze and the feeling of their feet sinking into the sand.[51] The sea seems to them to smooth the sand into a carpet; it wets their feet in a regular rhythm and then withdraws again. While they are walking, Octavius first recounts his ship voyage; on their way back, they notice the boats, which have been put on oaken blocks in order to protect them from the decay that emerges from the soil,[52] and they meet children who are skipping stones on the water. The child whose stone has gone farthest and skipped most often is declared

48. 6.16.16: "iam vero ipsa terra ita mihi parva visa est, ut me imperii nostri quo quasi punctum eius attingimus paeniteret." Cf. *Ac. Pr.* 2.41.127 and the analogous argument regarding the contemplation of immeasurable time, *Tusc.* 5.25.70 f.

49. 6.19.20. H.-J. Syberberg took up this idea at the end of his *Hitler. Ein Film aus Deutschland.*

50. The model is obviously a conversation recorded by Aulus Gellius (18.1), with Favorinus as judge.

51. 2.4: "ut et aura adspirans leniter membra vegetaret et cum eximia voluptate molli vestigio cedens harena subsideret."

52. 3.5: "ubi subductae naviculae substratis roboribus a terrena labe suspensae quiescebant."

the winner.[53] It is here that the discussion of religion begins. It is obvious that the one sea over which Octavius has traveled to Rome is to be interpreted as an illustration of the one God who laps around and courts the friends, but also withdraws. The children's stone throwing is an attempt to advance into the sea, and it cleverly makes the transition to the effort to approach through thinking God, whom one feels but cannot see. The analogy, which is used later on in order to illustrate this, is that of the wind;[54] and it is mentioned several times in the prologue.[55] Similarly, the boats that are protected from the earth and the decay that emerges from it probably allude to souls.[56] Of course, Minucius Felix's description of the walk along the beach is successful realistic literature independent of its relation to the later conversation; but in view of his admiration for Plato,[57] we can assume that he would have liked it to be read symbolically as well.

Cicero's depiction of nature remains anthropocentric insofar as he is chiefly concerned with its purifying or elevating effect on human beings. In contrast, in the work of Augustine, nature seems to be enjoyed as an end in itself—or rather, to be more precise, as the site of the manifestation of a divine order that is, for instance, mirrored in the animal world and whose sublimity paradoxically also shines through the actual ugliness. As they are going to the bath, Augustine and his friends come upon cocks fighting in front of the doorway; they have to wait until the battle is over. But the time is not wasted, because the beauty of reason manifests itself everywhere to the eyes of those who love, reason that guides all knowing and unknowing beings, and attracts its admirers in every way and everywhere it wants to be sought.[58] For reason rules even in what is without reason. The beauty of the cocks, the elegance and

53. 3.6: "is se in pueris victorem ferebat, cuius testa et procurreret longius et frequentius exsiliret."

54. 32.5.

55. The word *flatibus* is used in 3.3 and 32.5. See also *aura* in 2.4.

56. Cf. 34.9 ff.

57. 19.14, 23.2, 26.12, 34.6.

58. *Ord.* 1.8.25: "Quid enim non ambiunt, qua non peragrant oculi amantum, ne quid undeunde innuat pulchritudo rationis cuncta scientia et nescientia modificantis et gubernantis, quae inhiantes sibi sectatores suos trahit quacumque atque ubique se quaeri iubet?"

purposefulness of their movements, and the construction of the social hierarchy fascinate the friends; for them, even the formlessness of the cocks' cries and the movement of the defeated cock somehow correspond to natural laws and are therefore beautiful.[59] The basic philosophical problem of *De ordine,* which was discussed in chapter 3, also manifests itself here: it remains undetermined whether the order is characterized by specific axiological qualities or simply by the fact that it is order. The question raised shortly afterward as to where in the world there is no law and where the rule of the better is not found[60] is of a rhetorical nature (which it probably should be) only when "law" means "natural law" and "the better" means "the stronger." That is Spinoza's position, which is not very appropriate for a Christian Neoplatonist. Nonetheless, the immediately following terms *umbra* and *imitatio* point to a dimension of transcendence. But the relationship of the latter to the law, which governs the distribution of power among organisms as well as among men, remains just as unclear as that between sense perception and reason, on which the friends reflect in view of their experience.[61]

In *De legibus,* Atticus agrees with Cicero that physical proximity to a place revives the memory of what occurred there, and acknowledges that in Athens what fascinates him even more than the artworks is the memory of the important men who had lived, sat, and argued there; he eagerly contemplates their gravestones.[62] Cicero returned to this idea in the prologue to the fifth book of *De finibus bonorum et malorum*—in a passage that David Hume, a connoisseur of Cicero, used to support his own theory of the association of ideas, which is based on the three factors of similarity, proximity in space and time, and causal connection.[63] The conversation in *De finibus* V takes place in the year 79 B.C., on the grounds of the Academy, which had been abandoned since Athens was

---

59. 1.8.25: "et in uoce atque motu deforme totum et eo ipso naturae legibus nescio quo modo concinnum et pulchrum." Cf. the analogous passage on stupidity, 2.4.11.

60. 1.8.26: "ubi non lex? ubi non meliori debitum imperium?"

61. 1.8.26: "quid in nobis esset, quod a sensibus remota multa quaereret, quid rursum, quod ipsorum sensuum inuitatione caperetur."

62. 2.2.4.

63. Treatise 1.3.8. (supplement from the "Appendix").

plundered by Sulla's army in 86. Marcus Pupius Piso begins by asking whether nature or a delusion is the reason we are fascinated more by the sight of places where famous people have resided than by their writings—so great is the power of reminding that inhabits places.[64] Quintus, Atticus, Cicero, and finally his cousin Lucius Tullius Cicero all agree and add examples that characterize their respective interests. Cicero even believes he has seen Carneades himself, but then the place seems to him to have been robbed of his own voice.[65] What is important is that the five visitors are not mere tourists. Piso emphasizes that such efforts are intellectually demanding only if they aid the imitation of the greatest men; if it is simply a matter of seeking traces of past ages, they are just signs of curiosity.[66] "Imitari" is the crucial concept,[67] and once again we must read this passage reflexively: *De finibus* is itself an expression of the claim that Cicero has succeeded in turning into a productive imitation the associations connected with the places where Plato and the other scholarchs of the Academy lived.

The depiction of a *locus amoenus* as the appropriate setting for a philosophical conversation does not end with Plato and Cicero; it is found, for instance, in Methodius's *Symposion* (7 f.), in Eberhard's *Dialogus Ratii et Everardi* (251), in Shaftesbury's *The Moralists*,[68] and at the beginning of the first of Berkeley's *Three Dialogues between Hylas and Philonous*.[69] Characteristically, it is Philonous who describes the attraction of the place, just as it is he who in the second dialogue praises the more dramatic duties of the earth, which has an "agreeable wildness" and fills our mind with "pleasing horror."[70] Why is it he and not Hylas who says this? It signals from the outset that Berkeley's empirical immaterialism does not make it more difficult to enjoy nature. It is probably directed against Malebranche, the philosopher who, apart from

64. 5.1.2: "tanta vis admonitionis inest in loci."
65. 5.2.4.
66. 5.2.6: "ista studia, si ad imitandos summos viros spectant, ingeniosorum sunt; sin tantum modo ad indicia veteris memoriae cognoscenda, curiosorum."
67. It is repeated in the next sentence and again two sentences later.
68. (1999), 40, 95 ff. See also the dream that foreshadows the actual meeting, 26 f.
69. (1977), 149.
70. (1977), 195.

Locke, had the greatest influence on Berkeley; at the beginning of Male-branche's *Entretiens sur la métaphysique et sur la religion,* Theodore suggests to Ariste that they leave the places outside, which are enchanting but do not promote concentration, and go inside; one has to withdraw into oneself and track down the inner truth. "Mais pour cela il est necessaire que je quitte ces lieux enchantez qui charment nos sens, & qui par leur varieté partagent trop un esprit tel que le mien. . . . Allons nous renfermer dans vôtre cabinet, afin de rentrer plus facilement en nous-mêmes. Tâchons que rien ne nous empêche de consulter l'un & l'autre nôtre maître commun, la Raison universelle. Car c'est la verité interieure qui doit présider à nos entretiens."[71] In contrast, the frame conversation in Solger's aesthetic dialogue *Erwin* takes place outside, in beautiful nature; and when Adelbert asks him with concern whether the rushing brook will not drown out his voice, his friend replies, "I think it should instead, like a musical accompaniment, maintain the soul in the cheerful enjoyment of this nature, which is what first makes us really receptive to the beautiful."[72]

In Shaftesbury, the observation of purposefulness in the structure of individual organisms leads to reflections on the teleology of the whole world: Theocles asks Philocles, "Who better than yourself can show the structure of each plant and animal body, declare the office of every part and organ, and tell the uses, ends, and advantages to which they serve? How therefore should you prove so ill a naturalist in this whole, and understand so little the anatomy of the world and Nature, as not to discern the same relation of parts, the same consistency and uniformity in the universe!"[73] At the beginning of the decisive third part, Theocles allows himself to be inspired by the *genius loci:* "Here, Philocles, we shall find our sovereign genius, if we can charm the genius of the place (more chaste and sober than your Silenus) to inspire us with a truer song of Nature, teach us some celestial hymn, and make us feel divinity present in the solemn places of retreat."[74] He then addresses a kind of hymn

---

71. (1965), 29. The last sentence alludes to Augustine, vera rel. 39.72.

72. (1971), 4.

73. (1999), 62. In Lessing's *Ernst und Falk,* the observation of ants leads to a discussion of civil society (1966; II 695).

74. (1999), 97.

to nature—"supremely fair and sovereignly good! all-loving and all-lovely, all-divine! whose looks are so becoming and of such infinite grace; whose study brings such wisdom, and whose contemplation such delight"[75]—entirely in accord with Shaftesbury's notion that God's existence (which is, he claims, presupposed by every theory of revelation, and thus cannot be grounded in revelation) can be proven only by the beauty and harmony of nature. However, Shaftesbury is more a Platonist than a Spinozist; in his hymn the address to nature as "impowered creatress" is followed by an address to God as "impowering Deity, supreme creator." For the skeptically inclined Philocles, who only at the end allows himself to be infected by Theocles' enthusiasm,[76] the real problem is the existence of human beings with all their faults; and when Theocles turns toward him after ending his hymn, Philocles remarks ironically that he would have preferred that Theocles had been even more caught up in his ecstasy and had not noticed him at all.[77] However, such an absolute enthusiasm for nature would be hostile to the intersubjective occurrence of a conversation; and we begin to understand why Socrates only seldom went out of the city. At least with Philocles, Shaftesbury introduced an ironic counterweight to his own enthusiasm for nature; the critical sense of the Enlightenment protected him from slipping into kitsch. On the other hand, there is no irony whatever in Heidegger's invocation of the healing expanse of Russian forests in his *Abendgespräch in einem Kriegsgefangenlager in Rußland zwischen einem Jüngeren und einem Älteren.*[78]

Early on it was realized that the topos of the *locus amoenus* can easily come to seem hackneyed. In the frame conversation in Plutarch's

---

75. (1999), 98.

76. (1999), 125: "Your genius, the genius of the place, and the Great Genius have at last prevailed." Accordingly, Philocles fears that on leaving this place and Theocles he will suffer a relapse (145).

77. (1999), 99. To this corresponds Theocles' enthusiastic description of the beauties of the desert and of a lonely forest (122 ff.).

78. (1995), 205 ff. Later in the conversation, a role is played by the category of the desert, "the geographical idea" being translated "to the event of the desolation of the world and of human existence" (212). As always in Heidegger, generalities from the philosophy of history replace the analysis of concrete moral and political responsibilities: the world wars are "for their part already and only a consequence of the desolation that has been eating away at the earth for centuries" (211).

Erōtikos Flavian demands from the narrator, Plutarch's son Autobulos, that he give up meadows, shadows, ivy, and the other props that Plato's imitators use.[79] But no one has dealt with the *locus amoenus* more wittily than Oscar Wilde, in his dialogue *The Decay of Lying*. The conversation between Vivian and Cyril takes place in the library of a manor in Nottinghamshire—we think of the third and fourth book of *De finibus*. But whereas Cicero makes fun of the bookworm Cato, Wilde obviously indentifies with Vivian, who rejects Cyril's request that they go outside on a beautiful afternoon and enjoy nature. "Enjoy nature! I am glad to say that I have entirely lost that faculty. People tell us that Art makes us love Nature more than we loved her before; that it reveals her secrets to us; and that after a careful study of Corot and Constable we see things in her that had escaped our observation. My own experience is that the more we study Art, the less we care for Nature. What Art really reveals to us is Nature's lack of design, her curious crudities, her extraordinary monotony, her absolutely unfinished condition." Cyril says that Vivian need not look at the landscape, he can just lie in the grass, smoke, and talk—thus the reminiscence of Plato's *Phaedrus,* which is caricatured, of course, by the introduction of the reference to smoking. But Vivian refuses this as well. "But Nature is so uncomfortable. Grass is hard and lumpy and damp, and full of dreadful black insects. Why, even Morris's poorest workman could make you a more comfortable seat than the whole of Nature can."[80] Instead, Vivian wants to stay in the library and correct the proofs of his essay, which he finally reads to Cyril and discusses with him. The basic theses of his aesthetic essay fully justify his behavior: Vivian makes a radical break with the theory of mimesis. The basis of art, he says, is conscious lying. Wilde is thus in functional agreement with Plato but with a different evaluation: Nothing explains America's vulgarity better than the fact that it celebrates as a national hero a man who was not able to lie, as the well-known story of the cherry tree assumes, which is of course itself an invention.[81] Far from being an imitation of reality, as the naturalists imagined, great art is a product of the imagination's revolt against

79. *Mor.* 749A.
80. (1966), 970.
81. (1966), 980.

reality. "In literature we require distinction, charm, beauty and imaginative power. We don't want to be harrowed and disgusted with an account of the doings of the lower orders."[82] The only real persons are those who have never existed; they are an expression of the artist's creativity. "The justification of a character in a novel is not that other persons are what they are, but that the author is what he is."[83] If it is possible to speak of imitation, then it would be in the opposite direction: it is life that imitates art. "Schopenhauer has analyzed the pessimism that characterizes modern thought, but Hamlet invented it. The world has become sad because a puppet was once melancholy. . . . Robespierre came out of the pages of Rousseau."[84] Various witty anecdotes are told to confirm this thesis, Vivian implying that they are good inventions[85]—how could it be otherwise? Cyril finds his thesis interesting, but he wants to know whether it holds only for (human) life or also for nature. Vivian affirms the latter, in the mode of Berkeley's subjective idealism, but with the additional twist that our perception is a function of our artistic education:

> Nature is no great mother who has borne us. She is our creation. It is in our brain that she quickens to life. Things are because we see them, and what we see, and how we see it, depends on the Arts that have influenced us. To look at a thing is very different from seeing a thing. One does not see anything until one sees its beauty. Then, and then only, does it come into existence. At present, people see fogs, not because there are fogs, but because poets and painters have taught them the mysterious loveliness of such effects. There may have been fogs for centuries in London. I dare say there were. But no one saw them, and so we do not know anything about them. They did not exist till Art had invented them.[86]

82. (1966), 974.
83. (1966), 975.
84. (1966), 983.
85. Think of the story of a friend named Hyde who, as in R. L. Stevenson's famous story, tramples a child, though inadvertently, and is pursued by a mob before finally being saved by a surgeon. "As he passed out, the name on the brass door-plate of the surgery caught his eye. It was 'Jekyll.' At least it should have been" (1966; 984).
86. (1966), 986.

Wilde's paradox can be defused if we note that he distinguishes between being and existence. But then constructivism is false on the level of being: nature was always there, but it first appears in existence when it is perceived in its beauty, which was obviously already there. But by his own admission, Vivian is not concerned with consistency; like his author, he wants to stimulate and provoke, not set forth a fully elaborated aesthetic theory.[87] After he has reinterpreted nature as an imitation of art, he finally deigns to appear on the terrace, quoting Alfred Tennyson: "At twilight nature becomes a wonderfully suggestive effect, and is not without loveliness, though perhaps its chief use is to illustrate quotations from poets. Come! We have talked long enough."[88]

So far as I can see, the sole philosophical dialogue that takes place in a moving, enclosed space is Leibniz's *Dialogue entre Poliandre et Theophile*—in a coach. It ends with the arrival at the inn.[89] (Part of Jean-Baptiste Clamence's verbal outpouring in Albert Camus's *La Chute* occurs on a ship; but the work is not a dialogue, if only because Clamence's victim only listens.) The decline of the genre of the dialogue in the early nineteenth century is probably the main reason that a railway compartment or a row of seats in an airplane is the site of interesting conversations in some novels and short stories—think of the beginning of Dostoyevsky's *The Idiot* or Tolstoy's "Kreutzer Sonata"—but unless I am mistaken, they have not yet been used in philosophical dialogues. That is lamentable; the accidental nature of the encounter, in trains the getting on and getting off of potential conversation partners, the possible reference to places that one passes by or flies over, the particularities of modern technology, and finally the length of the conversation determined more or less by the length of the journey, are all capable of being imbued with poetry and philosophy.

87. (1966), 971. "Who wants to be consistent?" Vivan asks, like Nietzsche and utterly unlike the Platonic Socrates.

88. (1966), 992.

89. (1999), 2227.

CHAPTER 12

The Time of Conversation

A dialogue, as I have discussed, can abstract from the spatial location of a conversation. Analogously, it can abstract from the point in time at which the conversation is supposed to have taken place—or to be more precise, from the points in time between which it is supposed to have occurred. Even the attempt to establish a precise, fictional—even only relative—chronology for all of Plato's dialogues is doomed to fail (consider only the *Philebus*),[1] although most are scenic in nature and contain numerous allusions to past and even present events (which cannot always be made consistent, however).[2] Nonetheless, the appearance of certain characters often establishes a certain temporal framework within which the fictional conversation has to take place; we must assume correspondences between the chronology of the real world and that of literary universes in which counterparts of historical persons appear: the Socrates of a literary dialogue generally lives in an equivalent of the fifth century B.C. (unless he appears in a dialogue of the dead). Leaving the date open within a progressive series, for example, of years, is compatible with giving information about the point in time within a recurring temporal unit, for instance, a day of the week or month or an hour of the day, and vice versa.

---

1. The author of the anonymous *Prolegomena* already knows this (16.10 ff.).
2. See the reconstruction in D. Nails (2002), 307–30, 357–67.

But what the dialogue cannot abstract from is the *duration* of the conversation. Even if it is not mentioned, the length of time involved is inevitably shown. In direct dialogue, at least insofar as it does not mention or imply interruptions,[3] it corresponds at first sight to the period of time that the receiver needs to read the text out loud, which in some cases allows for silent reflection, for instance, before answering. This has to do with the nature of the literary work of art, which must be briefly examined here. Buildings, sculptures, and pictures are *spatial* works of art; music, on the other hand, necessarily takes time. Of course, a painter painted his picture at a certain point in time, and a composer wrote his symphony at a specific place. Naturally, the contemplation of a painting also takes time, and musical scores and a fortiori concert halls have spatial extension. But what enters into the production and reception of a work of art must be distinguished from what is inherent in it as such. The visual arts shape space; music organizes time (and also other things such as colors and tones, respectively). Literature shapes language, and since in its original form language is speech, it is just as temporal as music. Indeed, it gives time even more space than music does, because literature is not merely temporal but also represents temporal events. Time is thus its object as well as its medium. In the case of dramas that observe the unity of time, the time represented and the time of the representation do not coincide—no performance of Racine's *Britannicus* took place in A.D. 55—but the represented length of time and the duration of the representation do (at least approximately, since the doctrine of the unity of time allowed a whole day to be represented). Even in a drama in which the unity of time is not respected, this means only that the scenes represented do not immediately follow one another; if we add up the duration of the scenes represented and subtract the time that passes between them, we arrive at the duration of the representation. This also holds for a play like Thornton Wilder's *The Long Christmas Dinner,* whose action extends over a period of ninety years in the same room, as soon as we understand that despite the lack of scene changes,

---

3. For instance, in Aeneas's *Theophrastus,* when Aegyptus and Euxitheus go to the eponymous hero's residence (3.25 Colonna); an analogous situation in Nicholas of Cusa's *Idiota de mente* is bridged by a brief narrative insertion.

the represented time is discrete; that is, it constantly jumps over whole years. However, the point of the play is that the spectator does not immediately notice this, because certain rites are repeated every year.

This relationship holds, as mentioned, for direct dialogues. Indirect dialogues are, like novels, not subject to this rule, since on the one hand they can briefly summarize long stretches of conversation[4] and on the other, by introducing the narrator's reflections, for example, concerning the speaker's hidden motives, the time necessary for reading out loud can be extended beyond the duration of the active conversation represented. Descriptions of interruptions do both at the same time—that is, they abbreviate the length of time consumed by the interruption and the conversation but extend it beyond that of the conversation itself. Two classic examples of such representations of preparatory silence are found in Plato's *Symposium* (174d ff.), where Socrates stops dead on the way to Agathon's house, as if in a kind of cataleptic fit, and in Cicero's *De oratore*, where Crassus retires to a daybed for two hours before delivering his long speech, but Cotta can tell by the look in his eyes that he is in deep concentration.[5] However, the situation is more complicated because some direct dialogues can be enjoyed only if the reader abstracts from the fact that the conversation represented is supposed to have taken the same amount of time as reading it. No Stakhanov of discourse could endure an uninterrupted conversation of the length of that represented in Plato's *Republic* or his *Laws,* even as only a listener, not to mention as a speaker or narrator. With respect to temporal length, these dialogues are therefore to be considered nonrealistic; at least it is not claimed that such conversations lasted only five hours. On the other hand, *Le neveu de Rameau* begins in the late afternoon—the text suggests around 5:00 P.M.—and ends around 5:30, when Rameau leaves for the opera;[6] and while the duration indicated certainly makes sense for a brief conversation, even a rapid reader cannot read this extensive text out loud in so short a time. Thus here, in contrast to the *Republic,* the impossibility has to do not with the length of time but with what has to be done in it. A simple solution for

---

4. One example among many is Pl. *Smp.* 223d.
5. 3.5.17.
6. (1972), 31 f., 131.

those who are writing long dialogues but do not want to represent something nomologically impossible is to divide the conversation into several days. For instance, Cicero originally planned to write *De re publica* in nine books corresponding to nine days,[7] but finally organized the discussions in his six books into three days.[8] *De oratore* has three books, but the conversation takes place on only two days, the second day having two sessions—the impatience of Crassus's friend, depicted at the end of the second book, not allowing his speech to be postponed until the following day.[9] Despite their brevity, Augustine's Cassiciacum dialogues take place on several days, and conversely to *De oratore*, each of the dialogues takes place on more days than it has books (see above, p. 27). Licentius expressly requests a break in order to reflect on a question; the interlocutors change the subject and go to the baths, taking up the question again only on the following day.[10] Later on, Augustine also suggests that they pursue a question on the following day; as in the case of bodily nourishment, so in that of intellectual nourishment excess is detrimental.[11] Each of Berkeley's *Three Dialogues between Hylas and Philonous* takes a day; and at the end of both the first and the second day it is said that Hylas can or will devote the time that he is now going to spend alone to solitary reflection on what has been discussed up to this point. Typically, Philonous is the first to suggest this; the second time it is Hylas, who announces it on his own.[12] He has evidently internalized the conviction that common speaking and solitary reflection are both required in order to introduce a philosophical change in perspective;[13] and the form of a dialogue in three books, that is, without continuous time, corresponds exactly to this insight. The six books of Bodin's *Colloquium heptaplomeres* are divided into four days: the first book describes an

---

7. *QF* 3.5.1.

8. *De rep.* 6.8.8.

9. 2.90.367.

10. *C. acad.* 1.4.10. Licentius's mental absence as a result of intensive reflection reminds us of the passage in the *Symposium* just mentioned.

11. *Beat. vit.* 2.13. The comparison of both forms of nourishment runs throughout the work (2.14ff., 3.17, 20, 22).

12. (1977), 192, 215.

13. Cf. Shaftesbury (1999), 28: "Society itself cannot be rightly enjoyed without some abstinence and separate thought."

evening meal; the second and third, like the fourth and fifth, describe a midday and evening meal, respectively, of the two following days, while the sixth book describes only a single meal, to which the Catholic Coronaeus invites his guests on a Friday.[14] It is hardly an accident that the harshest criticism of religious persecution and the general decision in favor of religious tolerance take place on the day of Christ's death, and that special intellectual insights compensate for the smaller amount of food consumed. (The same holds analogously for the main conversation in Bruno's *Cena de le ceneri,* which takes place on Ash Wednesday.) A nuance of this kind is in agreement with the positive picture that Bodin draws of Coronaeus; like the latter, Bodin identifies with an ideal of spirituality to which some Catholic customs contribute. Analogously, Plato dates the conversation in the *Republic* to the Bendis festival (327a1 ff., 354a11), and that in the *Timaeus* (21a ff.) and the main conversation in the *Parmenides* to the Panathenaic festival.[15] On the one hand, the mood of a religious festival is supposed to inspire philosophical conversation; on the other, Plato naturally wants to suggest that philosophy is the highest form of religious service. Socrates' execution could take place, we are told in the *Phaedo* (58a ff.), only after the arrival of Theseus's ship from Delos. Thus Socrates' last conversation is "a reenactment in logos of Theseus's victory over the Minotaur, dramatically embedded in the context of the Athenian reenactment of the same heroic myth."[16] The fear of death corresponds to the Minotaur; and overcoming it by argument is more religious than the city's periodic and temporary renunciation of executions, whose resumption leads to the death of its most righteous citizen.

The tradition of philosophical conversation has lasted two and a half millennia, and an end is not in sight. When people gather together in order to discuss philosophical questions, they have significantly less time. Of course, having leisure is part of the ideal of the ancient and medieval intellectual. "Ne propera, otiosi sumus," Reason tells Augustine.[17]

14. (1857), 238: "Die consequenti tardius solito convenerant, quoniam dies erat Veneris jejunio sancta, qua non nisi semel cibum capiebat Coronaei domus."
15. This is already emphasized in the *Prolegomena* (16.43 ff).
16. According to R. Burger in her admirable monograph on the *Phaedo* (1984; 20).
17. *Soliloq.* 1.4.9. After the impression made on him by Reason, however, Augustine will later hasten (2.7.13).

Even Roman statesmen set aside periods, spent mainly at their villas, during which they could have at least some leisure. Little shows the modernity of Campanella's *La Città del Sole* more clearly than the abrupt end of the dialogue, at the end of which the Hospitaller wants still more information from the Genoese, but the latter has to get back to his ship.[18] The age of voyages to all corners of the earth, from which the utopian spirit drew so much inspiration—as is well known, early modern utopias were described in the framework of fictional travel reports—has transformed our relationship to time no less than our relationship to space; if there are more places to travel to or even to study, we have less time to philosophize at leisure in the same place. After he has told the Hospitaller for the second time that he must now leave, since he has things to do, the Genoese adds that the residents of the City of the Sun have discovered the art of flying, which the world still lacks. In the Latin version of 1637, it is added that they are working on a telescope in order to see hidden stars, and on a hearing device that will allow them to listen to the harmony of planetary movements.[19] The allusion to the Pythagorean harmony of the spheres as well as the many astrological observations show, of course, how far Campanella still was from modern science; but it is a sign of modernity that his City of the Sun is not satisfied with theory, the observation of and listening to the stars, but also wants to fly—perhaps even, the context seems to suggest, as far as the stars. It goes without saying that such perspectives announce the end of leisure; and so the last two sentences are the Hospitaller's plea not to depart and the Genoese's negative reply: "Non posso, non posso."[20]

But although the decline of leisure—among the upper classes, we must add—in an accelerated life-world is one of the hallmarks of modernity, ancient intellectuals were also unable to abstract from the fact that their time was not unlimited. We have to distinguish between the

18. In the Italian version of 1602: "perdo la nave, se non mi parto" (1998; 116).

19. "Questo sappi, ch'hanno trovato l'arte del volare, che sola manca al mondo"; "et in proximo ocularia expectare quibus occultae stellae videantur, et auricularia quibus coeli audiatur harmonia" (1998; 122).

20. (1998), 138. Immediately before, the Latin version mentions new inventions for traveling by water. This abrupt conclusion may have been deliberately imitated by E. Tugendhat (1997), 143: "The ship whistled again and began to get under way; he embraced me, sprang onto the deck, and disappeared."

duration of a conversation and the subjective awareness that we do not always have time for conversations, and even when we do, it is only for a certain length of time, and this kind of knowledge can also be found in ancient dialogues. Despite Friedländer's authority,[21] I cannot consider the *Theages* a work of Plato's because of its many anecdotes and philosophical thinness, even loquacity;[22] but there is something Platonic and Socratic about it. It begins with the following sentence from Demodocus: "Socrates, I have to speak with you privately, if you have the time; if you're busy, but not too, please take a few minutes for my sake."[23] Socrates, it turns out, has time, partly in general, partly especially for Demodocus's sake. The historical Socrates probably found time for a conversation in most cases; in Plato's work Socrates never flatly refuses a request for a conversation. In the *Protagoras,* despite the fact that he has other business to attend to, he remains until his opponent declares the conversation over.[24] Indeed, in the *Crito* as well he takes the necessary time, even though the context suggests that his chance to escape will not last long. But for him, far more important than haste is coming to the morally right decision (46b ff.); and at the end he invites Crito to make any objection he wishes (54d7). Even though Crito has nothing to say, it is never assumed that because of the external pressure of time—for example, the imminent changing of the guard—they have to hurry. In contrast, to withdraw from a conversation in which they are in danger of being defeated, Socrates' interlocutors either use lack of time as a pretext, like Euthyphro,[25] or stipulate that they need private time to reflect, like Hippias.[26]

---

21. (1964), II 135 ff., which maintains that it is an early work, like the *Hipparchus* (II 116).

22. The allusion to characters familiar from the *Laches* at 130a points to an imitator. The objection that Goethe, for example, also wrote weak works is not convincing because the pressure to publish in Goethe's time was quite different from what it was in Plato's, who in addition was not a courtier.

23. 121a1 ff. *Ō Sōkrates, edeomēn atta soi idiologēsasthai, ei scholē; kan ei ascholia de mē panu tis megalē, homōs emou heneka poiēsai scholēn.*

24. 335c5 f., 362a1 ff., with a compliment to the handsome host, for whose sake he has remained.

25. *Euthphr.* 15e3 f.

26. *Hp. ma.* 295a 4 ff., 297e1 f. The question of the dialogue's authenticity may be left open here; it certainly has its origin in the Old Academy.

However, there are dialogues in which the end of the conversation is imposed from outside: in the *Lysis,* Socrates is about to ask one of the older boys something when the teachers appear "like demons" and lead the youths off despite their resistance.[27] And yet a glance at the related *Charmides* shows that the persistence of the aporia is not due to the appearance of the barbarian slaves; on the contrary, this persistence is precisely the result the artist Plato wanted to achieve. The end of the *Lysis* anticipates the end of Feyerabend's "First Dialogue," when the philosophers are driven out of the university lecture hall by a scholarly-looking person (the modern equivalent of a barbarian slave?) because their time has run out: "You are philosophers? No wonder you can't finish in time."[28] The end of a conversation can also be determined by the weather or the time of day, or again an end based on objective grounds may coincide happily with such an external break. Cicero, who wants to return by boat from Hortensius's villa to his own,[29] says at the end of his speech in *Lucullus* that the boatman is signaling and even the West Wind itself—on which his departure depends—is whispering that it is time to leave; in any case, he has spoken long enough.[30] The day's end leads to Tacitus's *Dialogus de oratoribus* being broken off.[31] At the end of the first of Berkeley's *Three Dialogues between Hylas and Philonous,* the college clock calls the faithful to prayer.[32] In Diderot's *Entretien d'un père avec ses enfants,* the father puts his nightcap on and sends the children to bed;[33] in his *Paradoxe sur le comédien,* the desire for an evening meal leads to the end of the conversation.[34]

Sometimes the position of the sun is mentioned in the course of the conversation. In the preceding chapter I referred to the sunrise in the *Protagoras.* The *Laws*—whose approximate year of composition is not

27. 223a f. The conclusion of the *Symposium* (223b2 ff.) is similar, even if it is not an aporetic dialogue.
28. (1991), 45.
29. *Ac. Pr.* 2.3.9.
30. 2.48.147.
31. 42.1.
32. (1977), 192.
33. (1972), 279.
34. (1994), 120. "Mais il se fait tard. Allons souper" (But it's getting late. Let's go have supper).

easy to determine[35]—alludes to the summer solstice (683c4 f.), that is, to the longest day of the year, and the moment when noon comes is noted (722c7 f.). However, since from the beginning of the dialogue up to this point, less than a third of the total number of Stephanus pages has been reached,[36] the conversation must have continued into the night—at least if we assume that it began not too long after sunrise—which would fit well with the concluding discussion of the Nightly Council (962c ff.). Philosophical passion can also turn night into day—just consider Augustine's *De ordine,* in which the discussion begins at night. Indeed, the stillness of the night, which reveals the beauty of nature and does away with people's talkativeness, can be particularly suitable for philosophical depth. "I took notice," Philocles writes in Shaftesbury's *The Moralists* to his misanthropic friend Palemon, "that the approaching objects of the night were the more agreeable to you for the solitude they introduced, and that the moon and planets which began now to appear were in reality the only proper company for a man in your humour. For now you began to talk with much satisfaction of natural things, and of all orders of beauties, man only excepted."[37] And in fact Palemon himself is quoted: "The gaudy scene is over with the day. Our company have long since quitted the field; and the solemn majesty of such a night as this, may justly suit with the profoundest meditation or most serious discourse."[38]

The most fundamental temporal boundary comes from impending death. Death does not interrupt a conversation; it breaks it off. The temporality of the natural is intensified in the mortality of the organic; it culminates in humans' awareness of death. But it is precisely from this

---

35. If this Megillus is identical with the historical ambassador of Sparta in Athens who also ratified the truce with Tissaphernes (as Nails maintains [2002; 197 f.]), given the advanced age of the character in Plato's dialogue, we can assume a date in the first half of the fourth century.

36. The well-known argument that since frg. 5 from the fifth book mentions that the sun had just passed the zenith, Cicero's *De legibus* must have been divided into eight books—two more than *De re publica,* just as, in its division into books (which does not go back to Plato), the *Laws* has two more than the *Republic*—assumes that Cicero not only imitated Plato but also differed from him in the composition of his work and made the conversation stop before sundown.

37. (1999), 12.

38. (1999), 20.

awareness of death that philosophy and thus the turn toward the timeless emerge. Therefore it is no accident that several philosophical dialogues are played out in the shadow of imminent death. In the (nondialogic) Platonic *Apology*, Socrates says that he has been condemned because he and his judges talked with one another for too short a time.[39] A speech that one gives before people who have the power to execute one and which is subject to very stringent temporal limits is not free of domination; but Socrates shows the greatest composure. What is important for him is that the judges investigate the case, whether they do so now or later.[40] He is aware that the second alternative could cost him his life; but he is concerned less about that than about the comprehension of his fellow citizens. And the latter is not subject to the same deadline as the imminent judgment; people can still learn after they have made a mistake. Even after he has been condemned to death, Socrates wants to use the time that remains to him in conversation with those who voted for him: "As for you who voted for my acquittal, I should very much like to say a few words to reconcile you to the result, while the officials are busy *(ascholian agousi)* and I am not yet on my way to the place where I must die. I ask you, gentlemen, to spare me these few moments. There is no reason why we should not exchange fancies while the law permits."[41] This passage is found in the third speech, which may contain a few Socratic ideas but cannot be considered historical, since a man who had been condemned to die was no longer allowed any further opportunity to speak. What is fascinating in these two sentences is the combination of composure and the awareness that not much time remains. In three successive lines, "not yet" (*oupō*, e3), "these few moments" (*tosouton chronon*, e4), and "while" (*heōs*, e5) point to the temporal limitation that is most unmistakably indicated by the last word of the first sentence, "die" (*tethnanai*, e3). And yet it is the officials who are said to be busy *(ascholia)*, not Socrates, who is implied to have time on his hands, despite his impending execution. Precisely this attitude, that he is not under the pressure of time, also emerges from the *Phaedo*, which takes place on the day of

39. *Ap.* 37a6f.
40. 24b1.
41. 39e1–5.

Socrates' execution. It is his companions who are painfully aware that they will soon no longer be able to ask Socrates questions;[42] not for a moment does Socrates fear a loss of his ability to philosophize: right up to the end he remains as calm as his friends are upset.[43] For instance, approximately in the middle of the dialogue,[44] Simmias objects that he wants to express his reservations (which are for us only too justified), because he does not want to reproach himself later on for having not said what he thought[45]—implicitly suggesting that this is the last opportunity to do so. Cebes later makes this idea explicit,[46] for the hour of death is now closer. Interestingly, Socrates himself finally takes up the idea, although only in relation to the final myth, which he can no longer describe in all the desired detail.[47] Since the epistemological status of the myth is obviously subordinated to that of the proofs of immortality,[48] Socrates does not communicate the impression that his pupils will miss anything essential because of the now immediately imminent execution.

Socrates' third speech in the *Apology* is delivered, and the *Crito* and *Phaedo* take place, in the expectation of imminent death. The *Euthyphro* takes place after Socrates has been charged, that is, somewhat earlier but still within the horizon of the possibility of execution. Plato considered this condition so interesting that in the fictional chronology of his universe he probably situated the *Theaetetus*—whose frame conversation takes place while its eponymous hero is dying—immediately before the *Euthyphro,*[49] and the *Sophist* and *Statesman* on the following day.[50] The

---

42. Analogously, Gregory of Nyssa wants to have a few objections concerning the Resurrection discussed by his sister Macrina before she dies (129A).

43. Although in the *Crito* Socrates attributes greater objectivity with regard to the judgment to be made, since it does not directly concern him (*Cri.* 46e3 ff.), the irony is unmistakable.

44. In the precise center we find Socrates' calm remark, which makes the transition from Simmias's criticism to that of Cebes (86d5 ff.). In Plato, the middle of a dialogue is often an especially important place; cf. below, chapter 18 (p. 432).

45. 85d4 ff.

46. 107a5 ff.

47. 108d7 ff., 114c5 f.

48. 114d1 ff.

49. *Tht.* 210d1 ff. See the controversial discussion of this background in Feyerabend's first dialogue: (1991), 11 ff.

50. *Sph.* 216a1; *Plt.* 258a3 f.

point of this dating is to show that the true philosopher does not allow himself to be confused by accusations and holds firm to the laborious task of giving politics an epistemological and ontological foundation, even if it will not much help him with his judges.

Thus we have moved from the problem of the duration of a conversation to the point in time at which it takes place. In choosing it, Plato liked to evoke the background of death. The *Charmides* is one of Plato's most erotic dialogues, but at the beginning Socrates is coming straight from the siege of Potidaea and the battle at Spartolus (in 429), and the first questions concern those who have died there.[51] In addition, Plato presupposes that the reader knows that Critias and Charmides, who is obviously under Critias's influence, died in 403 at the battle of Munychia, in which the democrats under Thrasybulus defeated the Thirty Tyrants, one of whom Critias was and whom Charmides supported. Indeed, he alludes explicitly to this in the final sentences of the dialogue, which correspond symmetrically to the remarks at the beginning—one of numerous examples of Plato's often-used technique of ring composition. Charmides wants Socrates to teach him, and Critias supports him in this, which is a special reason for his ward to stick to his plan.[52] In this we see that for Charmides, Critias remains more important than Socrates; and when the latter ironically asks whether he is also prepared to use force to achieve this end, Charmides says he is, especially since Critias commands him to do so.[53] Socrates seems to accept this, but the reader of Plato knows that Socrates is not someone who can be forced—one has to convince him.[54] With his next-to-last sentence, Charmides shows that his natural temperance will not really help him;[55] he remains captive to familial bonds and to an ideal of violence which was to lead to his death immediately after the Peloponnesian War, at the beginning of which our dialogue takes place.

In *De oratore*, which is set in 91 B.C. and was written in 55 B.C., when he could not yet foresee his own imminent death, Cicero obviously also

51. 153b4 ff.
52. 176b9 ff.
53. 176c7 f.
54. Cf. *R.* 327c.
55. This was already said, 175d6 ff.

chose his interlocutors from the point of view that several of them—
Marcus Antonius (the grandfather of Cicero's murderer, whose head was
cut off and displayed on the speaker's platform, just as Cicero's later was),
Publius Sulpicius Rufus, Quintus Lutatius Catulus, and Caius Julius Caesar Strabo—lost their lives in the civil war that followed soon after the
conversation (Catulus avoided being murdered by committing suicide).
Despite his own political sympathies for Sulla, it is important for Cicero
that these men were later on different sides and were victims of both
parties; three were the victims of Marius and Cinna, but Sulpicius was a
supporter of Marius and was killed on Sulla's orders. (Quintus Mucius
Scaevola Augur also supported Marius but had already died in 88, so that
he was spared Sulla's revenge.) In the proem to the third book, Cicero describes the later fate of most of the interlocutors and some of their relatives in impressively gloomy tones; and he counts as fortunate Crassus,
who had died before the outbreak of war ten days after the fictional conversation represented and only a week after his historical speech against
the consul Lucius Marcius Philippus, which took the political crisis as its
subject and completely exhausted him. Crassus is to be counted fortunate
because he was spared a violent death or, had he escaped the latter, the
sight of the blood of his relatives and even that of his enemies: in his love
for his fatherland, he also should have been depressed by the death of his
worst enemy, Gaius Carbo,[56] not only by the violent rule of the bad, but
also by the bloodbath of citizens that accompanied the victory of the
good.[57] This is Cicero's point of view in the last—dialogue-external—
preface; but he increases the attractiveness of his dialogue considerably
by transforming—unlike Plato in the *Charmides*—his own knowledge
into clear premonitions of his conversation partners. The prologue to
the dialogue describes how Scaevola and Antonius visited Crassus at his
Tusculan estate and on the first day spoke only about politics, proving to
be astonishingly good prophets: "ut nihil incidisset postea civitati mali,
quod non impendere illi tanto ante vidissent."[58] Crassus's humanity was

56. 3.3.10: "cui maerori, qua mente ille in patriam fuit, etiam C. Carbonis, in-
imicissimi hominis, eodem illo die mors fuisset nefaria."
57. 3.3.12: "neque solum tibi improborum dominatus, sed etiam propter ad-
mixtam civium caedem bonorum victoria maerori fuisset."
58. 1.7.26.

shown, the reader is told, by the fact that during dinner he no longer talked about the tragic subject but rather evinced the cheeriness and wit suitable to a country estate.[59] The following morning they went for a walk together, and sat down under a plane tree, where, in order to provide a rest from the previous day's discussion, Crassus directed the conversation to the subject of eloquence.[60] *De re publica* also stands in the shadow of death—partly the alleged murder of Scipio, to which the latter alludes at the end,[61] partly the already raging civil war, of which the initial apparently purely astronomical discussion about the two suns is a metaphor.[62] Laelius's complaint that they should talk about the heavens only when the problems at home and in the state have been investigated (1.13.19) overlooks on the one hand that an interest in theoretical phenomena constitutes the intellectual freedom on the basis of which politics must be practiced, and which Cicero's model Plato possessed in such a large measure; and on the other hand, that a few categories extend to nature and society equally—in particular, the fundamental Platonic principles of unity and duality. The two suns in the heavens correspond to two Senates and two peoples in Rome.[63]

Obviously, the date at which a dialogue was written must be clearly distinguished from the date of the conversation it represents. Indeed, as a rule it is not part of the literary universe of the dialogue itself: an interesting exception is Augustine's Cassiciacum dialogues, which refer to their own transcription. However, the nature of a dialogue is determined in an essential way by whether it is set in the present of its author or in the past. (Philosophical dialogues that are set in the future seem just as conceivable as novels set in the future, such as those of Jules Verne or Edward Bellamy's *Looking Backward: 2000–1887*. But so far as I know, there are

---

59. 1.7.27: "Eo autem omni sermone confecto, tantam in Crasso humanitatem fuisse, ut, cum lauti accubuissent, tolleretur omnis illa superioris tristitia sermonis eaque esset in homine iucunditas et tantus in loquendo lepos, ut dies inter eos curiae fuisse videretur, convivium Tusculani." Sigonio praises this passage (1993; 202).

60. 1.8.29.

61. 1.12.12. *Laelius* takes place immediately after this death.

62. 1.10.15 ff.

63. 1.19.31 f. In Hobbes's dialogue *Behemoth* the analogous passage reads: "And consequently there must be two kingdoms in one and the same nation, and no man be able to know which of his masters he must obey" (1990; 8).

none, and there is an obvious reason for this. One can postulate techno-logical innovations even if one does not know in detail how they func-tion, because the purpose exists independently of the means for realizing it. But a philosophical theory does not exist independently of the argu-ments that support it; and if the author already knows them, then we are dealing with a contemporary philosophy, and it is not clear what would be gained by setting it in the future.) If the author himself is one of the interlocutors, then the dialogue must be set during his lifetime, in some cases in his youth; but even if this is not the case, the dialogue may be set in a contemporary frame. If an author does not introduce himself into the dialogue, setting the conversation in the past has the advantage that it need not harm any contemporary person. Cicero—who wrote only four dialogues in which he himself does not appear (including *De ora-tore*, which is set in his youth), and a fifth, in which he listens silently *(De natura deorum)*—considered setting *De re publica* in the present as well.

In a famous letter to Quintus written at the end of October or the be-ginning of November, 54 B.C., Cicero says that he has already changed the organization of the whole work several times. When the first two of nine planned books, in which the characters familiar to us from the final ver-sion already appeared, and whose rank gave their speeches weight, were read out loud at Cicero's estate in Tusculum before his friend Cnaeus Sal-lustius, the latter suggested that Cicero should himself be one of the inter-locutors. This would allow him, Sallustius said, to speak about politics with much greater authority, especially since he is not, after all, a mere theorist like Heraclides Ponticus but a former consul, and one who had moreover been involved in the most important political affairs; what he ascribes to people from a time so far in the past will appear to be a fiction. Although in *De oratore* he has shown the good taste to distance himself from the speakers' discourses because they were dedicated to rhetoric, he has attributed them to people he still could have known personally; and finally, Aristotle himself speaks in the first person when he writes about the state and eminent statesmen. Sallustius persuaded him, Cicero tells us, especially since with his present plan he could not discuss the enor-mous turmoil in his country, because it occurred long after the time of the characters in his dialogue. However, at first he sought primarily not to offend any of his contemporaries. He will now avoid that, he says, and be a speaker along with Quintus, but he will bring him the original version of the text the next time he comes to Rome. He believes that Quintus can imagine that he has not abandoned these books without a certain chagrin.[64] It is well known that this chagrin continued, and Cicero changed his mind again (but in the end he allotted Scipio and his friends only six books instead of nine); and we can only congratulate him on not having followed this flatterer's advice to make himself a speaker in the dialogue. He would have been able to avoid the main danger of a dialogue set in the present, namely, directly offending contemporaries,[65] but hardly the danger of pandering to his vanity. And Sallustius's objections are easy to reject. As a statesman, Scipio was certainly not inferior to Cicero; the fictional nature of the dialogue contributes to the genre's appeal, and in fact is more clearly manifest in dialogues set in the past; moreover, Cicero was able to provide a credible chain of transmission in *De re publica* as well; Aristotle should not be preferred to Plato—at least as a writer of dialogues; allusions to the present are entirely possible from a fictional point in the past, indeed they present a special challenge to the reader's intelligence; and furthermore, the time of the conversation in *De re publica* is connected with Cicero's present by an almost uninterrupted civil war

64. *QF* 3.5.1 f.: " . . . ii libri cum in Tusculano mihi legerentur audiente Sallustio, admonitus sum ab illo multo maiore auctoritate illis de rebus dici posse si ipse loquerer de re publica, praesertim cum essem non Heraclides Ponticus sed consularis et is qui in maximis versatus in re publica rebus essem; quae tam antiquis hominibus attribuerem, ea visum iri ficta esse; oratorum sermonem in illis nostris libris, quod esset de ratione dicendi, belle a me removisse, ad eos tamen rettulisse quos ipse vidissem; Aristotelem denique quae de re publica et praestanti viro scribat ipsum loqui.

"Commovit<me>, et eo magis quod maximos motus nostrae civitatis attingere non poteram, quod erant inferiores quam illorum aetas qui loquebantur. ego autem id ipsum tum eram secutus, ne in nostra tempora incurrens offenderem quempiam. nunc et id vitabo et loquar ipse tecum et tamen illa quae institueram ad te, si Romam venero, mittam. puto enim te existimaturum a me illos libros non sine aliquo meo stomacho esse relictos."

65. The notion (which goes back to L. Parmentier, and which is occasionally invoked for the purpose of the absolute chronology of Plato's dialogues) that Plato put only deceased persons into his dialogues is based on a presumed analogous desire of Plato's (cf. H. Thesleff [1982], 32). It is contradicted, for example, by the case of characters like Callias and Isocrates, who were certainly still alive when the corresponding dialogues, the *Protagoras* and the *Euthydemus,* appeared. In other cases it remains unproven and even improbable.

that allows common traits to emerge. In *Laelius*, Cicero himself emphasizes that dialogues set in the past have, in a way that is hard to explain,
more dignity because of the authority of earlier figures, especially significant ones.[66]

By a fortunate accident, a complementary letter by Diderot has come
down to us, in which he tells Mme de Maux that he originally conceived
what became *Le rêve de d'Alembert* more magnificently, as a dream of
Democritus's. His interlocutors were to be his beloved Leucippe—
fictional, but alluding by name to his famous fellow atomist—and the
physician Hippocrates. But then he would have had to limit himself to
the area of ancient philosophy, and that would have cost him too much.
Therefore he sacrificed the grandeur of the form to the richness of the
substance.[67] Diderot made the right choice. His problem was not vanity
(in the trilogy he plays only the role of a stimulus, and certainly not the
central role), and he could endure the wrath of d'Alembert and Mlle
de l'Espinasse. But how would an ancient materialist have been able to
take up the challenge of Cartesianism? Scipio and Cicero belonged to the
same culture; Democritus and Diderot did not. An abundance of anachronisms would have been inevitable.

Anachronisms often occur in dialogues set in the past, but they take
three different forms.[68] The naive form is the one in which the author
blithely contradicts the historical facts, for example, by having people

66. 1.4: "genus autem hoc sermonum positum in hominum veterum auctori
tate et eorum inlustrium plus nescio quo pacto videtur habere gravitatis." Cf. Sigonio
(1993), 172.
67. *Correspondance*, IX 129 f.: "J'avois vu la chose bien plus en grand. C'étoit le
rêve de Démocrite; et les interlocuteurs, Démocrite, Hyppocrate et Leucippe, maîtresse
de Démocrite. Mais il eût fallu se renfermer dans la sphère de la philosophie ancienne,
et j'y aurois trop perdu. J'ai sacrifié la noblesse de la forme à la richesse du fond."
68. In his *Dialogue between Alexander the Great and Diogenes the Cynic*, Henry
Fielding is guilty of a strange didactic pedantry. Diogenes talks to Alexander of "extending thy Arms to the farthest Limits of the World," and thus avoids anachronism, but in
a dialogue-external footnote Fielding adds for the benefit of the contemporary reader,
of whose education he seems not to have a high opinion: "Which was then known to
the *Greeks*" (1972; 233 [original emphasis]). This does not affect the high literary and
psychological value of the dialogue, which in its unmasking of Diogenes' resentment,
has almost Nietzschean characteristics, as does Diderot's *Le neveu de Rameau*. The
more one studies the eighteenth century, the less original Nietzsche appears.

meet whose lifetimes hardly overlap, or by attributing to someone knowledge of events that happened only after his death or at least after the fictional point in time when the conversation took place. Plato's dialogues are full of such anachronisms, as the ancients already realized.[69] Socrates never met Parmenides, and it may very well be that such a meeting was chronologically impossible. In any case, it is inadvisable to base a dating of the historical Parmenides on Plato's eponymous dialogue. The main conversation of the *Symposium* is set in 416, but at 193a3 very probably refers to Sparta's destruction of Mantinea in 385. This is a *terminus post quem* for the composition of the dialogue; and it is pointless to speculate as to whether Plato committed this anachronism immediately after the event, when his audience was still aware of it, or considerably later, when it was no longer so striking. The blending of events is especially remarkable in the *Gorgias;* Nails therefore discusses it as well as with the *Republic,* under the rubric "Dialogues with Problematic Dramatic Dates," in both cases giving as the time frame "throughout the Peloponnesian War."[70] We know of only one occasion on which Gorgias visited Athens, namely, in 427, although he may have been there more than once. At 503c2 f. it is said that Pericles has recently died, which points to the early 420s; 470d ff. alludes to Archelaus of Macedonia, who first came to power in 413; 485e3 f. quotes Euripides' *Antiope,* which was not performed before 411; 473e6 ff. probably refers to the trial in 405 of the generals who had been in command at the battle of Arginusae as an event that took place the preceding year. After citing these passages, Dodds rightly notes, "We must conclude either that Plato did not care how his readers situated his fictions in time or . . . that he deliberately lifted the present fiction 'out of the historical sphere of actual circumstances and the course of party politics at Athens.'"[71] The fact is that Plato constructs a fictional uni-

69. Macrobius appeals to Plato to excuse his own anachronisms: "nec mihi fraudi sit, si uni aut alteri ex his quos coetus coegit matura aetas posterior saeculo Praetextati fuit: quod licito fieri Platonis dialogi testimonio sunt" (*Sat.* 1.1.5). There follow examples from the *Parmenides, Timaeus,* and *Protagoras.* See also Athenaeus, V 217c and XI 505 f./506a, who inveighs against this with scholarly narrow-mindedness, and Sigonio (1993), 174.

70. (2002), 324 ff.

71. (1959), 18. The passage at 519a7 f. is dialogue-internally a prophecy, and thus does not contradict the other information.

verse, and in such a universe events can in good conscience be ordered very differently from the way they are ordered in reality. To that extent at least Plato would have agreed with Wilde: "There is such a thing as robbing a story of its reality by trying to make it too true, and *The Black Arrow* is so inartistic as not to contain a single anachronism to boast of."[72]

The second form of anachronism presupposes a sense of history. How can Machiavelli take a stand with regard to Napoleon III? By means of a dialogue of the dead. One of the reasons for the popularity of this subgenre is surely that it makes it possible to satisfy, without contravening the historical consciousness, the need for the authority of significant figures from the past at the same time as the need to come to terms with one's own time. In Valéry's *Eupalinos*, Phèdre quotes a well-known verse by Mallarmé—"Gloire du long désir, Idées!"—and, when Socrate asks him which poet wrote it, he answers, "Le très admirable Stephanos, qui parut tant de siècles après nous."[73] In view of the nature of the dialogue, the relative clause seems pedantic; but first, even the most witless schoolmaster can no longer point out the anachronism and interpret it as a sign of his author's historical ignorance; and second, the expression of this relative clause suggests that the writer, whose surname is not given, could easily be considered to be an ancient poet, partly because of his first name and partly because of his praise of the Ideas. Thereby reference is made to the constancy of certain basic concepts in the tradition, no matter how much Phèdre wants to criticize Plato's theory of Ideas. But this criticism can be made by an ancient as well as by a modern.

The third form is the provocative one. We have seen in chapter 10 that the anachronism of the *Menexenus* differs so strikingly from the others in Plato's work that it has to be seen as the real point of the dialogue. Iris Murdoch's *Acastos* also makes intentional use of anachronisms. Both her dialogues are supposed to take place in the late fifth century—the information about Socrates' and Plato's ages allows us to fix the date in the last decade[74]—and yet they quite clearly deal with philosophical problems of the late twentieth century in the latter's peculiar conceptual framework. In the first dialogue, which is concerned

72. (1966), 973, with reference to R. L. Stevenson's historical novel.
73. (1945), 23.
74. (1986), 9, 68.

with art, the friends have just emerged from the theater. Callistos says how pleased he was with the play, and asks Acastos whether he also liked it. Acastos is indecisive (Plato will not even dignify the same question by answering it), and Callistos reacts by remarking: "You must know what you feel, who else could?"[75] Thereby he presupposes the theory that every individual has privileged access to his own states of consciousness, which is in essence a theory that first became commonly held with Descartes. We can, however, find its first seed in Augustine's *Contra academicos,* where in the preface to the second book Augustine declares, just like Descartes, that he wants to free himself from vain and pernicious opinions,[76] and later points out that assertions about subjective appearances are infallible.[77] But in classical Greek philosophy, at least, such a view is not to be found, and so its attribution to Socrates' friends is anachronistic. The same holds for numerous concepts and theories that occur on the following pages, from the expression "just us intellectuals" to the claim that "Art is all in the mind. It's not in the play" or even that theater is mere "escape,"[78] and the assertion, which alludes to Wittgenstein's well-known concept of family resemblances, that "We speak . . . of 'the arts' as a *family*" to the demand, unimaginable before Hegel and Marx, that "Art must overcome the *alienation* of men from each other."[79] Much the same holds for *Above the Gods,* a dialogue on the philosophy of religion, in which for instance Plato seems to know the ontological proof of God's existence.[80] Murdoch is so conscious of the anachronistic nature of her dialogue that she gives the central scene, in which the friends ask a servant or slave about his religious feelings, in two different versions. *"The dialogues are designed to be performed either in modern dress or in period costume. In a period performance the servant in* Above the Gods *will of course be a slave, and the following text may be preferred."*[81]

75. (1986), 11.
76. 2.3.9. "Ego enim nunc aliud nihil ago, quam me ipse purgo a uanis perniciosisque opinionibus."
77. 3.11.24 and 26, as well as 3.12.27.
78. (1986), 12 f. Cf. 33 on the "intellectuals."
79. (1986), 18, 31.
80. (1986), 100.
81. (1986), 122. Original emphasis.

However, the version with the slave is also profoundly un-Greek: the humanitarian interest in the slave would have been alien to Plato, but might still pass, especially when combined, in Timonax's case, with a sexual interest. But the connection with economic observations such as "I think slavery is retarding our economy"[82] is completely anachronistic.

What is the purpose of these anachronisms? Murdoch obviously wants to indicate that the age of Socrates and Plato and our own are essentially related. "We're living in a period of intellectual and psychological *shock*, a time of deep change, an interregnum, a *dangerous interim*."[83] At the same time, she is concerned to make certain types appear to be timeless—the politician Mantias, the cynical Antagoras, the absolutist Plato, the wise Socrates, with whom and with whose unhistorical pupil Acastos she mostly sympathizes. But despite his fallibilism, her Socrates represents, just as she herself does in her theoretical writings, a rudimentary Platonism: "You see, we want to be certain that goodness rests upon reality. And as this desire will never go away, we shall always be searching for the gods."[84]

---

82. (1986), 130.
83. (1986), 76. Original emphasis.
84. (1986), 40.

CHAPTER 13

The Number of Persons
in the Conversation

A conversation is an intersubjective event; therefore it presupposes at least two conversation partners. There seems at first to be no maximum number, though the latter is in fact determined partly by real factors grounded in human psychology and partly by the limited number of possible philosophical positions. But for conceptual reasons it appears that there cannot be fewer than two if the work is to be a dialogue. On the one hand, this is correct: if there are not two conversation partners, usually designated by different names, there is by definition no dialogue. On the other hand, the degree of the conversation partners' ontological independence can be very small. The Platonic Socrates already repeatedly invented, although always within a real conversation, fictional interlocutors. The personification of the laws in the *Crito* was mentioned in chapter 10. In the *Hippias major*, in order to force Hippias to continue the conversation, Socrates imagines the objections that might be made by a third party; this allows him to soften his criticism of Hippias, precisely because he claims that he himself is not making them.[1] In the *Ion*,

---

1. This is particularly clear at 292c3 ff. Fictional interlocutors are also found in *Prt.* 330c2 ff.; in Augustine, *C. acad.* 3.14.31; and in Shaftesbury's *The Moralists* (1999;

Socrates makes an objection to himself in Ion's name.[2] In the *Theaete-tus,* Socrates imagines what Protagoras would say in reply to the criti-cism that has been directed at him in absentia,[3] a reply that is nevertheless voiced by Socrates, who ironically stresses the ineptness of the defense he makes on behalf of the great sophist.[4] With regard to Callicles' unwill-ingness to engage in conversation, Socrates emphasizes that he could continue his argument to the end even in a monologue.[5]

I have also discussed the role played by Philosophy in Boethius's *Consolatio philosophiae.* Initially, she is clearly a power superior to Bo-ethius who is experienced as another person; but in the course of the con-versation she becomes increasingly the voice of reason, which is onto-logically not an Other to the same extent that another person would be; it is, as it were, Boethius's better self.[6] This lack of otherness is still more obvious in the case of Augustine's unfinished *Soliloquia,* the last of his works written in Cassiciacum, already in 387. It represents a conversation between Augustine and Reason *(ratio).*[7] The first sentence immediately notes that it is unclear—no matter how much Augustine would like to be certain—whether this interlocutor who suddenly spoke to him, after he had long reflected alone on many and manifold problems and for several days sought himself as well as what was good for him and what was an

---

103 ff.), where Theocles seeks to anticipate, as it were, the objections of his real inter-locutor Philocles. In the thirteenth book of *Dichtung und Wahrheit,* Goethe tells how he transformed "even solitary thinking into companionable entertainment"; viz , "when he found himself alone, he commonly called to mind some person he knew. He asked this person to sit down, went back and forth to him, remained standing in front of him, and discussed with him some subject that he had in mind" (9.576; cf. 9.591 on Goethe's prose dialogues).

2. 538d f.
3. 162d ff., esp. 165e ff.
4. 168c2 ff.
5. *Grg.* 505e1 f., 519e1 f.
6. Much the same can be said about the soul in the Old Egyptian *Conversation of a World-Weary Man with His Soul.*
7. In his typology of early Christian Latin dialogues, P. L. Schmidt (1977) men-tions Augustine's *Soliloquia* and Boethius's *Consolatio* as examples of the self-reflexive dialogue (124 ff.), a fifth group alongside dogmatic-controversial, philosophical-theological, didactic, and hagiographic dialogue. Isidore of Seville's *Synonyma* is also placed in this category (180).

evil to be avoided, was himself or someone else, and in the latter case, if it was an external or internal Other. "Volventi mihi multa ac varia mecum diu ac per multos dies sedulo quaerenti memetipsum ac bonum meum, quidve mali evitandum esset, ait mihi subito sive ego ipse sive alius quis, extrinsecus sive intrinsecus, nescio; nam hoc ipsum est quod magnopere scire molior."[8] It is fascinating how the doubling of the "I," from which the conversation with objectivized Reason springs, is already implied in the first-person singular pronouns with which the period begins: "mihi," "mecum," "mememtipsum" constitute the subject-object structure peculiar to reflective thinking. In chapter 1 we saw that conversation with other people would not be possible at all without the mind's ability to "converse with itself," to privately anticipate others' possible objections, and thus, if they are justified, to anticipate common reason. Augustine was probably familiar with the well-known passages in Plato's *Theaetetus* (189e6f.) and *Sophist* (263e3ff.) that characterize thinking in this way; as early as *Contra academicos* he says that Carneades conversed with himself, as if this were commonly done.[9] In her first remark, Reason asks in whom Augustine would confide if he had found something. Augustine says he would confide in his memory; but he has to concede that this is not good enough and that he must therefore write down his ideas. But how? His present state of health does not allow him to do this; neither can he dictate his thoughts, because his current project demands complete solitude. "Nec ista dictari debent; nam solitudinem meram desiderant."[10] He follows Reason's advice to pray to God for good health, and to do so in writing, since he still has enough strength for that and writing will make him more resolute. Obviously, from this point on, the conversation with Reason and its transcription must be considered simultaneous[11]—just as the conversations in the three earlier dialogues

---

8. 1.1.1. In the *Retractiones*, the question is answered; he was alone: "me interrogans mihique respondens, tamquam duo essemus ratio et ego, cum solus essem" (1.4.1).

9. 3.10.22: "secum ipse, ut fit, loquens." See also *Ord.* 2.18.48: "ita secum loquetur."

10. 1.1.1.

11. This is indicated by passages like 1.15.27: "Concludamus, si placet, hoc primum volumen"; and 2.19f., 33f.; cf. also *Ord.* 1.11.33. Anselm probably had these passages in mind when he wrote something analogous at the end of the first book of *Cur deus homo* (1.25)—but there it is extremely inappropriate, since there is no mention of a simultaneous transcription of the conversation.

were partly written down at the same time, although by a secretary who was not himself a participant in them. This secretary is also absent as a real interlocutor in the *Soliloquia*. This fundamentally distinguishes the mood in which the *Soliloquia* originates from the attitude on which the earlier dialogues were based. Even though Augustine uses the *tu* form in addressing Reason and distinguishes her from himself,[12] the *Soliloquia* are, as Augustine was well aware, not a normal dialogue. In the second book Augustine expresses his shame at having too rapidly conceded something false; but Reason consoles him. They have chosen this form of discussion—for which she coins the hard but objectively appropriate neologism "soliloquia," that is, "conversation with oneself"—precisely because there is no better way of seeking the truth than by question and answer, even though it is rare to find a person who is not ashamed to be proven wrong in a disputation; indeed, it even happens that uncontrolled, noisy pigheadedness may destroy an argument that was being discussed competently, and even do it mainly with disguised, but also sometimes overt, injury to the Other; therefore it has seemed to her that the most peaceful and appropriate way of seeking truth with God's help is for her, Reason, to be questioned by herself and to answer herself.[13] The last phrase is remarkable; one would expect it to be expressed instead by Augustine, since questioning oneself is more characteristic of real individuals than of reason. (Is that why we find the surprising masculine "interrogatum"?) However, Augustine may have deliberately had Reason say this, namely, in order to show that she is only an aspect of himself, for it is precisely in this sentence that we learn that the whole conversation is in fact a conversation with himself. When it is published,

---

12. 1.15.30: "ista mecum atque adeo tecum, quando in silentio sumus, diligenter cauteque tractabo."

13. 2.7.14: "Ridiculum est, si te pudet, quasi non ob idipsum elegerimus huiusmodi sermocinationes; quae, quoniam cum solis nobis loquimur, Soliloquia vocari atque inscribi volo, novo quidem et fortasse duro nomine, sed ad rem demonstrandam satis idoneo. Cum enim neque melius quaeri veritas possit quam interrogando et respondendo et vix quisquam inveniatur, quem non pudeat convinci disputantem, eoque paene semper eveniat, ut rem bene inductam ad discutiendum inconditus pervicaciae clamor explodat, etiam cum laceratione animarum plerumque dissimulata, interdum et aperta, pacatissime, ut opinor, et commodissime placuit a meipso interrogatum mihique respondentem deo adiuvante verum quaerere."

it enters an intersubjective dimension, though a limited one; the text is not meant to be read by a large number of people but only by a few fellow citizens.[14]

The *Soliloquia* can thus be called dialogues only in a very formal sense, because Reason—unlike God, to whom Augustine turns in prayer and whose aid he hopes to receive[15]—is not really an Other; she must do what Augustine requires.[16] Instead, the *Soliloquia* foreshadows Descartes's *Meditationes de prima philosophia in qua Dei existentia et animae immortalitas demonstratur,* the title of the first edition. This holds first of all thematically: Augustine as well wants to know God and the soul.[17] Second, it holds on the level of its foundational ideas. As Antoine Arnauld already noted in the fourth set of Objections to the *Meditationes,*[18] no one had come closer to the cogito argument than Augustine had. This statement remains true even if the differences between the two arguments and their functions in the respective intellectual constructs must not be underestimated. An early form of the Augustinian version is found precisely in the *Soliloquia,*[19] along with a defense of the body-mind dualism.[20] In addition, the Platonist Augustine nonetheless uses the self-cancellation argument in order to arrive at eternal truths that Descartes, as a radical theological voluntarist, has to neglect.[21] This can be regarded as a step backward on Descartes's part, no matter how obvious his superiority in conceiving the mental—in the *Soliloquia* Augustine fails in this regard, as he seems himself to acknowledge.[22] Third, however, from a literary point of view the *Soliloquia* probably comes closer than any

14. 1.1.1: "Nec modo cures invitationem turbae legentium; paucis ista sat erunt civibus tuis."

15. Cf. esp. 1.15.30, but also, e.g., 2.6.9.

16. 2.13.24.

17. 1.2.7: "A. Deum et animam scire cupio. R. Nihilne plus? A. Nihil omnino." Cf. already *C. acad.* 1.8.23 and *Ord.* 2.7.24, 2.9.30, 2.18.47.

18. VII 197.

19. 2.1.1. See also *C. acad.* 3.11.26 and *Beat. vit.* 2.7, as well as the later canonical versions in *lib. arb.* 2.3.7 and *civ. dei* 11.26.

20. 2.3.3. Contrafactually, 2.5.7 is reminiscent of Berkeley.

21. 2.2.2, 2.15.28. In 2.11.21 dialectic is said to be self-grounding.

22. Concerning the nondialogic sketch *De immortalitate animae,* written immediately after the *Soliloquia,* Augustine writes in the *Retractiones* (1.5.1) that it is so obscure that he himself no longer understands it.

other ancient text to the genre of the meditation. But the fact that Augustine's text, unlike Descartes's, is full of second-person endings as well as personal and possessive pronouns shows that Augustine remained an Ancient. As such he could, paradoxically, break out of the form of the dialogue only within a structure that remained a dialogue in a very formal sense.[23]

Petrus Alfonsi's *Dialogus* is an original variation on the conversation with oneself,[24] because in it something unusual happens: after his conversion from Judaism to Christianity at the age of forty-three, the author—known, before his baptism, as Rabbi Moyses—represents a conversation between a certain Moyses and himself as "Petrus," in which the reasons for changing religions are discussed. Anyone who reads only the prologue to the dialogue learns that this Moyses was supposed to be a friend from Petrus's early childhood and a classmate.[25] But the prologue is preceded by a prayer and a two-part preface. The first part tells the story of Petrus Alfonsi's conversion, in which the "discovery" of the Trinity in the Prophets plays a role, and also describes his baptism (on June 29, 1106, St. Peter's Day, in Huesca, with King Alfonso VI as his godfather). The second part describes the three Jewish reactions to his falling away from the belief of the fathers: he despises God and the Law; he has incorrectly interpreted the Prophets and the Law; he has acted out of a desire for fame and opportunism because of the Christians' great power. Thereupon Petrus Alfonsi explains that he has written the following book so that everyone might know his true motives as well as his arguments. The refutation of objections to Christianity is based on reason

---

23. On the other hand, Eberhard's *Dialogus Ratii et Everardi* is a living dialogue, even if Ratius, the interlocutor of Everardus, who plays the role of the "I," is "a fictional figure resulting from the splitting of the *persona auctoris,* a 'better self' " (P. von Moos [1989], 175), who stands for reason: "Ratius rationabiliter secum ratiocinans" (258). But he remains a concrete person with a distinctive sense of humor.

24. Since the new edition by K.-P. Mieth (diss., FU Berlin, 1982) is not easily accessible, I quote the old Migne edition, in which the work still bears the title *Dialogi;* today it is still mostly quoted in this form (sometimes with the addition "contra Iudaeos"). But Ricklin's argument has convinced me that *Dialogus* was the original title (1999; 153).

25. "A tenera igitur pueritiæ ætate quidam mihi perfectissimus adhæserat amicus, nomine Moyes, qui a primæva ætate meus consocius fuerat et condiscipulus" (537 D).

and authority *(ratione et auctoritate).* He has written a dialogue so that the reader can grasp the ideas more easily,[26] and in defending Christianity he has used his present Christian name, but he has given his partner the name that he himself bore before his baptism, Moyses.[27] T. Ricklin interprets this as indicating that the *Dialogus* is "nothing other than a conversation between the baptized Petrus Alfonsi and his unbaptized 'predecessor' Moses."[28] Ricklin is surely aware of the anomaly involved in such a doubling of the personality before the age of Romanticism, but he sees a possible model in the Jewish doctrine of the two inclinations *(yetzer),* even more than in the Pauline discourse about the "old self" (Romans 6:6). According to him, the relation to the Jewish background also explains why "the identification of the figure of Moses with the prebaptismal author ... is only temporary, limited to the *prologus,* and to that extent highly precarious."[29] It can be objected against Ricklin that the preface says only that the interlocutor has Petrus's prebaptismal name; it does not say that he represents the person who the prebaptismal Petrus was. The introduction of Moyses in the prologue also counts against this supposition. And yet it is interesting that here he is described with a superlative—*perfectissimus ... amicus* (the most perfect friend)—and in a certain sense everyone is that to himself. Petrus and Moyses have studied together; they are both philosophically trained and recognize the right of reason to test traditions and deviate from them.[30] To that extent they are really very close to each other, and we can admit that Petrus Alfonsi has deliberately turned the conversation between two friends into something close to a conversation with himself: it is an explanation that Petrus owes to his old Jewish self no less than to his Jewish friends.

26. "Librum autem totum distinxi per dialogum, ut lectoris animus promptior fiat ad intelligendum" (538 B).

27. "In tutandis etiam Christianorum rationibus, nomen quod modo Christianus hebeo *[sic!],* posui: rationibus vero adversarii confutandis, nomen quod ante baptismum habueram, id est Moysen" (538 B/C).

28. (1999), 147.

29. 149; cf. 152.

30. "Tu vero in philosophiæ cunis enutritus, philosophiæ uberibus lactatus, qua fronte me potes inculpare, donec ea quæ fecerim, justa an injusta valeas probare?" (539 A).

We can interpret in a similar way another medieval philosophical dialogue, Ramon Llull's autobiographical poem on his despair titled *Desconhort*. While one of the conversation partners is the first-person narrator, who bears the name and several of the characteristics of the author, in this work Ramon, who has retired into a wood, meets by chance not an old friend but rather an unknown hermit,[31] but the conversation that develops between them soon becomes a kind of self-examination—for instance, when the hermit asks Ramon, whose failures torment him, whether he is perhaps too careless,[32] and conversely later on urges him to rest, which Ramon declines to do.[33] These are questions that Llull will have asked himself, or temptations to which he will have exposed himself; the dialogue thus casts in a dramatic form what must have in large part been a conversation with himself.[34] In the literary universe of the work the hermit remains a different person, and there is nothing that corresponds to the reference in the preface to Petrus Alfonsi's *Dialogus*. But since the hermit is not a clearly drawn individual and especially since the conversation is chiefly concerned with Ramon, the interpretation of the work as Ramon's conversation with himself is natural not only from a genetic but also from a work-immanent point of view. The *Desconhort* is self-observing in a more radical sense than the *Soliloquia* and even the *Consolatio philosophiae*, since the latter get down relatively quickly to the issues at hand; its central theme is the author. (In Petrus Alfonsi the author's conversion is the starting point but not the main theme of the conversation.) Much the same can be said for Petrarch's *Secretum*, which is also concerned with soul-searching, the book allegedly not being intended to exercise any external influence at all.[35] That Augustine the interlocutor is

---

31. V. 49 ff.
32. V. 145 ff.
33. V. 393 ff.
34. Cf. V. Hösle (1996) and the introduction to R. Llull (1998), 39 ff.
35. (1955), 26: "Ubi multa licet adversus seculi nostri mores, deque comunibus mortalium piaculis dicta sint, ut non tam michi quam toti humano generi fieri convitium videretur, ea tamen, quibus ipse notatus sum, memorie altius impressi.... Tuque ideo, libelle, conventus hominum fugiens, mecum mansisse contentus eris, nominis proprii non immemor. *Secretum* enim *meum* es et diceris." This is clearly an intensification with regard to the passage quoted above from *Soliloquia* 1.1.1.

a figure from the past increases the impression that a self-analysis is being carried out in the process of writing the book.

Two forms of self-observation in the dialogue must be distinguished. They are logically independent of each other; in one the author speaks with himself (on some subject), in the other he speaks about himself (with someone else). The latter structure begins with Llull's *Desconhort* and reaches its culmination in Jean-Jacques Rousseau's three dialogues *Rousseau juge de Jean-Jacques*. Here Rousseau's interlocutor is "Le Français," who is certainly another person; but this self-centered work is about Jean-Jacques, who shares essential traits with the author of this book and indeed stands for him. On the other hand, the dialogue character Rousseau cannot be identified either with the author or with Jean-Jacques.[36] But not only does he also come from Geneva;[37] he has a mysterious soul affinity with Jean-Jacques.[38] In the preface, "Du sujet et de la forme de cet écrit," the author claims that he has taken back his family name, of which the public has deprived him, using his first name, by which alone he is known to the public, to refer to himself in the third person—that is, as a subject of discussion: "J'ai pris la liberté de reprendre dans ces entretiens mon nom de famille que le public a jugé à propos de m'ôter, et je me suis désigné en tiers à son exemple par celui de baptême auquel il lui a plu de me réduire."[39] By this means he seeks to show how he would see someone like himself if he were another person—"de quel oeil, si j'étais un autre, je verrais un homme tel que je suis."[40] The dialogue character Rousseau thus shares the moral sensitivity of Rousseau the author, while Jean-Jacques shares his outward life. This splitting of the personality is on the one hand an attempt to make objectivity with regard to himself prevail (succeeding best in the judgment of the dialogue character Rousseau at the beginning of the second dialogue) and on the basis of this objectivity to provide a justification of Jean-Jacques. Rousseau as a

---

36. The author speaks directly only in the footnotes; one such note refers to "Rousseau qui parle ici" in a distancing third-person form (1999; 327).

37. (1999), 179.

38. Cf., e.g., (1999), 72, 78, 82, 90, 98, 132 f., 164. Differences are rarely mentioned (e.g., 140, 151).

39. (1999), 60.

40. (1999), 62.

moral observer—represented by Rousseau the dialogue character—
wants to absolve Rousseau as a human being with a life that has been
lived—represented by Jean-Jacques in the conversation—and reestab-
lish his social reputation. On the other hand, this split probably corresponds to a desperate need, grounded in the author's self-hatred, to
distance himself not only from his public image but also from himself.
Indeed, it is hard to avoid connecting it with Rousseau's advanced para-
noia outside the dialogue, which the work confirms in a depressing but
almost classical way. In a fascinating passage the dialogue character Rousseau transfers within the dialogue the split to Jean-Jacques himself: the
author of the books attributed to him could not, he says, be identical
with the author of the deeds he has allegedly committed.[41] At least Rousseau the author senses that it would be too much if he appeared three
times—in the first, second, and third persons, for instance, in a "Solilo-
quium" about himself; the Frenchman thus stands, up to the end, for an
alterity, the public perception of Rousseau, at least as he himself con-
strues it.[42] In his last work, the *Rêveries du promeneur solitaire*, which begins with the famous words, "Me voici donc seul sur la terre," the dialogue
form is avoided.[43] However, it also appears to be forced upon the earlier
work, because Rousseau, convinced of the absolute uniqueness of Jean-
Jacques' sufferings,[44] ultimately does not believe that he can make his position comprehensible to anyone except those to whom it need not be
communicated.[45] But then conversation becomes superfluous; the important "I" is a closed monad that turns around itself while crying out
into the void for the recognition on which it remains dependent, even if
it loudly rejects it.

---

41. (1999), 90 f.

42. Using the categories "I," "Self," and "Me" (see V. Hösle [1997], 288 ff., 320
ff.), one could say that in the dialogue Rousseau represents the "I," Jean-Jacques the
"Self," and the Frenchman the "Me" of Rousseau the author.

43. A recent philosophical analysis of this book is found in E. Friedlander (2004).

44. (1999), 141, 174. Cf. 119. In a pamphlet handed out to passersby in April
1776, mentioned in the *Histoire du précèdent écrit*, Rousseau describes his suffering
as deeper than that of Job (1999; 425)—just as Llull does in *Desconhort* (V. 591 ff.,
601 ff.).

45. (1999), 66.

Fichte's *Die Bestimmung des Menschen* is not entirely a dialogue; only the second book, titled "Wissen," is in dialogue form. The interlocutor here is not a real Other but rather "a marvelous figure" that appears to the first-person narrator at midnight and is referred to as "the Spirit" *(Der Geist)* in the following pages.[46] In the context of the work, the Spirit's task is to make the "I," who in the first book, "Doubt," is unable to escape the arguments in favor of a deterministic naturalism, familiar with the position of subjective idealism. However, this is only a transitional stage, because the dissolution of the world, and even of the "I," into pure images is no less disturbing than the objectivist vision modeled on Spinoza.[47] Instead of helping him overcome this conception, the Spirit abandons the "I," who in the third book, "Belief," will recognize on his own that the power of practical reason is the sole basis for resolving ontological questions: we believe in the existence of a reality independent of us because we are morally obligated to do so. "There is only one point toward which I must constantly direct my reflection: what I should do, and how I can most effectively meet this obligation. All my thinking must be related to my doing."[48] "The present world is there for us absolutely only through the command of duty; similarly, the other world will emerge for us only through another command of duty: for in no other way is there a world for any rational being."[49]

At the beginning, the Spirit had already told the "I" that he could not teach him anything but only remind him of something he already knew, nor could he deceive him, "for you yourself will think I am right about everything, if you were deceived, you would be deceived by yourself."[50] And at the end he emphasizes that he has sought to free the "I" from false views, not to teach him true knowledge. "And this then is the sole merit I claim for the system that we have just discovered together: it destroys and annihilates error. It cannot provide truth." He finally urges the narrator to seek another intellectual organ, and bids him farewell with the words: "I leave you with yourself alone."[51] Evidently the "I" has to find

---

46. 2.199.
47. 2.245.
48. 2.257.
49. 2.288.
50. 2.199.
51. 2.247.

the crucial philosophical idea by himself; and this holds not only dialogue-internally but also dialogue-externally. In the preface Fichte himself speaks, and he expressly warns the reader that the "I" must not be identified with the author; on the contrary, the reader himself should identify with this "I": "[The reader] should not merely conceive what is said here historically, but instead really and actually speak with himself while he is reading, reflect here and there, draw conclusions, make resolutions, like his representative in the book, and through his own work and reflection, purely by himself, develop and build up the way of thinking of which a mere image is presented in the book."[52] The word *image (Bild)* is used advisedly; it foreshadows the fundamental category of the second book, which proves to be insufficient; instead, it is a matter of autonomous and spontaneous action. The demand that the reader be autonomous is absolutely paradoxical when it comes from an external source, although according to the famous third paragraph of the *Grundlage des Naturrechts* an alternative path to self-consciousness can hardly be imagined.

The demand that the interlocutor be autonomous and the reference to morally responsible action distinguish Fichte's Spirit from the Genius who speaks with the imprisoned Tasso in Leopardi's *Dialogo di Torquato Tasso e del suo Genio Familiare*. The Genius's point is that Tasso should withdraw into his love fantasies and dreams, since the sole difference between what is true and what is dreamed is that the latter—and only the latter—can sometimes be beautiful and tender;[53] therefore one should encourage one's dreams and cultivate one's love relationships only in imagination, because real enjoyment exists only in hope and in a fancied and even dishonest memory, never in the present. Only in this respect can the Genius offer Tasso the consolation, namely, that the boredom he feels in prison will abate; being separated from people rejuvenates and, in the absence of renewed experience, leads to a transfiguration of reality. Tasso should spend his life dreaming and imagining, and if he needs his Genius, he can be found in a liquor bottle.[54]

No matter how superior Fichte's active attitude may be to Leopardi's melancholy, it nonetheless becomes intolerable when it takes the form

52. 2.168.
53. (1956), 522.
54. (1956), 526 f.

of "an attempt to force the reader to understand"—as he puts it in the subtitle to his *Sonnenklarer Bericht an das grössere Publicum, über das eigentliche Wesen der neuesten Philosophie* (A Crystal Clear Report to the General Public Concerning the Actual Essence of the Newest Philosophy: An Attempt to Force the Reader to Understand). What is unusual about this dialogue, which becomes direct from the "First Lesson" on, is that it represents a conversation between "the Author"—D. A. *(der Autor)*—and "the Reader"—D. L. *(der Leser);* the latter, the dialogue-external addressee, becomes a dialogue-internal interlocutor, who is supposed to be the "representative" of all readers[55]—or rather, to be more precise, of readers who are not academically trained, "popular" readers,[56] whom Fichte treats with condescension[57] but always better than professional philosophers, who have only their particular interests in view;[58] like Berkeley, Fichte thinks that his philosophy corresponds to common sense.[59] Thus from a literary point of view this text is intermediate between the second and third subgenres of intersubjectivity as they were distinguished in chapter 1 above. The Reader's present reading of the book becomes the starting point for the Author's observations: "You are now sitting there, for instance, holding this book in your hand, you see its letters, you read its words."[60] After the Author has formally become an interlocutor, it is on the conversation—which, because of the peculiar determination of the interlocutors, is real both on the dialogue-internal and dialogue-external levels—that he asks the Reader to reflect, instead of on a dialogue-internal fictional conversation with a third party: "in order not to accept anything fabricated, but rather to lead you directly into your present true state of mind, while you reason with me as you have earlier reasoned."[61] It is true that in the "Introduction" an appeal is

55. 2.374.

56. 2.326 ff., 385.

57. Cf., e.g., 2.403.

58. Cf. the "Nachschrift an die Philosophen von Profession" (2.410 ff.), and also 2.388 f., with significant insights into the sociology of knowledge.

59. The passage at 2.371 reminds us in a very concrete way of Berkeley's critique of abstract ideas.

60. 2.335.

61. 2.340.

again made to the autonomy of the Reader, who is expected not merely to observe, but rather to participate *intentione recta* in the process of philosophizing and to learn on his own: "What you will read from now on, I have of course thought; but it is of concern neither to you or me that you too now know what I thought. No matter how much you may otherwise be used to reading works simply to find out what the authors of these works thought and said, I want you not to deal with this one in the same way. I do not address your memory, but rather your understanding: my goal is not that you remember what I said, but rather that you yourself think, and if Heaven grants it, think just as I have thought."[62] And yet at least a modern reader cannot escape the impression that the only exercise of the Reader's autonomy that Fichte can imagine is to agree with *his* philosophy; in any event, the Reader is not invited to criticize it. At the end of the first lesson, "the Reader" is suddenly replaced by "a reader (who may moreover be a locally famous philosopher)"; the objection that the latter makes is surely not an immanent criticism. But instead of ironically pointing out, as Plato and Hume do, that this response sheds more light on the receiver than on the author, the Author reacts indignantly: "Put the book down: it is not written for you." At that point, this reader vanishes; in his stead appears "A second fair-minded reader" whose limited agreement the Author accepts—because he is his own creation.[63] Basically, the autonomy of the Reader is already infringed upon precisely because he has been made an interlocutor, for thereby Fichte claims to be able to anticipate his objections. The following passage is typical. After answering a question the Author has asked him, the Reader remarks, "you surely wanted me to answer you in this way," and then adds, "But in this connection I still have the following doubt."[64] The first sentence would make sense dialogue-internally in normal dialogues as well, but here it is also meaningful dialogue-externally, since the interlocutor is actually identical with the author. However, then the "but" in the second sentence makes no sense, since this doubt also corresponds to the author's intentions and thus to those of the interlocutor. It is true

62. 2.329.
63. 2.343.
64. 2.381.

that every writer of dialogues is open to the reproach that he has re-placed the real Other in his work by a construct; but at least the real Other retains his right as a receiver—that is, as someone who can make his own judgment about whether the dialogue is successful or not. But as a thinker of subjectivity, Fichte also wants to absorb completely this Other who has remained external. This didactic dialogue, whose frontal approach is made still more forceful by including the reader, cannot be distinguished sharply enough from the elegance of Plato's writings—though its philosophical quality is not thereby put in doubt. Plato's di-alogues demand a level of independent cooperative thinking on the part of the reader entirely different from that demanded by the *Sonnenklare Bericht,* which hardly raises hermeneutic questions. The price that Plato pays for proceeding in this way is high; only a few readers can really un-derstand what he wants. As an elitist aristocrat, he was willing to pay this price; and it is in accord with modern, universalist ethics that Fichte in contrast addresses the largest possible number of readers. But he overlooks the fact that a modern person's will to autonomy reacts sen-sitively when he is confronted by another person's performatively self-contradictory wish to force him to be autonomous—as autonomy is understood by this other person, of course.[65]

In the normal case, dialogue represents a conversation between at least two different people. "Nothing is better than thinking out loud with a friend."[66] "But the best philosophizing is and always remains compan-ionable."[67] Nicholas of Cusa demonstrated only his inadequate knowledge of Greek when he titled one of his dialogues with three interlocutors *Tri-alogus de possest,* because *dialogos* does not have directly to do with *duo.*[68]

65. To be sure, Fichte admits that attentiveness is something that cannot be forced (2.329f.), and in the conversation the Author constantly emphasizes, "you have to find it yourself" (336); "everything that can be done for you here is to guide you, so that you encounter what is right; and this guiding is absolutely all that any philosophical training can achieve" (337). But the criterion of success is agreement with the Author.

66. G. E. Lessing (1966), II 690.

67. K. W. F. Solger (1971), 3.

68. In *De venatione sapientiae,* Nicholas of Cusa analogously speaks of *De li non aliud* as a "tetralogo"; in the famous Parisina edition of 1514 this is corrected to read "dialogo quadrilocutorio" (XII, 41). In Bruno's *La cena de le ceneri,* it is the pedant Prudenzio who uses the terms "tetralogo," "trilogo," "pentalogo," "eptalogo"—"ed

And yet he at least instinctively sensed that a dialogue between two persons is qualitatively different from a dialogue with more persons. The reason for this is to be found in the essential differences between dual and plural intersubjectivity. A third interlocutor already irrevocably changes the qualitative nature of intersubjectivity—because Ego and Alter are then no longer speaking only to one another but rather, if they speak with one another, they are also implicitly speaking to the third party.[69] It is no accident that existentially intensive dialogues are often dual in nature. Consider the conversation in Plato's *Crito*, which by its very nature could not take place in the presence of many witnesses. But still more important is the fact that Crito has to learn to overcome his dependency on the judgment of the many—for at first he is driven at least as much by this as by his sincere friendship for Socrates; he does not want people to speak badly about him, Crito.[70] In contrast, Socrates shows his lack of interest in the opinion held by the *polloi* and opposes it to that of a single expert.[71] This idea corresponds perfectly to the framework of a dialogue in which Socrates is the sole conversation partner. That only two interlocutors are involved in the erotic discussion in the *Phaedrus* is obviously essential, even though, or precisely because, it is clearly shown that Socrates does not take advantage of the situation, despite his physical proximity (243e7 f.). Clitophon begins his harsh criticism of Socrates by expressly observing that they are alone.[72] Hieron, in

---

altri, che abusivamente si chiamano dialogi" (1985; I 24); one cannot determine with certainty whether the author also endorsed the false etymology. It seems to me likely that he did, since Prudenzio is supposed to be made ridiculous more because of his erudition than because of an error.

69. Cf. V. Hösle (1997), 422–31.

70. 44b6 ff.

71. 44c6 f., d6 ff., 46c2 ff., 47a13–b11, c11 ff., 48a5 ff. Cf. *La.* 184d5 ff. and *Phd.* 64b1 ff. However, in *Prt.* 353a7 ff. Protagoras shows himself to be arrogant with regard to the many, whereas here it is Socrates who takes them more seriously. A similar ironic inversion of the usual opposition is found in *Grg.* 488d5 ff. and 491d10 ff.

72. *Cli.* 406a9 f. I consider this dialogue Platonic; cf. (1984a), 335 f., n. 225. Its authenticity has also recently been defended by S. R. Slings (1999). The dialogue is certainly untypical of Plato, but that is also true of the *Menexenus*, which no one now considers inauthentic. Plato is extremely innovative, and the *Clitophon* is far too complex and dense, and the creation of an anti-Socratic voice far too skillful, for it to be ascribed to someone else.

Xenophon's dialogue that bears his name, would not speak so openly about the burden of his power if Simonides were not his sole interlocutor; the Marshal's wife in *Entretien d'un philosophe avec la Maréchale de **** would not question Diderot with such curiosity were others present. Rameau's moral self-exposure in Diderot's *Le neveu de Rameau* might be much more difficult for him if this were a nondual dialogue; and anyone who, in view of his cynicism, denies that this is so must at least admit it with regard to Rameau's genuine despair over the loss of his wife.[73] The two clerics in Voltaire's second "Dialogue chrétien" would not reveal their malice in such an ininhibited way before a larger audience; and daring theses like those in Diderot's *Suite de l'entretien précédent,* Leo - pardi's "Dialogo di Plotino e di Porfirio," or Gide's *Corydon* can best be discussed in dual dialogues. Significantly, the two friends in Lessing's *Ernst und Falk. Gespräche für Freymäurer* interrupt their discussion when guests arrive.[74] The essentially dual character of Wieland's "Gespräche unter vier Augen" is already indicated by its title.

In a generalized sense of the word, most of Plato's dialogues are dual—at least most of those whose titles are the names of one of Socrates' main interlocutors.[75] Dialogues with other kinds of titles, such as the *Symposium,* the *Republic* (with the exception of the first, probably independently composed book), and the *Laws* are typically not dual. In the *Sophist* and the *Statesman,* Theaetetus and the Young Socrates are only pupils, not adversaries. On the other hand, despite the audience's constant interruptions, the *Protagoras* represents basically a conversation between Socrates and Protagoras. In the *Lysis* as well, the eponymous hero is obviously superior to Menexenus, not to mention Hippo - thales. In the *Gorgias,* Socrates converses with three interlocutors, but he does so one at a time;[76] indeed, Polus and Callicles are under the spell of the statements made by the previous speaker, Gorgias, which

73. (1972), 129 f. The other people in the café, who are following the conversation only occasionally, seem not to notice this scene.

74. (1966), II 713.

75. The *Philebus* is also dual, even if the eponymous hero is not the main interlocutor. On the irony of Plato's title, see chap. 17 below (p. 423 f.).

76. We find something similar in Abelard's *Collationes* and Llull's *Llibre del gentil e dels tres savis* but not in Bodin's *Colloquium,* whose compositional achievement is particularly awe-inspiring.

they try to make consistent. Analogously, in the two parts of the *Parmenides,* the old sage from Elea first questions Socrates, then Aristotle; thus Parmenides, not Socrates, is the dominant figure here (this foreshadows several later dialogues, though only the *Timaeus* and the *Critias* take their titles from the name of the main speaker, as the *Parmenides* does). In the *Gorgias,* the positions taken by Gorgias, Polus, and Callicles appear in a logical sequence—the later ones radicalize and make explicit what was already implicit in the earlier ones. Thus Socrates battles three forms in which one and the same anti-philosophy appears; the opposition in the dialogue is clearly dual in nature. However, we have to grant that this is not always the case—at least not in the superficial structure. Thus two of Plato's dialogues have a "Hegelian" structure, that is, introduce the Socratic position as a synthesis of the other two—namely, the *Cratylus* and the *Laches.* In the latter, Socrates appears as a synthesis of the two generals Laches and Nicias, who have complementary strengths and weaknesses; thus here there are three independent positions. In chapter 3 I mentioned that Laches is the more forceful, Nicias the more intellectual of the two generals. And yet Socrates is not simply one of three interlocutors: he is the one truth opposed to two deficient forms. Hence we can see him as opposed to the two generals as one pole. The unity of this pole, even if it is twofold, is also emphasized by the fact that a further duality appears in the personal force field of the dialogue, that between Lysimachus and Melesias, who stand for a single principle, that of a lovable but degenerate old nobility. This twofold duality is a characteristic trait of the dialogue; on the one hand, it has a comic effect;[77] on the other, it allows the single Socrates to be opposed to a twofold duality. This is related to the *Euthydemus,* in which, however, the two Sophists do not oppose and complement each other, as Laches and Nicias do, but are instead representatives of a single position, and in which there is only one duo.[78]

77. Consider the analogous function of the structure in John Ford's film *Young Mister Lincoln,* where the great man is repeatedly opposed to pairs.

78. Cf. Glaucon and Adimantus in the *Republic,* on whose opposition *R.* 396b ff. and 372b ff. shed light, as well as that between Cebes and Simmias in the *Phaedo,* who are also not of the same rank. On the differences between the two, especially Simmias's

Elsewhere,[79] I have tried to show that it is plausible that the opposition of unity and duality in the *Euthydemus* is connected with Plato's doctrine of the two principles, which it illustrates in the structural form of the dialogue. In the *Crito*, the opposition between One and the Many is *discussed;* in the *Euthydemus*, the opposition between unity and duality—to which, according to Plato's unwritten doctrine, plurality can be traced— is *represented*.[80] In the case of the *Laches*, the duality is doubled and thus intensified.

However, the young Plato already took advantage of the opportunities offered by the introduction of a third party, even if the latter remains marginal. In the *Hippias major*, the third party is, as I have said, fictional; but he is needed to motivate Hippias to further efforts, which sheds a significant light on Hippias's intrinsic motivations as well as on his respect for the conversation partner: the third person is more important to him than the first and second. The *Ion* and the *Hippias minor* are very probably among Plato's earliest dialogues, and they have striking dramatic similarities in their ironic destruction of pseudoknowledge, the comedy consisting in the fact that both the bearers of this pseudoknowledge consider themselves nearly omniscient (thus grotesquely distorting, in Plato's view, the ideal of the true philosopher). The difference between the two is that Ion the rhapsode represents the prephilosophical

---

more persistent skepticism, which Plato regards as unjustified, cf. Sedley (1995), 14 ff. The *Phaedo* is of course named after its narrator, since Phaedo himself hardly contributed to the conversation (however, cf. 89a9 ff.; 89c5 ff. assumes an equality between Socrates and Phaedo in the face of death that is denied, using the same mythologeme—Heracles and Iolaus—between Socrates and Ctesippus in *Euthyd.* 297b9 ff.). Also, Phaedo's assertion that fourteen men were present at the death of Socrates is hardly an accident; it alludes to the companions of Theseus, whose ship is mentioned at 58a ff. Cf. R. Burger (1984), 19 f.

79. (2004c), 268 ff.

80. Bruno's *La cena de le ceneri* has the same principle of construction as the *Euthydemus* (in addition, both are mixed dialogues): the single sage—Socrates or Bruno—is opposed to two charlatans—Euthydemus and Dionysodorus or Nundinio and Torquato. Naturally, I am not claiming that Bruno deliberately imitated Plato; the parallel is typological, not genealogical. The title page of the *Cena* (1985; I 3) shows no less than the beginning of its first dialogue (I 19 ff., esp. 22) that Bruno also had a strong interest in numbers.

claim to knowledge, while Hippias the Sophist represents the philosophical claim. Hippias is therefore more reflective, thus conceited, and hence
more vulnerable. That is why this dialogue, in contrast to the *Ion,* needs a
third party. At the critical point in the conversation, 373a2 ff., Socrates insists that Hippias answer his questions instead of making a long speech
(*makron . . . logon,* 373a2) and then turns to the host, Eudicus, to ask
him to urge Hippias to reply. The latter, who had spoken only briefly at
the beginning, considers participation on his part to be superfluous, but
he reminds Hippias of his promise to answer all the questions asked of
him. This is a crucial function of the third party—tò act as an umpire
and see to it that the rules of the game are respected and commitments
honored, too.[81] When there is no third party, as in the *Euthyphro,* the interlocutor can simply leave. In contrast, in the *Gorgias* and the *Protagoras,*
it is the intervention of third parties that makes it possible to continue
the conversation. In the *Gorgias,* it is the defeated Gorgias who twice commands Callicles to continue.[82] Typically, between these two demands
Callicles speaks *about* Socrates in the third person (as he does already in
489b7: "this fellow") rather than speaking *to* him in the second person—
the classical way of objectivizing another person, which is possible only
when there are more than two interlocutors.

In the *Protagoras,* at the decisive turning point in the conversation,
which occurs in the middle of the work, no less than five third parties
speak up—because "third party" is obviously a qualitative term even
more than it is a quantitative one. Protagoras refuses to give up long
speeches and to engage in a conversation conducted by short questions
and answers *(brachylogia):* he wants to remain master of the process,
because his reputation ultimately depends on it.[83] That is why Socrates
starts to leave; he says he is incapable of long speeches, whereas Protagoras claims to be capable of both long and short speeches; therefore

81. It may be that "Eudicus" ("the just") is in this sense an aptronym; cf. Friedländer (1964), II 133. Friedländer thinks that a third party is necessary in this di -
alogue also because at least one person has to see through Socrates' deception.

82. 497b4 f., 8 ff. Cf. also 506a8 ff.

83. 335a4 ff. Already in 328a8 ff. Protagoras had suggested that all people are
alike, but he is nonetheless a little different *(oligon)* from the rest.

Protagoras must adapt to the weaker party. There is a difference between the give-and-take of conversation and public speeches.[84] But Socrates is first prevented from leaving by the host, Callias, who says that Protagoras is right: everyone has the right to speak as he sees best. Alcibiades contradicts him, and repeats Socrates' argument, whereas Critias scolds both the preceding speakers for being partisan, and simply asks Socrates and Protagoras not to break off the conversation in the middle. Then the two other Sophists speak up, Prodicus with his famous conceptual distinctions, for instance. between friendly "discussion" and hostile "disputation," and then Hippias, sarcastically styled "wise," who rides *his* hobbyhorse, initially opposing nature and law, *phusis* and *nomos*. Then, in a speech that is lofty or even stilted, Hippias begs the two opponents to adopt a middle way, that is, to speak neither too lengthily nor too briefly, and to choose an umpire who will see to it that the speeches are kept to the proper length. Both Hippias and Prodicus are praised by those present who want to elect an umpire. But Socrates opposes this suggestion. There are three possibilities, he says. The umpire may be worse than the speakers to be monitored, but it is not good that a worse man should have the supervision of a better. Or he is just as good; but then he is superfluous. Or he is better; but there can be no man wiser than Protagoras, and to set someone with such a claim over him would be to offend him—though it would not offend him, Socrates. He recommends instead that they continue to proceed by short questions and answers but make the questioning symmetrical: Protagoras must also have the right to question Socrates, just as Socrates has questioned him.[85] When he has finished, however, Socrates must also have the right to ask questions again; if Protagoras then refuses to answer, everyone must beg him not to let the conversation break down. Thus supervision is not to be exercised by a single individual, but by everyone.

This passage is of great importance for understanding Plato's conception of the nature of a successful philosophical conversation. On the one hand, it is a particularly detailed example of a procedural meta-discourse of the kind that characterizes many Platonic dialogues. In reality, the discourse in the *Protagoras* leads to a concrete result: first,

---

84. 334c ff. This passage is reflected in Cic. *Fin.* 2.1.1 ff.
85. Socrates proceeds similarly with regard to Polus, *Grg.* 465e6 ff.

the conversation is continued, and second, there is an important change, namely, that Protagoras attempts, though without much success, to question Socrates. On the other hand, this passage is an extremely witty representation of tendencies that are not very productive philosophically but are natural in an escape into the procedural, even today. Callias and Alcibiades merely repeat on the meta-level the positions taken by the two opposing sides. Critias is completely right when he points to this fact—but his own constructive recommendation, the simple demand that the conversation not be allowed to break down, is similarly inadequate and does not help resolve the opposition. Prodicus and Hippias, second-rate Sophists pushed into the background, finally see an opportunity to speak up;[86] but they are more interested in disseminating their favorite philosophical ideas than in analyzing the conflict. Hippias's declamatory speech ends with a demand that one constantly hears in similar situations—that a compromise be found and a middle road followed (the word *meson* occurs in 338a1 and 6). This is interesting because Plato himself teaches that virtue is a medium between extremes. This doctrine, which is known through Aristotle, is most clearly articulated in the *Statesman;* and in view of the work done by the Tübingen school it is very tempting to see the discussions in the *Statesman* as being foreshadowed by the *Protagoras,* which is concerned at the end with the art of measurement, and where at 357b5 f. one of the gaps in the text discovered by Hans Joachim Krämer[87] occurs.[88] Thus Hippias expresses an important insight but in a trivialized form.[89] In Plato's objective idealism error partakes in truth, though in a distorted form.[90] But it remains error, for giving speeches of middling length would not overcome the methodological opposition between Socrates and Protagoras but only blunt it.

86. Cf. also 347a6 ff.

87. (1959), 490 f.

88. The term used is *eis authis*. In the dialogue, it also appears at 347b3 and 361e5 (cf. *Euthphr.* 6c8). There, however, further discussions ought to be hindered by Alcibiades and Protagoras, respectively; thus reference is made to a time beyond the present conversation, a time that may never come. In contrast, Plato refers through Socrates to something beyond the dialogue, and even perhaps beyond the dialogue form itself.

89. Cf. the analogous passage in *Euthd.* 305c ff. See below, chapter 17, n. 30.

90. This holds a fortiori for unreflective popular wisdom, behind which Socrates ironically suspects a hidden philosophy (*Prt.* 342a ff.). It is expressed through proverbs such as *Mēden agan* (343b3).

With regard to such third parties, Socrates insists on the autonomy of the two opponents. His decisive argument is related ironically to Protagoras's alleged superiority; but naturally Plato thinks that someone with the capacity of being his own measure, which Socrates has (and which he himself has), must not be subject to the judgment of an inferior third party. There is something in this that is undemocratic and hostile to due process; and Socrates' argument, that an umpire who is as good as those to be judged is superfluous, is obviously fallacious: it overlooks the anthropological truth that people are more biased in judging their own cases than those of others. (However, Plato might have denied this is so in the case of exceptional people.) Consider the *Apology of Socrates*, where it was essentially the refusal to subject himself to the judgment of inferior judges that led to his condemnation. However, Socrates' last words to his judges, telling them that they should treat his sons just as he has treated them,[91] represents a certain symmetricalization. And something similar occurs in the *Protagoras* when Socrates offers to allow his opponent to question him. In any case, two points are crucial. First, Socrates succeeds; he remains in control of the process and makes no compromises. The procedure that he considers appropriate remains in force—although in part because Protagoras had boasted that he was capable of following it; thus nothing heteronomous is forced upon him. It is just that the roles are symmetricalized; the outcome must not depend on the persons concerned—but instead on the correct procedure. Second, Socrates rejects the idea of appointing an umpire; but insofar as he cleverly makes everyone present—and thus no one—a supervisor, he can present as a matter of recognizing a general equality that would be violated by naming an umpire what is in reality only an awareness of his own special role.

Later works that were not written by such a unique person as Plato have a considerably more developed consciousness of the need to have a conversation leader who grants speakers the floor,[92] and even an

---

91. *Ap.* 41e–f.

92. Sometimes the position of conversation leader produces itself, so to speak (thus in the Cassiciacum dialogues Augustine enjoys a natural authority, and he decides who may speak: *C. acad.* 1.3.8 and *Ord.* 2.7.22); sometimes someone is appointed to it, and sometimes someone simply seeks to seize it (e.g., Camilla in Schlegel [1967], 311; in the second edition the passage was, not surprisingly, changed).

umpire—significantly, this is especially true of interreligious dialogues. Minucius Felix appears as such an umpire in the dialogue "Octavius," which has three interlocutors and is named after its most important participant; or rather, at the beginning he is appointed to serve as umpire. This is shown even by his physical position: he sits between the pagan Caecilius and the Christian Octavius—not as a sign of his special rank, since there can be no friendship between those who are not equals, but rather as an umpire to listen to the two opponents and keep them separate.[93] His only contribution comes in the middle of the conversation, after Caecilius has completed his attack on Christianity and turned triumphally and arrogantly to Octavius. Minucius limits himself to warning Caecilius not to gloat before the other side has spoken, especially since it is a matter not of glory but of truth.[94] He compliments him on the rhetorical qualities of his speech but points out that these are no guarantee of truth. Therefore it is important to learn to distinguish between brilliant rhetoric and compelling arguments. Caecilius is disappointed, and even accuses Minucius of violating his duty as umpire; it is Octavius's task, he says, not the umpire's, to refute him. Minucius replies that Octavius in fact has the floor; he has only pointed out in the general interest that elegant and true speeches are two different things.[95] Since Caecilius ultimately converts to Christianity, Minucius does not have to judge between them, and this delights him because of the ill will that the exercise of this office often entails.[96]

In Abelard's four-party conversation *Collationes*—which like Plato's *Gorgias* remains dual insofar as the philosopher speaks with the Jew and the Christian in turn and there is never a conversation among four or even three interlocutors—the first-person narrator hesitates to accept

93. 4.6: "nec hoc obsequi fuit aut ordinis aut honoris, quippe cum amicitia pares semper aut accipiat aut faciat, sed ut arbiter et utrisque proximus aures darem et disceptantes duos medius segregarem."

94. 14.2: "neque enim prius exsultare te dignum est concinnitate sermonis, quam utrimque plenius fuerit peroratum, maxime cum non laudi, sed veritati disceptatio vestra nitatur."

95. 15.1: "'Id quod criminaris,' inquam, 'in commune, nisi fallor, conpendium protuli, ut examine scrupuloso nostram sententiam non eloquentiae tumore, sed rerum ipsarum soliditate libremus.'"

96. 40.3: "cum maxima iudicandi mihi invidia detracta sit."

the role of *judex* he has been offered. He is flattered by the request, and he ultimately agrees to play this role, but he emphasizes that in choosing him the opponents have chosen a foolish rather than a wise man.[97] At the end of the first part, he declares that he does not want to judge but to hear and listen to both rounds of the discussion before he makes a judgment, so that he will become wiser,[98] and the work finally ends without his judgment—probably because he did not complete the book, but perhaps also because of a deliberate decision in favor of a fragmentary character that leaves the definitive statement to be made by the reader.[99] Similarly, at the end of Llull's *Llibre del gentil e dels tres savis,* the pagan, who is the functional equivalent of Abelard's *judex,* does not tell the three wise representatives of the monotheistic religions to which one he has converted. However, in this case it is not that he refuses to tell them but rather that the three wise men do not want to know his decision. His factual decision is not to influence their discussion of the normative question as to which decision he *should* make on the basis of reason and the nature of the understanding—a discussion that will be helpful to them in their quest for truth. "E majorment con sia a nos materia que·ns esputem enffre nos per veer, segons fforsa de rahó e de natura de enteniment, qual deu eser la lig que tu triarás. E si tu denant nos manifestaves aquella lig que tu mes ames, no auriem tan be materia con nos esputasem, ni con la veritat atrobasem."[100] Of course, this statement is just as valid dialogue-externally: the reader's decision should also not be influenced by the pagan's decision. And the reader must understand that factual conversion stories belong to another order than the normative dimension of reasons.

The third party is not always an umpire. In *De legibus,* Cicero is so dominant that a judge who would have the last word against him is

97. (2001), 4 ff.

98. "Ego uero, cupidus discendi magis quam iudicandi, omnium prius rationes me uelle audire respondeo, ut tanto essem discretior in iudicando quanto sapientior fierem audiendo" (2001; 76).

99. In my opinion, the question cannot be definitively answered; see Marenbon's careful reflections, lxxxvi ff. However, today there is unanimous agreement that the work does not stem, as was earlier supposed, from the last years of Abelard's life but was probably written around 1130.

100. (1993), 206.

inconceivable; at least the two accompanying characters, Quintus and Atticus, have more or less equal rights with respect to each other. In the *Academica*, however, the exchange between Cicero and Varro seems fairly symmetrical; but what the function of poor Atticus is supposed to be cannot be determined. In the extant part of the text he is utterly superfluous (if not a ludicrous foil like Simplicio in Galileo's *Dialogo sopra i due massimi sistemi*). Such a third party is less significant than an umpire. However, the umpire is less significant than a third party who represents an independent third position. In Hume's *Dialogues Concerning Natural Religion*, Demea, Cleanthes, and Philo represent, as shown in chapter 9, three possible positions in the area of the philosophy of religion: a negative rationalistic theology, a positive empiricist theology, and a thoroughgoing skepticism. (Pamphilus remains silent or exercises an umpire's role only in the framework of his letter to Hermippus; in any case he does not represent any position of his own.) Since the difference between the positions of the dialogue partners is considerable, Hume's compositional achievement is particularly great; it could be described as a high degree of polyphony. Plato's most polyphonic dialogue is undoubtedly the *Symposium*, because it presents seven different conceptions of love. (The title alone indicates that it cannot be understood as dual.) But this plurality of voices does not cause the work to explode, thanks to a brilliant artistic device that establishes unity: the first six speeches demonstrate the movement of ascension that is the subject of the central speech that Socrates ascribes to Diotima; the latter is the culmination of the ascent, which is followed by an intellectual descent in Alcibiades' speech, which provides, however, an existential test of the Socratic way of life.[101] How paltry Marsilio Ficino's commentary on the *Symposium*, which is cast in dialogue form, seems in comparison! There are no relevant differences among the conceptions of love set forth by his speakers, and none of them grasps the difference between the conceptions of the speakers in Plato's *Symposium*. In contrast, Romanticism is concerned with differences and a multiplicity that is not hierarchically ordered, as in Plato, but rather enjoyed in its irreducibility; accordingly,

101. Similarly, the overall structure of the *Republic* reflects the "upward" and "downward" movement of the cave allegory. Cf. below chap. 18, p. 434.

a conclusion to human striving is inconceivable.[102] This is un-Platonic, as is Schlegel's rejection of the primacy of reason with regard to poetry. Precisely because poetry is not general, but instead does justice to individual differences, it is noble. "Reason is only one and the same in all: but as everyone has his own nature and his own love, everyone also carries his own poetry within him. This poetry must and should remain to him, as certainly as he is who he is, as certainly as something original was in him; and no criticism can or may deprive him of his most essential being, his innermost power, in order to reform and purify him into a general image without spirit or meaning, as fools endeavor who do not know what they want."[103] At least Schlegel acknowledges that individuality is also a limitation that contradicts human beings' spiritual nature, and that one function of conversation is precisely to outgrow one's own limitation: "But since his poetry, precisely because it is his, must be limited, his view of poetry, too, cannot be other than limited. The spirit cannot bear this, no doubt because without knowing it, it nonetheless knows that no human being is simply a human being, but also can and must be at the same time, really and in truth, the whole of humanity. Therefore the human being, sure that he will always rediscover himself, again and again goes out of himself in order to seek and find the completion of his innermost being in the depths of another being."[104] In this train of thought we recognize the influence of Aristophanes' speech in the *Symposium,* which is, however, generalized: the completion of the self through others is no longer dual and erotic but general and intellectual.

Regarding the representation of different positions, questions inevitably arise: Why did the author present, for instance, only three positions and not four or five? Are there in fact no others? Or are more simply not possible? In medieval dialogues on the philosophy of religion the fact that there are three great monotheistic religions is responsible for the number of interlocutors in Llull's work (and in Abelard, if we see the philosopher as an Islamic rationalist).[105] However, Nicholas of Cusa

---

102. F. Schlegel (1967), 284 f., 286. On Schlegel's dialogue, see V. Hösle (2010).
103. (1967), 284.
104. (1967), 285 f.
105. This is suggested by (2001), 48. On this, see Marenbon's introduction, l–liv.

already includes in his conversation on religion representatives of poly-theistic religions (in *De pace fidei,* there are seventeen mortal inter-locutors in all). In the late sixteenth century, Bodin used as the basis of his *Colloquium heptaplomeres* the three forms of Western Christianity. With the Jew, the Moslem, and the two philosophers—a Platonist and a Skeptic—he thus arrives at seven characters. This number, which gives his work its title, is familiar from Plato's *Symposium;* and there are prob-ably group psychology grounds for not going beyond it if each of the conversation partners is to speak at length. There are dialogues with more interlocutors—I have mentioned *De pace fidei,* and Feyerabend's "First Dialogue" also comes to mind. Ancient deipnon and symposium litera-ture provides the rule, which Kant still makes his own,[106] that a good ban-quet should have no fewer participants than the number of the Graces, and no more than the number of the Muses, that is, between three and nine—according to Evangelus in Macrobius's *Saturnalia.*[107] But in the latter work, with the arrival of Evangelus and two other uninvited guests the number of participants in the conversation rises to twelve (not to mention the enormous number in Athenaeus's *Deipnosophistai*). How-ever, in dialogues with so many interlocutors the contributions made by some of them are inevitably reduced to brief comments that do not allow either a characterization of the individual or a vivid elaboration of his position; otherwise, the work would lose its coherence.

I first distinguished between whether a certain number of philo-sophical positions is merely a fact or whether it can be seen as necessary. So far as I can see, Schelling's *Bruno* (1802) is the first philosophical di-alogue that claims to represent all the basic positions that are possible in philosophy. This is a new and fascinating idea; it continues the attempt made at the end of Kant's *Critique of Pure Reason,* in the fourth chapter of the "Transcendental Doctrine of Method," and anticipates Hegel's program of a philosophical history of philosophy and Trendelenburg's and Dilthey's efforts to arrive at a typology of possible philosophies. In Schelling, there are four interlocutors, one more than in Hume. One of

---

106. However, in both the *Metaphysik der Sitten* (8.561) and the *Anthropologie in pragmatischer Hinsicht* (12.617) he quotes it from Chesterfield.

107. 1.7.12, with reference to Varro's Menippean satire "Nescis quid vesper vehat."

them, Anselmo, whose position is based on Leibniz's,[108] accuses contemporary philosophy of many faults: a reduction of the legitimate forms of knowledge to insight into cause-and-effect relationships, diffidence with regard to the absolute and to categorical and apodictic knowledge, a dualistic conception of the absolute that opposes it to something else and thereby deprives it of its absoluteness, and in general the tendency "to make the innate and insuperable diremption of its own nature into philosophy itself."[109] To be sure, this is true only of "the rabble that 'philosophizes' today"; but the better contemporary philosophy is also disappointing, because it is only idealism in the formal sense, in that it declares, and rightly so, that the world of the senses is nothing. Thereupon Anselmo comes to speak of true philosophy and turns to his three interlocutors:

> But the grand and true forms of philosophy have disappeared, more or less. Philosophy's subject matter is by its nature perfectly simple and indivisible, and only to the extent that a given form of philosophy embodies this simplicity will its contents be true and correct. Just as the earth's one center of gravity can be viewed from four different directions of the compass, and just as the one primal matter shows itself in four metals, equally noble and equally indissoluble, so also has reason preeminently expressed its indivisible simplicity in four forms, which demarcate, as it were, the four directions of the world of philosophy. For the doctrine our contemporaries have labeled materialism seems to belong to the western hemisphere, while what they call intellectualism pertains to the Orient; and the southerly regions we can call the territory of realism, the northerly ones, that of idealism. But the task which calls for our greatest efforts is that of recognizing the one metal of philosophy, self-identical in all these forms, in the purity of its native state. And I believe it is crucial for someone who would transcend

108. (1976), 228.
109. (1976), 205. Translation here and in the following taken from *Bruno, or, On the natural and the divine principle of things,* trans. M. G. Vater (Albany, 1984), 204 and 205, respectively.

them to become acquainted with these particular forms of philosophy and with their fate, though the review of these positions would be pleasant for anyone who has already surpassed them. And so, if it is to your liking, here is what I propose: Alexander should trace the history of that philosophical doctrine that recognizes the eternal and divine principle in matter, while I shall relate the essentials of the doctrine of the intellectual world; then Lucian and you, Bruno, can bring the contrasting positions of idealism and realism into our inquiry.[110]

The program sounds fascinating; but its execution is deeply disappointing. First, the number four is not really grounded; it is merely made plausible by the reference to the four regions of the world (whose number is natural only if we assume two-dimensionality and a division into two). Second, the passage quoted comes only toward the end of the dialogue; the exchange between Lucian and Bruno regarding idealism and realism fills only the last pages,[111] and it cannot be said that the contrast dominates the dialogue from the outset and even less that it is its generating principle. Third, in the earlier part, after an introductory conversation between Anselmo and Alexander on truth and beauty, Bruno is the dominant character; and no matter how fascinating and even brilliant his sketch of natural philosophy may be, his long speech without any interruption,[112] which obviously has its model in Plato's *Timaeus,* is hardly suitable to the dialogue form. Fourth, however, the four positions are only further differentiations of a philosophy common to the four friends, since the "philosophical rabble" and even a position such as Kant's transcendental idealism are expressly excluded. Plato proceeded differently in his dialogues, which therefore have a dramatic quality entirely different from Schelling's *Bruno.* Characters like Thrasymachus and Callicles, and also Protagoras and even Laches, guarantee a high degree of polyphony in Plato's dialogues at least up to the *Republic.* In *Bruno,* in contrast, there

110. (1976), 205 f.
111. Right at the beginning it is said, without any further explanation, "Already the time is coming that summons us away" (1976; 217).
112. (1976), 153–81.

is too little diversity among the various interlocutors on the theoretical level, and no relevant character differences among them are made clear. Alexander responds to Anselmo's proposal with a long speech,[113] to which Anselmo makes no objection, since he obviously can agree with everything in it. In addition, the concluding exchange between Lucian and Bruno, who are clearly supposed to stand for Fichte and Schelling, does not establish a contrast even at the beginning. Lucian emphasizes: "Above all it seems necessary to say how we can distinguish at all between idealism and realism. They cannot be distinguished by their object, if both of them seek the highest kind of knowledge, for this is necessarily one and the same. If either or both of them are not of a speculative kind, however, then in the first case no comparison is possible, and in the other case it would be not be worthwhile to seek to determine their difference. The One of all philosophy is the absolute."[114] We do not need to inquire at length into how a conversation among people will go if it abominates any real otherness, because a comparison of the true and the false is not possible, and a comparison of falsities with one another is not worthwhile. Bruno takes over the leadership of the conversation,[115] and Lucian's contribution is reduced to agreeing, usually with clichés such as "necessarily," "I think," "so it is," "obviously," "doubtless," "certainly," "it goes without saying," "absolutely," "undeniably," "well-said," "precisely," "this is evident," "without reservations," "here, too, we are in agreement," "so it must be," "surely."[116] But in that case the dialogue form is clearly superfluous, and if Schelling thought that *Bruno* could be a model for a conversation between himself and Fichte, he was mistaken—doubtless, undeniably, and without reservations. Another writer of dialogues comes closer to *Bruno* than Plato does—and he is, naturally, Giordano Bruno himself, to whom the title of the dialogue already alludes, and to whose dialogue

113. (1976), 206–17.
114. (1976), 217.
115. This already occurred at the beginning, when he chose Lucian as his junior partner (1976; 131; see also 190).
116. K. Rosenkranz writes sarcastically about *Bruno* (1843), 200: "If we take away these manifold ways of expressing affirmation and the turns of phrase borrowed from Plato that the apparently conversing characters use in addressing each other— 'O best of men, excellent man'—we will have taken away the whole conversation."

De la causa, principio e uno, Schelling refers in his notes.[117] It is possible to differ regarding the quality of Bruno's lyrics; but it is certain that the dramatic life of his dialogues, with the exception of *La cena de le ceneri,* is not very developed. Schelling's *Bruno,* however, has a still lower degree of polyphony than *De la causa, principio e uno.*

The failure of Schelling's *Bruno* as a dialogue does not mean that the work is philosophically insignificant. On the contrary; anyone who reads it for the first time is surprised to find how much Hegel's *Naturphiloso-phie* owes to it. The brilliance of the idea that the integration of temporality into things is a criterion of their perfection[118] still needs to be deepened into a form of objective idealism that approaches the relation between being and time differently than does Heidegger, whose criticisms of modern natural sciences and technology, indeed, whose thesis regarding the "oblivion of Being" *(Seinsvergessenheit),* are anticipated by Schelling.[119] But however much these anticipations are worthy of a Schelling, they are not promoted by the use of the dialogue form. Hegel's critical judgment on the dialogue as a form of philosophy may have been codetermined by his reading of *Bruno.* But his criticism bears only on the defective version of the philosophical dialogue, not the perfect form it takes in Plato and whose philosophical potential Hegel misses in theory and Schelling in practice. When Hegel writes that Plato's and Aristotle's writings could easily be transformed into one another (11.270 f.), he merely demonstrates his faulty grasp on Plato's art of dialogue. But he rightly senses that *Bruno* could be transformed into his *Naturphilosophie* without losing anything essential.

117. (1976), 226 ff. On p. 129 a certain Polyhymnio is mentioned who is supposed to have taken part in the previous day's conversation. That is the name of one of the interlocutors in *De la causa, principio e uno,* from the second dialogue onward.
118. (1976), 170.
119. (1976), 202, 211, 225.

CHAPTER 14

The Initial Conditions of Conversation

Arranged and Accidental Conversations—Symmetrical and
Asymmetrical Conversations—Authority and Autonomy

People can encounter one another with force; they can limit their verbal exchange to practical discussions in order to achieve a certain goal;
they can ignore one another. That they have a discussion about a subject or even a philosophical conversation is not a matter of course. On
the one hand, people can come together for the express purpose of philosophizing with one another; on the other, such a conversation can be
a kind of gift resulting from an accidental meeting or grow out of an
everyday chat. (Moreover, accidents such as surprising associations and
insights can arise during both kinds of conversation.)[1] A good example
of the first case is provided by Plato's *Sophist* and *Statesman,* in which
the interlocutors meet by previous arrangement or have already met;
the *Philebus* even begins at a point when the philosophical conversation
is already under way. The *Hippias minor, Gorgias,* and *Parmenides* take
as their point of departure already delivered speeches, though Socrates
has missed hearing the second of these. The *Cratylus* begins abruptly

1. Plato's Socrates says that he still does not know where the conversation, like
the wind, will lead (*R.* 394d7 ff.).

with Hermogenes asking Socrates, after Cratylus has given his permission, the question which is the whole subject of the conversation; an analogous opening is found in the *Meno*.[2] We can also adduce a few dialogues by Nicholas of Cusa in which he himself appears: as Cardinal (since 1448), Prince-Bishop of Brixen (since 1450), and Vicar-General of the Papal States (since 1459), he was very busy, and special periods of free time had to be set aside in order to carry out philosophical discussions with friends and pupils. At the beginning of *De possest*, Nicholas's friend Bernardus (Bernhard of Kraiburg) tells Nicholas's secretary, Ioannes (Giovanni Andrea Bussi), to ask the Cardinal, who is sitting by the fire, a question, in order to engage him in a philosophical and theological conversation; the long-awaited opportunity has finally presented itself. Ioannes in turn tells Bernardus to ask Nicholas, who suggests in a friendly way that the two of them sit down with him and let him take part in their reflections.[3] Analogously, at the beginning of the *Directio speculantis seu de non aliud*, Bussi tells Nicholas about the interest he and his two conversation partners have in Plato, Proclus, and Aristotle.[4] Thus in both cases the philosophical conversation begins immediately. In *De apice theoriae*, Petrus (Peter of Erkelenz) hesitates to burden Nicholas with questions, but only because he sees that he is sunk in deep contemplation; thus here it is not a question of moving on to philosophy but rather of philosophizing being transformed from a subjective into an intersubjective phenomenon. Petrus finally musters the courage to ask Nicholas a question because it seems to him that Nicholas is now less tense, as if he had discovered something important and is happy about it.[5]

The first book of *De ludo globi* opens quite differently, with chance playing a role. Nicholas of Cusa is tired after playing the game of spheres, and Duke John asks him about the game's symbolic meaning. Thus a

---

2. See already Sigonio (1992), 192 ff.

3. XI 2, 3.

4. XIII 3.

5. XII 117: "Video te quadam profunda meditatione aliquot dies raptum adeo quod timui tibi molestior fieri, si te quaestionibus de occurrentibus pulsarem. Nunc, cum te minus intentum et quasi magni aliquid invenisses laetum reperiam, ignosces spero, si ultra solitum te interrogavero."

life-world activity, a game, becomes an occasion for philosophical speculations.[6] However, the transition to philosophy takes place very quickly,
too quickly; constructing it in a literary way would have been an artistic
task of which Nicholas was not capable. In *Idiota de sapientia* the layman turns to the speaker, and in *Idiota de mente* the orator turns to the
philosopher with a directness that may be likable enough but is not very
subtle from a human point of view and without art from a point of view
external to the dialogue.[7] In contrast, no one is as talented as Plato for
representing, especially in the dialogues preceding the *Republic,* the gradual entry into conversation of people who, to their own astonishment,
end up engaged in a process of philosophical questioning from which
they were initially very remote. Naturally, Socrates does not share this
astonishment, since he pulls the strings almost as much as Plato, the
puppet master of the dialogue, which in this case receives a dialogue-
internal proem,[8] a prologue which, like the overture to a good opera, foreshadows the themes that will subsequently be treated in the body of the
work.[9] Here we can distinguish dialogues such as the *Crito, Phaedo,* and
Symposium, where the encounter is not accidental but where the intensity
of the philosophical exchange that results is at least not foreseen by everyone, from the dialogues that begin with an accidental encounter: the *Ion,
Euthyphro, Lysis, Charmides, Euthydemus, Menexenus,* and probably also
Hippias major (whose beginning is not unambiguous), the *Phaedrus,* and
especially and paradoxically, in view of its length, the *Republic.* Indeed,
even the *Laches* can be counted among this second group of dialogues, because although Lysimachus and Melesias turn to Nicias and Laches with a
specific concern, they are not aware that Socrates is with them and will
soon dominate it. Among later dialogues, only a few belong to the cate-

---

6. IX 3. Analogously, in *De possest* children's playing with a top is interpreted
philosophically (XI 2 23 ff.); but here the game remains external to the conversation.

7. V 3 f., 45.

8. Sigonio compares it with the prologue in tragedy and comedy, whereas he
compares the argument proper with the *agōn* (1992; 165).

9. Following Basil (see above, chap. 4, n. 27), Sigonio (1993; 192) writes about
the Platonic prologue: "Quae pars quia mirificum quendam ingenii leporem et quandam quasi morum festivitatem desiderat, propterea ab Aristotele et Theophrasto in
suis dialogis repudiata est."

gory of those that begin with an accidental encounter or at least with an accidental event—for example, Augustine's *De ordine,* which was discussed in chapter 3, Aeneas of Gaza's *Theophrastus,* Leibniz's "Dialogue entre Poliandre et Théophile," and Diderot's *Entretien d'un philosophe avec la Maréchale de **** . They are relatively rare because they presuppose a leisure and a public life such as existed preeminently in ancient Greece. For example, the conversation described in Diderot's *Entretien d'un philosophe avec la Maréchale de **** results from the accident that the Marshal happens not to be at home, and Diderot can therefore pay his wife a courtesy visit. However, he has not entered his mansion by chance; he has a specific though quite different purpose in mind. From a philosophical-theological point of view, even an accident behind which no ulterior *human* motive is concealed may nonetheless appear as part of a *divine* intention—this holds, as we saw, for Augustine.[10] No one has expressed this more eloquently than Aeneas. The *Theophrastus* begins with the description of a voyage made against the Syrian Euxitheus's will: his ship is on its way from Syria to Athens when a storm drives it to Alexandria, the second intellectual center of the Greek world of late antiquity, where he meets by chance his old schoolmate Hierocles of Egypt. When the latter hears that Euxitheus's intention was to pursue philosophical studies in Athens, he takes him to meet the Athenian philosopher Theophrastus, who is sojourning in Alexandria. However, the Christian Euxitheus proves to be superior to the learned pagan who constantly cites ancient philosophers as authorities; but that is not what concerns us here. What is fascinating about the beginning of this dialogue is that Aegyptus praises the wind that has brought Euxitheus to him; an accident that cooperates with him has, contary to all expectation, driven to him a longed-for friend of whom he has continued to be fond, despite all the time that has gone by. Euxitheus also rejoices in the accident. The wind is thus not hostile but instead full of goodwill and

---

10. In addition to *De ordine,* we can also mention *De beata vita,* where God guides the conversational flow that is unforeseeable for the participants in it (3.17). Even before the development of Christian monotheism an accident that constitutes a conversation can be connected with the divine—for instance, *Euthd.* 272e1 ff., with the *daimonion.*

friendly to love, since it has brought the beloved to the lover. Since providence is one of the dialogue's themes, it is hard not to read the initial exchange in light of it;[11] indeed, since in addition to the defense of belief in the Resurrection, the rejection of the doctrine of the preexistence of the soul is a subject of the conversation, the opening sentence— "Whither and whence, Euxitheus?"[12]—can even have, in addition to its realistic meaning, a metaphysical second meaning,[13] despite the obvious Platonic models.[14]

A classic Platonic example of what might be called the "dialogue of the accidental conversation" is the *Euthyphro*: Socrates and the eponymous hero meet by chance in the portico of the Archon Basileus, Socrates because he has been accused and Euthyphro because he has filed a lawsuit. That this suit is against his own father—whom Euthyphro holds responsible for the death of a day laborer who, because he committed manslaughter, was bound, thrown into a pit, and died there of cold and hunger—offends the ethical feelings not only of his contemporaries, an offense of which Euthyphro is proud, but also those of Socrates and with him Plato, who consider it self-evident that one may not bring a lawsuit against one's father on behalf of an outsider.[15] (The "may" refers to what is morally permissible; a lawsuit like Euthyphro's, although unusual, seems to have been legally permissible.)[16] Today, on the basis of a universalist ethics, we would be more likely to agree with Euthyphro, who insists that it is not a matter of the degrees of nearness between Euthyphro on the one hand and the person killed and the killer on the other, but rather exclusively of the question whether the killing is in accord with the law or not.[17] But however much Euthyphro seems to us moderns—at least to the author of this book—to be defending an

11. Cf. 4.11 Colonna.

12. *Poi dē kai pothen, Euxithee;* (2.2 Colonna).

13. The *pothen* is perhaps repeated in the *hothen* connected with the demiurges (17,2 Colonna). See also 36,5/10/20 and 37,2.

14. *Phdr.* 227a1 and *Ly.* 203a6 f. Because of the dialogue's myth of the soul, a metaphysical dimension may also be intended in the initial question of the *Phaedrus*.

15. 4b5. Cf. *Cri.* 51c f.

16. A good overview of the corresponding controversy in legal history is offered by P. Stemmer (1992), 27 f.

17. 4b7 ff., 5d8 ff.

important material ethical insight, we must nonetheless agree with Plato that this ethical revolutionary, even if he represents a higher principle, is not personally very credible, and especially that he does not do justice to the argumentative duty of care to which every ethical reformer is subject. (This holds only for Plato's Euthyphro. Whether Plato did justice to the historical figure is an entirely different question that can no longer be answered—not even Plato's admirers should answer it too quickly in the affirmative.) Euthyphro's crucial argument is that he is dealing with his father as Zeus dealt with Kronos, and he reproaches his critics for the contradiction between what they say about the gods and what they say about him.[18] It might be objected that the contradiction can be erased by assuming that the standards are different for gods and humans, but it is clear that Plato joins in Euthyphro's criticism of the inconsistencies of naive religious people.[19] His and his Socrates' problem is something else: Euthyphro's own ideas are no less contradictory. Not only does he find it difficult to understand the general question about the nature of holiness; his attempt at a definition—the holy is what the gods love—fails both because it is possible that not all the gods agree and, even in the corrected version—the holy is what *all* the gods love—because it encounters the fundamental problem of any religious voluntarism (which also concerns the monotheistic variant): the gods love something because it is holy and not the other way around.[20] In addition, despite his boastful claims, Euthyphro is incapable of explaining why his behavior is justified by his criterion;[21] indeed he finds it difficult to understand that the controversy cannot be resolved by an appeal to generalities such as "whoever has illegally killed someone must be punished," but rather that the illegality of killing this laborer is what is at issue.[22] In the *Euthyphro*, Plato makes it clear that a religious foundation of moral norms cannot be achieved without a metaphysical clarification of ethical concepts, without a theory of the ideas that are directly addressed in the

18. 5e5 ff.
19. 6a6 ff. See also 8d11 ff. on the moral agreement between gods and humans.
20. 10a ff.
21. 9b4 f.
22. 8b7 ff.

dialogue.[23] But since the claim to act morally is peculiar to every person, and especially to religiously inspired moralists, Socrates needs only to use this claim as a springboard for his philosophical investigations. Similarly, in the *Lysis* he uses Hippothales' erotic desire, in the *Laches* the pedagogical concerns of Lysimachus and Melesias, in the *Charmides* the eponymous hero's headache, in the *Menexenus* his interlocutor's political ambition, and in the *Republic* Cephalus's reflections on his waning life as the starting point for philosophical questioning that goes beyond these matters in an almost dizzying way.[24] In D. Lewis's *Holes,* to launch a general attack on materialism Bargle uses the example of the holes in the Swiss cheese that he maliciously offers his materialistic guest.[25]

　　It is remarkable how the leitmotifs of the dialogue are already discernible in the prologue to the *Euthyphro*. Socrates and Euthyphro meet in a building in which trials take place; but Socrates is an accused, Euthyphro a plaintiff. That alone points to the difference between the two, a difference on which Socrates insists despite Euthyphro's attempts to curry his favor. Plato obviously considered it important to distinguish Socrates' rational morality from the self-righteous morality of the priest (just as Schiller wants to distinguish Wilhelm Tell from Johannes Parricida in the second scene of the fifth act of *Wilhelm Tell,* or as Kierkegaard wants to distinguish himself from Adler in his posthumous *Bogen om Adler* [Book on Adler]). Socrates' ironic comments on the wisdom and moral seriousness of his accuser Meletus (2c ff.) anticipate his ironic praise of Euthyphro's behavior (5a ff.). It is also tempting to connect his surprised question to Euthyphro, who has just boasted that others consider him mad to prosecute such a man—namely, the question whether Euthyphro's boast involves someone who has wings to fly with[26]—not only with the ironically assumed supernatural abilities of the soothsayer

---

23. 5d1 ff., 6d9 ff.

24. At the end of his sixtieth discourse ("Nessus or Deianeira"), Dio Chrysostom referred to Socrates' peculiar way of using every opportunity, in the wrestling school, at banquets, and in the agora, to move into philosophy, and to do so without introducing a theme of his own, but always making use of the current subject of conversation, which he guided toward philosophy: "*all' aei tēi parousēi chrōmenos kai tautēn prosagōn pros philosophian*" (174, 11 ff. de Budé).

25. (1983), 3.

26. 4a1 f.

but also with the later aporia. For Socrates describes himself as a descendant of Daedalus whose statements run off and will not stay put; indeed, he gives the same power to the statements of others.[27] Daedalus's art of flying is not explicitly mentioned, but his flight with Icarus is so closely connected with Daedalus's name[28] that Socrates' question is probably intended to anticipate his own behavior: he is the one who, like another Daedalus, will fly away intellectually from Euthyphro. Particularly witty is the passage at 3e4 f., where Euthyphro predicts that Socrates will win his case as he desires *(kata noun)*. It is typical that he begins the sentence with a "perhaps" *(isōs);* he does not want to make a firm commitment, and this makes his claim that all his predictions have thus far proven correct (3c ff.) seem not particularly remarkable, since they were probably all similarly qualified and thus resistant to falsification, like the Delphic oracle's prophecies. If we abstract from the qualification, the prediction is, of course, false, which casts light on Euthyphro's talent. But is it really false? In a certain sense it is not Socrates but the Athenians who lose; to his own way of thinking, he wins his case.[29] Naturally, Euthyphro did not have that in mind, but he states—involuntarily, as it were—an important truth, just as in their sophisms Euthydemus and Dionysodorus allude to connections that are considerably more profound than they themselves realize.[30] C. F. von Weizsäcker has rightly proposed a principle for interpreting Plato whose application ought in my opinion at least to be tried out: "For every claim that Plato puts into the mouths of his characters, there is an interpretation in which that claim, according to Plato's own opinion, is true."[31]

27. 11b9–e1. On the comparison with Daedalus's works of art, see also *Men.* 97d ff. The central verb *menein,* "to stay," occurs, in addition to *Euthphr.* 11b8, c4, c9, and d8, several times in a row in the complementary dialogue *Crito* (48b5, 7, and 10.)

28. Cf. Xen. *Mem.* 4.2.33.

29. Cf. *Ap.* 38d3 ff.

30. That even the perverse reflects the lofty, as in a distorted mirror, is an insight that we find not only in Plato but also in Dante and Goethe—in the countertrinity of the last circle of Hell as well as in Mephistopheles' erotic feelings with regard to the angels in the penultimate scene of *Faust II.* Agnes's remark to Leonhardt in Schleiermacher's *Weihnachtsfeier* is wholly Platonic: "And if you really want to do it well, then just start mocking; then surely the true will from you despite what you wanted, as it did before" (1869; 132).

31. (1981), 24. Cf. 53.

In the same way, early in the dialogue a theme is announced that appears in many of the so-called aporetic dialogues, and which must be kept constantly in view while interpreting them. Socrates declares that the distinction between the hatred that he himself provokes and the mere mockery that Euthyphro suffers is based on the fact that he, Socrates, teaches his wisdom and says everything he thinks, whereas Euthyphro makes himself scarce and conceals his wisdom.[32] This is obviously to be read just as ironically as his praise of Euthyphro; for in reading the dialogue we do not at all have the impression that Euthyphro has much to conceal, even if he alludes self-importantly to his secret knowledge regarding mythical events.[33] Conversely, however, this means that the Platonic Socrates does not say everything he knows. This does not mean that the statement that Socrates provokes hatred because he tries to teach his wisdom is false. "More artistic varieties of irony do not put the intended meaning in an abstract relationship of opposition to the literal meaning of what is said."[34] The former statement is correct for the historical Socrates as well as for the Platonic Socrates, and precisely in the *Euthyphro:* at the end, Euthyphro flees—physically, not intellectually—because he cannot bear the idea that Socrates—who does not thereby exactly increase Euthyphro's affection for him—will destroy his pretension to knowledge. But since Socrates does not resolve the aporia, which is easy to resolve, he keeps something hidden, whereas at the same time he uses arguments that compellingly refute the other's position: he shows the *pars destruens* of his wisdom but does not reveal the *pars construens.*

The masterly talent with which Plato sounds the later themes in the very first remarks of a dialogue is shown not only by the *Euthyphro.* The introduction to the *Laches,* regarding fencing in full armor, is the longest in any Platonic dialogue; it is aesthetically justified only if it foreshadows the true philosophical conversation. In fact, its theme anticipates the following philosophical battle in the armor of conceptually trained thinking; and the anecdote about Stesilaus's scythe-spear getting caught in the

---

32. 3c7 ff. The idea is repeated several times: 11b1 f., 14b9 ff., 15d1 ff., and e2. On this, see Szlezák (1985), 107–16.

33. 6b5 f., c5 ff.

34. W. Wieland (1982), 62. Even if I cannot agree with the context in which this statement appears, it is in itself precisely true for Plato's irony.

rigging (183c ff.) only anticipates the aporia of the dialogue, the getting-caught of the conversation. The argument made by the conservative Laches, that the new art of fencing cannot be worth much because it is not recognized precisely in Sparta, which is the place for fencing, just as Athens is the place for tragedy (182e ff.), must be read reflexively: the art of dialectic that Plato offers is the true military art, its representation in dialogue is the legitimate heir of tragedy, and thus Plato's philosophical-literary work is a synthesis of the two most important city-states of Greece.

With unsurpassable grace, the prologue to the *Phaedrus* outlines the theme of the dialogue as well as the nature of the relationship between the two interlocutors. Socrates meets Phaedrus, who is going for a walk outside the city after he has listened to a speech given by Lysias, which maintained that a beautiful boy ought to be inclined more toward someone who is not in love with him than toward someone who is. Socrates is curious, but Phaedrus is coy; he claims he cannot retrieve the speech from his memory. But Socrates does not believe him: he knows Phaedrus as well as he knows himself. And the Phaedrus he knows must certainly have asked Lysias to read him the speech several times, and Lysias would have been glad to do so; he would then have secured the text, parts of which he has learned by heart, and is now going outside the city to practice them; he had rejoiced to see in Socrates a possible victim, but when Socrates asked him to present the speech, he pretended not to want to, even though he was so eager to give it that he would finally have even resorted to violence in order to do so. "So beg him, Phaedrus, to do straightway what he will soon do in any case."[35] Phaedrus now agrees to present the speech he has learned by heart, but Socrates wants first to see what he has concealed under his cloak; it is the written text, which Phaedrus finally has to read. The proem is so successful because it demonstrates Socrates' character at the outset: he is a master of the psychology of everyday life, who knows Phaedrus and even Lysias very well, and immediately sees through Phaedrus's little lies; thus he is qualified to present a philosophical psychology such as we find especially in the first part of the dialogue on eros (245c ff.), and also in the second part on rhetoric

---

35. 228c3 ff: *su oun, ō Phaidre, autou deēthēti hoper takha pantōs poiēsei nun ēdē poiein.*

(269e ff.). His superiority over Phaedrus is full of irony, but no less full of goodwill; Socrates knows himself no better than he knows Phaedrus.[36] When he asks him to ask Phaedrus to be reasonable right away, he is appealing to a better Phaedrus, and thus already presupposes a multileveled model of the soul as it is later presented in mythical garb and to which 230a also alludes. The discussion regarding an oral presentation of the speech versus a reading of it naturally refers to the conclusion concerning the relationship between orality and scripturality. Phaedrus's behavior is no less characteristic. We see that he has just learned a lesson—he tries to conceal his eagerness to present and discuss Lysias's speech, just as the cunning lover in Lysias's speech conceals his love; Socrates will later note that the latter, even if he pretends to remain "cool," is in fact driven by sexual desire.[37] By revealing Phaedrus's real intention, Socrates anticipates the later unmasking of Lysias's lover; he shows that among friends one may certainly ask for something appropriate. Moreover, his first speech, which seems to surpass Lysias, contains nothing false; it limits itself to criticizing the passionate lover and deliberately breaks off before the praise of the person who is allegedly not in love (241d). And rightly, because the Platonic Socrates does not respect a person in the grip of passionate sexual desire any more than Lysias does (consider the *Lysis*). It is just that the alternative proposed by Plato and his Socrates is not the cool dandy but the philosophical lover, and the *Phaedrus* shows how such a lover behaves, how intelligently and empathetically he educates his beloved. He educates him in conversation, and this also deals with written texts; hence the erotic and rhetoric are the two interconnected themes of the dialogue. And naturally the rhetorical statements should also be read dialogue-externally, that is, reflexively.

Up to the *Republic,* Socrates towers over his interlocutors. In fact, one of the most important divisions of forms of conversation concerns whether the conversation takes place between equals or unequals, whether it is symmetrical or asymmetrical. In symmetrical dialogues the inter-

36. This foreshadows 255d3 ff.; the theme of the connection between self-knowledge and knowledge of the Other is pursued further in the "First Alcibiades." The *epilelēsmai* of 228a6 anticipates the doctrine of anamnesis.

37. 257b3 ff.

locutors ideally want to investigate something together or at least learn from one another. In asymmetrical dialogues one of the partners is the one who knows, the one (in the simplest case, that of the dual dialogue) who either teaches the other or, sometimes ironically, uncovers the interlocutor's lack of knowledge; the other is at least at the beginning still unknowing and at the end recognizes at least the untruth of his previous views, or even a positive truth. The knowing conversation partner may play the institutionalized role of the teacher, or in some cases even that of a father—to a son who may initially be arrogant, as in the sixth chapter of the *Chandogya-Upanisad,* or not, as in Augustine's *De magistro*—but this is not always the case, as remains to be shown. In conversations about religion, the knowing person is at the same time the one who has the right belief, whereas his interlocutor is initially unbelieving (in the sense that he does not share the right belief, even if he may have a false one). However, a conversation about religion is philosophical only when arguments are exchanged; and this means that the believer must at the same time be a knower. Although the recognition of religious truth may ultimately demand more than an act of the intellect, this also holds for those philosophical truths that compel us to adopt a new relationship to ourselves and to the world.

Plato's early and middle dialogues, and also the *Phaedrus,* the *Theaetetus,* the *Philebus,* and the *Laws,* are paradigmatic asymmetrical dialogues. Since asymmetry is offensive, it is hardly surprising that it is usually concealed—partly through blunt irony that is not hard to see through and partly by clichés of commonality, which are seriously meant in the sense that the insight of the Other is called upon. But when Socrates asks Crito to help him investigate the question whether the recommended escape from prison is moral or not,[38] this can scarcely blind the reader to the fact that the investigation is conducted almost completely by Socrates. The asymmetry is differently arranged in the various Platonic dialogues; the interlocutor may be a glittering but intellectually inferior rival (such as the Sophists are), a young man, sometimes with

---

38. *Cri.* 48d8: *Skopōmen . . . koinēi.* Cf. *Prt.* 330b6 f.: *koinēi skepsōmetha* and *Grg.* 506a4: *zētō koinēi meth' humōn.* In *Ly.* 218e1 ff. Socrates explains that through conversation he will learn how to understand better what he himself says.

his father, who is concerned about his son's education, or a politically interested but philosophically untrained layman of the same age. The *Theaetetus* comes closest to the two following dialogues in which the mature Socrates is confronted for the first time by an interlocutor who is of the same or even superior rank, since Theaetetus is a young man, though more intelligent than all the others who had appeared in Plato's dialogues up to this point[39]—a promising youth like the young Socrates with regard to Parmenides who, in the dialogue that bears his name, is superior to him only in age.[40] Here we probably get a glimpse of the nature of the conversation with younger members within the Academy, whereas the *Timaeus* probably reflects the didactic lectures given by older colleagues.

The Platonic dialogues mentioned first are not the only asymmetrical dialogues in the history of philosophy; but in chapter 4 we noted that in them the distance between the figure of Socrates and the other interlocutors is unique. This has to do on the one hand with the fact that the historical Socrates was truly a world historical individual—the first moral innovator who, unlike prophets such as Zarathustra and Amos, sought to found his message on the *logos* alone—and on the other hand with the fact that the author of the corresponding literary character was no doubt by far the greatest of these people who were both philosophers and artists, and moreover probably the greatest philosopher and one of the greatest artists of all time. The Platonic Socrates will therefore always remain, at least for people with a certain hermeneutic sensitivity and philosophical intelligence, one of the most humbling figures, and the self-confidence that he radiates and that his real model may have lacked, but which his author certainly had, is simply breathtaking: Plato considers the true philosopher divine.[41] The only other possible candidate for a similar and similarly justified sense of self-worth is Dante, but the fact that he explicitly expressed it, whereas Plato only alluded to it and concealed himself behind the figure—ironic, moreover—of his Socrates,

39. *Tht.* 142c5 ff., 143e ff.
40. *Prm.* 130e, 135d.
41. Cf. *La.* 196a6 f., *Euthd.* 219a3 f., *Sph.* 216a5 f. On the other hand, this is qualified in *Phdr.* 278d3 ff.

suggests that his feeling of self-worth was still greater. The recognition of his contemporaries evidently meant little to him, and the consciousness of sin, which so strongly characterizes the Christian Dante, was presumably alien to him as well.

Indeed, the asymmetry that characterizes the relationship of at least the young men to Socrates reaches a degree of intensification that is almost unbearable in that, disconcertingly, he secures for himself even the superiority that is usually the privilege of the younger—to be the beloved rather than the lover. The asymmetry that makes a love unhappy is often more painful than even the greatest intellectual asymmetry, and in a homoerotic culture an obvious way for the younger interlocutor to avenge himself would be to make the intellectually superior older man fall in love with him. Being desired by him could increase the younger man's sense of self-worth; rejecting the lover's advances produces asymmetry and thus reestablishes symmetry on a higher level. The Platonic Socrates can hardly be blamed for not being seducible (so that, for instance, in the *Lysis* the unhappy love of poor Hippothales is described with cold irony) and thus not exactly corresponding to the stereotype of the highly intellectual man longing for life that is drawn by Hölderlin in "Sokrates und Alkibiades" or by Thomas Mann, from *Tonio Kröger* to *Doktor Faustus*. However, what is problematic is that the point of Diotima's speech reported by Socrates is that love for a person appears to be a deficient form of love for an idea—the idea of the beautiful.[42] A happy marriage cannot be founded on the basis of such a view, but since Plato accords Socrates' marriage no great importance and he himself was unmarried, we can let this pass. What is morally questionable and, from the point of view of a universalist ethics, even shocking about Socrates' eroticism is that he lures young people into a kind of trap: he pretends to be in love with them when he is not, and makes them fall in love with him.[43]

In any case, that is the point of Alcibiades' speech at the end of the *Symposium*, which seems to be a descent from the philosophical heights of the Socrates-Diotima speech back into a more mundane realm, and

42. This has been emphasized by G. Vlastos (1969; esp. 31).
43. In *Thg.* 128b2 ff., Socrates claims that all he really knows about is the erotic.

yet represents only a confirmation of the speech's ideas. Alcibiades begins by saying that from Socrates as from no other radiates an existential challenge—for his own part, Alcibiades felt he simply shouldn't live, if he continued to be the kind of person he was.[44] Socrates, he says, is the only person who can make him feel ashamed; and thus he sometimes wishes Socrates were dead, even though he knows full well that then he would suffer still more. But Alcibiades goes on to describe Socrates' interest in beautiful young men and unmasks it as a game and disguise. He tells how he once believed that Socrates was sexually interested in him, and confesses, despite the attendant humiliation, that when he tried to yield to him, Socrates ignored him, arguing with unutterable arrogance that he would not exchange gold for copper, true moral beauty for beauty that was merely apparent because it was only physical.[45] The humiliation of this rejection is all the greater because it makes Alcibiades admire Socrates still more. His speech ends with a warning: The way Socrates treated him, he also treated Charmides and Euthydemus, son of Diocles; he deceived them, making them think he was the lover, but in truth he had become the beloved instead of the lover: *hous houtos exapatōn hōs erastēs paidika mallon autos kathistatai ant' erastou.*[46] The following scene is extremely witty and proves once again how important the connection between the subject of the conversation and the conversational procedure is for Plato. After Alcibiades, to the laughter of all those who understand how much he is still in love with Socrates, has warned Agathon that Socrates is playing the same game with him, Socrates says that Alcibiades obviously wants to separate him from Agathon. Thus on the one hand he diverts attention from himself, though he was the true subject of Alcibiades' speech, and on the other hand shows a serious interest in Agathon, who in fact feels courted and lies down again next to Socrates, after Alcibiades had pushed himself between the two. Thus Socrates confirms in fact what Alcibiades had predicted—at least the first part, that he is now behaving toward Agathon the way a lover does (just as the Jesuit in the well-known joke, asked whether Jesuits are trained to react

---

44. 216a1 f. *hōste moi doxai mē biōton einai echonti hōs echō.*
45. 218e3 ff., 219c3 ff.
46. 222b3 f.

to unpleasant questions with another question, replies, "Now, who told you that?"—thus answering precisely by refusing to answer). However, Agathon seems not to see that the second part of Alcibiades' prognosis—that Socrates is only playing with him—is true, too, even though the cross-examination to which Socrates subjected him at 199c ff. clearly shows that Socrates' interest in him is also primarily intellectual.

It is well known that the Platonic Socrates manipulates and deceives his interlocutors even when he is not speaking ironically.[47] But what justifies his behavior, not in the eyes of a Kantian, but in those of Plato, is that this manipulation is always in the interest of the person manipulated. The interlocutor is supposed to be brought to insight and morally improved, so far as it is possible for him; we saw this first in the *Phaedrus,* which ends, as was already noted (p. 127), with a common prayer (279b f.). The sexual humiliation of the interlocutor whom Socrates has caused to fall in love with him is supposed to lead him to think of something higher than the sexual; and Socrates does not withdraw his friendship from those whose sexual offers he rejects. However, since this friendship is shared with many others, one who hoped for a dual relationship may nonetheless feel offended and deceived—but given the different sensibilities of the ancient world, this supposition may be an anachronism. Moreover, Socrates' play is in one respect less asymmetrical than it seems: by inverting the usual direction of love he overcomes—even if only in a playful way—precisely the asymmetry that so essentially characterized male homosexuality among the Greeks, and triggers an impulse to activity in the otherwise passive beloved. It is among other things this asymmetry that is adduced in Plutarch's *Erōtikos* as an argument for the superiority of heterosexual over homosexual love.[48]

Other examples of dialogues that are asymmetrical, though to a significantly lesser degree, are provided by Cicero, especially those in which he himself appears. However, this does not hold for all of them—in

47. Consider, e.g., *Chrm.* 155eff.
48. 768Eff. Plutarch's dialogue, in contrast to which the mixed dialogue *Erōtes* ascribed to Lucian defends the traditional view that homosexuality is better for philosophical men, is one of the most influential texts in the history of morals. P. Singer (2004; 19 ff., esp. 28 f.) has described impressively how his grandparents David Oppenheim and Amalie Pollak fell in love while reading Pseudo-Lucian together.

chapter 7 (p. 140 f.), I discussed the pains Cicero took in the *Academica* to represent Varro's position as on the same level as his own. Neither is the converse true: although *De oratore* is a generally symmetrical dialogue, in *De re publica* Scipio is obviously dominant, and despite the many gaps in the extant text we can presume that the role of a *primus inter pares* that he plays in the conversation was supposed to be reflected in the role attributed in the lost books to the ideal statesman acting during the crisis in the Roman republic.[49] Augustine's and Nicholas of Cusa's dialogues in which they themselves appear are also asymmetrical, even if in the Cassiciacum dialogues we can discern a genuine spirit of mutual searching that tempers Augustine's unmistakable superiority. The whole subgenre of the didactic dialogue, in which someone who knows the truth teaches one or more pupils, is by definition asymmetrical; many medieval dialogues belong to this subgenre, but so do, for example, the *Milindapañha* and Berkeley's *Three Dialogues between Hylas and Philonous*. Even if "subversive" dialogues such as Bodin's *Colloquium heptaplomeres* and most of Diderot's[50] are often symmetrical, this is not the case for all of them: Gide's *Corydon* is an asymmetrical dialogue—"a tract," F. Porché contemptuously calls it[51]—and so is the second of Feyerabend's *Three Dialogues on Knowledge*. Regarding this second dialogue (which was in fact his first attempt in the genre, written in 1976), Feyerabend remarks self-critically: "It is not really a dialogue but a diatribe directed at a helpless victim" (1991; 165). Only the dialogue that appears first in the published version but which was written last, in 1990, is a symmetrical dialogue, and it alone corresponds formally to Feyerabend's pluralistic message; a teacher-pupil dialogue, on the other hand, is hardly suitable for an epistemological anarchist. But since an asymmetrical dialogue is easier to write, it is not surprising that Feyerabend found a form suitable for his message only on the third try. The third di-

---

49. Cf. Hösle (2004b), 155 n. 10.

50. This does not hold for the *Supplément au voyage de Bougainville*—neither for the frame conversation nor for the main conversation. In the former, A. remarks dejectedly: "Il semble que mon lot soit d'avoir tort avec vous jusque dans les moindres choses; il faut que je sois bien bon pour vous pardonner une supériorité aussi continue!"

51. Gide (1935), 334.

alogue, written in 1990 and chronologically the second, occupies an interesting intermediate position: it is dual in nature, like the second one, and takes place between the same A and B as in the latter, B standing for Feyerabend. But B's unprejudiced examination of the commonplaces of his own time is this time directed not only against critical rationalism but also against his own earlier position; he frankly acknowledges that he himself has changed: "In 1970, when I wrote the first version of *Against Method*, the world was different from what it is now and I was different from what I am now, not only intellectually, but also emotionally."[52] To A's first question, "Do you still believe in astrology?" he replies with the counter question, "Who told you I believed in astrology?" and to A's assurance that he himself told him, he responds with, "I don't remember what I said." And when A makes further attempts to hold him to his earlier position, he replies only with short questions such as "My position?" and "Who told you I had a 'philosophy'?"[53] This is surely a kind of self-distancing; but since this gift is positively valued and A completely lacks it, B remains overwhelmingly superior.

On the other hand, in the first dialogue, Arthur, who comes closest to representing Feyerabend's position, is really only one of several participants, and the contributions of the Korean student Charles and the Chinese student Lee Feng are at least as remarkable as his own, even if they point in different directions. The funny thing is that the second dialogue is formally a didactic dialogue, even though it does not represent a teaching situation, whereas the first dialogue is anything but a teacher-pupil dialogue, even though it represents a class discussion on Plato's *Theaetetus.* But it is a postmodern kind of class, if only because the group is extremely heterogeneous with regard to age, nationality, gender, and educational background. The professor, Dr. Cole, is "intelligent in a narrow way," and the student Jack is "a logician with the casual habits and precise diction of the US version of that profession";[54] but there are also more interesting persons in the class, including an elderly auditor from Central Europe named Seidenberg, a vagrant—or a student who looks

52. (1991), 129.
53. (1991), 127.
54. (1991), 3.

like a vagrant—named Leslie, a red-haired woman named Maureen who has accidentally signed up for the course thinking it was "the class on postmodern cooking,"[55] and finally Arthur, a historian of science, who listens at the door and then enters the room uninvited and takes part in the conversation.[56]

Despite his function, Cole is not the intellectually most fascinating participant in Feyerabend's dialogue. Even asymmetrical dialogues can acquire a certain complexity precisely when the intellectually superior interlocutor is not the one we would normally expect, given his position or his appearance: the initial relationships may deceive us as to the true relationships. We can speak here of an inversion of roles. In both the Platonic dialogues that are named after him, Hippias is a far more famous figure than Socrates, and in fact a pompous ass. Protagoras has more style, but in the dialogue named after him he is at least initially the courted star, and even after Socrates has refuted him he cannot resist insisting on his superiority—by praising Socrates in a way that is as such condescending and all the more so because he patronizingly refers to the relative youth of Socrates, who at the presumed time of the dialogue was approaching forty. "I hope I am not too bad a character, and I am the last man to be jealous. I have told a great many people that I never met anyone I admire nearly as much as you, certainly not among your cohort."[57] When someone has to base his sense of self-worth on his age, he is in a bad way; and therefore nothing reveals Protagoras's defeat more than this remark. Of course, Plato wants to give the impression that his Socrates really does not need this compliment; it is rather Protagoras who, defeated in argument, needs to hand out compliments.[58]

In contradistinction to the Sophists, Socrates occasionally calls himself a "layman" *(idiōtēs)*;[59] the Greek term persists in our word *idiot*. Analogously, Nicholas of Cusa puts a layman at the center of his three *Idiota* dialogues, a layman whose common sense proves to be superior to the knowledge of the rhetorician and the philosopher. The *Idiota de sapi-*

55. (1991), 4.
56. (1991), 5.
57. 361d8 ff.
58. In his elegy on Eudemus, Aristotle already said that not everyone has the right to praise everybody, precisely with reference to Plato (*Carmina*, frg. 2 Ross).
59. Cf. *Ion* 532e1 and *Euthd.* 278d5, 282d6, and 295e2.

entia begins with the layman remarking to a very rich rhetorician that it is astonishing that despite his constant reading of written works he has still not been led to humility. The rhetorician accuses him in turn of arrogance because he sets little store by scholarly study. Like Descartes's Eudoxe speaking to Epistemon, the layman insists that one should not be guided by the opinions of traditional authorities; for then one would be like a horse, which is free by nature but through art has been attached by a halter to a manger, where it eats only what is given it. Such an intellect nourishes itself on foreign and not natural foods, because it is bound to the authority of the writers.[60] To be sure, the food of wisdom is to be found in the books of the philosophers as well, but the first philosophers could not have learned from books; they must therefore have improved themselves by feeding on natural food. This is reminiscent, as was said, of Descartes, but it is specific to Nicholas of Cusa in two respects. On the one hand, the layman stresses that his criticism of the rhetorician is not the result of arrogance, but rather of love; and on the other hand, the knowledge of his lack of knowledge leads to humility. He does not want to learn from the rhetorician's books, but rather from the books of God; and these books are found everywhere, even in the marketplace. Wisdom calls in the streets—that is, the starting point for philosophy is to be found in the observation of the everyday activities of ordinary people. However, this is only its starting point: it is a matter of ascending from the observation of activities of measurement to the principle of number and finally to divine wisdom.[61] The rhetorician is impressed, and as is reported at the beginning of the second book, he seeks out the layman on his own in order to receive further instruction from him.[62]

In the *Idiota de mente,* he brings a philosopher whom he has met in Rome during the jubilee year to meet his new friend. The rhetorician recognizes the philosopher, who proves to be a Peripatetic, by his paleness and the astonishment with which he observes the pilgrims passing by. He speaks to him, and the philosopher acknowledges that he was astonished by the one faith that fills these many bodies. The rhetorician refers to the

60. V 4: "Traxit te opinio auctoritatis, ut sis quasi equus natura liber, sed arte capistro alligatus praesepi, ubi non aliud comedit, nisi quod sibi ministratur. Pascitur enim intellectus tuus auctoritati scribentium constrictus pabulo alieno et non naturali."
61. V 6 ff.
62. V 24.

divine origin of the fact that these pilgrims conceive more clearly through faith than the philosophers do through reason.[63] The philosopher agrees; in his reflection on the immortality of the spirit he has not arrived at the same understanding as these ignorant people. He came to Rome, he says, because he hoped to find in the temple of Mens on the Capitol—which is in fact historically attested—writings of wise men about the spirit. The rhetorician cannot help him, given the extensive destruction in Rome, but he suggests that they visit his friend the layman—in a very Platonic way, oral exchange is supposed to replace the reading of texts as the true medium of philosophy. The rhetorician has also learned this lesson; but the philosopher will approach the layman timidly: when he seeks out a wise man, he usually presents him with texts and asks him about their meaning. Since that is now not possible, he does not know how he should proceed in order to make the layman speak. The layman emphasizes that precisely because he is uneducated, he is not afraid to answer, whereas famous people are afraid to imperil their reputations. The three men sit down on stools. The rhetorician sees this as a violation of the customary ways of receiving an important man; but he promises the philosopher that he will not be sorry that he came here.[64] The rhetorician himself was embarrassed when on entering the layman's house they found him whittling a wooden spoon: the rhetorician feared that the philosopher would think he could learn nothing theoretical from a man whom he has seen occupying himself with such ordinary work.[65] But the layman is not ashamed; he is proud of his work, which allows him to feed himself but which he also interprets allegorically. In fact, the creative aspect that is peculiar to human *poiesis* and leads to the revaluation of craft activity, which comes closer to divine art than the imitation of things already existing in nature,[66] is transferred by the layman to the human faculty of

63. V 46: "Certe Dei donum esse necesse est idiotas clarius fide attingere quam philosophos ratione."
64. V 48.
65. V 47: "Erubeo idiota, inquit, te per hunc maximum philosophum hiis rusticis operibus implicatum reperiri; non putabit a te se theorias aliquas auditurum."
66. V 51: "Tales enim formae cocleares, scutellares et ollares sola humana arte perficiuntur. Unde ars mea est magis perfectoria quam imitatoria figurarum creatarum, et in hoc infinitae arti similior."

knowledge; the constructivist reconception of epistemology begins in the *Idiota de mente* and finds its point of departure in the spoon-whittling craftsman-philosopher.

We owe to Diderot the most provocative inversion of the expected roles in an asymmetrical dialogue. In the *Supplément au voyage de Bougainville*, the chaplain is not merely unable to persuade the Polynesian Orou to adopt his values; in defending them he cuts a very poor figure.[67] The old man had already described the misfortune that the arrival of the Europeans had been for the natives and rejected their apparent right to conquer, using an argument reminiscent of Francisco de Victoria,[68] to the effect that the Europeans would scarcely have considered a Polynesian conquest right if the natives had crossed the oceans first.[69] Diderot does not attribute the conquerors' greed to the chaplain, who is a good but limited man.[70] His attempts at missionary work fail miserably, partly because Orou proves to be not exactly a natural man but rather a talented naturalistic philosopher who, for example, immediately sees through the problematics of a voluntaristic conception of God,[71] and also shows that he can operate on the reflective level of a *philosophe* in dealing with ethical questions, for example, when he demands a moral standard that transcends culture[72]—surprisingly, if one

---

67. His argumentative awkwardness reminds us of the the first remarks made by the abbé Couet in Voltaire's dialogue *Le dîner du comte de Boulainvilliers* (1767), one of the most acerbic criticisms of Christianity written in the eighteenth century; however, since Couet changes his mind with amazing celerity and ends up speaking of "mon secret" (s.d., 210), it is possible that his banal remarks were meant ironically from the outset. But then his behavior is not well represented, because he gives no hint that he is speaking ironically. However, a quick change of mind would not be well motivated either, so that in both cases the dialogue is psychologically disappointing. In addition to the abbé and Henri comte de Boulainvilliers, the famed historian and defender of feudalism, the countess and the polymath Nicolas Fréret, whose hatred for Christianity was generally assumed, also take part in the conversation. Right at the end other guests turn up, including the abbé de Saint-Pierre, who reads from his *Pensées du matin.*

68. *De Indis,* II 3 (1917; 244). Montezuma's last words in his conversation with Fernand Cortez in Fontenelle's *Nouveaux dialogues des morts* are very similar (1971; 399).

69. (1972), 292.

70. On several occasions, he is called "le bon aumônier" (1972; 323, 324, 336).

71. (1972), 304, 306 f.

72. It is said to be the common good and individual interest (1972; 305, 317).

agrees with B's remark that a Polynesian certainly could not describe a Western society, because he would lack the language to do so.[73] The psychological remark, which is not inaccurate, that prohibitions often create an incentive to violate them,[74] is hardly to be expected from a member of a culture to which we owe the word *taboo* but rather from its Western theorists. Orou's casual acceptance of incest is not in accord with modern anthropological knowledge, however awkward the chaplain's efforts to ground the incest taboo, which he finally concludes with a condemnation and a demand that the subject be changed: "l'inceste est un crime abominable, et parlons d'autre chose."[75] Orou's superiority with regard to the chaplain is ultimately demonstrated not only in theory but also in practice, when the latter finally dedicates himself to the Polynesians' promiscuity—though he cannot help shrieking, "Mais ma religion! mais mon état!"[76] The defense of promiscuity is the real message of the meta-conversation, which even trivializes rape[77] and in appealing to the natural man draws on Plato's allegory of the cave.[78] Diderot's dialogue is witty, and his criticism of Europe, for example, the many small meannesses of civilization that certainly counterbalance the few great crimes of primitive cultures, is often instructive.[79] Since this dialogue is one of the reasons we have Paul Gauguin's pictures of Tahiti, we can forgive it some things. But this is the most ideological of Diderot's dialogues; it gives no hint of the negative sides of promiscuity and completely ignores the theoretical problem of how anything at all can be described as unnatural within the framework of a naturalistic philosophy.[80] As a dialogue, it is much less subtle than Diderot's other ones, because it presents in the chaplain a good-natured fool and in Orou anything but a Polynesian. The Other, whose representation is

---

73. (1972), 289.

74. (1972), 319, 328.

75. (1972), 318. The chaplain's answer to a question about the reasons for celibacy is equally precise: "Cela serait trop long et trop difficile à t'expliquer" (323).

76. (1972), 300f., 323.

77. (1972), 330.

78. (1972), 331 ff.

79. (1972), 333.

80. Bordeu is fully aware of the problem; cf. (1972), 245.

generally Diderot's achievement, is not at all brought out here; instead, he offers us a cardboard figure and an instrumentalization of a newly discovered culture for his own ends.

Nicholas of Cusa's layman essentially answers the questions of the philosopher; that is the normal procedure in the didactic dialogue, which can be followed as well when the roles expected on the basis of outward appearance are inversed. The *Milindapañha* makes use of the same procedure—Menander asks, Nāgasena answers to his satisfaction, and the king always reacts with the sentence, "Kallo si bhante Nāgasenāti," "You are clever, worthy Nāgasena." But sometimes the asymmetrical dialogue also makes use of the variant in which the superior partner does not answer but rather asks.[81] That is the role Socrates plays, especially in the early dialogues, and it is easy to see that it is pedagogically more interesting and better suited to the dialogue form. It is pedagogically more interesting because it demands more from the conversation partner: he cannot limit himself to listening, but must make an effort to present his own position, to explain it and defend it against attacks. For example, in *Contra academicos*, Augustine expressly helps Trygetius only a little, offering him no more than a definition of wisdom; Trygetius must learn for himself how to use it for his own ends.[82] The disciple's autonomy is thereby taken seriously to a quite different extent than when he has only to ask and always receives the answer. Since in such a dialogue an alternative position is at least tentatively sketched out, a certain polyphony is achieved even if the secondary voices ultimately fail and have to be abandoned. But in a dialogue in which only the master provides answers, the pupil can easily be dispensed with, since the master himself can ask the questions, the answers to which he already knows; and that means that the dialogue form is ultimately superfluous. Of course, the procedure in which the superior speaker is the one who asks the questions is never adopted dialogue-internally for literary reasons and only seldom for pedagogical reasons. Instead, it is usually adopted for reasons having to do with

81. Drawing on the important differentiation between teaching *(didaskein)* and conversing *(dialegesthai)* that we find in Arist. *SE* 171a38 ff., we could call this type of dialogue "dialectical," because according to Aristotle the dialectician asks, but not the teacher.

82. 1.6.16.

the sociology of knowledge: when the intellectually superior speaker is not yet recognized as such, he has to challenge a person with authority, and the latter is seldom as quick to retreat to the role of a pupil as are Nicholas of Cusa's rhetorician and his philosopher. Socrates cannot expect Protagoras and his entourage to listen to his own opposing speech;[83] he has to destroy Protagoras's claim to know the truth before people are willing to examine his own constructive ideas. Socrates earns the right to give the long concluding speech in the *Gorgias* (523a–527e) only after he has refuted no less than three interlocutors. Something analogous holds not only dialogue-internally but also dialogue-externally, and in fact for the whole of Plato's work. Plato had first to write aporetic dialogues whose goal is to challenge the false knowledge of established authorities,[84] including precisely respected critics such as the Sophists, before he could reasonably expect his audience to read him when he asked them to entertain, as in the *Republic,* metaphysical, ethical, and political theories that were in sharp conflict with common sense. This does not, of course, constitute proof that at a relatively early stage Plato already had in mind the theory that he later laid out; but it does answer the question why Plato, if he did already have that theory, did not immediately publish it: he had to prepare his audience for it. His Socrates had to ask questions before he and the other conversation leaders in the late works could give answers. In a smaller framework and in relation to a narrower subject, we see the same change in Berkeley's *Three Dialogues between Hylas and Philonous.* In the first dialogue Philonous limits himself essentially to asking Hylas questions and thereby making clear the difficulties, and even, as he thinks, the inconsistencies of Hylas's belief in the existence of matter; in the second dialogue, Hylas begins to ask Philonous questions, even if Philonous himself repeatedly asks counterquestions; in the third dialogue, finally, it is Hylas who asks most of the questions. Philonous's contributions are correspondingly longer in the second and third parts than in the first.

---

83. Even Hippias cannot impose his wish to give a speech (*Prt.* 347a6 ff.).

84. Cf. Arist. *SE* 171b4 ff. on the examining conversation, which is directed against those who are ignorant but claim to know and is a form of dialectical conversation: *hē gar peirastikē esti dialektikē tis kai theorei ou ton eidota alla ton agnoounta kai prospoioumenon.*

The existence of a superior partner does not exclude the possibility of the conversation partners being treated equally on a formal level. In the previous chapter we already noted that at the critical point in their conversation Socrates and Protagoras agree to take turns questioning each other.[85] This is a symmetrical procedure, even if Socrates more or less forces Protagoras to agree to it; thus the meta-level is asymmetrical. In the *Llibre del gentil,* the representatives of the three monotheistic religions agree to the same rules for all, and the pagan respects them strictly as umpires. Since at the beginning none of them wishes, out of respect for the others, to be the first to speak, the pagan suggests that the three wise men should present their respective religions in the order of their historical emergence. Further, he stipulates that they must not interrupt each other while the presentation is being made, because that might damage their mutual goodwill and thus their understanding.[86] Only he will be allowed to ask questions. Later in the conversation he does in fact not allow interlocutors to interfere, against the original agreement, in each other's presentations; interestingly, first the Christian, then the Christian and the Jew are the ones who want to contradict the Saracen.[87] The pagan's conversion to one of the three religions is in no way prevented by this neutrality; and conversion does not lead him to reject procedural equality in the future. This is absolutely compatible with inequality of substance, so far as knowledge of the truth goes; and someone who, like the Saracen, does not violate the procedural rules even once may be the one most distant from the truth, while someone who, like the Christian, twice infringes the rules may nonetheless be right. Procedures are for Llull indispensable, and they must be based on a spirit of equality and symmetry. But since according to him of several mutually incompatible positions at most one can be true, that is, an asymmetry of substance can exist, the question of truth cannot be reduced to the problem of the procedure to be followed.

85. *Prt.* 338c f.

86. (1993), 46: "per volentat del gentil ffo ffet ordenament enfre·ls .iii. savis que la .i. no contrastás al autre dementre que recomtaria sa raó; cor per contrast es engenrrada mala volentat en humá coratge, e per la mala volentat es torbat l'enteniment a entendre."

87. (1993), 160, 180.

The asymmetrical dialogue is a philosophical dialogue only when the inferior partner adopts the position of the superior one, not because of the latter's authority, but solely because he presents better arguments. The autonomy of the individual is indispensable where philosophy is concerned—though certainly someone can see autonomously that another person is argumentatively superior to him. But this insight at least remains his own. Despite his superiority, Socrates never tires of insisting that his interlocutor should agree only if he is himself convinced. Nothing is less pleasing to him than when someone concurs with him only because he thinks he is thereby doing him a favor. Typical of this is the passage in which Socrates tells Crito that if he has an objection, he should express it, and he, Socrates, will follow him; but he must not constantly repeat that Socrates should leave this place against the will of the Athenians. Socrates would very much like to leave after he has convinced Crito, but not against Crito's will.[88] The last sentence is a masterpiece of irony, but as such points to a deeper truth. Socrates acts as if he absolutely wanted to get away but could do so in good conscience only if he convinced Crito and the latter agreed. In reality, the situation is precisely the reverse: it is Crito who wants to take him away and would willingly forego a more precise investigation of the question. But this sentence is not entirely false either, because, to begin with its first half, as a human being with a normal desire to live, Socrates would naturally be glad to flee—but in his case this inclination is subject to a moral reservation; he will yield to it only if it proves to be morally permissible. And the criterion of this investigation, the second half of the sentence says, is the rational agreement that a disinterested person would give him. Perhaps I will be forgiven for giving in to the temptation to use Kantian categories

88. The text in Burnet's edition, and also in the new edition by E. A. Duke et al. reads: *hōs egō peri pollou poioumai peisas se tauta prattein, alla mē akontos* (48e3 ff.). Burnet did not yet know any manuscript with the reading *peisas* (he bases himself on a conjecture of Buttmann's); Duke et al. adduce Cod. Vat. Gr. 225. Most manuscripts have *peisai;* Cod. Vind. suppl. Gr. 7 even has *me* instead of *se,* which seems to be the basis for Schleiermacher's translation ("For I would very much like to do so if you persuaded me to do it, only not against my will"); but in this text as well, and even if we add *se,* the translation is linguistically impossible because of the genitive at the end. An excellent interpretation of this passage is offered by G. Calogero (1960; 23).

(which may be justified because no work of the ancients comes so close to the spirit of Kant's ethics as the *Crito*): The first half of the sentence speaks, as it were, of the phenomenal Socrates, the second of the noumenal Crito; and that is obviously ironic because the essence of the phenomenal Socrates was precisely that he corresponded to the morally obligatory. But that Socrates attributes a moral rationality to Crito as well, and appeals to his better self, means that he demands of his best friend more than the mere acceptance of his authority—even in such a personal decision, which seems to concern primarily Socrates himself. But insofar as the decision claims to be moral, it must also be shareable by others. It is true that an individual can also make the right decision, and it remains right even if the *hoi polloi*, that is, the many, contradict him, indeed, even if not a single other person agrees with him. But it must in principle be acceptable by others. Whether they can do justice to their potential, however, is their concern, and does not affect the validity of the arguments on which a decision is based. This is true even when it is precisely the appeal to the other's autonomous reason that triggers a negative reaction. This sounds paradoxical, but it can be understood psychologically. Although only reason constitutes an ideal symmetry, the use of reason is in reality unequally distributed; and therefore the demand for autonomy may be experienced as an especially insidious use of power because it is almost impossible to combat. This holds on the level of the individual as well as on that of culture; a symmetrical intercultural conversation might be experienced as asymmetrical on the meta-level because, for example, it forces a traditional culture that gives priority to asymmetrical relationships to adapt in a way that ensures its defeat (e.g., when only Christians are able to write interreligious dialogues). And yet there is no valid alternative to autonomy and symmetry, even if there remains a duty not to emphasize the impossibility of circumventing rational autonomy in a way that makes the intellectual asymmetry between the interlocutors too obvious and thus is felt to be performatively contradictory.

The *Gorgias* shows how much Socrates wants his interlocutor's agreement to be based on insight—and only on that. After Polus has adduced the Macedonian king Archilaus as an example of someone who is unjust but not unhappy, Socrates makes the central distinction between rhetoric and discussion; I shall return briefly to this in chapter 17 (p. 416 f.). Here we are concerned with the fact that Socrates refuses to allow appeals to witnesses external to the conversation: this kind of refutation does not contribute to truth.[89] It is true that almost everyone, Athenians and foreigners, would agree with Polus; in an exceptionally witty satire of name-dropping, Socrates himself names several respectable contemporaries, such as the whole family of Pericles, who would certainly say that Polus is right. But Socrates himself would not agree with him, because Polus has not compelled him to, but has instead merely ranged many false witnesses against him and attempts to drive him out of his property, the truth. "But if I cannot produce in you yourself a single witness in agreement with my views, I consider that I have accomplished nothing worth speaking of in the matter under debate; and the same, I think, is true for you also, if I, one solitary witness, do not testify for you and if you do not leave all these others out of account."[90] Here again the symmetry on the personal level is noteworthy; even if Socrates imposes his criterion,[91] he does so not out of a will to power but rather because it is the only correct one: it does not delegate the responsibility to absent witnesses but rather appeals to the interlocutor's autonomous insight.[92] The individual can escape his uncircumventable responsibility neither by subjecting himself to the superior insight of his interlocutor nor by adducing many authorities who, because they are absent, cannot be validated in the forum of critical examination. Indeed, following tradition is natural precisely when one has no interlocutor with whom one can question it; this is suggested by a passage in Aeneas's *Theophrastus.*[93] On reading Socrates' critique of external authorities in the *Gorgias,* it is hard not to think of Bruno's *La cena de le ceneri* and Galileo's *Dialogo sopra i due massimi sistemi.* It is true that because of the massive social change that had occurred in the interim, the authorities to which the know-it-all Prudenzio

---

89. *Grg.* 471e.

90. 472b6 ff.; 473e6 ff. and 475e7 ff. are very similar. See also 473a 2. This passage probably influenced Rousseau (1999), 99 f.

91. 472c2 ff.

92. "Don't answer counter to your real belief" *(mē para doxan apokrinou),* Socrates says to Thrasymachus, *R.* 346a3.

93. 16.21 f. Colonna: *tōn de patriōn aidōs kai summachountos aporia kateirgousa epeichen.*

and Simplicio appeal are not oral but written, not powerful politicians
and their entourage but rather a philosopher who comes, moreover, from
the school of Plato; however, for Prudenzio and Simplicio appealing to
Aristotle also offers a way of escaping their own responsibility to undertake critical examination. Right at the beginning, Prudenzio declares that
he remains a friend of antiquity, since so many important wise men cannot have been ignorant of the truth,[94] while Simplicio defends Aristotle's
philosophical arguments for the three-dimensionality of space as compelling; for if there were a better argument he would certainly not have
failed to make it. However, Sagredo adds: insofar as he knew about it.[95]
Simplicio then rejects Salviati's mathematical "proof" on the ground that
mathematical necessity should not be sought in nature,[96] and repeatedly
insists pompously that one must speak with respect of Aristotle.[97] In
short, he is a heteronomous spirit, and his ludicrousness is not diminished by the fact that Salviati's "proof" is in fact no advance beyond Aristotle but is instead circular: Plato and his pupil had a clearer understanding of the dependency of mathematics on undemonstrable axioms than
Galileo did. In Leopardi's *Dialogo di Plotino e di Porfirio*, in which the
prohibition on suicide is discussed and whose mood of world-weariness
is completely anachronistic, Plotino cites his beloved Plato, but emphasizes that he does not want to appeal to the latter's authority but rather
to discuss matters on the basis of reason, especially with Porfirio and concerning such an important question: "Porfirio, veramente io amo Platone, come tu sai. Ma non è già per questo, che io voglia discorrere per
autorità; massimamente poi teco e in una questione tale: ma io voglio
discorrere per ragione."[98]

The use of the term *witness* in the *Gorgias* might be criticized; in
questions of empirical fact the statements of credible witnesses are an important argument in discovering the truth, even if they cannot appear in
court. But normative investigations are not in fact decided by counting

94. (1985), I 41.
95. (1998), 11 f.
96. (1998), 14.
97. (1998), 37 f.
98. (1956), 652.

votes. However, one might again object that statements regarding the happiness of specific people are empirical in nature and that even if self-deceptions and especially deceptions of others are possible, such statements cannot abstract completely from self-attributions of the kind that Polus puts into play with reference to Archelaus.[99] On the one hand, Plato would react to this by referring to the eschatological dimension of the soul, which qualifies the self-attributions during this life; on the other, it is obvious that his conception of happiness, like that of the whole premodern eudaemonistic tradition, is normatively loaded. Here lies, in my opinion, the crucial weakness of this tradition, which Kant was the first to grasp and to overcome.[100] But since even Callicles accepts normative limits to the concept of pleasure,[101] Socrates' refutation is largely immanent. The same appeal to the intellectual autonomy of the Other is made against Callicles: Callicles' identification of the pleasant with the good is rejected not only by Socrates but also by Callicles himself—if he were only to observe himself correctly.[102] It is possible to see this as paternalism, but it is a kind of paternalism that calls for rational autonomy and in no way seeks to get around it.

An expression of this attitude is that Socrates, the son of a midwife, compares himself to a midwife who is able only to elicit from others insights to which they themselves must give birth. However, as an intellectual midwife, he can be helpful in the choice of the right interlocutors, which corresponds to the preparation for conception, the treatment of intellectual birth pains, and the testing of the insights expressed.[103] It is hardly surprising that other writers of dialogues have also made use of this comparison; at least it is extremely natural to draw a parallel between a creative intellectual process, on the one hand, and procreation and birth, on the other, since in both cases it is a matter of forms of creation.

99. 471b6 f.
100. However, no ancient thinker comes closer to Kant's critique of eudaemonism than Plato does; see N. White (2002).
101. 499b4 ff.
102. 495e1 f. Cf. 482b4 ff. and 488a46 ff. on the importance of consistency (including between life and theory).
103. *Tht.* 149a–151d. The remarks make especially good sense against the background of the doctrine of anamnesis.

In Shaftesbury's *The Moralists,* Theocles wants Philocles to tell him which products of the human mind are still more beautiful than works of art; and Philocles cannot come up with the answer: "I am barren, said I, for this time; you must be plainer yet, in helping me to conceive." And when Theocles asks only counterquestions that exclude any further assistance— "How can I help you? . . . Would you have me be conscious for you, of that which is immediately your own, and is solely in and from yourself?"— he helps him along precisely thereby: Philocles understands that what is at stake is his own feelings. However, in order to train them he needs Theocles' help: "But 'tis you, Theocles . . . must help my labouring mind, and be as it were the midwife to those conceptions; which else, I fear, will prove abortive."[104] Theocles praises Philocles because he allocates to him only the role of midwife; the pregnancy of the intellect stems from its own nature alone. The human mind can be impregnated only by the divine mind. This is certainly a thesis that deviates from Plato and fits well with the contemporary metaphysics of Malebranche and Leibniz. Moral concepts as intellectual children lead to the problem of innate ideas, and even if Shaftesbury did not yet know Kant's sharp distinction between "synthetic *a priori*" and "innate," Locke's critical pupil clearly understands that the empirical question as to whether certain ideas are innate is of little importance. What is crucial is whether they are developed "by nature"—at whatever time: thereby Shaftesbury approaches, though using clumsy terms, the dimension of validity.

Even the most important—and that inevitably means rationalist— Christian authors of philosophical dialogues have always appealed to the autonomy of their readers and/or conversation partners. In Augustine, Trygetius avers that in the freedom to which philosophy in particular promises to lead, he has thrown off the yoke of authority.[105] Indeed, at the end of *De ordine,* it is said that at the beginning of instruction, authority is inevitable; but it precedes reason only temporally, not with regard to the subject matter. "Ad discendum item necessario dupliciter ducimur, auctoritate atque ratione. Tempore auctoritas, re autem ratio

104. (1999), 134.
105. *C. acad.* 1.3.9: "iam enim libertate, in quam maxime nos uindicaturam se philosophia pollicetur, iugum illud auctoritatis excussi."

prior est." Since humans are initially so ignorant that they do not even know how they could educate themselves, the doors to knowledge can be opened to them only by authority; but retrospectively they can see the reason in what they have followed before they acquired reason. Of course, knowledge of the highest principle can be achieved in this life by only a few people; however, those who live ethically but rely on authority and do not educate themselves can hardly be called happy in this life.[106] Nonetheless, in the following Augustine recognizes a special role for divine as distinct from human authority, as well as for the Incarnation,[107] and he sees in the authority of the sacraments something superior to the beating around the bush characteristic of disputations. However, first he introduces a criterion for the evaluation of human authority, which often deceives us—the agreement of life and doctrine;[108] and second, he emphasizes that his friends should believe him only insofar as he provides an argumentative justification for what he says.[109] In Anselm's *Cur deus homo*, it is Boso who insists on hearing rational arguments;[110] but Anselm takes his desire very seriously, and he refers only to his own weaknesses, not to the inadequate legitimacy of Boso's desire, who is never simply referred to the master's authority.[111] A dramatic high point of the dialogue occurs when Boso has to confront fear and would like to abandon the rationalistic method. But Anselm reminds him that he called for reason, and must now find a way to cope with it: "Rationem postulasti; rationem accipe."[112] In the *Quaestiones naturales*, Adelard of Bath admonishes his

---

106. 2.9.26. Cf. 2.5.15 f. This reminds us of the intellectualism of the *Phaedo* (69a ff., 82a f.), but unlike Plato, Augustine counts on there being, at least for the time after death, a state that corresponds to morality, not to the intellectual level achieved: "tamen inconcusse credo, mox ut hoc corpus reliquerint, eos, quo bene magis minusue uixerunt, eo facilius aut difficilius liberari."

107. At the end of *Contra academicos*, Augustine accordingly acknowledges the authority of Christ (3.19 f., 42 f.) but defends a model of the *fides quaerens intellectum* that anticipates Anselm.

108. 2.9.27: "non uiuunt aliter, quam uiuendum esse praecipiunt." But cf. p. 55 f.

109. 2.10.28: "Nam mihi omnino illos nolo credere nisi docenti rationemque reddenti."

110. Cf. 2.16.

111. 1.1, 1.3, 1.4, 1.25.

112. 1.24.

nephew to follow reason; only those who have followed reason, he says, have ever gained authority.[113]

Analogously, at the beginning of *De non aliud*, Nicholas of Cusa tells his friend Ferdinandus that he will speak with him only on the condition that Ferdinand rejects as unimportant everything he will hear from him unless he is forced by reason to accept it.[114] It goes without saying that interreligious dialogues cannot function if one side appeals to its own authorities.[115] Malebranche's Christian philosopher says to his Chinese interlocutor, "Mais laissant maintenant à part l'autorité divine de nos livres sacrez, & celle de vos Docteurs."[116] Berkeley's Philonous says to Hylas at the end of the first dialogue: "Have you not had the liberty of explaining yourself all manner of ways? . . . Hath not every thing you could say been heard and examined with all the fairness imaginable? In a word, have you not in every point been convinced out of your own mouth?"[117]

But although the only asymmetry that can and should be recognized from normative points of view is the one that is based on intellectual superiority, the authors of philosophical dialogues repeatedly show very realistically the actual power relationships that limit discourse. The position of lesser power may be individually or even collectively grounded. The classical example of the latter case, especially in the context of dialogues on the philosophy of religion, is the Jews. For example, the Jew in Abelard's *Collationes* outdoes himself in showing his servility. He even goes so far as to see the function of circumcision as that of making Jews repulsive to the non-Jewish women they sometimes long for, and thus prevent miscegenation. However, in the next sentence a further explanation is offered: even if a non-Jewish woman were to desire a Jew, the latter would be ashamed to connect with her his member devoted to God[118]—thus now the Jew is the one who rejects advances. But if the

---

113. (1998), 102 ff.
114. XIII 3: "Dicam et tecum, Ferdinande, hoc pacto colloquar, quod omnia, quae a me audies, nisi compellaris ratione, ut levia abicias."
115. Cf. Abelard (2001), 89, 97, 99; and Llull (1993), 12.
116. (1958), 26.
117. (1977), 192.
118. (2001), 40.

arguments in the philosophy of religion made by Abelard's Jew have very little to do with contemporary Jewish self-interpretation, his character traits presumably represented what had struck Abelard in the Jews with whom he had become acquainted. Although the Jew speaks first, since his religion is older than the Christian religion, he immediately adds that armed with two horns—the two Testaments—the Christian, whom he more imploringly than sincerely calls "brother," will be able to mount a better defense against the rationalistic philosopher than he can. And he tells the latter that if he should fail argumentatively in the debate with him, he should not celebrate this as a victory over all Jews, or make the weakness of a small man into the disgrace of a whole people.[119] The Jew wants only to show that the possibility that the Jews were given their Law by God cannot be excluded; and he is content to fall back on an intentionalist ethics whose elaboration in *Scito teipsum (Ethica)* is known to be one of Abelard's greatest achievements and that certainly was not widespread among Jews in the twelfth century. (Similarly unhistorical is the fact that the philosopher interprets the Old Testament literally, whereas the Jew—like the Christians of the time in their polemics against the Jews—points to the spiritual meaning of the text, and even explains the meaning of earthly rewards and punishments in the Old Testament by referring to the developmental stage of the Jews immediately after the Exodus.)[120] If a servant believes he is obeying his lord because his fellow servants have told him that the master has given the command and they themselves obey it, we cannot blame him, even if the lord has not in fact given him that command.[121] The description of the suffering of the Jewish people, which has endured far more for the sake of God than any other people, is particularly moving; the Jew remarks that in the burnt offering of their pains the rust of their sins has been burned away. People who treat them unjustly believe that they are making a sacrifice to God, because the misfortune of the Jews is interpreted as a sign of God's hatred. In persecuting the Jews, the Christians, for instance, appeal to the

119. (2001), 12: "ne, si forte simplicitatem meam philosophicarum uirtute rationum superare uidearis, te nostros ideo uicisse glorieris, nec imbecillitatem unius homunculi ad totius populi conuertas ignominiam."
120. (2001), 56.
121. (2001), 14 ff.

crucifixion of Jesus, which they blame on the Jews. Jews have to fear even in their sleep that they will be murdered. God would have to be very cruel, the Jew concludes, if he did not reward the Jews' perseverance in their faithfulness.[122] It is obvious that Abelard has compassion for the Jews; but it also seems to me clear that he—not very differently from Plato with regard to Euthyphro (3c6 f.)—wants to reject the view that mere suffering by itself makes a person right. When the philosopher emphasizes in response that the Jews' zeal is undeniable, but the question is whether an intention is right or not,[123] he is reflecting Abelard's own ideas.[124] Although Abelard can also understand why a member of a people that has suffered so much lapses into this kind of defensive strategy, that does not mean that he shares it in substance. At the same time, he vividly depicts the arrogance with which the philosopher treats the Jew and that sharply differs from the respect that he shows the Christian, at least after the conversation with the latter has gotten under way: the Jews follow their senses like animals, are not philosophically trained, and can be led to belief only through miracles—which in reality can be performed by demons as well.[125]

The Jew Salomo in Bodin's *Colloquium heptaplomeres* is subject to a similar hatefulness—not only on the part of the Lutheran Grobian Fridericus, who even brutally rejects Jewish prayers for Christians,[126] but also on that of the skeptic Senamus.[127] At least, Salomo shares this fate with the Muslim Octavio; when the latter cites the works of Islamic theologians, they are described by Fridericus, who has never read them, as feces.[128] We understand why Salomo hesitates so long before entering

122. (2001), 18 ff.
123. (2001), 22: "sed plurimum refert utrum hec intentio recta sit an erronea."
124. (1971), 54: "Non est itaque intentio bona dicenda quia bona uidetur, sed insuper quia talis est, sicut existimatur."
125. (2001), 86: "Iudei quippe tantum, quod animales sunt ac sensuales, nulla imbuti philosophia qua rationes discutere queant, solis exteriorum operum miraculis mouentur ad fidem, quasi hoc facere solius Dei sit et nulla in eis demonum illusio fieri possit."
126. (1857), 157, 194, 211 ff., 269. Lutheran animosity toward Jews goes back to the Reformer himself.
127. (1857), 118, 159: "Vos Judaei tetrici ac tristes."
128. (1857), 319.

into the conversation about religion, and we must admire his courage when he finally presents openly his criticism of Christianity. On the other hand, we must also admire the host, the Catholic Coronaeus, who for the sake of the freedom of speech he had promised expressly forgoes replying to a speech very offensive to Catholics.[129] The apostate Octavio, who has converted from Catholicism to Islam, later refers to the love with which Coronaeus surrounds him,[130] and the dialogue presents in fact the perfect formality, indeed the sincere heartiness with which this man treats his guests; thus, for instance, he does not hesitate to cite Luther.[131] Remarkable is his argument that one should also pray for the souls of the dead if one is not, unlike himself, sure whether this might help them, since in any case it does them no harm.[132] The paradox here is that Coronaeus theoretically rejects religious freedom[133] but sets an example of it like no one else, and thereby shows that he really is "religiosissimus."[134] Obviously, Bodin knew that there are people who are better than what they believe in theory (even if the opposite case is more common). Presumably the fact that he had met people like Coronaeus explains why Bodin wanted to be buried as a Catholic—despite his mani - fest doubts about Christology, his strong sympathy for Judaism, which may have been the background of his mother's family, and his understanding for the Huguenots. As a model for Coronaeus, he may have had in mind Gasparo Contarini, a Venetian aristocrat, diplomat, and finally cardinal, whose understanding for the Reformation went very far, since he worked tirelessly for the institutional and moral reform of the church, and indeed accepted Luther's doctrine of justification, which he himself had even partly anticipated.

I mentioned Salomo's courage. In the early modern period inter-religious discussions were not really free, but as late as the eighteenth century even the limited tolerance Jews could now count on was still denied to atheists or those who were considered atheists: Locke, for instance, in

129. (1857), 160.
130. (1857), 184.
131. (1857), 347.
132. (1857), 350.
133. (1857), 356.
134. (1857), 354.

his *Epistula de tolerantia,* expressly excluded atheists from tolerance.[135] In *The Moralists,* his pupil Shaftesbury has Theocles grant that some-one who denied God's existence might be punished but radically denies that those who only doubt God's existence should also be punished. Someone who doubts may perhaps be willing to be taught something better, and in any case the power of the authorities does not extend to ideas—and thus overt doubt, this seems to imply, must not be inter-preted as secret denial. To the sarcastic remark, intended as a provoca-tion within the framework of the conversation, that no one writes so well against atheists as the person who signs their death warrant, the pious Theocles replies angrily: "If this were the true writing, replied he, there would be an end of all dispute or reasoning in the case. For where force is necessary, reason has nothing to do. But on the other hand, if reason be needful, force in the meanwhile must be laid aside; for there is no enforcement of reason but by reason. And therefore if atheists are to be reasoned with at all, they are to be reasoned with like other men, since there is no other way in Nature to convince them."[136]

When the power position is based merely individually on the pres-tige of an office or a name and no physical sanctions are threatened, the intellectually superior interlocutor can be expected, a fortiori, not to give in easily. In such a situation, irony is the best proven means of appearing to recognize the authorities while at the same time undermining them. Socrates' flattery of Hippias, for example, is almost shameless, but for that very reason immediately perceptible as ironic.[137] Irony was not Llull's strong suit; but his challenge to an archdeacon whom he, a layman, met on the way to the Council of Vienne in 1311, recounted in *Liber disputa-tionis Petri et Raimundi sive Phantasticus* (from which Nicholas of Cusa made several excerpts still extant in his library in Berkastel-Kues), is nevertheless wittily described. Of course, this dialogue does not represent a real conversation; for that, the cleric Petrus is too schematically depicted as an anti-Llull, and moreover, according to all the laws of human psy-chology, he would have broken off the conversation with Llull far earlier

135. On Locke's theory of tolerance, cf., e.g., R. Forst (2003; 276 ff.).
136. (1999), 48.
137. Cf. esp. *Hp. mi.* 368a ff. and *Hp. ma.* 282e9 ff.

The Universe of the Philosophical Dialogue

in the dialogue than he does, because no one, and certainly not a cleric, willingly allows himself to be threatened with hellfire, as Raimundus does several times here, by anyone whom he does not take seriously. But Llull must have frequently met people with some characteristics of this Petrus, who is a caricature. After he has introduced himself to Petrus, the latter tells him that he has already heard of him, and he knows that he is a "phantast," and asks him what his request to the Council would be. Raimundus names three goals: the foundation of mission schools in which the relevant foreign languages would be taught, the unification of all Catholic military orders, and the fight against Averroism. At this, Petrus laughs loudly and calls him "phantasticissimum." Perhaps, Raimundus replies, he may be that; but it does not seem to him so. What he is recommending is as feasible as it is morally obligatory. It is rather Petrus who is a phantast, because he does not listen to him as he should but scorns him in a phantastical way, even though as a cleric it is he who should devote himself to these matters. At this point the cleric gets nasty; he insults and threatens him, but Raimundus cares not a whit.[138]

Llull had not read Plato, only a few of whose works had at that time been translated into Latin; and yet his depiction of Petrus's conversational behavior reminds us of the one that Plato gives of that of Polus and Callicles (but, typically, not of the noble Gorgias). Polus laughs,[139] Callicles is condescending,[140] and even becomes aggressive[141]—modes of behavior that are widespread among those who no longer can find arguments for their own position.[142] Nonetheless, Petrus accepts Raimun -

138. *ROL* XVI 14: "Hic clericus Raimundo multa conuicia dixit minasque intulit. Raimundus de conuiciis minisque clerici perparum curauit."
139. *Grg.* 473e2. In contrast, at 509b3 ff. it is emphasized that something must be laughed at *with good reason;* thus even laughter is subject to a normative authority. Cf. *R.* 517d ff., where *katagelastos ho gelōs* is referred to. Similarly, Aug. *C. acad.* 1.5.13: "risu inrisione dignissimo."
140. *Grg.* 491e2: *Hōs hēdus ei;* "how sweet you are."
141. *Grg.* 490c8 f.
142. In the *Meno* (94e3 ff.), Anytus, the later accuser of Socrates, descends to explicit threats. According to 92b7 f., his knowledge of the Sophists is just as profound as the Catholic priest's knowledge of the Encyclopedists in Voltaire (s.d., 72), or the Frenchman's knowledge of Jean-Jacques in Rousseau (1999; 79, 95, 99); in the third dialogue, however, the Frenchman has finally read Jean-Jacques.

dus's suggestion that they engage in conversation to see which of the two of them is a phantast, and Petrus begins to refer to his own successes. He is the son of a farmer, he says, who financed his study by begging; but after studying both canon and civil law he achieved prosperity as an archdeacon by accumulating benefices. He spends a great deal, and he has provided well for his siblings and their children, who form part of his retinue, along with horses, servants, cooks, and so on. He travels to Vienne with the prospect of becoming a prelate. Thus he is no phantast but rather a prudent man with good judgment. In contrast, Raimundus, who conceals his antipathy for social climbers as little as Plato conceals his for money-grubbing Sophists, points out that his career has been just the opposite: he began as a rich man, married, and had children; now he is old and poor because he has devoted himself entirely to his plan of spreading the Christian faith, which he hoped, as is well known, to put on a rational foundation. Is such behavior phantastical? Raimundus appeals to Petrus's conscience and recommends that they prepare to decide the question by clarifying concepts.

The main part of the dialogue, then, is concerned with the concept of phantasy or imagination, the four causes, honor, pleasure, and order. The most original section is certainly the first one, in which Llull distinguishes between natural and moral imagination; the latter exists, he says, in a correct and a deviant form. Thanks to the former, man makes himself just and prudent; through the latter, the intellect acquires vicious habits (*habitus*) that are not true but fictitious. The unusual term "phantasia moralis" is fascinating; an important step in the history of the concept of "Imagination" is owed to the accusation of being a phantast. In Llull, the imagination is not only a theoretical but also a practical faculty; and even if he was presumably familiar with the moral evaluation widespread in contemporary Scholasticism, for example, of dream phantasies, the context seems to suggest that he had more in mind: the contrafactual element of moral action that must have had a special appeal for an innovator and writer of utopian novels like Llull was probably subsumed under the concept of the moral imagination.[143] Petrus accuses Raimundus of

---

143. That is why it is unfortunate that M. R. Pagnoni-Sturlese took no notice of this work of Llull's in her valuable article (1989).

being a phantast because he cannot realize his goals and yet does not change them; Raimundus replies that he is alone, but he is the only one who is concerned with the common good. And only a phantast can advise him to abstain from it. Petrus makes fun of Raimundus, because he debated as a single person with a large group of academic philosophers in Paris without being able to convince any of them;[144] but Llull knows, like the Platonic Socrates, about the special position of the one against the many. It is impressive that as a Catholic layman he retains his composure when confronted with the clerical dignity of his interlocutor; even if Petrus became pope, he would be a bad pope; the higher the office, the greater the sin that consists in misusing it.[145] Llull's reproaches become increasingly aggressive; and when at the end he asks Petrus whether it is in accord with the divinely willed order that a few clerics eat at tables loaded with fine dishes while the poor cry out at their doors, Petrus angrily breaks off the conversation. We will not be inclined to recognize any delicate sensitivity in Raimundus, but to be fair we have to remember three things: first, it is Petrus who began the mocking of the opponent; second, Raimundus's interest in the salvation of Petrus's soul is genuine; and third, Raimundus emphasizes that his opponent has just as much right to address moral reproaches to him.[146] The asymmetry in the positions of power is replaced by an asymmetry in moral value; but moral obligations are generally valid, and both sides have the right to demand that these obligations be fulfilled.

144. *ROL* XVI 17 f.
145. *ROL* XVI 19, 21.
146. *ROL* XVI 24: "Et quia praeceptum est, diligere suum proximum, et ego tuus proximus sum, ideo super te contristor, quod uisibilibus, ut debes, non utaris"; XVI 26: "tu uero, si in me prauas deprehendas phantasias, placet mihi, ut me reprehendas."

CHAPTER 15

The Goal of Conversation

Learning From versus Learning About—Dissent, Consensus,
Aporia—Total versus Partial Communication

What are the goals of philosophical conversation? Obviously these can be
very different in nature; indeed, they can be evaluated morally in different ways, even when there is a formal equality of treatment for both parties. Everyone who has reflected on the principles of ethics knows that
symmetry is a necessary but not sufficient condition of moral behavior.
Mutual instrumentalization—abuse, for instance—is hardly moral; and
even the bargaining behavior on which economic activities thrive is of
no help in philosophy, because haggling and compromising contribute
nothing to the search for truth. It may be prudent, if one does not want
to alienate the Other emotionally, to communicate the position that one
considers the right one in such a way that it does not seem too distant
from the Other's position; but that does not change the fact that truth
cannot be understood as a function—for instance, as an arithmetic or
geometric mean—of factual opinions.

An absolutely symmetrical conversation can be conducted by both
sides with the goal of humiliating the Other and displaying one's own
knowledge. Opposition, not collaboration, competition, not cooperation,
characterize such a conversation, in which what is in the foreground is

not the common discovery of the truth but rather—as in a legal proceeding, from which Laches distinguishes the philosophical conversation[1]—winning. Especially when a third party is present, a degeneration of the conversation in this way is always a danger, as we saw in chapter 13 (p. 273). In their discussions with Socrates, Hippias and Protagoras constantly also have the broader audience in view; and even if the latter can act beneficially as a referee, that only partly resolves a problem that it itself has created. The literary representation of two sides that crave recognition has a satirical potential, but it is seldom elevating; positive philosophical insights can hardly be communicated in such a dialogue. The reader will as a rule try to learn from a dialogue character, only if he also personally admires him; and for that reason a successful philosophical dialogue, when it represents conversational behavior whose chief goal is to triumph over the interlocutor, will oppose to him a behavior that is focused on the issue at hand. In such a behavior, a defeat that liberates someone from an error is seen as a common victory.[2]

The first passage in the *Gorgias* where Socrates abandons direct conversation and engages in a meta-discourse is famous. He senses that Gorgias's statements have become entangled in inconsistencies; but before he reveals them, he remarks that Gorgias has certainly often noticed that people do not easily end their discussions by making a common decision about their topic, having learned from one another, and taught one another; instead, when they have not agreed about a question, and one

---

1. *La.* 196b4 ff. See also the opposition *agōnistai-philosophoi* in *Tht.* 164c9 f. In 164c7, the adverb *antilogikōs* is used (cf. also 197a1, *Phd.* 101e1 f.), in which the preposition expresses the conflict. An eristic disputant (*eristikos*, cf. *Ly.* 211b8) is a person who wants to win an agonistic conversation, sometimes at any price; the weapons used may include logically dishonest means (cf. Arist. *SE* 171b22 ff.). In Plato, however, the use of such means is not always the mark of the eristic; in my opinion it is not in the passage just mentioned from the *Lysis* or, for example, in *Sph.* 225c7 ff. and 231e1 f., where the eristic appears as a subcategory of the agonistic; the Socratic manner of conducting a conversation clearly falls into the eristic too (225d7 ff.). The other subcategory of the eristic is the sophistic, which is basically concerned with money (225e1 ff.; cf. Arist. *SE* 171b25 ff.).

2. Cf. Caecilius at the end of *Octavius*, 3.8: "vicimus, et ita ut inprobe usurpo victoriam. nam ut ille mei victor est, ita ego triumphator erroris" (40). Cf. also Aug. *C. acad.* 1.3.8: "Non paruum in philosophia profectum puto, inquit, cum in comparatione recti uerique inueniendi contemnitur a disputante uictoria," and 3.14.30; *Ord.* 1.10.29.

of them has accused the other of being wrong or unclear, they get angry and claim that their interlocutor is speaking out of resentment and because he wants to win, instead of seeking to resolve the basic question at hand; and they finally separate in a shameful fashion, since they insult each other in such a way that someone who has only listened to them feels humiliated because he has not deemed listening to such people beneath his dignity.[3] Therefore Socrates is afraid to contradict Gorgias, he says, for fear that Gorgias might think he is doing so not to clarify the matter at hand but rather because he wants to make him look bad. Only if Gorgias is the same kind of man as he is, Socrates says, does he want to continue to question him; he himself is the kind of man who is glad to be refuted when he says something untrue, but also gladly refutes someone else's untrue opinion, and is no less happy to be refuted than to refute. It is a greater good to be freed from the greatest evil than to free another person from it; but he considers nothing a greater evil for human beings than a false opinion about the questions that are the topic of their conversation. Thereupon Gorgias declares that he is just like Socrates; but he refers to the audience, which may be weary, especially since he has already spoken at great length before Socrates arrived. However, Chaerephon and Callicles assure Gorgias that those present are eager to hear more, and Gorgias can then no longer retreat.[4] I say "can no longer retreat" because the reader cannot shake the feeling that Gorgias had hoped that by using the audience as a pretext he might be able to escape the refutation that he senses— to his dismay—is coming, even if he subsequently accepts it with great dignity.

This passage is so fascinating because it does two things. First, it elaborates two distinct ideal-typical attitudes, which are in fact to be found in most conversations among different interlocutors—even if mostly not in a pure form but rather in various degrees; as in many other situations, here too we grasp reality better with comparative than with classificatory concepts. Second, however, Plato would have been merely an abstract moralist and not the sublime philosopher that he is had he not

3. The same idea is found in the last verse of the thirtieth canto of the *Inferno*, where Virgil humbles Dante because the latter has listened too long to an undignified quarrel: "chè voler ciò udire è bassa voglia."
4. *Grg.* 457c–458e.

recognized that this conceptual distinction does not by itself resolve the true problem: which conversational behavior is to be subsumed under which category. No one will explicitly deny that he is concerned with the topic and nothing but the topic. And he will not behave in this way with the intention of deceiving others; he will believe in his own interest in the topic.[5] The people from whom Socrates distinguishes himself do not say that they are not concerned with the topic; on the contrary, they accuse others of not being concerned with the topic but acting instead solely out of personal motives such as envy.[6] The declaration, however sincere, that one is concerned only with the topic, whereas the opponent is acting out of personal motives, thus does not answer the question whether one is really only concerned with the topic. Like the perfect artist he is, Plato not only has this theory developed by his Socrates but also represents it in Gorgias's reaction. The latter admits that his feeling is the same as that of Socrates, but at the same time he shows his readiness to withdraw from the debate. Of course he does not say that, but he obviously hopes that one of those present will get him out of the fix he is in by expressing a lack of interest in further discussion; this he would find less embarrassing. However, it would be false to say that Gorgias hides behind his courtly consideration for the audience; as his subsequent conversational behavior shows, he is, in a way different from Polus and Callicles—but also from Socrates, who cares only about the argument—truly a polite and considerate person; his statement is thus doubly motivated. Why does Socrates force him to admit the principle of objectivity if there is in any case no alternative to it? Because making the implicit explicit is a kind of progress; only after making an express promise can one no longer go back.[7]

What is fascinating and at first surprising about the objectively oriented attitude is that it provides a better foundation for a successful

5. Such statements are legion in philosophical dialogues; one example is "Quasi ergo victoriae causa pugnem potiusquam veritatis" (Valla [1987], 90).

6. Cf., for example, the accusation Critias directs against Socrates in *Chrm.* 166c5 f. The latter replies that he treats everyone else just as he treats himself, by destroying false knowledge everywhere (c7 ff.), and he challenges Critias to abstract from the personal dimension and concentrate on the subject at issue (d8 ff.).

7. Cf. *Grg.* 458d7 ff. with *Hp. mi.* 373a9 ff., c1 ff., and *Prt.* 348b f., where, however, it is Eudicus and Alcibiades, respectively, who have to remind Hippias and Protagoras of their promises. The latter thus prove to be more heteronomous than Gorgias.

philosophical intersubjectivity than the attitude that seeks primarily the Other's recognition; respect is normally not gained precisely when it is striven for *intentione recta*—in any case, the respect of those who matter. (Vain people may prefer to be courted rather than to see people trying to resolve a problem.) A fruitful conversation always centers on a topic, and the only people who are interesting as persons are those who are animated by an interest in such a topic. On such a basis they may then reflect on their interlocutors and even on themselves; and inevitably they will strive to validate arguments that they consider compelling, and thus to refute others. However, this striving is subject to the condition that what is to be communicated must be confirmed to be true and irrefutable. And Socrates sincerely tries to meet this condition. He hunts after Being and wants to educate people, whereas Euthydemus and Dionysodorus hunt after people.[8] However, as we saw in the previous chapter, Plato can be accused of having interpreted real intersubjectivity as only a stage in the ascent toward the idea of the beautiful. But the Other ought not to be interesting only because we can learn from him; and also not because we consider it our duty to disseminate our own ideas, independently of the benefit which we ourselves may derive from their dissemination; instead, the production of a community should be seen as an end in itself, even if only common insights can guarantee such a community's longevity.

Furthermore, it is problematic that Plato never shows us Socrates being refuted; the omniscience he ascribes to Socrates prevents the latter from exemplifying the virtue that he claims for himself in the abstract— responding gratefully to a refutation. We never see him act in conflict with this claim, but also never in accord with it; and perhaps that explains why Socrates has a credibility gap with some readers. He is too perfect to embody certain virtues that are not found either in him or in charlatans like Euthydemus and Dionysodorus, or in men obsessed with power, like Callicles, but instead in someone like Gorgias, who for that reason radiates a kind of sad dignity. This observation is not invalidated by the many mistakes that Socrates makes. The ones Plato does not recognize, because they are his own, do not cloud—from his point of view, which is all that concerns us here—the omniscience of his Socrates. And when he does

8. Contrast *Euthd.* 290c1 f. and 295d2.

make mistakes that Plato recognizes as such, he always seems to make them intentionally. Socrates' reinterpretation of the word *hekōn* (willingly) in Simonides' poem, which has been moved from the subordinate clause to the main clause on the absurd ground that the poet could not have implied that someone intentionally acted badly,[9] is of course not a seriously meant attempt to find a confirmation of his own ethical theory in a lyric poet, because immediately afterward he claims that he is not interested in any confirmation external to the conversation; instead, it is intended to make recourse to interpretation where it is a matter of substantive issues appear ridiculous, to discredit it, and to throw light on Hippias, who applauds Socrates' interpretation.[10] The famous passage *Protagoras* 349e ff. does not prove that Socrates has committed any logical error either; what happens is rather that Socrates tries to get Protagoras to accept a statement that does not follow from his preceding statements, and would lead to an inconsistency. Protagoras is clever enough not to accept the statement; but according to the usual understanding of the practice of disputation at that time, Socrates has the right to lure him into a trap, and the error is Protagoras's when he accuses Socrates of not correctly remembering his words—which, given Socrates' superhuman memory, is not a plausible explanation.[11]

Perhaps still more disturbing than Socrates' omniscience is the way in which he treats a certain figure in the universe of the Platonic dialogues. We can hardly blame him for addressing pompous asses like Hippias, Ion, and Euthyphro or reactionaries like Anytus with heavy-handed irony; after all, that is his only—still very slim—chance of making something clear to people like them, and they have only themselves to blame for their arrogance. But the way he treats the young slave in the *Meno* is dismaying. There is no commonality between him and Socrates, who is examining him; he is not a real interlocutor but a mere guinea pig whom Socrates uses to demonstrate the theory of anamnesis to Meno.[12]

9. *Prt.* 345d ff.
10. *Prt.* 347b ff.
11. 350c6 ff. I owe this analysis to a splendid but unpublished work by my student Miriam Ossa.
12. On the deficiency of the pedagogical and a fortiori the rhetorical question as opposed to the shared investigation, cf. Gadamer (1960), 345 ff.

Socrates' request that Meno choose any one his many slaves, so that he can use the latter to show Meno something,[13] demonstrates his complete lack of interest in the individuality of the person to be questioned, and in contrast to his depiction of Meno and Anytus, Plato makes no effort whatever to characterize the boy. Socrates does ask whether the boy knows Greek—but he asks Meno, not the boy, and the answer interests him only because it is the presupposition for his experiment.[14] It is well known that in the "conversation"—or rather the test—it is a question of constructing the side of a quadrangle whose surface is twice as great as the one initially given, whose side is two feet long. Socrates limits himself to simple questions (which often more or less predetermine the answer)[15] intended to show that the boy has knowledge which is not learned, which he must therefore have glimpsed before his birth, and which he now recalls.[16] The boy at first believes that the side of the quadrangle sought must be four feet long, and then he proposes three feet. In each case Socrates refutes his guess by counterquestions, and the boy then admits that he does not know the answer. This is progress, because previously— Socrates remarks in an aside to Meno—the boy believed he knew the answer (82e5) but in reality did not know it (82e8 ff.). The substance of Socrates' aside is important: it points to the difference between belief and knowledge, implies that knowledge presupposes truth,[17] and shows with what skill Plato is able to attribute a mixed epistemic status such as "to think one knows."[18] At the same time, the remark is performatively interesting: Socrates himself does not say that the boy does not know the answer but instead asks Meno whether he knows it. Meno's insight is thus gained in the same way as the boy's—through autonomous answers to questions. In the second intermezzo, Socrates emphasizes, once again

13. 82a8 ff.

14. Contrast the way Socrates in the *Theages* directs the conversation between himself and Demodocus about the education of Theages to the latter himself (122d2 ff.).

15. 84c10 ff.

16. However, the mythical explanation's claim to truth is limited by Socrates, 86b6 ff.

17. That is explicitly said in *Grg.* 454d4 ff.

18. This is intensified in *Euthphr.* 15d8 f., where Socrates declares that he now knows that Euthyphro believes he knows exactly what the holy and the unholy are. We observe that Socrates thereby ascribes knowledge to himself and denies it to Euthyphro.

addressing only Meno, that the boy now no longer believes he knows what he really does not know; a correct assessment of his own condition has thus been achieved, and that is better, because he will now really try to find out the truth.[19] Socrates is able to bring the boy to see that the diagonal of the given quadrangle is the side they are looking for (its irrational character is not thematized). The use of the technical term *diametros* is the only information that Socrates gives as a kind of gift to the boy (who is never addressed by his own name but is now addressed for the first time by his master's name);[20] but he then turns back to Meno, with whom he discusses the epistemological consequences of his psychological experiment.

An entirely different sensibility—which certainly has to do with the transition to a Christian society that had occurred in the meantime—becomes clear in the dialogue that most closely rivals the *Meno,* Leibniz's *Dialogus de arte computandi.* I have already mentioned its weaknesses (p. 129); basically, this text is more a mathematical than a philosophical work.[21] But epistemological ideas also play a role in it, even if they are not central; and in particular, the questioning of a boy is modeled on the *Meno*—but with what differences! The conversation represented begins among friends in Aretaeus's garden; one of them is the mathematician Charinus, who obviously stands for Leibniz. They are joined by Eusebius, who in his old age is devoting himself, after an active life, to the contemplation of divine and human things. In his piety he reminds us of old Cephalus at the beginning of the *Republic;* but he does not leave to look after the sacrifices but rather talks about his own reading of Plato's dialogues, which are so different from the exaggerations of the pseudo-Platonists. He says that he has just read the *Phaedo*—an obvious choice for a man nearing death who is, unlike Cephalus, a philosophically reflective man—and even if he is not entirely convinced by the arguments given there, he thinks they contain the germs of better ones that remain to be developed. In particular, the argument based on reminiscence

19. 84a3 ff. This passage influenced Alc. 1 116e ff.
20. 85b5 f. In 82b9 he was called only *ō pai.*
21. The criticism of Descartes is important; according to Leibniz, Descartes erroneously believed he had perfected mathematics: (1976), 85 ff. However, Leibniz agrees with Descartes in defending more than three dimensions (99 ff.) and in using algebra to solve geometric problems.

shows that the nature of the soul does not depend on the body and the senses. Charinus replies that he has not yet sufficiently examined what might be inferred from reminiscence, but the phenomenon is undeniable. He mentions the *Meno,* and just at that moment Aretaeus's son comes in, "a boy with a generous countenance whose curiosity and desire for knowledge suggested that he might achieve great things; his father had him educated in such a way that he would be guided more by shame and the encouragement of praise than by fear and whippings."[22] Eusebius requests that they try out the *Meno'*s thesis on him, and after some hesitation, Charinus agrees—but any failure of the conversation must, he says, be blamed on his own weaknesses, not those of the method or the human soul. The boy wants to get away; but Charinus praises his appearance—in a Platonic way, he calls him *bellissime puer*—and wins his trust by means of friendly gestures and short questions. He tells him about a wager he claims to have made with a friend: if the boy proves himself by his answers to Charinus's arithmetic questions, Charinus will win a great deal of money; but if he does not prove himself—but there he breaks off, because he does not want to consider this possibility. Thus he appeals—by means of a lie that Leibniz, like Plato but unlike Kant, considers legitimate in such a situation—not to the desire for gain but rather to the boy's willingness to help, and shows him trust. Despite his shyness, the boy is motivated, because his teacher has explained that he will teach him the art of drawing only when he has mastered the art of calculation, and he is very interested in drawing. Hence he is motivated by an intellectual striving—even if it is not primarily mathematical. Charinus uses this aboriginal interest differently than does Socrates. The boy's self-confidence steadily increases; laughing, he sees that he knows more than he had thought, when it turns out that he has mastered numbering. This even holds, Charinus goes on, for part of algebra. The boy does not know what this monstruous word means, but Charinus proves to him that he can carry out certain algebraic operations.[23] Indeed, the boy quickly understands that the problem he has been set can be more

22. (1976), 9: "liberali facie puer, et ipsa curiositate ac discendi cupiditate egre-gium aliquid promittens. Hunc ita educari curabat pater, ut magis pudore et laudum stimulis, quam metu et virgis duceretur."
23. (1976), 27.

easily solved. Charinus praises him but emphasizes the importance of following a method rather than a natural impulse in solving mathematical problems.[24] He grants Eusebius that the boy is particularly bright, but with further intermediate questions that are in this case unnecessary, anyone can be led to the right answers. Again and again the boy asks a question when he does not understand; and Charinus chooses examples that are familiar to the boy from his everyday experience.[25] When the boy finally proves a proposition all by himself, he adds, "Quod erat demonstrandum," and Charinus now recognizes him as a geometrician; Eusebius admires his metamorphosis.[26] The boy has thus developed into a full-fledged partner; from the outset, he is taken seriously by adults who do not command him to do anything but rely on his own motivation.

The instrumentalization of the slave in Plato is not nice, but since all that is involved is mathematical knowledge, it is perhaps bearable. On the other hand, simple objectifying observation from outside, as in the case of Antagoras's behavior in Murdoch's *Above the Gods,* the other modern dialogue that takes up the slave scene in the *Meno* (and of course harks back to the appearance of the drunken Alcibiades at the end of the *Symposium*), is unacceptable. The host of the friends who are discussing religion lacks religious feelings himself. The Sophist Antagoras, who is in love with the young Timonax, considers religion a superstition and man the measure of all morality, but religion is socially useful and has to be used by the political elites for their own ends. Timonax views this attitude as cynical; religion is immoral because it prevents people from reflecting on the transformation of society. In his antireligious feelings he nonetheless adheres to an absolute norm: "It isn't relative, it's absolute, we can't be relaxed about all this."[27] Antagoras sees a self-contradiction in this and remarks, with the condescension of a postmodernist addressing a Marxist: "Timonax contradicts himself, he is taking up a religious attitude, his 'absolute' is just God, it can't be anything else!"[28] Acastos, through whom Murdoch the adherent to value Platonism herself speaks,

---

24. (1976), 35 ff.
25. (1976), 73, 119 ff.
26. (1976), 135.
27. (1986), 81.
28. (1986), 83.

now chimes in; he sees the rational foundation of religion in the autonomous recognition of the moral as a sphere that we discover, not invent, even if it is clearly an error to reify it. Traditional religion is full of defects; but there is a danger that its decline would lead to a decline of all religiousness. The latter consists, not in a belief in immortality, but rather in "that sort of—absolute seriousness." Antagoras sarcastically paraphrases: "Religion is just morality plus tragic feeling."[29] Acastos does not agree: religion is the belief that life is a whole and that the good is everywhere; it is a feeling of reverence for things. But he can only speak the language of "as if,"[30] and is not able to express himself clearly. In the following pause in the conversation, a servant (or in the alternative version, a slave)—"a graceful youth"—serves wine. The friends' behavior toward him is characteristic: *"Socrates is relaxed and amiable, Acastos would-be friendly but awkward, Timonax perfunctory, Antagoras indifferent. Plato observes and frowns."*[31] Timonax suggests with ethnological interest that they ask the slave about his religious convictions; Acastos is finally persuaded by Socrates to do this. The servant, whom Antagoras describes in his presence as not very smart and as not understanding the language well, does not know the word *religion;* and when Acastos finally asks him whether he *thinks* there might be a God, he replies in the negative, to Timonax's delight. But then he adds: "Not like that—I don't think—I *know* there is God." He has an absolute trust in God, to whom he will go when he dies; he does not love God because he does good things for him, but because he is God; and he is satisfied with his lot because he knows that he is inside God's love and because he is aware of his own sins. Regardless of his deficient intellectuality and knowledge of the language, the servant is far superior at least to Antagoras and Timonax in the depth of his feeling and in the tact of his behavior. Antagoras is happy that his servant's religion at least prevents him from stealing from him; in the second version, Timonax calls him a "beautiful animal."[32] Even Plato, who now speaks up and presents his rationalistic interpretation of religion, in which, however, eros also plays a major role,

29. (1986), 87.
30. (1986), 89. Cf. 105 and 110, where Plato rejects the category of "as if."
31. (1986), 92. Italics in the original.
32. (1986), 97, 129.

is inferior to the servant in one respect: his philosophy manifests itself in explosive hatred for Alcibiades and the Heraclitean philosophy of unity of opposites that he presents. Murdoch named her dialogues after the purely fictional character of Acastos, whose conception of religion comes closest to her own, though it is more sketched out than fully elaborated. Acastos is no great thinker, but he has subtle intuitions. However, he is too intellectual to live them out entirely; only the slave succeeds in doing that, and someone like Plato is far from sharing his reverence for things.

With their slave or servant, Plato's *Meno* and Murdoch's *Above the Gods* introduce a character *about whom,* not *from whom,* the other interlocutors want to learn. Therein lies an offensive asymmetry. But this attitude is not necessarily connected with asymmetry; it can also be mutual, especially in a dual dialogue. Diderot's *Le neveu de Rameau* provides the most perfect representation of an encounter whose goal is not to find the truth, as in a true conversation, but rather to find out about the other person. That is what is uncanny about the dialogue, far more than Rameau's immoralism. Thrasymachus in the first book of the *Republic* and Callicles in the *Gorgias* are also immoralists, but, first, they represent an objective position to which they want to convert Socrates— and here there is a problem, as we shall see later—and second, Socrates never abandons the attempt to convince his interlocutors.[33] The opponents recognize a common horizon of truth within which they meet one another; and even if their conceptions of truth are incompatible, which explains the violence of their debate, the appeal to truth continues to bind them together. But it is precisely this horizon that is lacking in the case of Diderot's dialogue, in which neither of the participants has any passionate interest in "converting" the other. Instead, what is predominant is each man's indifference to the person of the other, who is interesting only as an object of detached observation—like the butterfly for the lepidopterist or the "primitive" for the ethnologist. Someone who wants to persuade his interlocutor to see things as he does may do

---

33. Cf. only *Grg.* 513c8 f. and *R.* 354a12 ff. The difference consists in the fact that Thrasymachus appears to accept his refutation by Socrates, or at least listens with interest (cf., e.g., 450a5 f. and b3 f.), whereas Callicles lets it roll off of him.

this in a way that offends the latter's autonomy; but that is ultimately less insulting personally than when the interlocutor is no longer a co-subject but only an object of investigation. Such a change in attitude may be natural, however, when one no longer believes in the possibility of resolving controversial questions rationally and has become happily resigned to the notion that people have certain views for no reason other than that that is just the way they are; philosophy is then replaced by psychology. The first-person narrator of *Le neveu de Rameau* is, like Constantin Constantius in Kierkegaard's *Gjentagelsen* (Repetition) or the narrator of Grillparzer's *Der arme Spielmann* (The Poor Fiddler), an observer by nature: "regardant beaucoup, parlant peu, et écoutant le moins que je pouvais" (looking hard, saying little, and listening the least amount possible).[34] He is sitting in the Café de la Régence, watching the chess players, whose intellectual abilities vary considerably, as he knows well—some are clever, others stupid—when Jean-François Rameau comes up to him and offers him his own observations regarding the chess players. The two men have known each other for a long time; that is, they have already observed one another on numerous occasions; the first-person narrator describes in particular the eating habits of Rameau, who is admitted to certain societies on the condition that he may eat with them but may not speak: "Il se taisait, et mangeait de rage. Il était excellent à voir dans cette contrainte. S'il lui prenait envie de manquer au traité, et qu'il ouvrît la bouche; au premier mot, tous les convives s'écriaient, ô Rameau! Alors la fureur étincelait dans ses yeux, et il se remettait à manger avec plus de rage" (He kept quiet and ate with fury. He was remarkable to see under that restraint. If he had the inclination to break the treaty and open his mouth, at the first word all the guests would shout "Why Rameau!" The rage would blaze in his eyes and he fell to eating with greater fury still).[35] A fellow human who can only eat but may not speak is no longer a co-subject but is reduced to the level of animality. Despite extensive observation, the narrator *(Moi)* therefore has no deep interest in his interlocutor *(Lui):* "Je ne pense guère à vous,

---

34. (1972), 32 (7). Here and below, parenthetical numerals refer to page numbers in Barzun (Anchor, 1956).

35. (1972), 33 (8).

quand je ne vous vois pas" (I don't think about you very much when I don't see you), he tells Rameau condescendingly.[36] Conversely, when he is able to speak, Rameau repeatedly stresses that eating comes first, then morality.[37] In fact, there is a clear gradient between the two interlocutors who are observing each other: *Moi* is the more detached observer, while *Lui* needs his recognition,[38] and at the same time completely reveals himself: "Après ce que je viens de vous révéler, j'ignore quel secret je puis avoir pour vous" (After what I've told you, I can't imagine what secret I could withhold from you).[39] Therein lies something that wins from the reader a sympathy that *Moi* does not elicit.

Rameau is the nephew of the famous composer Jean-Philippe Rameau, whose musical talent he cannot rival, and this is all the sadder because he has a great musical sensitivity. Even if his defense of the music of Egidio Romoaldo Duni does not show that Diderot had a refined musical taste (because here the author is speaking through *Lui*), his reflections on the priority of vocal music over instrumental music and his interpretation of song as an imitation of the expressive sounds of passion are interesting.[40] In any case, a certain "reprimitivization" with the goal of achieving more immediate expression has proven beneficial twice in the history of modern music—around 1600 and around 1750. But more important than the aesthetic discussions are the ethical and pedagogical discussions in the work, and they are so fascinating because they are an expression of Rameau's uncanny personality. In essence the dialogue is the tragedy of the person with only a middling talent who owes even the name he is usually known by, "Rameau's nephew," to someone superior in whose shadow he lives. One of *Lui*'s first remarks is, "A quoi bon la médiocrité dans ces genres" (What's the use of mediocrity in these genres), and in his next to last utterance he sarcastically notes that although Dauvergne's music has some fine things in it, he was not the first to write them; there is always someone dead who drives the

36. (1972), 34 (10).
37. (1972), 64, 74, 80, 87, 125.
38. (1972), 79.
39. (1972), 95 (59).
40. (1972), 101 ff. "Je vous aime mieux musicien que moraliste" (I prefer you as a musician rather than as a moralist," 77), says *Moi* to Rameau (116).

living to despair.[41] However, middling talent and a lack of originality become tragic only under specific, typically modern conditions. First, it is no longer sharing in truth or beauty that makes a fulfilled life but rather one's own contribution to their discovery or creation; if the former still counts as the highest value, even the unoriginal pupil of a master can be satisfied with his life: Boso seems not to have suffered from the fact that he was no Anselm, because he had access to Anselm's insights. Second, someone who can no longer see the talented individual as a model is condemned to increased dissatisfaction, because he sees talent as something that does not permeate the latter's whole personality, but represents, as it were, something external to an individual who as a person is no better than the untalented individual. Jean-Philippe Rameau—at least as he is described by his nephew, whose objectivity we have in general reason to doubt, but whose character would hardly be as deformed as it is had he had real models—appears in his stinginess not to be a commendable person; and also *Moi* is no Socrates (and, unlike his author, no genius). One could maintain that moral mediocrity is easier to bear in the highly talented, because the inequality exists in only one respect; but in truth it is just the other way around. Since the core of a person is moral in nature and nothing so unconditionally commands respect as moral value, the recognition of moral superiority has something uplifting about it, except in the case of pathological characters; and if the morally superior person is distinguished by intellectual or other gifts, we find this just. (In addition, we are glad that he has greater chances of realizing his moral goals.) In contrast, a simple talent seems a matter of chance, and the distribution of extramoral gifts can easily seem unjust. Still more shocking than an unequal distribution of talents is an unequal distribution of wealth that is not correlated with moral gifts; if one depends for one's living on wealthy people whom one despises on moral grounds, the outrage becomes a painful humiliation, because one inevitably despises oneself as well—and precisely to the extent that one is intelligent and not self-deceiving, even if one tries repeatedly to console oneself with the idea that the dilapidation of the limited talent one did have is not so much one's own fault as a result of general social

41. (1972), 130 f.

decay.[42] The world in which Rameau lives is such that it contains no common values—no "fatherland"—but only tyranny and slaves, and in it people's only goal is money.[43] The people on whom he lives parasitically are opponents of the "philosophes," which allows the author to settle accounts with his personal and intellectual enemies. Rameau is the court jester of the rich,[44] and plays with the holiest forms of Christianity,[45] indeed recites the most abominable tirades of Christian anti-Judaism in a tone of hypocritical piety in which, however, his admiration for the brutal predatory spirit that drives that anti-Judaism is quite sincere.[46]

Rameau begins by complaining that in history geniuses have caused nothing but trouble and therefore should be done away with while still children; but he knows very well that this complaint arises from resentment. *Moi* first sarcastically remarks that the enemies of genius all claim to have genius themselves, and reminds Rameau that he had earlier been in despair because he was only an ordinary person.[47] However, after a while *Lui,* who constantly contradicts himself and knows it (and for that very reason is impossible to refute), admits that he absolutely wants to be someone else, even at the peril of being a genius, a great man. For he is, he says, as mediocre as he is envious; and out of envy he rejoices when he hears something that depreciates those who are generally praised.[48] Envy is the vice that people most rarely acknowledge having,[49] because it is connected with the confession of an inferiority that they themselves feel (and in fact Rameau later accuses *Moi* of being himself envious, indeed, of despising him solely out of envy—his modesty merely cloaking his pride, and his sobriety being imposed on him

42. (1972), 120, 124.
43. (1972), 65 f.
44. (1972), 85.
45. (1972), 105.
46. (1972), 99.
47. (1972), 37.
48. (1972), 42. "Je suis envieux. Lorsque j'apprends de leur vie privée quelque trait qui les dégrade, je l'écoute avec plaisir. Cela nous rapproche: j'en supporte plus aisément ma médiocrité" (When I hear something discreditable about their private lives, I listen with pleasure: it brings me closer to them; makes me bear my mediocrity more easily, 16).
49. As H. Melville rightly says (1986; 327).

by necessity).[50] Even if on the one hand Rameau's awareness of his own weaknesses ennobles him, on the other hand a person who does not respect moral ideas even by being hypocritical and self-deceiving[51] is capable of anything. More than once, Rameau says with pride that he knows himself very well;[52] and the interest in sincere self-knowledge is not the only Socratic element in this unfortunate man who considers himself better than those who know just as little as he does but imagine that they know something (and he bases his ignorance on interesting arguments drawn from the arsenal of epistemological holism).[53] His admission that he knows nothing does not prevent Rameau from offering explanations of human behavior that go very deep. Here are some observations recorded by Rameau the psychologist: ingratitude is natural to humans, because the obligation to thank people is a burden;[54] there are moral people who are unhappy as well as immoral people who are happy;[55] the severity of moralists stems from the fact that someone who is suffering wants to make others suffer as well;[56] the appearance of vice is worse than its reality;[57] even the savage wants to benefit from the blessings of civilization.[58] On the one hand, this reminds us of La Rochefoucauld; on the other, it lacks any moral foundation or intention: what *Lui* calls a vice

50. (1972), 64.
51. (1972), 70: "Heureusement, je n'ai pas besoin d'être hypocrite; il y en a déjà tant de toutes les couleurs, sans compter ceux qui le sont avec eux-mêmes" (I don't need to be a hypocrite; there are enough of them around, not counting those who deceive themselves, 38). The deception of others ends up in self-deception: "Il avait tant fait les mines, qu'il se croyait la chose" (so much mimicry had ended by seeming real, 39). The human tendency to self-deception is repeatedly emphasized (80). The narrator also acknowledges that Rameau is no hypocrite (115), and he himself declares that others do what he theoretically systematizes (116).
52. (1972), 39, 44: "Personne ne me connaît mieux que moi; et je ne dis pas tout" (No one knows me better than I and I haven't said all I know, 18). The contrary statement, however, is not long in coming: "Que le diable m'emporte si je sais au fond ce que je suis" (The devil take me if I know what I am like at bottom, 47).
53. (1972), 58. At the end Rameau alludes to Socratic maieutics (120).
54. (1972), 65.
55. (1972), 68.
56. (1972), 69f.
57. (1972), 84.
58. (1972), 117.

Moi may count a virtue, and vice versa.[59] Tradition had not yet formalized and demoralized the concept of greatness so much that it could conceive the phenomenon not only of amoral, but even immoral greatness; but that is precisely what concerns Rameau. At the outset, *Moi* says that malice and genius do not necessarily go hand in hand;[60] and he argues, quite in the mode of Leibniz, that certain weaknesses of major intellects fulfill an absolutely positive function. But in response Rameau asks why a powerful and wise Nature has not always correlated greatness with goodness.[61] According to him, malice is not only a necessary means for achieving the good but also an end that Nature seeks for its own sake; and in this antiteleological perspective the question quite naturally arises as to whether there can be greatness in evil. Rameau realizes that his interlocutor despises him, and he admits that he sometimes despises himself as well, but only seldom; he congratulates himself on his vices more often than he reproaches himself for them. His discussion partner is more consistent in his contempt. *Moi* agrees, but asks why Rameau is revealing all his turpitude to him. *Lui* replies that by doing only so can he win: "S'il importe d'être sublime en quelque genre, c'est surtout en mal. On crache sur un petit filou; mais on ne peut refuser une sorte de considération à un grand criminel. Son courage vous étonne. Son atrocité vous fait frémir. On prise en tout l'unité de caractère" (If there's one realm in which it is essential to be sublime, it is in wickedness. You spit on ordinary scum, but you can't deny a kind of respect to a great criminal: his courage amazes, his ferocity overawes. People especially admire integrity of character).[62] Augustine already knew that great and successful criminals enjoy more prestige in this world than petty ones,[63] but Rameau goes further: he ascribes moral value (insofar as this concept still makes sense in his case) to consistent rogues and recognizes sublimity chiefly in evil. It is true that he has to concede that he himself does not possess the consistency of character he aims at, but for him this objection becomes merely an opportunity to tell the story of the renegade

59. (1972), 85.
60. (1972), 38.
61. (1972), 40f.
62. (1972), 95.
63. *De civ. dei* 4.4.

of Avignon, one of the greatest rogues one can imagine and in whom Rameau sees a model. *Moi* is repulsed no less by the teller of this story than by its object, and Rameau is happy to force him to admit that he, Rameau, is at least original in his moral degradation: "que j'étais au moins original dans mon avilissement" (that I am at least original in my vileness).[64] Better to be a great criminal than an "espèce," which is "de toutes les épithètes la plus redoutable, parce qu'elle marque la médiocrité, et le dernier degré du mépris" (the ones we call "types," of all descriptions the worst, because it indicates mediocrity and the lowest degree of contempt).[65] Rameau admits that he dreams of doing something for which everyone would admire him;[66] and if the only way he could achieve that was a great bit of roguery or a great crime, then he is willing—at least theoretically. Rameau has thus become a predecessor of literary figures such as Raskolnikov, real philosophers such as Nietzsche, and well-known historical actors of the twentieth century (to name them would be superfluous and merely confirm their way of thinking). It may be that such people are psychologically beyond the reach of a rational refutation; thus we can only say that an exchange with people like them is no more than a perversion of conversation.

As mentioned earlier, the goal of a good discussion is the common discovery of the truth. When this goal is abandoned, conversations become pathological and the Other inevitably becomes an object—because only a person who can make a truth claim is a subject, and a truth claim is necessarily intersubjective. However, this does not imply that the only successful conversation or representation of a conversation in a dialogue is one in which the interlocutors agree at the end. Not all, perhaps, but many of our insights are hypothetical in nature: we can grasp that p is the case if q is the case without already knowing whether q and therefore p is in fact the case. Mutual understanding often enough consists in seeing why the Other thinks the way he thinks: if we assume his premises, his other assumptions seem rational, even if they are incompatible with our own. It is this case of mutual understanding without agreement that

64. (1972), 99 (63).
65. (1972), 112 (74).
66. (1972), 121. Cf. 78: "je crois qu'on m'accorderait quelque génie" (no one could deny me a touch of genius, 45).

a satisfactory theory of the philosophical conversation and dialogue must take into account, and if criticism of the imperative of consensus in the ethics of discourse had limited itself to this type of conversation, we would have to admit that it was correct.[67] But if on the contrary dissension is from the outset taken as the goal of conversation, the latter is denatured; and it is of course overlooked that at least regarding the following point a consensus is presupposed, namely, that dissension is something good. (On a level that is not transcendental but instead psychological, the human need for consensus is also shown by the fact that the theoreticians of dissension prefer to invite to their meetings those who think as they do.) In the case of mutual understanding without agreement there exists on an intermediate level an analogous agreement, namely, that a certain assumption follows from another, even if there is disagreement with regard to these assumptions considered separately.

To Plato, the goal of mutual understanding without agreement would certainly have seemed too modest, though it seems to play an important role in three classical authors of philosophical dialogues— Cicero, Bodin, and Diderot. In the representation of the warm friendship that can bind together people who have learned to live with the fact that they have different philosophical views, the point is implicit that certain virtues are possible only when disagreement is not entirely resolved—just as only mortals can be courageous in the full sense of the word. The tolerance of disagreement may have so high a moral value that it compensates for the failure to achieve theoretical truth. Bodin's *Colloquium heptaplomeres* seems to suggest that God is best served by a plurality of religions; and it is hardly an accident that the conversation on the fourth day, when the discussion of the philosophy of religion begins, opens with a discussion of musical harmony, which presupposes

67. D. Nikulin (2005), 99 ff., coined the term *allosensus* and distinguished it from *heterosensus:* whereas in the second case incompatibility among the views expressed in a conversation occurs, in allosensus different but not mutually exclusive opinions are involved. Such an exchange of opinions is surely characteristic of every conversation; but in a discussion the point is usually to find out which of the contradictory positions is the true one. However, as I said, a consensus regarding implications is compatible with continuing dissension; and for this situation a neologism that went beyond "consensus" and "dissension" would be useful.

that there are different tones.[68] At the end of the last day, the conversation returns to this topic when Coronaeus asks the boy to sing the first verse of Psalm 133, "ecce, quam bonum et iucundum, cohabitare fratres in unum," and not diatonically or chromatically but enharmonically. And in fact the seven friends decide never to speak about religion again but only to confirm their religion through the holiness of their way of life.[69] Theoretical dissonances are dissolved in the practical consonance of living together as brothers.

Diderot shows a similar respect for the religious Other in his two *Entretiens*. We recognize that despite the loss of his faith he retained a liking for some—not all—representatives of Catholicism, a liking he could not feel toward immoralism, even though he might have found the latter more intellectually exciting. The first lines of the *Entretien d'un philosophe avec la Maréchale de* *** (published in 1777) depict the lady of the house, the wife of Victor-François, duke de Broglie, with unconcealed affection. By her very outward appearance she is the opposite of Rameau: "C'est une femme charmante; elle est belle et dévote comme un ange; elle a la douceur peinte sur son visage; et puis, un son de voix et une naïveté de discours tout à fait avenants à sa physionomie" (She is a charming lady; she is as beautiful and devout as an angel; sweetness is written on her face; and then, a tone of voice and a naiveness in speaking completely in accord with her appearance). Since the duke is not at home, Diderot seeks her out; and she begins by asking him whether he is the one who doesn't believe in anything, and whether his morality is nonetheless that of a believer. "Pourquoi non, quand il est un honnête homme?" (Why not, if he is a decent man?), her visitor replies.[70] The subject of the conversation, which had concerned all educated Europeans since at least the time of Bayle and Shaftesbury (Diderot had freely translated the latter's *Inquiry Concerning Virtue and Merit* into French), is thereby already opened up: Can there be a binding morality without Christian belief, and in particular without the prospect of a beyond? With enchanting naturalness, which the reader soon realizes is in part

---

68. (1857), 112 ff.
69. (1857), 358.
70. (1972), 339.

used deliberately, the Marshal's wife asks Diderot what benefit he derives from not believing, if he lives morally anyway. None, Diderot replies, and asks whether people believe in order to gain some benefit. The Marshal's wife is uncertain but suggests—she is, after all, a granddaughter of Samuel Bernard, count de Coubert, Louis XIV's famous banker, who financed his wars and left behind him an enormous estate—that self-interest could not harm the affairs of either this world or the next. Diderot says that this is a view somewhat humiliating for the poor human race; and the Marshal's wife, who perhaps feels targeted, goes on the offensive and asks Diderot a second time whether he really doesn't steal. She finds his denial inconsistent and admits that if she had nothing to hope for or to fear, she would not forego certain pleasures—which ones, she will not tell Diderot, but only her confessor. Diderot says that his moral actions are "à fonds perdu"; and when the banker's granddaughter patronizingly remarks that this is the recourse of the poor, Diderot asks—as gentleman, taking the question as being related only to himself—whether she would rather he were a usurer. Her answer is: "Mais oui; on peut faire l'usure avec Dieu tant qu'on veut: on ne le ruine pas. Je sais bien que cela n'est pas délicat, mais qu'importe?" (Of course; one can practice usury with God all one wants; one won't bankrupt him. I know that isn't very delicate, but what does that matter?).[71] If Diderot is not expecting there to be a beyond, then he must be either evil or stupid. Diderot tries to point out an alternative: an unbeliever can act morally if his nature, education, and experiences have led him to find happiness in moral action. The Marshal's wife agrees with him, but she counters very cleverly by asking what would happen in the case of those who are motivated by bad principles and passions. Diderot's answer is not exactly satisfactory: people are inconsistent, and there is nothing more common than inconsistency. The Marshal's wife concedes that someone might believe and yet act as if he did not, and Diderot adds that someone might not believe and yet act as if he did.[72] The two mirror symmetrical comments correspond to the picture that Diderot draws of the sexes: in the *Suite de l'entretien précédent,* Bordeu emphasizes, before he enters into risky ethical discussions,

71. (1972), 341.
72. (1972), 342.

the purity of his morals.[73] That women, in contrast, think the opposite of what they say, is the famous last statement in the *Supplément au Voyage de Bougainville*.[74] If we relate this to the present text, it could suggest that the Marshal's wife does not believe what she claims to believe, even if she does not claim to always act accordingly.

This would not erode her charm, however, because the latter depends precisely on her lack of consistency and reflectiveness. It is delightful how, after admitting that she has read nothing but her book of hours and concerned herself with nothing other than living in accord with the Gospels and bearing children,[75] she discovers to her surprise that she has herself philosophized in proposing a definition of good and evil by relating them to the beneficial and the harmful, respectively: "Et j'ai fait de la philosophie!" she cries, not unlike Monsieur Jourdain in Molière's *Le bourgeois gentilhomme*.[76] On the basis of her definition, Diderot now seeks to show that religion is bad because its benefit is more than outweighed by the hatred that it arouses among people of different faiths. The Marshal's wife sees in this merely an abuse—but Diderot replies that it is an abuse inseparable from the thing, since it follows from the unknowability of God.[77] This consequence holds only for stupid people—but they are in the majority. When Diderot refers to the moral weaknesses of the ancient divinities, the Marshal's wife emphasizes that that is precisely what differentiates them from the Christian God; whereupon Diderot, who is himself inconsistent, responds that with the ancient gods we would at least be somewhat more cheerful. In addition, he has never seen any Christians. "Et c'est à moi que vous dites cela, à moi?" (Are you saying that to me?) the Marshal's wife asks. "No," Diderot answers, using the classical evasive maneuver that consists in inventing a third party, "c'est à une de mes voisines qui est honnête et pieuse comme vous l'êtes, et qui se croyait chrétienne de la meilleure foi du monde, comme vous vous le croyez" (I said it to one of

73. (1972), 244.
74. (1972), 336.
75. We learn later that she has six children (1972; 356).
76. (1972), 343. See the similar remark made by Mlle de l'Espinasse (1972; 197).
77. See the related exchange in Voltaire (s.d., 200). For quoted passage below, (1972), 345.

my neighbors, who is good and beautiful and pious, just as you are, and
believed very sincerely that she was a Christian, just as you do). Despite
her piety, this neighbor is aware of her beauty, especially her bosom, into
which she likes to allow others little glimpses, although the Gospel describes even the conceiving of indecent thoughts as adultery, and she is
therefore encouraging adultery (as Christ understands it). Confronted
by this objection, the neighbor pointed out to him that the cut of her
clothes was a matter of fashion—as if calling oneself a Christian but not
being one were also a fashion. The Marshal's wife is aware of this and all
the other excuses that cannot withstand examination; for they would
also have been her own. "Mais elle et moi nous aurions été toutes deux
de mauvaise foi" (But she and I would have both been insincere),[78] says
the talented naive philosopher in an anticipation of Sartre. She wants to
know how Diderot's neighbor reacted to his curtain lecture: he saw her
the following day as she was going to church—with the same décolleté
as before, and they smiled at each other. Diderot is entirely satisfied with
this contempt for religion, because strict Christian ethics is contrary to
nature and suitable only for melancholics, a category to which—it is
implied—his beautiful and lovable interlocutor fortunately does not
belong. As a further objection to a religious ethic, Diderot adds—urged
on by the Marshal's wife, who does not want to let him go—that priests
often see violations of specific religious obligations such as fasting as
worse than violations of general moral norms such as the prohibition of
adultery. The Marshal's wife does not know how she should reply to this,
but she remains nonetheless unpersuaded. Diderot assures her that he is
not trying to persuade her. Religions are like marriages, and she is evidently as happily married to Catholicism as she is to her husband. "La
religion, qui a fait, qui fait et qui fera tant de méchants, vous a rendue
meilleure encore; vous faites bien de la garder. Il vous est doux d'imag-
iner à côté de vous, au-dessus de votre tête, un être grand et puissant,
qui vous voit marcher sur la terre, et cette idée affermit vos pas. Contin-
uez, madame, à jouir de ce garant auguste de vos pensées, de ce specta-
teur, de ce modèle sublime de vos actions" (Religion, which has made,
makes, and will make so many evil persons, has made you still better;

78. (1972), 347.

you do well to keep it. You like to imagine alongside you, over your head, a great and powerful being who sees you tread the earth, and this idea makes you tread with more assurance. Continue, Madame, to enjoy this august guarantor of your thoughts, this spectator, this sublime model for your actions).[79]

Religion seems to become a purely private matter, a means of living happily without any claim to truth. The Marshal's wife is taken with the idea that Diderot does not want to convert her—"vous n'avez pas ... la manie du prosélytisme" (you don't have ... the mania for proselytizing)—but she cannot let the conversation end that way; in the second part it is a question of the inner grounds of religion and no longer its social benefits. The Marshal's wife wants to know whether Diderot is not disturbed by the idea that he will be nothing after death. Diderot answers that he would have nothing against an extension of his existence, but wonders why a being who was able to make him unhappy for no reason should not amuse himself by doing it a second time. If there is a God, he implies, there is hardly any reason to pin one's hopes on his kindness. He also has an easy time refuting the Marshal's wife's awkward attempts to argue for the existence of God; and the mortality of animal souls seems disturbing enough if humans are only more perfect animals.[80] However, the Marshal's wife is unshakable in her belief and asks whether Diderot is really calm, in view of the possibility of his damnation. Diderot does not want to vouch for what he might do if his mental powers declined; but if he remains fully conscious, he will approach death with composure. Indeed, extinction seems to him a lesser evil than the damnation likely for most people, given the demands of the Christian God. But the Marshal's wife emphasizes that she is not a Jansenist, indeed, she does not even believe that good pagans like Socrates or Marcus Aurelius would be damned. "Fi donc! Il n'ya que des bêtes féroces qui puissent le penser" (Fie! Only savage beasts could think that).[81] However, in Diderot's case she is not so sure, because he rejects the light of

79. (1972), 349 f.
80. (1972), 351.
81. (1972), 353. Contrast this with abbé Couet in Voltaire's "Le dîner du comte de Boulainvilliers" (s.d.; 185 f.).

which he is well aware. Diderot points out that belief is not under the control of the will, and finally resorts to a story. A Mexican did not believe his grandmother, who had told him about a realm beyond the sea. But having fallen asleep on the coast, he finds that he has been carried across the sea on a plank and meets the aged ruler of the realm of the beyond in which he had not believed. Is it plausible to assume that he will now be punished with eternal torments? The Marshal's wife would certainly not do that, and the Marshal is also not a tiger; he would finally forgive. But, the Marshal's wife responds, the Marshal and the Old Man are different. Diderot asks whether the Marshal is better than God. God forbid, his wife answers; but God's justice is different. Diderot points out, as Philo does to Demea in Hume's dialogue, that such an answer is fatal to any theology because it deprives us of the possibility of knowing God. The Marshal's wife feels dizzy, but she thinks it is in any case safer to live as if the Old Man existed, and not to count too much on his kindness. Finally, she asks how Diderot would act before the magistrates, or on his deathbed. He will do his best to spare the magistrates a cruel act, he says, and he will submit himself to the rites of the church. "Fi! le vilain hypocrite" (Fie! The wicked hypocrite), are the last words of the Marshal's wife and of the whole dialogue.[82]

The gracefulness of this work certainly depends on the fact that the two interlocutors are not trying to convince each other but rather respect and even like each other in their alterity—and not only feel Christian *agape*, but quite consciously play with the means of erotic attraction. To the Marshal's wife's remark that they will see each other again—she means in another world—Diderot replies that he truly hopes so; for wherever it is, he will always be honored to court her.[83] The flirtation with the pious beauty, prolonged in imagination into the beyond—a beauty who allows even atheists glimpses of her well-endowed bosom—has the lightness of a comedy by Marivaux; the price to be paid is that neither of the protagonists is distinguished by philosophical or moral consistency. The pious lady is, as a banker's granddaughter, a religious utilitarian in the fashion of William Paley, who partly hopes to receive something from

82. (1972), 357.
83. (1972), 355.

God and partly loves religion only because it suits her, and also lives it only as far as it suits her. The atheist is imbued with the intrinsic value of virtue and pins his hopes not on the kindness, but on the inconsistency, of human nature, in order to pull through with his own inconsistency in not being able to say what the source of the validity of moral norms is for those who are not drawn to them by their natures. In pagan religion he praises only what corresponds to his own secularized Christian norms, and not, like Nietzsche, also its violations of universal values. Whoever agrees with Kant that "to be consistent is the greatest duty of a philosopher"[84] will be disappointed by Diderot's dialogue and accuse him of never having really understood the impossibility of a naturalistic ethics that does justice to our intuitions (even if his late debate with Helvétius shows that the problem bothered him). But anyone who values the artful representation of people will surrender to the enchantment of the dialogue and let pass in review before his mind the neither morally nor intellectually outstanding but nonetheless lovable Catholic women whom he has had the good fortune to encounter and who, like the Marshal's wife, are good wives and mothers, are active in charities, and at the same time have a coquettish curiosity with regard to hard-bitten atheists who suddenly begin to wish that their grandmothers might be right after all, so that they could flirt with such women for all eternity. Diderot shows the reader that the Marshal's wife is a good and benevolent person, because she is blessed with external happiness through wealth and beauty, but especially with inner happiness through her nature and her kind of religiousness. To deprive such a person of her religious foothold would be, as Diderot well knows, against all morality, including secular morality.

It speaks for Diderot's fairness that he also erected a monument to an existentially deeper understanding of Catholicism—the monument to that of his own father, Didier, constituted by the *Entretien d'un père avec ses enfants ou du danger de se mettre au-dessus des lois* (written in 1770 and first published in 1773, though in a somewhat shorter version than that published in 1798). The author of sentimental family dramas that are no longer of any interest managed in this dialogue to provide a depiction of his family that describes its personal force field psychologically with

---

84. *Kritik der praktischen Vernunft,* A 44.

as much care as it describes the religious and philosophical opposi-
tions that divide its individual members. In addition to his prudent and
pious father, a knifesmith generally respected by both rich and poor because of his righteousness, about whom Diderot, despite all the contradictions of their worldviews and their personal conflicts, still speaks
with deep love eleven years after his death in 1759, and Denis himself,
his brother the sanctimonious abbé Didier-Pierre, and his sister Denise
all take part in the conversation. A few visitors also join in: the physician Bissei, a magistrate, an obliging prior, a geometrician, and a hatmaker, that is, representatives of the three higher faculties (respectively,
two of whom also stand for the governmental and ecclesiastical powers) and intellectual and manual labor; at the end, another lady notori-
ous for her loose way of life appears. The conversation begins with
the father telling his famous son that they have both made noise in the
world, but he, the father, had disturbed the peace of others while the
son had disturbed his own peace. The narrator leaves open the question
whether the old knifesmith's witticism is good or bad—but this reflection of his own is excellent because it begins the dialogue in a spirit of
hesitation and indecision that continues right to the end. And even
if the witticism may not have been exciting, it nonetheless characterizes Didier, for whom fame is considerably less important than inner
peace. We are reminded of Cephalus, who mentions at the beginning of
Plato's *Republic* (330d ff.), as a major advantage of wealth, that it makes
it easier for a well-disposed person to act righteously, which becomes
increasingly important as death approaches. However, there are important differences between the ways righteousness is understood by the
Christian Didier and the pagan Cephalus. Didier begins to indulge in
dreamy memories, from which the abbé tears him away by asking what
he is thinking about. Didier replies that he is thinking that the reputation for respectability, the one to be desired most, has its dangers too,
even for someone who deserves it. He trembles when he thinks how he
once almost led his whole family to ruin. And he tells how after the
death of a very old, wealthy priest, the impoverished relatives, who had
been reduced to beggary, asked him to ensure the security of the estate.
He does not want to reject the request, and goes to the place, where he
has the authorities put seals on the property and awaits the arrival of

the heirs. He makes an inventory of all the objects. In an old chest he comes across some hoary letters and bills, and under them a will. The will is ancient; the executors named in it have been dead for more than twenty years. And it names a rich Paris bookseller as the sole heir. Didier spent a whole night trying to find a way to set aside the will as no longer valid, or even to burn it, until he finally decided to ask the advice of the Oratorian priest Father Bouin. But before he can go on with his story, the family physician comes in; he has just treated a criminal who will probably be sentenced to death in the near future. Why should he treat such a person? Didier and Denis ask. The physician takes refuge in professional ethics: "Mon affaire est de le guérir, et non de le juger; je le guérirai, parce que c'est mon métier; ensuite le magistrat le fera pendre, parce que c'est le sien" (My job is to treat, not to judge; I will heal him because that is my job; then the magistrate will have him hanged because that is his job).[85] Denis objects that there are general civic duties, such as the promotion of the common good, which do not include the preservation of a criminal. But the physician replies that it is not for him to declare someone a criminal or to find out what he has done. *Moi* now offers a different version of the case: what would the physician do if he had to treat a robber generally recognized to be a criminal? Bissei hesitates but finally answers that he would treat him as well; for anyone who even allows himself such reflections must ultimately accept that a Jansenist would refuse to treat a Molinist, and a fanatical theist would refuse to treat an atheist. It is hard enough to determine the right dose of drugs without having to determine the moral worth of the potential patient. How would he feel, *Moi* goes on, if the criminal he healed then murdered a friend of his physician? Bissei's answer is very beautiful: he would certainly suffer pains, but he would feel no remorse; "assurément, je serai consumé de douleur; mais je n'aurai point de remords."[86] Diderot repeats his point of view, which he tries to support with Galen's authority; but Bissei withdraws from the conversation with the remark: "Cher philosophe, j'admirerai votre esprit et votre chaleur, tant qu'il vous plaira; mais votre morale ne sera ni la mienne, ni celle de l'abbé,

85. (1972), 255.
86. (1972), 256.

je gage" (Dear philosopher, I shall admire your mind and your warmth as much as you like; but your morality will not be mine, nor that of the abbé, I'll wager).[87]

After his departure, Didier allows himself to joke that one could count on the physician killing his criminal patient despite his good intentions, and continues with his own story. The priest whose advice he asked emphasized the sacredness of the will; if he wants to help the poor relatives, he must do so at his own cost. Here Didier shivers; and even if the occasion is the door left open by the physician, we see that the memory of the meeting with the priest has contributed to it.[88] To all his questions Bouin always replied with a counterquestion that began with the words: "Qui est-ce qui vous a autorisé . . . ?" (Who authorized you to . . . ?). That is precisely what is at issue: under cross-examination Didier has to admit that he himself has no moral authority but instead must submit to that of the church. With a heavy heart Didier returned and at least gave the poor relatives something to eat and drink (the abbé protests, because in doing so his father had already misappropriated someone else's property). Then he told the relatives about the existence of a will that disinherited them; and never in his life had he suffered more than on seeing their reaction. He had hoped to move the heir, who had in the meantime been informed, to make a generous gesture; but in vain. The heir did not even look at the poor relatives and took complete possession of the legacy. Didier is nauseated when he thinks about him. However, one thing is clear to him: had he initially ignored the will and distributed the property among the relatives, and then sought out Bouin and heard his judgment, he would have made full restitution to the designated heir, even though this would have inevitably meant that he and his children would be cast into poverty. "J'aurais restitué; oh! j'aurais restitué; rien n'est plus sûr, et vous étiez ruinés" (I would have made restitution; oh! I would have made restitution; nothing is more certain, and you would have been ruined).[89]

87. (1972), 258.
88. (1972), 259. The power of the memory is also shown by his gestures (1972; 262).
89. (1972), 261.

They then fall silent until the previously mentioned visitors arrive. The hatmaker has a request: he wants moral advice from those present whom he begs to stay—the prior, the magistrate, the geometrician, the philosopher, and Didier, who is famous for his honesty and uprightness. The hatmaker's wife, who had been seriously ill, has died a fortnight before, after he had cared for her for eighteen years and not only used for that purpose all the income he had earned by hard work but also went so far into debt that he is still not debt-free. Soon he will no longer be capable of working, and he has no children. He will be able to avoid ending up in the poorhouse only because after his wife's death he withheld part of the dowry that according to the law should have gone to distant relatives of hers. Now he is tormented by the question whether he must give this money back, even if it means the poorhouse for him, and asks the assembled wise men for their advice. Didier asks the prior to speak first; the latter says that he doesn't like scruples. Perhaps the hatmaker should not have withheld the money at the time, but his advice is that he should now keep it. The magistrate, on the other hand, urges him to follow the law, even if it means the poorhouse; even the option of not touching the capital and living off the interest is not legal. The mathematician asks how much he spent on his wife and how much he embezzled; since the two sums are approximately equal, nothing additional remains—and thus it is assumed that he can live with a good conscience. *Moi* refuses to comment; when the laws are in conflict with common sense, philosophy must keep silent. Didier refers the hatmaker to his conscience, which obviously gives him no peace; he would be happier if he fulfilled his legal duty. However, the hatmaker brusquely replies that he will go to Geneva. Does he think he can leave his pangs of conscience behind him? He does not know, but he is going to move to Geneva. After his departure, the others discuss the question of whether it is possible to rid oneself of pangs of conscience by moving to another place and with the passage of time. The question is of great importance when a Kantian conception of ethics is not available; for Didier, the decisive answer to the question, "Why be moral?" is clearly, "Because otherwise one will suffer from the pangs of one's own conscience." In a sentence not ascribed explicitly to anyone, but which presumably reflects the father's position, we read: "My children, the wicked man's days are filled with worries. Tranquility is only for the good man. He alone lives and dies in peace."[90] We understand why someone who is not a Kantian has to cling to this psychological theory, and why someone who has doubts about this theory will find attractive the Kantian position that the validity of morality is not based on psychological assumptions but on a categorical imperative.[91]

After all the guests have left, Didier asks Denis why he kept quiet during the discussion with the hatmaker. His answer—because there is no good advice for a stupid person—is not untypical of the arrogance of French Enlightenment thinkers with regard to the classes that they wanted to liberate. The hatmaker is his wife's nearest relative, so her dowry would go to him. His father thinks that with this argument Denis is adhering only to the letter, not to the spirit, of the law. This is a comical reversal of the reaction that one might actually expect: it is after all the father who insists on following the law exactly—and normally that means the letter of the law—whereas Denis appeals to reason. Denis's siblings opine that without laws there would be no property and thus also no theft; but Denis disagrees and appeals to a theory of natural law reminiscent of Locke, according to which property is legitimated by labor. The highest court is that of the heart, reason, and the conscience, and natural equity. The father sarcastically remarks that he should preach these principles from the rooftops and then he would soon see what splendid consequences they have. Denis replies that he will not preach these principles, because they are not made for the stupid; but he will take them to heart himself. Because he is a wise man? his father asks. "Absolutely," *Moi* replies.[92] The idea that certain truths have to be kept hidden and are not for everyone returns twice: "c'était une affaire à n'être pas portée devant les juges" (it was a matter that should not be brought before the judge), Denis later says about that story about the inheritance;[93] and at the end he whispers in his father's ear—who begs him to speak still more softly—that strictly speaking, there are no laws

90. (1972), 267.
91. Cf. Kant's critique of Garve in the essay *Über den Gemeinspruch . . .* , 11.137.
92. (1972), 269.
93. (1972), 273.

for the wise man: "Mon père, c'est qu'à la rigueur il n'y a point de lois pour le sage."[94]

Since they are now fewer, Denis states, in response to his father's request, that in his opinion his father has acted badly just once in his life, and that was when he listened to the bigoted Father Bouin. Denise shows that she is of limited intelligence when she is not capable of analyzing the case in accord with general principles; worried, she asks her brother whether he wants to ruin them all. Didier, however, wants to hear his son's reasons for saying what he has said, on the condition that he does not abuse Father Bouin (which Denis has no intention of doing). Denis argues that the will was either invalid or unjust; in either case the father was not bound by it and should have burned it. He should have followed the urgings of his heart instead of those of the priest, whose decision demonstrates only the dreadful authority that religious opinions enjoy even among the most intelligent men. Didier tries to lure his son into a trap: what decision would he have made had he himself been made the sole heir? The same decision, Denis answers, and it would have been still easier to make. It speaks for the mutual respect between father and son that Didier tells Denis that he takes him at his word and asks whether in his son's opinion his decision will at least be absolved by his religion, that is, whether Denis thinks that Didier acted at least subjectively in accord with his conscience. "Je le crois; mais tant pis pour elle" (I believe so; but too bad for your religion), replies his son,[95] who condemns only his father's religion, not his father himself. Didier takes one of his son's recommendations very seriously: he should at least have contested the will in court. But the abbé thinks he would have lost the case, because judges do not act according to what is equitable in individual cases but according to general principles that cannot be disregarded without leading to much worse consequences—an argument that is reminiscent of Hume's theory of justice. Then, Denis says, his father should have avoided the courts and acted on the basis of the authority of reason. But his father disapproves of giving private reason precedence over public reason. Reason might be a soft pillow, but he would sleep better on that of religion

94. (1972), 279.
95. (1972), 272.

and the laws; and he refuses to discuss this question, because he doesn't need insomnia. Finally he asks whether his son would have prevented him from giving back the property if he had destroyed the will and only later learned Father Bouin's judgment. No, Denis answers, because his father's peace of mind is more important to him than all the goods in the world: "Non, mon père; votre repos m'est un peu plus cher que tous les biens du monde."[96] The father is pleased by this answer, partly because his conscientiousness in immediately announcing the death of an uncle who was a canon had cost Denis a canonry. Denis says that he would rather be a good philosopher, or nothing at all, than a bad canon. To Didier's dismay, the obliging prior, who suddenly reappears, asks whether there is such a thing as a bad canon. He is asked what he thinks about the case of the inheritance, and instead of proposing a solution, he tells how he himself, acting as legal advisor to the creditors of a money-changer who had gone bankrupt, destroyed a promissory note signed by a poor neighbor. Didier had been one of the creditors. Didier now agrees that the prior was generous at his expense but objects that this principle of sympathy is dangerous and could lead very far: "Justice . . . ," he begins, but the prior interrupts him, "is often a great injustice."[97] The conversation ends with a comic scene: a libertine woman comes in; she lives apart from her husband, who cheated on her first. The prior teases her, but Denis tries to prove to him that the spouse who first commits adultery frees his partner to do the same. This is too much for Didier; he breaks off the conversation and packs them all off to bed. He has the last word: it wouldn't bother him to live in a city with one or two citizens like Denis, but if all of them thought as he does, he would no longer want to live there.

The significance of this dialogue does not lie in the philosophical answers it gives. Even someone who solves the problem of the exceptions to prima facie norms (which is obviously the common subject of all three discussions in the dialogue) differently from the way Kant does cannot help feeling that *Moi* has it too easy; the appeal to one's own heart can hardly justify every violation of the law. Diderot provides nei-

96. (1972), 273.
97. (1972), 278.

ther a complex value-ethics nor a satisfactory theory of the function of positive law. But the impressive thing about this text is that its author is much better and more complex than *Moi*. With the knifesmith Didier, he has first of all presented a man whose integrity and readiness to sacrifice himself are beyond doubt. *Moi* also recognizes that Didier's decision to obey ecclesiastical authority is, given his assumptions, respectable and even compelling; indeed, he would have been willing to help bear the high costs of this decision. The fact that one may have moral respect for people whose values differ from one's own is one of the dialogue's crucial lessons. Second, Diderot shows that this lesson has been learned not only by an Enlightenment thinker but also by a traditional Catholic like his father who, despite traces of paternalism, treats him respectfully and even lovingly. Third, Diderot is fully aware of the breadth of the Catholic religion's spectrum. He sketches Father Bouin and his own clerical brother with unconcealed antipathy, and his father, whose good heart made his decision difficult, with admiration—indeed, with a greater admiration than the obliging, nameless prior, who agrees with Denis on most substantive questions. However, when the prior is said to know more about good wines than about moral questions, and to be fond of Béroalde de Verville's obscene Rabelaisian novel *Le moyen de parvenir*,[98] it is suggested that his amiability arises more from convenience than from a commitment to reason. In his existential seriousness Denis stands closer to his father than to the prior, who is certainly less religious than Didier and even than Denis, if we consider existential seriousness a *conditio sine qua non* of religion. The prior is likable, but he lacks the greatness of the Catholic layman Didier. Fourth, Diderot not only presents the argument for a strict adherence to the usual moral norms; he lets his father have the last word, and his warning sounds all the more persuasive because it comes not from a fanatic but from a man who is open-minded, who does not object to there being a few people like Denis, but whose life experience has enabled him to foresee the social consequences of a generalized enlightenment. Moreover, in his dialogue Diderot depicts very objectively the change that results from the decline of an ethos that has its center in the authority of the church. Didier may have made the

98. (1972), 264.

wrong decision; but because he obeyed Bouin's authoritative judgment, his conscience remains clear, and that is what matters to him most. The hatmaker is more open-minded; he does not turn to a father confessor but to five representatives of different ranks. Does that help? Hardly, because he does not receive an unambiguous reply. Indeed, even if it is especially the prior who accommodates him, he decides to venture onto new moral and religious ground—no matter how doubtful it seems that in Calvinistic Geneva he will find more sympathetic understanding for his behavior. Under the conditions of the pluralism then beginning, an ethical discourse does not provide the individual with the moral certainty he desires; and the wider range of choices offered by the possibility of traveling abroad—which in our time has increased exponentially in comparison with Diderot's period—does not make things easier. It is a mark of Diderot's greatness that he has no illusions regarding the cost of Enlightenment—and does not try to conceal it from his readers. Diderot might be justly accused of never having understood the arguments for the ontological difference between the mental and the physical, and for the irreducibility of moral obligation to nature; but he was no ideologue. Thanks to a father like Didier, he was aware that traditional Catholicism is an imposing worldview. As a philosopher, Diderot is not first-rate; but as a writer of dialogues he is. Since Plato, no one else has represented with such aesthetic perfection the drama constituted by different people philosophizing together.

Bodin's and Diderot's dialogues not only end without consensus but also recognize the fact that consensus will not be achieved. People learn to live with dissension. This should not be called an aporia, because that term suggests that somewhere beyond the current crisis there will be a consensus. That is precisely what Plato's use of the concept presupposes—otherwise the constantly repeated demand to continue searching would make no sense.[99] Nowhere in Plato do we find anything comparable to the end of the *Colloquium heptaplomeres;* nowhere is it said that it has been discovered that the questions or problems under discussion are undecidable, that approaches to them inevitably depend—at the level of theoretical validity—on one's own inclinations,

---

99. Cf., e.g., *Euthphr.* 15c11 f.; *La.* 201a1 ff.

and that an objective truth does not exist. This leaves open the possibility that in writing the aporetic dialogues Plato did not yet have an answer to the questions raised, and that the aporias arrived at in them are real, but not, Plato hopes, final. According to this line of interpretation, Plato is supposed to suggest that although the dialogue partners have in fact failed to achieve the goal, a legitimate goal nonetheless remains. But a priori such an interpretation is not very plausible. When someone reflects on a problem and arrives at no solution, he seldom writes a book about it—unless he can, for instance, prove why a solution cannot exist (as Kant claims to have done in the "Dialectic" of the *Critique of Pure Reason*), which is itself a solution on another level. However, as I have said, we find nothing of the sort in Plato, and he is hardly one to engage in the vain enterprise of reporting his own failure. The suspicion that the aporias at the end of the early dialogues—like those in book B of Aristotle's *Metaphysics*—were intended to awaken a sense that there was a problem, but did not reveal everything the author knew, and were thus for him merely apparent aporias, is strengthened when we examine Plato's later works. There we find, as I have already indicated in chapter 8, answers to most of the earlier aporias.[100]

Is it likely that Plato found these answers only later on? That is theoretically possible, but its probability becomes very slim if we consider the following. First, in a few dialogues—for example, *Hippias minor*, discussed in chapter 3—the aporia is easily resolved; the comic inversion of Socrates' and Protagoras's roles at the end of the *Protagoras*, regarding whether virtue can be taught, is not a sign of Socrates' embarrassment but rather results simply from different concepts of virtue: a virtue as Protagoras understands it cannot be teachable, whereas a virtue as Socrates understands it must be teachable.[101] This leads us to suspect that the same must hold for other dialogues in which the solution is not so easily found, especially when no difference in Socrates' treatment of the

100. On the interpretation of the aporias in the early dialogues as apparent aporias and on the *Republic* as the intellectual background of the earlier dialogues, M. Erler (1987) and C. Kahn (1996) are central. H. Gundert (1971; 6) has correctly noted that "The Socratic openness of these dialogues is not to be understood in a modern way, as if it taught us to live with the question, because the foundation cannot be known."

101. This is very clearly said at 361b3 ff.

aporias is discernible. (Here we are concerned only with Plato's view of the possibility of resolving an aporia. Whether he was right about this or underestimated problems is an entirely different question.) Second, the earlier dialogues are shot through with allusions to many of the theories developed in the *Republic* and the later dialogues. A few examples have already been mentioned;[102] another famous example is *Phaedo* 110b6 f., which points forward to *Timaeus* 55c4 ff. It is the dense web of these passages that makes a reconstruction of Plato's development so difficult, and even if, on the basis of everything we know about human psychology, we can assume that Plato developed intellectually in a continuous fashion, only little that is both interesting and certain can be said about this development due to the representation of his philosophy in dialogue form, and there are good reasons for thinking that at the time of the earliest dialogues Plato had worked out the basic structures if not the details of central theoretical elements of his later philosophy. Since we do not know when Plato published his first dialogue, it is in any case possible that he was aware of Eleatic and Pythagorean philosophy as well as Socratic philosophy at the time of his first publication; and even if he began publishing his dialogues in the fifth century, we cannot exclude the possibility that a man of his talents had made himself familiar with the essential features of the most important theories of his time and was already integrating them into his own synthesis. Third, an interpretation of the aporias as merely apparent aporias is also supported by the behavior of the Platonic Socrates, whose "pathos of distance" is far more marked than Nietzsche's, precisely because it is not blatantly pointed to. Every intelligent reader suspects that Socrates knows more than he says, that is, has an esoteric knowledge that he does not want to convey to just anyone, and this favors the assumption that Socrates knows a solution to his aporias, or rather he believes he does. But this, along with the thoroughly positive image of Socrates that Plato gives us, implies that Plato as well knew or thought he knew how to resolve the aporias. (The converse would of course not be valid: if an author has a solution dialogue-

102. Cf., e.g., above, chap. 3, notes 19 and 23 on *La.* 197e1 f. and 199a1 ff.; p. 161 on *Euthd.* 301a1 ff., which anticipates *Prm.* 130e4 ff.; and p. 279 on *Prt.* 357b5 f. Also, *Chrm.* 171e5 ff. obviously presupposes the conception developed in the *Republic*.

externally, none of his characters need have it dialogue-internally.) Socrates' dialogue-internal advantage in knowledge corresponds to Plato's dialogue-external knowledge that he withholds. In chapter 14 (p. 298), we saw that in the *Euthyphro* Socrates alludes to a secret knowledge. It is Thomas Szlezák's achievement (1985) to have assembled the numerous parallel passages and in the other dialogues subjected them to a com - prehensive interpretation. Lysimachus and Melesias in the *Laches,* for example, are certainly not people for whom a mode of presentation like that adopted by Socrates in the central books of the *Republic* would be suitable; accordingly, in response to Lysimachus's request for instruction, Socrates replies evasively; "God willing," are his last words,[103] and shortly before, Nicias has mentioned that he has not yet succeeded in persuading Socrates to undertake the instruction of his son Niceratus.[104] Being taught by Socrates is an honor that is not granted to everyone. However, only Nicias can say this so openly; Socrates hides behind his own alleged need for a teacher,[105] and points vaguely to an esoteric dimension: *oudeis gar ekphoros logos.*[106] And in addition his assertion that it would be horrible to refuse to help someone who wanted to become as good as possible[107] is certainly not a pretense incompatible with his factual refusal to act as a teacher; Socrates is simply of the opinion that not everyone has something to gain by studying with him.[108] Analogously, the author Plato believes that few readers would learn anything from him if he presented them at the outset with the metaphysical foundation of ethics that he offers in the *Republic;* he must first prepare the ground for such an encounter by challenging the prejudices of contemporary culture, partly encouraging formally the reader to think for himself by

103. *La.* 201c 5. Cf. *Hp. ma.* 286c 3.

104. 200c7 ff.

105. Granted that in the Platonic literary universe as a whole, Socrates later finds teachers in the Eleatic Stranger and in Timaeus; but even if at the time he wrote the *Laches,* Plato was already thinking of such encounters, he could not expect his reader to anticipate them; Socrates' search for a teacher must therefore have appeared, in view of the dialogues Plato had published up to that point, as ironic understatement.

106. 201a3.

107. 200e1 f.

108. Plato says much the same thing in the first person, *Ep.* 7 341d4 ff.

exposing him to the experience of aporias and partly helping him to see that on the level of content, his previous convictions did not constitute a consistent whole.

However, all these passages in which Socrates communicates only partly, not totally, prove only that according to Plato the true philosopher does not immediately reveal everything, but instead knows reasons on deeper levels and holds back knowledge that cannot benefit his present interlocutors. With the elaborated theory of Ideas, the *Republic* offers one level of these deeper reasons, but it is itself full of deliberate gaps, a few of which point to the late dialogues. But even in the late dialogues hints of something more remain, and it is more than tempting to connect them with reports regarding Plato's unwritten doctrine, especially his doctrine of the two principles. However, it is not easy to determine whether the allusions in the earliest dialogues to an esoteric doctrine[109] already have in view the doctrine of the two principles or central doctrinal components of the *Republic,* that is, theories that would later be published. The mere reference to a knowledge that is not (yet) communicated does not suffice to settle this question; references to the content of the later doctrines are indispensable. Such a reference is found in the passage in the *Protagoras* mentioned in note 102 in this chapter, and another in the *Euthydemus.*[110] These are certainly not the earliest of Plato's dialogues; and therefore the current state of research allows us to say scarcely more than that Plato was familiar at least since the *Protagoras* and the *Euthydemus* with the theory of the two principles, which Aristotle and other writers attribute to him and which is obviously a further development of the doctrine of Philolaus, which he encountered no later than his first trip to Sicily.[111] However, from his first dialogues on, Plato's image of the true philosopher included the notion that he communicates his knowledge very selectively.[112]

The resistance that the so-called Tübingen school of Plato interpretation has aroused has not always, indeed has even seldom, concerned

---

109. Cf., e.g., *Ion* 541e1 ff.

110. Cf. above, 275 f.

111. Cf. V. Hösle (2004e), 268 ff.

112. *Ap.* 33b6 ff., where Socrates denies that he teaches privately topics that he does not communicate to everyone; this may reflect a statement made by the historical Socrates.

substantive issues. It is often based on a disinclination to entertain eso-teric doctrines that goes back to the Enlightenment, that is, an opposition to strict control over the communication of certain insights that not everyone is deemed worthy of knowing. But however esoteric strategies may be evaluated on the basis of a universalist ethics—the author of this book adheres to the principle of publicity—it is a historical fact that esotericism in the previously mentioned sense played a central role in premodern cultures (in Plato's milieu, among the Pythagoreans, for instance). Later philosophical dialogues also show an awareness that in a conversation one may be well advised not to reveal everything one knows to everyone. Augustine, for example, assumes that because certain in-sights can be understood only by those who have freed themselves from all vices and have adopted a superhuman way of life, someone who seeks to convey them to just anyone has committed a sin.[113] Thus Alypius sus-pects that Augustine has access to secret knowledge that he has not yet shared with his friends.[114] Nicholas of Cusa makes his layman hesitate be-fore conveying his paradoxical views—only when the orator has taken what we would now call an existential interest *(ex affectu)* in them can he speak. And even when the orator explains that he is full of enthusiasm *(inflammor)*, the layman says that he does not know whether it is permis-sible to reveal such secrets and to lay bare such depths so easily: "Nescio, si liceat tanta secreta detegere et tam altam profunditatem facilem osten-dere."[115] But he communicates his conviction that the incomprehensible will be comprehended in an incomprehensible way. The orator reacts by saying that this view is strange and outlandish: "Mira dicis et absona." That, the layman replies, is the reason why one should not communicate the secret to everyone, precisely because it appears outlandish when it is revealed. But the self-contradictory will prove to be true because the principle is of a different kind from what is grounded in the principle. This argument that explains why one must be wary of sharing certain insights is familiar to us from Plato's *Seventh Letter;*[116] and in the sub-sequent passage Nicholas of Cusa shows in a fascinating way a certain

113. *C. acad.* 3.17.38.
114. *Ord.* 2.20.53: "quamuis suspicemur et credamus tibi esse adhuc secretiora."
115. V 8.
116. 341e3 ff.

knowledge of Plato's doctrine of the two principles.[117] Similarly, in
Bruno's *La cena de le ceneri,* Teofilo explains that one must not communicate especially complex truths to everyone; one should not cast pearls
before swine.[118] However, Bruno did not have his plebeian urge to communicate fully under control, and had to pay a high price for it. Here we
may find useful the distinction between *Geheimnis* and *Heimlichkeiten*
drawn by Falk in Lessing's *Ernst und Falk* in connection with his criticism of Freemasonry: "*Heimlichkeiten* are things that can be said and
that one conceals only at certain times, in certain countries, partly out
of envy, partly out of fear, and partly out of prudence."[119] In contrast, a
Geheimnis is something that cannot be so simply communicated, even if
one wants to; and if others are given not the exact idea, but only an approximate version of it, that is "useless or dangerous. Useless, if it does
not contain enough, and dangerous if it contains the smallest thing too
much."[120] According to Lessing, *Heimlichkeiten* are often ludicrous; but
it is an error to confuse the *Geheimnis* with them. Lessing skillfully inter-
weaves the subject of conversation with the conversational procedure
by making Falk capable of awakening Ernst's interest in his topic only
by making a fuss about secrecy; Ernst is so eager to know the secret that
he becomes a Freemason himself—and is dreadfully disappointed. In
this way he becomes free to realize that the Freemasons' true concern—
their *Geheimnis*—is not dependent on forms and is not conveyed by
their *Heimlichkeiten.* "Freemasonry is nothing arbitrary or dispensable,
but rather something necessary that is grounded in the nature of man
and civil society. Consequently, one must be able to hit upon it through
one's own reflection as well as be led to it by instruction."[121] One could

117. V 31 ff.
118. (1985), I 36; cf. 50.
119. "Heimlichkeiten sind Dinge, die sich wohl sagen lassen und die man nur
zu gewissen Zeiten, in gewissen Ländern, teils aus Neid verhehlte, teils aus Furcht ver-
biß, teils aus Klugheit verschwieg" (1966; II, 709).
120. "unnütz oder gefährlich. Unnütz, wenn er nicht genug, und gefährlich,
wenn er das Geringste zuviel enthielte" (1966; II 691).
121. "Die Freimäurerei ist nichts Willkürliches, nichts Entbehrliches, sondern
etwas Notwendiges, das in dem Wesen des Menschen und der bürgerlichen Gesellschaft
gegründet ist. Folglich muß man auch durch eignes Nachdenken ebensowohl darauf
verfallen können, als man durch Anleitung darauf geführet wird" (1966; II 691).

say much the same about Plato, who must have hoped that the intelligent reader of his dialogues who had undergone the program of education outlined in the *Republic* would hit upon the basic principles of Platonic philosophy by himself, precisely because they are grounded in reason. For just this reason it is ultimately superfluous to explicate them for the exceptionally talented.

The notion that not everything can be publicly discussed is a commonplace of the philosophical dialogue, as discussed in chapter 11 (p. 218 ff.). I already mentioned (p. 362 f.) that in Diderot's *Entretien d'un père avec ses enfants* it is said that it is unwise to say everything one thinks. However, in Diderot this concerns ethically audacious theories in an era of state censorship and persecution, whereas in Plato and Nicholas of Cusa it is a matter of complex metaphysical theories that would be beyond the understanding of most people. This form of esotericism is more subtle or at least different from the one that is connected with external persecution and that Leo Strauss has investigated; we fail completely to understand the specific nature of the former if we confuse it with the latter.

CHAPTER 16

The Ethics of Conversation

Jürgen Habermas distinguishes four validity claims made by every human utterance: comprehensibility, truth, truthfulness, and moral rightness.[1] It is an index of the empirical universality of these claims that they are thematized early on in philosophical dialogues, all of them occurring, for instance, in Plato. However, the situation is more complex insofar as we already find in Plato, in the form of irony, a behavior that is not exactly truthful; the ironist says something different from what he thinks. In chapter 7, we saw that the ironist, too, hopes to be understood—but only by people of a certain intelligence, and for that reason he puts obstacles in the way of comprehensibility that have to be overcome. Unlike a published work that can in principle be read by anyone, in universalist modernity as well a conversation can be successful only if the number of people is limited (see chap. 13); exclusion and inclusion are therefore inevitably strategies for conducting conversations. In the following pages, I analyze some of the norms that are obeyed and even explicitly formulated in dialogues.

The goal of every successful conversation is the sharing of an insight—and even if this insight is that a problem is temporarily or even permanently insoluble, or that on the basis of different premises

---

1. Cf., e.g., (1973), 219 ff.; and (1976).

different conclusions are inevitable. The first, necessary presupposition for such a common insight is that the conversation partners understand each other. They need not necessarily speak the same language (though I know of no multilingual philosophical dialogue); but everyone must speak a language that the others understand or can have translated for them. Having two deaf people speak completely at cross-purposes, as in Erasmus's innovative conversation dialogue *Aprosdionusa sive absurda,* which foreshadows the theater of the absurd,[2] is certainly a pathological exception. But even people who are not hard of hearing and are carrying on a philosophical conversation may speak at cross-purposes, because although they understand their interlocutors' words, they do not grasp their meaning—forcing it, for example, into the categories that they themselves use and which are precisely the ones being challenged. There are two conditions for understanding that must be met by both or by all sides: first, a great effort must be made to understand the inner logic of the other's line of thought; second, one must speak comprehensibly. Anyone who does not understand must frankly ask and not hesitate to admit his failure to understand (in order to be polite, he will also do this when he has the impression that the other has expressed himself un-clearly);[3] and the other must respond with the sincere intention of ex-pressing his thoughts precisely and in a language accessible to his inter-locutor(s). The contrast between Dionysodorus and the Eleatic stranger is enlightening. In the *Euthydemus,* Dionysodorus refuses to respond to Socrates' question requesting a clarification of what he really meant by his trick question;[4] and even if Dionysodorus could justify his refusal by appealing to the common practice of *elenchos,* he shows only that such an absolutized rule does not allow true understanding to emerge; that is, that it is eristic rather than dialectical. In the *Statesman,* in contrast, the Stranger from Elea emphasizes, in connection with the *dihairesis* of con-cepts, that it should be ensured that every *meros* has at the same time an *eidos* (262b1 f.). This and the following sentence are hard to understand, and Young Socrates has the stubbornness and honesty to ask what the

2. (1972), 610 f.
3. Cf. *Grg.* 458e4 f.
4. 295b4 ff.

Stranger means. The latter's answer is significant: he will try to speak more clearly because Socrates is the kind of person it is a pleasure to teach. However, in the following sentence he says that "A fully satisfactory demonstration is not possible now . . . but we must try for the sake of clearness to push the examination a little bit further *(smikrōi pleon)*." This limitation as well as the stereotypical formula *eis authis* (262a6) and, pointing beyond conversation and dialogue, the refusal to answer Socrates' further question (263a5 ff.), indicate that in this dialogue and perhaps in the whole dialogic work, Plato does not seek to provide an exhaustive discussion of the underlying problem of the distinction between artificial concepts and "natural" ones that grasp the essence of a thing.[5] But this stubbornness and honesty are partially rewarded: they show a more philosophical spirit than simply accepting the interlocutor's statements without understanding them. However, Young Socrates has to learn to postpone certain questions; sometimes one has to be satisfied with a partial understanding if one wants to progress far enough to be able really to fill in the earlier gaps in understanding.

Understanding can fail because of the intellectual operations used, but also because of the words used. In Leibniz's *Dialogus de arte computandi,* Charinus tells the boy that when he does not understand a question, he should not say it is too hard but rather that Charinus has formulated it poorly, for example, because he has used unfamiliar words; that is, the boy should shift the blame to him.[6] The use of undefined technical terms in a conversation is a discourtesy to the interlocutor and often only an attempt to impress that should be avoided by anyone who really wants to be understood. It is more dialectical, Socrates explains in the *Meno,* not only to say the truth, but to do so with the help of concepts with which the interlocutor says he is already familiar;[7] attention to the other's understanding is thus part of being a good dialectician. In general, a sense of whether a factual or verbal problem is involved is crucial for arriving at understanding; the warning issued by the Stranger from Elea is to be understood in this sense: Socrates should not take words too seriously if

---

5. Cf. T. A. Szlezák (2004), 170 ff.
6. (1976), 15: "ita culpam a te in me transferes."
7. 75d5 ff.

he wants to be richer in insight when he is old.[8] We find something analogous in Augustine: "Postea, inquam, de uerbo quaeremus fortasse diligentius; non enim hoc curandum est in conquisitione ueritatis."[9] Verbal distinctions that introduce conceptual differences are never harmful and often useful; the dying Socrates says to Crito, who thinks he will be burying him and not simply his body, that the use of false words corrupts the soul (*Phd.* 115e4 ff.). But insisting on the use of specific words does not advance philosophy. The inability to see that someone is using different words to refer to the same thing that we are referring to, and is using the same words to refer to things different from those we are referring to, is always an obstacle to conversation.

Analogously, it is essential to distinguish a hermeneutic discussion from a discussion about a substantial issue. Plato's Socrates repeatedly insists on this distinction. In chapter 15 (p. 336) I discussed the comic aspects of the interpretation of Simonides in the *Protagoras,* where Socrates moves from the poet's utterances, whose meaning cannot be definitively determined, to the truth and to the conversation partners themselves.[10] Analogously in the *Hippias minor,* Socrates asks Hippias, who is hiding behind an interpretation of Homer, "And is that your own opinion, Hippias?"[11] Socrates explains that it is not possible to ask Homer precisely what he meant by his words; thus if Hippias wants to defend the view that he believes was Homer's, he should assume responsibility for it and answer for himself and for Homer.[12] At the end of *Contra academicos,* Augustine concedes that his interpretation of the Academicians, that is, his assumption that in the Academy there was an esoteric doctrine, may be false; but that does not affect his objective refutation of skepticism.[13]

---

8. *Plt.* 261e5 ff.

9. *Beat. vit.* 4.31. See also *C. acad.* 2.11.25 f. (with reference to a fragment from the second book of Cicero's *Academici libri* [= 22,3 ff. Plasberg]) and 3.13.29 and *Ord.* 2.2.4.

10. 347e1–348a6.

11. 365c6. In *Ion* 531a an analogous transition from the *interpretandum* to the object of the *interpretandum* takes place, as a transition to that which is more important.

12. 365c8 ff. Jowett trans. in Hamilton and Cairns.

13. 3.20.43: "Hoc mihi de Academicis interim probabiliter, ut potui, persuasi. Quod si falsum est, nihil ad me, cui satis est iam non arbitrari non posse ab homine inueniri ueritatem."

And after a discussion of a difficult passage in Persius, Augustine tells Adeodatus that he has correctly interpreted it, but in any case it has no consequences for their own discussion. In substantial matters they are not bound by the authority of the poet: "Bene intelligis; sed quoquo modo se habeat Persiana sententia, quid ad nos? Non enim horum auctoritati subiecti sumus in talibus rebus."[14]

Understanding someone does not necessarily mean agreeing with him; indeed, it does not even imply a knowledge of whether or not what he says is true. But for someone to be really understood, he must not only speak comprehensibly; he must also say openly what he thinks. Otherwise, I understand what he says but not what he thinks, and therefore I do not understand the core of his person. Truthfulness thus proves to be a condition for understanding not a specific speech, of course, but a person. In Plato's *Laches,* Lysimachus is not a great mind, but when at the beginning of his speech he announces that he and Melesias want to speak openly *(parrēsiazesthai),*[15] he fulfills a necessary—even if not a sufficient—condition for a philosophical conversation. Even the slave in the *Meno* is urged by Socrates to say what he thinks.[16] We have already seen that a lack of truthfulness can prevent active understanding—for example, when someone is not sincere enough to ask when he has not understood something. Now it is a question of insufficient sincerity preventing someone from being understood. Often enough that is precisely the purpose of the corresponding behavior—but not always. Sometimes a participant in the conversation would like to be understood, but he is afraid of the consequences of being straightforward. In a society with an inquisition, for example, these consequences may be legal in nature, but they are often only social: someone who expresses certain opinions makes himself a pariah either morally, because he defends theses that decent people reject, or intellectually, because he defends, for instance, traditional moral beliefs from whose alleged refutation the critical intelligence derives its sense of self-worth. Feelings of shame repeatedly prevent people from being forthright, or at least make it more difficult

---

14. *De mag.* 9.28.
15. 178a4 f. Cf. 179c1 f.
16. 83d1 f. An analogous formulation is found in *Prt.* 319a9 f.

for them to be so.[17] This is suggested in the *Protagoras* (312a4 ff.); in the *Gorgias,* the topic is fully developed. Polus and Callicles accuse Socrates of having been able to refute Gorgias and Polus, respectively, only because he made unfair use of their sense of shame and forced them to be insincere; had they simply said openly what they thought, they could have preserved the consistency of their position.[18] Callicles also has difficulties being completely shameless; but in order to keep his position consistent he even denies his own intuitions (495a5 ff.). Socrates then says he is grateful to him for having defended the view that "might makes right" in its pure form, because if he (Socrates) succeeds in refuting Callicles, he can be sure that he has discovered the truth (487e1 ff.). Callicles says what others merely think (492d2 f.). Finally, Socrates claims that shame has led Gorgias and Polus to formulate true propositions (508b7 ff.); but it is understood that Callicles' sincere shamelessness has made it possible to arrive at the truth only because it has become necessary. Sincerity does not guarantee truth, nor does insincerity always lead to error; but if someone insincerely professes a truth, according to Socrates' and Plato's rationalism he can do so only if he has not really understood and justified it. But it is one of Callicles' contradictions that he not only accuses Socrates of using others' feelings of shame to succeed in refuting them, but even seeks to elicit feelings of shame in Socrates himself when the latter refers to the logical problems or morally repulsive consequences of Callicles' theory.[19] Socrates is repeatedly accused by his interlocutors of a lack of urbanity *(agroikia)*,[20] for instance, when he insists on precision, and he gladly agrees with this label[21]—one of many examples of the way someone proudly accepts a label that was initially intended as an insult (think of the Cynics). Truth is more important to Socrates than any etiquette, and he is ashamed only when he is refuted—no matter how large the audience.[22]

17. Cf., e.g., Aug. *Beat. vit.* 2.12, 2.16.
18. 461b4 ff., 482c5 ff., 487a7 ff. The theme of shame or timidity, which is constantly present in the dialogue, is also discussed: 463a5, 489a1 f., 494c5 f., d2 ff.
19. 489b7 ff., 494e7 f.
20. *Grg.* 461c3 f. Cf.—with different but semantically related terms—*Hp. ma.* 288d1 ff., 290e3.
21. *Grg.* 462e6, 509a1; *Hp. ma.* 288d4 f., 290e4; as well as *Ap.* 32d2 and *Phd.* 100d3 f.
22. 522d3 ff.

In order to find out whether a position is right or wrong, it is not necessary, however, for someone to actually defend it; it can be examined simply as a conceivable possibility. In fact, many philosophical dialogues include a character who plays the role of devil's advocate, that is, who strongly defends a position even if he is not truly convinced of its truth, or even considers its opposite true.[23] The discussion games played in the Academy already obviously presupposed this skill and willingness;[24] the latter are also manifested in many later dialogues.[25] In Shaftesbury's *The Moralists*, for example, the skeptical Philocles admits that he enjoys playing out opposed positions: "This, you said, was my constant way in all debates: I was as well pleased with the reason on one side as on the other; I never troubled myself about the success of the argument, but laughed still, whatever way it went, and even when I convinced others, never seemed as if I was convinced myself."[26] Later, Philocles explains that his attacks on the author of a recent ethical treatise—Shaftesbury himself—were intended only to provoke Theocles to reply to them;[27] a passage that makes good sense dialogue-externally as well, of course, since Shaftesbury has himself attacked only in order to provide a thorough defense of his position. But despite his admission that his objections were not meant seriously, the unnamed elderly gentleman who takes part in the conversation later considers that Philocles has been refuted—in the mistaken belief that an objection made only to broaden the conversation expressed Philocles' real conviction.[28]

No matter how important the readiness to play devil's advocate may be, there is still something about it that is contrary to conversation and thus to dialogue. Why? The answer is not hard to find and is implicit in what was said about the dialogue-external interpretability of the passage in Shaftesbury: someone who plays devil's advocate is superfluous as a

23. Cf. already Sigonio (1993), 183 ff.
24. Just consider the three ends that according to Aristotle his *Topics* serves: *pros gumnasian, pros tas enteuxeis, pros tas kata philosophian epistēmas* (101a27 f.). In addition to discussions and the philosophical sciences, these ends include a mental gymnastics that can be practiced by testing all possible statements.
25. Cf., e.g., Aug. *Ord.* 1.7.20.
26. (1999), 17 f.
27. (1999), 50.
28. (1999), 78.

real Other. Since as a person he does not stand behind what he says but only plays out a position, one might in principle do it oneself; but then such a thinking through of various possibilities can also be represented in a *quaestio disputata,* and even in a meditation, and the choice of the genre of the dialogue is a mistake. Someone who does not really stand behind what he says is irrefutable; and even if this irrefutability may seem worth striving for, the price to be paid for it is too high, because it makes the person disappear: standing for something is inevitably part of what it means to be a person. Someone who is not convinced of anything will not be able to convince others of anything—at least if he seems not convinced, that is, if he does not disguise his lack of conviction. Consider Philus in Cicero's *De republica:* precisely because he enjoys the reputation of being especially upright, but at the same time defends the thesis that truth is most easily discovered if both sides of a question are argued, he is entrusted with the defense of injustice, which he finally accepts, because for the sake of truth one must assume even more burdens than in searching for gold.[29] The result, of course, is that Cicero does not achieve an existentially gripping defense of the thesis that might makes right such as Plato puts into the mouths of Thrasymachus and Callicles in the first book of the *Republic* and in the *Gorgias,* respectively. On the contrary, the position critical of justice that Philus only pretends to assume culminates not in a cynical defense but rather in a critique of Roman imperialism—a critique which, because it comes from the point of view of "might makes right," seems to everyone present the quintessence of justice. One could hardly expect Roman politicians to see it otherwise, and this proves the old maxim that the refusal to discuss Machiavellianism seriously is especially marked among people who are Machiavellian in practice.

---

29. "et PHILVS: 'praeclaram vero causam ad me defertis, cum me improbitatis patrocinium suscipere voltis.' 'atqui id tibi' inquit LAELIVS 'verendum est, si ea dixeris quae contra iustitiam dici solent, ne sic etiam sentire videare! cum et ipse sis quasi unicum exemplum antiquae probitatis et fidei, nec sit ignota consuetudo tua contrarias in partis disserendi, quod ita facillume verum inveniri putes.' Et PHILVS: 'heia vero' inquit, 'geram morem vobis et me oblinam sciens; quod quoniam qui aurum quaerunt non putant sibi recusandum, nos cum iustitiam quaeramus, rem multo omni auro cariorem, nullam profecto molestiam fugere debemus'" (*De rep.* 3.5.8).

And yet there is also what we may call the sincere devil's advocate. At the beginning of the second book of the *Republic*, Plato's brothers Glaucon and Adimantus take over from Thrasymachus. Annoyed, Glaucon asks whether Socrates will be satisfied with merely seeming to convince or wants really to convince (357a4 ff.). Thrasymachus might have been refuted—but the position for which he stands has not. Thrasymachus gave up too soon, as if he were a serpent charmed by Socrates, and neither of the latter's two arguments has convinced him, Glaucon. Then, drawing on the story of the ring of Gyges, he develops the theory that only someone who is too weak to act unjustly falls back on justice; the unjust man leads a much better life than the just man. The elder brother, Adimantus, seconds this view, and even goes further by attacking the traditional conception of justice, on the ground that it values justice only because of its consequences, not in itself, and even if there are gods, they can be bribed by making sacrifices to them. Of course, it is Plato himself who is speaking through Adimantus's critique of tradition; he sees the "might makes right" doctrine as a necessary consequence of the contradictions of prephilosophical ethics and religion, and obviously concedes that it alone has led to the unprecedented enterprise of representing the intrinsic value of justice (366e5 ff.). Adimantus ends his presentation with the acknowledgment that he has spoken against his own convictions and only because he wants to hear the contrary proven by Socrates (367a8 ff.), who has devoted his whole life to thinking about these questions (d8 f.). Socrates' reaction is famous: he praises the two brothers' characters[30] and quotes a verse addressed to the sons of Ariston—one of whom is Plato, who thus makes a dialogue-external reference to himself.[31] It is divine that they are able to speak so well in favor of the superiority of injustice, yet are not convinced by their own arguments. What they have said shows why the two brothers are sincere devil's advocates: they are not playing with the doctrine that might makes right, as Philus does, but instead do everything they can to make the strongest case for it, because they really want to know what the truth about it is. They hope

30. *tēn phusin* (367e6), analogous to *tēs sēs phuseos* in the previously cited passage in the *Statesman*, 262c3 f.
31. Cf. below, p. 437.

with all their hearts that this doctrine is false, but their interest in it is
existential; their conviction could easily change if Socrates does not refute their arguments. A radical skeptic wants primarily to use his objections to test his conversation partners (i.e., to learn about them, not
from them); Glaucon and Adimantus thirst for the refutation they hope
Socrates will provide. Alypius is similarly grateful to Augustine for having refuted his skepticism.[32] Boso is also a sincere devil's advocate; even
if he is not really prepared to give up his faith,[33] his desire to understand
is obvious.

No one is more opposed to these men than Callicles, not only thematically, but also formally: he inwardly distances himself at the end of
his conversation with Socrates; his concessions are not sincere, because
he is not interested in his refutation.[34] It is true that from time to time an
interest in Socrates flickers, for example, when Callicles' own political
categories are discussed;[35] and Callicles deigns to remark that like many
people, he thinks Socrates seems to speak well, in a way, but he does not
believe him (513c4 ff.).[36] Socrates is admired the way one might admire
an item in a cabinet of curiosities—and precisely thereby the truth
claim that radiates from him is evaded. As a whole, the final part of the
Gorgias is an outstanding example of a conversation that is doomed
to fail because it is not sincere, and it is not sincere because it is not
founded on an interest in the truth, no matter how counterintuitive
and paradoxical it might be. In the *Protagoras,* the eponymous hero
grants Socrates' statement by saying, "if you like"; but Socrates is not
content with this answer. "It isn't this 'if you like' and 'if that's what you
think' that I want us to examine, but you and me ourselves. What I mean
is, I think the argument will be most fairly tested, if we take the 'if' out

32. *C. acad.* 3.20.44. On Socrates' gratitude to those who teach him things, see
Grg. 470c6 ff. and *R.* 338b4 ff.

33. *Cur deus homo,* 1.1, 2.15.

34. *Grg.* 499b4 ff., 501c7 f., 505c5 f., d4 f., and 8 f., 510a1 f.

35. 510a11 f., 511a5 ff.

36. Similarly, in Malebranche the Chinese philosopher says to the Christian, "Je
vous avoüe de bonne foi que je n'ai rien à répliquer à vôtre démonstration de l'existence de l'Etre infini. Cependant je n'en suis point convaincu" (I tell you honestly that
I have no response to your demonstration of the existence of the infinite Being. But
I'm not convinced) (1958; 7; cf. 11).

of it."[37] Without a commitment on the part of the interlocutors, a philosophical conversation is not possible, especially when it concerns ethical questions, which inevitably have consequences for the way we conduct our lives. Plato and his Socrates like play and irony; but the question as to how one should live must be examined with the greatest conceivable seriousness.[38] In ironic statements the primary meaning is not really meant; and it seems pedantic when the person addressed does not continue the ironic play and objects instead, emphasizing what was actually meant. However, someone who begins by pedantically emphasizing that what was said is not true, and then pursues a direction precisely opposite to what was meant, is making use of a meta-irony. Polus finds Socrates' new paradoxical statement even more difficult to refute than the preceding one—and means, naturally, that it is still easier to refute it. Socrates replies that it is not more difficult, but impossible; for the true can never be refuted (473a8 ff.). The use of this meta-irony to stress the idea that there is something absolute about truth, and especially ethical truth, that cannot be played with ironically, is somehow deeply shocking. We can understand the Corinthian farmer who sold his land after reading the *Gorgias* and went to study with Plato.[39] Iris Murdoch's Plato has nothing of the subtle ironic playfulness of the historical Plato, but she correctly sees that the core of this man was an unconditional moral seriousness. In *Art and Eros*, Callistos says: "Plato's so emotional and extreme, he gets so cross," and Deximenes corrects him: "You mean he takes it all seriously."[40] And in "Above the Gods" Plato explains that a religious foundation for morality is necessary because it involves something that we cannot choose: "This isn't something optional, we're not volunteers, we're conscripts."[41]

Existential commitment and openness are, as I said, not sufficient in the search for truth. A philosophical theory that can make a claim to

---

37. 331c5 ff. Guthrie's trans. in Hamilton and Cairns. Cf. 359c6 ff., where Protagoras refuses to take a position of his own and would like only to report the opinions of others. Parallel demands are found in other dialogues: *Cri.* 49c11 f. and *R.* 346a3 f.

38. *Grg.* 500b5 ff. Surprisingly, in *Prt.* 351d2 ff. Protagoras also shows a high moral seriousness in dealing with ethical questions.

39. Aristotle, *Nerinthus*, frg. 1 Ross.

40. (1986), 46.

41. (1986), 99.

truth is found only by someone who meets two conditions. First, the philosopher must be open to new ideas; only someone who is prepared to take risks will be creative. At the beginning he must not be afraid of inadequate clarity and precision, for in an initial phase of the investigation these qualities can hardly be already present, and anyone who feels a fundamental loathing for vagueness will cling to the commonplaces of his culture; he may perhaps further develop them, but he will make no contribution to charting out new directions. Licentius recognizes that he cannot express himself precisely, but he nonetheless asks his friends to try to understand what he wants to say.[42] In *Above the Gods*, Acastos is not able to articulate satisfactorily his philosophy of religion; he sometimes speaks in anacolutha, and the stage directions repeatedly emphasize the gestures that take over when he runs out of arguments or even becomes speechless.[43] To Socrates' demand that he muster his strength for a final attack, he helplessly responds: "I can't"—"I don't know!"—and finally, close to tears: *"I don't know!"*[44] And yet it speaks well of Socrates that he brings Acastos into the conversation and draws out his intuitions; even if they cannot be formulated in a clear theory, they are still the material for the thoughts of both his friends and the readers of the dialogue. Hegel famously praises the plasticity of Socrates' interlocutors in the Platonic dialogues—"so comfortable with the self-denial of their *own* reflections and ideas, with which *independent* thinking is impatient to prove itself"[45] Although I think that in the second part of the *Parmenides* Socrates means to criticize the passivity of the young Aristotle (which contrasts so strikingly with the intelligent questions asked by the young Socrates in the first part), we must certainly concede that those young interlocutors are not allowed the autonomy they enjoy in Murdoch's work; in Plato, they are led by Socrates the knowing conversation leader, whereas in Murdoch Socrates makes them grow by listening to them as much as he questions them. In doing so the superior partner can, depending on the situation, respect his interlocutor by helping him to express clearly what he really wanted to say, even when it is false; or he can support

42. Aug. *Ord.* 2.1.3. Cf. 2.7.20.
43. (1986), 84: *"expressive gestures"*; 85: *"with gestures"*; 89: *"expressive gestures."*
44. (1986), 90 f.
45. 5.31.

him, since he wanted after all to say what is true, by quietly guiding him
in the right direction, even if he ultimately says something which he did
not at all have originally in mind. The first way makes more sense if intellectual progress depends on clear insight into one's own errors.

Second, truth is concrete, and someone who never arrives at precise formulations can contribute nothing to philosophy. Accuracy and a
willingness to engage in self-criticism are just as important as the playful elaboration of hypotheses; heuristics must be restrained by criticism. Anyone who prematurely regards something as proven when this
is not at all the case may even fall victim to a fundamental skepticism
when he finally realizes his mistake; Plato,[46] Minucius,[47] and Augustine[48] had already understood this connection, which in recent decades
has manifested itself in the astonishing transformation of Marxists into
postmodernists. In any case, the conversational atmosphere must be
such that no one hesitates to admit mistakes and to correct his earlier
position—and that is something quite different from proposing theses
whose inconsistency with the preceding ones is not even noticed. Such
a hesitation may arise from a personal pigheadedness, but it can also
arise from an agonal orientation of the conversation that punishes every
self-correction with a loss of face. Charmides shows that he has at least
one of the presuppositions of good philosophizing when he says, after
Socrates has proven that according to his definition of temperance one
can be temperate without knowing it: "But that, Socrates, . . . is impossible, and therefore if this is, as you imply, the necessary consequence of
any of my previous admissions, I will withdraw them and will not be
ashamed to acknowledge that I made a mistake, rather than admit that a
man can be temperate who does not know himself."[49] In fact, Socrates
himself does not hesitate to withdraw statements, whether because he

46. *Phd.* 89c ff.
47. "Odio . . . sermonum" (14.6) is, of course, a quotation from Plato's *Phd.* 89d3.
48. *De mag.* 10.31. "Quare, ut aequum est, bene consideratis perspectisque rationibus cedere, ita incognita pro cognitis habere periculosum; metus est enim ne,
cum saepe subruuntur, quae firmissime statura et mansura praesumimus, in tantum
odium uel timorem rationis incidamus, ut ne ipsi quidem perspicuae ueritati fides
habenda uideatur."
49. *Chrm.* 164c7 ff.

had made them only to test others or because he no longer needs them in the present context.[50] He has the fairness to acknowledge that his interlocutor has the same right,[51] and even to suggest that his interlocutor had previously expressed an opinion only to test him, Socrates.[52] Analogous passages are found in Augustine's *Contra academicos*[53] and Berkeley's *Three Dialogues between Hylas and Philonous*. Hylas concedes that after his previous admissions he cannot avoid the conclusion that primary qualities cannot be interpreted differently from secondary qualities, so far as the impossibility of their existence outside the mind is concerned; but he believes that he has too hastily accepted something crucial. "But my fear is, that I have been too liberal in my former concessions, or overlooked some fallacy or other. In short, I did not take time to think." Philonous is generous: "For that matter, Hylas, you may take what time you please in reviewing the progress of our inquiry. You are at liberty to recover any slips you might have made, or offer whatever you have omitted, which makes for your first opinion."[54]

The need for self-correction is avoided when the thesis that one seeks to defend is from the outset presented with the necessary differentiations and restrictions, indeed, when the limits of one's own competence are indicated to the interlocutor at the very beginning. In *De libero arbitrio*, which from the sixteenth century on had a significant influence on theological discussion regarding the compatibility of freedom of the will with theism, Valla presented his central statement with great literary skill. His assertion is that divine omnipotence, but not divine omniscience, is incompatible with freedom of the will. But the difference is not immediately obvious, and at first Valla introduces it gradually. Right at the beginning of the conversation, Valla tells his friend Antonius Glarea that the problem he has raised is one of the most difficult,[55] and he hesitates for a long time to express himself regarding it, especially since it is inevitably bound up with a criticism of earlier authors, in particular

50. Cf. *Ly.* 219c6 f.
51. *Phd.* 95e2 f.
52. *Prt.* 349c5 ff.
53. 1.3.8.
54. (1977), 177. Cf. 192.
55. (1987), 65 ff.

Boethius. Finally he proceeds, but only on condition that Antonius promise him that he will not insist on being invited to dinner after he has already been invited to lunch.[56] Antonius does not understand what he means, and Valla explains that after he has answered Antonius's question, namely, whether divine foreknowledge contradicts freedom of the will, he should not raise a further one. Valla answers Antonius's question in the negative, and argues with bravura for this answer; foreknowledge is no more the cause of an event than knowledge of it after the fact, and one cannot decide against what is known by God in advance because one does not know God's foreknowledge. After this rejection of Antonius's two most important arguments, Valla illustrates his own theory by telling the story of Sextus Tarquinius, who could not accuse Apollo, who had predicted his crimes, of being responsible for them.[57] But could Tarquinius not blame Jupiter, who had made him what he was? Valla says he could, and explains that he switched to an ancient example because Roman polytheism allowed him to separate the creator and the knower of human affairs into two persons.[58] Antonius thinks he has been cast back into the same hole out of which Valla had drawn him; the same question arises all over again if human will is not canceled by God's foreknowledge but instead by God's will. But here Valla reminds Antonius of their agreement: after lunch he may not also demand dinner. Antonius feels that he has been tricked, and resorts to a deft comparison: Valla is like a host who forces his guest to vomit up what he has eaten—or at least sends him away as hungry as he was when he arrived.[59] But Valla defends himself: he cannot serve up any more, no matter how much he would like to, and if he knew someone who could be expected to provide an answer, he would go with Antonius to ask him. He compares philoso-

56. "Ut si te laute accepero in hoc prandio, ne iterum accipi velis in cena" (1987; 74).

57. (1987), 103 ff.

58. (1987), 116: "Hoc est quod pro mea probatione afferre volui, nam haec est vis huius fabulae, ut cum sapientia Dei separari non possit a voluntate illius ac potentia, hac similitudine separarem Apollinis et Iovis: et quod in uno Deo obtineri non valebat, id obtineretur in duobus, utroque suam certam naturam habente, altero quidem creandi ingenia hominum, altero autem sapiendi."

59. (1987), 118.

phy's inability to resolve these questions with Paul's Letter to the Romans. Why God elects one person and damns another is unknown even to the angels, and fundamentally beyond the reach of humans.[60] In his mistrust of philosophical reasoning, in his emphasis on the complete dependency of humans on God, in his attacks on the defects of pagan philosophy— which are formulated in the most elegant Humanistic Latin—Valla foreshadows Luther's sensibility. For that very reason he also contributes to the schism between theology and philosophy of religion; and therefore his dialogue is less philosophical than most of those of the Middle Ages.

So far as the moral rightness of conversational behavior is concerned, the respect shown the other is crucial. (For reasons that will later become clear, this subject will not be discussed in detail until the following chapter.) It is certainly not a presupposition of any conversation that the ideas of every participant contribute to the same degree to the discovery of the truth; as was shown in chapter 14, asymmetrical conversations are very common. But we have seen that in this case as well equal treatment at the level of procedures is obligatory; intellectual superiority must not be connected with an external status, or even with age.[61] Even in the didactic dialogue it must be assumed that the disciple is in principle capable of asking critical questions; and these must be taken seriously and carefully examined. At least it must be assumed that communicating a discovery is worthwhile; and that can hardly be the case if the person to whom it is communicated has no value. An expression of this respect is the avoidance of insulting expressions: "Suppose that we instruct him instead of abusing him," Socrates says to Laches, who has reproached Nicias for talking nonsense.[62] Taking the interlocutor seriously is absolutely compatible with a sense of what he is capable of; Socrates speaks to a brilliant mathematician like Theaetetus differently from the way he speaks to a general like Laches, and to the latter differently from the way he speaks to a boy like Lysis. But in Plato psychological and pedagogical considerations are always based on a previous familiarity with the field that is to be communicated; to this first

60. (1987), 133, 139 ff.
61. Cf. *La.* 189a6 ff.
62. *La.* 195a7: *Oukoun didaskōmen auton alla mē loidorōmen.*

and up to now unsurpassed philosophical educationist, a pedagogy that has become formalistic would have seemed a mistake. First of all, we read in the *Laches* (190d7 ff.), one must know what courage is; then one can test in what way it could be conveyed to young men, insofar as it can be taught by means of exercise and instruction. Analogously, in the *Phaedrus,* the true orator is first required to have a knowledge of his subject and then a familiarity with the human soul grounded in the nature of the whole.[63] It remains impressive how Socrates is capable of adapting to the age of his interlocutors in the *Lysis,* and especially how he takes the loving relationship between parents and child as his starting point (207d ff.). In his preface to *Contra academicos,* Augustine expressly acknowledges that he wanted to discover what his young interlocutors were capable of, given their age.[64] The Platonic conversational universe is extremely extensive so far as age is concerned—from the boy (in the *Lysis* and the *Meno*) to the old man (in the *Laws,* for instance), everyone is invited to philosophize. To be sure, youths are favored; we may leave open the question whether Plato and his Socrates were particularly interested in that age group on erotic grounds or, conversely, an erotic interest emerged secondarily from the fact that at that age an existentially sincere interest in the great questions is natural and, if it is correctly trained, can lead to important discoveries. But Socrates repeatedly emphasizes that even in old age it is not too late to begin philosophizing.[65] It is true that an ironic note is discernible in these passages—in the *Laches* with regard to the fellow students, in the *Euthydemus* with regard to the alleged teachers. The author of the seventh book of the *Republic,* with its years-long program of education in the mathematical sciences, which are seen as the presupposition of dialectic, certainly knew that certain insights can be gained only if one has been trained for them early on; these discoveries are therefore denied those who begin to take an interest in philosophy only when they are no longer young. But this does not hold for all discoveries, and everyone is urged to concern himself with philosophy in accord with his abilities and op-

---

63. 259e ff., 269e ff.
64. 1.1.4.: "uolui temptare pro aetate quid possent."
65. *La.* 201a2 ff., *Euthd.* 272b1 ff.

portunities, even in old age. "Philosophia est enim, a cuius uberibus se nulla aetas queretur excludi."[66]

No matter how impressive the range of ages that Plato covers in his dialogues, his universe of discourse is limited in two respects: the participants in the conversations are always male and Greek. The sexually and culturally Other appears only on the margins or in the form of masks. Thus Xanthippe and Socrates' children appear at the beginning and the end of the *Phaedo,*[67] but in both cases only to be led away. Socrates' immediate family is not allowed to witness either the philosophizing about immortality or Socrates' death. The modern reader—but surely not Plato—finds it particularly brutal that Socrates does not himself ask his wife to leave him but commands Crito to see to it that she is taken away; Xanthippe is not even on the emotional level a "Thou," but simply an object one has at one's disposal. Similarly, at the end of the *Lysis,* the teachers who speak only broken Greek,[68] and are therefore foreigners, appear as a force hostile to philosophy. Nonetheless, they are granted the honor of actively participating: they force their way into Socrates' conversation and are not simply ordered to leave, like Xanthippe. This is not in contradiction to the fact that the Platonic conversation leaders repeatedly appeal to foreign authorities. In the *Char-mides,* for example, Socrates appeals to a Thracian physician,[69] in the *Republic* to the Pamphlyian Er,[70] and in the *Phaedrus* to an Egyptian myth;[71] in the *Timaeus,* Solon, after Critias the elder's speech reported by his like-named grandson, also appeals to an Egyptian.[72] That in the first case the appeal is to a pure invention is clear from the context, and Phaedrus's cocky remark at 275b3 f. suggests that he too believes in one of Socrates' fictions.[73] In his dialogues, indeed in a single dialogue, namely, the *Parmenides,* Plato certainly assembled Greeks from all parts

---

66. Aug. *C. acad.* 1.1.4.
67. 60a1–b1, 116a7–b5.
68. *Ly.* 223a7.
69. 156d ff.
70. 614b ff.
71. 274c ff.
72. 21e ff.
73. On the dialogue-external function of this passage, see V. Hösle (2004b; 161 ff.).

of the Greek-speaking world; but at first he had little interest in bar-barians.[74] In the late Plato, this seems to have changed—consider the interest shown in Persian history in the *Laws*[75] and the connection be-tween Plato's two principles theory and Avestian dualism that was obvi-ously already seen in the Old Academy.[76] And yet the famous anecdote in Philodemos to the effect that the dying Plato was annoyed by the bar-barian music that a Chaldean—that is, a man well versed in Persian culture—who was living in his house had caused to be performed[77] shows both that the elderly Plato was in contact with non-Greeks and that he was convinced of their cultural inferiority—obviously so much so that his foreign guests thought it wise to agree with this opinion of his, and perhaps actually shared it. However, Alexander's campaign led to an intercultural interest that inevitably resulted in the inclusion of the cultural Other in the philosophical dialogue.[78] In his dialogue *Peri hup-nou*, Clearchus had his teacher Aristotle refer to a Jew who was intellec-tually descended from the Indian Gymnosophists;[79] however, Aristotle praises this Jew because he was Greek not only in his language but also in his soul.[80] Heracleides of Pontus went further in his dialogue *Zōroas-trēs*, in which he played off Zoroaster—the Greek name for the Persian founder of the Zoroastrian religion, Zarathustra—against Plato.[81] But we have no knowledge of the details of this dialogue, and the depiction

74. The *xenōn* in *La.* 186b4 is opposed to *Athēnaiōn*, and thus also surely in-cludes, perhaps exclusively, other Greeks. Nonetheless, in the passage at 186b3 f., in which slaves and freemen are mentioned along with Athenians and foreigners, there is a remarkable anticipation of Paul's Letter to the Galatians, 3:28—significantly, however, without referring to and overcoming the gender opposition. In the *Laches*, it is a matter of pupils, not of teachers. However, see *Phd.* 78a3 ff.

75. 693d ff.

76. Cf. Aristotle, *Peri philosophias,* frg. 6 Ross, and on this—somewhat exagger-ated—W. Jaeger (1955; 133 ff.). In the *Alcibiades I,* which is probably not by Plato but reflects Platonic ideas, Socrates refers to the Persians' religion and their theory of virtue (121e f.), and in the certainly inauthentic *Axiochus* to the magus Gobryas (371a ff.).

77. Cf. K. Gaiser (1988), 176 ff., as well as 421 f. and 434 ff.

78. Cf. Hirzel (1895), I 334 ff.

79. Frg. 5–10 Wehrli. In his work *Peri paideias,* frg. 13 Wehrli, the Gymno - sophists are themselves said to be the intellectual descendants of the Persian magi.

80. Frg. 6 Wehrli.

81. Frg. 68–70 Wehrli.

of a non-Greek remained a rare exception. Even someone who shares the view that the literary quality of the ancient dialogues was rarely achieved in the Middle Ages should recognize the broadening of the horizon for conversation and dialogue that the universalism of monotheistic religions necessarily produced. The Muslim in Llull's *Llibre del gentil e dels tres savis* and the Jew Salomo in Bodin's *Colloquium heptaplomeres* are depicted with particular sensitivity; we note that their authors were well acquainted with the corresponding religions. The fact that there were late antique and medieval dialogues between religions, that is, between cultures, resulted from the missionary impulse of the universal religions (including Buddhism), which did not stop at the boundaries of a language or a culture.

However, there are two dangers to which intercultural dialogues can easily succumb. On the one hand, the cultural Other can be merely an exotically disguised form of what one rejects in oneself. Malebranche's Chinese philosopher argues very much like a Spinozist; and even if we can recognize in the denial of transcendence something common to Spinoza and Confucianism, Malebranche makes not the slightest effort to grasp what is specific to the Chinese worldview or even its peculiar conceptuality; only the concept of the "Ly" is used. Malebranche's knowledge of China was very limited, and when in the same year that his dialogue was published, 1708, the Jesuit L. Marquer attacked him for incorrectly ascribing atheism to the Chinese philosopher (the Jesuits were well acquainted with China) Malebranche openly admitted, in the "Avis touchant l'entretien d'un philosophe chrétien avec un philosophe chinois," that this character could easily be called a "Japanese," a "Siamese," or still more easily a "Frenchman." "Il me paroît qu'il y a beaucoup de rapport entre les impietez de Spinoza, & celles de nôtre philosophe Chinois. Le changement de nom ne changeroit rien dans ce qui est essentiel à mon Ecrit" (It seems to me that there is a close relationship between Spinoza's impieties and those of our Chinese philosopher. Changing the name would change nothing that is essential to my work).[82] In one passage, Malebranche's fictional Chinese seems to argue more like Leibniz; in any case, the latter felt that he was being

82. (1958), 42.

attacked.[83] It is clear that Malebranche was never concerned with China but rather with settling accounts with alternative post-Cartesian metaphysics. On the other hand, in Voltaire's *Entretiens chinois*, the Mandarin who is supposed to have traveled in Europe represents a philosophy superior to that of the Jesuits, namely, Voltairean deism;[84] and here too no real interest is shown in the foreign culture. In chapter 14 (p. 311 ff.) it was mentioned that Diderot's Polynesian Orou has little to do with Polynesia but much to do with the French Enlightenment's ideas of sexual emancipation. If the genre of the philosophical dialogue is to bloom again, in the age of globalization, we can count on further intercultural dialogues on the model of Daniel Bell's important work *East Meets West*. May they avoid these two errors of constructing the culturally Other as what we regard as good or as bad in our own culture, because both are forms of instrumentalization.

The inclusion of the other sex in the philosophical conversation, which has so long been considered an exclusively male domain, has been slower and more difficult; even Iris Murdoch's *Acastos* presents only men.[85] Nevertheless, Plato's Socrates twice dons the mask of a woman—in the *Menexenos* and in the *Symposium*: Aspasia and Diotima, respectively. Aspasia had not only been mocked in comedy,[86] but was also familiar from other *logoi Sōkratikoi*: both Antisthenes and Aeschines wrote dialogues with the title *Aspasia*; Antisthenes' work was probably the earlier.[87] In the latter Pericles' love for the former courtesan from Miletus is subjected to acerbic criticism and condemned as an example

83. (1958), 14, with A. Robinet's footnote, which quotes from Leibniz's marginal notation on his copy of Malebranche's work: "Il semble que ce qui suit est dirigé contre mon système de l'harmonie préétablie" (The following seems to be directed against my system of preestablished harmony).

84. Even the Jesuit notices that a criticism of Christian monks is concealed behind the Mandarin's criticism of Chinese Buddhist monks (s.d.; 237).

85. The same holds for Edith Stein's *Was ist Philosophie? Ein Gespräch zwischen Edmund Husserl und Thomas von Aquin* (1993; 19–48). On the other hand, the heroine of John Perry's *A Dialogue on Personal Identity and Immortality*—Gretchen Weirob, a dying woman who argues *against* all arguments for a personal immortality—is entirely different from Socrates and Macrina.

86. Ar. *Ach.* 524 ff.

87. B. Ehler's arguments (1966; 33 f.) are not compelling, but plausible.

of the domination of pleasure over reason.[88] Dittmar suggests that Aspasia and Pericles did not take part in the conversation but were only its
topic; at least their conversation was reported by others.[89] In Aeschines'
like-named dialogue, Aspasia did not appear directly either;[90] instead,
Aeschines represented a conversation between Socrates and the Callias
familiar to us from Plato's *Protagoras* and other texts, who had asked
Socrates by whom he should have his son educated and had received the
surprising answer: by Aspasia.[91] According to Ehler's convincing reconstruction, the greater part of the conversation consisted in a justification
of this advice, partly by referring to other remarkable women such as
Rhodogyne and Thargelia, partly by describing Aspasia's cleverness in
dealing with Pericles and Lysicles and with Xenophon and his wife. The
longest extant fragment represents this conversation, in which Aspasia
embarrasses first Xenophon's wife and then Xenophon himself. She asks
whether, if their neighbor had better jewelry and clothes or a better horse
or estate, they would prefer these to their own, and they say they would.
Then she asks: What if they had a better spouse? Here Xenophon falls
silent, and his wife blushes; and Aspasia draws from this the conclusion
that since one inevitably wishes to have the best partner, they must each
seek to become the best partner.[92] What is interesting about this passage
is that Xenophon and his wife are treated in precisely parallel ways; no
trace of male superiority is discernible. In fact, the superior third party,
Aspasia, is a woman, and she ultimately shows the couple that instead of
desiring something else they should work on themselves in order to remain desirable. A subtle point is that desiring appears as a rather passive
process, whereas reflection on how one can become desirable leads to

88. Cf. the few fragments in Giannantoni II 373 f. H. Dittmar has probably correctly interpreted them: "Antisthenes igitur in dialogo illo Aspasia Milesia velut ex-
emplo utitur, quo id, quod dialogi summa esse videtur, demonstret amore libidinoso
rationem deleri" (1911; 9). But Aspasia may have gotten off better than Pericles; cf.
Hirzel (1895), I 127, n. 2.
89. (1911), 10.
90. On the other hand, this occurs in a modern dialogue—in Wieland's thirteenth and last "Göttergespräch."
91. Frg. XIV Krauss.
92. Frg. 8 Krauss.

genuine, that is, more moral, activity. There is no doubt that Aeschines' image of Aspasia was more positive than that of Antisthenes. And yet we cannot exclude the possibility of Socratic irony, precisely in the way a character like Callias is treated.[93] But this irony also cannot be proven, and thus it remains plausible to see Aeschines as a forerunner of Plato's demand for equal education for men and women and a proponent of the theory that they are born equal.[94]

But although the Platonic Socrates emphasizes this demand in the *Republic,*[95] Plato does not include women as real conversation partners in his literary universe. We can no longer tell how ironic Aeschines' *Aspasia* was; in the *Menexenus,* the irony is palpable. Socrates makes it clear that the story that he learned the speech from Aspasia is a fiction, and Menexenus understands that.[96] On the other hand, in the *Symposium,* the existence of Diotima is not explicitly put in doubt; but the notion that the priestess from Mantinea delayed the outbreak of plague in Athens for ten years[97] shifts her into a mythical dimension. Above all, however, Diotima is not really a sexual Other. She is a priestess of Reason—as a person, too, she is thus the counterpart of the courtesan and eroticist Aspasia[98]—and the central point of her speech is, as I have already said (p. 303), the ascent from a beloved person to the idea of the Good. Precisely because she deindividualizes Eros and thus a fortiori desexualizes it, whether she is male or female is actually a matter of indifference; indeed she is a woman precisely because having a male teach Socrates about erotic matters might suggest that they had a non-Platonic relationship. Diotima is not "a person but a mask, a 'feminine' costume designed from the start to

93. Ehlers expressly draws attention to this, refusing to see the work as making any contribution to the "woman question" (1966; 5 f., 41, 50).

94. Cf. O. Gigon (1947), 310 f.

95. 451c ff. The argumentation is complex; one of its presuppositions is that men are in general superior to women in all domains (455c f.). For precisely that reason, however, women cannot be limited to a single area of activity. On this, see M. S. Kochin (2002; 61 f.). An extensive equality between men and women is suggested in *Grg.* 470e9 ff.

96. 249d4: *ei gunē ousa;* d8 f.; e1: *ekeinēi ē ekeinōi.* See also above, chap. 10 (p. 186 f.) on the special ontological status of the universe of the *Menexenus.*

97. *Smp.* 201d3 ff.

98. As Ehlers rightly points out (1966; 135).

be worn by men";[99] she might just as well be a sexless angel. For that very reason she became the model for the virginal or at least widowed female teachers in early Christian dialogues.

Its contribution to raising the status of women is undoubtedly one of Christianity's greatest achievements, and this is particularly evident in dialogue literature. Methodius is no philosopher, and even as a theologian he is not particularly innovative or rigorous. But having written— probably in the second half of the third century—a *Symposion* in which all the participants are women remains a formal innovation of which he and the early church can be proud. It is true that his work lacks the polyphony that makes the Platonic model so fascinating; only Theo - phila's second speech, which tries to defend marriage, brings a divergent point of view into play. But she is also criticized: her argument that children are welcomed by God, and thus procreation must be pleasing to God, is refuted by the objection that it could also be used to prove the legitimacy of adultery, the offspring of which would also not be rejected by God.[100] By making use of an original adaptation of the Platonic allegory of the cave, Theophila is able to defend her view that human sins must be distinguished from divine effects; nonetheless, the dialogue consists more of sermonlike eulogies of virginity than an argumentative debate of the kind that is necessarily appropriate to philosophy. Men do not appear in this dialogue, even if Methodius himself is concealed behind the Eubulion in the frame conversation (in his dialogue *Agla - ophon,* which is directed against Origen, he calls himself "Eubulius");[101] men could endanger the ideal of virginity. On the other hand, Gregory of Nyssa's *On the Soul and the Resurrection* represents a conversation between a man and a woman, Gregory himself and his sister Macrina; here, too, from the outset the sibling relationship and clerical status keep both interlocutors at a distance from any eroticism. What is impressive about their conversation is the naturalness with which Gregory recognizes the intellectual superiority of his dying sister, who is represented as a kind of new Socrates. In the very first sentence Gregory calls Macrina "the sister

99. D. M. Halperin (1990), 293.
100. 34 ff.
101. His real name is given on p. 293.

and teacher" *(hē adelphē kai didaskalos),*[102] and she is called "teacher" throughout the conversation.[103] She shows first philosophical, then exegetical skills in her justification of belief in the Resurrection; and even someone who is no more convinced by her Platonizing arguments than by those made in the *Phaedo*—antiquity never grasped the special status of subjectivity—has to admire the exegetical courage with which she rejects the interpretation of Hell as a place and the idea of eternal damnation.[104] (On this last question, Gregory follows the admired Origen.) Macrina also shows psychological mastery in overcoming Gregory's sadness because of the recent death of their brother Basilius and her own impending death, which she confronts fearlessly. It is impressive how she is able to observe objectively the physician who is treating her and to evaluate epistemologically his diagnostic capabilities, without taking the slightest interest in his specific conclusions regarding herself.[105] She thereby shows in her own behavior the distance from the sensual that she discusses theoretically.

Monica's role in Augustine's Cassiciacum dialogues is more limited. Augustine, who had only a rudimentary knowledge of Greek, cannot have known Gregory's dialogue, which had appeared only a few years earlier; otherwise he would not have so proudly claimed—that is, dialogue-internally, through Monica's rhetorical question—that in the books that he and his friends had read women had never been included in this kind of disputation.[106] In *Contra academicos,* Monica appears only once, in order to call the men to dinner;[107] but in *De beata vita* and *De ordine,* she takes part in the conversation herself.[108] Augustine praises his mother's contribution as being worthy of Cicero, if not stylistically, at least in terms of substance; he says that one would have thought a

102. 12 A.

103. On the function of women as theological teachers in the early church, see R. Albrecht (1986), 221 ff.

104. 68B ff., 100 ff.

105. 29C ff.

106. *Ord.* 1.11.31: "Quid agitis? inquit; numquidnam in illis quos legitis libris etiam feminas umquam audiui in hoc genus disputationis inductas?"

107. 2.5.13.

108. Her first comment occurs in *Beat. vit.* 2.8. See also 2.10 f., 2.16, 3.19, 4.27, 4.35; and *Ord.* 2.7.21 f.

man had spoken (a compliment not likely to be appreciated by modern feminists), indeed that she was inspired by God.[109] To be sure, there is a certain condescension in these passages; when at the end of *De ordine*, Augustine thanks Monica for her prayers, to which he owes his existential devotion to philosophy, and asks her for more prayers,[110] it is assumed that philosophy proper is for men, whereas women are to provide, as it were, the infrastructure—ranging from preparing meals to intercession. But it is anachronistic to complain about this, because up to the nineteenth century this model prevailed in the West; and compared with their contemporary culture, Methodius, Gregory, and Augustine were progressive.[111]

We undoubtedly owe to the Renaissance progress in integrating women into the culture of conversation in general—but only to a limited extent into philosophy. The third book of Castiglione's *Cortegiano* is about the education of a lady of the court and contains a defense of the dignity of women, such as we also find at the same period in the work of Heinrich Cornelius Agrippa von Nettesheim, as well as eulogies of ancient and contemporary women. Even if most of the speeches are given by men, the focal point of the group gathered at the court of Urbino is Duchess Elisabetta Gonzaga; and an important role in the conversation is also played by her friend Emilia Pio. Women are also central in many of Erasmus's *Colloquia familiaria;* the intellectually most ambitious of these is the dialogue *Abbatis et eruditae*[112] between the Benedictine abbot Antronius and the educated Lady Magdalia, who reads Greek and Latin books and is far superior both intellectually and as a person to the dim and morally lax abbot. At the end of the conversation she warns the abbot that women will soon occupy the chairs of theology, preach in the churches, and ultimately claim the mitre, that is, the dignity of abbots and bishops. The world is changing fast—people must either take off their masks or really play the role to which they have

109. 2.10. On Monica's divine inspiration, see also *Beat. vit.* 4.27 and *Ord.* 2.1.1.
110. 2.20.52.
111. Within pagan philosophy, however, Musonius Rufus should be singled out; he demanded that daughters also be given a philosophical education (3 and especially 4).
112. (1972), 403–8.

been assigned.[113] However, women are scarcely to be found in the genuinely philosophical dialogues. In Giordano Bruno's *Spaccio de la bestia trionfante,* Sofia is an allegory; in his work real women—Laodomia and Giulia—are found in the fifth and last dialogue of the second part of *De gli eroici furori.* But their role is limited; they content themselves with interpreting an allegorical poem. In the summary preceding the work, Bruno writes that according to the mores of his country it is not for women to make comments, to argue, to decipher, to know much, and to be teachers, in order to claim the right to teach and to provide men with instruction, rules, and doctrine; instead, it is appropriate for them, if the spirit occasionally takes possession of their bodies, to foretell and prophesy; that is why it is enough for them to simply present the figure and leave to a male mind the intellectual work of explaining the connection signified.[114] We can hardly avoid concluding that at least Gregory of Nyssa, and perhaps also Augustine, had a higher opinion of the philosophical qualifications of women than did the radical innovator Bruno.

During the Enlightenment, women acquired a more important place in philosophical dialogues. In Fontenelle's *Entretiens sur la pluralité des mondes* (1686), a fictional Marquise is the first-person narrator's conversation partner. But she is his pupil; the dialogue belongs to the category of didactic dialogues. In the Préface, Fontenelle explains that by introducing a woman who is capable of following cosmological reflections even though she has no scientific training, he sought to encourage ladies (to whom Algarotti was to explain Newtonianism in 1737).[115] Under-

113. (1972), 407: "Quod nisi caueritis vos, res eo tandem euadet, vt nos praesideamus in scholis theologicis, vt concionemur in templis. Occupabimus mitras vestras. . . . Videtis iam inuerti mundi scenam. Aut deponenda est persona, aut agendae sunt suae cuique partes."

114. (1985), II 943.

115. (1955), 54: "J'ai cru que cette fiction me servirait, et à rendre l'ouvrage plus susceptible d'agrément, et à encourager les dames par l'exemple d'une femme qui, ne sortant jamais des bornes d'une personne qui n'a nulle teinture de science, ne laisse pas d'entendre ce qu'on lui dit, et de ranger dans sa tête, sans confusion, les tourbillons et les mondes" (I thought this fiction would serve me, and make the work more likely to please, and to encourage ladies by the example of a woman who, while never going beyond the limits of a person who has no tincture of science, nevertheless understands what is said to her, and finds a place in her head, without confusion, for vortices and worlds). Cf. Rendall (1971).

standing his work required no more attention, he claimed, than reading Mme de Lafayette's novel *La Princesse de Clèves*. In an introductory epistle he writes that having won the Marquise over to philosophy is an important acquisition, because beauty and youth are always very valuable.[116] Despite the remarkable pedagogical intention, this is no less condescending than Augustine's compliments to Monica; and in fact in the dialogues of the Enlightenment women are never the equals of men. We have already seen this in Diderot's two *Entretiens;* even if his admiration and liking for the Marshal's wife are sincere, she is not taken seriously as an intellectual. Although Mlle de l'Espinasse has an exceptional intellectual openness and curiosity (p. 203 f.), she remains Bordeu's pupil.

Even the Romantic ideal of love does not yet lead to granting the two sexes equal intellectual standing. Two women, Amalia and Camilla, take part in Schlegel's *Gespräch über die Poesie;* indeed, they suggest to the men that they should write essays and read them aloud.[117] But they themselves are only listeners; it is the four men who make presentations. One of the essays is actually a letter to Amalia, and it begins: "I have to say . . . that you are almost entirely wrong. At the end of the dispute, you recognize yourself that you were wrong to get so deeply involved, because it is contrary to feminine dignity to, as you rightly call it, descend from the cheerful element of banter and eternal poetry to the thorough or ponderous seriousness of men. . . . Furthermore, I think that it is not enough to recognize wrongdoing; one must also atone for it, and it seems to me that it would be a very appropriate penance for your having associated yourself with criticism for you to be compelled to read patiently this critical epistle on the subject of yesterday's conversation."[118] Women are

---

116. (1955), 58.
117. (1967), 287.
118. "Ich muß . . . Ihnen so gut als völlig unrecht geben. Sie selbst geben es sich am Ende des Streites darin, daß sie sich so tief eingelassen, weil es gegen die weibliche Würde sei, aus dem angeborenen Element von heiterm Scherz und ewiger Poesie zu dem gründlichen oder schwerfälligen Ernst der Männer sich, wie Sie es richtig nannten, herabzustimmen . . . Ja ich behaupte noch außerdem, daß es nicht genug sei, Unrecht anzuerkennen; man muß es auch büßen, und die wie mirs scheint, ganz zweckmäßige Buße dafür, daß Sie sich mit der Kritik gemein gemacht haben, soll nun sein, daß Sie sich die Geduld abnötigen, diese kritische Epistel über den Gegenstand des gestrigen Gesprächs zu lesen" (1967; 329).

402 *The Universe of the Philosophical Dialogue*

forbidden to engage in argumentative efforts—on pain of being obliged to read texts on literary theory written by men.

A similar image of women also determines *Die Weihnachtsfeier,* a dialogue published by Schlegel's close friend Schleiermacher a few years later, in 1806. The conversation develops, as the title indicates, after Christmas presents are given out; its participants fall into three different groups: children, among whom the somewhat precocious Sophie is the most significant, women, and men. The conversation gains depth through reflections on the preservation of the childlike in adults— reflections that lead to a discussion of the difference between the sexes. Ernestine says that in men the transition from childhood to adulthood takes place more abruptly and is connected with a period of passion and confusion; "in our sex the two are more imperceptibly united with one another. In that which attracts us to the games of childhood already lies our whole life; only the higher meaning of this and that is revealed gradually as we grow up."[119] The mocker Leonhardt draws from this the conclusion that men are more Christian than women, since Christianity preaches a conversion that women really don't need. But Christ did not convert either, Karoline replies. Friederike points out that women are the soul of such celebrations; and when Leonhardt, who represents the principle of reflection, asks the ladies present to tell stories having to do with Christmas, she sits down at the piano, because even a tale such as those the other women present is unsuited to her nature. After three edifying stories have been told, it is the men's turn. Telling stories is not their strong point, Ernst says, and he suggests that "following the English fashion, not to say the Greek fashion, but which is not entirely alien to us, either," they should select a subject, and then each of them will give a speech about it—a speech about "such a subject and in such a manner that we do not in any way forget the presence of women, but instead consider it the finest thing to be understood and praised by them."[120]

119. "bei unserm Geschlecht vereinigt sich beides unmerklicher miteinander. In dem, was uns in den Spielen der Kindheit anzieht, liegt schon unser ganzes Leben, nur daß sich, wie wir erwachsen, allmählich die höhere Bedeutung von dem und jenem offenbart" (1869; 121).

120. "nach Englischer Weise, um nicht zu sagen nach griechischer, und die uns doch auch nicht ganz fremd ist . . . und zwar einen solchen und so, daß wir dabei die

Friederike proposes, naturally enough, the subject of Christmas itself. Leonhardt—"the unbelieving rogue"[121]—refers with barely concealed irony to the highly questionable historical status of the Christmas story: "And since night is the historical cradle of Christianity, the birthday celebration of the same also takes place at night, and the candles with which it is resplendent are, as it were, the star over the inn and the halo without which the child would not be found in the darkness of the stable and in the otherwise starless night of history."[122] In contrast, Ernst does not attempt to trace Christmas back to historical facts—"the celebration does not depend on that, but rather on the necessity of the Redeemer and the experience of an intensified existence that is not to be traced back to any beginning other than this one."[123] Whereas Leonhardt appealed to the Synoptic Gospels, Eduard appeals to John; his interpretation of the Christmas holiday anticipates Hegel's speculations on the philosophy of religion. "But just in the same way every one of us sees in the birth of Christ his own higher birth, through which nothing other than deep devotion and love lives in him and the eternal son of God appears in him as well."[124] Finally, the mystic Joseph does not want to give an intellectual

---

Gegenwart der Frauen in keinem Sinn vergessen, sondern es für das Schönste achten, von ihnen verstanden und gelobt zu werden" (1869; 137 f.). The following sentence alludes still more directly to the *Symposium* (194a2 ff.): "Es ist schon von einem Bessern, als ich bin, bei einer ähnlichen Gelegenheit angemerkt worden, daß die letzten am übelsten daran sind, wo über einen Gegenstand, welcher es auch sei, auf diese Weise geredet wird" (It has already been noted on a similar occasion by a better man than I that the last speakers are worst at this when a subject, whatever it may be, is spoken about in this way) (1869; 152).

121. "der ungläubige Schalk" (1869; 145).

122. "Und wie die Nacht die historische Wiege des Christenthums ist, so wird auch das Geburtsfest desselben in der Nacht begangen, und die Kerzen, mit denen es prangt, sind gleichsam der Stern über der Herberge und der Heiligenschein, ohne welchen man das Kind nicht finden würde in der Dunkelheit des Stalles und in der sonst unbesternten Nacht der Geschichte" (1869; 144 f.).

123. "das Fest hängt nicht daran, sondern wie an der Notwendigkeit des Erlösers, so an der Erfahrung eines gesteigerten Daseins, welches auf keinen andern Anfang als diesen zurückzuführen ist" (1869; 150).

124. "Ebenso aber auch jeder von uns schaut in der Geburt Christi seine eigene höhere Geburt an, durch die nun auch nichts anderes in ihm lebt als Andacht und Liebe und auch in ihm der ewige Sohn Gottes erscheint" (1869; 156).

speech: "The speechless object requires or produces in me a speechless joy."[125] He shows that not every man is an intellectual; but all women may still be nonintellectuals. The dialogue depends on the assumption that the polarity of man and woman enlivens and brightens reality—and one consequence of this polarity is that abstract reflection, without which philosophy is not possible, is denied women.

The inclusion of women in philosophical conversation is a process that got under way late and is not yet concluded. Although openness to the Other is a criterion of good conversation, the number of interlocutors must inevitably be limited if a fruitful exchange is to be possible. I already discussed this matter from the quantitative point of view in chapter 13. Something analogous also holds so far as quality is concerned: at the end of chapter 15 esoteric techniques were discussed. Inclusion and exclusion go hand in hand; indeed, the greater the number of people with potential access to the conversation, the more rigorous the selection has to be. The decision as to whether one wants to engage in a conversation with a certain person is not obvious—precisely because, in view of the limited time available to us, a positive decision usually decreases the probability of being able to conduct a conversation with someone else. Someone who has begun a conversation can also decide at any time to break it off and withdraw; even the Platonic Socrates threatens on two occasions to withdraw if Protagoras is not willing to respond to his questions.[126] And sometimes it is desirable that those who are not capable of participating in a conversation or even hinder it withdraw from a group. Had Anytus remained past *Meno* 95a1, Meno, and with him the reader, would have been deprived of Socrates' epistemological explanations. Cephalus represents the best aspect of Greek mores; but he is incapable of clear and precise philosophical discussion, not only because of his great age, but also constitutionally. The great conversation of the *Republic* could not have begun while he was still present; and therefore the reader must be thankful for the religious duties that call him away.[127] Cicero refers to this departure when Atticus asks him

---

125. "Der sprachlose Gegenstand verlangt oder erzeugt auch mir eine sprachlose Freude" (1869; 157).

126. Cf., e.g., *Prt.* 335c3 ff. and 353b5. See also *Grg.* 489d7 f.

127. *R.* 331d6 ff.

with surprise why he had Scaevola leave at the end of the first book of *De oratore*.[128] He did not send him away without reason, Cicero replies, but instead did the same thing that "our god Plato" did in the *Republic*. Like Cephalus, Scaevola is too old and fragile to participate in a very long conversation, and the second and third books of *De oratore* deal with subjects that are too technical for him.[129]

Someone may be unsuited for a conversation on intellectual grounds; he may also be so cynical that one refuses to engage in conversation with him on moral grounds; consider Bärlach's refusal to engage in philosophical debate with the sadistic doctor Emmenberger in Friedrich Dürrenmatt's *Der Verdacht*. A rationalist like Socrates, however, considers it his duty to refute immoralists; and he proceeds with his argumentation even when the latter are, like Callicles, no longer really listening to him. The danger of the conversation being broken off out of indignation is obvious: people cling to their opinions, even when the latter cannot be rationally grounded, and therefore according to the criteria of a rationalistic ethics are perhaps not moral at all. In his *Corydon*, Gide expressed this attitude in the last words spoken by the first-person narrator, of whose intellectual and also moral superiority the reader is not really convinced. After Corydon's final speech the narrator leaves him, almost without saying a word and aware that after certain assertions a good silence is better than any rejoinder: "Après qu'il eut fini, il demeura quelque temps dans l'attente d'une protestation de ma part. Mais, sans rien ajouter qu'un adieu, je pris mon chapeau et sortis, bien assuré qu'à de certaines affirmations un bon silence répond mieux que tout ce qu'on peut trouver à dire."[130] In this way he may be able to convince himself, but hardly those who think differently. For we can recognize as true only that which has withstood the test of conversation.

128. 1.62.265.

129. *Att.* 4.16.3: "Quod in iis libris quos laudas personam desideras Scaevolae, non eam temere demovi, sed feci idem quod in '*Politeiai*' deus ille noster Plato.... et erat primi libri sermo non alienus a Scaevolae studiis; reliqui libri [technologian] habent, ut scis."

130. (1935), 318.

CHAPTER 17

The Logic of Conversation

The goal of conversation is to arrive at a consensus, even if only with re-gard to implications: anyone who accepts *p* has a duty to accept *q*. How do we arrive at such a consensus? Whereas in the didactic dialogue the pupil generally follows the teacher's deductions—insofar as they are really deductions—the dialogues that are more interesting from a liter-ary and philosophical standpoint present interlocutors who have differ-ent views. The dramatic quality of the conversational event is a function of the collision of their divergent views and their gradual convergence. So far as its validity is concerned, the process of convincing each other is rational in nature, but since all rational beings that we know are also emotional beings, a more comprehensive analysis of the phenomenon cannot ignore the human psyche's resistance to the intellect's insight.

Among the sources of the conversational practice depicted in Plato's dialogues and first conceptualized in Aristotle's *Topics* are the elenchic argumentative games that had probably been widespread among the educated since the Sophists.[1] The term *argumentative game* is used ad-visedly, because the very special game of elenchus has a few of the char-

1. On the nature of these games, see in particular the eighth book of the *Topics*. For secondary literature, see the classical presentation in E. Kapp (1942), esp. 12 ff., and, more recently, P. Stemmer (1992), 96 ff.

acteristics that we associate with games—no matter how notoriously difficult it is to define what a game is. First, it is an intelligent pastime enjoyed for its own sake. Second, it functions only thanks to certain rules whose violation makes one a spoilsport. Third, it presupposes— like many if not all games—a plurality of players. This game requires precisely two players—one who makes a statement (the proponent) and another who questions him and tries to draw conclusions from his answers but does not himself make statements (the opponent).[2] Fourth, the game can be won or lost. The answerer loses if his initial statement proves to be inconsistent with other propositions he has accepted, and the questioner loses if he does not succeed in demonstrating such an inconsistency. However, as we have seen, the defeat may be mitigated if the answerer has defended the questionable thesis only as a devil's advocate and thus playfully.

Not every claim to have proven an inconsistency in another person's position was objectively justified, as is shown in particular by the *Euthydemus;* and the desire for more precise rules of deduction and refutation in these games led to the development of logic within the Platonic Academy—and crucially as the work of the young Aristotle. "Plato had undoubtedly mastered this logical structure of the elenchic procedure; otherwise he could not have composed the dialogues as he did. He had mastered it as had everyone who took part in an elenchus as a questioner or as an answerer. But Plato did not expressly thematize the logical structure of the elenchus; he never discussed it, never made it an object of his philosophizing. For that reason he coined no fixed linguistic terms for the individual elements of this procedure and their connection with each other; he was far from having formulated a terminology."[3] Logic has its historical origin in pragmatics; as Robert Brandom puts it, it makes explicit rules that are already being followed.[4] The *Topics* are prior to the *Analytics,* at least genetically. However, the *topoi* that are

2. Cf. *Chrm.* 163e5 ff.
3. P. Stemmer (1992), 128. See also 138.
4. Cf. R. Brandom (1994), whose categories and terminology I repeatedly draw on in the following pages, even though I doubt that his pragmatic starting point really solves the validity problem of the justification of logic. Cf. V. Hösle (2005b).

discussed by Aristotle and his many successors, such as Cicero, and that structure argumentations, are no more the subject of this book than the rhetorical figures that ornament them verbally.[5]

Its development into logic shows, moreover, that the elenchus is not merely a game. The rules of deduction are not arbitrary; they have to guarantee the very essence of logic—that true propositions lead only to further true propositions. It is this relationship to truth that distinguishes dialectic from eristic.[6] Aristotle does not yet consider a plurality of possible logical systems, a plurality that has given the problem of grounding logic an entirely new acuteness. Pursuing the question of whether certain rules of deduction, and thus a certain logic, could be said to make possible a superior form of conversation[7] would take us far beyond the framework of this book and the competence of its author. In the following pages it is presupposed that classical logic is the most appropriate for a philosophical conversation. In any case, among the philosophical di - alogues written up to this point I know of none that is based on a different logic. I shall concentrate instead on the way, assuming classical logic, refutation and persuasion take place.

As a rule, we are motivated to change our own views only when we have been shown that they are false or at least questionable. This not only results from the natural fact of inborn inertia but also has a substantial basis. Someone who changes his opinions for no reason is even more threatening than the obstinate person, because it can be assumed

5. The best modern discussion of this subject is by C. Perelman and L. Olbrechts-Tyteca (1988).

6. Plato repeatedly contrasts eristic and dialectic; cf. *Men.* 75c8 ff. and *R.* 454a8 f. In Aristotle dialectic is distinguished from philosophy (*Top.* 155b7 ff.) and thus devalued; but the distinction between it and eristic remains, though now as part of a triad the first member of which is *apodeixis: Top.* 100a25 ff. See also 161a33 f. and *SE* 171b34 ff.

7. On this, cf. Lorenzen in P. Lorenzen and K. Lorenz (1978), 1–8, esp. 8: "In Plato's mode of expression a dialectic, a search for truth in conversation, in which each person disinterestedly conveys his knowledge, has already developed out of eristic. And this dialectical game leads us precisely to classical logic. Intuitionist and classical logic could therefore also be contrasted with each other as 'eristic' and 'dialectical' logic. This makes it clear that the operative interpretation of logic makes simultaneously comprehensible the legitimacy of the standpoints of both the intuitionist and the classical camps. Either *eristic* or *dialectical* logic can be the appropriate logic, depending on whether the conversation partners want to speak *against each other* or *with each other.*"

that he will abandon his new conviction just as quickly. It becomes clear that something really is a mistake only after one has sought at length to defend it and has failed. The most appropriate way of stabilizing opinions is to ground them, which can transform them into knowledge;[8] the best way to put them in question is to prove that a certain number of convictions are inconsistent. Only in the rarest cases will someone hold a view that is contradictory in itself;[9] in general, contradiction can be concluded only from a plurality of opinions. The derivation of the contradiction is usually possible only if propositions can be deduced of which the proponent was at first not aware, but which follow from his explicit convictions as well as from the underlying logic. Such processes can in principle be pursued by the individual himself, perhaps partly preverbally. However, in a conversation, which is what we are necessarily concerned with in a book on the dialogue, views must be formulated verbally and communicated; in particular, they must be defended. The interlocutors must undertake commitments and attribute them to one another. In elenchus, these two roles are often allocated to the proponent and the opponent; in a normal conversation each person is engaged in both activities, making his own claims and ascribing claims to others. Naturally, such an ascription is itself a commitment that makes a truth claim: A asserts that B is committed to p, and such an assertion can be falsified if, for example, A has misunderstood B. But A's assertion of "B has committed himself to p" is something entirely different from his own assertion of p. Not only are the truth conditions different; the intellectual capacities that are necessary to ground the ascription "B has committed himself to p" are often, if not always, of a different kind than those required to ground the assertion of p, because they are always—or at least also—hermeneutic in nature, whereas this does not hold for every p. Thus p can be an epistemological or an ethical proposition. However, p can also be a hermeneutic proposition (e.g., "Plato believes in the possibility of an ultimate justification"); then the capacities presupposed

---

8. Cf. *Men.* 97a ff.

9. More common is the defense of meaningless propositions and concepts such as—according to Berkeley's Philonous (who confuses *noēsis* and *noēma*, however)—the concept of matter (1977; 208 ff.).

by commitment and attribution are the same. But of course the truth conditions remain different.

In the previous chapter, I discussed mutual understanding as a presupposition for conversation. If one wants to prove an inconsistency to the other person, it generally does not suffice, as mentioned, to understand every individual statement; one must have an overview of the totality of the statements made. One must, "keep score," to use one of Brandom's central categories.[10] This requires memory. It is considered one of Thomas Reid's greatest achievements, for example, in the *Essays on the Intellectual Powers of Man,* to have stressed the central importance of memory for the theory of knowledge. Only through memory do humans transcend being lost in time, which never endures but is always passing; only through memory do they raise themselves, even if always only partially, to the timeless sphere in which *noēmata* exist and are connected by arguments. Anyone who was completely absorbed in the present, without either retention or protention, could no more draw logical conclusions than he could perceive a melody. It is hardly surprising that Plato was already well aware that memory is the central presupposition of conversation; indeed, given the multitude of cross-references in his dialogues and between them, we may presume that he himself had a monstrous memory and that an almost unimaginable plenitude of material—his own as well as that of others—was simultaneously present to him. In any case, he constantly emphasizes the indispensable importance of memory for philosophy, and not only in the framework of the mythical theory of anamnesis. In addition to courage, magnanimity, and a capacity for learning, the true philosopher needs a good memory;[11] in fact, only the memory seems to guarantee personal identity, given the change of states of consciousness in every person.[12] In the *Philebus,* in which the phenomenon of the pleasure taken in expectation shows that hedonism is

---

10. (1994), 180 ff. Brandom borrows the concept "scorekeeping" from D. Lewis (1983; 233–49).

11. *R.* 490c9 ff.; the latter virtue is itself presupposed in the sentence, whose first word appeals to the conversation partners' memory *(memnēsai).*

12. *Smp.* 208a4 ff. in the context of what is probably the first discussion of the identity problem that has tormented modern philosophy since Locke. Cf. also *Lg.* 732b7 ff., as well as the alleged etymology of *mnēmē* in *Cra.* 437b3 ff. (from *monē,* persisting).

considerably more complex than it at first seems, *anamnēsis,* which is distinguished from *mnēmē,* does not presuppose the theory of the pre-existence of the soul; what distinguishes it from passive memory is its active, spontaneous element.[13] But Plato does not merely theorize regarding the memory—he shows it in action, as it were, in the figure of his Socrates. For instance, Socrates reproaches Polus for not remembering well, despite his youth, the definition that he, Socrates, gave of rhetoric;[14] and he later ironically acts as though he himself had a poor memory, asking Polus to remind him of something.[15] In view of other kinds of addressees, the analogous demand in the *Phaedo*—"First remind me of what you said, if you find my memory inaccurate"[16]—is not sarcastic; but it is ironic, because in this situation it is superfluous, even if it correctly refers to the memory as a general presupposition of conversation. Someone like Lysimachus, who concedes that because of his age he can remember neither what he wanted to ask nor what he heard in the interim, especially if much has been said,[17] thereby shows that he is not suited for the business of philosophy.

Plato knows, of course, that a good memory is only a necessary, not a sufficient, condition for a successful conversation; understanding is more than simply remembering.[18] But it remains a necessary condition

13. 34a10 ff.

14. *Grg.* 466a6 ff. See also *Ion* 539e7 ff. Cf. the very similar passage in Berkeley (1977), 183: "Either, Hylas, you are jesting, or have a very bad memory." Conversely, Augustine praises Adeodatus because he remembers very well everything he has admitted (*De mag.* 9.28).

15. 473d4. Similarly ironic is the question he asks Callicles, 488b6. Appeals to memory are also found, for example, in 495d3, 499e7, 500a8. In the *Protagoras,* Socrates declares that he is forgetful (334c8 ff.), but Alcibiades points out to the less intelligent participants in the conversation (and dialogue-externally to less attentive readers) that this is a jest (336d2 ff.). The sarcasm of Socrates' remark in praise of Hippias, to the effect that he has almost forgotten his mnemotechnical discoveries (*Hp. mi.* 368d5 ff.; cf. *Hp. ma.* 285e9 f.) is insurpassable. Of course the fact that Simmias has to be reminded of the proofs for the theory of anamnesis (*Phd.* 73a5 f., b6 f.—with a dialogue-external allusion to the *Meno*) is also amusing, and corresponds to the Platonic distancing from his person mentioned in chapter 13, n. 78. Augustine remembers the discussion of memory, *Ord.* 2.2.7.

16. 91c6 f.: *prōton me hupomnēsate ha elegete, ean mē phainōmai memnēmenos.*

17. *La.* 189c6 ff.

18. *Phd.* 103b1 f.

not only because it is the presupposition for the identity of the speaker
but also because it alone makes it possible to retain the proposition to
be tested. Without the identity of the proposition there would be no
persuasion; a Heraclitean ontology like that of Cratylus collides with
this transcendental presupposition of every conversation.[19] Socrates' reproach that Callicles has deceived him by asserting first one thing, then
the opposite, indeed, that he has treated him as if he were a child,[20] corresponds to the pride with which he replies to Callicles' condescending
criticism that he always says the same thing: "Not only that, Callicles, but
about the same matters."[21] Callicles himself had shown the spark of reason that is denied no human being who seeks at least temporarily to
participate seriously in a conversation when he asserted that his view
was the same as it was earlier.[22] Because of this assertion he contradicts
himself when he later criticizes Socrates for his constant repetitions; but
such a contradiction does him more honor (because he at least momen-
tarily shows some insight) than avoiding contradictions by refusing
stable statements can do him. Dionysodorus's refusal to stand by his
earlier statements is connected with his reproach that Socrates is old-
fashioned;[23] but first of all, this does not prevent him from being refuted,[24]
and second, his refusal and his reproach show that this man is simply
laughable—unlike Callicles, who at least tries to be consistent and thus
has a certain tragic greatness. In view of such passages, it is hard to avoid
the impression that long before the *Sophist* Plato already had a "Platonizing" ontology of propositions, which according to him is the transcendental condition of the possibility of conversation. Anyone who recalls
that Plato was obviously familiar with the Megarian school before the
death of Socrates[25]—otherwise he would hardly have retired to Megara

19. *Cra.* 439b10 ff. See also *Tht.* 182c9 ff.

20. *Grg.* 499b9 ff.

21. *Grg.* 490e10 f.: *Ou monon ge, ō Kallikleis, alla kai peri tōn autōn.* Cf. 491b5 ff.,
508e6 ff., 527b2 ff., d5 ff., *Smp.* 221e5 f. See also chap. 14, n. 27, on the *Euthyphro* and
the *Crito.*

22. 488b7.

23. *Euthyd.* 287b2 ff. Cf. 295c11.

24. 288a1 f.

25. D. L. 3.6., according to Hermodorus.

after Socrates' execution—will not find this surprising. However, it is Socratic that Plato evidently connected the logical problem of the self-identity of a proposition with the problem of human self-identity, which is not only a psychological but also an ethical one. The latter presupposes the former, because only someone who commits himself—especially in the case of moral questions—can develop a stable identity, and such a commitment is possible only if there is a timeless realm of ideas and propositions that is independent of change in our minds. Logical Platonism is the presupposition for a moral realism.

The identity of meanings and propositions and their grasping through memory are, as I have said, not sufficient conditions for a productive conversation. In a conversation in which the participants oppose one other, the person who seeks to prove that his interlocutor has contradicted himself will try to get him to agree to propositions whose implication of a result that is incompatible with the thesis to be defended is not immediately evident; like a good chess player, the opponent will be wary of allowing the proponent to foresee his next moves.[26] But this is more a matter of psychology than of logic per se. What follows, however, is a fundamentally logical problem. Even if someone is proven to have been inconsistent, this only means that the conjunction of the statements made must be false. Which one or which ones of these statements must be considered false is—according to the Duhem-Quine thesis—not thereby proven. It is well known that even protocol statements are not so simple to identify, because every observation is shaped by a theory;[27] and "philosophical facts" can often be interpreted in different ways. Since philosophy, which is all we are concerned with here, is not an empirical enterprise, a holistic theory of knowledge is unavoidable at least with respect to it, so long as we do not wish to appeal simply to intuitions. If, as seems sensible, one is allowed to take back earlier moves, then an

26. Cf. Arist. *Top.* 156a7 ff., b4 ff.

27. This holds a fortiori if certain classes of observations are considered improper, for then an ethical theory restricts "pure observation" (cf. Gide [1935; 248 ff.]). But one can free oneself from such theories (or rather prejudices) more easily than from scientific ones. Bruno already realized that theory determines which observations are allowed (1985; I 145).

interlocutor can usually avoid refutation by withdrawing one of his preceding statements. Plato's Socrates already knows this; he permits Polus
either to withdraw premises that entail counterintuitive consequences or
else to accept these consequences.[28] For the most part, there are various
possibilities to choose from the premises; and it is not logic that commands us to sacrifice a certain statement. Someone who does not really
desire to be consistent is not an interesting interlocutor; in a certain sense
he cannot be refuted, but it is also not worthwhile trying to do so: confronted by Euthydemus and Dionysodorus, Socrates finally gives up.[29]
But this desire for consistency is absolutely compatible with a plenitude
of different argumentative strategies.

This holds a fortiori if the contradiction was only the result of an
assumption that one's opponent, but not oneself, has made—that is, if
the criticism was external, not immanent. In Malebranche's dialogue, the
Chinese philosopher, who is in reality a Spinozist, seeks to draw from contradictory effects the conclusion that "Ly" is not wise—for example, by
pointing to the fact that "Ly" causes corn to grow and then destroys it
by storms. But the Christian philosopher contradicts him: "I conclude
demonstratively exactly the contrary."[30] Such events, he maintains, result
from God's will to allow general, simple, and fertile natural laws to govern the world. Malebranche argues exactly the way Leibniz and Berkeley
argue: these three thinkers believe, like Spinoza, that a rational theology
must attribute a special role to natural laws but consider this notion compatible with a conception of God as an intelligent being who wants what is
good. In fact, the existence of things contrary to the assumed ends is compatible with the thesis that this is a necessary part of the best of all possible
worlds—or more precisely, of a world that could not be better. This holds
especially if it is maintained, as Malebranche (and Leibniz) did, that
human happiness is not the crucial criterion of such a world: "Man's happiness is not God's goal, I mean his principal goal, his ultimate goal."[31]

28. *Grg.* 480e1 ff.

29. *Euthd.* 303a9. The related passage at *Hp. ma.* 301e6 is similarly ironic.

30. "Moy j'en conclus démonstrativement tout le contraire" (1958; 28).

31. "Le bonheur de l'homme n'est pas la fin de Dieu, j'entends sa fin principale,
sa derniere fin" (1958; 31).

Even Hume's Philo admits this compatibility, perhaps only for the sake of the argument; but he immediately adds that God's attributes of omnipotence and perfect goodness cannot be deduced from Nature as we experience it.[32] The philosophical problem is thus whether there are a priori arguments for ascribing these attributes to God.

Logic shows only that certain conclusions follow from certain premises; someone who wants to deny a conclusion therefore has to deny only the conjunction of the premises. A good example of this is found in Gide's *Corydon*. A picture of Walt Whitman on Corydon's desk leads his visitor to remark that it is out of place there, because Bazalgette (the author of *Walt Whitman, l'homme et l'oeuvre*, published in 1908) has shown that Whitman was not a homosexual. Corydon reconstructs the syllogism (whose remarkable confusion of descriptive and normative statements does not seem to bother him): homosexuality is contrary to nature; Whitman was healthy; therefore he was not a homosexual.[33] But he correctly points out that the argument, while maintaining the second premise, can be turned around: from Whitman's homosexuality and his healthiness it could just as well be deduced that homosexuality is not contrary to nature. The visitor recognizes that in each case an unproven premise has been posited whose negation appears as the conclusion in the other case; neither argument is thus logically superior. However, he says, his own premise is less contrary to common sense. But Corydon, who is concerned with truth, questions the validity of common sense, for it is not common sense but only truth that one ought not to offend: "Ce n'est pas le sens commun, c'est la vérité qu'il importe de ne pas heurter."[34] Appealing to common sense as a guarantee for premises is in any case quite different from appealing to logic. Indeed, it is even implausible to claim that the burden of proof always rests on the person who maintains something contrary to common sense. For example, Philonous sees the burden of proof as being on the person who maintains the existence of

---

32. (1947), 201.
33. We may add that the unnaturalness of a thing does not determine its moral permissibility. In Pseudo-Lucian Charicles emphasizes that heterosexuality corresponds more to nature (*Am.* 20), but Callicratidas replies that that shows only that homosexuality is a late cultural achievement (35).
34. (1935), 188.

something—even if it is something as unquestioned as matter.[35] On this subject the opposite but formally similar (because it seeks to make do with the most economical ontology possible) case is Argle's materialism. Bargle, who takes holes as his first example against a materialistic ontology, is finally forced to lay down his arms faced with Argle's ingenious resistance: "I see that I can never hope to refute you, since I no sooner reduce your position to absurdity than you embrace the absurdity." Argle replies: "Not absurdity; disagreement with common opinion."[36]

One of the essential differences between Plato's and Aristotle's philosophical profiles is that the latter sees the dialectical syllogism's starting point in the *endoxa,* that is, in the opinion of all or most people or the most famous and respected wise men[37]—and thus also the starting point of normal conversation. Because of the normative dignity Aristotle accords to the *endoxa,* he has to define the eristic syllogism as one that takes its point of departure either really from apparent *endoxa* or only apparently from real or apparent *endoxa* (and thus in the latter case it is not a genuine syllogism).[38] Plato's Socrates, in contrast, is well aware that some of his theses—for instance, the one about the philosopher-kings—are paradoxical, that is, that they conflict with the *doxa;* but this does not disqualify them in general, even if it makes special efforts to ground them as necessary.[39] He considers as simply rhetorical, and thus not valid, a refutation that appeals to the fact that one's own opinion is shared by many and respected persons; although such a refutation might be taken into account in law courts, it does not contribute to the discovery of the truth.[40] Plato never sees factual consensus as a criterion of truth; and we can hardly disagree when we see how many generally recognized convictions, both descriptive and normative in nature, have

35. Berkeley (1977), 205.
36. Lewis (1983), 8.
37. *Top.* 100b21 ff.
38. 100b23 ff. In addition, he mentions the apodeictic syllogism as a third form (a27 ff.).
39. Cf. *R.* 472a1–7. The second sentence ends with *ededoikē houtō paradoxon logon legein te kai epicheirein diaskopein.*
40. *Grg.* 471e2 ff. In 471d4 f., rhetoric *(tēn rhētorikēn)* is opposed to the art of discussion *(tou . . . dialegesthai).* This influenced Cic. *Fin.* 2.6.17, where, however, a philosophical rhetoric is distinguished from a forensic rhetoric.

been falsified in the course of history. It is true that appeals to others flatter them, and this may explain their success in law courts. But this only confirms Socrates' thesis that rhetoric is a form of flattery.[41]

Philosophers who have the courage to question the commonplaces of their culture and tradition are certainly more fascinating; but they are also more dangerous: Nietzsche, for example, belongs to this group, along with Plato. For such a philosopher, there is an obvious temptation to present his new view in a declamatory fashion, as it were. But people may react to it with indifference: one assurance is merely exchanged for another, and new fashions are no better than the old ones. One has to accept the decisive premises before one follows such a philosopher; someone who is not prepared to do so cannot engage in a productive exchange. In fact, in several dialogues we find the idea that without common assumptions a conversation is not possible at all. Socrates urges Crito to carefully examine the proposition that we may not respond to wrongdoing with wrongdoing, and that we may treat no one badly, no matter how he has offended us, and not to accept it contrary to his conviction; he knows that this seems and will seem true only to a few people: "between those who do think so and those who do not there can be no agreement on principle; they must always feel contempt when they observe one another's decisions."[42] Similarly, in Llull's *Declaratio Raimundi*, Socrates says that he is prepared to engage in discussion with Raimundus if they can agree on a few true principles recognized by both sides, to which they can appeal and with whose help they can discover who is saying the truth and who is saying something false.[43]

In actuality, it is not difficult to see that without such commonalities each party can appeal only to his own premises, which are precisely not recognized by the other. It is obvious that such discussions and "refutations" are unproductive; Bruno, for example, claims to refute opposing views immanently, that is, using the principles on which they

41. *Grg.* 463aff.
42. *Cri.* 49d2 ff. Translation from H. Tredennick in Hamilton and Cairns.
43. *ROL* XVII 255: "Consentit tamen Socrates, quod si ipsi in aliquibus ueris principiis et utrique parti communibus possent ad inuicem conuenire, ad quae unanimiter recurrerent, in quibus cognoscerent, quis eorum ueritatem diceret aut errorem, sibi placeret."

themselves are based.[44] In interreligious debates in which the specific assumptions of one's own religion are precisely what is at issue, appeal to these assumptions is ridiculous. The same goes for theses that can be made plausible only if one shares the controversial assumptions, which are, however, supposed to be used to ground these assumptions; then we are dealing with a *petitio principii*. In the third act of the *Prabodhacandrodaya* by Kṛṣṇa Miśra this is already used for comic effect: a Buddhist monk and a Jain monk squabble with each other and argue for their own religions in an obviously circular fashion. The Jain wants to ask the Buddhist something, but the latter treats him arrogantly. Who gave him his commands? The all-knowing Buddha. How does he know that the Buddha is all-knowing? It says so in his writings. The Jain correctly points out that if the Buddha is all-knowing only because he himself has said so, then he, the Jain, is all-knowing as well. But this critical attitude breaks down when it is a matter of justifying his own position. He urges the Buddhist to convert to Jainism, and when the Buddhist asks who recognizes the authority of the Jina, the Jain refers to the Jina's knowledge of the planets. But the Buddhist denies such knowledge. Their mutual spiteful remarks end when a Kapalika, who belongs to a Shivaite sect, appears and, because his religion is being criticized, would like to kill the Jain. Finally he refrains from doing so and enjoys the subtler triumph of seeing the two monks allow themselves to be seduced by a female member of his sect.[45]

Kṛṣṇa Miśra's drama first became known in Europe in the nineteenth century; thus only a typological affinity is involved when we find a similar passage in the central fourth book of Bodin's *Colloquium heptaplomeres*. This is not surprising because appealing to one's own premises in conversations with members of other religions is human, all too human. When the friends have finally gotten so far as to begin discussions of religious questions, the skeptic Senamus predicts that such discussions will not lead to anything. Who is to be the referee? With disarming naïveté

44. "per desiderio, che tiene, di mostrar la imbecillità di contrari pareri per i medesimi principii, co' quali pensano esser confirmati" (1985; I 50). Conversely, he accuses his opponents of not grasping the crucial principle of immanent criticism (138).
45. In Nambiar's edition of 1971, cf. 70 ff.

the Lutheran Fridericus cries out: "Christus Deus!" But Senamus points out that Christians, Jews, and Muslims do not agree as to whether Christ is God. The Calvinist Curtius is subtler: he refers to appropriate witnesses and texts. But here, too, there is absolutely no agreement as to what is to be recognized as appropriate.[46] The Catholic Coronaeus refers, characteristically, to the church. But which is the true church? The Jew Salomo points out that both Christians and Muslims recognize the Jews as God's people—but Fridericus adds: up to the advent of Christ. When the Muslim Octavius emphasizes that although Mohammed did in fact cite the Gospels he considered the New Testament to be corrupted by the Christians, the rationalist Toralba introduces the wise men as referees. However, here, too, Senamus skeptically remarks: "But it is doubted, too, who the wise men are."[47] And when Toralba refers to God, Senamus promptly replies: "It is in fact necessary that the religion that has God as its author is true, but therein lies the labor and the difficulty, namely to discover whether he is the author of this religion or that one."[48]

It is not difficult to see that a conversation in which the participants appeal to premises that they alone recognize is doomed to failure. Even if someone succeeds in proving by means of immanent criticism that there is an inconsistency, for example, in the religion of one of his interlocutors, he is still far from having proven that his own religion is the right one, because the two religions do not exhaust all the logical possibilities. However, it remains true that of two positions, if one and only one is refuted, the other one must be given priority—so long as a consistent third position has not been found. The refusal to commit oneself to a position that is the only one that has survived the elenchus, because contradictions might still be found in it as well, is not acceptable. Philonous rightly reacts to Hylas's reservation that objections to immaterialism might later be found as follows: "Pray, Hylas, do you in other cases, when a point is once evidently proved, withhold your assent on account of objections or difficulties it may be liable to? . . . If this be a sufficient

46. (1857), 131; cf. 140.
47. (1857), 132: "Sed etiam illud dubitatur, qui sint sapientes?"
48. (1857), 132: "Vera profecto sit religio, quae Deum auctorem habet, necesse est, sed num hujus legis aut illius auctor sit, hoc opus, hic labor est."

pretence for withholding your full assent, you should never yield it to any proposition, how free soever from exceptions, how clearly and solidly soever demonstrated."[49] Hylas agrees, and Philonous gives him an important piece of advice: he should carefully examine every later objection to see if it does not count just as much against the contradictory position: for such an objection could have no effect on either of the two positions.[50]

In comparing two positions, for example, two religions, people obviously act unfairly—even if this behavior is widespread—when they presuppose an ideal image of their own religion and contrast it with the historical reality of other religions.[51] We cannot move beyond a positional, dogmatic conversation in that way. Obviously, in such a situation there are only two possibilities. Either one abandons the attempt to convince the other with objective arguments; that is what happens, in fact, at the end of the *Colloquium heptaplomeres,* as was foreseen by Senamus. (The use of rhetorical persuasive and propagandistic arts is compatible with such a decision.) Or else one does not appeal to premises that are peculiar to one's own religion, but instead to premises that are connected with the rational nature of human beings and that one hopes might make possible a rational evaluation of the various religions that transcends particular religions. This is the strategy that Abelard, Llull, and Nicholas of Cusa all use to different degrees. In *De pace fidei,* the latter begins the discussion with a reflection on the one wisdom that every-

49. (1977), 254 f.

50. This idea has already appeared earlier in the conversation: "In short, by whatever method you distinguish *things* from *chimeras* on your own scheme, the same, it is evident, will hold also upon mine. For it must be, I presume, by some perceived difference, and I am not for depriving you of any one thing that you perceive" (1977; 226). Original emphasis.

51. In the prophetic second of Wieland's *Gespräche unter vier Augen* (1798), in which he anticipates Napoleon's monocracy (which began with the coup d'état of November 9, 1799), Wilibald analogously asks the republican Heribert, who has referred to the bad way in which most kings exercise their office: "Do you want to convince yourself that you, on just the same grounds and according to just the same way of inferring, are obliged to swear the most sincere hatred for *democracy* itself?" (Wollen Sie sich überzeugen, daß Sie, aus ebendenselben Gründen und nach eben derselben Art zu schließen, der *Demokratie* selbst den herzlichsten Haß zuzuschwören schuldig sind?) (1970; 197; cf. 203).

one loves and presupposes.[52] This is not a presupposition that is merely factually shared, as would be the case if the interlocutors happened to belong to the same religious community. Instead, it is a question of something transcendentally given—something that is the condition of possibility for every conversation that is concerned with truth claims. The concession that there is a transcendental given does not yet mean that the question as to which religion is the true one can be decided, or is even a meaningful question; instead, it may be that one can, on the basis of such givens, prefer this in one religion, that in another, without being able to establish a clear hierarchy of the factually given religions. But the assumption of a reason that transcends factual beliefs is indeed a necessary presupposition for a conversation about religion that seeks to be more than an exchange of mutual assurances that each is sure he is right and the other is mistaken. However, Senamus's radicalness consists in the fact that he questions the possibility of such a reason as well. In his view, the attempt to resolve the conflict of religions and denominations through a withdrawal to the allegedly neutral level of reason cannot succeed because the same plurality emerges on this level as on that of religions. Every philosophical school claims to be reasonable, and it is no more possible to decide among these claims than between those made by the various religions. Senamus obviously mirrors the French skepticism of the late sixteenth century; in his case, Bodin might have been thinking of Montaigne, who at the end of the "Apology for Raymond Sebond" brings up the epistemological problem of the criterion *(rouet)* familiar to us from Sextus Empiricus. In order to be valid, an argument must meet the requirements of a criterion; but we need an argument for this criterion. The circle seems inescapable. Skepticism seems radical and liberating, but Montaigne shows that fideism—that is, the appeal to one's own faith and the refusal to try to justify it or even to consider justification a desideratum—is its natural consequence. Anyone who does not like this outcome should hesitate to adopt skepticism as a philosophy.

That Plato can be given the honorary title of "the father of rationalist philosophy" is due in part to the fact that he was the first to have understood the problem of securing the first principles of philosophy,

52. VII 11 ff.

that is, its ultimate ground, and to have recognized in this the central difference between philosophy and mathematics, which proceeds on the basis of axioms.[53] This is not the place to reconstruct his ideas on this subject, which are only partly set forth in the dialogues; obviously Plato believed that in the esoteric theory of the two principles he had found the ultimate foundation of metaphysics. Why did he believe that? Well, because neither the Eleatic grounding in the One nor the Ionian assumption of an unlimited Many could lead to an intelligible world: this seems to me to be the real point of the *Parmenides,* and it had already taken shape in the work of Philolaus.[54] In opposition to Gorgias, Plato wants to show that there is an absolute existent, that it is knowable, and that it is communicable—indeed, according to Plato, the knowability of its object and the communicability of the corresponding theory are restrictive conditions for meaningful philosophy. A theory can, in Plato's view, be true if only one person or even no one considers it true; but it cannot be true if it entails the consequence that it cannot be communicated, or that communicating it works against its goal. One of the many burdens we have inherited from Heidegger is the disastrous opposition between objective thinking about Being and subjective transcendental philosophy—an opposition that is historically determined and proceeds from Heidegger's hostility to contemporary neo-Kantianism. In reality, Plato shows that the use of transcendental arguments in no way implies a forgetfulness of Being; on the contrary, it is the only way to develop a rational theory of Being. In this book, which is more concerned with matters of literary theory, I cannot investigate the possibility of grounding transcendentally theories in the areas of the philosophy of language, epistemology, and ontology, as Plato does in the *Cratylus, Parmenides, Theaetetus,* and *Sophist.* However, I would like to refer briefly to the ideas on the foundation of ethics that are not so much thematized as dramatically presented in Plato's work.[55] Even if Plato does not distinguish terminologically between semantic and performative contradic-

53. *R.* 509d ff.
54. *DK* 44 B 3 and 6.
55. On this, cf. V. Hösle (1984a), 330–59; and especially the fine books by C. Jermann (1986) and R. Geiger (2006).

tion, he obviously knows both forms; indeed, he seems to assume the priority of the latter,[56] which he never tires of representing.

It has often been emphasized that the oddest dialogue title in Plato is that of the *Philebus,* which tries to ground the priority of reason over pleasure. The title is odd because the eponymous hero of the dialogue says almost nothing, indeed, he very quickly opts out of the conversation. He has spoken before the beginning of the conversation represented,[57] but we are hardly inclined to think he did more than state his hedonistic thesis. His first comment at 11c4 consists of four particles and a vocative; in 12a7 f. he declares that he thinks and will continue to think that pleasure is victorious, and asks Protarchus to look into the question;[58] in 12b1 f. he solemnly declares that he is washing his hands of his own approval or refutation. In 18a1 f. Philebus makes a single comment, and in 18d3–e7 makes five more, three of which, however, once again consist only of particles. In 22c3 f. he makes a brief protest, in 27e4–28b6 he makes four more short remarks, the last of which again assigns Protarchus to carry on the discussion—then Philebus disappears from the conversation, and not because he is withdrawing, as do Anytus or Cephalus in other dialogues, but presumably because he has fallen asleep; in 15c8 we read that he is lying down peacefully and that he should not be disturbed with questions. What is the point of naming a dialogue after someone who contributes so little to the conversation? By his behavior, Philebus obviously exemplifies the principle of a pleasure that is not illuminated by reason; and against such a person one can in fact not argue, because he is not open to reason. On the other hand, according to Plato someone like Protarchus, who is open to reason, has thereby already recognized the intrinsic value of reason. He will lose in the discussion, but he will win through the discovery of the truth, which will be found through the explication of his own rational activity. It is no accident that Philebus's last statement comes in the context of the

56. Cf. G. Damschen (1999).
57. 11a1 ff., b4 ff.
58. Note the opposition beetween the present and future forms of *dokein* used in relation to Philebus, and *gnōsēi* used in relation to Protarchus. Philebus remains the captive of opinion because he does not engage in the discussion to see what results from it, but instead already knows what he will continue to opine.

discussion of the status of reason as a principle. His sole philosophically interesting statement is his accusation, which anticipates the hermeneutics of suspicion of a Nietzsche, that by honoring reason Socrates seeks to glorify his own goddess.[59] Socrates' retort is not slow in coming: "And you your own goddess, my friend; still we ought to give an answer to our question"; as is well known, psychologizing contributes nothing to the clarification of the truth, and it can always be reversed. And yet it seems to me that as so often happens in analogous cases in Plato, behind Philebus's fatuous criticism, which springs from the resentment felt by a person incapable of argument, a correct insight is concealed. The philosopher does in fact want to glorify his own activity, but not because he is in love with his particular self, but rather because this activity and its explication are the sole way of arriving at the truth; one may, indeed should, reflect on them. And if reason proves to be the real essence of humans, then it is no disgrace to combine praise of reason with praise of one's true self and to take pleasure in and through reason. It is not possible to argue against reason without presupposing it; for the sake of performative consistency, an irrationalist would do better to keep quiet. Then, however, he is no longer a relevant conversation partner, and is more like a jellyfish or a mussel, which seem to be the quintessence of life forms that lack reason.[60] Aristotle must have had this passage in mind, at least unconsciously, when writing the famous section in his justification of the law of noncontradiction as the condition of the possibility of any discourse, in which he says that anyone who asserts something recognizes it, but someone who does not assert anything is, insofar as he does not assert anything, no better than a vegetable.[61]

It is worthwhile to contrast Philebus with the might-makes-right theorists Thrasymachus and Callicles. The latter argue for their position; indeed, they do so in a social context. However, this involves a paradox, and even a performative contradiction: what they are doing presupposes principles different from the ones that they propose. In the first book of the *Republic*, after praising injustice (which he continues to designate by this word), that is, the tyrant's way of life, Thrasymachus wants to

59. 28b1. Cf. 22c3 f.
60. 21c4 ff.
61. *Metaph.* 1006a11 ff.

leave. But Socrates urges him to stay, because something essential is at stake, namely, how one ought to lead one's life: "Well, do I deny it, said Thrasymachus. —You seem to, said I, or else to care nothing for us and so feel no concern whether we are going to live worse or better lives in our ignorance of what you affirm that you know."[62] The irony is unmistakable, for how, given Thrasymachus's speech, could Socrates believe that he cared about his interlocutors? But however much this presupposition contradicts what Thrasymachus has said, it nonetheless follows from the fact that he has communicated his convictions at all—and is now prepared to engage in discussion with them. But Socrates still has to get him to do so, and he does this skillfully by first appealing to the relevance of the question for every individual, and thus also for Thrasymachus, and only then moving on to the others present. Even if disinterested concern for others appears to be the presupposition of any genuine conversation—as in the following argument it is the presupposition of any art—Socrates nonetheless entices Thrasymachus by telling him that he wants to test his argument. If Thrasymachus really wants to know the best way to live one's life, that is, if his ethical theory makes a claim to be valid, then he can hardly refuse.

Callicles defends a way of life similar to the one defended by Thrasymachus, but he at least has taken the revaluation of language so far that he can describe this way of life as the naturally just one.[63] After his long speech, which culminates in his advising Socrates to keep away from philosophy, Socrates is so delighted that he can hardly control himself. Callicles, he says, has three qualities that everyone must have who is examining the question of the right way to lead one's life: knowledge, benevolence, and truthfulness.[64] Naturally, the ascription of this first quality is ironic. On the other hand, we have already seen in chapter 16 (p. 379) that the ascription of the third quality is seriously meant; only Callicles' *parresia* (frankness), which is almost shameless, opens the way for deeper reflections on the foundation of ethics.[65] But what about

---

62. *R.* 344e4 ff.
63. This is evidence for the later composition of the *Gorgias*.
64. 486e5 ff.
65. See also 491e7 f., 492d1 ff., 521a6 f., where the verbal derivative of the term is used.

benevolence *(eunoia)*? In his conversation with Polus, Socrates had already asked him to do something good for him, as a friend, by refuting something he has said;[66] and he also tells Callicles that he considers him a friend.[67] In fact, since Callicles says what other people only think, and tries to take care of Socrates in his own way, he acts in accord with fundamental norms and has thereby recognized them. The truly radical adherent to the might-makes-right thesis, Plato seems to suggest, does not set forth his theory in discourse; but for that very reason it is not a philosophical challenge. Anyone who conveys his theory in discourse and subjects it to testing by others is always already caught up in the web of an ethics implied by conversation; he cannot avoid at least claiming to be sincere and well intentioned. How far Plato saw in this idea the central argument is hard to decide; it may certainly be that he gave greater weight to the explicit arguments, which are not always good ones because they operate in the framework of eudaemonism.[68] But first of all, the interpreter does not have to evaluate an author's arguments the way the author himself does; someone who rejects eudaemonism and is interested in a foundation of ethics in terms of discourse theory will pay special attention to this passage. Second, Plato sought to draw the reader's attention to this contradiction by elaborating it twice; and there can be no doubt that he himself perceived it.[69]

Callicles remains unconvinced by Socrates. Although Plato believed in an ultimate ground of philosophy and tried to provide it by means of transcendental arguments, he knows that the recognition of an argument is more than an intellectual act, especially when this recognition has consequences for the way one leads one's own life or for one's own self-respect, thus especially in the case of ethical theories. Even if there is a self-grounding of reason, we have to be willing to subject ourselves to it; and even if this will is not interesting from the point of view of justification, it is psychologically central. In Fichte's *Sonnenklarer Bericht*,

66. 470c7 f. 473a 3 corresponds to it.
67. 499c3 f.
68. Cf. *Grg.* 507c9 f. and e1.
69. In antiquity, a related argument is found in the work of Epictetus (2.20). However, Rousseau argues the opposite thesis, namely, that an immoralist must not feign, because he has to find allies (1999; 88).

the author wants to demonstrate a contradiction "to anyone who just has sound understanding, and the good will to be reasonable."[70] This goodwill is not always a given; for instance, Salomo and Coronaeus have the honesty to admit that they will not give up their religions under any circumstances;[71] thus we can hardly be surprised that the *Colloquium heptaplomeres* does not end with a consensus. Certain views are so related to identity that their refutation does not suffice; people will cling to them even if they are proven to be inconsistent, for instance, because they believe they have a duty to be faithful to the teachers who have conveyed these views to them. In this connection the well-known psychic mechanisms dealing with cognitive dissonances begin to operate. The causal explanation of a conviction contributes nothing to the analysis of its validity; but if a view is refuted, an explanation of how it came about, or even an understanding of the error as an obvious conclusion drawn from false premises, can be helpful in overcoming psychic resistance to accepting this refutation. The error is then no longer an isolated fact but is understood as part of one's self that one can grow out of. This is often easier than the demand for a break with one's own past, which has something violent about it.

Even if a fundamental will to be reasonable is present, emotions repeatedly play a disturbing role in conversations that is not easy to overcome. In the face of death, for example, fear is of course especially strong.[72] In their dialogues about death, both Plato and Gregory show how pupils must learn first to control their fear before they are capable of testing arguments.[73] Plato's subtle ability to hint at a connection between the conduct of a conversation and its subject manifests itself in the fact that not only does he give a literary representation of Socrates' control over his affects, but also his Socrates uses such control as an argument against the theory of the soul as an "attunement" of the body.[74] At the same time, Plato sees in the emotions not merely something that

70. 2.406.
71. (1857), 127 f., 158.
72. Aug. *Ord.* 1.11.32.
73. Cf. *Phd.* 77d5 ff., 83c5 ff., 84a2 ff.; Gregory, *De anima,* 12 A ff.
74. 94b ff.

endangers the work of the *logos;* I already discussed on several occasions his positive evaluation of eros and friendship as driving forces of conversation. Augustine seems not to be ashamed of his wrath against skepticism, which he accuses of having paralyzed humans' capacity for moral judgment.[75] The role of the emotions is particularly interesting in Anselm's *Cur deus homo.* Boso, who insists on reason, is driven into fear and despair in the course of the conversation,[76] in which the possibility of atonement for sins seems to recede ever further; only at the end does he break out in a jubilation that is so sweet because it is so reasonable.[77] By revealing the emotions to which Boso is subject in the course of the conversation, Anselm is able to integrate into his absolutely rationalistic theology elements of a theology that concentrates on human moods, such as has been developed by Kierkegaard, for example.[78]

The numerous myths in Plato's works, which appear especially at the end of a conversation, are an expression of his recognition of the necessity of appealing in a reasonable way to the nonrational as well.[79] In the Platonist Shaftesbury's *The Moralists,* Theocles rightly does not want to exploit the enthusiasm that he has aroused in Philocles: "I scorn to take the advantage of a warm fit and be beholden to temper or imagination for gaining me your assent. Therefore ere I go yet a step farther, I am resolved to enter again into cool reason with you."[80] But after he has developed his arguments, he responds to Philocles' request not only to convince him but also to confirm and strengthen him in his belief. In the process of argumentation, one may never yield to an inclination, but after the argument is concluded, one may strengthen the result and help reason with the heart. "It had been indeed shameful for you to have yielded without making good resistance. To help oneself to be convinced is to prevent reason, and bespeak error and delusion. But upon fair con-

75. *C. acad.* 3.15.34. In *Beat. vit.* 2.14, Trygetius acknowledges that his antipathy to the theory preceded his familiarity with the arguments directed against it.

76. 1.20 and 22.

77. 2.19.

78. Cf. B. Goebel and V. Hösle (2005).

79. For just this reason Plato rejects a sharp opposition between *mythos* and *logos* (*Grg.* 523a1 ff., 526d3, 527a5 ff.).

80. (1999), 107.

viction to give our heart up to the evident side, and reinforce the impression, this is to help reason heartily. And thus we may be said honestly to persuade oneself."[81] Similarly, at the beginning Boso criticizes Anselm's reasons of convenience as merely attractive, without solid truth; however, he recognizes that such reasons may be adduced as images of reality, as it were, so that the reality of truth shines forth more brightly—if in fact the truth has been discovered in an argumentatively rigorous way.[82] Boso praises Anselm's later arguments as images that are both reasonable and beautiful.[83]

It would be one-sided, however, to interpret beauty solely as a post facto embellishment of truth. Precisely when the concern is not a special technical problem, when instead a comprehensive change in perspective is to be introduced—at least a new research program, perhaps even a philosophical conversion such as Licentius, for instance, experiences[84]—an elenchus, or even a constructive argument, cannot suffice. A vision must be outlined that can necessarily be based only partly on arguments, because their concrete elaboration will be the work of a lifetime. That vision must possess what can be designated by no better name than the word *beauty*. It necessarily includes a reference to a principle of unity that is sensed behind a plurality, but is also concealed behind it, and can be brought to light only through a slow process of approximation. Only someone who already believes in it can work his way up to reason; and its credibility is increased by beauty. Reason rightly teaches Augustine that the three theological virtues, philosophical equivalents of faith, hope, and charity, are required. For knowledge is sought only by someone who already believes in its possibility.[85]

81. (1999), 138.
82. 1.4: "Monstranda ergo prius est veritatis soliditas rationabilis ...; deinde, ut ipsum quasi corpus veritatis plus niteat, istae convenientiae quasi picturae corporis sunt exponendae."
83. 2.8.
84. Cf. *Ord.* 1.8.23: "ita totus in quaedam magna et mira subuehor. Nonne hoc est uere in deum conuerti?"
85. *Soliloq.* 1.6.12.

CHAPTER 18

The Aesthetics of the Dialogue

One of the reasons research programs are persuasive, as I said, is that they are beautiful. Also, deliberately embellishing a philosophical dialogue by rhetorical and aesthetic means is not dishonorable; in fact it is an obligation if an effect is sought.[1] To be sure, rhetorical set pieces cannot replace arguments. That is one of the points of Plato's *Gorgias*. But we cannot accept the idea that it was not until the *Phaedrus* that Plato recognized the importance of a philosophically justified rhetoric and thus the artistic character of his own dialogues. The exceptional literary qualities of the *Gorgias* and the early dialogues, which could hardly have escaped so reflective a thinker as Plato,[2] already speak against such a view; and so does the fact that from the beginning—from the *Ion* onward—Plato's image of poetry is ambivalent, because he distinguishes different forms depending on the conversational context, and in all his criticisms of the deficient forms of poetry he is constantly aware of the possibility of a philosophically grounded poetry, or a poetically formed philosophy; indeed, as he well knows, this possibility is realized in his own work.[3] It cannot be an accident that "the sole legitimate way of communicating phi-

---

1. On the quasi-transcendental role of the rhetorical, see the fine book by P. L. Oesterreich (2003).
2. Cf. D. Roochnik (1995).
3. Cf. above, chap. 9, p. 164 ff.

losophy in writing that Plato allows and practices is poetry."[4] Moreover, in the *Gorgias* we already find enough passages that point to a rhetoric subordinated to philosophical ends.[5]

However, it is true that such a rhetoric first becomes an explicit theme in the *Phaedrus,* which is one of the most important texts of antiquity for literary studies and contains the main key to understanding the Platonic literary universe and its relation to Plato's oral teachings. Not only does Plato declare here that true rhetoric must be based on factual knowledge and familiarity with the addressee's soul, but he also clearly implies that even from a purely literary point of view his works are superior to those of his competitors. Of special importance for the history of aesthetics, but also for the hermeneutics of Plato's work, is the thesis set forth in connection with a criticism of the beginning of Lysias's erotological speech, to the effect that in a speech nothing must seem haphazard, but instead everything must be in its proper order; like an animal, a speech must have a head and feet, that is, a middle and extremities that are worked out in relation to each other and to the whole.[6] The comparison of the work of art to an organism—which reaches a certain high point in Kant's *Critique of Judgment,* where the faculty of aesthetic judgments is connected with the faculty of teleological judgments—probably begins with this passage in the *Phaedrus;* and it goes without saying that Plato thereby calls upon his reader to analyze the connection of the parts of his work with each other and with the whole. The text does not force the reader to extend this way of seeing things to the whole of Plato's work; but the additional allusions discussed in chapter 8 at least suggest that this should be done. But it is undeniable that Plato invites us to read each of his dialogues as an organic whole. There must be a connection between the themes of a dialogue; in chapter 14 (p. 299 f.) it was noted that the erotic and rhetoric, the two themes of the *Phaedrus,* are connected through the idea of a philosophical intersubjectivity that is constituted in the process of education. In the same chapter we saw

---

4. Gundert (1971), 5.

5. Cf. *Grg.* 480c, 502e, 504d5 f., 508c1–3, 517a5, 527c3 f.

6. 264b f.; cf. 268d3 ff. In *Pol.* 1284b7 ff., 1309b21 ff. Aristotle even compares constitutions with works of art.

that in Plato the relationship between the secondary actions in the prologue and the topic of the main conversation is no less tightly woven.[7] Finally, the connection between characters and ideas is, if possible, even more carefully worked out in Plato. The same goes for all aesthetically successful dialogues; organicity is a general aesthetic criterion.[8] The more comprehensive and polyphonous a dialogue is, the more difficult it becomes to make the connection between the various themes and characters clear; but the aesthetic achievement is all the greater when the writer succeeds in producing such a connection. Because of their numerous characters and their apparently disparate themes, the *Charmides* and the *Euthydemus* are among Plato's most perfect works from a literary point of view. Indeed, they are so perfect that one is sometimes astonished that a human being was able to compose them.

The architectonic principles of Plato's dialogues are many and diverse; and there are good reasons for thinking that some of them have not yet been discovered.[9] In a literary culture in which spacing and italicization were not possible and tables of contents and indexes did not exist, such architectonic ideas naturally played a more important role; but Plato's artistic nature made an outstanding aesthetic virtue out of a necessity. In a thinker who conceived the One as a mean between deficiency and excess, it is hardly surprising that the midpoint of a dialogue is an excellent place for central statements regarding the subject. I have already discussed the *Phaedo* in this respect (chap. 12, p. 247); other well-known examples occur in the *Euthydemus* (280b4–6) and the *Statesman* (284d1 f.).[10] In the *Theaetetus,* the excursus (173c–177c) on the true philosopher is also located almost exactly at the midpoint of the dialogue; but this excursus comes in the first of the three parts that discuss Thea - etetus's three serious attempts at definition, since these parts become shorter and shorter. Obviously these parts are an elaborate commentary,

---

7. What Bruno claims for his *Cena de le ceneri* is true of Plato's dialogues: "Non v'è parola ociosa" (1985; I 15).

8. Cf. the clever defense in M. Roche (2002), 29 ff.

9. For example, W. T. Schmid's analyses of the structure of the *Laches* are convincing, especially regarding the parallelism between the introduction and the philosophical part (1992; 38 ff.).

10. For details, see E. A. Wyller (1970), 62 ff., 82 ff., 119 ff.

referring only allusively to the *nous*,[11] on the four-part division of the cognitive faculties in the Allegory of the Line;[12] they become increasingly shorter because this corresponds to the ascent to the *nous* as the principle of unity. We owe Péter Várdy (2004; 292 n. 48) an important recent discovery: in terms of length, the third part (201c–210b) is related to the second (187b–201c) as the third and the second together are related to the first (151d–187b). This can hardly be an accident, and the impression becomes a certainty when Várdy notes that the twice expressed proportion in question is approximately that of the Golden Section. The proof of the theorems on this section in Euclid XIII 1 ff. probably goes back to Eudoxus, who was following a suggestion made by Plato;[13] the latter probably took a special interest in them because the diagonals of a regular pentagon divide each other into the Golden Ratio (Euclid XIII 8), and Hippasus of Metapontus's discovery of incommensurability by using the reciprocal substraction method *(antanairesis)* was probably carried out on the regular pentagon.[14] How could Plato better honor Theaetetus, the mathematician to whom we owe a comprehensive theory of irrationalities and the Platonic solids, which include the pentadodecahedron, than by adopting this structural principle? Nonetheless, one wonders how many people in the Academy perceived the tribute implicit in this structural principle—Theaetetus himself was already dead. But it would not have escaped Eudoxus. It is debated whether the Golden Section, which is repeatedly recognizable in Greek architecture—for example, in the Parthenon's facade—was intentionally produced or appeared by chance; but in the case of the founder of the Academy an accident in this matter can be excluded.

11. 202d ff.

12. Cf. V. Hösle (1984a), 397 ff. The proportion of the twice bisected line in *R.* 509d, a : b = c : d = (a + b) : (c : d) implies b = c; thus there are only three different lengths, but this is the only similarity with the structure of the *Theaetetus.* The Golden Section is only one of infinite ways to realize that proportion.

13. This is the most plausible interpretation of the passage Procl. *in Euc.* 67, 6 f. Friedlein.

14. See K. von Fritz (1971), 545–75. In Luc. *Laps.* 5, the pentagram is said to be the Pythagoreans' badge of recognition. I have shown that Plato alludes almost explicitly to the Golden Section, which structures also the *Phaedrus,* in a new essay (2008b).

I have just discussed the ascent to the principle of unity. In chapter 13 (p. 283) we saw how in the *Symposium* Plato placed the intellectual thematization of the movement of ascent in the last part of the Socrates-Diotima speech (209e ff.), which itself represents the keystone of a real ascent extending over six speeches. Complementing the movement of ascent is the movement of descent in the level of sophisms in the *Euthydemus*—the first sophisms refer to problems with philosophical content, but the last (303a6 ff.) is of an unsurpassable stupidity. Movements of both ascent and descent characterize the magnificent ring composition of the *Republic.* In chapter 12 (p. 248) I noted the casual use of this principle in the *Charmides,* and it is well known that it had structured the *Iliad,* the first large composition of the Western world, and it is also familiar from contemporary vase painting. But unlike the *Charmides,* the thematics of the *Republic* is structured in a circular composition: an ascent from individual ethics to epistemology and metaphysics takes place via poetry and politics; and on the basis of epistemology and metaphysics a further, intellectually deepened descent to politics, poetry, and ethics (and something like this also holds very approximately for the whole of Plato's work). The third of the three allegories found at the center of the *Republic,* the Allegory of the Cave, discusses precisely this movement upward out of the cave and down into it; the work's architectonic principle is thus represented in the work itself.

However, this does not take place directly. In fact, alongside orga - nicity Plato recognized indirectness of communication as the second essential mark of great art. In the *Lysis* (214d3 ff.) and the *Republic* (332b9 f.), Socrates says that poets speak in riddles and allusions—that is the meaning of *ainittontai.* In the nonauthentic *Alcibiades II,* this becomes a statement on essential properties of poetry: "All poetry has by nature an enigmatical character, and it is by no means everybody who can interpret it."[15] On the one hand, this may be applied to the Platonic dialogues themselves; on the other hand, it follows from this that Plato himself formulated indirectly his statements about the poetic character of his own work, including precisely those on the indirect communication

---

15. *estin te gar phusei poiētikē hē sumpasa ainigmatōdēs kai ou tou prostuchontos andros gnōrisai* (147b 9 f.). Translation from. B. Jowett.

employed in it. A well-known example is found in Alcibiades' speech in the *Symposium,* in the comparison of Socrates to a Silenus statue, which is ugly on the outside but conceals splendid divine images within. Certainly Albidiades intends, and Plato intends through him, to sing the praises of the historical Socrates, indeed, of the idea of the true philosopher. But Plato also believes he has done justice to this idea, and thus it would not be surprising if a few of his statements, for instance, those about Socrates' erotic behavior, also applied to Plato. But as we know, the dialogues never discuss the man Plato. But they do discuss his dialogues themselves. In any case, it is almost impossible not to connect the next-to-last paragraph of the speech, which seems to be added on to it—Alcibiades explains that he had earlier skipped over a point, and only now begins to speak about Socrates' speeches (221d7 ff.)—with Plato's dialogues, which represent these speeches.[16] These speeches—and accordingly, the reader is thus indirectly called upon to add, these dialogues—which often seem laughable at first, deal with beasts of burden, blacksmiths, cobblers, and tanners and seem to say the same thing through the same examples, so that an inexperienced person without understanding might easily ridicule them. But anyone who glances at them after having opened them and penetrates into them finds first that they alone of all the speeches have sense and then that they are divine, containing most images of virtue and extending to most, indeed all of what must be examined, by someone who wants to be good and beautiful. Plato can certainly claim to have sense, and his dialogues are characterized by a thematic universality even more than the speeches of the historical Socrates. In view of the reflexive meaning of the conclusion of the *Symposium* (223d), the dialogue-external interpretation of this passage is compelling: Plato invites his reader to read his dialogues on several levels, and thus engage in a reading that plumbs the depths to apply, for example, what is said about Socrates to Plato's dialogues themselves. This invitation is discreet and precisely indirect, as befits the nature of great and noble art.

But isn't it outlandish to say of Plato, the faithful pupil of Socrates, that he referred to himself through the master? No. This would have been unseemly only if it took place directly; indirectly, Plato does it all the

16. Cf., e.g., K. Gaiser (1984), 55 ff., esp. 70.

time. In chapter 8 (p. 157) we saw that in the *Phaedo* Plato has Socrates expressly deny that he has knowledge about natural philosophy; in the universe of Plato's dialogues, this knowledge is subsequently communicated by Timaeus, that is, by a Pythagorean. Plato was well aware of which elements in his philosophy were of Socratic, Eleatic, and Pythagorean origin, and in his late work he made this quite clear through his choice of the main conversation leaders. But it appears that he did so only in the late work, starting with the Eleatic dialogues, which push Socrates into the background for the first time. Certainly up to the *Republic,* Socrates is the dominant character; but the tension between the two functions of the Platonic Socrates—to be an ideal image of the philosopher and to refer to the historical figure of this name—repeatedly leads to slight contradictions in Plato's literary universe. Thus the previously discussed passages in the *Phaedo* show that already before the *Sophist* Plato had pointed to the limits of his Socrates. Another passage is found in Diotima's speech in *Symposium* 210a1 f., in which Diotima expresses her doubts as to whether Socrates will be able to ascend to the most perfect and highest mysteries, for the sake of which the erotic mysteries accessible to him took place. Concerning this, Stenzel rightly observes that "Diotima very clearly indicates the most that could be expected from Socrates' powers of understanding. She doubts whether Socrates could follow her to the last stage of the path to knowledge, to the vision of unified beauty in itself. In this reference to that which, by its form of representation, exceeds Socrates' powers of understanding we certainly find an allusion to Plato's real doctrine of the Ideas, and therefore hardly anyone will think to interpret the otherwise ubiquitous equation of Socrates and Plato as suggesting that this 'more' that is beyond Socrates conceals not the writer's true philosophical seriousness, but only poetic playfulness."[17] A related passage is *Euthydemus* 290e—where in my opinion Plato seeks to point out that the determination of the relationship between mathematics and dialectic, which the Allegory of the Divided Line in the *Republic* first hints at and which was explained only in the unwritten teachings, is not a Socratic but rather an original Platonic achievement.[18] D. Sedley has drawn attention to two similar passages in which

17. (1956), 34 f.
18. Cf. V. Hösle (2004b), 164 ff.

Plato discreetly draws attention to himself.[19] The effusive praise, which can hardly be justified dialogue-internally, that Socrates showers on Adimantus in *Republic* 427c6 f. and on Glaucon in *Republic* 580b8 ff. is formulated in both passages with reference to "the son of Ariston"; but this is Plato himself, Adimantus's and Glaucon's brother, and he has really constructed the ideal city and demonstrated the correlation between happiness and morality. The repeated use of the patronymic in similar contexts shows—just like the repetition of the Golden Section in the *Theaetetus*—that it must be intentional. Finally, in a brilliant article G.W. Most has proposed new and strong arguments for the position that the famous last words of the Platonic Socrates, that a cock is owed to Asclepius (*Phaedo* 118a7 f.), are related to the healing of Plato (the only sick person mentioned in the dialogue), which the dying Socrates perceives clairvoyantly; thus Plato is subtly and discreetly installed as Socrates' true heir.[20] In such passages Plato lifts his mask, as it were; in them we find a form of poetic *sphragis,* in which Plato allows himself to be recognized and abandons the anonymity behind which he likes to conceal himself.

Such dialogue-external references are so skillfully introduced that we can easily overlook them behind their dialogue-internal function— still more easily than we can overlook Michelangelo's portrayal of himself in the flayed skin displayed by Saint Bartholomew in *The Last Judgment.* One might even stubbornly refuse to recognize those references, and reject the corresponding interpretations as overinterpretations, perhaps with the argument that they are too modern and presuppose our familiarity with illusion-breaking theater in the mode of Brecht. But this argument is ridiculous on two grounds. First, it would only show that Plato was much more modern than we had previously thought; this

19. (1995), 4 f.

20. "In the end, Plato turns out not to be absent from Socrates' dying hours after all, but—by a typically Platonic irony—where he is named it is to assert his absence, and where he is present he is not named: in a buried *sphragis,* Plato's hidden signature silently names him as the author of the *Phaedo*" (Most [1993], 107). The only problem with Most's interpretation is that it does not solve the question what the historical Socrates may have intended by his last words, whose authenticity Most does not doubt. If one concedes that in the *Phaedo* Plato wanted to authorize himself as Socrates' heir, it is tempting to see in the passage 78a3–9 a hidden reference to himself. David O'Connor suggested to me that *plattonti Ap.* 17c5 and *platanon Phdr.* 229a8 may be allusions by paronomasia to the name of the real author of the two works.

holds for his artistic means no less than for his philosophy. And second, contemporary art was obviously familiar with the device of breaking illusions—consider the *parabasis* in Old Comedy. E. Heitsch has pointed out that the *pepaisthō metriōs*, "now there should have been enough play," at the end of the *Phaedrus* (278b7) repeats a classical concluding verse of comedy (e.g., Aristophanes, *Thesmophoriazusae*, 1227: *pepaistai metriōs*), by which the chorus takes leave of the audience, and rightly emphasized that Socrates' use of these words is really very strange.[21] Dialogue-internally, it has just been decided that written work is a play, conversation serious;[22] thus there has been enough play only if one adopts the dialogue-external perspective and reflects that the whole is a written work by Plato. By means of this illogical statement, Plato thus once again refers to himself as the creator of the whole.

The literary universe—this is the main thesis of this long and crucial part—is closed in on itself; it represents a possible world. And yet nothing prevents counterparts of objects in this world (or, depending on the theory, objects that have a transworld identity to them) from also existing in the real world, or, conversely, prevents the author of the work and his audience from having counterparts in that possible world. The work can refer to them either directly or indirectly; and to that extent it is, though a monad, at least not a windowless monad. The dialogue seeks to be read, and it can certainly encourage its reading by mentioning or at least anticipating the transformation of the conversation into a written form. In chapter 9 (p. 168) I discussed the repeated changes in medium described by the frame conversation between Eucleides and Terpsion in the *Theaetetus*. The conclusion of the *Phaedrus* has been so often interpreted that here I can limit myself to repeating the obvious point that in it Socrates, and through him Plato, discusses in paradigmatic form the relation between oral and written communication. In my opinion, there is no doubt that Plato's own dialogues are among the *suggrammata* criticized[23]—but there is also hardly any doubt

---

21. (1993), 213. Cf. 65, n. 72.
22. Cf. 276b5, d2, e5, 277e6, 278a5. However, in 265c8 f. spoken words are also treated as a joke.
23. Cf. Szlezák (1985), 376 ff.

that one of the reasons that Plato wrote dialogues is that they come closer to conversation than other literary genres. It is true that this is not said at the end of the *Phaedrus,* and in fact cannot be said dialogue-internally, because Socrates does not know of any dialogues; but it is simply natural to assume that it is so. Plato was, of course, aware of the exceptional literary achievement made by his dialogues. No esotericist should deny that. But neither should anti-esotericists deny that Plato quite clearly saw the center of his philosophical existence not in his written work but rather in personal conversations with his fellow philosophers, including the communication of the doctrines based on the two principles theory, which was reserved for these conversations. This may seem surprising, and we may wonder how such a conversation took place—presumably with an art that was still greater than that of the dialogues. But even if that sounds incredible, given the perfection of the dialogues, Plato is always good for surprises, and we have every reason to think that encountering the man personally was even more overwhelming than encountering his dialogues still is.

While the *Phaedrus* emphasizes the deficiency of the dialogue compared with conversation, several dialogues seek to thematize, within the conversation they represent, the transition from conversation to dialogue.[24] At the end of the *Tusculan Disputations,* Cicero announces that he believes that he will write down the conversation they have just had and send the transcript to Brutus.[25] At the end of *De libero arbitrio,* Antonius suggests to Valla that the conversation just concluded be written down, so that others can benefit from this good event,[26] and Valla agrees; like Cicero, he also announces that he will then have the dialogue sent

---

24. In chapter 2, I discussed Augustine's twenty allusions to the transcription of the Cassiciacum dialogues, not only in the prefaces to them, but in the body of the text as well (p. 26 ff.); and there too we distinguished the probable historical content of these statements from the fictionality of the corresponding passages in de Maistre's *Les soirées de Saint-Pétersbourg.* Anselm's statement at the end of the first book of *Cur deus homo* (1.25) to the effect that he will now pause in order to spare the reader excessive efforts is awkward because it is not reconciled with the conversation, and thus he steps outside his role. See above, chap. 13, n. 11.

25. 5.41.121.

26. (1987), 146: "Ceterum hanc disputationem quam inter nos habuimus nonne mandabis litteris, et in commentarium rediges? ut huius boni alios participes facias."

to the person to whom it is dedicated and who has already been mentioned in the preface.[27] On the other hand, in his *Ernst und Falk,* Lessing emphasized a deficiency of conversation as compared with the possibilities offered by written expression. "Everything that I tell you here only briefly and perhaps not with the appropriate precision, I take it upon myself to prove black on white the next time I am in the city with you, among my books," Falk says to Ernst in reference to his historical observations regarding the Freemasons, which, by the way, are not correct. Ernst becomes very curious and asks Falk whether he will soon have to go into the city; Falk's penultimate sentence sounds as un-Platonic as it could conceivably be: "Among my books you shall see and grasp."[28] The reference from the conversation to the dialogue is particularly subtle at the end of Valéry's *Eupalinos.* This is a dialogue of the dead, and the ontological status of the dead is, as we know, not easy to conceive. Do they develop? Or are they frozen fast in the decisions they once made? Do they perhaps exist only in the memory and imagination of the living, in the works of art dedicated to them? Socrate wants to change, but the shade of Phèdre, accustomed to routine, wants to remain true to the old Socrate. Fidelity, Socrate says, means following him even when he changes, and when Phèdre asks him whether he wants to take back for all eternity the words that made him immortal, he replies that down here his immortality exists only relative to mortals; but here—but there is no here— everything that they say is both a natural play of the silence of this Underworld and something imagined by a speaker in the other world who is using them as marionettes. "That is, strictly speaking, what immortality consists in,"[29] Phèdre replies at the end. The conversation partners recognize that they are only characters in a dialogue, and that means that they owe their being to the creative activity of a living person.

27. Cf. also the beginning and the end of F. De Sanctis's *Schopenhauer e Leopardi* (1986), 117, 160.
28. "Unter meinen Büchern sollst du sehen und greifen" (1966; II 717 ff.).
29. "C'est en quoi rigoureusement consiste l'immortalité" (1945; 106).

PART III

The Reception of
the Philosophical Dialogue

At the beginning of this book, a central distinction was drawn between conversation and dialogue. On the one hand, there is nothing to change in this. The representation—especially an artistic representation—of a conversation must not be confused with the conversation itself. Conversation is a dynamic, living process; the dialogue is a dead work of art. But one could just as well say that conversation is burdened with the contingencies of life; dialogue abstracts from them and puts the stamp of the eternal form of beauty on an event that would otherwise sink into the abyss of time. Conversation and dialogue are related to each other as life and the work of art; and it is well known that it is not easy to determine which is the more important. Alcidamas already compared written discourses with images of real bodies that are pleasant to look at but have no use for human life;[1] and the greatest philosophical artist that human-ity has seen or ever will see followed his example.[2] And yet this judgment is one-sided insofar as the work of art also remains part of the process of life and of reality. Art transcends reality by moving into an ideal dimen-sion; but human reality consists in large part of participating in this tran-scendence. Anyone who rejects this glimpse of transcendence as hostile to life poisons life, which is *human* life only insofar as it is spiritual life. But the spirit is openness to the ideal.

On the other hand, this means that dialogue itself remains embed-ded in the conversation that is human culture. Socrates and Phaedrus do not really speak in the Platonic dialogue, but through them Plato truly speaks to us, and he can speak to us because the historical Socrates ac-tually taught him. The history of the philosophical dialogue is a form of real conversation, even if it deviates from normal conversation in one re-spect: it lacks mutuality. In his dialogues, Cicero replies to what he thinks he has heard in Plato's dialogues, but Plato can no longer react to what he says. However, other people can take up Cicero's suggestions, and even the type of answer he makes to Plato; the conversation of tradition takes the form of a cascade. In view of the kind of questioning pursued in this book it seems natural to distinguish, within the reception history of the philosophical dialogue, between the effect that consists in creating a new philosophical dialogue and the effect that remains nondialogic in nature. The first form of reception is at the same time the production of a philo-sophical dialogue, and the second is, at least insofar as the philosophical dialogue is concerned, pure reception. .

---

1. *Sph.* 27 f.
2. *Phdr.* 275d ff

CHAPTER 19

Conversation between
Different Dialogic Universes

The subject of this chapter cannot be an analysis of all the references among particular philosophical dialogues. A complete analysis of this kind would coincide with a history of Western philosophy that would be selective but still thousands of pages long; further, several examples have already been given in the preceding chapters. Here I am concerned solely with a categorization of the possible relationships between different dialogic universes, and in fact only formal relationships.[1] The reader will hardly be surprised to learn that most of these references are to Plato: there is probably in no other genre such an unambiguous classic, and competing with him is no easy task. However fascinating reading Plato is, it nonetheless lays upon the intelligent reader the burden of realizing that there is not the slightest prospect of equaling the master, at least aesthetically.

An initial, natural division is based on whether the specific form of intertextuality taken by one philosophical dialogue's reference to

---

1. References to an author's own works were discussed in chapter 4 and will not be taken up again here. A systematization of various forms of intertextuality can be found in Hösle (2008c).

another is dialogue-internal or dialogue-external, that is, whether only the author is aware of it or the characters in the literary universe deliberately establish it. For example, it would be psychologically incredible to have a literary figure as hostile to authority as Nicholas of Cusa's "idiota" refer to literary models. In the following passage from his *Entretien d'un père avec ses enfants,* Diderot is clearly playing with Cephalus's departure to participate in the sacrifices at the beginning of Plato's *Republic* (331d7 ff.): "*Mon père haussa les épaules, et se retira pour quelques devoirs pieux qui lui restaient à remplir*" (My father shrugged and withdrew for some religious duties which remained for him to perform). Didier is obviously not thinking about Plato, whom he cannot have read; but Denis has read him, and he expects or at least hopes that the reader will recognize the allusion. Very similarly, the anti-intellectual Joseph in Schleiermacher's Christian symposium plays a role analogous to that of Plato's Alcibiades, that of the late-arriving guest;[2] but of course he is not aware of this; only the author of the text, who thus winks to the reader, knows it.

In contrast, Cicero's cultivated Roman senators draw plausibly on ancient models; in a beautiful countryside, for instance, Scaevola and Atticus expressly cite Plato's *Phaedrus.*[3] But in Cicero as well such a citation is not always comprehensible dialogue-internally; in such a case it may have another function.[4] No less learned than Cicero's statesmen are Eusebius and Charinus at the beginning of Leibniz's *Dialogus de arte computandi,* who cite the *Phaedo* and *Meno.* What the author intends by such a reference is not always immediately clear. Hume's Philo refers twice to Cicero's *De natura deorum;*[5] and since Hume's work corresponds both thematically and in the number of characters to Cicero's, it is natural to

---

2. Diderot (1972), 274. Schleiermacher (1869), 156. *Smp.* 223b corresponds in Schleiermacher to the "cheerful foray of some acquaintances" (lustige Streifpartie von einigen Bekannten [1869; 136]), which precedes, however, the actual speeches.

3. *De or.* 1.7. 28; *De leg.* 2.3.6.

4. Cf. *De rep.* 2.1.21 f.; and on it, Hösle (2004b), 156 ff.

5. (1947), 165 (with an explicit quotation from 1.8.19), and 168 (with a generic reference to Cicero; apparently the passage at 1.23 ff. 65 ff. is meant). Philo probably also took the anecdote about Simonides and Hiero (149) from *De natura deorum* (1.22.60).

pay attention to the analogies. In the personal dynamics of Hume's work, the negative theologian Demea corresponds to Cicero's Epicurean Velleius even if he thinks quite differently, but Balbus and Cleanthes or Cotta and Philo represent strikingly similar positions. Since in his function as a listener, Cicero at that time awarded the palm to Balbus, this might seem to suggest to Hume's readers that Hume analogously preferred Philo to Cleanthes; and we have already seen (p. 111 f.) that in the nineteenth century this suggestion was widely accepted. However, as an admirer of Cicero, Hume presumably understood the ambivalence of his text, which was discussed in chapter 7 (p. 143 f.); in fact, the preface to the work implies that the position of Cicero the author is close to Cotta's. However, Hume did not write a similar preface but instead had Pamphilus speak in a way that misleads the reader, precisely if he allows himself to be deceived by a superficial comparison with Cicero.

The extreme case of dialogue-internal reference is that of the commentary. In Ficino's *In convivium Platonis, de amore,* nine Platonists meet, at the invitation of Lorenzo de' Medici, on Plato's supposed birth and death day, November 7, 1475, at the country estate of Careggi, the seat of the so-called Academy, which was in reality not an institution but merely a loose group of friends.[6] The number of guests was chosen advisedly; it corresponds to that of the muses as well as to the square root of Plato's alleged life span of eighty-one. The guests are received in a princely fashion by Lorenzo's plenipotentiary, Francesco Bandini, and they dine together in the solemn awareness that they are resuming a tradition that existed from Plato's death to Plotinus and Porphyry but was interrupted twelve hundred years ago. After they have finished their meal, one of the guests, Bernardo Nuzzi, reads Plato's *Symposium* to the group; then he requests each of the others to comment on one of the seven speeches in the dialogue. Who comments on which speech is determined by lot; the author of the book, Marsilio, comes up empty, while Giovanni Cavalcanti must comment on three speeches, because Marsilio's father, a physician, and the bishop Antonio degli Agli are called away on urgent business.[7] Ficino is evidently basing himself on a historical event. In 1476

6. Cf. A. Chastel (1954), 7.
7. (1984), 10 ff.

an analogous banquet was held at Bandini's home in Florence; whether the custom was continued, we do not know. Ficino's text certainly does not represent the real speeches that were made on that occasion; instead, it merges these speeches with his own commentary, which was already prepared, "so as to compose a kind of collective manifesto of the new doctrine."[8] Commentary and dialogue are not genres that are easy to combine with each other; and the genesis of the work sheds light on its limited polyphony, which so strongly and so detrimentally distinguishes it from the famous Platonic model, as we saw in chapter 13 (p. 283).

In contrast, Paul Feyerabend's "First Dialogue on Knowledge," which represents a conversation in a seminar on Plato's *Theaetetus,* is polyphonous to the point of cacophony. I have noted the extreme heterogeneity of the participants in the conversation (p. 307 f.); it contrasts fundamentally with the cultural and social homogeneity of the participants in Ficino's symposium, who are all educated, upper-class male Italians with a predilection for Plato. No less marked is the opposition between the strict rituals of Ficino's academy and the arbitrary nature of forms in Feyerabend's seminar room. The beginning of the conversation—Cole is not able to make himself heard because of the loud sounds of machines outside the window, and they have to change classrooms—is an apt symbol of the difficulties of communication in a postmodern world that is the inevitable result of the technological reshaping of communication: people from all parts of the world come together, and it is not clear whether what will develop is merely background noise or an especially interesting form of global philosophizing. All kinds of questions are raised. The Chinese mathematics or physics student Lee Feng suddenly begins to talk about Einstein-Podolsky-Rosen correlations and the problem of measurement in quantum physics, taking *Theaetetus* 153d3 ff. as his point of departure.[9] Donald protests—what does that have to do with Plato? But the Korean, Charles, replies that that depends on how one wants to discuss a philosopher. Did they want to talk about his arguments in relation to the state of knowledge in his time, or did they want to analyze to what extent his ideas returned later on? Given recent argumentative weapons,

8. Chastel (1954), 11.
9. (1991), 28 ff.

positions that had been defeated could certainly be defended anew. The passage is hermeneutically interesting and shows that at least the later Feyerabend was not a radical historicist; he starts out, in the manner of the traditional history of philosophical problems, from questions that range over different periods and that explain why studying classical writers is so productive when we are trying to solve problems. In fact, it is misguided to try to understand Feyerabend's philosophy on the basis of *Against Method;* that book was a provocation, and Feyerabend reached the top of his form by using the dialogue, a genre that is congenial to him. In the "First Dialogue," cultural relativism is clearly rejected because of its negative moral and political consequences;[10] Plato's spirit and the spirit of his criticism of relativism transform Feyerabend's original insights into something consistent.

A classification of the references between dialogues that is uncorrelated to this one depends on whether the reference is positive or critical in nature. Of course, every intelligent reference is both: even someone who wants to criticize a philosophical dialogue considers it worthy of criticism, and thus in some way wants to be judged on the basis of his innovations with regard to it; and even someone who sees himself primarily as a successor at the same time claims to be innovating because otherwise he would limit himself to simply copying the work that is his model. And yet despite the existence of a wide spectrum the ideal-typical difference is obvious. In *De re publica* and *De legibus,* Cicero wants to compete with Plato's *Republic* and *Laws,* and on the basis of the Roman sense for practice, for history, and for legal institutions, even to surpass him, but Plato remains his model admired more than anything else— that divine man whom Cicero, moved by a certain admiration, perhaps praises more often than necessary.[11] In contrast, with his Salomo, Bodin considers the approach of Justin's interreligious dialogue fundamentally flawed; this was discussed earlier, in chapter 7 (p. 141). Indeed, he presumably also wants to distance himself from Nicholas of Cusa's *De pace*

10. (1991), 42.
11. *De leg.* 3.1.1: "divinum illum virum, quem quadam admiratione commotus saepius fortasse laudo quam necesse est." Cf. *Att.* 4.16.3, above, chap. 16, n. 129. "We both want to be Socratics and Platonists," Cicero writes to his son Marcus at the beginning of *De officiis* (1.1.2).

fidei, which could hardly have been unknown to him. Senamus's criticism of the circularity of Nicholas's justification of the Christian church[12] was directed against *De concordantia catholica,* I 2;[13] but it seems likely that Bodin was implying a similar accusation against *De pace fidei* as well. To be sure, we have already seen (p. 420 f.) that Nicholas of Cusa recognized in the striving for wisdom a ground common to all representatives of religions; but the heavenly topography that he thinks up, and especially the introduction of the Word of God and of Peter and Paul as leaders of the conversation destroy the neutrality of the place. Anyone who thinks through and feels the problem of circular foundation as Bodin did must be deeply annoyed by the framework of *De pace fidei;* and in fact instead of a consensus achieved under divine guidance he represents the untranscendable dissension of finite men with all their weaknesses, though he also represents their capacity for friendship with members of other religions. We see the difference between the dialogue-internal, that is, direct, criticism of Justin and the chiefly dialogue-external debate with *De pace fidei* reflected in the different arrangement of the dialogues. If a dialogue is set in the distant past or in foreign cultures, a dialogue-internal criticism of other dialogues can often not be *told* at all; instead, criticism must be *shown.* If dialogues of other Socratic thinkers were extant, we would probably see how in his own works Plato subjected them to criticism through particular deviations, even without naming them, a criticism all the subtler because not carried out explicitly, as in a treatise. Conversely, there is an explicit criticism of the theses and arguments of an author of dialogues that remains entirely within the limits of his categories, allegories, and formal means; we have already seen (p. 98) that this holds for Aeneas and Zacharias.

The criticism of a model may be unconscious, so to speak, but it may also be deliberate. In chapter 15 we saw how both Leibniz and Murdoch imitate the slave scene in the *Meno* and at the same time subtly transform it. There is no reason to assume that Leibniz deliberately intended to criticize Plato; but his Christian sensitivity made him instinc-

12. (1857), 131.
13. XIV 33. In an earlier study (2004c; 80 n. 53) I did not recognize the direct quotation.

tively avoid in his own presentation of Charinus's relation to the boy what was shocking in Plato's depiction of the scene. In contrast, Murdoch very consciously distinguishes herself from Plato. That is shown very clearly by the fact that although Plato is one of her conversation partners, both her dialogues are named after Acastos. Murdoch depicts her character Plato as ambivalent, and this mirrors her ambivalence toward the real Plato and his work, whose absolutism presumably seemed to her politically dangerous as well. Her Plato becomes almost frightening when at the end of the second dialogue he turns against Alcibiades, who conceives God as beyond good and evil: "That's a damned lie, the worst lie of all, Good must *never* make peace with evil, never, never! It must *kill* evil!"[14] Alcibiades says that Plato is bloodthirsty, with respect to others as well as himself: "Why be always tearing yourself to pieces?" Plato proves that Alcibiades' criticism is not wrong by physically attacking him; but naturally Alcibiades is stronger. Even Socrates slaps Plato, who repeats that he would like to kill Alcibiades' ideas.[15] Plato's fanaticism is not very attractive; but it is based in an existential seriousness that thirsts for the absolute and that Socrates seeks to calm in the manner of the later Wittgenstein: "Everything is in a way less deep and in a way deeper than you think."[16] But Acastos senses that Plato's dualistic resistance to reality is itself an attractive part of this reality, and therefore at the end he leaves the room with him in a friendly, affectionate way.

Between positive continuation and criticism we can locate what might be called further development. Methodius's *Symposion* remains philosophically within the horizon of the Platonic model, but its subject is transposed, as it were, into another key, since women speak instead of men, and the erotic ideal is replaced by an ideal of virginal life. The same goes for Gregory of Nyssa's *On the Soul and the Resurrection,* in which the Platonic model is partly imitated, partly modulated by the introduction of a female teacher as well as the defense of the Christian belief in the Resurrection. To continue with musical metaphors, we might speak of a reversal that loosely resembles a retrograde sequence

14. (1986), 116.
15. (1986), 117.
16. (1986), 119.

of notes, when the equivalent of a secondary role pushed aside at the beginning of a dialogue has the last word in a later dialogue. Didier Diderot, as discussed earlier (p. 358), has some characteristics of the aged Cephalus in the *Republic;* but unlike the latter, he remains the dominant figure right up to the end. It is true that he also leaves to go to evening prayers, but he returns in a good mood[17] and resumes control of the conversation, to which he finally puts an end, in full possession of the *patria potestas.* This reversal is especially amusing in an anti-Platonist with revolutionary tendencies. We can speak of an inversion when the ascending movement in the model dialogue is replaced by a descending movement. The model dialogue par excellence, because of its formal perfection, is probably Plato's *Symposium;* its influence is seen in Methodius, Ficino, Schleiermacher, and Kierkegaard. Whereas Ficino comments on it and Methodius and Schleiermacher transpose it into the Christian key—the church father into a sphere of feminine chastity, the most important Reformed theologian into the realm of intact family life—Kierkegaard offers a sarcastic satire on his model; through its depiction of decadent luxury his work is somehow related to the highlight of Petronius's *Satiricon,* the *Cena Trimalchionis,* even if only one of Kierkegaard's characters, the fashion designer, is truly vulgar, that is, thinks chiefly about money (because the reduction of questions of value to questions of price is the true shibboleth of vulgarity). It remains noteworthy that Kierkegaard achieves his satire precisely by remaining outwardly more faithful to his model than do Methodius and Schleiermacher; for whereas the latter introduced women, Kierkegaard's banquet is exclusively masculine, like Plato's (and Ficino's). Victor explicitly states, during a meeting at a confectioner's before the banquet proper, that women should never be present at a banquet, or at most in the Greek style, in the form of a chorus of dancers.[18] But for two reasons it is precisely the external similarity that creates an internal distance from Plato's work that we do not find in Methodius's and Schleiermacher's dialogues. In them, the introduction of women went hand in hand with the rejection of pre-Christian homo - eroticism. But if one continues this rejection and if the banquet consists

17. (1972), 277.
18. 7.26 f.

only of men, first, the object of love remains outside the community, and second, the romantic ideal of love, which is perceived as the sole alternative to cynicism and hedonism, largely excludes the beloved woman from the immediate horizon. Love can no longer be lived; the subject of the conversation and the conversational procedure are completely separated. I already discussed (p. 115 f.) how the literary form of *Stadier paa livets vei*, in which that of the anti-*Symposium* "In vino veritas" is embedded, is essentially antidialogic and thus anti-Platonic. We must add that in "In vino veritas" the triumph of subjectivity is already represented by the fact that it is an indirect dialogue, in which the narrator, William Afham, devotes a great deal of time to his subjective reflections at the beginning and at the end describes himself as "nothing" and thus causes himself and the participants in the symposium to disappear, as it were.[19] The point of what follows is to refer to the inversion of the sequence of speeches with respect to Plato's work.

As mentioned already several times, the first six speeches in Plato's *Symposium* present a movement of ascent—that is, in Plato's interpretation, with which someone who sees in the love of a person something higher than the love of a quality may disagree, and therefore prefer Aristophanes' speech to that of Diotima. With charming naïveté, in part by resorting to myths, Phaedrus praises Eros as a life-world power that leads us to sacrifice even our own lives. What is new in Pausanias's speech is that he introduces a normative difference, as it were, by distinguishing between the common and the heavenly Aphrodite. The crucial statement is that there is more than one kind of Eros.[20] This implies, though still in the language of myth, a distinction between appearance and Idea. A central metaphysical theory of Plato's—that virtue is a midpoint between extremes—is just as much indicated by the interpretation of the strict qualifications underlying Attic pederasty as a midpoint between the Boeotians' acceptance of all forms of pederasty and the Ionians' just as one-sided, fundamental rejection of it. Paradoxically, however, it is

---

19. 7.79 f. This suggests that the narrator is not truthful within the literary universe. "We must distinguish pretending to pretend from really pretending," writes Lewis (1983; 280), and Afham is an example of the first case.

20. 180c6 f.: *nun de ou gar estin heis.*

precisely the middle, preferred position, Eros for the sake of virtue,[21] that is complex, whereas the other two are simple—in this context *poikilos,* best rendered here as "complex," is, contrary to what is usual in Plato,[22] a positive predicate.[23] What is new in Eryximachus's speech? Here for the first time Eros is explicitly conceived as a cosmic phenomenon. The physician Eryximachus expressly agrees with Pausanias that Eros is two-fold in nature; but he stresses that it is not limited to humans alone but instead is at work in animals and plants, indeed, in all beings, so to speak: *hōs epos eipein en pasi tois ousi.*[24] Eryximachus takes pre-Socratic natural philosophy, especially Heraclitus, as his starting point[25]—as does Plato himself, who had overcome the sophistical and Socratic reduction of philosophy to ethics and politics by going back to the pre-Socratics, and who thought he had found in the doctrine of the two principles the foundation of a general ontology. Aristophanes' hiccups are responsible for the fact that, contrary to the seating arrangement, he speaks after Eryximachus, who is able to demonstrate his medical knowledge in a way that corresponds to his name, which Plato probably interpreted as mean-ing "hiccups-fighter."[26] On the one hand, this allows Aristophanes to make an important contribution to the theory of laughter by distinguish-ing between the witty *(geloion),* which is an intellectual achievement, and the ridiculous *(katagelaston).*[27] On the other hand, Plato probably wants to indicate that poetry can delve even deeper into the nature of love than can the observations of natural science. What is really interesting about the famous myth of the original wholes that were split in half by the gods when they became a danger to them, the two halves henceforth seeking one another in love, is the emergence of the categories of unity and duality, which are central for Plato, and which Eryximachus had still avoided in his interpretation of Heraclitus. Eros is the desire to make two into one.[28] Why is Agathon's verbiage an advance over Aristophanes?

21. 184c3 ff.
22. Contrast with *R.* 557c5, 6, 8, for instance.
23. *Smp.* 182a7 ff.
24. 186a6 f.
25. 187a3 ff.
26. 185c4 ff., 189a1 ff.
27. 189b4 ff.
28. 191c8 ff., d5, 192e1 ff., e8 f.

The second sentence in his speech indicates the progress it signifies: it praises the god Eros and not humans for what the god has given them.[29] It is just too bad that his eulogy is not correct, as Socrates shows by his questions.[30] As desire, Eros is not itself beautiful; instead it is a striving toward beauty and wisdom. Indeed, Diotima—introducing her allows Socrates to disguise his criticism of Agathon as self-criticism[31]—has taught Socrates that Eros is neither the striving toward another half nor a striving toward a whole, insofar as its goal is not something good:[32] ontological categories have to be interpreted ethically; the true One is the Good. Despite all his use of pre-Socratic speculation regarding the *arkhē*, Plato remains a Socratic, insofar as he conceives theoretical and practical philosophy together.

In Kierkegaard, in contrast, the speeches represent a deeper and deeper descent into a meaningless and immoral understanding of love. Although five, not seven, speeches are given, we know from his diaries that Kierkegaard originally planned to have seven participants in his banquet—including, however, the silent narrator.[33] They are old acquaintances from Kierkegaard's early works, who come together in the *Stadier* and achieve a kind of merger of literary universes that were once independent.[34] Victor Eremita is the editor of *Either/Or;* "Johannes med Tilnavn Forføreren" is the author of A's collected works, the famous "Diary of

---

29. 194e5 ff. This is expressly praised by Socrates, 199c3 ff.
30. 199c ff.
31. 201e3 ff.
32. 205e1 ff.
33. (1913), 286 (= Papirer B 172, 1).
34. Judge Vilhelm from the second part of *Enten-Eller* (Either/Or) appears in the second part of *Stadier;* Johannes de Silentio, the author of *Frygt og Baeven* (Fear and Trembling), probably corresponds to Frater Taciturnus in the third part of *Stadier*. "Thus only two characters are missing in *Stadier*, Johannes Climacus, the author of the *Philosophical Fragments,* and the A who is supposed to have written most of the first part of *Either/Or.* Kierkegaard saved Johannes Climacus . . . for his final philosophical work, the *Concluding Unscientific Postscript.* Thus only A from the first volume of *Either/Or* is really missing. Kierkegaard intended to have him appear as well at the banquet. The unhappy lover of memory who appears in the original draft is, of course, a condensation of this A" (E. Hirsch [1982; V]). According to Hirsch, "A" was omitted, among other reasons, because he would have become too similar to the Quidam in the passion story of the third part of *Stadier*.

a Seducer"; Constantin Constantius is the author of *Gjentagelsen* (Repetition). The unnamed young man in the latter work is its hero, in whom Constantin took in the earlier work an interest as a psychological voyeur; new, however, is the fashion designer ("Modehandeleren"), who remains anonymous as well, and who represents, in contrast to the idealized other figures, the banality of everyday life. Constantin, who organized the banquet in a hall in a forest near Copenhagen—as an aesthetically bracketed event; after it is concluded, the room will be destroyed by hired laborers[35]—explains at the outset that the speeches will begin only after the meal, and only when so much has been drunk that people will be in a condition to say many things that they would not otherwise wish to say—without the speech having to be interrupted by hiccups.[36] This is, of course, an allusion to Plato's *Symposium,* as is Johannes's remark that he never gets drunk but instead becomes increasingly sober the more he drinks. This last reminds us of Socrates, who at the end of the banquet remains sober, whereas Aristophanes and Agathon are nodding off.[37] But here, too, the contrast in the parallel is crucial: Socrates demonstrates the power of the philosophical *logos,* Johannes the seducer's cold-bloodedness. Victor's comment that experimental reflection that aims at intoxication is precisely an obstacle to getting drunk refers to Kierkegaard's basic insight that immediacy cannot be intentionally produced.

The young man whose purity of soul was initially praised[38] is the first to speak, around midnight, but he is no longer as beautiful as he was before the meal;[39] obviously the destruction of his noble naïveté is one of the results, and perhaps one of the goals, of the sumptuous banquet. His central statement is that he has never been in love, and even if unhappy love is the deepest kind of pain, he himself is perhaps still more unhappy because of his inability to love. This inability is, however, peculiar to him, because in the love that he has never experienced but on which he has reflected, he sees nothing but contradictions—between its ideal and its reality; one does not want to prattle like people in love who go on

35. 7.29 and 75.
36. 7.32.
37. 223d6 ff.
38. 7.24.
39. 7.32. After his speech is over, however, he is even more beautiful than before the meal (7.46)—just like Charmides, *Chrm.* 158c5 f.

about a beatitude that they do not really feel. To Constantin's objection that someone who has never had a love affair has no right to talk about the subject, the young man replies that precisely for this reason it can be said that he has a relationship to the whole (feminine) sex and not to an individual: "fordi han i sin Tanke kunde siges at forholde sig til hele Kjønnet, og ikke til de Enkelte."[40] No doubt this is also an ironic reversal of the Socratic ascent from the individual beloved to the Idea of the Good—in Kierkegaard as a thinker of individuality this "ascent" takes the form of a flight from concrete responsibility. The young man sees contradictions in love; that is why it is comic; and with this category as well an incidental theme of the *Symposium* is taken up, although in Plato it is not connected with Eros. Love is comic, the young man says, at least for a third party; and his problem is that in reflection he is always for himself a third party: "Derfor kan jeg ikke elske uden tillige i min Reflexion at være mig selv Trediemand."[41] He says explicitly that when love is connected with the Good one has moved beyond the sphere of the erotic; love for a person cannot be explained as love for the person's qualities; thus it is inexplicable and attacks its victims in an inexplicable way. The transformation of the mental into the bodily is also comic;[42] indeed, erotic pleasure is selfish, even if it is oriented toward another person, since in the loving union only one self is constituted.[43] But since the bourgeois already expects to constitute a whole himself before he begins to love, man and woman together are really one and a half beings: "han og Qvinden bliver halvanden."[44] But what is especially ridiculous— and here again the evaluation is opposite the one made by Diotima and Socrates[45]—is the triumph of the species that takes place in reproduction, which leads to a new existence, and not for the loves themselves. The debt of gratitude that one owes the progenitor cannot be paid off; and nothing is more dreadful than to be a father in such a way that the son cannot free himself from the father's nature—here, of course, Kierkegaard himself is speaking through the young man. From the former the latter

40. 7.34.
41. 7.35.
42. 7.39.
43. 7.42.
44. 7.43.
45. *Smp.* 207c ff.

also derives the crucial character trait that makes his thought everything for him; he cannot abandon it in order to attach himself to a wife.[46] Even a woman who followed his thoughts could not help him, because she would thereby be not lovable and would not understand him.

The young man has a grave dignity in that he does not know whether he should laugh, cry, or fall in love. This observation is made by Constantin, who in his own speech sheds any tragic undertone and recommends that women be subsumed under the category of fun. Man is absolute, whereas women's nature resides in relationship; between such different beings there can only be disparity, and that is precisely the fun of it.[47] Women talk and contradict themselves, they prattle; a man cannot really take them seriously, and the notion that Socrates, for instance, would become jealous because of Xanthippe is simply laughable. One can take women seriously only for the sake of fun; and a man will have the most fun when women try to emancipate themselves.[48] Victor Eremita adds the further criticism that women are content in their contradictions, because the gallantry of suitors conceives them under imaginary categories. To be sure, woman inspires man, who through her can become a hero or a poet—but solely a woman he does not get. Only a negative relation to a woman can be made infinite, and if she is even unfaithful to the man— it is well known that Kierkegaard saw Regine Olsen's engagement to Frederik Schlegel as a breach of faith, which hardly does him credit—she helps him achieve increased ideality. Marriage is even bizarre, since it has a little of everything; but seducing women or experimenting with them is also only a form of dependency on them.[49] The fashion designer knows women, whom he studies in a frenzied way, from their weak sides. Women are slaves to fashion, and thus a man who does not get involved with any woman is lucky.[50] The fashion designer's pleasure—which has nothing to do with his profits—consists in making women dependent on fashion, and thus, as he puts it, in using it to prostitute them, as they deserve.[51] Paradoxically, however, misogyny is carried to its furthest point by the

46. 7.45.
47. 7.47.
48. 7.53 f.
49. 7.61.
50. 7.65.
51. 7.67.

womanizer Johannes the Seducer, who recognizes only one categorical imperative: to enjoy. He wants to do that with the largest possible number of women, whom he regards as more perfect than men. Like Aristophanes, he, too, recites a myth. In the beginning, the gods created only the male, but when they felt threatened by him, they gave him woman, who was supposed to draw him into the vast detours of the finite world. This she succeeded very well in doing—except in the case of the eroticist. Whereas other men are captured by women, the eroticist only plays with them. Eroticists set very great store by women, and the latter sense this. Whereas an individual man corresponds to the idea of Man, the idea of Woman is not exhausted by any individual woman; therefore the eroticist wants to love as many women as possible. The idea of Woman is a workshop of possibility, and this fills the eroticist with enthusiasm. What is particularly desirable in woman is her naïveté and innocence, behind which her own desire is concealed in an enigmatic way. Woman is a fraud perpetrated by the gods; a sign of this is that she wants to be seduced, and the eroticist wants to seduce as many women as he can: "Som Qvinden er et Bedrag af Guderne, saa er dette det sande Udtryk, at hun vil forføres; og som Qvinden ikke er en Idee, saa er Sandheden heraf, at Erotikeren vil elske saa mange, som muligt."[52] With marriage, the gods triumph and humans become temporal. In seduction, however, both partners move into the extratemporal realm.

With this last idea, Kierkegaard turns against Plato in what is perhaps the most radical way. The escape from time is for the Christian thinker—as it was later for Hans Jonas, the most important ethicist among Heidegger's students—precisely irresponsibility; it is the acceptance of our temporality that constitutes the ethical stage. Judge Vilhelm, whom the participants in the symposium glimpse with his wife after they get up from the table, and whose manuscript "Some Reflections on Marriage to Answer Objections" (Adskilligt om Ægteskapet mod Insigelser) was purloined by Victor Eremita, from whom Afham then stole it,[53] points out in this text that true beauty is the one that develops for the husband's grateful glance only over the course of years.[54]

52. 7.73.
53. 7.79.
54. 7.120.

CHAPTER 20

Conversation between
Author and Reader

The reception of a philosophical dialogue that leads to the production of another philosophical dialogue is not the normal case. There are receptions that end without any further production of a work but may perhaps lead to a new culture of conversation,[1] and there are receptions at whose end stand works that are not philosophical dialogues—whether they are philosophical works in another genre, or interpretations of the history of philosophy, or something entirely different. The reception of a philosophical dialogue always begins with an interpretation, and we have already seen, in chapter 7, what has to be taken into account in reconstructing the *mens auctoris*. Part II attempted an approach to the literary universe of the dialogue, for only through this universe can the reader penetrate the author's intended meaning. However, in this process the reader necessarily encounters views that do *stem* from the author but *are not his* but rather those of his literary characters. The autonomy of the lit-

---

1. Consider G. Heckmann's theory, influenced by L. Nelson, of the Socratic conversation (1981), which cannot, however, be dealt with in this book devoted to dialogue. On this, see D. Horster (1994) and the essay collection edited by D. Birnbacher and D. Krohn (2002).

erary universe and its characters implies that these views can be understood independently of the value the author attached to them and that their truth value can be tested. A reader of the *Llibre del gentil e dels tres savis* may come to the conclusion that the Muslim's arguments are the best. That is not necessarily a false interpretation, if it is not accompanied by the assertion that it was Llull's own evaluation. An author may have demonstrated something different from what he intended to demonstrate; just as the famous golem may escape the control of his creator. Diderot's Rameau has his own life, quite independently of the not easily answered question of what Diderot the author (i.e., not Diderot Rameau's conversation partner) thought of him. The reader respects this independent life by thinking thoughts that may go beyond those of the author.

Any philosophical work may suggest things that the author himself was not thinking about but that follow, more or less, from what he said and meant. The progress of intellectual history is largely based on this mechanism: Berkeley had good reasons to believe that his own position followed from the premises of Malebranche's and Locke's positions—especially the assumption that we know only ideas—even though he was aware that neither of them would have shared his conclusions. However, what distinguishes the philosophical dialogue from other literary genres of philosophy is that the reader cannot avoid the impression that a critical effort is expressly expected from him, precisely because it is presented to him. "Whatever one makes of these common experiences, the fact remains that Plato's dialogues have some kind of intrinsic power to elicit the active involvement of an attentive reader. The reader engages in the flow of the developing argument, and learns more about its topic with each repeated engagement."[2] Thus one can argue that the elucidation of a philosophical dialogue that deliberately deviates from the *mens auctoris* and takes seriously the invitation to seek out the truth—even if this means breaking with the author—is more faithful to the author than an interpretation that seeks to reconstruct a *noēsis* instead of grasping *noēmata*. This kind of elucidation responds, as it were, to the author's

2. K. Sayre (1992), 239.

invitation to engage in conversation by carrying his reflection further, and transfers into reality the conversation that is played out in a fictional universe. The elucidator's readiness to take risks continues that of the literary figures who seek not only to understand one another but also to learn from one another. It is well known that the interpretations of Plato made by middle and neo-Platonism, and by the Christian Platonism of the Middle Ages and the Renaissance, quite often failed to grasp the true meaning of Plato's dialogues (even if less often and to a lesser extent than was thought before Plato's unwritten doctrines were rediscovered); but they would certainly have disturbed Plato less than the purely philological approach to his work that abstracts from the question of truth and wants to learn everything about him, but no longer from him. A mistaken interpretation that is philosophically productive is a more important achievement than a correct interpretation without philosophical ideas. Nonetheless, the magnificent example of Schleiermacher shows that precise philological interpretation is absolutely compatible with further philosophical development in the same spirit. But these remain two different tasks.

Deconstructionist hermeneutics has often crassly failed to meet philological standards, but it correctly points out the contradictions in most *interpretanda*—which certainly exist, because of human fallibility. In this sense the Hegel of *Vorlesungen über die Geschichte der Philosophie* (Lectures on the History of Philosophy) was the first deconstructionist— though a consistent deconstructionist only because he held fast to an absolute standpoint for himself. In philosophical dialogues two kinds of contradictions can be observed that are not found in other philosophical texts. First, there are contradictions between the various views held by the various characters. Such contradictions must, of course, be rigorously distinguished from contradictions in the author's position; A does not contradict himself when he claims that B and C contradict each other. Sometimes the author actually has a theory that makes it clear where truth lies; but it may also happen that he himself does not know exactly who is right. The charm of Diderot's *Entretiens* consists precisely in the fact that the author seems to have a subtler sense of the problem than the like-named participant in the conversation; in any case, the author shows problems in the position taken by the literary character that the latter himself seems not to perceive clearly. Indeed, it is not even obvious that Diderot the author really sees them clearly. To be sure, he represents them, but an artist can show more than he himself understands. This leads to the second point. Precisely because philosophical dialogues are works of art, it may happen that the author expresses, as an artist, ideas that he cannot think through as a philosopher. Plato is certainly one of the most reflexive thinkers of all time; yet he, too, sometimes depicts contexts that he was not able to conceptualize theoretically. No aspect of Plato's philosophy is more alien to us than the lack of a plausible theory of subjectivity; the last great renascence of his objective idealism, German idealism, is distinguished from Plato most essentially by its integration of the Cartesian discovery of the subject. And yet with his Socrates, Plato had presented a concrete subject who still remains the most impressive figure of an ideal philosopher; indeed, he thereby anticipated the insights of existentialism—that reduced form of Cartesianism stripped of all theological elements—in an astonishing way. Plato subordinated love for a person to love for an idea, but by having this idea expressed in an intersubjective context in the *Symposium,* whose grace still enchants us almost 2,400 years later, he provided a powerful incentive to seek an alternative theory of love and intersubjectivity. Plato doubtless considered the institution of slavery justified; but by showing that the slave in the *Meno* is capable of anamnesis, he unintentionally forces the reflective reader to ask why some people may be held as slaves, even if their intellectual gifts are not essentially different from those of free persons.

The fate of the philosophical dialogue and presumably also of a culture of philosophical conversation, without which that genre lacks a soil in which it can thrive, depends crucially on the following problem. We owe not only the abolition of slavery and the inclusion of sexual and cultural Others into philosophical conversation to the slow rise of ethical universalism; to the latter we also owe the preference for symmetrical conversation over asymmetrical conversation. This preference is so natural that it has repeatedly found expression in the history of the philosophical dialogue—think of Cicero after Plato, Bodin after Nicholas of Cusa, Diderot after Leibniz and Hume. A philosopher and interpreter as important as Gadamer errs when he misunderstands his own philosophical hermeneutics as Platonist, writing, for example, that "in emphasizing the hermeneutic phenomenon's relationship to the question, we can also appeal to Plato."[3] Gadamer is mistaken, because for Plato the question is a means to an answer, which is what really matters for him, even if he is all too aware that it becomes an answer for the *educandus* only when he has independently made it his own, that is, when he has appropriated it on the basis of the failure of alternative attempts of his own in the *elenchus*. But Gadamer's error is more than natural in a culture that is constitutionally incapable of coping with the ideas of such an enormously superior figure as the Platonic Socrates and therefore has to render him harmless by taking at face value his ironic statements about his own ignorance. As I have said, the effort to achieve equality is understandable and reasonable. But a successful conversation must be at least as much concerned with answering substantial questions, and if someone who makes a superior contribution to answering them meets with resentment instead of gratitude, there is something wrong with the conversation; indeed, even the correctness of philological interpretations is compromised when the Platonic Socrates is conceived as someone who is supposed to be as baffled as we ourselves and the hosts of present-day talk shows are. In a situation in which every claim to be in search of something that is more than mere opinion is taken primarily as an affront to equality and not as an ascent into an intellectual sphere that precisely ignores personal differences, philosophical conversation and philosophical dialogue do not have an easy time of it. Only in universalist cultures that provide a place for meritocratic elitism and in which selected individuals show mutual respect for each other by seeking to learn from one another can conversation that has substance bloom.

What must be done in such a situation? Writing dialogues is difficult,[4] but perhaps a contribution to the revival of this genre could be made by the form of reception that attempts to understand not only conversation within literary universes but also the conversation of tradition that takes place between these universes. Such an attempt has been presented here; and since it has interwoven the manifold historical voices

3. "So können wir uns auf Plato berufen, wenn wir auch für das hermeneutische Phänomen den Bezug auf die Frage in den Vordergrund stellen" (1960; 350).
4. See my attempts (2007) and (2009b).

that dialogues themselves represent, it has itself the characteristics of a historical dialogue, and because the selection has been made using aesthetic criteria, among others, perhaps it even has a few characteristics of a fictional dialogue.

If this inadequate attempt has sharpened our perception of the subtlety of the philosophical and artistic means that have been used in the history of the genre, and may encourage those making further attempts not to fall beneath their level, then it, too, may have a modest place in the great conversation of tradition that consists of dialogues. And if such a contribution can even motivate people to engage in real philosophical conversations, then its author may hope to have shown ways of becoming happy. Philosophizing in community, which connects the glimpses into the transcendence of the intellectual world with the experience of friendship, is the source of the most profound happiness. Augustine's young and graceful friend Licentius knew this: "Nam ne longius abeam, si nobis ipsis, ut heri licuit, cotidie uiuere liceret, nihil mihi occurrit, cur nos beatos appellare dubitaremus:"[5] "In order not to stray, if we were allowed to live each new day as we were allowed to live yesterday, I see no reason why we should hesitate to call ourselves happy."

5. *C. acad.* 1.4.11.

BIBLIOGRAPHY

Primary Literature (including Classical Secondary Literature)

I have not always cited the latest critical editions, preferring sometimes to stay with proven older editions. I quote Plato in Burnet's edition, but I have repeatedly consulted the more recent, not yet completed edition in the Oxford Classical Texts series. When I have referred to a passage but have not explicitly quoted it (e.g., from Xenophon), I have not always indicated the edition used.

Peter Abelard. 1971. *Ethics*. Ed. D. E. Luscombe. Oxford.
———. 2001. *Collationes*. Ed. and trans. J. Marenbon and G. Orlandi. Oxford.
Adelard of Bath. 1998. *Conversations with His Nephew*. Ed. and trans. C. Burnett. Cambridge.
Aeschinis Socratici reliquiae. 1911. Ed. H. Krauss. Leipzig.
Albinus. *Prologos*. Quoted according to B. Reis; see Secondary Literature, below.
B. Flacci Albini seu Alcuini. 1863. *Opera omnia*. Vol. 2. Acc. J.-P. Migne. Paris. (= *PL* 101.)
Ammonius in Aristotelis Categorias Commentarius. 1895. Ed. A. Busse. Berlin. (= *CAG* IV.)
Anonymi contra philosophos. 1975. Ed. D. Aschoff. Turnhout.
Anonymus dialogus cum Iudaeis saeculi ut videtur sexti. 1994. Ed. J. H. Declerck. Turnhout.
Anselm of Canterbury. 1963. *Pourquoi Dieu s'est fait homme (Cur deus homo)*. Latin text, ed. R. Roques. Paris.
Antiphontis orationes et fragmenta adiunctis Gorgiae Antisthenis Alcidamantis declamationibus. 1908. 2nd ed. Ed. F. Blass. Leipzig.
Aristotelis Topica et Sophistici Elenchi. 1958. Rec. W. D. Ross. Oxford.
Aristotelis Metaphysica. 1957. Rec. W. Jaeger. Oxford.
Aristotelis de arte poetica liber. 1965. Rec. R. Kassel. Oxford.
Aristotelis fragmenta selecta. 1955. Rec. W. D. Ross. Oxford.
Die Schule des Aristoteles. Texte und Kommentar. 1944–69. 10 vols. Ed. F. Wehrli. Basel.
Athenaei Navcratitae Dipnosophistarum libri XV. 1887–95. Rec. G. Kaibel. Stuttgart.

S. Aurelii Augustini Confessionum libri XIII. 1969. 2nd ed. Ed. M. Skutella. Stuttgart.

Aurelii Augustini Contra Academicos De beata vita De ordine De magistro De libero arbitrio. 1970. 2nd ed. Ed. W. M. Green and K.-D. Daur. Turnhout.

Sancti Aurelii Augustini Retractationum libri II. 1984. Ed. A. Mutzenbecher. Turnhout.

Sancti Aureli Augustini Opera, sect. I pars IV: Soliloquiorum libri duo. De inmortalitate animae. De quantitate animae. 1986. Rec. W. Hörmann. Vienna.

Bell, D. 2000. *East Meets West: Human Rights and Democracy in East Asia.* Princeton.

Berkeley, G. 1977. *The Principles of Human Knowledge: Three Dialogues between Hylas and Philonous.* Ed. G. J. Warnock. Glasgow.

Bodin, J. [1857] 1966. *Colloquium Heptaplomeres: Faksimile-Neudruck der Ausgabe von L. Noack.* Schwerin; Stuttgart–Bad Cannstatt.

Boethius. 2000. *De consolatione philosophiae. Opuscula theologica.* Ed. C. Moreschini. Munich and Leipzig.

Bruno, G. 1985. *Dialoghi italiani, nuovamente ristampati con note da G. Gentile.* 2 vols. 3rd ed. Ed. G. Aquilecchia. Florence.

Campanella, T. 1998. *La Città del Sole: Civitas solis.* Ed. T. Tornitore. Milan.

Castiglione, B. *Il Cortegiano.* 2 vols. Ed. A. Quondam. Milan.

M. Tulli Ciceronis Rhetorica. n.d. and 1903. 2 vols. Rec. A. S. Wilkins. Oxford.

M. Tullius Cicero. 1979. *De legibus.* 3rd ed. Ed. K. Ziegler, rev. W. Görler. Freiburg and Würzburg.

M. Tulli Ciceronis Hortensius. 1962. Ed. A. Grilli. Milan and Varese.

M. Tulli Ciceronis De finibus bonorum et malorum. 1998. Rec. L. D. Reynolds. Oxford.

M. Tulli Ciceronis De officiis. 1994. Rec. M. Winterbottom. Oxford.

M. Tulli Ciceronis scripta quae manserunt omnia. 1969. Fasc. 39: *De re publica.* Rec. K. Ziegler. Leipzig.

M. Tulli Ciceronis scripta quae manserunt omnia. 1922. Fasc. 42: *Academicorum reliquiae cum Lucullo.* Rec. O. Plasberg. Stuttgart.

M. Tulli Ciceronis scripta quae manserunt omnia. 1918. Fasc. 44: *Tusculanae disputationes.* Rec. M. Pohlenz. Stuttgart.

M. Tulli Ciceronis scripta quae manserunt omnia. 1961. Fasc. 45: *De natura deorum.* Post O. Plasberg, ed. W. Ax. Stuttgart.

M. Tulli Ciceronis scripta quae manserunt omnia. 1975. Fasc. 46: *De divinatione. De fato. Timaeus.* Ed. R. Giomini. Leipzig.

M. Tulli Ciceronis scripta quae manserunt omnia. 1917. Fasc. 47: *Cato Maior. Laelius.* Rec. K. Simbeck. *De gloria.* Rec. O. Plasberg. Leipzig.

M. Tulli Ciceronis Epistulae ad Atticum. 1987. 2 vols. Ed. D. R. Shackleton Bailey. Stuttgart.

M. Tulli Ciceronis Epistulae ad familiares. 1988. Ed. D. R. Shackleton Bailey. Stuttgart.

M. Tulli Ciceronis Epistulae ad Quintum fratrem. Epistulae ad M. Brutum. . . 1988. Ed. D. R. Shackleton Bailey. Stuttgart.

Clavier, P. 2002. *Dieu sans barbe.* Paris.

Démétrios. 1993. *Du style*. Ed. and trans. P. Chiron. Paris.

De Sanctis, F. 1986. *Scelta di scritti critici e ricordi*. Ed. G. Contini. Torino.

Œuvres de Descartes. 1897–1913. Rpt. 1964–74. 13 vols. Ed. C. Adam and P. Tannery. Paris.

Diderot, D. 1972. *Le neveu de Rameau et autres dialogues philosophiques*. Ed. J. Varloot. Paris.

———. 1994. *Paradoxe sur le comédien*. Paris.

———. 1955–70. *Correspondance*. 16 vols. Ed. and annot. G. Roth. Paris.

Diogenis Laertii vitae philosophorum. 1964. 2 vols. Rec. H. S. Long. Oxford.

Dionis Chrysostomi Orationes. 1919. Vol. 2. Ed. G. de Budé. Leipzig.

Libellus de sublimitate Dionysio Longino fere adscriptus. 1968. Rec. D. A. Russell. Oxford.

Eberhard of Ypres. *Dialogus Ratii et Everardi*. Cited according to N. M. Haring; see Secondary Literature, below.

Enea di Gaza [Aeneas of Gaza]. 1958. *Teofrasto*. Ed. M. E. Colonna. Naples.

Engel, P. 1997. *La dispute: Une introduction à la philosophie analytique*. Paris.

Epicteti dissertationes ab Arriano digestae. 1894. Rec. H. Schenkl. Leipzig.

Erasmus. 1972. *Opera omnia Desiderii Erasmi Roterodami, ordinis primi tomus tertius*. Amsterdam.

Feyerabend, P. K. 1991. *Three Dialogues on Knowledge*. Oxford and Cambridge.

Fichtes Werke. 1971. 11 vols. Ed. I. H. Fichte. Rpt. Berlin.

Ficino, M. 1984. *Über die Liebe oder Platons Gastmahl*. Ed. P. R. Blum. (German/Latin.) Hamburg.

Fielding, H. 1972. *Miscellanies by H. Fielding, Esq.* Vol. 1. Ed. H. K. Miller. Middletown, CT.

Fontenelle. 1955. *Entretiens sur la pluralité des mondes: Digression sur les anciens et les modernes*. Ed. R. Shackleton. Oxford.

———. 1971. *Nouveaux dialogues des morts*. Crit. ed. Ed. J. Dagen. Paris.

Foster, B. R. 1993. *Before the Muses: An Anthology of Akkadian Literature*. 2 vols. Bethesda, MD.

Frege, G. 1976. *Logische Untersuchungen*. 2nd ed. Ed. and introd. G. Patzig. Göttingen.

Gadamer, H.-G. 1960. *Wahrheit und Methode. Grundzüge einer philosophischen Hermeneutik*. Tübingen.

Gadamer, H.-G., and S. Vietta. 2002. *Im Gespräch*. Munich.

Galilei, G. 1998. *Dialogo sopra i due massimi sistemi del mondo tolemaico e copernicano*. I: *Testo*. Crit. ed. and comm. O. Besomi and M. Helbing. Padua.

Gide, A. 1935. *Œuvres complètes*. Vol. 9. Paris.

Goethes Werke. Hamburger Ausgabe in 14 Bänden. 1989. 11th ed. Ed. E. Trunz. Hamburg.

Grammatici Latini. 1857. Vol. 1. Rec. H. Keil. Leipzig.

S. P. N. Gregorii episcopi Nysseni opera quae reperiri potuerunt omnia. 1863. Vol. 3. Acc. J.-P. Migne. Paris (= *PG* 46.)

Hegel, G. W. F. 1969–71. *Werke in zwanzig Bänden*. Frankfurt.

Heidegger, M. 1995. *Feldweg-Gespräche (1944/45)*. Frankfurt.

Heisenberg, W. 1969. *Der Teil und das Ganze. Gespräche im Umkreis der Atom-physik.* Munich.

Hermogenis Opera. 1913. Ed. H. Rabe. Leipzig.

Hobbes, T. 1990. *Behemoth or the Long Parliament.* Ed. F. Tönnies. Chicago.

Home, H., Lord Kames. 1851. *Elements of Criticism.* New York.

Hume, D. 1947. *Dialogues Concerning Natural Religion.* Indianapolis.

———. 1987. *Essays Moral, Political, and Literary.* Ed. E. F. Miller. Indianapolis.

———. 1932. *The Letters of D. Hume.* 2 vols. Ed. J. Y. T. Greig. Oxford.

Hut, P., and B. van Fraassen. 1997. "Elements of Reality: A Dialogue." *Journal of Consciousness Studies* 4 (2): 167–80.

Isidori Hispalensis episcopi Etymologiarum sive Originum libri XX. 1911. 2 vols. Rec. W. M. Lindsay. Oxford.

Iustini philosophi et martyris opera quae feruntur omnia. Rec. I. C. T. eques de Otto, tomi I. pars I., 3rd ed. 1876, pars II., 3rd ed. 1877. Rpt. Wiesbaden, 1969.

Ja'far b. Mansur al-Yaman. 2001. *Kitab al-'Alim wa'l-ghulam.* Arabic ed. and English trans. J. W. Morris. London.

Kant, I. 1976–77. *Werkausgabe.* 12 vols. Ed. W. Weischedel. Frankfurt.

Kierkegaard, S. 1991. *Samlede Værker.* Vols. 7 and 8: *Stadier paa Livets Vei.* Copenhagen.

———. [1913] 1968. *Søren Kierkegaards Papirer.* Vol. 5. Ed. P. A. Heiberg and V. Kuhr. Rpt. Copenhagen.

Kṛṣṇa Miśra. 1971. *Prabodhacandrodaya* (Sanskrit text with English translation). S. K. Nambiar. Delhi, Patna, and Varanasi.

Lakatos, I. 1976. *Proofs and Refutations: The Logic of Mathematical Discovery.* Ed. J. Worrall and E. Zahar. Cambridge.

Leibniz, G. W. 1976. *Ein Dialog zur Einführung in die Arithmetik und Algebra.* Ed. E. Knobloch. Stuttgart–Bad Cannstatt.

———. 1999. *Sämtliche Schriften und Briefe.* Ed. Berlin-Brandenburgische Akademie der Wissenschaften und Akademie der Wissenschaften in Göttingen. 6th ser., vol. 4 of *Philosophische Schriften.* Berlin.

Leopardi, G. 1956. *Opere.* Vol. 1. Ed. S. Solmi. Milan and Naples.

Lessing, G. E. 1966. *Gesammelte Werke in zwei Bänden.* 2 vols. Gütersloh.

Lewis, D. 1983. *Philosophical Papers.* Vol. 1. New York and Oxford.

Llull, R. 1993. *Llibre del gentil e dels tres savis.* Ed. A. Bonner. Palma de Mallorca.

———. 1998. *Lo desconhort/Der Desconhort.* Ed and trans. J. Hösle and V. Hösle. Munich.

Raimundi Lulli Opera Latina. 1975. Vol. VII: 168–77. Ed. H. Harada. Turnhout. (= *ROL* VII.)

Raimundi Lulli Opera Latina. 1988. Vol. XVI: 190–200. Ed. A. Oliver, M. Senellart, and F. Domínguez-Reboiras. Turnhout. (= *ROL* XVI.)

Raimundi Lulli Opera Latina. 1989. Vol. XVII: 76–81. Ed. M. Pereira and T. Pindl-Büchel. Turnhout. (= *ROL* XVII.)

Luciani Samosatensis Opera. 1896– . 4 vols. Rec. C. Iacobitz. Leipzig.

T. Lucreti Cari de rerum natura libri sex. 1953. Rec. J. Martin. Leipzig.

Ambrosii Theodosii Macrobii Saturnalia. 1963. Instr. I. Willis. Leipzig.

Maistre, J.-M. de. 1850. *Les soirées de Saint-Pétersbourg.* 2 vols. Paris.

Malebranche. 1958– . *Œuvres complètes.* Vol. XV: *Entretien d'un philosophe chrétien et d'un philosophe chinois.* Paris.

——. 1965. *Œuvres complètes.* Vol. XII: *Entretiens sur la métaphysique et sur la religion.* Vol. XIII: *Entretiens sur la mort.* Paris.

Maximus Tyrius Dissertationes. 1994. Ed. M. B. Trapp. Stuttgart and Leipzig.

Melville, H. 1986. *Billy Budd, Sailor, and Other Stories.* New York.

Methodius of Olympus. 1963. *Méthode d'Olympe: Le Banquet.* Introd. and crit. ed. H. Musurillo. Trans. and notes V.-H. Debidour. Paris.

The Milindapañho, the Pali Text. [1880] 1962. Ed. V. Trenckner. London.

M. Minuci Felicis. *Octavius.* Ed. B. Kytzler. Leipzig.

Murdoch, I. 1986. *Acastos: Two Platonic Dialogues.* New York.

Nicolai de Cusa Opera omnia. 1959. Vol. IV: *Opuscula I,* ed. P. Wilpert. Hamburg.

Nicolai de Cusa Opera omnia. 1937. <Vol. V>: *Idiota de sapientia de mente de staticis experimentis,* ed. L. Baur. Leipzig.

Nicolai de Cusa Opera omnia. 1959. Vol. VII: *De pace fidei cum epistula ad Ioannem de Segobia,* ed. R. Klibansky and H. Bascour. Hamburg.

Nicolai de Cusa Opera omnia. 1998. Vol. IX: *Dialogus de ludo globi,* ed. I. G. Senger. Hamburg.

Nicolai de Cusa Opera omnia. 1973. Vol. XI 2: *Trialogus de possest,* ed. R. Steiger. Hamburg.

Nicolai de Cusa Opera omnia. 1982. Vol. XII: *De venatione sapientiae. De apice theoriae,* ed. R. Klibansky and I. G. Senger. Hamburg.

Nicolai de Cusa Opera omnia. 1944. <Vol. XIII>: *Directio speculantis seu de non aliud,* ed. L. Baur and P. Wilpert. Leipzig.

Nicolai de Cusa Opera omnia. 1963. Vol. XIV: *De concordantia catholica libri tres,* ed. G. Kallen. Hamburg.

Nietzsche, F. 1988. *Kritische Studienausgabe in 15 Einzelbänden.* 2nd ed. Ed. G. Colli and M. Montinari. Munich.

Entretien d'Origène avec Héraclide. 1960. Introd., text, trans., and notes J. Scherer. Paris.

The Oxyrhynchus Papyri. 1912. Part IX. London.

The Oxyrhynchus Papyri. 1977. Part XLV. London.

Perry, J. 1978. *A Dialogue on Personal Identity and Immortality.* Indianapolis.

Petrarca, F. 1955. *Prose.* Ed. G. Martellotti, P. G. Ricci, E. Carrara, and E. Bianchi. Milan and Naples.

Petri Alphonsi ex Judaeo christiani dialogi. 1898. In *Goffridi Abbatis Vindocinensis opera omnia,* 535–671, acc. J.-P. Migne. Paris. (= *PL* 157.)

Poetarum philosophorum fragmenta. 1901. Ed. H. Diels. Berlin.

Platonis Opera. 1900–1907. 5 vols. Rec. I. Burnet. Oxford.

Platonis Opera. 1995. Vol. I. Rec. E. A. Duke et al. Oxford.

Plutarchi Moralia. 1938. Vol. IV. Rec. C. Hubert. Leipzig.

Popper, K., and J. C. Eccles. 1977. *The Self and Its Brain.* New York.

Procli Diadochi in Platonis Cratylum Commentaria. 1908. Ed. G. Pasquali. Leipzig.

Procli Diadochi in Platonis rem publicam commentarii. 1899–1901. 2 vols. Ed. G. Kroll. Leipzig.

Procli Philosophi Platonici Opera Inedita. 1864. Ed. V. Cousin. Paris.

Prolégomènes à la philosophie de Platon. 1990. Ed. L. G. Westerink, trans. J. Trouillard. Paris.

Purtill, R. L. 1975. *Philosophically Speaking.* Englewood Cliffs, NJ.

Rosenberg, J. F. 2000. *Three Conversations about Knowing.* Indianapolis.

Rousseau, J.-J. 1999. *Dialogues de Rousseau juge de Jean-Jacques suivis de Le Lévite d'Éphraïm.* Ed. É. Leborgne. Paris.

Tyrannii Rufini Opera. 1961. Rec. M. Simonetti. Turnhout.

Schelling, F. W. J. 1976. *Schriften von 1801–1804.* Darmstadt.

Schlegel, F. 1967. *Charakteristiken und Kritiken I (1796–1801).* Ed. H. Eichner. Munich.

Schleiermacher, F. 1869. *Monologen. Eine Neujahrsgabe. Die Weihnachtsfeier. Ein Gespräch.* Ed. C. Schwarz. Leipzig.

———. 1988. *Dialektik (1814/15). Einleitung zur Dialektik (1833).* Ed. A. Arndt. Hamburg.

———. 1996. *Über die Philosophie Platons.* Ed. T. Steiner. Hamburg.

Schopenhauer, A. 1977. *Zürcher Ausgabe. Werke in zehn Bänden.* Zürich.

Scruton, R. 1993. *Xanthippic Dialogues.* London.

Shaftesbury, Earl of. 1999. *Characteristics of Men, Manners, Opinions, Times, etc.* Vol. II. Bristol.

Shelley, P. B. 1977. *Shelley's Poetry and Prose.* Ed. D. H. Reiman. New York.

Sigonio, C. 1993. *Del dialogo.* Ed. F. Pignatti. Rome.

Sillographorum graecorum reliquiae. 1885. Rec. C. Wachsmuth. Leipzig.

Socraticorum Reliquiae. 1983–85. 4 vols. Ed. G. Giannantoni. Rome.

Solger, K. W. F. 1971. *Erwin. Vier Gespräche über das Schöne und die Kunst.* Munich.

———. 1972. *Philosophische Gespräche. Erste Sammlung.* Darmstadt.

Speroni, S. 1989. *Opere.* Introd. M. Pozzi. Rome.

Spinoza, B. 1925. *Opera.* 4 vols. Ed. C. Gebhardt. Heidelberg.

Stein, E. 1993. *Werke.* Vol. XV: *Erkenntnis und Glaube.* Freiburg.

P. Cornelii Taciti libri qui supersunt: Germania. Agricola. Dialogus de oratoribus. 1962. Ed. E. Koestermann. Leipzig.

Tasso, T. 1586. *Discorso dell'arte del dialogo.* Rpt. in T. Tasso, *Prose,* ed. E. Mazzali, 331–46. Milan and Naples, 1959.

Tóth, I. 2000. *Palimpseste: Propos avant un triangle.* Paris.

Tugendhat, E. 1997. *Dialog in Leticia.* Frankfurt.

Valéry, P. 1945. *Eupalinos: L'Âme et la Danse. Dialogue de l'Arbre.* Paris.

Valla, L. 1987. *Über den freien Willen. De libero arbitrio.* Ed. E. Keßler. Munich.

Victoria, F. de. 1917. *De Indis et de iure belli relectiones.* Ed. E. Nys. Washington, DC.

Voltaire. n.d. *Dialogues et anecdotes philosophiques.* Ed. R. Naves. Paris.

Die Fragmente der Vorsokratiker, Griechisch und Deutsch von H. Diels. 1954. 3 vols. 7th ed. Ed. W. Kranz. (= DK.)

Weizsäcker, C. F. von. 1981. *Ein Blick auf Platon. Ideenlehre, Logik und Physik.* Stuttgart.

Wetzel, M. 2001, 2005. *Prinzip Subjektivität. Allgemeine Theorie.* 2 vols. Würzburg.

Wieland, C. M. 1970. *Aufsätze zu Literatur und Politik.* Ed. D. Lohmeier. Reinbek.

Wilde, O. 1966. *Complete Works.* Introd. V. Holland. London.
Wittgenstein, L. 1980. *Schriften 1. Tractatus logico-philosophicus; Tagebücher 1914–1916; Philosophische Untersuchungen.* 4th ed. Frankfurt.
Zacharias Scolastico. 1973. *Ammonio.* Ed. M. Minniti Colonna. Naples.

Secondary Literature

Albrecht, R. 1986. *Das Leben der Heiligen Macrina.* Göttingen.
Alster, B. 1990. "Sumerian Literary Dialogues and Debates and Their Place in Ancient Near Eastern Literature." In *Living Waters,* ed. E. Keck, S. Søndergaard, and E. Wulff, 1–16. Copenhagen.
Auerbach, E. 1946. *Mimesis. Dargestellte Wirklichkeit in der abendländischen Literatur.* Bern.
Barnes, J. 1987. "Plato." In *The New Encyclopædia Britannica,* 15th ed., vol. 25, 880–87. Chicago.
De Bary, W. T., W. Chan, and B. Watson, comps. 1960. *Sources of Chinese Tradition.* New York.
Bernays, J. 1863. *Die Dialoge des Aristoteles in ihrem Verhältnis zu seinen übrigen Werken.* Berlin; rpt. Darmstadt 1968.
Birnbacher, D., and D. Krohn, eds. 2002. *Das sokratische Gespräch.* Stuttgart.
Booth, W. C. 1983. *The Rhetoric of Fiction.* 2nd ed. Chicago.
———. 1988. *The Company We Keep: An Ethics of Fiction.* Berkeley.
Brandom, R. 1994. *Making It Explicit.* Cambridge, MA.
Brown, P. 1969. *Augustine of Hippo: A Biography.* Berkeley.
Burger, R. 1984. *The Phaedo: A Platonic Labyrinth.* New Haven.
Burton, J. H. 1846. *Life and Correspondence of David Hume.* 2 vols. Edinburgh; rpt. New York, 1983.
Büttner, S. 2000. *Die Literaturtheorie bei Platon und ihre anthropologische Begründung.* Tübingen and Basel.
Calogero, G. 1960. *Platone, Il Critone.* 3rd ed. Introd. and comm. G. Calogero. Florence.
Casale, R. 2005. "Erziehung vor der Moralerziehung: Konversation versus Kom - munikation." In *Pädagogik und Ethik,* ed. D. Horster and J. Oelkers, 25–48. Wiesbaden.
Chastel, A. 1954. *Marsile Ficin et l'art.* Geneva.
Cox, V. 1992. *The Renaissance Dialogue: Literary Dialogue in Its Social and Political Contexts, Castiglione to Galileo.* Cambridge.
Curtius, E. R. 1961. *Europäische Literatur und lateinisches Mittelalter.* 3rd ed. Bern and Munich.
Dambre, M., and M. Gosselin-Noat, eds. 2001. *L'Éclatement des genres au XXe siècle.* Paris.
Damschen, G. 1999. "Das Prinzip des performativen Widerspruchs. Zur epistemologischen Bedeutung der Dialogform in Platons Euthydemos." *Methexis* 12: 89–101.
Dancy, J. 1995. "'For Here the Author Is Annihilated': Reflections on Philosophical Aspects of the Use of the Dialogue Form in Hume's *Dialogues*

Concerning Natural Religion." In *Philosophical Dialogues: Plato, Hume, Wittgenstein,* ed. T. Smiley, 63–83. Oxford. (= *Proceedings of the British Academy* 85.)

Dittmar, H. 1911. *De Aspasia Aeschinis Socratici dialogo. Quaestionum Aeschinearum Specimen.* Göttingen.

Dodds, E. R. 1959. *Plato, Gorgias: A Revised Text with Introduction and Commentary by E. R. Dodds.* Oxford.

Donohue, J. J. 1943. *The Theory of Literary Kinds: Ancient Classifications of Literature.* Dubuque, IA.

Döring, K. 2006. *Die Kyniker.* Bamberg.

Dover, K. J. 1989. *Greek Homosexuality.* Cambridge, MA.

Edelstein, L. 1962. "Platonic Anonymity." *American Journal of Philology* 83: 1–22.

Ehlers, B. 1966. *Eine vorplatonische Deutung des Sokratischen Eros. Der Dialog Aspasia des Sokratikers Aeschines.* Munich.

Else, G. F. 1986. *Plato and Aristotle on Poetry.* Ed. P. Burian. Chapel Hill.

Erler, M. 1987. *Der Sinn der Aporien in den Dialogen Platons.* Berlin.

Forno, C. 1992. *Il «libro animato»: Teoria e scrittura del dialogo nel Cinquecento.* Turin.

Forst, R. 2003. *Toleranz im Konflikt. Geschichte, Gehalt und Gegenwart eines umstrittenen Begriffs.* Frankfurt.

Forster, E. M. 1974. *Aspects of the Novel and Related Writings.* London.

Fowler, A. 1982. *Kinds of Literature: An Introduction to the Theory of Genres and Modes.* Cambridge, MA.

Frede, M. 1992. "Plato's Arguments and the Dialogue Form." *Oxford Studies in Ancient Philosophy,* suppl., vol. 1992: *Methods of Interpreting Plato and His Dialogues,* ed. J. C. Klagge and N. D. Smith, 201–19. Oxford.

Friedlander, E. 2004. *J.-J. Rousseau: An Afterlife of Words.* Cambridge, MA.

Friedländer, P. 1964. *Platon.* 3rd ed. 3 vols. Berlin.

Friedlein, R. 2004. *Der Dialog bei Ramon Llull. Literarische Gestaltung als apologetische Strategie.* Tübingen.

Fries, C. 1933. "Zur Vorgeschichte der platonischen Dialogform." *Rheinisches Museum für Philologie* 82: 145–61.

Fries, T. 1993. *Dialog der Aufklärung. Shaftesbury, Rousseau, Solger.* Tübingen and Basel.

von Fritz, K. 1971. *Grundprobleme der Geschichte der antiken Wissenschaft.* Berlin.

Furbank, P. N. 1992. *Diderot: A Critical Biography.* New York.

Gabriel, G. 1975. *Fiktion und Wahrheit. Eine semantische Theorie der Literatur.* Stuttgart–Bad Cannstatt.

———. 1997. *Logik und Rhetorik der Erkenntnis. Zum Verhältnis von wissenschaftlicher und ästhetischer Weltauffassung.* Paderborn.

Gaiser, K. 1963. *Platons ungeschriebene Lehre.* Stuttgart.

———. 1964. "Platons *Menon* und die Akademie." *Archiv für Geschichte der Philosophie* 46: 241–92.

———. 1984. *Platone come scrittore filosofico: saggi sull'ermeneutica dei dialoghi platonici.* Naples.

———. 1985. "Ein Gespräch mit König Philipp. Zum 'Eudemos' des Aristoteles." In *Aristoteles. Werk und Wirkung,* I: 457–84. Ed. J. Wiesner. Berlin.

472   Bibliography

———. 1987. *Aristoteles. Werk und Wirkung.* Vol. II. Ed. J. Wiesner. Berlin

———. 1988. *Philodems Academica. Die Berichte über Platon und die Alte Akademie in zwei herkulanensischen Papyri.* Stuttgart–Bad Cannstatt.

Gale, M. R. 2001. *Lucretius and the Didactic Epic.* Bristol.

Galle, R. 1980. "Diderot—oder die Dialogisierung der Aufklärung." In *Europäische Aufklärung III,* ed. J. von Stackelberg, 209–47. Wiesbaden.

Gaukroger, S. 1995. *Descartes: An Intellectual Biography.* Oxford.

Geiger, R. 2006. *Dialektische Tugenden. Untersuchungen zur Gesprächsform in den Platonischen Dialogen.* Paderborn.

Gigon, O. 1947. *Sokrates. Sein Bild in Dichtung und Geschichte.* Bern.

Gilman, D. 1993. "Theories of Dialogue." In *The Dialogue in Early Modern France, 1547–1630: Art and Argument,* ed. with prologue C. H. Winn, 5–76. Washington, DC.

Goebel, B., and V. Hösle. 2005. "Reasons, Emotions and God's Presence in Anselm of Canterbury's Dialogue *Cur deus homo.*" *Archiv für Geschichte der Philosophie* 87: 189–210.

Gómez, J. 1988. *El diálogo en el Renacimiento español.* Madrid.

Görgemanns, H. 1997. "Dialog." In *Der neue Pauly. Enzyklopädie der Antike,* ed. H. Cancik and H. Schneider, 3:517–21. Stuttgart.

Gottschalk, H. B. 1980. *Heraclides of Pontus.* Oxford.

Guellouz, S. 1992. *Le dialogue.* Paris.

Gundert, H. 1968. *Der platonische Dialog.* Heidelberg.

———. 1971. *Dialog und Dialektik. Zur Struktur des platonischen Dialogs.* Amsterdam.

Habermas, J. 1973. "Wahrheitstheorien." In *Wirklichkeit und Reflexion. Walter Schulz zum 60. Geburtstag,* ed. H. Fahrenbach, 211–65. Pfullingen.

———. 1976. "Was heißt Universalpragmatik?" In *Sprachpragmatik und Philosophie,* ed. K.-O. Apel, 174–272. Frankfurt.

Hadamard, J. 1996. *The Mathematician's Mind.* Princeton.

Halperin, D. M. 1990. "Why Is Diotima a Woman? Platonic Eros and the Figuration of Gender." In *Before Sexuality: The Construction of Erotic Experience in the Ancient Greek World,* ed. D. M. Halperin, J. J. Winkler, and F. I. Zeitlin, 257–308. Princeton.

Haring, N. M. 1953. "A Latin Dialogue on the Doctrine of Gilbert of Poitiers." *Mediaeval Studies* 15: 243–89.

Heal, J. 1995. "Wittgenstein and Dialogue." In *Philosophical Dialogues. Plato, Hume, Wittgenstein,* ed. T. Smiley, 63–83. Oxford. (= *Proceedings of the British Academy* 85.)

Heckmann, G. 1981. *Das sokratische Gespräch. Erfahrungen in philosophischen Hochschulseminaren.* Hannover.

Heitsch, E. 1993. *Platon Phaidros.* Trans. and comm. E. Heitsch. Göttingen.

———. [2000] 2001. "Beweishäufung in Platons Phaidon." Rpt. in *Gesammelte Schriften II: Zur griechischen Philosophie,* 175–217. Munich and Leipzig.

Hirsch, E. 1982. "Anmerkungen des Übersetzers." In S. Kierkegaard, *Stadien auf des Lebens Weg,* vol. 1, I–XX. Gütersloh.

Hirzel, R. [1885] 1963. *Der Dialog. Ein literarhistorischer Versuch.* 2 vols. Leipzig; rpt. Hildesheim.

Hoffmann, M. 1966. *Der Dialog bei den christlichen Schriftstellern der ersten vier Jahrhunderte.* Berlin.

Horster, D. 1994. *Das sokratische Gespräch in Theorie und Praxis.* Opladen.

Hösle, V. 1984a. *Wahrheit und Geschichte. Studien zur Struktur der Philosophiegeschichte unter paradigmatischer Analyse der Entwicklung von Parmenides bis Platon.* Stuttgart–Bad Cannstatt.

———. 1984b. *Die Vollendung der Tragödie im Spätwerk des Sophokles.* Stuttgart–Bad Cannstatt.

———. 1996. "Rationalismus, Intersubjektivität und Einsamkeit: Lulls Desconort zwischen Heraklit und Nietzsche." In *Constantes y fragmentos del pensamiento luliano,* ed. F. Domínguez and J. de Salas, 39–57. Tübingen.

———. 1997. *Moral und Politik.* Munich. [*Morals and Politics.* Trans. S. Rendall. Notre Dame, 2004.]

———. 2001. Review of M. Wetzel, *Prinzip Subjektivität: Allgemeine Theorie. Erster Halbband: Ding und Person, Dingbezugnahme und Kommunikation, Dialektik* [Würzburg, 2001]. *Wiener Jahrbuch für Philosophie* 33: 233–36.

———. 2004a. *Platon interpretieren.* Paderborn.

———. 2004b. "Eine Form der Selbsttranszendierung philosophischer Dialoge bei Cicero und Platon und ihre Bedeutung für die Philologie." *Hermes* 132: 152–66.

———. 2004c. "Interreligious Dialogues during the Middle Ages and Early Modernity." In *Educating for Democracy: Paideia in an Age of Uncertainty,* ed. A. M. Olson, D. M. Steiner, and I. S. Tuuli, 59–83. Lanham, MD.

———. 2004d. "Wahrheit und Verstehen. Davidson, Gadamer und das Desiderat einer objektiv-idealistischen Hermeneutik." In *Logik, Mathematik und Naturphilosophie im objektiven Idealismus. Festschrift für Dieter Wandschneider,* ed. W. Neuser and V. Hösle, 265–83. Würzburg. [English version in *Between Description and Interpretation: The Hermeneutic Turn in Phenomenology,* ed. A. Wiercinski, 376–91. Toronto, 2005.]

———. 2004e. "Platons 'Protreptikos,' Gesprächsgeschehen und Gesprächsgegenstand in Platons *Euthydemos.*" *Rheinisches Museum für Philologie* 147: 247–75.

———. 2005a. "Die Philosophie und ihre literarischen Formen—Versuch einer Taxonomie." In *Das Geistige und das Sinnliche in der Kunst,* ed D. Wandschneider, 41–55. Würzburg.

———. 2005b. "Inferentialismus bei Brandom und Holismus bei Hegel—Eine Antwort auf Richard Rorty und einige Nachfragen an Robert Brandom." In *Diskurs und Reflexion,* ed. W. Kellerwessel, W.-J. Cramm, D. Krause, and H.-C. Kupfer, 463–86. Würzburg. [English version in *Graduate Faculty Philosophy Journal* 27 (2): 61–82.]

———. 2007. "Encephalius." *Mind and Matter* 5 (2): 135–65.

———. 2008a. "Cicero's Plato." *Wiener Studien* 121: 145–70.

———. 2008b. "Did the Greeks Deliberately Use the Golden Ratio in an Artwork? A Hermeneutical Reflection." *La Parola del Passato* 63: 415–26.

———. 2008c. "Über den Vergleich von Texten." *Orbis litterarum* 63: 381–402.

———. 2009a. "Poetische Poetiken in der Antike: Horaz' Ars Poetica und Pseudo-Longinos' *Peri hupsous.*" *Poetica* 41: 55–74.

————. 2009b. "Die Einheit des Wissens und die Wirklichkeit der Universität." *Scheidewege* 39: 43–57.

————. 2010. "Poetische Poetiken in der Neuzeit: Boileau, Pope, Friedrich Schlegel und Adorno." *Zeitschrift für Ästhetik und allgemeine Kunstwissenschaft* 55: 25–47.

Huff, T. 1993. *The Rise of Early Modern Science: Islam, China, and the West.* Cambridge.

Israel, J. 2001. *Radical Enlightenment: Philosophy and the Making of Modernity, 1650–1750.* Oxford.

Jacobi, K. 1999. "Einleitung." In *Gespräche lesen. Philosophische Dialoge im Mittelalter,* ed. K. Jacobi, 9–22. Tübingen.

Jaeger, W. 1955. *Aristoteles. Grundlegung einer Geschichte seiner Entwicklung.* 2nd ed. Berlin.

Jansen, T. 2000. *Höfische Öffentlichkeit im frühmittelalterlichen China. Debatten im Salon des Prinzen Xiao Ziliang.* Freiburg.

Jermann, C. 1986. *Philosophie und Politik. Untersuchungen zur Struktur und Problematik des Platonischen Idealismus.* Stuttgart–Bad Cannstatt.

Kahn, C. 1996. *Plato and the Socratic Dialogue.* Cambridge.

Kalmbach, G. 1996. *Der Dialog im Spannungsfeld von Mündlichkeit und Schriftlichkeit.* Tübingen.

Kapp, E. 1942. *Greek Foundations of Traditional Logic.* New York.

Kerschensteiner, J. 1945. *Platon und der Orient.* Stuttgart.

Kochin, M. S. 2002. *Gender and Rhetoric in Plato's Political Thought.* Cambridge.

Kosman, L. A. 1992. "Silence and Imitation in the Platonic Dialogues." *Oxford Studies in Ancient Philosophy,* suppl. vol.: *Methods of Interpreting Plato and his Dialogues,* ed. J. C. Klagge and N. D. Smith, 73–92. Oxford.

Krämer, H. J. 1959. *Arete bei Platon und Aristoteles.* Heidelberg.

Lachmann, R. 1982. *Dialogizität.* Ed. R. Lachmann. Munich.

Landfester, M., with H. Cancik and H. Schneider. 1999. "Dialog." In *Der neue Pauly. Enzyklopädie der Antike. Rezeptions- und Wissenschaftsgeschichte,* Bd. 13, 830–36. Stuttgart and Weimar.

Laqueur, T. 2003. *Solitary Sex: A Cultural History of Masturbation.* New York.

Leonhardt, J. 1999. *Ciceros Kritik der Philosophenschulen.* Munich.

Lombard, C. M. 1976. *Joseph de Maistre.* Boston.

Lorenzen, P., and K. Lorenz. 1978. *Dialogische Logik.* Darmstadt.

Lukács, G. 1971. *Die Theorie des Romans.* Neuwied and Berlin.

Marsh, D. 1980. *The Quattrocento Dialogue: Classical Tradition and Humanist Innovation.* Cambridge, MA.

Martin, J. 1931. *Symposion. Die Geschichte einer literarischen Form.* Paderborn.

Mayr, E. 1997. *This Is Biology: The Science of the Living World.* Cambridge, MA.

McDonald, J. M. S. 1931. *Character-Portraiture in Epicharmus, Sophron, and Plato.* Sewanee, TN.

McDowell, J. 1994. *Mind and World.* Cambridge, MA.

Meissner, H. M. 1991. *Rhetorik und Theologie. Der Dialog Gregors von Nyssa De anima et resurrectione.* Frankfurt.

Moos, P. von. 1989. "Literatur-und bildungsgeschichtliche Aspekte der Dialog-form im lateinischen Mittelalter. Der Dialogus Ratii des Eberhard von Ypern zwischen theologischer disputatio und Scholaren-Komödie." In *Tradition und Wertung. Festschrift für F. Brunhölzl zum 65. Geburtstag,* ed. G. Bernt, F. Rädle, and G. Silagi, 165–209. Sigmaringen.

———. 1997. "Gespräch, Dialog und Dialogform nach älterer Theorie." In *Gattungen mittelalterlicher Schriftlichkeit,* ed. B. Frank, T. Haye, and D. Tophinke, 235–59. Tübingen.

Most, G. W. 1993. "'A Cock for Asclepius.'" *Classical Quarterly* 43: 96–111.

Nails, D. 1995. *Agora, Academy, and the Conduct of Philosophy.* Dordrecht.

———. 2002. *The People of Plato: A Prosopography of Plato and Other Socratics.* Indianapolis.

Natorp, P. 1893. "Alexamenos von Teos." In *Paulys Realencyclopädie der classischen Altertumswissenschaft,* ed. G. Wissowa. Erster Halbband, Stuttgart, 1375.

Nikulin, D. 2005. "Dialogue versus Discourse: On the Possibility of Disagreement in Human Communication." *Graduate Faculty Philosophy Journal* 26 (1): 89–105.

Nüsser, O. 1991. *Albins Prolog und die Dialogtheorie des Platonismus.* Stuttgart.

O'Donnell, J. J., ed. 1992. *Augustine: Confessions.* 3 vols. Oxford.

Oesterreich, P. L. 2003. *Philosophie der Rhetorik.* Bamberg.

O'Meara, J. J. 1951. "The Historicity of the Early Dialogues of Saint Augustine." *Vigiliae Christianae* 5: 150–78.

———. 1954. *The Young Augustine: The Growth of St. Augustine's Mind up to His Conversion.* London.

Ong, W. 1979. *Ramus: Method, and the Decay of Dialogue.* New York.

———. 1982. *Orality and Literacy: The Technologizing of the Word.* London.

Pagnoni-Sturlese, M. R. 1989. "Phantasia III." In *Historisches Wörterbuch der Philosophie,* ed. J. Ritter and K. Gründer, vol. 7: 516–35. Basel.

Parkinson, R. B. 1996. "Types of Literature in the Middle Kingdom." In *Ancient Egyptian Literature: History and Forms,* ed. A. Loprieno, 297–312. Leiden.

Pavel, T. G. 1986. *Fictional Worlds.* Cambridge, MA.

Pearce, L. 1994. *Reading Dialogics.* London.

Perelman, C., and L. Olbrechts-Tyteca. 1988. *Traité de l'argumentation: la nouvelle rhétorique.* Brussels.

Perger, M. von. 1999. "Vorläufiges Repertorium philosophischer und theologischer Prosa-Dialoge des lateinischen Mittelalters. Von Minucius Felix bis Nikolaus von Kues." In *Gespräche lesen. Philosophische Dialoge im Mittelalter,* ed. K. Jacobi, 435–94. Tübingen.

Pinto Colombo, M. 1934. *Il mimo di Sofrone e di Senarco.* Florence.

Rallo Gruss, A. 1996. *La escritura dialéctica: estudios sobre el diálogo renacentista.* Málaga.

Reis, B. 1999. *Der Platoniker Albinos und sein sogenannter Prologos. Prolegomena, Überlieferungsgeschichte, kritische Edition und Übersetzung.* Wiesbaden.

Reisman, D. C. 2004. "Plato's *Republic* in Arabic: A Newly Discovered Passage." *Arabic Sciences and Philosophy* 14: 263–300.

Rendall, S. 1971. "Fontenelle and His Public." *MLN* 86: 496–508.

Reydams-Schils, G. 2005. *The Roman Stoics: Self, Responsibility, and Affection.* Chicago.

Ricklin, T. 1999. "Der 'Dialogus' des Petrus Alfonsi. Eine Annäherung." In *Gespräche lesen. Philosophische Dialoge im Mittelalter,* ed. K. Jacobi, 139–55. Tübingen.

Roche, M. 1997. *Tragedy and Comedy.* Albany, NY.

———. 2002. *Die Moral der Kunst. Über Literatur und Ethik.* Munich.

Roochnik, D. 1995. "Socrates' Rhetorical Attack on Rhetoric." In *The Third Way: New Directions in Platonic Studies,* ed. F. Gonzalez, 81–94. Lanham, MD.

Rosenkranz, K. [1843] 1969. *Schelling.* Danzig; rpt. Aalen.

———. 1866. *Diderot's Leben und Werke.* 2 vols. Leipzig.

Ruch, M. 1958. *Le préambule dans les œuvres philosophiques de Cicéron. Essai sur la genèse et l'art du dialogue.* Paris.

Ruggiu, L. 1975. *Parmenide.* Venice.

Ryle, G. 1966. *Plato's Progress.* Cambridge.

Sayre, K. 1992. "A Maieutic View of Five Late Dialogues." *Oxford Studies in Ancient Philosophy,* supp. vol. 1992: *Methods of Interpreting Plato and His Dialogues,* ed. J. C. Klagge and N. D. Smith, 221–43. Oxford.

Schacht, J. 1964. "An Early Murci'ite Treatise: The *Kitabal -'Alim wal-Muta'allim.*" *Oriens* 17: 96–117.

Schildknecht, C. 1990. *Philosophische Masken. Literarische Formen der Philosophie bei Platon, Descartes, Wolff und Lichtenberg.* Stuttgart.

Schildknecht, C., and D. Teichert, eds. 1996. *Philosophie in Literatur.* Frankfurt.

Schmid, W. T. 1992. *On Manly Courage: A Study of Plato's Laches.* Carbondale.

Schmidt, P. L. 1977. "Zur Typologie und Literarisierung des frühchristlichen lateinischen Dialogs." In *Christianisme et formes littéraires de l'antiquité tardive en occident,* ed. A. Cameron et al., 101–80. Geneva.

Schmidt-Glintzer, H. 1976. *Das Hung-ming chi und die Aufnahme des Buddhismus in China.* Wiesbaden.

Schmölders, C., ed. 1986. *Die Kunst des Gesprächs. Texte zur Geschichte der europäischen Konversationstheorie.* 2nd ed. Munich.

Sedley, D. 1995. "The Dramatis Personae of Plato's Phaedo." In *Philosophical Dialogues: Plato, Hume, Wittgenstein,* ed. T. Smiley, 3–26. Oxford. (= *Proceedings of the British Academy* 85.)

———. 2004. *The Midwife of Platonism: Text and Subtext in Plato's Theaetetus.* Oxford.

Singer, P. 2004. *Pushing Time Away.* New York.

Slings, S. R., ed. 1999. *Plato, Clitophon.* Cambridge.

Snyder, J. R. 1989. *Writing the Scene of Speaking: Theories of Dialogue in the Late Italian Renaissance.* Stanford.

Söll, L. 1980. *Gesprochenes und geschriebenes Französisch.* 2nd ed. Berlin.

von Staden, H. 1999. "Metaphor and the Sublime: Longinus." In *Desde los poemas homéricos hasta la prosa griega del siglo IV d. C.,* ed. J. A. López Férez, 359–80. Madrid.

Stemmer, P. 1992. *Platons Dialektik. Die frühen und mittleren Dialoge.* Berlin.

Stenzel, J. 1956. *Kleine Schriften zur griechischen Philosophie.* Darmstadt.

Stierle, K. 1984. "Gespräch und Diskurs. Ein Versuch im Blick auf Montaigne, Descartes und Pascal." In *Das Gespräch,* ed. K. Stierle and R. Warning, 297–334. Munich.

Szlezák, T. A. 1985. *Platon und die Schriftlichkeit der Philosophie. Interpretationen zu den frühen und mittleren Dialogen.* Berlin.

———. 1988. "Gespräche unter Ungleichen. Zur Struktur und Zielsetzung der platonischen Dialoge." *Antike und Abendland* 34: 99–116.

———. 2004. *Das Bild des Dialektikers in Platons späten Dialogen. Platon und die Schriftlichkeit der Philosophie.* Part II. Berlin.

Thesleff, H. 1982. *Studies in Platonic Chronology.* Helsinki.

Thompson, D. B. 1960. "The House of Simon the Shoemaker." *Archaeology* 13: 234–40.

Todorov, T. 1981. *Mikhaïl Bakhtine: le principe dialogique.* Paris.

———. 1987. *La notion de littérature et autres essais.* Paris.

Trapp, M. 2000. "Plato in the *Deipnosophistae.*" In *Athenaeus and His World,* ed. D. Braund and J. Wilkins, 353–63, 577–78. Exeter.

Várdy, P. 2004. "Das Lächerliche und das Absolute. Anmerkungen zu Platons *Euthydemos.*" In *Logik, Mathematik und Naturphilosophie im objektiven Idealismus,* ed. W. Neuser and V. Hösle, 285–95. Würzburg.

G. Vlastos, G. [1969] 1981. "The Individual as an Object of Love in Plato." In *Platonic Studies,* 2nd ed., 3–42. Princeton.

Volgers, A., and C. Zamagni, eds. 2004. *Erotapokriseis: Early Christian Question-and-Answer Literature in Context.* Leuven.

Voss, B. R. 1970. *Der Dialog in der frühchristlichen Literatur.* Munich.

Wertheimer, J. 1990. *"Der Güter Gefährlichstes, die Sprache." Zur Krise des Dialogs zwischen Aufklärung und Romantik.* Munich.

Westermann, H. 2002. *Die Intention des Dichters und die Zwecke der Interpreten. Zur Theorie und Praxis der Dichterauslegung in den platonischen Dialogen.* Berlin.

White, N. 2002. *Individual and Conflict in Greek Ethics.* Oxford.

Wieland, W. 1982. *Platon und die Formen des Wissens.* Göttingen.

Wilamowitz-Moellendorff, U. von. 1879. "Phaidon von Elis." *Hermes* 14: 187–93.

Wildberg, C. 2002. *Hyperesie und Epiphanie. Ein Versuch über die Bedeutung der Götter in den Dramen des Euripides.* Munich.

Wilkerson, T. E. 1995. *Natural Kinds.* Aldershot.

Wyller, E. A. 1970. *Der späte Platon.* Hamburg.

Zoll, G. 1962. *Cicero Platonis aemulus. Untersuchungen über die Form von Ciceros Dialogen, besonders von De oratore.* Zürich.

INDEX

Abelard, Peter, 420
  and Christianity, 324–25
  Collationes, 47, 99, 197–98, 199, 219,
    274n.76, 281–82, 282nn.98–99,
    284, 323–25, 324n.119,
    325nn.123–25
  on the Jews, 323–25
  Scito teipsum (Ethica), 324
  vanity of, 198
abstraction, 210, 237
Abū Muqātil, 73n.5
Academy, 111, 380
  and Cicero, 90, 143, 230–31
  of Plato, 84, 87, 90, 125, 152, 160,
    231, 243n.26, 302, 392, 407, 433
  and skepticism, 90, 96, 143, 377
  See also Augustine, works of, *Contra
    academicos*
accidental conversations, 290, 292–94,
  293n.
Adelard of Bath: *Quaestiones naturales,*
  322–23
Aeneas of Gaza: *Theophrastus,* 98,
  144n.15, 238n., 293, 318, 318n.93,
  448
Aeschines, 79, 166n.16
  Aspasia, 394–96
Aeschylus: *Oresteia,* 155
aesthetic analysis, 2–4, 430–40
aesthetic bracketing, 38, 143, 144, 145
aesthetic dialogues, 51–52, 154, 232
aesthetic norms, 25n.12, 101
  as genre-specific, 9
Agrippa von Nettesheim, Heinrich
  Cornelius, 399

Albinus
  dialogue taxonomy of, 163, 164n.5
  Prologos, 39n.49, 163
Alcidamas, 75, 78, 441–42
  *On the authors of written speeches or
    on the Sophists,* 78n.19
Alcuin
  De dialectica, 98, 98n.94
  *Disputatio de rhetorica et de
    virtutibus,* 98
Alexamenus of Teos, 78–79, 78n.21
Algarotti, Francesco, 400
allegory, 189–90, 196, 212–14, 215,
  219
Ambrosiaster, 16n.22
anachronisms, 187, 253–57
Anaxagoras, 170
Anselm of Canterbury, 21, 322n.107
  Cur deus homo, 98, 127, 260n.11, 322,
    383, 428, 429, 429n.82, 439n.24
  Meditations, 15
  Proslogion, 17n.
  on reason, 322
Antiochus of Ascalon, 90
Antiphon, 75n.10
Antisthenes, 79
  Aspasia, 394–95, 395n.88, 396
Apel, Karl-Otto, 128
Aquinas, Thomas, 3, 132
Arcesilaus, 90
architectonic ideas, 432
argumentative analysis, 2–4, 6
  argumentative games, 406–8
Aristippus, 81
Aristo of Ceos, 188, 188n.10

VITTORIO HÖSLE

is Paul G. Kimball Chair of Arts and Letters in the Department
of German Languages and Literatures and concurrent professor of
philosophy and political science at the University of Notre Dame.
He founded the Notre Dame Institute for Advanced Study. He is the
author or editor of many books, including *Darwinism and Philosophy*
(coedited with Christian Illies, 2005) and *Morals and Politics* (2004),
both published by the University of Notre Dame Press.